CONTEMPORARY
AMERICAN POETRY

CONTEMPORARY AMERICAN POETRY

EIGHTH EDITION

Edited by

A. Poulin, Jr.

Late of State University of New York,
College at Brockport

and

Michael Waters

Salisbury University,
Maryland

HOUGHTON MIFFLIN COMPANY   BOSTON   NEW YORK

in memory of A. *Poulin, Jr.*
1938–1996

for Boo and Daphne   — A. P., Jr.

for Mihaela and Kiernan   — M.W.

Publisher: Patricia A. Coryell
Executive Editor: Suzanne Phelps Weir
Sponsoring Editor: Michael Gillespie
Associate Editor: Bruce Cantley
Editorial Assistant: Lindsey Gentel
Associate Project Editors: Rachel Zanders and Teresa Huang
Editorial Assistants: Kristen Truncellito and Michelle O'Berg
Senior Photo Editor: Jennifer Meyer Dare
Senior Composition Buyer: Sarah Ambrose
Senior Manufacturing Coordinator: Renée Ostrowski
Senior Marketing Manager: Cindy Graff Cohen

Cover image: Richard Pousette-Dart. Top painting: *Primordial Movement*, 1939. Oil on linen, 36 × 48 inches. Collection of the artist. Bottom painting: *East River*, 1939. Oil on masonite panel, 36½ × 48¼ inches. Collection of the artist.

Acknowledgments begin on page 681.

Printed in the U.S.A.

Library of Congress Control Number: 2005927704

ISBN: 0-618-52785-0

123456789-CRS-09 08 07 06 05

AMERICAN POETRY

Whatever it is, it must have
A stomach that can digest
Rubber, coal, uranium, moons, poems.

Like the shark, it contains a shoe.
It must swim for miles through the desert
Uttering cries that are almost human.

— Louis Simpson

A. Poulin, Jr.

Michael Waters

Contents

Preface   xxiii

AI
The Mother's Tale   3
The Mortician's Twelve-Year-Old Son   4
Twenty-Year Marriage   4
Why Can't I Leave You?   5
I Have Got to Stop Loving You So I Have Killed My Black Goat   5
Finished   6
Riot Act, April 29, 1992   8

JOHN ASHBERY
Self-Portrait in a Convex Mirror   11

MARVIN BELL
The Self and the Mulberry   25
To Dorothy   25
The Mystery of Emily Dickinson   26
To an Adolescent Weeping Willow   26
White Clover   27
Drawn by Stones, by Earth, by Things That Have Been in the Fire   28
Sevens (Version 3): In the Closed Iris of Creation   29
Ars Poetica at the Window   31

JOHN BERRYMAN
from *The Dream Songs*
4 [Filling her compact & delicious body]   33
14 [Life, friends, is boring]   33
26[The glories of the world]   34
29 [There sat down, once]   34
47 April Fool's Day, or, St Mary of Egypt   35
89 Op. posth. no. 12   36
91 Op. posth. no. 14   36
129 [Thin as a sheet]   37
172 [Your face broods]   37
366 [Chilled in this Irish pub]   38
382 [At Henry's bier]   38
384 [The marker slants]   39

ELIZABETH BISHOP
The Fish   41
At the Fishhouses   43
In the Waiting Room   45
One Art   47

CONTENTS

ROBERT BLY

An Empty Place	49
Snowbanks North of the House	49
The Resemblance Between Your Life and a Dog	50
Warning to the Reader	50
Six Winter Privacy Poems	51
Driving to Town Late to Mail a Letter	52
After Long Busyness	52
The Dead Seal	52
Looking into a Tide Pool	53
The Yellow Dot	54
The Russian	54
Pitzeem and the Mare	55

GWENDOLYN BROOKS

from *A Street in Bronzeville*

the mother	57
a song in the front yard	58
A Lovely Love	58
The Lovers of the Poor	59
Beverly Hills, Chicago	61
We Real Cool	62
The Egg Boiler	63

OLGA BROUMAS

The Choir	65
Caritas	66
Calypso	71

LUCILLE CLIFTON

[i was born with twelve fingers]	73
at the cemetery, walnut grove plantation, south carolina, 1989	73
the lost baby poem	74
[at last we killed the roaches]	75
homage to my hips	75
wishes for sons	76
poem to my uterus	76
lumpectomy eve	77
scar	77
lorena	78
moonchild	78
the gift	79

CONTENTS

BILLY COLLINS

Litany	81
Sonnet	82
Japan	82
Osso Buco	83
Man in Space	85
By a Swimming Pool Outside Siracusa	85
Writing in the Afterlife	86

ROBERT CREELEY

I Know a Man	89
After Lorca	89
The Figures	90
The Language	91
The Flower	92
Something	92
The Warning	93
The Act of Love	93

JAMES DICKEY

The Heaven of Animals	97
The Sheep Child	98
The Poisoned Man	100
The Hospital Window	101
Adultery	102

STEPHEN DOBYNS

Long Story	105
Bowlers Anonymous	106
How to Like It	107
Fragments	108
Tenderly	109
Tomatoes	110
Cemetery Nights	111

RITA DOVE

American Smooth	113
Crab-Boil	114
Wingfoot Lake	114
The Breathing, the Endless News	115
After Reading *Mickey in the Night Kitchen* for the Third Time Before Bed	116
Parsley	117
Testimonial	119

STEPHEN DUNN

The Stairway	121
Instead of You	121
The Routine Things Around the House	123
Cohabiting	124
The Insistence of Beauty	125
Landscape at the End of the Century	127

LOUISE ERDRICH

Jacklight	129
The Strange People	130
I Was Sleeping Where the Black Oaks Move	131
Indian Boarding School: The Runaways	132
Dear John Wayne	132
Mary Magdalene	134
Christ's Twin	134
New Vows	135

CAROL FROST

Chimera	137
Homo Sapiens	137
Sexual Jealousy	138
Laws	138
Fury	139
Scorn	139
To Kill a Deer	140
The St. Louis Zoo	141
Telling the Bees	142
The Part of the Bee's Body Embedded in the Flesh	142
The Undressing	143

ALLEN GINSBERG

from *Howl*	145
America	150
Ode to Failure	152

LOUISE GLÜCK

Nostos	155
The Mirror	155
Mock Orange	156
Retreating Wind	156
The White Rose	157
Midnight	158
Parable of Flight	158

CONTENTS

The Balcony   159
Vespers   160
Celestial Music   160

ALBERT GOLDBARTH
The Talk Show   163
Ancestored-Back Is the Overpresiding Spirit of This Poem   164
Reality Organization   166
Arguing Bartusiak   168
The Whole Earth Catalogue   169

KIMIKO HAHN
The Izu Dancer   173
The Older Child   178
The Shower   179
The Artist's Daughter   180
Reckless Sonnet   181

DONALD HALL
Maple Syrup   183
In the Kitchen of the Old House   184
When the Young Husband   186
The Porcelain Couple   187
Ardor   188
Digging   189

MICHAEL S. HARPER
We Assume: On the Death of Our Son, Reuben Masai Harper   191
Reuben, Reuben   192
Dear John, Dear Coltrane   192
Love Medley: Patrice Cuchulain   194
This Is My Son's Song: *"Ungie, Hi Ungie"*   194
Studs   195
Here Where Coltrane Is   197

ROBERT HASS
The Image   199
Meditation at Lagunitas   199
A Story About the Body   200
Privilege of Being   200
Happiness   202
Our Lady of the Snows   202
Spring Drawing 2   203
Faint Music   204

CONTENTS

ROBERT HAYDEN
Those Winter Sundays   207
Night, Death, Mississippi   207
Middle Passage   209

WILLIAM HEYEN
The Return   215
The Pigeons   215
Witness   216
Simple Truths   218
Blackbird Spring   220
Yellowjackets   221

ANDREW HUDGINS
The Chinaberry   223
One Threw a Dirt Clod and It Ran   224
Heat Lightning in a Time of Drought   225
Grandmother's Spit   227
In   227
Ashes   228
Supper   229

RICHARD HUGO
Living Alone   231
Degrees of Gray in Philipsburg   231
A Map of Montana in Italy   233
The Lady in Kicking Horse Reservoir   234
Death in the Aquarium   235
Langaig   236

DONALD JUSTICE
Early Poems   239
First Death   239
Children Walking Home from School Through Good Neighborhood   241
Psalm and Lament   242
Absences   243
Men at Forty   243
Variations on a Text by Vallejo   244
In Memory of the Unknown Poet, Robert Boardman Vaughn   245

GALWAY KINNELL
Blackberry Eating   247
After Making Love We Hear Footsteps   247
The Bear   248

CONTENTS

The Fundamental Project of Technology   251
Flower of Five Blossoms   252

CAROLYN KIZER

Thrall   257
The Intruder   258
A Widow in Wintertime   259
from *Pro Femina*
   One [From Sappho to myself, consider the fate of women]   259
Semele Recycled   260
The Skein   263

YUSEF KOMUNYAKAA

Audacity of the Lower Gods   265
Blackberries   265
Work   266
In the Background of Silence   267
Tu Do Street   268
Thanks   269
Boys in Dresses   270
Ode to the Maggot   271

MAXINE KUMIN

Morning Swim   273
To Swim, to Believe   274
Heaven as Anus   274
Requiem on I-89   275
The Grace of Geldings in Ripe Pastures   276
Woodchucks   276
The Highwaymen   277
In the Pea Patch   278
In the Park   278
Nurture   279

STANLEY KUNITZ

The Layers   281
Robin Redbreast   282
The Wellfleet Whale   283
The Abduction   286
The Portrait   287
Touch Me   288
The Long Boat   289

LI-YOUNG LEE

The Gift	291
Persimmons	292
Eating Alone	294
Eating Together	295
My Indigo	295
This Room and Everything in It	296
You Must Sing	297

DENISE LEVERTOV

The Acolyte	299
The Poem Unwritten	300
Our Bodies	300
The Mutes	301
Wedding-Ring	303
Where Is the Angel?	303
Life at War	304

PHILIP LEVINE

The Simple Truth	307
On the Birth of Good & Evil During the Long Winter of '28	308
Animals Are Passing from Our Lives	308
You Can Have It	309
What Work Is	311
I Was Born in Lucerne	312
They Feed They Lion	313
The Two	314

ROBERT LOWELL

Memories of West Street and Lepke	317
"To Speak of Woe That Is in Marriage"	318
Skunk Hour	319
Eye and Tooth	320
For the Union Dead	321

WILLIAM MATTHEWS

Men at My Father's Funeral	325
Housework	325
In Memory of the Utah Stars	326
Pissing Off the Back of the Boat into the Nivernais Canal	327
Moving Again	328
Grief	329
The Cloister	330
Onions	330

CONTENTS

JAMES MERRILL

The Octopus	333
Laboratory Poem	333
Charles on Fire	334
The Mad Scene	335
A Renewal	335
The Kimono	335
Voices from the Other World	336
A Downward Look	337
b o d y	338
An Upward Look	338

W. S. MERWIN

The Poem	341
How We Are Spared	341
For the Anniversary of My Death	341
Dead Hand	342
The Chaff	342
Field Mushrooms	342
The Rose Beetle	343
Fog-Horn	344
St Vincent's	344
When You Go Away	346
Air	347

MARILYN NELSON

A Wreath for Emmett Till	349
Minor Miracle	355

NAOMI SHIHAB NYE

Vocabulary of Dearness	357
Steps	357
Arabic	358
The Small Vases from Hebron	359
The Shapes of Mouths at Parties	360
Morning Paper, Society Page	360
What Brings Us Out	361
The Last Day of August	362
The Traveling Onion	363

FRANK O'HARA

Why I Am Not a Painter	365
Poem [I don't know as I get what D. H. Lawrence is driving at]	366
Personal Poem	366
Steps	367

Poem [Lana Turner has collapsed!]   369
For Grace, After a Party   369
The Day Lady Died   370
Getting Up Ahead of Someone (Sun)   370

SHARON OLDS
Monarchs   373
A Woman in Heat Wiping Herself   373
Early Images of Heaven   374
The Pope's Penis   375
The Elder Sister   375
The Lifting   376
The Glass   377
May 1968   378
Good Will   379

MARY OLIVER
Where Does the Dance Begin, Where Does It End?   381
Sleeping in the Forest   381
Spring Azures   382
Little Owl Who Lives in the Orchard   383
University Hospital, Boston   384
In Blackwater Woods   385
The Summer Day   386
Singapore   387

MICHAEL PALMER
I Do Not   389
Sun   391
Dearest Reader   393
Untitled [O you in that little bark]   393
"or anything resembling it"   394

CARL PHILLIPS
Glads   397
Our Lady   398
Luna Moth   399
Toys   400
Parable   401
Aubade: Some Peaches, After Storm   402
Singing   403

SYLVIA PLATH
Stillborn   405
Crossing the Water   405

CONTENTS

Daddy   406
Cut   408
Lady Lazarus   409

ADRIENNE RICH
Power   413
Planetarium   413
Diving into the Wreck   415
The Novel   417
One Life   418
The School Among the Ruins   419

THEODORE ROETHKE
My Papa's Waltz   423
Root Cellar   423
Cuttings (*later*)   424
The Lost Son   424
In a Dark Time   429

ANNE SEXTON
Her Kind   431
With Mercy for the Greedy   431
To a Friend Whose Work Has Come to Triumph   432
The Abortion   433
Man and Wife   434
In Celebration of My Uterus   435
The Room of My Life   437

CHARLES SIMIC
Charles Simic   439
Poem Without a Title   439
February   440
Poem   440
Stone   440
Fork   441
Solitude   441
Fear   442
Classic Ballroom Dances   442
The Old World   443
Entertaining the Canary   443
Used Book Store   444
My Noiseless Entourage   444
errata   445

LOUIS SIMPSON

Working Late 447

Riverside Drive 448

Quiet Desperation 448

In the Suburbs 451

Physical Universe 451

DAVE SMITH

Fiddlers 455

Blowfish and Mudtoad 455

Night Fishing for Blues 455

2000 458

Pine Cones 459

Allegheny Happiness 460

The Tire Hangs in the Yard 461

W. D. SNODGRASS

Viewing the Body 465

from *Heart's Needle*

    9 [I get numb and go in] 465

"After Experience Taught Me . . ." 468

Old Apple Trees 469

Love Lamp 471

GARY SNYDER

"One Should Not Talk to a Skilled Hunter About What Is

    Forbidden by the Buddha" 473

Bubbs Creek Haircut 473

Hay for the Horses 477

The Bath 478

Axe Handles 481

GARY SOTO

Black Hair 483

Envying the Children of San Francisco 484

Oranges 485

Mexicans Begin Jogging 486

The Tale of Sunlight 487

Failing in the Presence of Ants 489

ELIZABETH SPIRES

The Beds 491

Sunday Afternoon at Fulham Palace 492

The First Day 494

The Celestial   495
"In Heaven It Is Always Autumn"   496
Glass-Bottom Boat   497
Cemetery Reef   498

DAVID ST. JOHN
Gin   501
The Swan at Sheffield Park   502
Lucifer in Starlight   506
Last Night with Rafaella   507

WILLIAM STAFFORD
How the Real Bible Is Written   511
At Fourth and Main in Liberal, Kansas, 1932   511
Growing Up   512
Ask Me   512
Ceremony   512
Traveling Through the Dark   513
Vocation   513
Adults Only   514
Fifteen   514
Widow   515
The Light by the Barn   516
A Wind from a Wing   516
With Kit, Age 7, at the Beach   517
Near   517

GERALD STERN
I Remember Galileo   519
The Dancing   519
Soap   520
The Bull-Roarer   522
Another Insane Devotion   525
Lilacs for Ginsberg   526
She Was a Dove   527

MARK STRAND
Keeping Things Whole   529
The Dress   529
The Prediction   530
My Life by Somebody Else   530
A Morning   531
The Idea   531
A. M.   532

from *Dark Harbor*
    XXX [There is a road through the canyon] — 532
    XXXIX [When after a long silence one picks up the pen] — 533
    XLV [I am sure you would find it misty here] — 533
The Night, The Porch — 534
A Piece of the Storm — 534
Leopardi — 535

JEAN VALENTINE
Annunciation — 537
December 21st — 537
American River Sky Alcohol Father — 538
The Messenger — 538
Snow Landscape, in a Glass Globe — 541
The Under Voice — 542
Skate — 542
Letter — 543

ELLEN BRYANT VOIGT
January — 545
The Hen — 545
The Trust — 546
Woman Who Weeps — 547
The Lotus Flowers — 548
Two Trees — 549
Harvesting the Cows — 550

RICHARD WILBUR
The Ride — 553
Love Calls Us to the Things of This World — 554
Playboy — 555
Cottage Street, 1953 — 555
The Writer — 556
In Trackless Woods — 557
The Lilacs — 558
Mayflies — 559

C. K. WILLIAMS
Blades — 561
From My Window — 562
The Gas Station — 564
Bone — 566
The Singing — 566

CONTENTS

C. D. WRIGHT
The Secret Life of Musical Instruments   569
Wages of Love   570
More Blues and the Abstract Truth   571
Why Ralph Refuses to Dance   572
Planks   573
So Far Off and Yet Here   574
Song of the Gourd   574
Girl Friend Poem #3   575

CHARLES WRIGHT
Reunion   577
Grace   577
Snow   577
Him   578
California Dreaming   578
Night Journal   581
Relics   582

JAMES WRIGHT
Autumn Begins in Martins Ferry, Ohio   585
Lying in a Hammock at William Duffy's Farm in
    Pine Island, Minnesota   585
The Minneapolis Poem   586
In Response to a Rumor That the Oldest Whorehouse in
    Wheeling, West Virginia, Has Been Condemned   588
The Young Good Man   589
The Old WPA Swimming Pool in Martins Ferry, Ohio   590
A Blessing   592
The Journey   592

Notes on the Poets   595
Criticism: A Selected Bibliography   675
Notes on the Editors   679
Acknowledgments   681

Preface

In *Tradition and the Individual Poem: An Inquiry into Anthologies* (2001), Anne Ferry acknowledges "the indisputable power of anthologies to influence the course of poetry and of criticism," dating such sway back to Richard Tottel's "earliest extant" anthology of 1557. A. Poulin, Jr., having shepherded *Contemporary American Poetry* through six editions, was aware of such influence, and he had a sense of humor. He'd sent his friends a *Peanuts* cartoon strip in which Sally complains to Charlie Brown, "We've been reading poems in school, but I never understand any of them. How am I supposed to know which poems to like?" Charlie Brown's reply in the final panel had been revised so that the words in the balloon read, simply, "Poulin tells you." Ferry quotes British Poet Laureate (1968–1972) Cecil Day-Lewis: "A satisfying arrangement of poems requires a special talent which can be fairly called 'creative.'" The anthologist's task here, then, is not to gather a representative sampling of poems written during a chosen period of time but rather, as Poulin understood it, to select work that leans toward the creation of "*the* central metaphor for the quality of our experience since World War II." No single poet had yet accomplished this, he argued in 1971. Instead, contemporary American poets had "described the deterioration and sterility of the individual self, thereby fabricating a cumulative metaphor for our own age." Poulin was describing the now out-of-fashion confessional mode.

More recent poetry, especially (though not exclusively) poetry by marginalized writers, focuses less on the individual self than on the generative and myth-making aspects of community, past and present, as well as on the spiritual resonance that informs our ongoing democratic experiment and defines our still-emerging national character. Such poetry asks who we are by delineating the spaces we inhabit and that inhabit us, and by ranging through vast privacies enacted against the backdrop of public discourse and citizenship. As this Eighth Edition demonstrates, contemporary American poetry still amplifies Ralph Waldo Emerson's belief in the "infinitude of the private man."

Any continuing anthology needs to remain *active*, and toward that end I have tried to rely less on the usual "anthology pieces" and to incorporate new and vital work. However, I trust that constant readers will find many favorite poems still on these pages. Another ongoing feature is the inclusion of several long poems (among them John Ashbery's "Self-Portrait in a Convex Mirror," Olga Broumas's "Caritas," the first section of Allen Ginsberg's seminal "Howl," Kimiko Hahn's self-generative "The Izu Dancer," Robert Hayden's harrowing "Middle Passage," Marilyn Nelson's crown of sonnets, "A Wreath for Emmett Till," and Gary Snyder's "Bubbs Creek Haircut" from *Mountains and Rivers without End*) demonstrating the persistent search for a form conducive both to our fluctuating American idiom and to the varieties of our daily experience. Once again,

I have had to drop several poets whose work I admire — always an unpleas-
ant task — in order to introduce new poets in the anthology. I have returned
Theodore Roethke and Mary Oliver to this edition and have added for the
first time the work of seven poets: Billy Collins, Stephen Dunn, Louise
Erdrich, Michael Palmer, Dave Smith, Jean Valentine, and C. D. Wright.

In his 1837 oration, Emerson insisted: "There is then creative reading
as well as creative writing. When the mind is braced by labor and invention, the page of whatever book we read becomes luminous with manifold
allusion. Every sentence is doubly significant, and the sense of our author
is as broad as the world." I hope this edition inspires such creative reading.

I remain grateful to Dr. Timothy O'Rourke, Dean of the Fulton School
at Salisbury University, for release time that enabled me to complete this
volume. To Mihaela and Kiernan, my gratitude and love, as ever . . .

Michael Waters
January 2005
Salisbury, Maryland

CONTEMPORARY
AMERICAN POETRY

Photo by Charlie M.D. Sirat of the Daily O'Collegian

Ai

THE MOTHER'S TALE

Once when I was young, Juanito,
there was a ballroom in Lima
where Hernán, your father,
danced with another woman
and I cut him across the cheek
with a pocketknife.
Oh, the pitch of the music sometimes,
the smoke and rustle of crinoline.
But what things to remember now
on your wedding day.
I pour a kettle of hot water
into the wooden tub where you are sitting.
I was young, free.
But Juanito, how free is a woman? —
born with Eve's sin between her legs,
and inside her,
Lucifer sits on a throne of abalone shells,
his staff with the head of John the Baptist
skewered on it.
And in judgment, son, in judgment he says
that women will bear the fruit of the tree
we wished so much to eat
and that fruit will devour us
generation by generation,
so my son,
you must beat Rosita often.
She must know the weight of a man's hand,
the bruises that are like the wounds of Christ.
Her blood that is black at the heart
must flow until it is as red and pure as His.
And she must be pregnant always
if not with child
then with the knowledge
that she is alive because of you.
That you can take her life
more easily than she creates it,
that suffering is her inheritance from you
and through you, from Christ,

3

who walked on his mother's body
to be the King of Heaven.

THE MORTICIAN'S TWELVE-YEAR-OLD SON

Lady, when you were alive
I'd see you on the streets,
the long green dress with the velvet flower
sewn dead center between your breasts
so tightly I could never get a look inside.

Now the gas lamps half-light the table,
washing the sheet that covers you with shadows.
A few strands of your dyed red hair
hang nearly to the floor,
as if all your blood had run there to hide.

I lift the sheet, rub the mole on your cheek
and it comes off black and oily on my hand.
I bend over your breasts and sing,
love, sister, is just a kiss away.——→ naïveté, not
I cover each nipple with my mouth.   taking it
Tonight, just a kiss away.   literally

TWENTY-YEAR MARRIAGE

You keep me waiting in a truck
with its one good wheel stuck in the ditch,
while you piss against the south side of a tree.
Hurry. I've got nothing on under my skirt tonight.
That still excites you, but this pickup has no windows
and the seat, one fake leather thigh,
pressed close to mine is cold.
I'm the same size, shape, make as twenty years ago,
but get inside me, start the engine;
you'll have the strength, the will to move.
I'll pull, you push, we'll tear each other in half.
Come on, baby, lay me down on my back.

AI

Pretend you don't owe me a thing
and maybe we'll roll out of here,
leaving the past stacked up behind us;
old newspapers nobody's ever got to read again.

WHY CAN'T I LEAVE YOU?

You stand behind the old black mare,
dressed as always in that red shirt,
stained from sweat, the crying of the armpits,
that will not stop for anything,
stroking her rump, while the barley goes unplanted.
I pick up my suitcase and set it down,
as I try to leave you again.
I smooth the hair back from your forehead.
I think with your laziness and the drought too,
you'll be needing my help more than ever.
You take my hands, I nod
and go to the house to unpack,
having found another reason to stay.

I undress, then put on my white lace slip
for you to take off, because you like that
and when you come in, you pull down the straps
and I unbutton your shirt.
I know we can't give each other any more
or any less than what we have.
There is safety in that, so much
that I can never get past the packing,
the begging you to please, if I can't make you happy,
come close between my thighs
and let me laugh for you from my second mouth.

I HAVE GOT TO STOP LOVING YOU
SO I HAVE KILLED MY BLACK GOAT

His kidney floats in a bowl,
a beige, flat fish, around whom parasites, slices of lemon,
break through the surface of hot broth, then sink below,

as I bend, face down in the steam, breathing in.
I hear this will cure anything.

When I am finished, I walk up to him.
He hangs from a short wooden post,
tongue stuck out of his mouth,
tasting the hay-flavored air.
A bib of flies gather at his throat
and further down, where he is open
and bare of all his organs,
I put my hand in, stroke him once,
then taking it out, look at the sky.
The stormclouds there break open
and raindrops, yellow as black cats' eyes, come down
each a tiny river, hateful and alone.

Wishing I could get out of this alive, I hug myself.
It is hard to remember if he suffered much.

FINISHED

You force me to touch
the black, rubber flaps
of the garbage disposal
that is open like a mouth saying, ah.
You tell me it's the last thing I'll feel
before I go numb.
Is it my screaming that finally stops you,
or is it the fear
that even you are too near the edge
of this Niagara to come back from?
You jerk my hand out
and give me just enough room
to stagger around you.
I lean against the refrigerator,
not looking at you, or anything,
just staring at a space which you no longer inhabit,
that you've abandoned completely now
to footsteps receding
to the next feeding station,
where a woman will be eaten alive

after cocktails at five.
The flowers and chocolates, the kisses,
the swings and near misses of new love
will confuse her,
until you start to abuse her,
verbally at first.
As if trying to quench a thirst,
you'll drink her
in small outbursts of rage
then you'll whip out your semiautomatic,
make her undress, or listen to hours
of radio static as torture
for being amazed that the man of her dreams
is a nightmare, who only seems happy
when he's making her suffer.

The first time you hit me,
I left you, remember?
It was December. An icy rain was falling
and it froze on the roads,
so that driving was unsafe, but not as unsafe
as staying with you.
I ran outside in my nightgown,
while you yelled at me to come back.
When you came after me,
I was locked in the car.
You smashed the window with a crowbar,
but I drove off anyway.
I was back the next day
and we were on the bare mattress,
because you'd ripped up the sheets,
saying you'd teach me a lesson.
You wouldn't speak except
to tell me I needed discipline,
needed training in the fine art
of remaining still
when your fist slammed into my jaw.
You taught me how ropes could be tied
so I'd strangle myself,
how pressure could be applied to old wounds
until I cried for mercy,
until tonight, when those years
of our double exposure end
with shot after shot.

How strange it is to be unafraid.
When the police come,
I'm sitting at the table,
the cup of coffee
that I am unable to drink
as cold as your body.
I shot him, I say, he beat me.
I do not tell them how the emancipation from pain
leaves nothing in its place.

RIOT ACT, APRIL 29, 1992

I'm going out and get something.
I don't know what.
I don't care.
Whatever's out there, I'm going to get it.
Look in those shop windows at boxes
and boxes of Reeboks and Nikes
to make me fly through the air
like Michael Jordan
like Magic.
While I'm up there, I see Spike Lee.
Looks like he's flying too
straight through the glass
that separates me
from the virtual reality
I watch everyday on TV.
I know the difference between
what it is and what it isn't.
Just because I can't touch it
doesn't mean it isn't real.
All I have to do is smash the screen,
reach in and take what I want.
Break out of prison.
South Central homey's newly risen
from the night of living dead,
but this time he lives,
he gets to give the zombies
a taste of their own medicine.
Open wide and let me in,
or else I'll set your world on fire,

but you pretend that you don't hear.
You haven't heard the word is coming down
like the hammer of the gun
of this black son, locked out of the big house,
while massa looks out the window and sees only smoke.
Massa doesn't see anything else,
not because he can't,
but because he won't.
He'd rather hear me talking about mo' money,
mo' honeys and gold chains
and see me carrying my favorite things
from looted stores
than admit that underneath my Raiders' cap,
the aftermath is staring back
unblinking through the camera's lens,
courtesy of CNN,
my arms loaded with boxes of shoes
that I will sell at the swap meet
to make a few cents on the declining dollar.
And if I destroy myself
and my neighborhood
"ain't nobody's business, if I do,"
but the police are knocking hard
at my door
and before I can open it,
they break it down
and drag me in the yard.
They take me in to be processed and charged,
to await trial,
while Americans forget
the day the wealth finally trickled down
to the rest of us.

John Ashbery

SELF-PORTRAIT IN A CONVEX MIRROR

As Parmigianino did it, the right hand
Bigger than the head, thrust at the viewer
And swerving easily away, as though to protect
What it advertises. A few leaded panes, old beams,
Fur, pleated muslin, a coral ring run together
In a movement supporting the face, which swims
Toward and away like the hand
Except that it is in repose. It is what is
Sequestered. Vasari says, "Francesco one day set himself
To take his own portrait, looking at himself for that purpose
In a convex mirror, such as is used by barbers . . .
He accordingly caused a ball of wood to be made
By a turner, and having divided it in half and
Brought it to the size of the mirror, he set himself
With great art to copy all that he saw in the glass,"
Chiefly his reflection, of which the portrait
Is the reflection once removed.
The glass chose to reflect only what he saw
Which was enough for his purpose: his image
Glazed, embalmed, projected at a 180-degree angle.
The time of day or the density of the light
Adhering to the face keeps it
Lively and intact in a recurring wave
Of arrival. The soul establishes itself.
But how far can it swim out through the eyes
And still return safely to its nest? The surface
Of the mirror being convex, the distance increases
Significantly; that is, enough to make the point
That the soul is a captive, treated humanely, kept
In suspension, unable to advance much farther
Than your look as it intercepts the picture.
Pope Clement and his court were "stupefied"
By it, according to Vasari, and promised a commission
That never materialized. The soul has to stay where it is,
Even though restless, hearing raindrops at the pane,
The sighing of autumn leaves thrashed by the wind,
Longing to be free, outside, but it must stay
Posing in this place. It must move

11

As little as possible. This is what the portrait says.
But there is in that gaze a combination
Of tenderness, amusement and regret, so powerful
In its restraint that one cannot look for long.
The secret is too plain. The pity of it smarts,
Makes hot tears spurt: that the soul is not a soul,
Has no secret, is small, and it fits
Its hollow perfectly: its room, our moment of attention.
That is the tune but there are no words.
The words are only speculation
(From the Latin *speculum*, mirror):
They seek and cannot find the meaning of the music.
We see only postures of the dream,
Riders of the motion that swings the face
Into view under evening skies, with no
False disarray as proof of authenticity.
But it is life englobed.
One would like to stick one's hand
Out of the globe, but its dimension,
What carries it, will not allow it.
No doubt it is this, not the reflex
To hide something, which makes the hand loom large
As it retreats slightly. There is no way
To build it flat like a section of wall:
It must join the segment of a circle,
Roving back to the body of which it seems
So unlikely a part, to fence in and shore up the face
On which the effort of this condition reads
Like a pinpoint of a smile, a spark
Or star one is not sure of having seen
As darkness resumes. A perverse light whose
Imperative of subtlety dooms in advance its
Conceit to light up: unimportant but meant.
Francesco, your hand is big enough
To wreck the sphere, and too big,
One would think, to weave delicate meshes
That only argue its further detention.
(Big, but not coarse, merely on another scale,
Like a dozing whale on the sea bottom
In relation to the tiny, self-important ship
On the surface.) But your eyes proclaim
That everything is surface. The surface is what's there
And nothing can exist except what's there.
There are no recesses in the room, only alcoves,

And the window doesn't matter much, or that
Sliver of window or mirror on the right, even
As a gauge of the weather, which in French is
Le temps, the word for time, and which
Follows a course wherein changes are merely
Features of the whole. The whole is stable within
Instability, a globe like ours, resting
On a pedestal of vacuum, a ping-pong ball
Secure on its jet of water.
And just as there are no words for the surface, that is,
No words to say what it really is, that it is not
Superficial but a visible core, then there is
No way out of the problem of pathos vs. experience.
You will stay on, restive, serene in
Your gesture which is neither embrace nor warning
But which holds something of both in pure
Affirmation that doesn't affirm anything.

The balloon pops, the attention
Turns dully away. Clouds
In the puddle stir up into sawtoothed fragments.
I think of the friends
Who came to see me, of what yesterday
Was like. A peculiar slant
Of memory that intrudes on the dreaming model
In the silence of the studio as he considers
Lifting the pencil to the self-portrait.
How many people came and stayed a certain time,
Uttered light or dark speech that became part of you
Like light behind windblown fog and sand,
Filtered and influenced by it, until no part
Remains that is surely you. Those voices in the dusk
Have told you all and still the tale goes on
In the form of memories deposited in irregular
Clumps of crystals. Whose curved hand controls,
Francesco, the turning seasons and the thoughts
That peel off and fly away at breathless speeds
Like the last stubborn leaves ripped
From wet branches? I see in this only the chaos
Of your round mirror which organizes everything
Around the polestar of your eyes which are empty,
Know nothing, dream but reveal nothing.
I feel the carousel starting slowly
And going faster and faster: desk, papers, books,

Photographs of friends, the window and the trees
Merging in one neutral band that surrounds
Me on all sides, everywhere I look.
And I cannot explain the action of leveling,
Why it should all boil down to one
Uniform substance, a magma of interiors.
My guide in these matters is your self,
Firm, oblique, accepting everything with the same
Wraith of a smile, and as time speeds up so that it is soon
Much later, I can know only the straight way out,
The distance between us. Long ago
The strewn evidence meant something,
The small accidents and pleasures
Of the day as it moved gracelessly on,
A housewife doing chores. Impossible now
To restore those properties in the silver blur that is
The record of what you accomplished by sitting down
"With great art to copy all that you saw in the glass"
So as to perfect and rule out the extraneous
Forever. In the circle of your intentions certain spars
Remain that perpetuate the enchantment of self with self:
Eyebeams, muslin, coral. It doesn't matter
Because these are things as they are today
Before one's shadow ever grew
Out of the field into thoughts of tomorrow.

Tomorrow is easy, but today is uncharted,
Desolate, reluctant as any landscape
To yield what are laws of perspective
After all only to the painter's deep
Mistrust, a weak instrument though
Necessary. Of course some things
Are possible, it knows, but it doesn't know
Which ones. Some day we will try
To do as many things as are possible
And perhaps we shall succeed at a handful
Of them, but this will not have anything
To do with what is promised today, our
Landscape sweeping out from us to disappear
On the horizon. Today enough of a cover burnishes
To keep the supposition of promises together
In one piece of surface, letting one ramble
Back home from them so that these
Even stronger possibilities can remain

Whole without being tested. Actually
The skin of the bubble-chamber's as tough as
Reptile eggs; everything gets "programmed" there
In due course: more keeps getting included
Without adding to the sum, and just as one
Gets accustomed to a noise that
Kept one awake but now no longer does,
So the room contains this flow like an hourglass
Without varying in climate or quality
(Except perhaps to brighten bleakly and almost
Invisibly, in a focus sharpening toward death — more
Of this later). What should be the vacuum of a dream
Becomes continually replete as the source of dreams
Is being tapped so that this one dream
May wax, flourish like a cabbage rose,
Defying sumptuary laws, leaving us
To awake and try to begin living in what
Has now become a slum. Sydney Freedberg in his
Parmigianino says of it: "Realism in this portrait
No longer produces an objective truth, but a *bizarria.* . . .
However its distortion does not create
A feeling of disharmony. . . . The forms retain
A strong measure of ideal beauty," because
Fed by our dreams, so inconsequential until one day
We notice the hole they left. Now their importance
If not their meaning is plain. They were to nourish
A dream which includes them all, as they are
Finally reversed in the accumulating mirror.
They seemed strange because we couldn't actually see them.
And we realize this only at a point where they lapse
Like a wave breaking on a rock, giving up
Its shape in a gesture which expresses that shape.
The forms retain a strong measure of ideal beauty
As they forage in secret on our idea of distortion.
Why be unhappy with this arrangement, since
Dreams prolong us as they are absorbed?
Something like living occurs, a movement
Out of the dream into its codification.

As I start to forget it
It presents its stereotype again
But it is an unfamiliar stereotype, the face
Riding at anchor, issued from hazards, soon
To accost others, "rather angel than man" (Vasari).

Perhaps an angel looks like everything
We have forgotten, I mean forgotten
Things that don't seem familiar when
We meet them again, lost beyond telling,
Which were ours once. This would be the point
Of invading the privacy of this man who
"Dabbled in alchemy, but whose wish
Here was not to examine the subtleties of art
In a detached, scientific spirit: he wished through them
To impart the sense of novelty and amazement to the spectator"
(Freedberg). Later portraits such as the Uffizi
"Gentleman," the Borghese "Young Prelate" and
The Naples "Antea" issue from Mannerist
Tensions, but here, as Freedberg points out,
The surprise, the tension are in the concept
Rather than its realization.
The consonance of the High Renaissance
Is present, though distorted by the mirror.
What is novel is the extreme care in rendering
The velleities of the rounded reflecting surface
(It is the first mirror portrait),
So that you could be fooled for a moment
Before you realize the reflection
Isn't yours. You feel then like one of those
Hoffmann characters who have been deprived
Of a reflection, except that the whole of me
Is seen to be supplanted by the strict
Otherness of the painter in his
Other room. We have surprised him
At work, but no, he has surprised us
As he works. The picture is almost finished,
The surprise almost over, as when one looks out,
Startled by a snowfall which even now is
Ending in specks and sparkles of snow.
It happened while you were inside, asleep,
And there is no reason why you should have
Been awake for it, except that the day
Is ending and it will be hard for you
To get to sleep tonight, at least until late.

The shadow of the city injects its own
Urgency: Rome where Francesco
Was at work during the Sack: his inventions
Amazed the soldiers who burst in on him;

They decided to spare his life, but he left soon after;
Vienna where the painting is today, where
I saw it with Pierre in the summer of 1959; New York
Where I am now, which is a logarithm
Of other cities. Our landscape
Is alive with filiations, shuttlings;
Business is carried on by look, gesture,
Hearsay. It is another life to the city,
The backing of the looking glass of the
Unidentified but precisely sketched studio. It wants
To siphon off the life of the studio, deflate
Its mapped space to enactments, island it.
That operation has been temporarily stalled
But something new is on the way, a new preciosity
In the wind. Can you stand it,
Francesco? Are you strong enough for it?
This wind brings what it knows not, is
Self-propelled, blind, has no notion
Of itself. It is inertia that once
Acknowledged saps all activity, secret or public:
Whispers of the word that can't be understood
But can be felt, a chill, a blight
Moving outward along the capes and peninsulas
Of your nervures and so to the archipelagoes
And to the bathed, aired secrecy of the open sea.
This is its negative side. Its positive side is
Making you notice life and the stresses
That only seemed to go away, but now,
As this new mode questions, are seen to be
Hastening out of style. If they are to become classics
They must decide which side they are on.
Their reticence has undermined
The urban scenery, made its ambiguities
Look willful and tired, the games of an old man.
What we need now is this unlikely
Challenger pounding on the gates of an amazed
Castle. Your argument, Francesco,
Had begun to grow stale as no answer
Or answers were forthcoming. If it dissolves now
Into dust, that only means its time had come
Some time ago, but look now, and listen:
It may be that another life is stocked there
In recesses no one knew of; that it,
Not we, are the change; that we are in fact it

If we could get back to it, relive some of the way
It looked, turn our faces to the globe as it sets
And still be coming out all right:
Nerves normal, breath normal. Since it is a metaphor
Made to include us, we are a part of it and
Can live in it as in fact we have done,
Only leaving our minds bare for questioning
We now see will not take place at random
But in an orderly way that means to menace
Nobody — the normal way things are done,
Like the concentric growing up of days
Around a life: correctly, if you think about it.

A breeze like the turning of a page
Brings back your face: the moment
Takes such a big bite out of the haze
Of pleasant intuition it comes after.
The locking into place is "death itself,"
As Berg said of a phrase in Mahler's Ninth;
Or, to quote Imogen in *Cymbeline*, "There cannot
Be a pinch in death more sharp than this," for,
Though only exercise or tactic, it carries
The momentum of a conviction that had been building.
Mere forgetfulness cannot remove it
Nor wishing bring it back, as long as it remains
The white precipitate of its dream
In the climate of sighs flung across our world,
A cloth over a birdcage. But it is certain that
What is beautiful seems so only in relation to a specific
Life, experienced or not, channeled into some form
Steeped in the nostalgia of a collective past.
The light sinks today with an enthusiasm
I have known elsewhere, and known why
It seemed meaningful, that others felt this way
Years ago. I go on consulting
This mirror that is no longer mine
For as much brisk vacancy as is to be
My portion this time. And the vase is always full
Because there is only just so much room
And it accommodates everything. The sample
One sees is not to be taken as
Merely that, but as everything as it
May be imagined outside time — not as a gesture
But as all, in the refined, assimilable state.

JOHN ASHBERY

But what is this universe the porch of
As it veers in and out, back and forth,
Refusing to surround us and still the only
Thing we can see? Love once
Tipped the scales but now is shadowed, invisible,
Though mysteriously present, around somewhere.
But we know it cannot be sandwiched
Between two adjacent moments, that its windings
Lead nowhere except to further tributaries
And that these empty themselves into a vague
Sense of something that can never be known
Even though it seems likely that each of us
Knows what it is and is capable of
Communicating it to the other. But the look
Some wear as a sign makes one want to
Push forward ignoring the apparent
Naïveté of the attempt, not caring
That no one is listening, since the light
Has been lit once and for all in their eyes
And is present, unimpaired, a permanent anomaly,
Awake and silent. On the surface of it
There seems no special reason why that light
Should be focused by love, or why
The city falling with its beautiful suburbs
Into space always less clear, less defined,
Should read as the support of its progress,
The easel upon which the drama unfolded
To its own satisfaction and to the end
Of our dreaming, as we had never imagined
It would end, in worn daylight with the painted
Promise showing through as a gage, a bond.
This nondescript, never-to-be defined daytime is
The secret of where it takes place
And we can no longer return to the various
Conflicting statements gathered, lapses of memory
Of the principal witnesses. All we know
Is that we are a little early, that
Today has that special, lapidary
Todayness that the sunlight reproduces
Faithfully in casting twig-shadows on blithe
Sidewalks. No previous day would have been like this.
I used to think they were all alike,
That the present always looked the same to everybody
But this confusion drains away as one

Is always cresting into one's present.
Yet the "poetic," straw-colored space
Of the long corridor that leads back to the painting,
Its darkening opposite — is this
Some figment of "art," not to be imagined
As real, let alone special? Hasn't it too its lair
In the present we are always escaping from
And falling back into, as the waterwheel of days
Pursues its uneventful, even serene course?
I think it is trying to say it is today
And we must get out of it even as the public
Is pushing through the museum now so as to
Be out by closing time. You can't live there.
The gray glaze of the past attacks all know-how:
Secrets of wash and finish that took a lifetime
To learn and are reduced to the status of
Black-and-white illustrations in a book where colorplates
Are rare. That is, all time
Reduces to no special time. No one
Alludes to the change; to do so might
Involve calling attention to oneself
Which would augment the dread of not getting out
Before having seen the whole collection
(Except for the sculptures in the basement:
They are where they belong).
Our time gets to be veiled, compromised
By the portrait's will to endure. It hints at
Our own, which we were hoping to keep hidden.
We don't need paintings or
Doggerel written by mature poets when
The explosion is so precise, so fine.
Is there any point even in acknowledging
The existence of all that? Does it
Exist? Certainly the leisure to
Indulge stately pastimes doesn't,
Any more. Today has no margins, the event arrives
Flush with its edges, is of the same substance,
Indistinguishable. "Play" is something else;
It exists, in a society specifically
Organized as a demonstration of itself.
There is no other way, and those assholes
Who would confuse everything with their mirror games
Which seem to multiply stakes and possibilities, or
At least confuse issues by means of an investing

JOHN ASHBERY

Aura that would corrode the architecture
Of the whole in a haze of suppressed mockery,
Are beside the point. They are out of the game,
Which doesn't exist until they are out of it.
It seems like a very hostile universe
But as the principle of each individual thing is
Hostile to, exists at the expense of all the others
As philosophers have often pointed out, at least
This thing, the mute, undivided present,
Has the justification of logic, which
In this instance isn't a bad thing
Or wouldn't be, if the way of telling
Didn't somehow intrude, twisting the end result
Into a caricature of itself. This always
Happens, as in the game where
A whispered phrase passed around the room
Ends up as something completely different.
It is the principle that makes works of art so unlike
What the artist intended. Often he finds
He has omitted the thing he started out to say
In the first place. Seduced by flowers,
Explicit pleasures, he blames himself (though
Secretly satisfied with the result), imagining
He had a say in the matter and exercised
An option of which he was hardly conscious,
Unaware that necessity circumvents such resolutions.
So as to create something new
For itself, that there is no other way,
That the history of creation proceeds according to
Stringent laws, and that things
Do get done in this way, but never the things
We set out to accomplish and wanted so desperately
To see come into being. Parmigianino
Must have realized this as he worked at his
Life-obstructing task. One is forced to read
The perfectly plausible accomplishment of a purpose
Into the smooth, perhaps even bland (but so
Enigmatic) finish. Is there anything
To be serious about beyond this otherness
That gets included in the most ordinary
Forms of daily activity, changing everything
Slightly and profoundly, and tearing the matter
Of creation, any creation, not just artistic creation
Out of our hands, to install it on some monstrous, near

Peak, too close to ignore, too far
For one to intervene? This otherness, this
"Not-being-us" is all there is to look at
In the mirror, though no one can say
How it came to be this way. A ship
Flying unknown colors has entered the harbor.
You are allowing extraneous matters
To break up your day, cloud the focus
Of the crystal ball. Its scene drifts away
Like vapor scattered on the wind. The fertile
Thought-associations that until now came
So easily, appear no more, or rarely. Their
Colorings are less intense, washed out
By autumn rains and winds, spoiled, muddied,
Given back to you because they are worthless.
Yet we are such creatures of habit that their
Implications are still around *en permanence*, confusing
Issues. To be serious only about sex
Is perhaps one way, but the sands are hissing
As they approach the beginning of the big slide
Into what happened. This past
Is now here: the painter's
Reflected face, in which we linger, receiving
Dreams and inspirations on an unassigned
Frequency, but the hues have turned metallic,
The curves and edges are not so rich. Each person
Has one big theory to explain the universe
But it doesn't tell the whole story
And in the end it is what is outside him
That matters, to him and especially to us
Who have been given no help whatever
In decoding our own man-size quotient and must rely
On second-hand knowledge. Yet I know
That no one else's taste is going to be
Any help, and might as well be ignored.
Once it seemed so perfect — gloss on the fine
Freckled skin, lips moistened as though about to part
Releasing speech, and the familiar look
Of clothes and furniture that one forgets.
This could have been our paradise: exotic
Refuge within an exhausted world, but that wasn't
In the cards, because it couldn't have been
The point. Aping naturalness may be the first step
Toward achieving an inner calm

JOHN ASHBERY

But it is the first step only, and often
Remains a frozen gesture of welcome etched
On the air materializing behind it,
A convention. And we have really
No time for these, except to use them
For kindling. The sooner they are burnt up
The better for the roles we have to play.
Therefore I beseech you, withdraw that hand,
Offer it no longer as shield or greeting,
The shield of a greeting, Francesco:
There is room for one bullet in the chamber:
Our looking through the wrong end
Of the telescope as you fall back at a speed
Faster than that of light to flatten ultimately
Among the features of the room, an invitation
Never mailed, the "it was all a dream"
Syndrome, though the "all" tells tersely
Enough how it wasn't. Its existence
Was real, though troubled, and the ache
Of this waking dream can never drown out
The diagram still sketched on the wind,
Chosen, meant for me and materialized
In the disguising radiance of my room.
We have seen the city; it is the gibbous
Mirrored eye of an insect. All things happen
On its balcony and are resumed within,
But the action is the cold, syrupy flow
Of a pageant. One feels too confined,
Sifting the April sunlight for clues,
In the mere stillness of the ease of its
Parameter. The hand holds no chalk
And each part of the whole falls off
And cannot know it knew, except
Here and there, in cold pockets
Of remembrance, whispers out of time.

by Ken Robbins

Marvin Bell

THE SELF AND THE MULBERRY

I wanted to see the self, so I looked at the mulberry.
It had no trouble accepting its limits,
yet defining and redefining a small area
so that any shape was possible, any movement.
It stayed put, but was part of all the air.
I wanted to learn to be there and not there
like the continually changing, slightly moving
mulberry, wild cherry and particularly the willow.
Like the willow, I tried to weep without tears.
Like the cherry tree, I tried to be sturdy and productive.
Like the mulberry, I tried to keep moving.
I couldn't cry right, couldn't stay or go.
I kept losing parts of myself like a soft maple.
I fell ill like the elm. That was the end
of looking in nature to find a natural self.
Let nature think itself not manly enough!
Let nature wonder at the mystery of laughter.
Let nature hypothesize man's indifference to it.
Let nature take a turn at saying what love is!

TO DOROTHY

You are not beautiful, exactly.
You are beautiful, inexactly.
You let a weed grow by the mulberry
and a mulberry grow by the house.
So close, in the personal quiet
of a windy night, it brushes the wall
and sweeps away the day till we sleep.

A child said it, and it seemed true:
"Things that are lost are all equal."
But it isn't true. If I lost you,
the air wouldn't move, nor the tree grow.
Someone would pull the weed, my flower.
The quiet wouldn't be yours. If I lost you,
I'd have to ask the grass to let me sleep.

MARVIN BELL

THE MYSTERY OF EMILY DICKINSON

Sometimes the weather goes on for days
but you were different. You were divine.
While the others wrote more and longer,
you wrote much more and much shorter.
I held your white dress once: 12 buttons.
In the cupola, the wasps struck glass
as hard to escape as you hit your sound
again and again asking Welcome. No one.

Except for you, it were a trifle:
This morning, not much after dawn,
in level country, not New England's,
through leftovers of summer rain I
went out rag-tag to the curb, only
a sleepy householder at his routine
bending to trash, when a young girl
in a white dress your size passed,

so softly!, carrying her shoes. It must be
she surprised me — her barefoot quick-step
and the earliness of the hour, your dress —
or surely I'd have spoken of it sooner.
I should have called to her, but a neighbor
wore that look you see against happiness.
I won't say anything would have happened
unless there was time, and eternity's plenty.

TO AN ADOLESCENT WEEPING WILLOW

I don't know what you think you're doing,
sweeping the ground. You
do it so easily, backhanded, forehanded.
You hardly bend. Really, you sway.
What can it mean
when a thing is so easy?

I threw dirt on my father's floor.
Not dirt, but a chopped green
dirt which picked up dirt.

MARVIN BELL

I pushed the pushbroom.
I oiled the wooden floor of the store.

He bent over and lifted the coal
into the coalstove. With the back of the shovel
he came down on the rat just topping the bin
and into the fire.

What do you think? — Did he sway?
Did he kiss a rock for luck?
Did he soak up water
and climb into light and turn and turn?

Did he weep and weep in the yard?

Yes, I think he did. Yes,
now I think he did.

So Willow, you come sweep my floor.
I have no store.
I have a yard. A big yard.

I have a song to weep.
I have a cry.

You who rose up from the dirt,
because I put you there
and like to walk my head in under
your earliest feathery branches —
what can it mean
when a thing is so easy?

It means you are a boy.

WHITE CLOVER

Once when the moon was out about three-quarters
and the fireflies who are the stars
of backyards
were out about three-quarters
and about three-fourths of all the lights
in the neighborhood

were on because people can be at home,
I took a not so innocent walk
out among the lawns,
navigating by the light of lights,
and there there were many hundreds of moons
on the lawns
where before there was only polite grass.
These were moons on long stems,
their long stems giving their greenness
to the center of each flower
and the light giving its whiteness to the tops
of the petals. I could say
it was light from stars
touched the tops of flowers and no doubt
something heavenly reaches what grows outdoors
and the heads of men who go hatless,
but I like to think we have a world
right here, and a life
that isn't death. So I don't say it's better
to be right here. I say this is where
many hundreds of core-green moons
gigantic to my eye
rose because men and women had sown green grass,
and flowered to my eye in man-made light,
and to some would be as fire in the body
and to others a light in the mind
over all their property.

DRAWN BY STONES, BY EARTH, BY THINGS
THAT HAVE BEEN IN THE FIRE

I can tell you about this because I have held in my hand
the little potter's sponge called an "elephant ear."
Naturally, it's only a tiny version of an ear,
but it's the thing you want to pick up out of the toolbox
when you wander into the deserted ceramics shop
down the street from the cave where the fortune-teller works.
Drawn by stones, by earth, by things that have been in the fire.

The elephant ear listens to the side of the vase
as it is pulled upwards from a dome of muddy clay.

The ear listens to the outside wall of the pot
and the hand listens to the inside wall of the pot,
and between them a city rises out of dirt and water.
Inside this city live the remains of animals,
animals who prepared for two hundred years to be clay.

Rodents make clay, and men wearing spectacles make clay,
though the papers they were signing go up in flames
and nothing more is known of these long documents
except by those angels who divine in our ashes.
Kings and queens of the jungle make clay
and royalty and politicians make clay although
their innocence stays with their clothes until unravelled.

There is a lost soldier in every ceramic bowl.
The face on the dinner plate breaks when the dish does
and lies for centuries unassembled in the soil.
These things that have the right substance to begin with,
put into the fire at temperatures that melt glass,
keep their fingerprints forever, it is said,
like inky sponges that walk away in the deep water.

SEVENS (VERSION 3):
IN THE CLOSED IRIS OF CREATION

A pair of heavy scissors lay across the sky
waiting for an affirmation,
waiting for the go-ahead of tragic love.
The sky, as always, was full of sobbing clouds
ready to rain down heavily on desire
wherever a hand opens or a leg stretches out
and life waits to begin —
the way everything, even scissors, waits to begin.
We who began in water, in clay,
in the ancient diggings of the word,
whitened by the chalk of dreams,
bloom in colors (everyone has noticed!)
blind toward scissors and clouds.
Within the sight of a pail of water,
our mothers pushed us away
for the good of our souls

MARVIN BELL

into a world where the sun had burned a hole
in the name of love.
Sleep in the sewers
descends, bringing an inner life
utterly at peace behind an in-turning iris —
crawling, pre-cadaverous, fetal.
To choose between knowing the truth
or, on the other hand, orgasm and repose,
always with the patience of a cricket on guard
in case Spring should arrive in disguise,
hiding its muscular body under rags,
its footsteps muffled by the mating of vines —
to choose at all, we have to crawl
on bare knees down alleys of pumice
and plead among the red columns of silos,
in the dust of exploding grains,
with shaking hands and trembling lips
plead for a severing of knives.
If now in the blackest hole we sometimes dance
like an orphan among loaves of black bread,
and lift plain water to our lips to toast
our good luck, and if in a thicket of almonds
with a smell of oil before it turns
to bitter wine,
we laugh so hard we lose our bodies momentarily,
we are also, at the same time, absorbing
the shivering of all cities
born of this baked earth, this chaste diamond
that flowered, reluctantly, absurdly,
into an eternity of ice
and descended through the decorations of the frost
to be shipwrecked in space.
And so each morning I throw a little chalk into my coffee
in memory of the blood and bones of the universe,
and each morning I eat some sacramental bread
as a prayer
not to become one of the thieves
but to save and keep my life for whenever I may need it,
perhaps when things are going better,
when everything is or isn't sevens,
and the planet is in perpetual motion
giving regular birth to the spaces behind her.
I myself swear never to be surprised
when someone elects to stay in the womb.

MARVIN BELL

True silence existed only before there was life
and was eaten in the first rain of the universe,
beaten into piles of grain and no grain
in the first silo, in the first air,
without a place to put a foot down, without an us,
all in a hole
that held (aloft? upside down?) as if in an iris
the thin tracings of the first wax,
and of the first delicate amoebic embracings,
and of the shapes to come when love
began to sever us.

ARS POETICA AT THE WINDOW

The history of this moment lengthens in shadow.
Trying to see the past, the light from a lamp is sucked up.
Leaving one in a field of static with a little music in the background.
This isn't hard to fathom after midnight.
There are whole sections of the brain without road traffic.
Domains where the mind is but a knapsack.
One needed little things, toiletries and the like, in the countryside.
The swirling of the river should have told us.
That whatever tries to move in a straight line shall be forced aside.
Shall be bent at every turn, creating a continuous arc.
And so that arcing shall draw a spiral, as it must.
This is clear after midnight, when striving shrivels.
I crave an intimacy too private to speak of.
Truly, one must close one's eyes to see.
True today, true tomorrow, true in the posthumous present.

John Berryman

from *THE DREAM SONGS*

4

Filling her compact & delicious body
with chicken páprika, she glanced at me
twice.
Fainting with interest, I hungered back
and only the fact of her husband & four other people
kept me from springing on her

or falling at her little feet and crying
'You are the hottest one for years of night
Henry's dazed eyes
have enjoyed, Brilliance.' I advanced upon
(despairing) my spumoni. — Sir Bones: is stuffed,
de world, wif feeding girls.

— Black hair, complexion Latin, jewelled eyes
downcast . . . The slob beside her   feasts . . . What wonders is
she sitting on, over there?
The restaurant buzzes. She might as well be on Mars.
Where did it all go wrong? There ought to be a law against Henry.
— Mr. Bones: there is.

14

Life, friends, is boring. We must not say so.
After all, the sky flashes, the great sea yearns,
we ourselves flash and yearn,
and moreover my mother told me as a boy
(repeatingly) 'Ever to confess you're bored
means you have no

Inner Resources.' I conclude now I have no
inner resources, because I am heavy bored.
Peoples bore me,
literature bores me, especially great literature,

Henry bores me, with his plights & gripes
as bad as achilles,

who loves people and valiant art, which bores me.
And the tranquil hills, & gin, look like a drag
and somehow a dog
has taken itself & its tail considerably away
into mountains or sea or sky, leaving
behind: me, wag.

26

The glories of the world struck me, made me aria, once.
— What happen then, Mr Bones?
if be you cares to say.
— Henry. Henry became interested in women's bodies,
his loins were & were the   scene of stupendous
    achievement.
Stupor. Knees, dear. Pray.

All the knobs & softnesses of, my God,
the ducking & trouble it swarm on Henry,
at one time.
— What happen then, Mr Bones?
 you seems excited-like.
— Fell Henry back into   the original crime: art, rime

besides a sense of others, my God, my God,
and a jealousy for the honour (alive) of his country,
what can get more odd?
and discontent with the thriving gangs & pride.
— What happen then, Mr Bones?
— I had a most marvellous   piece of luck. I died.

29

There sat down, once, a thing on Henry's heart
só heavy, if he had a hundred years
& more, & weeping, sleepless, in all them time
Henry could not make good.

Starts again always in Henry's ears
the little cough somewhere, an odour, a chime.

And there is another thing he has in mind
like a grave Sienese face a thousand years
would fail to blur the still profiled reproach of. Ghastly,
with open eyes, he attends, blind.
All the bells say: too late. This is not for tears;
thinking.

But never did Henry, as he thought he did,
end anyone and hacks her body up
and hide the pieces, where they may be found.
He knows: he went over everyone, & nobody's missing.
Often he reckons, in the dawn, them up.
Nobody is ever missing.

47

APRIL FOOL'S DAY, OR, ST MARY OF EGYPT

— Thass a funny title, Mr Bones.
— When down she saw her feet, sweet fish, on the threshold,
she considered her fair shoulders
and all them hundreds who have held them, all
the more who to her mime thickened & maled
from the supple stage,

and seeing her feet, in a visit, side by side
paused on the sill of The Tomb, she shrank: 'No.
They are not worthy,
fondled by many' and rushed from The Crucified
back through her followers out of the city ho
across the suburbs, plucky

to dare my desert in her late daylight
of animals and sands. She fall prone.
Only wind whistled.
And forty-seven years went by like Einstein.
We celebrate her feast with our caps on,
whom God has not visited.

89

OP. POSTH. NO. 12

In a blue series towards his sleepy eyes
they slid like wonder, women tall & small,
of every shape & size,
in many languages to lisp 'We do'
to Henry almost waking. What is the night at all,
his closed eyes beckon you.

In the Marriage of the Dead, a new routine,
he gasped his crowded vows past lids shut tight
and a-many rings fumbled on.
His coffin like Grand Central to the brim
filled up & emptied with the lapse of light.
Which one will waken him?

O she must startle like a fallen gown,
content with speech like an old sacrament
in deaf ears lying down,
blazing through darkness till he feels the cold
& blindness of his hopeless tenement
while his black arms unfold.

91

OP. POSTH. NO. 14

Noises from underground made gibber some
others collected & dug Henry up
saying 'You *are* a sight.'
Chilly, he muttered for a double rum
waving the mikes away, putting a stop
to rumours, pushing his fright

off with the now accumulated taxes
accustomed in his way to solitude
and no bills.
Wives came forward, claiming a new Axis,

fearful for their insurance, though, now, glued
to disencumbered Henry's many ills.

A fortnight later, sense a single man
upon the trampled scene at 2 a.m.
insomnia-plagued, with a shovel
digging like mad, Lazarus with a plan
to get his own back, a plan, a stratagem
no newsman will unravel.

129

Thin as a sheet his mother came to him
during the screaming evenings after he did it,
touched F.J.'s dead hand.
The parlour was dark, he was the first pall-bearer in,
he gave himself a dare & then did it,
the thing was quite unplanned,

riots for Henry the unstructured dead,
his older playmate fouled, reaching for him
and never will he be free
from the older boy who died by the cottonwood
& now is to be planted, wise & slim,
as part of Henry's history.

Christ waits. That boy was good beyond his years,
he served at Mass like Henry, he never did
one extreme thing wrong
but tender his cold hand, latent with Henry's fears
to Henry's shocking touch, whereat he fled
and woke screaming, young & strong.

172

Your face broods from my table, Suicide.
Your force came on like a torrent toward the end
of agony and wrath.
You were christened in the beginning Sylvia Plath
and changed that name for Mrs Hughes and bred
and went on round the bend

till the oven seemed the proper place for you.
I brood upon your face, the geography of grief,
hooded, till I allow
again your resignation from us now
though the screams of orphaned children fix me anew.
Your torment here was brief,

long falls your exit all repeatingly,
a poor exemplum, one more suicide
to stack upon the others
till stricken Henry with his sisters & brothers
suddenly gone pauses to wonder why he
alone breasts the wronging tide.

366

Chilled in this Irish pub I wish my loves
well, well to strangers, well to all his friends,
seven or so in number,
I forgive my enemies, especially two,
races his heart, at so much magnanimity,
can it at all be true?

— Mr Bones, you on a trip outside yourself.
Has you seen a medicine man? You sound will-like,
a testament & such.
Is you going? — Oh, I suffer from a strike
& a strike & three balls: I stand up for much,
Wordsworth & that sort of thing.

The pitcher dreamed. He threw a hazy curve,
I took it in my stride & out I struck,
lonesome Henry.
These Songs are not meant to be understood, you understand.
They are only meant to terrify & comfort.
Lilac was found in his hand.

382

At Henry's bier let some thing fall out well:
enter there none who somewhat has to sell,
the music ancient & gradual,

the voices solemn but the grief subdued,
no hairy jokes but everybody's mood
subdued, subdued,

until the Dancer comes, in a short short dress
hair black & long & loose, dark dark glasses,
uptilted face,
pallor & strangeness, the music changes
to 'Give!' & 'Ow!' and how! the music changes,
she kicks a backward limb

on tiptoe, pirouettes, & she is free
to the knocking music, sails, dips, & suddenly
returns to the terrible gay
occasion hopeless & mad, she weaves, it's hell,
she flings to her head a leg, bobs, all is well,
she dances Henry away.

384

The marker slants, flowerless, day's almost done,
I stand above my father's grave with rage,
often, often before
I've made this awful pilgrimage to one
who cannot visit me, who tore his page
out: I come back for more,

I spit upon this dreadful banker's grave
who shot his heart out in a Florida dawn
O ho alas alas
When will indifference come, I moan & rave
I'd like to scrabble till I got right down
away down under the grass

and ax the casket open ha to see
just how he's taking it, which he sought so hard
we'll tear apart
the mouldering grave clothes ha & then Henry
will heft the ax once more, his final card,
and fell it on the start.

Elizabeth Bishop

THE FISH

I caught a tremendous fish
and held him beside the boat
half out of water, with my hook
fast in a corner of his mouth.
He didn't fight.
He hadn't fought at all.
He hung a grunting weight,
battered and venerable
and homely. Here and there
his brown skin hung in strips
like ancient wallpaper,
and its pattern of darker brown
was like wallpaper:
shapes like full-blown roses
stained and lost through age.
He was speckled with barnacles,
fine rosettes of lime,
and infested
with tiny white sea-lice,
and underneath two or three
rags of green weed hung down.
While his gills were breathing in
the terrible oxygen
— the frightening gills,
fresh and crisp with blood,
that can cut so badly —
I thought of the coarse white flesh
packed in like feathers,
the big bones and the little bones,
the dramatic reds and blacks
of his shiny entrails,
and the pink swim-bladder
like a big peony.
I looked into his eyes
which were far larger than mine
but shallower, and yellowed,
the irises backed and packed

41

with tarnished tinfoil
seen through the lenses
of old scratched isinglass.
They shifted a little, but not
to return my stare.
— It was more like the tipping
of an object toward the light.
I admired his sullen face,
the mechanism of his jaw,
and then I saw
that from his lower lip
— if you could call it a lip —
grim, wet, and weaponlike,
hung five old pieces of fish-line,
or four and a wire leader
with the swivel still attached,
with all their five big hooks
grown firmly in his mouth.
A green line, frayed at the end
where he broke it, two heavier lines,
and a fine black thread
still crimped from the strain and snap
when it broke and he got away.
Like medals with their ribbons
frayed and wavering,
a five-haired beard of wisdom
trailing from his aching jaw.
I stared and stared
and victory filled up
the little rented boat,
from the pool of bilge
where oil had spread a rainbow
around the rusted engine
to the bailer rusted orange,
the sun-cracked thwarts,
the oarlocks on their strings,
the gunnels — until everything
was rainbow, rainbow, rainbow!
And I let the fish go.

ELIZABETH BISHOP

AT THE FISHHOUSES

physical description of place

Although it is a cold evening,
down by one of the fishhouses
an old man sits netting,
his net, in the gloaming almost invisible,
a dark purple-brown,
and his shuttle worn and polished.
The air smells so strong of codfish
it makes one's nose run and one's eyes water.
The five fishhouses have steeply peaked roofs
and narrow, cleated gangplanks slant up
to storerooms in the gables
for the wheelbarrows to be pushed up and down on.
All is silver: the heavy surface of the sea,
swelling slowly as if considering spilling over,
is opaque, but the silver of the benches,
the lobster pots, and masts, scattered
among the wild jagged rocks,
is of an apparent translucence
like the small old buildings with an emerald moss
growing on their shoreward walls.
The big fish tubs are completely lined
with layers of beautiful herring scales
and the wheelbarrows are similarly plastered
with creamy iridescent coats of mail,
with small iridescent flies crawling on them.
Up on the little slope behind the houses,
set in the sparse bright sprinkle of grass,
is an ancient wooden capstan,
cracked, with two long bleached handles
and some melancholy stains, like dried blood,
where the ironwork has rusted.
The old man accepts a Lucky Strike.
He was a friend of my grandfather.
We talk of the decline in the population
and of codfish and herring
while he waits for a herring boat to come in.
There are sequins on his vest and on his thumb.
He has scraped the scales, the principal beauty,
from unnumbered fish with that black old knife,
the blade of which is almost worn away. — *iambic pent.*

ELIZABETH BISHOP

Down at the water's edge, at the place
where they haul up the boats, up the long ramp
descending into the water, thin silver
tree trunks are laid horizontally
across the gray stones, down and down
at intervals of four or five feet.

Cold dark deep and absolutely clear,
element bearable to no mortal,
to fish and to seals . . . One seal particularly
I have seen here evening after evening.
He was curious about me. He was interested in music;
like me a believer in total immersion,
so I used to sing him Baptist hymns.
I also sang "A Mighty Fortress Is Our God."
He stood up in the water and regarded me
steadily, moving his head a little.
Then he would disappear, then suddenly emerge
almost in the same spot, with a sort of shrug
as if it were against his better judgment.
Cold dark deep and absolutely clear,
the clear gray icy water . . . Back, behind us,
the dignified tall firs begin.
Bluish, associating with their shadows,
a million Christmas trees stand
waiting for Christmas. The water seems suspended
above the rounded gray and blue-gray stones.
I have seen it over and over, the same sea, the same,
slightly, indifferently swinging above the stones,
icily free above the stones,
above the stones and then the world.
If you should dip your hand in,
your wrist would ache immediately,
your bones would begin to ache and your hand would burn
as if the water were a transmutation of fire
that feeds on stones and burns with a dark gray flame.
If you tasted it, it would first taste bitter,
then briny, then surely burn your tongue.
It is like what we imagine knowledge to be:
dark, salt, clear, moving, utterly free,
drawn from the cold hard mouth
of the world, derived from the rocky breasts
forever, flowing and drawn, and since
our knowledge is historical, flowing, and flown.

ELIZABETH BISHOP

IN THE WAITING ROOM

In Worcester, Massachusetts,
I went with Aunt Consuelo
to keep her dentist's appointment
and sat and waited for her
in the dentist's waiting room.
It was winter. It got dark
early. The waiting room
was full of grown-up people,
arctics and overcoats,
lamps and magazines.
My aunt was inside
what seemed like a long time
and while I waited I read
the *National Geographic*
(I could read) and carefully
studied the photographs:
the inside of a volcano,
black, and full of ashes;
then it was spilling over
in rivulets of fire.
Osa and Martin Johnson
dressed in riding breeches,
laced boots, and pith helmets.
A dead man slung on a pole
— "Long Pig," the caption said.
Babies with pointed heads
wound round and round with string;
black, naked women with necks
wound round and round with wire
like the necks of light bulbs.
Their breasts were horrifying.
I read it right straight through.
I was too shy to stop.
And then I looked at the cover:
the yellow margins, the date.

Suddenly, from inside,
came an *oh!* of pain
— Aunt Consuelo's voice —
not very loud or long,
I wasn't at all surprised;
even then I knew she was

ELIZABETH BISHOP

a foolish, timid woman.
I might have been embarrassed,
but wasn't. What took me
completely by surprise
was that it was *me*:
my voice, in my mouth.
Without thinking at all
I was my foolish aunt,
I — we — were falling, falling,
our eyes glued to the cover
of the *National Geographic*,
February, 1918.

I said to myself: three days
and you'll be seven years old.
I was saying it to stop
the sensation of falling off
the round, turning world
into cold, blue-black space.
But I felt: you are an *I*,
you are an *Elizabeth*,
you are one of *them*. ⟵ stranger, family member, woman
Why should you be one, too?
I scarcely dared to look
to see what it was I was.
I gave a sidelong glance
— I couldn't look any higher —
at shadowy gray knees,
trousers and skirts and boots
and different pairs of hands
lying under the lamps.
I knew that nothing stranger
had ever happened, that nothing
stranger could ever happen.
Why should I be my aunt,
or me, or anyone?
What similarities —
boots, hands, the family voice — *heredity*
I felt in my throat, or even
the *National Geographic*
and those awful hanging breasts —
held us all together
or made us all just one?
How — I didn't know any
word for it — how "unlikely" . . .

ELIZABETH BISHOP

in the waiting room,
in Worcester
or in the world?

How had I come to be here,
like them, and overhear
a cry of pain that could have
got loud and worse but hadn't?

The waiting room was bright
and too hot. It was sliding
beneath a big black wave,
another, and another.

Then I was back in it.   *time*
The War was on. Outside,
in Worcester, Massachusetts,
were night and slush and cold,
and it was still the fifth
of February, 1918.

ONE ART

villanelle
11-10-11

The art of losing isn't hard to master;
so many things seem filled with the intent
to be lost that their loss is no disaster.

Lose something every day. Accept the fluster
of lost door keys, the hour badly spent.
The art of losing isn't hard to master.

Then practice losing farther, losing faster:
places, and names, and where it was you meant
to travel. None of these will bring disaster.

I lost my mother's watch. And look! my last, or
next-to-last, of three loved houses went.
The art of losing isn't hard to master.

I lost two cities, lovely ones. And, vaster,
some realms I owned, two rivers, a continent.
I miss them, but it wasn't a disaster.

— Even losing you (the joking voice, a gesture   *12*
I love) I shan't have lied. It's evident   *10*
the art of losing's not too hard to master   *11*
though it may look like (*Write* it!) like disaster.   *11*

Robert Bly

AN EMPTY PLACE

The eyes are drawn to the dusty ground in fall —
pieces of crushed oyster shell
like doors into the earth made of mother-of-pearl,
slivers of glass,
a white chicken's feather that still seems excited by the warm blood,
and a corncob, all kernels gone, room after room in its endless palace . . .
this is the palace, the place of many mansions,
which Christ has gone to prepare for us.

SNOWBANKS NORTH OF THE HOUSE

Those great sweeps of snow that stop suddenly six feet from the house . . .
Thoughts that go so far.
The boy gets out of high school and reads no more books;
the son stops calling home.
The mother puts down her rolling pin and makes no more bread.
And the wife looks at her husband one night at a party and loves him no
    more.
The energy leaves the wine, and the minister falls leaving the church.
It will not come closer —
the one inside moves back, and the hands touch nothing, and are safe.

And the father grieves for his son, and will not leave the room where the
    coffin stands;
he turns away from his wife, and she sleeps alone.

And the sea lifts and falls all night; the moon goes on through the
    unattached heavens alone.
And the toe of the shoe pivots
in the dust. . . .
The man in the black coat turns, and goes back down the hill.
No one knows why he came, or why he turned away, and did not climb
    the hill.

ROBERT BLY

THE RESEMBLANCE BETWEEN YOUR LIFE AND A DOG

I never intended to have this life, believe me —
It just happened. You know how dogs turn up
At a farm, and they wag but can't explain.

It's good if you can accept your life — you'll notice
Your face has become deranged trying to adjust
To it. Your face thought your life would look

Like your bedroom mirror when you were ten.
That was a clear river touched by mountain wind.
Even your parents can't believe how much you've changed.

Sparrows in winter, if you've ever held one, all feathers,
Burst out of your hand with a fiery glee.
You see them later in hedges. Teachers praise you,

But you can't quite get back to the winter sparrow.
Your life is a dog. He's been hungry for miles,
Doesn't particularly like you, but gives up, and comes in.

WARNING TO THE READER

Sometimes farm granaries become especially beautiful when all the oats or wheat are gone, and wind has swept the rough floor clean. Standing inside, we see around us, coming in through the cracks between shrunken wall boards, bands or strips of sunlight. So in a poem about imprisonment, one sees a little light.

But how many birds have died trapped in these granaries. The bird, seeing the bands of light, flutters up the walls and falls back again and again. The way out is where the rats enter and leave; but the rat's hole is low to the floor. Writers, be careful then by showing the sunlight on the walls not to promise the anxious and panicky blackbirds a way out!

I say to the reader, beware. Readers who love poems of light may sit hunched in the corner with nothing in their gizzards for four days, light failing, the eyes glazed. . . . They may end as a mound of feathers and a skull on the open boardwood floor . . .

ROBERT BLY

SIX WINTER PRIVACY POEMS

I

About four, a few flakes.
I empty the teapot out in the snow,
Feeling shoots of joy in the new cold.
By nightfall, wind,
The curtains on the south sway softly.

II

My shack has two rooms; I use one.
The lamplight falls on my chair and table,
And I fly into one of my own poems —
I can't tell you where —
As if I appeared where I am now,
In a wet field, snow falling.

III

More of the fathers are dying each day.
It is time for the sons.
Bits of darkness are gathering around them.
The darkness appears as flakes of light.

IV *On Meditation*

There is a solitude like black mud!
Sitting in this darkness singing,
I can't tell if this joy
Is from the body, or the soul, or a third place!

V *Listening to Bach*

Inside this music there is someone
Who is not well described by the names
Of Jesus, or Jehovah, or the Lord of Hosts!

VI

When I woke, a new snow had fallen.
I am alone, yet someone else is with me,
Drinking coffee, looking out at the snow.

DRIVING TO TOWN LATE TO MAIL A LETTER

It is a cold and snowy night. The main street is deserted.
The only things moving are swirls of snow.
As I lift the mailbox door, I feel its cold iron.
There is a privacy I love in this snowy night.
Driving around, I will waste more time.

AFTER LONG BUSYNESS

I start out for a walk at last after weeks at the desk.
Moon gone, plowing underfoot, no stars; not a trace of light!
Suppose a horse were galloping toward me in this open field?
Every day I did not spend in solitude was wasted.

THE DEAD SEAL

1

Walking north toward the point, I come on a dead seal. From a few feet away, he looks like a brown log. The body is on its back, dead only a few hours. I stand and look at him. There's a quiver in the dead flesh: My God, he's still alive. And a shock goes through me, as if a wall of my room had fallen away.

His head is arched back, the small eyes closed; the whiskers sometimes rise and fall. He is dying. This is the oil. Here on its back is the oil that heats our houses so efficiently. Wind blows fine sand back toward the ocean. The flipper near me lies folded over the stomach, looking like an unfinished arm, lightly glazed with sand at the edges. The other flipper lies half underneath. And the seal's skin looks like an old overcoat, scratched here and there — by sharp mussel shells maybe.

I reach out and touch him. Suddenly he rears up, turns over. He gives three cries: Awaark! Awaark! Awaark! — like the cries from Christmas toys. He lunges toward me; I am terrified and leap back, though I know there can be no teeth in that jaw. He starts flopping toward the sea. But he falls over, on his face. He does not want to go back to the sea. He looks up at the sky, and he looks like an old lady who has lost her hair. He puts his chin back down on the sand, rearranges his flippers, and waits for me to go. I go.

2

The next day I go back to say goodbye. He's dead now. But he's not. He's a quarter mile farther up the shore. Today he is thinner, squatting on his stomach, head out. The ribs show more: each vertebra on the back under the coat is visible, shiny. He breathes in and out.

A wave comes in, touches his nose. He turns and looks at me — the eyes slanted; the crown of his head looks like a boy's leather jacket bending over some bicycle bars. He is taking a long time to die. The whiskers white as porcupine quills, the forehead slopes. . . . Goodbye, brother, die in the sound of the waves. Forgive us if we have killed you. Long live your race, your inner-tube race, so uncomfortable on land, so comfortable in the ocean. Be comfortable in death then, when the sand will be out of your nostrils, and you can swim in long loops through the pure death, ducking under as assassinations break above you. You don't want to be touched by me. I climb the cliff and go home the other way.

LOOKING INTO A TIDE POOL

It is a tide pool, shallow, water coming in, clear, tiny white shell-people on the bottom, asking nothing, not even directions! On the surface the noduled seaweed, lying like hands, slowly drawing back and returning, hands laid on fevered bodies, moving back and forth, as the healer sings wildly, shouting to Jesus and his dead mother.

ROBERT BLY

THE YELLOW DOT

God does what she wants. She has very large
Tractors. She lives at night in the sewing room
Doing stitchery. Then chunks of land at mid-
Sea disappear. The husband knows that his wife
Is still breathing. God has arranged the open
Grave. That grave is not what we want,
But to God it's a tiny hole, and he has
The needle, draws thread through it, and soon
A nice pattern appears. The husband cries,
"Don't let her die!" But God says, "I
Need a yellow dot here, near the mailbox."

The husband is angry. But the turbulent ocean
Is like a chicken scratching for seeds. It doesn't
Mean anything, and the chicken's claws will tear
A Rembrandt drawing if you put it down.

In memory of Jane Kenyon

THE RUSSIAN

"The Russians had few doctors on the front line.
My father's job was this: after the battle
Was over, he'd walk among the men hit,
Sit down and ask: 'Would you like to die on your
Own in a few hours, or should I finish it?'
Most said, 'Don't leave me.' The two would have
A cigarette. He'd take out his small notebook —
We had no dogtags, you know — and write the man's
Name down, his wife's, his children, his address, and what
He wanted to say. When the cigarette was done,
The soldier would turn his head to the side. My father
Finished off four hundred men that way during the war.
He never went crazy. They were his people.

He came to Toronto. My father in the summers
Would stand on the lawn with a hose, watering
The grass that way. It took a long time. He'd talk

To the moon, to the wind. 'I can hear you growing' —
He'd say to the grass. 'We come and go.
We're no different from each other. We are all
Part of something. We have a home.' When I was thirteen,
I said, 'Dad, do you know they've invented sprinklers
Now?' He went on watering the grass.
'This is my life. Just shut up if you don't understand it.'"

PITZEEM AND THE MARE

Let's tell the other story about Pitzeem and his horse.
When the One He Loved moved to the mountains,
He bought a mare and a saddle and started out.

He rode all day with fire coming out of his ears,
And all night. When the reins fell, the mare knew it right
Away. She turned and headed straight for the barn.

No one had told Pitzeem, but his horse had left
A new foal back in the stable. She thought of nothing
All day but his sweet face with its long nose.

Pitzeem! Pitzeem! How much time you've lost!
He put the mountain between the mare's ears again.
He slapped his own face; he was a good lover.

And every night he fell asleep once more. Friends,
Our desire to reach our true wife is great,
But the mare's love for her child is also great. Please

Understand this. The journey was a three-day trip,
But it took Pitzeem thirty years. You and I have been
Riding for years, but we're still only a day from home.

Thomas Victor

Gwendolyn Brooks

no ambiguity, unlike Rita Dove (see "Parsley" =?)

from *A STREET IN BRONZEVILLE*

the mother

Abortions will not let you forget.
You remember the children you got that you did not get,
The damp small pulps with a little or with no hair,
The singers and workers that never handled the air.
You will never neglect or beat
Them, or silence or buy with a sweet.
You will never wind up the sucking-thumb
Or scuttle off ghosts that come.
You will never leave them, controlling your luscious sigh,
Return for a snack of them, with gobbling mother-eye.

I have heard in the voices of the wind the voices of my dim killed
      children.
I have contracted. I have eased
My dim dears at the breasts they could never suck.
I have said, Sweets, if I sinned, if I seized
Your luck
And your lives from your unfinished reach,
If I stole your births and your names,
Your straight baby tears and your games,
Your stilted or lovely loves, your tumults, your marriages, aches, and your
      deaths,
If I poisoned the beginnings of your breaths,
Believe that even in my deliberateness I was not deliberate.
Though why should I whine,
Whine that the crime was other than mine? —
Since anyhow you are dead.
Or rather, or instead,
You were never made.
But that too, I am afraid,
Is faulty: oh, what shall I say, how is the truth to be said?
You were born, you had body, you died.
It is just that you never giggled or planned or cried.
Believe me, I loved you all.
Believe me, I knew you, though faintly, and I loved, I loved you
All.

a song in the front yard

I've stayed in the front yard all my life.
I want a peek at the back
Where it's rough and untended and hungry weed grows.
A girl gets sick of a rose.

I want to go in the back yard now
And maybe down the alley,
To where the charity children play.
I want a good time today.

They do some wonderful things.
They have some wonderful fun.
My mother sneers, but I say it's fine
How they don't have to go in at quarter to nine.
My mother, she tells me that Johnnie Mac
Will grow up to be a bad woman.
That George'll be taken to Jail soon or late
(On account of last winter he sold our back gate).

But I say it's fine. Honest, I do.
And I'd like to be a bad woman, too,
And wear the brave stockings of night-black lace
And strut down the streets with paint on my face.

A LOVELY LOVE

Lillian's

Let it be alleys. Let it be a hall
Whose janitor javelins epithet and thought
To cheapen hyacinth darkness that we sought
And played we found, rot, make the petals fall.
Let it be stairways, and a splintery box
Where you have thrown me, scraped me with your kiss,
Have honed me, have released me after this
Cavern kindness, smiled away our shocks.
That is the birthright of our lovely love
In swaddling clothes. Not like that Other one.
Not lit by any fondling star above.

Not found by any wise men, either. Run.
People are coming. They must not catch us here
Definitionless in this strict atmosphere.

Loathe-love

THE LOVERS OF THE POOR

arrive (The Ladies from the Ladies' Betterment
          League   *vs. "dirty light"*
Arrive in the afternoon, the late light slanting   *late light*
In diluted gold bars across the boulevard brag
Of proud, seamed faces with mercy and murder hinting
Here, there, interrupting, all deep and debonair,
The pink paint on the innocence of fear;)   *late light*
[They] Walk in a gingerly manner up the hall.)
Cutting with knives served by their softest care,
Served by their love, so barbarously fair.
Whose mothers taught: You'd better not be cruel!
You had better not throw stones upon the wrens!
Herein they kiss and coddle and assault
Anew and dearly in the innocence
With which they baffle nature. Who are full,
Sleek, tender-clad, fit, fiftyish, a-glow, all
unproductive Sweetly abortive, hinting at fat fruit,
Judge it high time that fiftyish fingers felt
Beneath the lovelier planes of enterprise.
To resurrect. To moisten with milky chill.
To be a random hitching-post or plush.
To be, for wet eyes, random and handy hem.
        Their guild is giving money to the poor.
The worthy poor. The very very worthy   *—dark-skinned*
And beautiful poor. Perhaps just not too swarthy?
Perhaps just not too dirty nor too dim
Nor — passionate. In truth, what they could wish
Is — something less than derelict or dull.
Not staunch enough to stab, though, gaze for gaze!
God shield them sharply from the beggar-bold!
The noxious needy ones whose battle's bald
Nonetheless for being voiceless, hits one down.   *tone changes*
        But it's all so bad! and entirely too much for them.
The stench; the urine, cabbage, and dead beans,
Dead porridges of assorted dusty grains,

why would they not give money to the passionate perpetuate the cycle — don't let them" his above by giving them the resources

The old smoke, *heavy* diapers, and, they're told,
Something called chitterlings. The darkness. Drawn
Darkness, or dirty light. The soil that stirs.
The soil that looks the soil of centuries.
And for that matter the *general* oldness. Old
Wood. Old marble. Old tile. Old old old.
Not homekind Oldness! Not Lake Forest, Glencoe.
Nothing is sturdy, nothing is majestic,
There is no quiet drama, no rubbed glaze, no
Unkillable infirmity of such
A tasteful turn as lately they have left,
Glencoe, Lake Forest, and to which their cars
Must presently restore them. When they're done
With dullards and distortions of this fistic
Patience of the poor and put-upon.
　　　They've never seen such a make-do-ness as
Newspaper rugs before! In this, this "flat,"
Their hostess is gathering up the oozed, the rich
Rugs of the morning (tattered! the bespattered. . . .)
Readies to spread clean rugs for afternoon.
Here is a scene for you. The Ladies look,
In horror, behind a substantial citizeness
Whose trains clank out across her swollen heart.
Who, arms akimbo, almost fills a door.
All tumbling children, quilts dragged to the floor
And tortured thereover, potato peelings, soft-
Eyed kitten, hunched-up, haggard, to-be-hurt.
　　　Their League is alloting largesse to the Lost.
But to put their clean, their pretty money, to put
Their money collected from delicate rose-fingers
Tipped with their hundred flawless rose-nails seems . . .
　　　They own Spode, Lowestoft, candelabra,
Mantels, and hostess gowns, and sunburst clocks,
Turtle soup, Chippendale, red satin "hangings,"
Aubussons and Hattie Carnegie. They Winter
In Palm Beach; cross the Water in June; attend,
When suitable, the nice Art Institute;
Buy the right books in the best bindings; saunter
On Michigan, Easter mornings, in sun or wind.
Oh Squalor! This sick four-story hulk, this fibre
With fissures everywhere! Why, what are bringings
Of loathe-love largesse? What shall peril hungers
So old old, what shall flatter the desolate?
Tin can, blocked fire escape and chitterling
And swaggering seeking youth and the puzzled wreckage

Of the middle-passage, and urine and stale shames *changes tone*
And, again, the porridges of the underslung
And children children children. Heavens! That
Was a rat, surely, off there, in the shadows? Long
And long-tailed? Gray? The Ladies from the Ladies'
Betterment League agree it will be better
To achieve the outer air that rights and steadies,
To hie to a house that does not holler, to ring
Bells elsetime, better presently to cater
To no more Possibilities, to get
Away (Perhaps the money can be posted.) *given publicly (so as not to see their lives?)*
Perhaps they two may choose another Slum!
Some serious sooty half-unhappy home! —
Where loathe-love likelier may be invested.
     Keeping their scented bodies in the center
Of the hall as they walk down the hysterical hall,
They allow their lovely skirts to graze no wall,
Are off at what they manage of a canter, *gallop*
And, resuming all the clues of what they were,
Try to avoid inhaling the laden air.

BEVERLY HILLS, CHICAGO

("and the people live till they have white hair")
          — E. M. Price

The dry brown coughing beneath their feet,
(Only a while, for the handyman is on his way)
These people walk their golden gardens.
We say ourselves fortunate to be driving by today.

That we may look at them, in their gardens where
The summer ripeness rots. But not raggedly.
Even the leaves fall down in lovelier patterns here.
And the refuse, the refuse is a neat brilliancy.

When they flow sweetly into their houses
With softness and slowness touched by that everlasting gold,
We know what they go to. To tea. But that does not mean
They will throw some little black dots into some water and add sugar and
    the juice of the cheapest lemons that are sold,

While downstairs that woman's vague phonograph bleats, "Knock me a
    kiss."
And the living all to be made again in the sweatingest physical manner
Tomorrow. . . . Not that anybody is saying that these people have no trouble.
Merely that it is trouble with a gold-flecked beautiful banner.

Nobody is saying that these people do not ultimately cease to be. And
Sometimes their passings are even more painful than ours.
It is just that so often they live till their hair is white.
They make excellent corpses, among the expensive flowers. . . .

Nobody is furious. Nobody hates these people.
At least, nobody driving by in this car.
It is only natural, however, that it should occur to us
How much more fortunate they are than we are.

It is only natural that we should look and look
At their wood and brick and stone
And think, while a breath of pine blows,
How different these are from our own.

We do not want them to have less.
But it is only natural that we should think we have not enough.
We drive on, we drive on.
When we speak to each other our voices are a little gruff.

WE REAL COOL

The Pool Players.
Seven at the Golden Shovel.

We real cool. We
Left school. We

Lurk late. We
Strike straight. We

Sing sin. We
Thin gin. We

Jazz June. We
Die soon.

GWENDOLYN BROOKS

THE EGG BOILER

Being you, you cut your poetry from wood.
The boiling of an egg is heavy art.
You come upon it as an artist should,
With rich-eyed passion, and with straining heart.
We fools, we cut our poems out of air,
Night color, wind soprano, and such stuff.
And sometimes weightlessness is much to bear.
You mock it, though, you name it Not Enough.
The egg, spooned gently to the avid pan,
And left the strict three minutes, or the four,
Is your Enough and art for any man.
We fools give courteous ear — then cut some more,
Shaping a gorgeous Nothingness from cloud.
You watch us, eat your egg, and laugh aloud.

Olga Broumas

THE CHOIR

I walk and I rest while the eyes of my dead
look through my own, inaudible
hosannas greet
the panorama charged serene
and almost ultraviolet with so much witness.
Holy the sea, the palpitating membrane
divided into dazzling fields and whaledark by the sun.
Holy the dark, pierced by late revelers and dawnbirds,
the garbage truck suspended in shy light,
the oystershell and crushed clam of the driveway,
the dahlia pressed like lotus on its open palm.
Holy the handmade and created side by side,
the sapphire of their marriage,
green flies and shit and condoms in the crabshell
rinsed by the buzzing tide.
Holy the light —
the poison ivy livid in its glare,
the gypsy moths festooning the pine barrens,
the mating monarch butterflies between the chic boutiques.
The mermaid's handprint on the artificial reef. Holy the we,
cast in the mermaid's image, smooth crotch of mystery and scale,
inscrutable until divulged by god
and sex into its gender, every touch
a secret intercourse with angels as we walk
proffered and taken. Their great wings
batter the air, our retinas bloom silver spots like beacons.
Better than silicone or graphite flesh absorbs
the shock of the divine crash-landing.
I roll my eyes back, skylights brushed by plumage of detail,
the unrehearsed and minuscule, the anecdotal midnight
themes of the carbon sea where we are joined:
zinnia, tomato, garlic wreaths
crowning the compost heap.

OLGA BROUMAS

CARITAS

> *Thank someone for being*
> *that one. Walk with her*
> *to the center of a place*
> *and back again*
> *singing a little song.*
> *Burn something.*
>
> — Seneca Tribe of
> Native Americans

1

Erik Satie, accused
once of formlessness, composed
a sonata titled: Composition in the Form
of a Pear. When I tell you
that it would take
more brilliance than Mozart
more melancholy precision than Brahms
to compose a sonata in the form of
your breasts, you
don't believe me. I lie
next to your infidel sleep, all night
in pain
and lonely with my silenced
pleasure. Your breasts
in their moonlit pallor
invade me, lightly, like minor
fugues. I lie
between your sappling thighs, tongue
flat on your double lips, giving
voice, giving
voice. Opulent
as a continent in the rising light, you sleep
on, indifferent
to my gushing praises. It is
as it should be. Atlantis,
Cyprus, Crete, the encircled
civilizations, serene
in their tidal basins, dolphin-
loved, didn't heed to the faint, the

riotous
praise
of the lapping sea.

2

Your knees, those pinnacles
competing with the finest
dimpled, five-
year-old chins are
dancing. Ecstatic as nuns
in their delirious habit, like
runaway needles on a multiple graph,
the first organic model of
seismographs, charting
the crest I keep you on
and on till all
the sensitive numbers on the
Richter scale ring out at
once, but
silently: a choir
of sundial alarums. You reach that place,
levitated by pleasure, the first
glimpse the melting
glacier must
have had, rounding the precipice,
of what came to be known as
Niagara Falls. After all this time,
every time,
like a finger inside
the tight-gummed,
spittle-bright, atavistic
suckle of
a newborn's fragile-lipped
mouth, I
embrace you, my heart
a four-celled embryo, swimming
a pulse, a bloodstream that becomes, month
to month, less
of a stranger's, more
intimate, her
own.

3

There are people who do not explore the in-
Sides of flowers . . .

— *Sandra Hochman*

With the clear
plastic speculum, transparent
and, when inserted, pink like the convex
carapace of a prawn, flashlight in hand, I
guide you
inside the small
cathedral of my cunt. The unexpected
light dazzles you. This flesh, my darling, always
invisible like the wet
side of stones, the hidden
hemisphere of the moon, startles you
with its brilliance, the little
dome a spitting
miniature of the Haghia Sophia
with its circlet of openings
to the Mediterranean sun.
A woman-made language would
have as many synonyms for pink / light-filled / holy as
the Eskimo does
for snow. Speechless, you
shift the flashlight from
hand to hand, flickering. An orgy
of candles. Lourdes in mid-August. A flurry of
audible breaths, a seething
of holiness, and
behold
a tear
forms in the single eye, carmine
and catholic. You too, my darling, are
folded, clean
round a light-filled temple, complete
with miraculous icon, shedding
her perfect tears, in touch
with the hidden hemispheres,
the dome
of our cyclops moon.

4

She's white and her shoulders sing
like a singular vein of marble
alive and kicking in the jagged hill.
Her eyes are wet heaps
of seaweed in the sullen dusk.
Eyes of shadow and latitudes. Eyes of slate,
eyes of flint, eyes the color of certain stones
prized above all by Georgia
O'Keeffe. Eyes of an agile
wilderness, wings of a desert
moth. Her handsome hands. Each
one a duchess in her splendid gardens, each
one a pastry cook at her pliable dough, each one
a midwife at her palpable labor, the referee
of our relay race.
Her belly lulls me like an immense coastline
of dunes beneath a floating gull.
Her belly lulls me in a lustrous bowl
so precious
all the Asiatic dynasties
roll in their gilded graves, tarnished
with envy. Skin like the awning of
a ceremonial tent, the cloth draped over
the bread and wine of
an ungodly marriage. Is not this love
also a tavern? Is this meal not also
a public meal? I am encircled like a pit
in the fruit's ripe stomach, an ovum in cilia-lined
amniotic space, a drunken satellite, home
at last from its dizzy orbit.
Strike
up the music, my
love will dance. The loaf
of bread held against her breasts, the blade
in her nimble fingers, her feet stamping patterns
like snakes in the circle of dust, her waist a
scorpion's, she'll
dance, dance
the bread dance, slicing
out flawless ovals from
her inexhaustible loaf.

5

Imagine
something so beautiful
your liver would swell with contraband
chemicals, laughter, the dangerous
and infectious song.
Something so fine
you'd need no alibi for
your avid enchantment. A small
thing to start with: a special hairline
on a special nape, bent
low towards you. Imagine now
how your fingertips throb. You follow
the spinal valley, dipping
its hollow core like a ladle of light
in your ministering fingers.
Intuit the face
like that of a woman's
inscribed upon the porous
tablets of the law, rich with an age,
with tenderness, various, and like a map
of recurring lives. Here the remnants of
an indefatigable anger, the jubilant
birth-yell, here the indelible
covens of pleasure, a web
of murmurs, a lace
mantilla of sighs.
Recapture
the fleshy mouth full of fissures, the tongue
on the sated lip, the residual flare
of a regal nostril, the purple shade
of an earlobe, the eyebrows meeting
squarely above the lids.
You laugh
at this like a daughter, a young
sprig of amaranth caught
in your gelding teeth, that fade-
less flower you call a pigweed, a prince's
feather, a love-
lies-bleeding. But
not this love. Laugh, lover, laugh
with me. In that side-
splitting reservoir, in the promised calm

of its heaving waters, you'll
bend, you'll see this woman's
beautiful
and familiar face.

CALYPSO

I've gathered the women like talismans, one
by one. They first came for tarot card
gossip, mystified
by my hands, by offers
cut with escape. They came

undone in my studio, sailing long eyes, heavy
with smoke and wet
with the force of dream: a vagina
folding mandala-like
out of herself, in full bloom. I used them. I used

the significance
of each card to uphold the dream, soon
they came back with others. I let the bitch
twitch in my lap. I listened. I let the tea steep
till the pot was black. Soon

there was no need for cards. We would use
stills from our daily lives, every woman
a constellation of images, every
portrait each other's chart.
We came together

like months
in a lunar year, measured in nights, dividing
perfectly into female phases. Like women anywhere
living in groups we had synchronous menses. And had
no need of a wound, a puncture, to seal our bond.

Lucille Clifton

[i was born with twelve fingers]

i was born with twelve fingers
like my mother and my daughter.
each of us
born wearing strange black gloves
extra baby fingers hanging over the sides of our cribs and
dipping into the milk.
somebody was afraid we would learn to cast spells
and our wonders were cut off
but they didn't understand
the powerful memory of ghosts.   now
we take what we want
with invisible fingers
and we connect
my dead mother   my live daughter   and me
through our terrible shadowy hands.

at the cemetery,
walnut grove plantation, south carolina, 1989

among the rocks
at walnut grove
your silence drumming
in my bones,
tell me your names.

nobody mentioned slaves
and yet the curious tools
shine with your fingerprints.
nobody mentioned slaves
but somebody did this work
who had no guide, no stone,
who moulders under rock.

LUCILLE CLIFTON

tell me your names,
tell me your bashful names
and i will testify.

*the inventory lists ten slaves
but only men were recognized.*

among the rocks
at walnut grove
some of these honored dead
were dark
some of these dark
were slaves
some of these slaves
were women
some of them did this
honored work.
tell me your names
foremothers, brothers,
tell me your dishonored names.
here lies — pun
here lies
here lies
here lies
hear

the lost baby poem

the time i dropped your almost body down
down to meet the waters under the city
and run one with the sewage to the sea
what did i know about waters rushing back
what did i know about drowning
or being drowned

you would have been born into winter
in the year of the disconnected gas
and no car   we would have made the thin
walk over genesee hill into the canada wind
to watch you slip like ice into strangers' hands
you would have fallen naked as snow into winter

if you were here i could tell you these
and some other things

if i am ever less than a mountain
for your definite brothers and sisters
let the rivers pour over my head
let the sea take me for a spiller
of seas   let black men call me stranger
always   for your never named sake

[at last we killed the roaches]

at last we killed the roaches.
mama and me. she sprayed,
i swept the ceiling and they fell
dying onto our shoulders, in our hair
covering us with red. the tribe was broken,
the cooking pots were ours again
and we were glad, such cleanliness was grace
when i was twelve. only for a few nights,
and then not much, my dreams were blood
my hands were blades and it was murder murder
all over the place.

homage to my hips

these hips are big hips
they need space to
move around in.
they don't fit into little
petty places. these hips
are free hips.
they don't like to be held back.
these hips have never been enslaved,
they go where they want to go
they do what they want to do.
these hips are mighty hips.
these hips are magic hips.

LUCILLE CLIFTON

i have known them
to put a spell on a man and
spin him like a top!

wishes for sons

i wish them cramps.
i wish them a strange town
and the last tampon.
i wish them no 7-11.

i wish them one week early
and wearing a white skirt.
i wish them one week late.

later i wish them hot flashes
and clots like you
wouldn't believe.   let the
flashes come when they
meet someone special.
let the clots come
when they want to.

let them think they have accepted
arrogance in the universe,
then bring them to gynecologists
not unlike themselves.

poem to my uterus

you   uterus
you have been patient
as a sock
while i have slippered into you
my dead and living children
now
they want to cut you out
stocking i will not need

LUCILLE CLIFTON

where i am going
where am i going
old girl
without you
uterus
my bloody print
my estrogen kitchen
my black bag of desire
where can i go
barefoot
without you
where can you go
without me

lumpectomy eve

all night i dream of lips
that nursed and nursed
and the lonely nipple

lost in loss and the need
to feed that turns at last
on itself   that will kill

its body for its hunger's sake
all night i hear the whispering
the soft

    love calls you to this knife
    for love   for love

all night it is the one breast
comforting the other

scar

we will learn
to live together.
i will call you

body/mind

ribbon of hunger
and desire
empty pocket flap
edge of before and after.

and you
what will you call me?

woman i ride
who cannot throw me
and i will not fall off.

lorena

it lay in my palm soft and trembled
as a new bird and i thought about
authority and how it always insisted
on itself, how it was master
of the man, how it measured him, never
was ignored or denied and how it promised
there would be sweetness if it was obeyed
just like the saints do, like the angels,
and i opened the window and held out my
uncupped hand. i swear to god,
i thought it could fly

moonchild

whatever slid into my mother's room that
late june night, tapping her great belly,
summoned me out roundheaded and unsmiling.
is this the moon, my father used to grin,
cradling my head. it was the moon
but nobody knew it then.

the moon understands dark places.
the moon has secrets of her own.
she holds what light she can.

LUCILLE CLIFTON

we girls were ten years old and giggling
in our hand-me-downs. we wanted breasts,
pretended that we had them, tissued
our undershirts. jay johnson is teaching
me to french kiss, ella bragged, who
is teaching you? how do you sigh; my father?

the moon remembers everything. *—cycles*
she rules the oceans, rivers, rain.
when i am asked whose tears these are
i always say; the moon's.

the gift

there was a woman who hit her head
and ever after she could see the sharp
wing of things   blues and greens
radiating from the body of her sister
her mother   her friends.   when she felt

in her eyes the yellow sting
of her mothers dying   she trembled
but did not speak.   her bent brain
stilled her tongue so that her life
became flash after flash of silence

bright as flame.   she is gone now
her head knocked again against the door
that opened for her only.
i saw her last in a plain box smiling,
behind her sewn eyes there were hints
of purple and crimson and gold

Billy Collins

LITANY

You are the bread and the knife,
The crystal goblet and the wine.

— *Jacques Crickillon*

You are the bread and the knife,
the crystal goblet and the wine.
You are the dew on the morning grass,
and the burning wheel of the sun.
You are the white apron of the baker
and the marsh birds suddenly in flight.

However, you are not the wind in the orchard,
the plums on the counter,
or the house of cards.
And you are certainly not the pine-scented air.
There is no way you are the pine-scented air.

It is possible that you are the fish under the bridge,
maybe even the pigeon on the general's head,
but you are not even close
to being the field of cornflowers at dusk.

And a quick look in the mirror will show
that you are neither the boots in the corner
nor the boat asleep in its boathouse.

It might interest you to know,
speaking of the plentiful imagery of the world,
that I am the sound of rain on the roof.

I also happen to be the shooting star,
the evening paper blowing down an alley,
and the basket of chestnuts on the kitchen table.

I am also the moon in the trees
and the blind woman's teacup.
But don't worry, I am not the bread and the knife.
You are still the bread and the knife.

BILLY COLLINS

You will always be the bread and the knife,
not to mention the crystal goblet and — somehow —
    the wine.

SONNET

All we need is fourteen lines, well, thirteen now,
and after this one just a dozen
to launch a little ship on love's storm-tossed seas,
then only ten more left like rows of beans.
How easily it goes unless you get Elizabethan
and insist the iambic bongos must be played
and rhymes positioned at the ends of lines,
one for every station of the cross.
But hang on here while we make the turn
into the final six where all will be resolved,
where longing and heartache will find an end,
where Laura will tell Petrarch to put down his pen,
take off those crazy medieval tights,
blow out the lights, and come at last to bed.

JAPAN

Today I pass the time reading
a favorite haiku,
saying the few words over and over.

It feels like eating
the same small, perfect grape
again and again.

I walk through the house reciting it
and leave its letters falling
through the air of every room.

I stand by the big silence of the piano and say it.
I say it in front of a painting of the sea.
I tap out its rhythm on an empty shelf.

I listen to myself saying it,
then I say it without listening,
then I hear it without saying it.

And when the dog looks up at me,
I kneel down on the floor
and whisper it into each of his long white ears.

It's the one about the one-ton
temple bell
with the moth sleeping on its surface,

and every time I say it, I feel the excruciating
pressure of the moth
on the surface of the iron bell.

When I say it at the window,
the bell is the world
and I am the moth resting there.

When I say it into the mirror,
I am the heavy bell
and the moth is life with its papery wings.

And later, when I say it to you in the dark,
you are the bell,
and I am the tongue of the bell, ringing you,

and the moth has flown
from its line
and moves like a hinge in the air above our bed.

OSSO BUCO

I love the sound of the bone against the plate
and the fortress-like look of it
lying before me in a moat of risotto,
the meat soft as the leg of an angel
who has lived a purely airborne existence.
And best of all, the secret marrow,
the invaded privacy of the animal

prized out with a knife and swallowed down
with cold, exhilarating wine.

I am swaying now in the hour after dinner,
a citizen tilted back on his chair,
a creature with a full stomach —
something you don't hear much about in poetry,
that sanctuary of hunger and deprivation.
You know: the driving rain, the boots by the door,
small birds searching for berries in winter.

But tonight, the lion of contentment
has placed a warm, heavy paw on my chest,
and I can only close my eyes and listen
to the drums of woe throbbing in the distance
and the sound of my wife's laughter
on the telephone in the next room,
the woman who cooked the savory osso buco,
who pointed to show the butcher the ones she wanted.
She who talks to her faraway friend
while I linger here at the table
with a hot, companionable cup of tea,
feeling like one of the friendly natives,
a reliable guide, maybe even the chief's favorite son.

Somewhere, a man is crawling up a rocky hillside
on bleeding knees and palms, an Irish penitent
carrying the stone of the world in his stomach;
and elsewhere people of all nations stare
at one another across a long, empty table.

But here, the candles give off their warm glow,
the same light that Shakespeare and Izaak Walton wrote by,
the light that lit and shadowed the faces of history.
Only now it plays on the blue plates,
the crumpled napkins, the crossed knife and fork.

In a while, one of us will go up to bed
and the other one will follow.
Then we will slip below the surface of the night
into miles of water, drifting down and down
to the dark, soundless bottom
until the weight of dreams pulls us lower still,
below the shale and layered rock,

beneath the strata of hunger and pleasure,
into the broken bones of the earth itself,
into the marrow of the only place we know.

MAN IN SPACE

All you have to do is listen to the way a man
sometimes talks to his wife at a table of people
and notice how intent he is on making his point
even though her lower lip is beginning to quiver,

and you will know why the women in science
fiction movies who inhabit a planet of their own
are not pictured making a salad or reading a magazine
when the men from earth arrive in their rocket,

why they are always standing in a semicircle
with their arms folded, their bare legs set apart,
their breasts protected by hard metal disks.

BY A SWIMMING POOL OUTSIDE SIRACUSA

All afternoon I have been struggling
to communicate in Italian
with Roberto and Giuseppe who have begun
to resemble the two male characters
in my *Italian for Beginners*,
the ones always shopping, eating,
or inquiring about the times of trains.

Now I can feel my English slipping away,
like chlorinated water through my fingers.

I have made important pronouncements
in this remote limestone valley
with its trickle of a river.
I stated that it seems hotter
today even than it was yesterday

and that swimming is very good for you,
very beneficial, you might say.
I also posed burning questions
about the hours of the archaeological museum
and the location of the local necropolis.

But now I am alone in the evening light
which has softened the white cliffs,
and I have had a little gin in a glass with ice
which has softened my mood or —
how would you say in English —
has allowed my thoughts to traverse my brain
with greater gentleness, shall we say,

or, to put it less literally,
this drink has extended permission
to my mind to feel — what's the word? —
a friendship with the vast sky
which is very — give me a minute — very blue
but with much great paleness
at this special time of day, or as we say in America, now.

WRITING IN THE AFTERLIFE

I imagined the atmosphere would be clear,
shot with pristine light,
not this sulfurous haze,
the air ionized as before a thunderstorm.

Many have pictured a river here,
but no one mentioned all the boats,
their benches crowded with naked passengers,
each bent over a writing tablet.

I knew I would not always be a child
with a model train and a model tunnel,
and I knew I would not live forever,
jumping all day through the hoop of myself.

I had heard about the journey to the other side
and the clink of the final coin

in the leather purse of the man holding the oar,
but how could anyone have guessed

that as soon as we arrived
we would be asked to describe this place
and to include as much detail as possible —
not just the water, he insists,

rather the oily, fathomless, rat-happy water,
not simply the shackles, but the rusty,
iron, ankle-shredding shackles —
and that our next assignment would be

to jot down, off the tops of our heads,
our thoughts and feelings about being dead,
not really an assignment,
the man rotating the oar keeps telling us —

think of it more as an exercise, he groans,
think of writing as a process,
a never-ending, infernal process,
and now the boats have become jammed together,

bow against stern, stern locked to bow,
and not a thing is moving, only our diligent pens.

Robert Creeley

I KNOW A MAN

As I sd to my
friend, because I am
always talking, — John, I

sd, which was not his
name, the darkness sur-
rounds us, what

can we do against
it, or else, shall we &
why not, buy a goddamn big car,

drive, he sd, for
christ's sake, look
out where yr going.

AFTER LORCA

for M. Marti

The church is a business, and the rich
are the business men.
                    When they pull on the bells, the
poor come piling in and when a poor man dies, he has a
        wooden
cross, and they rush through the ceremony.

But when a rich man dies, they
drag out the Sacrament
and a golden Cross, and go *doucement, doucement*
to the cemetery.

And the poor love it
and think it's crazy.

ROBERT CREELEY

THE FIGURES

The stillness
of the wood,
the figures formed

by hands so still
they touched it
to be one

hand holding one
hand, faces
without eyes,

bodies of wooden
stone, so still
they will not move

from that quiet
action ever
again. Did the man

who made them find
a like quiet? In
the act of making them

it must have been
so still he heard the wood
and felt it with his hands

moving into
the forms
he has given to them,

one by singular
one, so quiet,
so still.

ROBERT CREELEY

THE LANGUAGE

Locate *I*
love you some-
where in

teeth and
eyes, bite
it but

take care not
to hurt, you
want so

much so
little. Words
say everything,

I
love you
again,

then what
is emptiness
for. To

fill, fill.
I heard words
and words full

of holes
aching. Speech
is a mouth.

ROBERT CREELEY

THE FLOWER

I think I grow tensions
like flowers
in a wood where
nobody goes.

Each wound is perfect,
encloses itself in a tiny
imperceptible blossom,
making pain.

Pain is a flower like that one,
like this one,
like that one,
like this one.

SOMETHING

I approach with such
a careful tremor, always
I feel the finally foolish

question of how it is,
then, supposed to be felt,
and by whom. I remember

once in a rented room on
27th street, the woman I loved
then, literally, after we

had made love on the large
bed sitting across from
a basin with two faucets, she

had to pee but was nervous,
embarrassed I suppose I
would watch her who had but

ROBERT CREELEY

a moment ago been completely
open to me, naked, on
the same bed. Squatting, her

head reflected in the mirror,
the hair dark there, the
full of her face, the shoulders,

sat spread-legged, turned on
one faucet and shyly pissed. What
love might learn from such a sight.

THE WARNING

For love — I would
split open your head and put
a candle in
behind the eyes.

Love is dead in us
if we forget
the virtues of an amulet
and quick surprise.

THE ACT OF LOVE

for Bobbie

Whatever constitutes
the act of love,
save physical

encounter, you are
dear to me,
not value as

with banks —
but a meaning self-
sufficient, dry

ROBERT CREELEY

at times as sand,
or else the trees,
dripping with

rain. How shall
one, this so-
called person,

say it? He
loves, his mind
is occupied, his

hands move
writing words
which come

into his head.
Now here,
the day surrounds

this man
and woman
sitting a small

distance apart.
Love will not
solve it — but

draws closer,
always, makes
the moisture of their

mouths and bodies
actively
engage. If I

wanted
a dirty picture,
would it always

be of a
woman straddled?
Yes

ROBERT CREELEY

and no, these
are true opposites,
a you and me

of non-
sense,
for our love.

Now, one
says, the wind
lifts, the sky

is very blue, the
water just
beyond me makes

its lovely sounds.
How *dear*
you are

to me, how love-
ly all your
body *is*, how

all these
senses do
commingle, so

that in your very
arms I still
can think of you.

James Dickey

THE HEAVEN OF ANIMALS

Here they are. The soft eyes open.
If they have lived in a wood
It is a wood.
If they have lived on plains
It is grass rolling
Under their feet forever.

Having no souls, they have come,
Anyway, beyond their knowing.
Their instincts wholly bloom
And they rise.
The soft eyes open.

To match them, the landscape flowers,
Outdoing, desperately
Outdoing what is required:
The richest wood,
The deepest field.

For some of these,
It could not be the place
It is, without blood.
These hunt, as they have done,
But with claws and teeth grown perfect,

More deadly than they can believe.
They stalk more silently,
And crouch on the limbs of trees,
And their descent
Upon the bright backs of their prey

May take years
In a sovereign floating of joy.
And those that are hunted
Know this as their life,
Their reward: to walk

Under such trees in full knowledge
Of what is in glory above them,
And to feel no fear,
But acceptance, compliance.
Fulfilling themselves without pain

At the cycle's center,
They tremble, they walk
Under the tree,
They fall, they are torn,
They rise, they walk again.

THE SHEEP CHILD

Farm boys wild to couple
With anything   with soft-wooded trees
With mounds of earth   mounds
Of pinestraw   will keep themselves off
Animals by legends of their own:
In the hay-tunnel dark
And dung of barns, they will
Say   I have heard tell

That in a museum in Atlanta
Way back in a corner somewhere
There's this thing that's only half
Sheep   like a woolly baby
Pickled in alcohol   because
Those things can't live his eyes
Are open   but you can't stand to look
I heard from somebody who . . .

But this is now almost all
Gone. The boys have taken
Their own true wives in the city,
The sheep are safe in the west hill
Pasture   but we who were born there
Still are not sure. Are we,
Because we remember, remembered
In the terrible dust of museums?

JAMES DICKEY

Merely with his eyes, the sheep-child may

Be saying   saying

> I am here, in my father's house.
> I who am half of your world, came deeply
> To my mother in the long grass
> Of the west pasture, where she stood like moonlight
> Listening for foxes. It was something like love
> From another world that seized her
> From behind, and she gave, not lifting her head
> Out of dew, without ever looking, her best
> Self to that great need. Turned loose, she dipped her face
> Farther into the chill of the earth, and in a sound
> Of sobbing   of something stumbling
> Away, began, as she must do,
> To carry me. I woke, dying,
>
> In the summer sun of the hillside, with my eyes
> Far more than human. I saw for a blazing moment
> The great grassy world from both sides,
> Man and beast in the round of their need,
> And the hill wind stirred in my wool,
> My hoof and my hand clasped each other,
> I ate my one meal
> Of milk, and died
> Staring. From dark grass I came straight
>
> To my father's house, whose dust
> Whirls up in the halls for no reason
> When no one comes   piling deep in a hellish mild corner,
> And, through my immortal waters,
> I meet the sun's grains eye
> To eye, and they fail at my closet of glass.
> Dead, I am most surely living
> In the minds of farm boys: I am he who drives
> Them like wolves from the hound bitch and calf
> And from the chaste ewe in the wind.
> They go into woods   into bean fields   they go
> Deep into their known right hands. Dreaming of me,
> They groan   they wait   they suffer
> Themselves, they marry, they raise their kind.

JAMES DICKEY

THE POISONED MAN

When the rattlesnake bit, I lay
In a dream of the country, and dreamed
Day after day of the river,

Where I sat with a jackknife and quickly
Opened my sole to the water.
Blood shed for the sake of one's life

Takes on the hid shape of the channel,
Disappearing under logs and through boulders.
The freezing river poured on

And, as it took hold of my blood,
Leapt up round the rocks and boiled over.
I felt that my heart's blood could flow

Unendingly out of the mountain,
Splitting bedrock apart upon redness,
And the current of life at my instep

Give deathlessly as a spring.
Some leaves fell from trees and whirled under.
I saw my struck bloodstream assume,

Inside the cold path of the river,
The inmost routes of a serpent
Through grass, through branches and leaves.

When I rose, the live oaks were ashen
And the wild grass was dead without flame.
Through the blasted cornfield I hobbled,

My foot tied up in my shirt,
And met my old wife in the garden,
Where she reached for a withering apple.

I lay in the country and dreamed
Of the substance and course of the river
While the different colors of fever

JAMES DICKEY

Like quilt patches flickered upon me.
At last I arose, with the poison
Gone out of the seam of the scar,

And brought my wife eastward and weeping,
Through the copper fields springing alive
With the promise of harvest for no one.

THE HOSPITAL WINDOW

I have just come down from my father.
Higher and higher he lies
Above me in a blue light
Shed by a tinted window.
I drop through six white floors
And then step out onto pavement.

Still feeling my father ascend,
I start to cross the firm street,
My shoulder blades shining with all
The glass the huge building can raise.
Now I must turn round and face it,
And know his one pane from the others.

Each window possesses the sun
As though it burned there on a wick.
I wave, like a man catching fire.
All the deep-dyed windowpanes flash,
And, behind them, all the white rooms
They turn to the color of Heaven.

Ceremoniously, gravely, and weakly,
Dozens of pale hands are waving
Back, from inside their flames.
Yet one pure pane among these
Is the bright, erased blankness of nothing.
I know that my father is there,

In the shape of his death still living.
The traffic increases around me
Like a madness called down on my head.

JAMES DICKEY

The horns blast at me like shotguns,
And drivers lean out, driven crazy —
But now my propped-up father

Lifts his arm out of stillness at last.
The light from the window strikes me
And I turn as blue as a soul,
As the moment when I was born.
I am not afraid for my father —
Look! He is grinning; he is not

Afraid for my life, either,
As the wild engines stand at my knees
Shredding their gears and roaring,
And I hold each car in its place
For miles, inciting its horn
To blow down the walls of the world

That the dying may float without fear
In the bold blue gaze of my father.
Slowly I move to the sidewalk
With my pin-tingling hand half dead
At the end of my bloodless arm.
I carry it off in amazement,

High, still higher, still waving,
My recognized face fully mortal,
Yet not; not at all, in the pale,
Drained, otherworldly, stricken,
Created hue of stained glass.
I have just come down from my father.

ADULTERY

We have all been in rooms
We cannot die in, and they are odd places, and sad.
Often Indians are standing eagle-armed on hills

In the sunrise   open wide to the Great Spirit
Or gliding in canoes   or cattle are browsing on the walls
Far away   gazing down with the eyes of our children

JAMES DICKEY

Not far away   or there are men driving
The last railspike, which has turned
Gold in their hands. Gigantic forepleasure lives

Among such scenes, and we are alone with it
At last. There is always some weeping
Between us   and someone is always checking

A wrist watch by the bed to see how much
Longer we have left. Nothing can come
Of this   nothing can come

Of us: of me with my grim techniques
Or you who have sealed your womb
With a ring of convulsive rubber:

Although we come together,
Nothing will come of us. But we would not give
It up, for death is beaten

By praying Indians   by distant cows   historical
Hammers   by hazardous meetings that bridge
A continent. One could never die here

Never die   never die
While crying. My lover, my dear one
I will see you next week

When I'm in town. I will call you
If I can. Please get hold of   please don't
Oh God, Please don't any more I can't bear . . . Listen:

We have done it again   we are
Still living. Sit up and smile,
God bless you. Guilt is magical.

① cycles (this relates to Kinnell) ② vs. change
③ surreal, yet straightforward
③

Stephen Dobyns

(handwritten: matter-of-fact, plain tone? — journalistic?)

LONG STORY

There must have been a moment after the expulsion
from the Garden when the animals were considering
what to do next and just who was in charge.
The bear flexed his muscles, the tiger flashed
his claws, and even the porcupine thought himself
fit to rule and showed off the knife points
of his quills. No one noticed the hairless creatures,
with neither sharp teeth, nor talons, they were too puny.
It was then Cain turned and slew his own brother
and Abel's white body lay sprawled in the black dirt
as if it had already lain cast down forever.
What followed was an instant of prophetic thought
as the trees resettled themselves, the grass
dug itself deeper into the ground and all
grew impressed by the hugeness of Cain's desire.
He must really want to be boss, said the cat.
This was the moment when the animals surrendered
the power of speech as they crept home to the bosoms
of their families, the prickly ones, the smelly ones,
the ones they hoped would never do them harm.
Who could envy Cain his hunger? Better to be circumspect
and silent. Better not to want the world too much.
Left alone with the body of his brother, Cain began
to assemble the words about what Abel had done
and what he had been forced to do in return.
It was a long story. It took his entire life
to tell it. And even then it wasn't finished.
How great language had to become to encompass
its deft evasions and sly contradictions,
its preenings and self-satisfied gloatings.
Each generation makes a contribution, hoping
to have got it right at last. The sun rises
and sets. The leaves flutter like a million
frightened hands. Confidently, we step forward
and tack a few meager phrases onto the end.

(handwritten annotations: "there is no known motive — coming up w/ lies (?)"; "to dress up / primp / swell w/ pride"; "cycle"; "The Sun Also Rises"; "change"?; "Where does the Tower of Babel fit?")

105

BOWLERS ANONYMOUS

Here comes the woman who wears the plastic prick
hooked to a string around her waist, the man who
puts girls' panties like a beanie on his head,
the chicken molester, the lady who likes Great Danes,
the boy who likes sheep, the old fellow who likes
to watch turkeys dance on the top of a hot stove,
the bicycle-seat sniffer, grasshopper muncher,
the bubbles-in-the-bath biter — they all meet
each night at midnight and, oh lord, they bowl.
From twelve to six they take it out on the pins
as they discuss their foibles with their friends.
I'm trying to cut down, says the woman who nibbles
the tails of mice. I've thrown away my Zippo, says
the man who sticks matches between people's toes.
There is nothing that can't become a pleasure
if one lets it, and so they bowl. They think
of that oddly handsome German shepherd face
and they bowl. Their hands quiver at the thought
of jamming their fingers in a car door
and they bowl. These are the heroes, these
grocers and teachers and postmen and plumbers.
They bring snapshots of themselves and Scotch tape,
then fix their photos to the pins and they bowl.
They focus on their faces at the end of the alley
and they bowl. They see the hunger in their eyes,
the twist of anticipation in their lips, and oh
they bowl — bowl to remember, bowl to forget,
as the pins with their own bruised faces explode
from midnight to six. While in those explosions
of wood, in which each pin describes an exact arc,
they feast on those moments when the world seems to stop
and everything conspires to push some fleeting
beauty — ripening peach or blossoming rose —
to the queer brink of perfection, where it flames,
flickers, fades, and is never perfect again.

STEPHEN DOBYNS

HOW TO LIKE IT

These are the first days of fall. The wind
at evening smells of roads still to be traveled,
while the sound of leaves blowing across the lawns
is like an unsettled feeling in the blood,
the desire to get in a car and just keep driving.
A man and a dog descend their front steps.
The dog says, Let's go downtown and get crazy drunk.
Let's tip over all the trash cans we can find.
This is how dogs deal with the prospect of change.
But in his sense of the season, the man is struck
by the oppressiveness of his past, how his memories
which were shifting and fluid have grown more solid
until it seems he can see remembered faces
caught up among the dark places in the trees.
The dog says, Let's pick up some girls and just
rip off their clothes. Let's dig holes everywhere.
Above his house, the man notices wisps of cloud
crossing the face of the moon. Like in a movie,
he says to himself, a movie about a person
leaving on a journey. He looks down the street
to the hills outside of town and finds the cut
where the road heads north. He thinks of driving
on that road and the dusty smell of the car
heater, which hasn't been used since last winter.
The dog says, Let's go down to the diner and sniff
people's legs. Let's stuff ourselves on burgers.
In the man's mind, the road is empty and dark.
Pine trees press down to the edge of the shoulder,
where the eyes of animals, fixed in his headlights,
shine like small cautions against the night.
Sometimes a passing truck makes his whole car shake.
The dog says, Let's go to sleep. Let's lie down
by the fire and put our tails over our noses.
But the man wants to drive all night, crossing
one state line after another, and never stop
until the sun creeps into his rearview mirror.
Then he'll pull over and rest awhile before
starting again, and at dusk he'll crest a hill
and there, filling a valley, will be the lights
of a city entirely new to him.

[handwritten annotations: "surreal" (top left); "seasons changing but also cycle?" (top right); "change" (right, near line about change); "changes tone pretty radically, more serious" (left margin); "cycle" (right); "not sure where he is going" (right); "(this is how men deal with the prospect of change)" (bottom right); "(run away)" (bottom right)]

STEPHEN DOBYNS

you must understand where your comforts lie in the midst of chaos.

But the dog says, Let's just go back inside.
Let's not do anything tonight. So they
walk back up the sidewalk to the front steps.
How is it possible to want so many things
and still want nothing. The man wants to sleep
and wants to hit his head again and again
against a wall. Why is it all so difficult?
But the dog says, Let's go make a sandwich.
Let's make the tallest sandwich anyone's ever seen.
And that's what they do and that's where the man's
wife finds him, staring into the refrigerator
as if into the place where the answers are kept —
the ones telling why you get up in the morning
and how it is possible to sleep at night,
answers to what comes next and how to like it.

more serious

imperfection (in relationships?)

"change"

FRAGMENTS

Now there is a slit in the blue fabric of air.
His house spins faster. He holds down books,
chairs; his life and its objects fly upward:
vanishing black specks in the indifferent sky.

The sky is a torn piece of blue paper.
He tries to repair it, but the memory
of death is like paste on his fingers
and certain days stick like dead flies.

surreal

Say the sky goes back to being the sky
and the sun continues as always. Now,
knowing what you know, how can you not see
thin cracks in the fragile blue vaults of air.

imperfection

My friend, what can I give you or darkness
lift from you but fragments of language,
fragments of blue sky. You had three
beautiful daughters and one has died.

for Donald Murray

STEPHEN DOBYNS

TENDERLY

It's not a fancy restaurant, nor is it
a dump and it's packed this Saturday night
when suddenly a man leaps onto his tabletop,
whips out his prick and begins sawing at it

with a butter knife. I can't stand it
anymore! he shouts. The waiters grab him
before he draws blood and hustle him
out the back. Soon the other diners return

to their fillets and slices of duck. How
peculiar, each, in some fashion, articulates.
Consider how the world implants a picture
in our brains. Maybe thirty people watched

this nut attack his member with a dull knife
and for each, forever after, the image pops up
a thousand times. I once saw the oddest thing —
how often does each announce this fact?

In the distant future, several at death's door
once more recollect this guy hacking at himself
and die shaking their heads. So they are linked
as a family is linked — through a single portrait.

The man's wobbly perch on the white tablecloth,
his open pants and strangled red chunk of flesh
become for each a symbol of having had precisely
enough, of slipping over the edge, of being whipped

about the chops by the finicky world, and of reacting
with a rash mutiny against the tyranny of desire.
As for the lunatic who was tossed out the back
and left to rethink his case among the trash cans,

who knows what happened to him? A short life,
most likely, additional humiliation and defeat.
But the thirty patrons wish him well. They all
have burdens to shoulder in this world and whenever

one feels the strap begin to slip, he or she thinks
of the nut dancing with his dick on the tabletop
and trudges on. At least life has spared me this,
they think. And one — a retired banker — represents

the rest when he hopes against hope that the lunatic
is parked on a topless foreign beach with a beauty
clasped in his loving arms, breathing heavily, Oh,
darling, touch me there, tenderly, one more time!

straightforward

TOMATOES

A woman travels to Brazil for plastic
surgery and a face-lift. She is sixty
and has the usual desire to stay pretty.
Once she is healed, she takes her new face
out on the streets of Rio. A young man
with a gun wants her money. Bang, she's dead.
The body is shipped back to New York,
but in the morgue there is a mix-up. The son
is sent for. He is told that his mother
is one of these ten different women.
Each has been shot. Such is modern life.
He studies them all but can't find her.
With her new face, she has become a stranger.
Maybe it's this one, maybe it's that one.
He looks at their breasts. Which ones nursed him?
He presses their hands to his cheek.
Which ones consoled him? He even tries
climbing into their laps to see which
feels most familiar but the coroner stops him.
Well, says the coroner, which is your mother?
They all are, says the young man, let me
take them as a package. The coroner hesitates,
then agrees. Actually, it solved a lot of problems.
The young man has the ten women shipped home,
then cremates them all together. You've seen
how some people have a little urn on the mantel?
This man has a huge silver garbage can.
In the spring, he drags the garbage can
out to the garden and begins working the teeth,
the ash, the bits of bone into the soil.

Then he plants tomatoes. His mother loved tomatoes.
They grow straight from seed, so fast and big
that the young man is amazed. He takes the first
ten into the kitchen. In their roundness,
he sees his mother's breasts. In their smoothness,
he finds the consoling touch of her hands.
Mother, mother, he cries, and flings himself
on the tomatoes. Forget about the knife, the fork,
the pinch of salt. Try to imagine the filial
starvation, think of his ravenous kisses.

CEMETERY NIGHTS

Sweet dreams, sweet memories, sweet taste of earth:
here's how the dead pretend they're still alive —
one drags up a chair, a lamp, unwraps
the newspaper from somebody's garbage,
then sits holding the paper up to his face.
No matter if the lamp is busted and his eyes
have fallen out. Or some of the others
group together in front of the TV, chuckling
and slapping what's left of their knees.
No matter if the screen is dark. Four more
sit at a table with glasses and plates,
lift forks to their mouths and chew. No matter
if their plates are empty and they chew only air.
Two of the dead roll on the ground,
banging and rubbing their bodies together
as if in love or frenzy. No matter if their skin
breaks off, that their genitals are just a memory.

The head cemetery rat calls in all the city rats,
who pay him what rats find valuable —
the wing of a pigeon or ear of a dog.
The rats perch on tombstones and the cheap
statues of angels and, oh, they hold their bellies
and laugh, laugh until their guts half break;
while the stars give off the same cold light
that all these dead once planned their lives by,
and in someone's yard a dog barks and barks
just to see if some animal as dumb as he is
will wake from sleep and perhaps bark back.

Rita Dove

AMERICAN SMOOTH

We were dancing — it must have
been a foxtrot or a waltz,
something romantic but
requiring restraint,
rise and fall, precise
execution as we moved
into the next song without
stopping, two chests heaving
above a seven-league
stride — such perfect agony
one learns to smile through,
ecstatic mimicry
being the *sine qua non*
of American Smooth.
And because I was distracted
by the effort of
keeping my frame
(the leftward lean, head turned
just enough to gaze out
past your ear and always
smiling, smiling),
I didn't notice
how still you'd become until
we had done it
(for two measures?
four?) — achieved flight,
that swift and serene
magnificence,
before the earth
remembered who we were
and brought us down.

RITA DOVE

CRAB-BOIL

(Ft. Myers, 1962)

Why do I remember the sky
above the forbidden beach,
why only blue and the scratch,
shell on tin, of their distress?
The rest

imagination supplies:
bucket and angry pink beseeching
claws. Why does Aunt Helen
laugh before saying "Look at that —

a bunch of niggers, not
a-one get out 'fore the others pull him
back." I don't believe her —

just as I don't believe *they* won't come
and chase us back to the colored-only shore
crisp with litter and broken glass.

"When do we kill them?"
"Kill 'em? Hell, the water does *that*.
They don't feel a thing . . . no nervous system."

I decide to believe this: I'm hungry.
Dismantled, they're merely exotic,
a blushing meat. After all, she *has*
grown old in the South. If
we're kicked out now, I'm ready.

[handwritten annotation: poets tell us when someone/something is unreliable... crabs!]

WINGFOOT LAKE

(Independence Day, 1964)

On her 36th birthday, Thomas had shown her
her first swimming pool. It had been
his favorite color, exactly — just
so much of it, the swimmers' white arms jutting
into the chevrons of high society.
She had rolled up her window
and told him to drive on, fast.

Now this *act of mercy*: four daughters
dragging her to their husbands' company picnic,
(white families) on one side and (them)
on the other, unpacking the same
squeeze bottles of Heinz, the same
waxy beef patties and Salem potato chip bags.
So he was dead for the first time
on Fourth of July — ten years ago

had been harder, waiting for something to happen,
and ten years before that, the girls
like young horses eyeing the track.
Last August she stood alone for hours
in front of the T.V. set
as a crow's wing moved slowly through
the white streets of government.
That brave swimming

scared her, like Joanna saying
Mother, we're Afro-Americans now!
What did she know about Africa?
Were there lakes like this one
with a rowboat pushed under the pier?
Or Thomas' Great Mississippi
with its sullen silks? (There was
the Nile but the Nile belonged

to God.) Where she came from
was the past, 12 miles into town
where nobody had locked their back door,
and Goodyear hadn't begun to dream of a park
under the company symbol, a white foot
sprouting two small wings.

THE BREATHING, THE ENDLESS NEWS

Every god is lonely, an exile
composed of parts: elk horn,
cloven hoof. Receptacle

for wishes, each god is empty
without us, penitent,
raking our yards into windblown piles. . . .

Children know this: they are
the trailings of gods. Their eyes
hold nothing at birth then fill slowly

with the myth of ourselves. Not so the dolls,
out for the count, each toe pouting from
the slumped-over toddler clothes:

no blossoming there. So we
give our children dolls, and
they know just what to do —

line them up and shoot them.
With every execution
doll and god grow stronger.

AFTER READING *MICKEY IN THE NIGHT KITCHEN* FOR THE THIRD TIME BEFORE BED

I'm in the milk and the milk's in me! . . . I'm Mickey!

My daughter spreads her legs
to find her vagina:
hairless, this mistaken
bit of nomenclature
is what a stranger cannot touch
without her yelling. She demands
to see mine and momentarily
we're a lopsided star
among the spilled toys,
my prodigious scallops
exposed to her neat cameo.

And yet the same glazed
tunnel, layered sequences.
She is three; that makes this
innocent. *We're pink!*
she shrieks, and bounds off.

Every month she wants
to know where it hurts

and what the wrinkled string means
between my legs. *This is good blood*
I say, but that's wrong, too.
How to tell her that it's what makes us —
black mother, cream child.
That we're in the pink
and the pink's in us.

PARSLEY

1. *The Cane Fields*

There is a parrot imitating spring
in the palace, its feathers parsley green.
Out of the swamp the cane appears

to haunt us, and we cut it down. El General
searches for a word; he is all the world
there is. Like a parrot imitating spring,

we lie down screaming as rain punches through
and we come up green. We cannot speak an R —
out of the swamp, the cane appears

and then the mountain we call in whispers *Katalina*.
The children gnaw their teeth to arrowheads.
There is a parrot imitating spring.

El General has found his word: *perejil*.
Who says it, lives. He laughs, teeth shining
out of the swamp. The cane appears

in our dreams, lashed by wind and streaming.
And we lie down. For every drop of blood
there is a parrot imitating spring.
Out of the swamp the cane appears.

2. *The Palace*

The word the general's chosen is parsley.
It is fall, when thoughts turn
to love and death; the general thinks

of his mother, how she died in the fall
and he planted her walking cane at the grave
and it flowered, each spring stolidly forming
four-star blossoms. The general

pulls on his boots, he stomps to
her room in the palace, the one without
curtains, the one with a parrot
in a brass ring. As he paces he wonders
Who can I kill today. And for a moment
the little knot of screams
is still. The parrot, who has traveled

all the way from Australia in an ivory
cage, is, coy as a widow, practising
spring. Ever since the morning
his mother collapsed in the kitchen
while baking skull-shaped candies
for the Day of the Dead, the general
has hated sweets. He orders pastries
brought up for the bird; they arrive

dusted with sugar on a bed of lace.
The knot in his throat starts to twitch;
he sees his boots the first day in battle
splashed with mud and urine
as a soldier falls at his feet amazed —
how stupid he looked! — at the sound
of artillery. *I never thought it would sing*
the soldier said, and died. Now

the general sees the fields of sugar
cane, lashed by rain and streaming.
He sees his mother's smile, the teeth
gnawed to arrowheads. He hears
the Haitians sing without R's
as they swing the great machetes:
Katalina, they sing, *Katalina*,

mi madle, mi amol en muelte. God knows
his mother was no stupid woman; she
could roll an R like a queen. Even
a parrot can roll an R! In the bare room
the bright feathers arch in a parody

of greenery, as the last pale crumbs
disappear under the blackened tongue. Someone

calls out his name in a voice
so like his mother's, a startled tear
splashes the tip of his right boot.
My mother, my love in death.
The general remembers the tiny green sprigs
men of his village wore in their capes
to honor the birth of a son. He will
order many, this time, to be killed

for a single, beautiful word.

TESTIMONIAL

Back when the earth was new
and heaven just a whisper,
back when the names of things
hadn't had time to stick;

back when the smallest breezes
melted summer into autumn,
when all the poplars quivered
sweetly in rank and file . . .

the world called, and I answered.
Each glance ignited to a gaze.
I caught my breath and called that life,
swooned between spoonfuls of lemon sorbet.

I was pirouette and flourish,
I was filigree and flame.
How could I count my blessings
when I didn't know their names?

Back when everything was still to come,
luck leaked out everywhere.
I gave my promise to the world,
and the world followed me here.

Stephen Dunn

THE STAIRWAY

The architect wanted to build a stairway
and suspend it with silver, almost invisible
guy wires in a high-ceilinged room,
a stairway you couldn't ascend or descend
except in your dreams. But first —
because wild things are not easily seen
if what's around them is wild —
he'd make sure the house that housed it
was practical, built two-by-four by
two-by-four, slat by slat, without ornament.
The stairway would be an invitation
to anyone who felt invited by it,
and depending on your reaction he'd know
if friendship were possible.
The house he'd claim as his, but the stairway
would be designed to be ownerless,
tilted against any suggestion of a theology,
disappointing to those looking for politics.
Of course the architect knew
that over the years he'd have to build
other things the way others desired,
knew that to live in this world was to trade
a few industrious hours for one beautiful one.
Yet every night when he got home
he could imagine, as he walked in the door,
his stairway going nowhere, not for sale,
and maybe some you to whom nothing
about it need be explained, waiting,
the wine decanted, the night about to unfold.

INSTEAD OF YOU

I place a dead butterfly on the page,
this is called starting
with an image from real life.

STEPHEN DUNN

It is gold and black
and, as if in some embalmer's dream,
a dusting of talc on its wings.
I have plans
for these wings. I will not let them
slip through my hands.
And if anyone is worried about how
the butterfly died, I'll tell them
my cat swatted it out of the air,
I just picked it up
and brought it to this page
with a notion of breathing
a different life into it. And I confess:
the cat's gesture was more innocent than mine.

The wings suggest nothing I want,
they are so lovely
I simply like the way they distract,
how my eye turns away from the living-
room, and the mind spins
into the silliness of spring.
I don't want much.
Just for certain private places
to remain open to me, that's all.
But this is no time to get ethereal.
Already, in a far corner of the page,
something dark is tempting me
to pull it into the poem. One tug
and it's a bat
trapped in sunlight, rabid with fear.

There's no way to keep the ugliness out,
ever. Drops of blood
beautiful, say, on the snow,
always lead to a wound.
Can this still turn out to be a love poem?
Can I still pull you from the wreckage
and kiss your bruises, so black and gold?
Is it too late to introduce you
who were always here, the watermark,
the poem's secret?
From the start all I wanted to explain
was how things go wrong,
how the heart's an empty place
until it is filled,

and how the darkness is forever waiting
for its chance.
If I have failed, know that I was trying
to get to you in my own way,
know that my cat never swatted a butterfly,
it was I who invented and killed it,
something to talk about
instead of you.

THE ROUTINE THINGS AROUND THE HOUSE

When Mother died
I thought: now I'll have a death poem.
That was unforgivable

yet I've since forgiven myself
as sons are able to do
who've been loved by their mothers.

I stared into the coffin
knowing how long she'd live,
how many lifetimes there are

in the sweet revisions of memory.
It's hard to know exactly
how we ease ourselves back from sadness,

but I remembered when I was twelve,
1951, before the world
unbuttoned its blouse.

I had asked my mother (I was trembling)
if I could see her breasts
and she took me into her room

without embarrassment or coyness
and I stared at them,
afraid to ask for more.

Now, years later, someone tells me
Cancers who've never had mother love
are doomed and I, a Cancer,

feel blessed again. What luck
to have had a mother
who showed me her breasts

when girls my age were developing
their separate countries,
what luck

she didn't doom me
with too much or too little.
Had I asked to touch,

perhaps to suck them,
what would she have done?
Mother, dead woman

who I think permits me
to love women easily,
this poem

is dedicated to where
we stopped, to the incompleteness
that was sufficient

and to how you buttoned up,
began doing the routine things
around the house.

COHABITING

There's not a nude in a museum
or a person anywhere, taking a bath,
nearly as naked as that French girl,
stripped of all but her socks,
head shaved, being spat upon
by her own townspeople
in one of history's sunlit
cobblestone squares. I've only
read about her, but somehow,
for me, she's permanently fixed,
a scaffolding of awful

yet understandable righteousness
surrounding her, accentuating
the stark paleness of her skin,
the big war finally over,
and behind it, for centuries,
those without pity
with their saliva and their stones.

I imagine how it began
between them, a man in a uniform
she had to have been wary of,
a man, in fact, dressed to kill,
touching her in some exactly
right place in a wrong time.
And I see her resisting for as long
as she can — minutes, weeks —
her mind searching for principles
her body doesn't seem to have.
Perhaps she thinks it's the end
of her world, what has she to lose?
Or she just falls
into those irrevocable tomorrows
like someone who knows
only what she feels, the enemy slowly
transformed into a man as lonely
as she is, with beautiful hands.

I can see the picture clearly now.
Terrified, she rushes forward,
which makes no sense, but I remember
when I did the same. Everything
in my education said, no, go back,
and I went headlong into the flames.

THE INSISTENCE OF BEAUTY

The day before those silver planes
came out of the perfect blue, I was struck
by the beauty of pollution rising
from smokestacks near Newark,

gray and white ribbons of it
on their way to evanescence.

And at impact, no doubt, certain beholders
and believers from another part of the world
must have seen what appeared gorgeous —
the flames of something theirs being born.

I watched for hours — mesmerized —
that willful collision replayed,
the better man in me not yielding,
then yielding to revenge's sweet surge.

The next day there was a photograph
of dust and smoke ghosting a street,
and another of a man you couldn't be sure
was fear-frozen or dead or made of stone,

and for a while I was pleased
to admire the intensity — or was it the coldness? —
of each photographer's good eye.
For years I'd taken pride in resisting

the obvious — sunsets, snowy peaks,
a starlet's face — yet had come to realize
even those, seen just right, can have
their edgy place. And the sentimental,

beauty's sloppy cousin, that enemy,
can't it have a place too?
Doesn't a tear deserve a close-up?
When word came of a fireman

who hid in the rubble
so his dispirited search dog
could have someone to find, I repeated it
to everyone I knew. I did this for myself,
not for community or beauty's sake,
yet soon it had a rhythm and a frame.

STEPHEN DUNN

LANDSCAPE AT THE END OF THE CENTURY

The sky in the trees, the trees mixed up
with what's left of heaven, nearby a patch
of daffodils rooted down
where dirt and stones comprise a kind
of night, unmetaphysical, cool as a skeptic's
final sentence. What this scene needs
is a nude absentmindedly sunning herself
on a large rock, thinks the man fed up
with nature, or perhaps a lost tiger,
the maximum amount of wildness a landscape
can bear, but the man knows and fears
his history of tampering with everything,
and besides to anyone who might see him
he's just a figure in a clearing
in a forest in a universe
that is as random as desire itself,
his desire in particular, so much going on
with and without him, moles humping up
the ground near the daffodils, a mockingbird
publishing its cacophonous anthology,
and those little Calvinists, the ants,
making it all the more difficult
for a person in America
to close his office, skip to the beach.
But what this scene needs are wisteria
and persimmons, thinks the woman
sunning herself absentmindedly on the rock,
a few magnificent words that one
might want to eat if one were a lover
of words, the hell with first principles,
the noon sun on my body, tempered
by a breeze that cannot be doubted.
And as she thinks, she who exists
only in the man's mind, a deer grazes
beyond their knowing, a deer tick riding
its back, and in the gifted air
mosquitoes, dragonflies, and tattered
mute angels no one has called upon in years.

Louise Erdrich

JACKLIGHT

*The same Chippewa word is used both for flirting and hunting game,
while another Chippewa word connotes both using force in intercourse
and also killing a bear with one's bare hands.*

> — R. W. Dunning, *Social and Economic Change
> Among the Northern Ojibwa* (1959)

We have come to the edge of the woods,
out of brown grass where we slept, unseen,
out of knotted twigs, out of leaves creaked shut,
out of hiding.

At first the light wavered, glancing over us.
Then it clenched to a fist of light that pointed,
searched out, divided us.
Each took the beams like direct blows the heart answers.
Each of us moved forward alone.

We have come to the edge of the woods,
drawn out of ourselves by this night sun,
this battery of polarized acids,
that outshines the moon.

We smell them behind it
but they are faceless, invisible.
We smell the raw steel of their gun barrels,
mink oil on leather, their tongues of sour barley.
We smell their mothers buried chin-deep in wet dirt.
We smell their fathers with scoured knuckles,
teeth cracked from hot marrow.
We smell their sisters of crushed dogwood, bruised apples,
of fractured cups and concussions of burnt hooks.

We smell their breath steaming lightly behind the jacklight.
We smell the itch underneath the caked guts on their clothes.
We smell their minds like silver hammers
cocked back, held in readiness
for the first of us to step into the open.

We have come to the edge of the woods,
out of brown grass where we slept, unseen,

out of leaves creaked shut, out of hiding.
We have come here too long.

It is their turn now,
their turn to follow us. Listen,
they put down their equipment.
It is useless in the tall brush.
And now they take the first steps, now knowing
how deep the woods are and lightless.
How deep the woods are.

THE STRANGE PEOPLE

*The antelope are strange people . . . they are beautiful to
look at, and yet they are tricky. We do not trust them.
They appear and disappear; they are like shadows on the
plains. Because of their great beauty, young men sometimes follow the antelope and are lost forever. Even if
those foolish ones find themselves and return, they are
never again right in their heads.*

— Pretty Shield, Medicine Woman of the Crows
transcribed and edited by Frank Linderman (1932)

All night I am the doe, breathing
his name in a frozen field,
the small mist of the word
drifting always before me.

And again he has heard it
and I have gone burning
to meet him, the jacklight
fills my eyes with blue fire;
the heart in my chest
explodes like a hot stone.

Then slung like a sack
in the back of his pickup,
I wipe the death scum
from my mouth, sit up laughing
and shriek in my speeding grave.

Safely shut in the garage,
when he sharpens his knife
and thinks to have me, like that,

I come toward him,
a lean gray witch
through the bullets that enter and dissolve.

I sit in his house
drinking coffee till dawn
and leave as frost reddens on hubcaps,
crawling back into my shadowy body.
All day, asleep in clean grasses,
I dream of the one who could really wound me.
Not with weapons, not with a kiss, not with a look.
Not even with his goodness.

If a man was never to lie to me. *Never lie me.*
I swear I would never leave him.

I WAS SLEEPING WHERE THE BLACK OAKS MOVE

We watched from the house
as the river grew, helpless
and terrible in its unfamiliar body.
Wrestling everything into it,
the water wrapped around trees
until their life-hold was broken.
They went down, one by one,
and the river dragged off their covering.

Nests of the herons, roots washed to bones,
snags of soaked bark on the shoreline:
a whole forest pulled through the teeth
of the spillway. Trees surfacing
singly, where the river poured off
into arteries for fields below the reservation.

When at last it was over, the long removal,
they had all become the same dry wood.
We walked among them, the branches
whitening in the raw sun.
Above us drifted herons,
alone, hoarse-voiced, broken,
settling their beaks among the hollows.
Grandpa said, *These are the ghosts of the tree people
moving among us, unable to take their rest.*

Sometimes now, we dream our way back to the heron dance.
Their long wings are bending the air
into circles through which they fall.
They rise again in shifting wheels.
How long must we live in the broken figures
their necks make, narrowing the sky.

INDIAN BOARDING SCHOOL: THE RUNAWAYS

Home's the place we head for in our sleep.
Boxcars stumbling north in dreams
don't wait for us. We catch them on the run.
The rails, old lacerations that we love,
shoot parallel across the face and break
just under Turtle Mountains. Riding scars
you can't get lost. Home is the place they cross.

The lame guard strikes a match and makes the dark
less tolerant. We watch through cracks in boards
as the land starts rolling, rolling till it hurts
to be here, cold in regulation clothes.
We know the sheriff's waiting at midrun
to take us back. His car is dumb and warm.
The highway doesn't rock, it only hums
like a wing of long insults. The worn-down welts
of ancient punishments lead back and forth.

All runaways wear dresses, long green ones,
the color you would think shame was. We scrub
the sidewalks down because it's shameful work.
Our brushes cut the stone in watered arcs
and in the soak frail outlines shiver clear
a moment, things us kids pressed on the dark
face before it hardened, pale, remembering
delicate old injuries, the spines of names and leaves.

DEAR JOHN WAYNE

August and the drive-in picture is packed.
We lounge on the hood of the Pontiac
surrounded by the slow-burning spirals they sell

at the window, to vanquish the hordes of mosquitoes.
Nothing works. They break through the smoke screen for blood.

Always the lookout spots the Indians first,
spread north to south, barring progress.
The Sioux or some other Plains bunch
in spectacular columns, ICBM missiles,
feathers bristling in the meaningful sunset.

The drum breaks. There will be no parlance.
Only the arrows whining, a death-cloud of nerves
swarming down on the settlers
who die beautifully, tumbling like dust weeds
into the history that brought us all here
together: this wide screen beneath the sign of the bear.

The sky fills, acres of blue squint and eye
that the crowd cheers. His face moves over us,
a thick cloud of vengeance, pitted
like the land that was once flesh. Each rut,
each scar makes a promise: *It is
not over, this fight, not as long as you resist.*

Everything we see belongs to us.

A few laughing Indians fall over the hood
slipping in the hot spilled butter.
The eye sees a lot, John, but the heart is so blind.
Death makes us owners of nothing.
He smiles, a horizon of teeth
the credits reel over, and then the white fields

again blowing in the true-to-life dark.
The dark films over everything.
We get into the car
scratching our mosquito bites, speechless and small
as people are when the movie is done.
We are back in our skins.

How can we help but keep hearing his voice,
the flip side of the sound track, still playing:
*Come on, boys, we got them
where we want them, drunk, running.*
They'll give us what we want, what we need.
Even his disease was the idea of taking everything.
Those cells, burning, doubling, splitting out of their skins.

LOUISE ERDRICH

MARY MAGDALENE

I wash your ankles
with my tears. Unhem
my sweep of hair
and burnish the arch of your foot.
Still your voice cracks
above me.

I cut off my hair and toss it across your pillow.
A dark towel
like the one after sex.
I'm walking out,
my face a dustpan,
my body stiff as a new broom.

I will drive boys
to smash empty bottles on their brows.
I will pull them right out of their skins.
It is the old way that girls
get even with their fathers —
by wrecking their bodies on other men.

CHRIST'S TWIN

He was formed of chicken blood and lightning.
He was what fell out when the jug tipped.
He was waiting at the bottom
of the cliff when the swine plunged over.
He tore out their lungs with a sound like ripping silk.
He hacked the pink carcasses apart, so that the ribs spread
like a terrible butterfly, and there was darkness.
It was he who turned the handle and let the dogs
rush from the basements. He shoved the crust
of a volcano into his roaring mouth.
He showed one empty hand. The other gripped
a crowbar, a monkey wrench, a crop
which was the tail of the ass that bore them to Egypt,
one in each saddlebag, sucking twists
of honeyed goatskin, arguing
already over a woman's breasts.
He understood the prayers that rose

in every language, for he had split the human tongue.
He was not the Devil nor among the Fallen —
it was just that he was clumsy, and curious,
and liked to play with knives. He was the dove
hypnotized by boredom and betrayed by light.
He was the pearl in the mouth, the tangible
emptiness that saints seek at the center of their prayers.
He leaped into a shadow when the massive stone
rolled across the entrance, sealing him with his brother
in the dark as in the beginning.
Only this time he emerged first, bearing the self-
    inflicted wound, both brass halos
tacked to the back of his skull.
He raised two crooked fingers; the extra die
tumbled from his lips when he preached
but no one noticed. They were too busy
clawing at the hem of his robe and planning
how to sell him to the world.

NEW VOWS

The night was clean as the bone of a rabbit blown hollow.
I cast my hood of dogskin
away, and my shirt of nettles.
Ten years had been enough. I left my darkened house.

The trick was in living that death to its source.
When it happened, I wandered toward more than I was.

Widowed by men, I married the dark firs,
as if I were walking in sleep toward their arms.
I drank, without fear or desire,
this odd fire.

Now shadows move freely within me as words.
These are eternal, these stunned, loosened verbs.
And I can't tell you yet
how truly I belong

to the hiss and shift of wind,
these slow, variable mouths
through which, at certain times, I speak in tongues.

Carol Frost

CHIMERA

By the verge of the sea a man finds a gelatinous creature,
parching, thick as a shoe, its head a doubtful dark green
that leans toward him as he bends near in some dark
wonderment of his own. The sky is haunted by pure light,

the sea a rough mixture of blue, and green, and black. Suddenly
he hears the air rent with loud cries and looks to see
pelicans on the piers raising their wings then falling, changing shape
to dive into the sea. He thinks of Bosch's rebellious angels
changing shape as they are pursued out of the immaculate sky.

Who are they? Angels who accept the hideous
and monstrous. Fallen, they make up a nightmare fauna.
Say the sea is to be questioned. Below the bounds
of this estate, through rainbowed cold, the rockheaded and cored

of bone, the chimera our madness does not cease to reinvent
and which we dare not think alive, crawls in a thick ooze.
Yet even this one, torn to the plain insides and leaking dyes,
exudes a gentle unrest of the soul. Is it not good? The man pauses,
looks around — the sea undulated, sharpening and smoothing

all the grooves that history has graven on the sand —
then he puts his hands under the terrible flesh and heaves it
as far as he can back into the Atlantic, as if it were the mirror
of a lost estate, the dawn-time of the world's first season.

HOMO SAPIENS

In this lonely, varying light of dawn with the residue of desire
like mist departing, I am walking. Was it in your eyes,
where my elongated face shone, I saw for the first time —
as if all the transparent fire in these trees had become palpable —

a hunger that was not wholly animal?
The need to tremble like dogwood, feeling the rain touch down.
My strange blood rises, and I may see you, fair leaves slipping over you,
    half-hidden
in the morning. With the beasts beside a pond,
I conjure the inward sun to leap into my brain. What remains?
Wild, beautiful petals all around.
A beast's face. And something, something else.

SEXUAL JEALOUSY

Think of the queen mole who is unequivocal,
exuding a scent to keep the other females neuter
and bringing forth the colony's only babies, hairless and pink in the dark
of her tunneled chamber. She may chew a pale something, a root,
find it tasteless, drop it for the dreary others to take away, then demand
more; she must suckle the young. Of course
they all hate her and are jealous of the attention given her
by her six bedmates. In their mutual dream she is dead and her urine
no longer arrests their maturing. As irises infallibly unfold,
one of their own will feel her sex grow quickest and greatest. As they dig
together, their snouts full of soil, they hope this and are ruthless in their
    waiting.

LAWS

She knows of doom only what all women know,
deciding not to speak of it, since speech pretends
its course can be made to bend: — someone fleeing hot and sweating
and the victors close behind, then two roads all at once in a wood.
    Which one leads
farther away? Under cover of silence
she goes along as if perhaps nothing would happen to her,
seeming to be swayed by breezes — dazed, her friends say in their
    concern,
after, when they've thought of it, having called or dropped by.

Once, though, late in her illness, in the heat of a morning walk,
she raises her wig and shows us this surge of white back from the fore-
    head. The tablets
Moses carried, with his guesses, in the end could not have been more
    blinding or more lawful.

FURY

And the whole night she had told herself to be pleasant
as she lay by the sleeping man, and she'd gladly have listened to herself,
but as the enormous dawn sneaked into their darkness
and seized them in its paws, she found herself with the old fury,
past her carefullest politeness. She saw she'd need millennia to find a
    way
to comprehend the reason for the difference between their early
    ideals —
a garden where plums and peaches grew well and tasted wild
and they were unembarrassed by genitals — and what had become of
    them.
This apple-pose. It was no good blaming God or Adam, she knew, but
    she couldn't help herself — :
Why hadn't the one spoken forthrightly and had the other caved in?
Then, hardly allowing him to fully awaken, she said her first sarcasm.
    Then another.

SCORN

She thought of no wilder delicacy than the starling eggs she fed him for
    breakfast,
and if he sat and ate like a farmhand and she hated him sometimes,
she knew it didn't matter: that whatever in the din of argument
was harshly spoken, something else was done, soothed and patted away.
When they were young the towering fierceness
of their differences had frightened her even as she longed for physical
    release.
Out of their mouths such curses; their hands huge, pointing, stabbing
    the air.

How had they *not* been wounded? And wounded they'd convalesced in
     the same rooms
and bed. When at last they knew everything without confiding — fears,
     stinks,
boiling hearts — they gave up themselves a little so that they might both
     love and scorn
each other, and they ate from each other's hands.

TO KILL A DEER

Into the changes of autumn brush
the doe walked, and the hide, head, and ears
were the tinsel browns. They made her.
I could not see her. She reappeared, stuffed with apples,
and I shot her. Into the pines she ran,
and I ran after. I might have lost her,
seeing no sign of blood or scuffle,
but felt myself part of the woods,
a woman with a doe's ears, and heard her
dying, counted her last breaths like a song
of dying, and found her dying.
I shot her again because her lungs rattled like castanets,
then poked her with the gun barrel
because her eyes were dusty and unreal.
I opened her belly and pushed the insides
like rotted fruit into a rabbit hole,
skinned her, broke her leg joints under my knee,
took the meat, smelled the half-digested smell
that was herself. Ah, I closed her eyes.
I left her refolded in some briars
with the last sun on her head
like a benediction, head tilted on its axis
of neck and barren bone; head bent
wordless over a death, though I heard
the night wind blowing through her fur,
heard riot in the emptied head.

CAROL FROST

THE ST. LOUIS ZOO

The isle is full of noises, / Sounds, and sweet air . . . sometimes voices.
— The Tempest

High, yellow, coiled and weighting the branch like an odd piece of fruit,
      a snake slept
by the gate, in the serpent house. I walked around the paths hearing

hushed air, piecemeal remarks, and the hoarse voice of the keeper
      spreading cabbage
and pellets in the elephant compound — "Hungry, are you? There's a
      girl.

How's Pearl?" — A clucking music, then silence again crept past me
on the waters of the duck pond. Birds with saffron wings in the flight
      cage

and flamingos the color of mangoes, even their webbed feet red-orange,
      made so
"by the algae they ingest," as angels are made of air — some bickered,

some were tongue-tied, some danced on one leg in the honeyed light.
I thought of autumn as leaves scattered down. Nearby, closed away

in his crude beginnings in a simulated rain forest, the gorilla pulled out
      handfuls
of grass, no Miranda to teach him to speak, though he was full of noises

and rank air after swallowing. Smooth rind and bearded husks lay about
      him.
His eyes were ingots when he looked at me.

In late-summer air thick with rose and lily, I felt the old malevolence;
the snake tonguing the air, as if to tell me of its dreaming: — birds of
      paradise

gemming a pond; the unspooling; soft comings on, soft, soft
gestures, twisted and surreptitious; the shock; the taste; the kingdom.

In something more than words, *You are the snake, snake coils in you,*
it said. Do you think anyone knows its own hunger as well as the snake?

Why am I not just someone alive? When did Spirit tear me
to see how void of blessing I was? The snake hesitated, tasting dusk's
     black honey,

to feel if it was still good. And through its swoon
it knew it. Leaf, lichen, the least refinements, and the perfection.

TELLING THE BEES

Will we tell the bees or bees tell us it's no sadder — another fall whose
     ever fall it is?

It's as if they felt for us: the sting, the swarming in the mind,

the sugar tear to probe for, or a mood to dance on air. If there were
     overblown roses

and a child spilled root beer, the bees would seem to know the difference,
     flying there,

but not care, evening too swift, autumnal. I say only listen to the hum
     behind the trees

where the white bee boxes burn in evening. Drink in the air. There's
     more moving

in the season's heart — seconds of snow on the steep part of the wind —

than can be stopped. The bees, small jewels, however, hand themselves
     over

to us. It's all right to cry, I tell myself. But it isn't sadder than it was before.

THE PART OF THE BEE'S BODY EMBEDDED IN THE FLESH

The bee-boy, *merops apiaster*, on sultry thundery days
filled his bosom between his coarse shirt and his skin
with bees — his every meal wild honey.

CAROL FROST

He had no apprehension of their stings or didn't mind
and gave himself — his palate, the soft tissues of this throat —
what Rubens gave to the sun's illumination
stealing like fingers across a woman's thigh
and van Gogh's brushwork heightened.
Whatever it means, why not say it hurts —
the mind's raw, gold coiling whirled against
air currents, want, and beauty? I *will* say beauty.

THE UNDRESSING

They took off their clothes 1000 nights
and felt the plaster of the moon
sift over them, and the ground roll
them in its dream. Little did they know
the light and clay and their own sweat
became a skin they couldn't wash away.
Each night bonded to the next,
and they grew stiffer. They noticed this
in sunlight — there were calluses,
round tough moons on their extremities,
shadows under their eyes,
and sometimes a faint sour smell they hadn't had as children.
It worried them, but at night the animal
in their bodies overcame their reluctance
to be naked with each other,
and the mineral moon did its work.
At last when they woke up and were dead,
statues on their backs in the park,
they opened their mouths
and crawled out, pitifully soft and small,
not yet souls.

Arthur Furst

Allen Ginsberg

Handwritten annotations:
like whitman, focused on community, no one (person) is particular to blame

Whitman-esque (long-winded)
repetitious "who", "america"
self-reflective
referential(?) - "timely" and/or "dated"
specific
explicit - sexual
war-torn
Marx! communism
trance-like(?)

from HOWL

for Carl Solomon

I

I saw the best minds of my generation destroyed by madness, starving
    hysterical naked,
dragging themselves through the negro streets at dawn looking for an
    angry fix,
angelheaded hipsters burning for the ancient heavenly connection to the
    starry dynamo in the machinery of night,
who poverty and tatters and hollow-eyed and high sat up smoking in the
    supernatural darkness of cold-water flats floating across the tops of
    cities contemplating jazz,
who bared their brains to Heaven under the El and saw Mohammedan
    angels staggering on tenement roofs illuminated,
who passed through universities with radiant cool eyes hallucinating
    Arkansas and Blake-light tragedy among the scholars of war,
who were expelled from the academies for crazy & publishing obscene
    odes on the windows of the skull,
who cowered in unshaven rooms in underwear, burning their money in
    wastebaskets and listening to the Terror through the wall,
who got busted in their pubic beards returning through Laredo with a
    belt of marijuana for New York,
who ate fire in paint hotels or drank turpentine in Paradise Alley, death,
    or purgatoried their torsos night after night
with dreams, with drugs, with waking nightmares, alcohol and cock and
    endless balls,
incomparable blind streets of shuddering cloud and lightning in the
    mind leaping toward poles of Canada & Paterson, illuminating all
    the motionless world of Time between,
Peyote solidities of halls, backyard green tree cemetery dawns, wine
    drunkenness over the rooftops, storefront boroughs of teahead
    joyride neon blinking traffic light, sun and moon and tree vibrations
    in the roaring winter dusks of Brooklyn, ashcan rantings and kind
    king light of mind,
who chained themselves to subways for the endless ride from Battery to
    holy Bronx on benzedrine until the noise of wheels and children

brought them down shuddering mouth-wracked and battered bleak
of brain all drained of brilliance in the drear light of Zoo,
who sank all night in submarine light of Bickford's floated out and sat
through the stale beer afternoon in desolate Fugazzi's, listening to
the crack of doom on the hydrogen jukebox,
who talked continuously seventy hours from park to pad to bar to
Bellevue to museum to the Brooklyn Bridge,
a lost battalion of platonic conversationalists jumping down the stoops
off fire escapes off windowsills off Empire State out of the moon,
yacketayakking screaming vomiting whispering facts and memories and
anecdotes and eyeball kicks and shocks of hospitals and jails and
wars,
whose intellects disgorged in total recall for seven days and nights with
brilliant eyes, meat for the Synagogue cast on the pavement,
who vanished into nowhere Zen New Jersey leaving a trail of ambiguous
picture postcards of Atlantic City Hall,
suffering Eastern sweats and Tangerian bone-grindings and migraines of
China under junk-withdrawal in Newark's bleak furnished room,
who wandered around and around at midnight in the railroad yard wondering where to go, and went, leaving no broken hearts,
who lit cigarettes in boxcars boxcars boxcars racketing through snow
toward lonesome farms in grandfather night,
who studied Plotinus Poe St. John of the Cross telepathy and bop kaballa
because the cosmos instinctively vibrated at their feet in Kansas,
who loned it through the streets of Idaho seeking visionary indian angels
who were visionary indian angels,
who thought they were only mad when Baltimore gleamed in supernatural
ecstasy,
who jumped in limousines with the Chinaman of Oklahoma on the
impulse of winter midnight streetlight smalltown rain,
who lounged hungry and lonesome through Houston seeking jazz or sex
or soup, and followed the brilliant Spaniard to converse about
America and Eternity, a hopeless task, and so took ship to Africa,
who disappeared into the volcanoes of Mexico leaving behind nothing
but the shadow of dungarees and the lava and ash of poetry scattered
in fireplace Chicago,
who reappeared on the West Coast investigating the F.B.I. in beards and
shorts with big pacifist eyes sexy in their dark skin passing out
incomprehensible leaflets,
who burned cigarette holes in their arms protesting the narcotic tobacco
haze of Capitalism,
who distributed Supercommunist pamphlets in Union Square weeping
and undressing while the sirens of Los Alamos wailed them down,
and wailed down Wall, and the Staten Island ferry also wailed,

who broke down crying in white gymnasiums naked and trembling before the machinery of other skeletons,

who bit detectives in the neck and shrieked with delight in policecars for committing no crime but their own wild cooking pederasty and intoxication,

who howled on their knees in the subway and were dragged off the roof waving genitals and manuscripts,

who let themselves be fucked in the ass by saintly motorcyclists, and screamed with joy,

who blew and were blown by those human seraphim, the sailors, caresses of Atlantic and Caribbean love,

who balled in the morning in the evenings in rosegardens and the grass of public parks and cemeteries scattering their semen freely to whomever come who may,

who hiccupped endlessly trying to giggle but wound up with a sob behind a partition in a Turkish Bath when the blonde & naked angel came to pierce them with a sword,

who lost their loveboys to the three old shrews of fate the one eyed shrew of the heterosexual dollar the one eyed shrew that winks out of the womb and the one eyed shrew that does nothing but sit on her ass and snip the intellectual golden threads of the craftsman's loom,

who copulated ecstatic and insatiate with a bottle of beer a sweetheart a package of cigarettes a candle and fell off the bed, and continued along the floor and down the hall and ended fainting on the wall with a vision of ultimate cunt and come eluding the last gyzym of consciousness,

who sweetened the snatches of a million girls trembling in the sunset, and were red eyed in the morning but prepared to sweeten the snatch of the sunrise, flashing buttocks under barns and naked in the lake,

who went out whoring through Colorado in myriad stolen night-cars, N.C., secret hero of these poems, cocksman and Adonis of Denver — joy to the memory of his innumerable lays of girls in empty lots & diner backyards, moviehouses' rickety rows, on mountaintops in caves or with gaunt waitresses in familiar roadside lonely petticoat upliftings & especially secret gas-station solipsisms of johns, & hometown alleys too,

who faded out in vast sordid movies, were shifted in dreams, woke on a sudden Manhattan, and picked themselves up out of basements hungover with heartless Tokay and horrors of Third Avenue iron dreams & stumbled to unemployment offices,

who walked all night with their shoes full of blood on the snowbank docks waiting for a door in the East River to open to a room full of steamheat and opium,

who created great suicidal dramas on the apartment cliff-banks of the
Hudson under the wartime blue floodlight of the moon & their
heads shall be crowned with laurel in oblivion,

who ate the lamb stew of the imagination or digested the crab at the
muddy bottom of the rivers of Bowery,

who wept at the romance of the streets with their pushcarts full of
onions and bad music,

who sat in boxes breathing in the darkness under the bridge, and rose up
to build harpsichords in their lofts,

who coughed on the sixth floor of Harlem crowned with flame under the
tubercular sky surrounded by orange crates of theology,

who scribbled all night rocking and rolling over lofty incantations which
in the yellow morning were stanzas of gibberish,

who cooked rotten animals lung heart feet tail borsht & tortillas dreaming of the pure vegetable kingdom,

who plunged themselves under meat trucks looking for an egg,

who threw their watches off the roof to cast their ballot for Eternity outside of Time, & alarm clocks fell on their heads every day for the
next decade,

who cut their wrists three times successively unsuccessfully, gave up and
were forced to open antique stores where they thought they were
growing old and cried,

who were burned alive in their innocent flannel suits on Madison
Avenue amid blasts of leaden verse & the tanked-up clatter of the
iron regiments of fashion & the nitroglycerine shrieks of the fairies
of advertising & the mustard gas of sinister intelligent editors, or
were run down by the drunken taxicabs of Absolute Reality,

who jumped off the Brooklyn Bridge this actually happened and walked
away unknown and forgotten into the ghostly daze of Chinatown
soup alleyways & firetrucks, not even one free beer,

who sang out of their windows in despair, fell out of the subway window,
jumped in the filthy Passaic, leaped on negroes, cried all over the
street, danced on broken wineglasses barefoot smashed phonograph
records of nostalgic European 1930's German jazz finished the
whiskey and threw up groaning into the bloody toilet, moans in their
ears and the blast of colossal steamwhistles,

who barreled down the highways of the past journeying to each other's
hotrod-Golgotha jail-solitude watch or Birmingham jazz incarnation,

who drove crosscountry seventytwo hours to find out if I had a vision or
you had a vision or he had a vision to find out Eternity,

who journeyed to Denver, who died in Denver, who came back to Denver
& waited in vain, who watched over Denver & brooded & loned in
Denver and finally went away to find out the Time, & now Denver
is lonesome for her heroes,

who fell on their knees in hopeless cathedrals praying for each other's
salvation and light and breasts, until the soul illuminated its hair for
a second,

who crashed through their minds in jail waiting for impossible criminals
with golden heads and the charm of reality in their hearts who sang
sweet blues to Alcatraz,

who retired to Mexico to cultivate a habit, or Rocky Mount to tender
Buddha or Tangiers to boys or Southern Pacific to the black loco-
motive or Harvard to Narcissus to Woodlawn to the daisychain or
grave,

who demanded sanity trials accusing the radio of hypnotism & were left
with their insanity & their hands & a hung jury,

who threw potato salad at CCNY lecturers on Dadaism and subsequently
presented themselves on the granite steps of the madhouse with
shaven heads and harlequin speech of suicide, demanding instanta-
neous lobotomy,

and who were given instead the concrete void of insulin metrasol elec-
tricity hydrotherapy psychotherapy occupational therapy pingpong
& amnesia,

who in humorless protest overturned only one symbolic pingpong table,
resting briefly in catatonia,

returning years later truly bald except for a wig of blood, and tears and
fingers, to the visible madman doom of the wards of the madtowns
of the East,

Pilgrim State's Rockland's and Greystone's foetid halls, bickering with
the echoes of the soul, rocking and rolling in the midnight solitude-
bench dolmen-realms of love, dream of life a nightmare, bodies turned
to stone as heavy as the moon,

with mother finally ******, and the last fantastic book flung out of the
tenement window, and the last door closed at 4 a.m. and the last
telephone slammed at the wall in reply and the last furnished room
emptied down to the last piece of mental furniture, a yellow paper
rose twisted on a wire hanger in the closet, and even that imaginary,
nothing but a hopeful little bit of hallucination —

ah, Carl, while you are not safe I am not safe, and now you're really in
the total animal soup of time —

and who therefore ran through the icy streets obsessed with a sudden
flash of the alchemy of the use of the ellipse the catalog the meter
& the vibrating plane,

who dreamt and made incarnate gaps in Time & Space through images
juxtaposed, and trapped the archangel of the soul between 2 visual
images and joined the elemental verbs and set the noun and dash
of consciousness together jumping with sensation of Pater Omni-
potens Aeterna Deus

to recreate the syntax and measure of poor human prose and stand
before you speechless and intelligent and shaking with shame,
rejected yet confessing out the soul to conform to the rhythm of
thought in his naked and endless head,
the madman bum and angel beat in Time, unknown, yet putting down
here what might be left to say in time come after death,
and rose reincarnate in the ghostly clothes of jazz in the goldhorn shadow
of the band and blew the suffering of America's naked mind for love
into an eli eli lamma lamma sabacthani saxophone cry that shivered
the cities down to the last radio
with the absolute heart of the poem of life butchered out of their own
bodies good to eat a thousand years.

San Francisco, 1955–56

AMERICA

America I've given you all and now I'm nothing.
America two dollars and twentyseven cents January 17, 1956.
I can't stand my own mind.
America when will we end the human war?
Go fuck yourself with your atom bomb.
I don't feel good don't bother me.
I won't write my poem till I'm in my right mind.
America when will you be angelic?
When will you take off your clothes?
When will you look at yourself through the grave?
When will you be worthy of your million Trotskyites?
America why are your libraries full of tears?
America when will you send your eggs to India?
I'm sick of your insane demands.
When can I go into the supermarket and buy what I need with my good
looks?
America after all it is you and I who are perfect not the next world.
Your machinery is too much for me.
You made me want to be a saint.
There must be some other way to settle this argument.
Burroughs is in Tangiers I don't think he'll come back it's sinister.
And you being sinister or is this some form of practical joke?
I'm trying to come to the point.
I refuse to give up my obsession.

8 America stop pushing I know what I'm doing.

9 America the plum blossoms are falling.

I haven't read the newspapers for months, everyday somebody goes on trial
for murder.

10 America I feel sentimental about the Wobblies.

11 America I used to be a communist when I was a kid I'm not sorry.

I smoke marijuana every chance I get.

I sit in my house for days on end and stare at the roses in the closet.

When I go to Chinatown I get drunk and never get laid.

My mind is made up there's going to be trouble.

You should have seen me reading Marx.

My psychoanalyst thinks I'm perfectly right.

I won't say the Lord's Prayer.

I have mystical visions and cosmic vibrations.

12 America I still haven't told you what you did to Uncle Max after he came
over from Russia.

I'm addressing you.

Are you going to let your emotional life be run by Time Magazine? *media*

I'm obsessed by Time Magazine.

I read it every week.

Its cover stares at me every time I slink past the corner candystore.

I read it in the basement of the Berkeley Public Library.

It's always telling me about responsibility. Businessmen are serious.
Movie producers are serious. Everybody's serious but me.

It occurs to me that I am America.

I am talking to myself again.

Asia is rising against me.

I haven't got a chinaman's chance.

I'd better consider my national resources.

My national resources consist of two joints of marijuana millions of genitals
an unpublishable private literature that jetplanes 1400 miles an hour
and twentyfive-thousand mental institutions.

I say nothing about my prisons nor the millions of underprivileged who live
in my flowerpots under the light of five hundred suns.

I have abolished the whorehouses of France, Tangiers is the next to go.

My ambition is to be President despite the fact that I'm a Catholic.

13 America how can I write a holy litany in your silly mood?

I will continue like Henry Ford my strophes are as individual as his automobiles more so they're all different sexes.

14 America I will sell you strophes $2500 apiece $500 down on your old
strophe

15 America free Tom Mooney

America save the Spanish Loyalists
America Sacco & Vanzetti must not die
America I am the Scottsboro boys.
America when I was seven momma took me to Communist Cell meetings
    they sold us garbanzos a handful per ticket a ticket costs a nickel and
    the speeches were free everybody was angelic and sentimental about
    the workers it was all so sincere you have no idea what a good thing
    the party was in 1835 Scott Nearing was a grand old man a real
    mensch Mother Bloor the Silk-strikers' Ewig-Weibliche made me cry
    I once saw the Yiddish orator Israel Amter plain. Everybody must
    have been a spy.
America you don't really want to go to war.
America it's them bad Russians.
Them Russians them Russians and them Chinamen. And them Russians.
The Russia wants to eat us alive. The Russia's power mad. She wants to take
    our cars from out our garages.
Her wants to grab Chicago. Her needs a Red *Reader's Digest*. Her wants
    our auto plants in Siberia. Him big bureaucracy running our filling-
    stations.
That no good. Ugh. Him make Indians learn read. Him need big black
    niggers. Hah. Her make us all work sixteen hours a day. Help.
America this is quite serious.
America this is the impression I get from looking in the television set.
America is this correct?
I'd better get right down to the job.
It's true I don't want to join the Army or turn lathes in precision parts
    factories, I'm nearsighted and psychopathic anyway.
America I'm putting my queer shoulder to the wheel.

Berkeley, January 17, 1956

ODE TO FAILURE

Many prophets have failed, their voices silent
ghost-shouts in basements nobody heard dusty laughter in family attics
nor glanced them on park benches weeping with relief under empty sky
Walt Whitman viva'd local losers — courage to Fat Ladies in the Freak
    Show! nervous prisoners whose mustached lips dripped sweat on
    chow lines —
Mayakovsky cried, Then die! my verse, die like the workers' rank & file
    fusilladed in Petersburg!

Prospero burned his Power books & plummeted his magic wand to the
   bottom of dragon seas
Alexander the Great failed to find more worlds to conquer!
O Failure I chant your terrifying name, accept me your 54 year old
   Prophet
epicking Eternal Flop! I join your Pantheon of mortal bards, & hasten
   this ode with high blood pressure
rushing to the top of my skull as if I wouldn't last another minute, like the
   Dying Gaul! to
You, Lord of blind Monet, deaf Beethoven, armless Venus de Milo, head-
   less Winged Victory!
I failed to sleep with every bearded rosy-cheeked boy I jacked off over
My tirades destroyed no Intellectual Unions of KGB & CIA in turtle-
   necks & underpants, their woolen suits & tweeds
I never dissolved Plutonium or dismantled the nuclear Bomb before my
   skull lost hair
I have not yet stopped the Armies of entire Mankind in their march
   toward World War III
I never got to Heaven, Nirvana, X, Whatchamacallit, I never left Earth,
I never learned to die.

Boulder, March 7 / October 10, 1980

Louise Glück

NOSTOS

There was an apple tree in the yard —
this would have been
forty years ago — behind,
only meadow. Drifts
of crocus in the damp grass.
I stood at that window:
late April. Spring
flowers in the neighbor's yard.
How many times, really, did the tree
flower on my birthday,
the exact day, not
before, not after? Substitution
of the immutable
for the shifting, the evolving.
Substitution of the image
for relentless earth. What
do I know of this place,
the role of the tree for decades
taken by a bonsai, voices
rising from the tennis courts —
Fields. Smell of the tall grass, new cut.
As one expects of a lyric poet.
We look at the world once, in childhood.
The rest is memory.

THE MIRROR

Watching you in the mirror I wonder
what it is like to be so beautiful
and why you do not love
but cut yourself, shaving
like a blind man. I think you let me stare
so you can turn against yourself
with greater violence,
needing to show me how you scrape the flesh away
scornfully and without hesitation
until I see you correctly,

as a man bleeding, not
the reflection I desire.

MOCK ORANGE

It is not the moon, I tell you.
It is these flowers
lighting the yard.

I hate them.
I hate them as I hate sex,
the man's mouth
sealing my mouth, the man's
paralyzing body —

and the cry that always escapes,
the low, humiliating
premise of union —

In my mind tonight
I hear the question and pursuing answer
fused in one sound
that mounts and mounts and then
is split into the old selves,
the tired antagonisms. Do you see?
We were made fools of.
And the scent of mock orange
drifts through the window.

How can I rest?
How can I be content
when there is still
that odor in the world?

RETREATING WIND

When I made you, I loved you.
Now I pity you.

I gave you all you needed:
bed of earth, blanket of blue air —

As I get further away from you
I see you more clearly.
Your souls should have been immense by now,
not what they are,
small talking things —

I gave you every gift,
blue of the spring morning,
time you didn't know how to use —
you wanted more, the one gift
reserved for another creation.

Whatever you hoped,
you will not find yourselves in the garden,
among the growing plants.
Your lives are not circular like theirs:

your lives are the bird's flight
which begins and ends in stillness —
which *begins* and *ends*, in form echoing
this arc from the white birch
to the apple tree.

THE WHITE ROSE

This is the earth? Then
I don't belong here.

Who are you in the lighted window,
shadowed now by the flickering leaves
of the wayfarer tree?
Can you survive where I won't last
beyond the first summer?

All night the slender branches of the tree
shift and rustle at the bright window.
Explain my life to me, you who make no sign,

though I call out to you in the night:
I am not like you, I have only
my body for a voice; I can't
disappear into silence —

And in the cold morning
over the dark surface of the earth
echoes of my voice drift,
whiteness steadily absorbed into darkness

as though you were making a sign after all
to convince me you too couldn't survive here

or to show me you are not the light I called to
but the blackness behind it.

MIDNIGHT

Speak to me, aching heart: what
ridiculous errand are you inventing for yourself
weeping in the dark garage
with your sack of garbage: it is not your job
to take out the garbage, it is your job
to empty the dishwasher. You are showing off again,
exactly as you did in childhood — where
is your sporting side, your famous
ironic detachment? A little moonlight hits
the broken window, a little summer moonlight, tender
murmurs from the earth with its ready sweetnesses —
is this the way you communicate
with your husband, not answering
when he calls, or is this the way the heart
behaves when it grieves: it wants to be
alone with the garbage? If I were you,
I'd think ahead. After fifteen years,
his voice could be getting tired; some night
if you don't answer, someone else will answer.

PARABLE OF FLIGHT

A flock of birds leaving the side of the mountain.
Black against the spring evening, bronze in early summer,
rising over blank lake water.

Why is the young man disturbed suddenly,
his attention slipping from his companion?
His heart is no longer wholly divided; he's trying to think
how to say this compassionately.

Now we hear the voices of the others, moving through the library
toward the veranda, the summer porch; we see them
taking their usual places on the various hammocks and chairs,
the white wood chairs of the old house, rearranging
the striped cushions.

Does it matter where the birds go? Does it even matter
what species they are?
They leave here, that's the point,
first their bodies, then their sad cries.
And from that moment, cease to exist for us.

You must learn to think of our passion that way.
Each kiss was real, then
each kiss left the face of the earth.

THE BALCONY

It was a night like this, at the end of summer.

We had rented, I remember, a room with a balcony.
How many days and nights? Five, perhaps — no more.

Even when we weren't touching we were making love.
We stood on our little balcony in the summer night.
And off somewhere, the sounds of human life.

We were the soon to be anointed monarchs,
well disposed to our subjects. Just beneath us,
sounds of a radio playing, an aria we didn't in those years know.

Someone dying of love. Someone from whom time had taken
the only happiness, who was alone now,
impoverished, without beauty.

The rapturous notes of an unendurable grief, of isolation and terror,
the nearly impossible to sustain slow phrases of the ascending figures —

they drifted out over the dark water
like an ecstasy.

Such a small mistake. And many years later,
the only thing left of that night, of the hours in that room.

VESPERS

In your extended absence, you permit me
use of earth, anticipating
some return on investment. I must report
failure in my assignment, principally
regarding the tomato plants.
I think I should not be encouraged to grow
tomatoes. Or, if I am, you should withhold
the heavy rains, the cold nights that come
so often here, while other regions get
twelve weeks of summer. All this
belongs to you: on the other hand,
I planted the seeds, I watched the first shoots
like wings tearing the soil, and it was my heart
broken by the blight, the black spot so quickly
multiplying in the rows. I doubt
you have a heart, in our understanding of
that term. You who do not discriminate
between the dead and the living, who are, in consequence,
immune to foreshadowing, you may not know
how much terror we bear, the spotted leaf,
the red leaves of the maple falling
even in August, in early darkness: I am responsible
for these vines.

CELESTIAL MUSIC

I have a friend who still believes in heaven.
Not a stupid person, yet with all she knows, she literally talks to god,
she thinks someone listens in heaven.
On earth, she's unusually competent.
Brave, too, able to face unpleasantness.

LOUISE GLÜCK

We found a caterpillar dying in the dirt, greedy ants crawling over it.
I'm always moved by weakness, by disaster, always eager to oppose
    vitality.
But timid, also, quick to shut my eyes.
Whereas my friend was able to watch, to let events play out
according to nature. For my sake, she intervened,
brushing a few ants off the torn thing, and set it down across the road.

My friend says I shut my eyes to god, that nothing else explains
my aversion to reality. She says I'm like the child who buries her head in
    the pillow
so as not to see, the child who tells herself
that light causes sadness —
My friend is like the mother. Patient, urging me
to wake up an adult like herself, a courageous person —

In my dreams, my friend reproaches me. We're walking
on the same road, except it's winter now;
she's telling me that when you love the world you hear celestial music:
look up, she says. When I look up, nothing.
Only clouds, snow, a white business in the trees
like brides leaping to a great height —
Then I'm afraid for her; I see her
caught in a net deliberately cast over the earth —

In reality, we sit by the side of the road, watching the sun set;
from time to time, the silence pierced by a birdcall.
It's this moment we're both trying to explain, the fact
that we're at ease with death, with solitude.
My friend draws a circle in the dirt; inside, the caterpillar doesn't move.
She's always trying to make something whole, something beautiful, an
    image
capable of life apart from her.
We're very quiet. It's peaceful sitting here, not speaking, the composition
fixed, the road turning suddenly dark, the air
going cool, here and there the rocks shining and glittering —
it's this stillness that we both love.
The love of form is a love of endings.

Albert Goldbarth

THE TALK SHOW

*. . . in 1930, The Bell Telephone Company commissioned one of their
employees, Karl Jansky, to find out why the new car radios suffered
from static. Jansky set up radio antennae, and heard a steady hiss
coming from the direction of the Milky Way. Radio astronomy was
born thirty years later.*

— James Burke

A woman "heard angels." The paper says angels
sussurra'd her body, rang their praises daylong
through its reedy places, stirred her
smallest water. And elsewhere, Larry
"Dude Man" Chavez raises his #2 wrench
indifferently overhead on the C-track tightening line,
and feels something like lightning — only
there isn't lightning — beam to the wrench head,
branch down his arm, make all of his muscles
electric feathers, then exit his other arm out
its guttering candelabrum fingers and into
the frame of the Ford. It's stored

there. It happens. We all know it happens.
The cops and the hospital nightshift crew know
what a full moon means, and
if their decades of statistics don't cut diddlysquat
with you, here's someone being wheeled in
from a 3-car smashup while the universe hums
its lunar kazoo, and adrenalin everywhere dervishes.
And statistics on sunspots, and suicides.
And statistics on lines of magnetic pull,
and conception. We're the few but beautiful
units of the first day of the cosmos
densed-up over time; when the lady I love

flaps suddenly in sleep like a wire discharging, it
makes sense as much as anything — bad dreams,
zinged nerves — to simply say *we're* where
the Big Bang ripples to the limits of a continuous medium,
flickers a little, kicks. I've disappointed her

sometimes; and so, myself. I've left the house then,
while she slept, and while my neighbors slept, as if
I could walk noise out of myself
through darkness, finally dialing-in
the talk show where the blood calls with its question,
and the "sky," whatever that is, whatever portion we are
of it or once were, answers. And

I've walked past where the university's planetarium
dish-ear swivels hugely for the far
starcrackle Karl Jansky more primitively
dowsed. It happens any size; that woman? picked up
cop calls on her IUD, the paper adds, in bubble-bursting
glee. Although if angels are voices beyond us
in us, everyone's umbles are singing hosannahs
under their everyday wamble and gab. I've
slipped back into bed some nights and clasped her
till I slept, then woke to her heart
in my ear, that mysterious sound,
on earth as it is in heaven.

ANCESTORED-BACK
IS THE OVERPRESIDING SPIRIT OF THIS POEM

If only somebody would drill with a finger-long rig down
into my skull, and saw a tiny circle out of its bone,
so pools of acid antsiness and angst can steam away;
so all of the great in-gnarling, all of the bunched-up
broodiness can breathe; and so at least the day's
accumulated ephemera, its fenderbender squabbles,
its parade of petty heartache can evaporate in writhes
of sour mist — this spatting couple, for example,
in the booth across the aisle as I'm chowing on a burger
and their every more-than-whispered perturbation is,
this afternoon, a further furrow worked into my mind. . . .
You know I'm kvetching metaphorically. But literalist
Amanda Fielding, wielding a scalpel and electric drill,
bored a hole in her skull in 1970, filming that self-surgery,

and zealously thereafter promoting the benefits of this
third eye, finally "running for Parliament on a platform
of trepanation for national health." The operation

was successfully conducted in the Stone Age (72%
of the skulls we've found reveal that the patients far survived
that crisis moment), and the Chinese medico Thai Tshang Kung
(150 B.C.) was said "to cut open the skulls of the sick
and arrange their brains in order." A Roman physician's
effects from the second century A.D. include a trepanation kit
in bronze, its tooth-edged bit and driving-bow
as finely produced as any machine-tooled apparatus
a surgeon in 1996 would wish for — when the bow unfolds
it's as intricate in its simplicity as a line of true haiku.
I've read a book whose major pleasure is its breathlessness

in gasping at the ancientness of various devices,
flushing toilets(!) condoms(!) hand grenades(!) — the book
is a grove of invisible exclamation points. These
green glass beads like rain-splats on a leaf
— 4,000 years ago. Bone dice, the same. The ribbed vault
in this early Gothic church is a masterly hollowing-out
of space — but houses of *literal* ribs, of mammoth bones,
were sturdy dwellings 15,000 years ago. Rhinoplasty(!)
soccer(!) odometers(!) "Butter" (a favorite sentence)
"spread everywhere, once it was discovered." Though we don't know
poot about the urgent stirrings in our own hearts
or the dreams irrupting nightly in our own heads,
we've been diagramming stars on plaques
of tortoise plate and antler, we've made sky maps,

from before we even understood the link of sex
to birth. And if our coin-op slot machines
can be ancestored-back to that Greco-Egyptian
contrivance of Heron of Alexandria (by which
a dropped-in-place five-drachma bronze piece
starts the portioned flow of a worshiper's ablution-water) . . .
if *ancestored-back* is the overpresiding spirit
of this poem . . . we *are* the progeny of stars,
we *are* their original core-born elements
in new recombination, densed and sizzled into
sentience and soul. I can't imagine the interior tumult
driving Amanda Fielding and her followers, but
I'm not surprised our smallest human units were created
in explosion, speed, and void. My friends

are not the kind to drill their heads and rid themselves
of troubles by decanting. Even so, I've seen them consider

their restless faces in the mirror and wish for *some* release.
Our daily dole of woe is unrelenting. In this burger joint,
in the Booth of a Thousand Sorrows across the aisle,
they're arguing still. Outside, the snow provides each tree
with a clerical collar — this couple is arguing. Outside,
the setting summer sun makes each tree a flambeau
— this couple is arguing, they'll never stop, their joys
have been prodigious and their anti-joy will balance this
or more, the hands with which they make their hard points
in the air are hands of oxygen and nitrogen and argon
older than dust or salt. It's midnight. How
emphatic we can be. How long they've been at it.

REALITY ORGANIZATION

1.

4:30 a.m. with the woe adding up
in notches on your gut-wall,
guilts, indignities, whatever, there's no sleep,
you're bright, you "keep up," you know what's what, but
this isn't the time when you want to know everything's nothing

but some few subatomic elements skeetering
through emptiness, what seem the solid edges of things
are hazinesses of particle give-and-take and "really"
must look like continual maelstrom, and people you love
are whole new sets of cells each 7 years — no,

that's all fine to know but now you simply want
to walk with some dignity to the shed, and
press your forehead to the russian olive there, its trunk
unyielding, a thing not you but able to texture you,
a hardness to hold to, a firm true specific event.

2.

Zen and the Art of Computer Management Systems.
Holistic Bioengineering: A Home Cassette Series.
Alternate Consciousness and Corporation Profile — A Symposium.

By now it's no secret: scientific method,
the Newtonian / Cartesian paradigm, isn't hauling ass

and soul in happy tandem very well. And so
(as one book says) "to use an obvious example," war
we calibrate down to the leastmost ladybug's-waist-sized
chainmail link and up to megaton trajectory, we
artfully assemble, Trojan H and H-bomb, but

what makes us make war, what demanding psyche-ghosts
howl down the spiral staircase
of our genes — "we are no closer to this
understanding now than, say, in Hellenistic times." They
had *Lysistrata*. We have biofeedback and we have *Lysistrata*.

3.

We have biofeedback. We know there are levels
where light's too large to land, so "being" anything isn't
being visible or countable — levels where dream is
logic, levels where you could fall lost in the space
between your own hand and its shadow. Maybe a God,

even a God of terrible vengeance, is less frightening
than floating through physics. The God says:
Here are boundaries; this and this are real, this not.
The God says: Things actually do add up. We love
to add. The name of Allah was *26,000*

times stitched into a 16th century Turkish warship's pennant.
There are an estimated *4 million* mummified ibises
in an Egyptian labyrinth offered unto Thoth.
We love to tally. The rosary's abacus beads.
The first worked stones are scored.

4.

It was nearly dawn when I found you. By then
you were calm. That tree had punished you or healed you
or simply been a symbol of something reliably
beyond the tormenting refinements of human confusion.
Your skin was moire from the bark — your sadness,

leached out by that contact. I led you back
into the house. Or you could have been leading me — that's
not the point. I know we can't approach the universe
as if its secrets are quantifiable, not any more. And even
so, I know we all deserve the reassurance

of weight and number, perimeter, durability. Some
days both of those opposing knowings pull, and early
sun in a slant through the basketball net
mandalas the shed — my eyes can spin in there,
electronwise, wholegalaxyclusterwise, and not be wiser.

ARGUING BARTUSIAK

*Space-time simply doesn't exist where loop lines are absent, any more than a
blanket exists between the weave of its threads.*

> — Marcia Bartusiak, in a science article

The idea is, the marriage still exists
when they're at different coasts for the summer:
her job, his ailing parents. Some weeks
even fax- and phone-chat thins
to a nebular frizzle the instruments barely acknowledge.
Even so, she knows she knows she's married and
she *thinks* she knows he knows it too.
She imagines him now, he's walking through the garden
of the house in Palo Verde, in the dawnlight there
that always looks so unsoiled, so
historically uninhabited-through; and in the face
of the coffee and its seemingly prescient tentacles of steam,
he sees the day ahead, a day of salt baths
and colostomy bags, of people one loves monolithically
going grain by grain to something
a son can only sift through, shaking his head.
In a way, although the thought is shameful, she
envies him this: the lug and grunt of working
human necessities — enormous grand pianos
of human distress and their human solutions — across
the convolute rooms of a day. For her, the world is all abstraction
and the iffiness of quarkish nonevents, for her

it's less than air, since air of course is elements
imperturbable and ponderous by her standards
— she's a theoretician of quantum gravity models, and
she uses a machine the size of a shopping mall
to track the ghostly geysering of particles that exist
so far in hypothesis only. It's *beautiful*,
                    it's *consummatory*, labor; but some mornings
when she walks along the squabble of Atlantic water
and Jersey shore, she feels the need
to hug herself, to keep herself
from suddenly evaporating into the between-states
of her studies. Or to have *somebody*
hug her. That night, at Kelly's Reef,
as a patchwork jazz quartet is into its last set,
Mr. Silk-'n-Sip — a friend of a friend
of a friend, who's magically latched on to their party —
makes the thousand invisible signs of availability.
His hands are shapely and capable. His stories
encompass plasma physics, Van Gogh connoisseurship,
Tantric sex techniques. She's crazy
to say no, but she says no. It's 4 a.m.
and in the rumple of her by-the-month
efficiency apartment, in her sleeplessness,
she idly works the gold ring off her finger, lets the light
trace its solidity, then puffs a single
breath through its empty center. It's late,
she's sleepy at last, she
wraps herself in her blanket, and
if some of it, *somewhere* in it, isn't blanket,
she wraps herself in that too.

THE WHOLE EARTH CATALOGUE

Plate tectonics: like blackened pieces
of sweet pork crackling, the continents slide
on their underside greases. Night; outside,
the sad moon drags the sea behind, a washerwoman
her bucket. The moon
and her crimp-rimmed craters.
The maestro moon and her ever-attentive
oyster castanet orchestra. The atmosphere

ALBERT GOLDBARTH

of Earth weighs, oh, 5,000
million million tons but a ladybug
bears it untroubled, and

I'm stroking Skyler's back,
the rolling fold between her shoulders,
down the serial rings of the spine and
up again, just lightly, up
and down, and

70 billion neutrinos pass through our bodies
this moment and every moment
and through the lava and through the iron core.
The moon and her purely cosmetic light.
That skyhigh silversmith plating us sterling.
At the vent slits of the Mid-Atlantic Ridge
are sea worms 10 feet long
with no eyes, mouth or gut. And
there are shards of stone with
ferns inside so it looks as if Time is
waiting to be unzipped and entered. And

I'm beside Skyler, almost not touching
her eyelids and her trusting
upturned wrists, but touching them,
figure 8-ing them spiderily with my fingers.
In some Paul Klee

watercolors, as in certain Chinese landscape scrolls,
abstracted hills and sky fill space
to the edges, and it's only
on a second look we see
a minuscule man or a woman is one stroke
of deliberation dabbed in a corner,
going about its own
important business — maybe

setting up, for all we know, an easel for an afternoon
of landscape painting. Getting
the serpent of wind in the wheat
just right. The dusk
rum-coloring the chalk cliffs. Then the moon.
Anchovies gleaming like a miser's hoard
beneath the moon. The moon

and her two Martian stepsisters.
Moon in the rain forests,
moon in the arctic ice, and
mayflies stippling air, and elk
switchbacking eluding pursuing wolves, and
kelp in drift, and galaxies in drift, and

Skyler drifting to sleep, her nipples
tucked under my thumbs, and then the whorled
availability of an ear until she's under. You know
the Eskimo of Greenland voyaged with beautiful
carvings always in their canoes,
a foot long, maybe 18 inches. They look like
spinal columns of angels or troll lords, long
and knobbed and coved. They're maps
of several hundred miles of the coastline
most worth knowing. They fondled them over
and over. On nights with no moon,
in such dark there's no planet,
the eyes in their fingers knew these by heart.

Colleen McKay

Kimiko Hahn

THE IZU DANCER

The story was almost too simple:
a student from Tokyo
travelling along the coast during summer break
hooks up with a dance troupe.
They move from one cheap hotel to another,
accepting him as waves accept sand and small animals.
He falls in love.
Spring buds never quivered so lightly
as his skin when he heard her drum.
Though not a difficult text
every few words I was stuck
flipping through water radicals
水　　氵　　氺
so I could resume the journey inside words
I had begun as a child, as when Kawabata wrote
雨脚が杉の密林を白く染めながら
"while the shower bleached the cedars"

I did not know
I did not want to know Japanese
so much as a way back to, say, salt
and to him in his heaven.
(Or to him, in such a rush to pick me up
he forgot his shoes, stood at my door in red woolen socks.)
Yet from the fragrance of his lines I struggled to raise:
"I thought for a moment of running out barefoot to look for her.
It was after two." from
跣で湯殿を抜け出して行ったって、どうにも出来ないのだと
思った。二時を過ぎていた。
I needed the information locked in ink —
each stroke, a signal; each kanji, a panorama.
And barbed fence.

There are over 2,000 species of fireflies,
each with its own mating signal
so as not to crossover.

If you catch one they will not burn a hole in your hand
or explode in your face.
They call out: hey baby. They say: wait up, girl.
まって
With closed eyes I imagine her thoughts:
I swept my hair up off my back,
waded in from the heat of the road,
stuffy towns and constant companions
and sat down in the surf.
The air stung with a smell of iodine.
When I returned to my towel
my legs were bright red
from the concentration of salt.
For lunch we ate squid, rice, green tea.
I wanted to lick the beads of sweat
from his temples.
The afternoon forecast a meeting,
clouds thickening offshore
but at fourteen my heart was not as willing
as my body. And too, I was afraid my body
looked funny.

The Heian poet wrote about sleeves soaked with tears.
But I know even young girls break into a sweat
in passion or terror;
a terror, as if mother left the house one morning
to buy milk and never returned.
As if you could no longer speak to her.
As if a lover said: *Goodbye.*
The season's blooms turn to fruit,
And you do see persimmons fragrant among the branches
sweat in the morning heat as the blossoms before them.
Would we run around the house looking for mother?
Would we find the suitcase gone,
drawers empty, closets
vacant, heart
lost?
But isn't everything about loss:
the pin cushion of pins, the branch
knocking against the window,
Kawabata's swiveling chair.

In time we belong to what the objects mean.
Then around 2 am the stomach sours from all the coffee.

The strokes blur into the mess of lines and noises they really are.
Though in some respects the characters are astonishingly simple:

tree 木   forest 森

woman 女   mischief; noisy; assault 姦

But the complex unfolding of a single sentence
with whole sentences modifying a noun
at the end of the line baffled, humiliated
and toughened my spirit.

I persevered in my search for the fragrance of words
in this modest story — the only Kawabata story I could read.
Where did he unearth
不自然な程美しい黒髪が私の胸に触れそうになった。

("Her hair, so rich it seemed unreal, almost brushed against my chest.")
Where did I find the hands on my shoulders, sliding down my arms
then up under my t-shirt, into my bra,
squeezing my breasts, pinching my nipples so hard
I blinked to hold back tears.
He watched my expression as a meteorologist reads delicate instruments.
If the body is a map, a weathermap, summer vacations or winter holidays
all begin here. Something a student may not realize.

Later the dancer combed the puppy's fur
with the pink comb, the one
he thought he would ask for
to prove to himself on the boat back to Tokyo
that the lengths of hair were real.
Outside this window the magnolia under the street lamp
appears as artificial as the light.

The arrangement interrupts my train of thought
as details of her life crazed him like musk.
In my search did I look for the writer
or the boy? for mother
to take me in her arms and not let go?
or father to praise the poem without:
yes, but
yes, if
yes, perhaps

The character for house is roof over pig

家

for peace, roof over woman

安

for wife, woman with a broom

婦

Then there's adulteress:

姦 婦

If I had slept with that professor
betrayal might have become real
as the magnolia in the street —
delicate, sooty and pink.

Branches open. Petals full and moist.
I wanted to cross that fence
with the passion of leaving home,
the need for certain loss
that means constructing something for oneself —
roof with pig.
To write and never discover the scent
is to signal a firefly behind the stone wall.
In looking for mother do I admit I've failed
to make these rooms home
or does she also dream of grandma sitting on the beach
her chignon unravelling in the sea breeze?
When she opens her eyes
snow covers the early blooms.
Then there he is: Kawabata pulls off a spray laden with snow
and gently carries it inside.
We enjoy the beauty of its predicament
as snow melts all over the mahogany.
Why not buckle down and learn the language cold;
why not remember

思   field over heart means remember

If I give in to every desire
will oil spills suffocate the hemisphere,
will the ozone layer evaporate like a marriage.
Why this settling in to study
versus the constant urge to leave,
to walk in the night air free of dictionaries and parents.
The student didn't know what to say

to the little dancer, what would ease the calf-like movements
that increased her charm — ease his own breath
racing against his heart at the thought of her.
If he read her a story,
if she laughed or blushed but didn't run away
that would mean something.

The story is so clear I can dream his lines:
Stepping out of the waves
I noticed a rash spread over my legs,
the color of boiled lobster or genitals.
It embarrassed her. She turned and ran away
as if I had said something amiss.
To kiss me there.

If I saw a red Volkswagen my heart would roll like a tsunami
toward a man smoking a cigarette, leaning against the chalkboard.
Tall. Graying. In no time all lessons will be forgotten.
But not a memory of no memory.
Perhaps I did not want the language enough
or wanted something else —
— to leave a laundry-filled dormitory room
and press my whole body against the professor's doorbell
till he came downstairs and invited me inside.
Cooked me dinner. Fucked in the guest room.
Perhaps I didn't want any language. Any marriage.

Even Kawabata's snowscapes steamed in the winter light.
Is all betrayal really of father or mother?
In the kanji for mother
母
the two nipples reduce it to a primitive symbol.
I reach to touch a lover with the confidence
of a child burying into a breast;
a tangible connection but also the perfume
or stench that is language. Ah,
the irregular verbs. Oh, the conditional.
An occasional classical phrase
nestled into the vernacular.
The lullabies: should, would, could. I need
the knowledge from a peach floating downstream:
domburikokkosukkou —
of saying the right words without thinking.

When he saw her in the public bath the student was delighted
the dancer was too young to consummate his

fever　　　　　　　　

He could sit beside her at dinner or the movies
finally.

*

A waitress pours me a warmup and I look over
to catch the back of a man's neck,
his heavy black hair in a severe razor-cut style.
I imagine he is B. D. Wong
the incredibly handsome actor in *M. Butterfly.*
His moist white cotton shirt
hangs a bit off his shoulders
and he holds a cup of cappuccino in one hand
and a slim hard-cover book in the other.
I imagine he turns around to ask for —
an ashtray
and ends up at my table
talking about contemporary poetry, mutual friends
and international affairs.
But as the man gathers his belongings he turns
and instead of the aristocratic profile and rakish glow
it's an older Italian man, moustached and serious.
But briefly that fragrance!

THE OLDER CHILD

What will become her earliest memory —
the sperm whale battling the giant squid
in the dark exhibition at the museum?
looking up at 3 am
to see her sister pressed against two white breasts?
or maybe her yellow room
filled with the noise of boys in the vacant lot:
bang, boom-boom, fuckyoufuckyoufuck you.

KIMIKO HAHN

THE SHOWER

The hot spray softens her neck muscles
as she swings her head side to side
raises an arm and spirals fingertips
from arm pit to aureola firmly firmly —
the legacy of twentieth century females,
a fact even brown rice, an underwire bra,
or low-impact aerobics cannot
cauterize. She recalls the nurse
who told a dormitory of freshmen about
self-examinations, about a farmer's wife
in Oxford, Iowa, whose breast tripled in size,
festered, stank, and still she hid
the awful message: what was meant to nourish,
what had nourished half a dozen babies,
poisoned the whole system. While soaping
beneath her breasts she remembers
an Ariyoshi novel from Japanese Lit:
the mother and daughter-in-law
in grotesque competition for the son / husband
to anesthetize and sever experimentally.
Now the left side and thoughts of nursing
at two then four in the morning.
Her own daughters are tucked
into their collective unconscious, perhaps
images of the breast, pillow-like: sweet
or so large as to suffocate. Which dream?
Which dream for me? No lumps
detected while showering she wraps
a terry cloth robe around her self,
thinks, nursing was precious and erotic, both
and it is over. What to make of these
ornaments, these empty chambers
that sting with pleasure even as
the skin begins to loosen? How to take care?
How to see these breasts as flesh
and emblem? What about her mother's breasts —
those things that finally belonged to her younger sister;
things she wanted, wanted to possess completely
like two suns emanating from her own chest.

KIMIKO HAHN

THE ARTIST'S DAUGHTER

In her lover's studio, the walls,
smeared and splattered

in half a dozen versions of black,
his brushes in discarded tomato cans —

here, her body is light

as if shafts of light cut limbs
off her torso, as if the air

pricked the recollection:
gripping his finger when she crossed the street

to his first and last gallery show — not
the lover but the father. Light,

her gut light not

from the stunning sun
but from the redolence of turpentine —

which is all she needs to
fall in love. He, the lover,

knows this and although is not figurative,
pulls her skirt up, tears her stockings off

and licks her sex, his tongue —
soft as a brush. The lover

knows the truth about this light

and its attachment to tissue.

She knows the truth about history
is not some fact but an image

teased from nerve endings. Hers,

she surmises, no different from
his watching his sister in their parents' bathroom

disrobe so gingerly he was sure

each gesture was performed for a god.

Did that sister notice him in the misted mirror
and pretend she did not

so he could, decades later,
never paint the body as a body

and always love oils
thickly applied to canvas the size of a door?

Did she? And does the artist's daughter

finally cast off what

she herself can't form into a subject

to be seized by this particular fragrance
on the floor half-covered in tarp?

RECKLESS SONNET

Not all insects but certain insects
spiral above bodies of water in their courtship,
the male carrying a stone fly or mayfly in his legs.
The female will follow him,
alighting on a petal or stem,
then accept the prey
and consume it during their consummation.
How pleasant,
though different from fellatio or kissing,
to eat, say, a square of bitter chocolate
filled with a creamy nougat
while the male pulses inside.
How *sweet*.
How exquisite a bribe for the bride.

Donald Hall

MAPLE SYRUP

August, goldenrod blowing. We walk
into the graveyard, to find
my grandfather's grave. Ten years ago
I came here last, bringing
marigolds from the round garden
outside the kitchen.
I didn't know you then.
                 We walk
among carved names that go with photographs
on top of the piano at the farm:
Keneston, Wells, Fowler, Batchelder, Buck.
We pause at the new grave
of Grace Fenton, my grandfather's
sister. Last summer
we called on her at the nursing home,
eighty-seven, and nodding
in a blue housedress. We cannot find
my grandfather's grave.
                 Back at the house
where no one lives, we potter
and explore the back chamber
where everything comes to rest: spinning wheels,
pretty boxes, quilts,
bottles, books, albums of postcards.
Then with a flashlight we descend
firm steps to the root cellar — black,
cobwebby, huge,
with dirt floors and fieldstone walls,
and above the walls, holding the hewn
sills of the house, enormous
granite foundation stones.
Past the empty bins
for squash, apples, carrots, and potatoes,
we discover the shelves for canning, a few
pale pints
of tomato left, and — what
is this? — syrup, maple syrup
in a quart jar, syrup

my grandfather made twenty-five
years ago
for the last time.
                    I remember
coming to the farm in March
in sugaring time, as a small boy.
He carried the pails of sap, sixteen-quart
buckets, dangling from each end
of a wooden yoke
that lay across his shoulders, and emptied them
into a vat in the saphouse
where fire burned day and night
for a week.
                    Now the saphouse
tilts, nearly to the ground,
like someone exhausted
to the point of death, and next winter
when snow piles three feet thick
on the roofs of the cold farm,
the saphouse will shudder and slide
with the snow to the ground.
                    Today
we take my grandfather's last
quart of syrup
upstairs, holding it gingerly,
and we wash off twenty-five years
of dirt, and we pull
and pry the lid up, cutting the stiff,
dried rubber gasket, and dip our fingers
in, you and I both, and taste
the sweetness, you for the first time,

the sweetness preserved, of a dead man
in the kitchen he left
when his body slid
like anyone's into the ground.

IN THE KITCHEN OF THE OLD HOUSE

In the kitchen of the old house, late,
I was making some coffee
    and I daydreamed sleepily of old friends.

Then the dream turned. I waited.
    I walked alone all day in the town
where I was born. It was cold,
    a Saturday in January
when nothing happens. The streets
    changed as the sky grew dark around me.
The lamps in the small houses
    had tassels on them, and the black cars
at the curb were old and square.
    A ragman passed with his horse, their breaths
blooming like white peonies,
    when I turned into a darker street
and I recognized the house
    from snapshots. I felt as separate
as if the city and the house
    were closed inside a globe which I shook
to make it snow. No sooner
    did I think of snow, but snow started
to fill the heavy darkness
    around me. It reflected the glare
of the streetlight as it fell
    melting on the warmth of the sidewalk
and frozen on frozen grass.
    Then I heard out of the dark the sound
of steps on the bare cement
    in a familiar rhythm. Under
the streetlight, bent to the snow,
    hatless, younger than I, so young that
I was not born, my father
    walked home to his bride and his supper.
A shout gathered inside me
    like a cold wind, to break the rhythm,
to keep him from entering
    that heavy door — but I stood under
a tree, closed in by the snow,
    and did not shout, to tell what happened
in twenty years, in winter,
    when his early death grew inside him
like snow piling on the grass.
    He opened the door and met the young
woman who waited for him.

DONALD HALL

WHEN THE YOUNG HUSBAND

When the young husband picked up his friend's pretty wife
in the taxi one block from her townhouse for their
first lunch together, in a hotel dining room
        with a room key in his pocket,

midtown traffic gridlocked and was abruptly still.
For one moment before klaxons started honking,
a prophetic voice spoke in his mind's ear despite
        his pulse's erotic thudding:

"The misery you undertake this afternoon
will accompany you to the ends of your lives.
She knew what she did when she agreed to this lunch,
        although she will not admit it;

and you've constructed your playlet a thousand times:
cocktails, an omelet, wine; the revelation
of a room key; the elevator rising as
        the penis elevates; the skin

flushed, the door fumbled at, the handbag dropped; the first
kiss with open mouths, nakedness, swoon, thrust-and-catch;
endorphins followed by endearments; a brief nap;
        another fit; restoration

of clothes, arrangements for another encounter,
the taxi back, and the furtive kiss of goodbye.
Then, by turn: tears, treachery, anger, betrayal;
        marriages and houses destroyed;

small children abandoned and inconsolable,
their foursquare estates disestablished forever;
the unreadable advocates; the wretchedness
        of passion outworn; anguished nights

sleepless in a bare room; whiskey, meth, cocaine; new
love, essayed in loneliness with miserable
strangers, that comforts nothing but skin; hours with sons
        and daughters studious always

to maintain distrust; the daily desire to die
and the daily agony of the requirement
to survive, until only the quarrel endures."
            Prophecy stopped; traffic started.

THE PORCELAIN COUPLE

When Jane felt well enough for me to leave her
a whole day, I drove south by the river
to empty my mother's house in Connecticut.
I hurried from room to room, cellar to attic,
looking into a crammed storeroom, then turning
to discover a chest with five full drawers.
I labeled for shipping sofas and chairs,
bedroom sets, and tables; I wrapped figurines
and fancy teacups in paper, preserving
things she had cherished — and in late years dreaded
might go for a nickel at a sale on the lawn.
Everywhere I saw shelves and tabletops
covered with glass animals and music boxes.
In closets, decades of finery hung in dead air.
I swept ashtrays and blouses into plastic sacks,
and the green-gold dress she wore to Bermuda.
At the last moment I discovered and saved
a cut-glass tumbler, stained red at the top,
Lucy 1905 scripted on the stain. In the garage
I piled bags for the dump, then drove four hours
north with my hands tight on the steering wheel,
drank a beer looking through the day's mail,
and pitched into bed with Jane who slept fitfully.
When I woke, I rose as if from a drunken sleep
after looting a city and burning its temples.
All day, while I ate lunch or counted out pills,
I noticed the objects of our twenty years:
a blue vase, a candelabrum Jane carried on her lap
from the Baja, and the small porcelain box
from France I found under the tree one Christmas
where a couple in relief stretch out asleep,
like a catafalque, on the pastel double bed
of the box's top, both wearing pretty nightcaps.

DONALD HALL

ARDOR

Nursing her I felt alive
in the animal moment,
scenting the predator.
Her death was the worst thing
that could happen,
and caring for her was best.

After she died I screamed,
upsetting the depressed dog.
Now I no longer
address the wall covered
with many photographs,
nor call her "you"
in a poem. She recedes
into the granite museum
of JANE KENYON 1947–1995.

I long for the absent
woman of different faces
who makes metaphors
and chops onion, drinking
a glass of Chardonnay,
oiling the wok, humming
to herself, maybe thinking
how to conclude a poem.
When I make love now,
something is awry.
Last autumn a woman said,
"I mistrust your ardor."

This winter in Florida
I loathed the old couples
my age who promenaded
in their slack flesh
holding hands. I gazed
at young women with outrage
and desire — unable to love
or to work, or to die.

Hours are slow and weeks
rapid in their vacancy.

DONALD HALL

Each day lapses as I recite
my complaints. Lust is grief
that has turned over in bed
to look the other way.

DIGGING

One midnight, after a day when lilies
lift themselves out of the ground while you watch them,
and you come into the house at dark
your fingers grubby with digging, your eyes
vague with the pleasure of digging,

let a wind raised from the South
climb through your bedroom window, lift you in its arms
— you have become as small as a seed —
and carry you out of the house, over the black garden,
spinning and fluttering,

and drop you in cracked ground.
The dirt will be cool, rough to your clasped skin
like a man you have never known.
You will die into the ground
in a dead sleep, surrendered to water.

You will wake suffering
a widening pain in your side, a breach
gapped in your tight ribs
where a green shoot struggles to lift itself upwards
through the tomb of your dead flesh

to the sun, to the air of your garden
where you will blossom
in the shape of your own self, thoughtless
with flowers, speaking
to bees, in the language of green and yellow, white and red.

Michael S. Harper

WE ASSUME: ON THE DEATH OF OUR SON,
REUBEN MASAI HARPER

We assume
that in 28 hours,
lived in a collapsible isolette,
you learned to accept pure oxygen
as the natural sky;
the scant shallow breaths
that filled those hours
cannot, did not make you fly —
but dreams were there
like crooked palmprints on
the twin-thick windows of the nursery —
in the glands of your mother.

We assume
the sterile hands
drank chemicals in and out
from lungs opaque with mucus,
pumped your stomach,
eeked the bicarbonate in
crooked, green-winged veins,
out in a plastic mask;

A woman who'd lost her first son
consoled us with an angel gone ahead
to pray for our family —
gone into that sky
seeking oxygen,
gone into autopsy,
a fine brown powdered sugar,
a disposable cremation:

We assume
you did not know we loved you.

MICHAEL S. HARPER

REUBEN, REUBEN

I reach from pain
to music great enough
to bring me back,
swollenhead, madness,
lovefruit, a pickle of hate
so sour my mouth twicked
up and would not sing;
there's nothing in the beat
to hold it in
melody and turn human skin;
a brown berry gone
to rot just two days on the branch;
we've lost a son,
the music, *jazz*, comes in.

DEAR JOHN, DEAR COLTRANE

a love supreme, a love supreme
a love supreme, a love supreme
Sex fingers toes
in the marketplace
near your father's church
in Hamlet, North Carolina —
witness to this love
in this calm fallow
of these minds,
there is no substitute for pain:
genitals gone or going,
seed burned out,
you tuck the roots in the earth,
turn back, and move
by river through the swamps,
singing: *a love supreme, a love supreme*;
what does it all mean?
Loss, so great each black
woman expects your failure
in mute change, the seed gone.
You plod up into the electric city —

MICHAEL S. HARPER

your song now crystal and
the blues. You pick up the horn
with some will and blow
into the freezing night:
a love supreme, a love supreme —

Dawn comes and you cook
up the thick sin 'tween
impotence and death, fuel
the tenor sax cannibal
heart, genitals and sweat
that makes you clean —
a love supreme, a love supreme —

Why you so black?
cause I am
why you so funky?
cause I am
why you so black?
cause I am
why you so sweet?
cause I am
why you so black?
cause I am
a love supreme, a love supreme:

So sick
you couldn't play *Naima*,
so flat we ached
for song you'd concealed
with your own blood,
your diseased liver gave
out its purity,
the inflated heart
pumps out, the tenor kiss,
tenor love:
a love supreme, a love supreme —
a love supreme, a love supreme —

MICHAEL S. HARPER

LOVE MEDLEY: PATRICE CUCHULAIN

"Stirrups, leggings, a stainless
steel slide, a dishpan, sheet,
a thread spool, scissors,
three facemasks, smocks, paper
overshoes, a two-way mirror, dials":
the head and left arm
cruise out, almost together,
and you drop into gloves,
your own ointment
pulling your legs
binding your cord; the cheesed
surface skin, your dark
hairless complexion, the metallic room,
orchestrate and blow up your lungs,
clogged on protein and vitamins,
for the sterile whine of the delivery
room and your staff of attendants.
It is free exercise when the cord's
cut; you weigh in for the clean up
as your mother gets her local
for her stitches: boy, 6 lbs 13 oz.

As you breathe easily, your mother's
mother is tubed and strapped,
hemorrhaging slowly from her varices;
your two dead brothers who could
not breathe are berries
gone to rot at our table:
what is birth but death
with complexity: blood, veins,
machinery and love: our names.

THIS IS MY SON'S SONG: *"UNGIE, HI UNGIE"*

A two-year-old boy
is a blossom in the intensive
care aisle, small as
a ball-bearing,

MICHAEL S. HARPER

round, open and smooth;
for a month, in his first
premature hours, his shaved
head made him a mohawk Indian
child, tubes the herbs
for his nest, a collapsed lung
the bulbous wing of a hawk.
Slivered into each sole
is an intravenous solution
to balance his losses
or what they take out
for the lab; the blue spot
on his spine is a birth
mark of needle readings;
the hardened thighs immune
from 70 shots of various
drugs of uneven depth; the chest
is thick with congestion: bad
air and mucus — good air and pure
oxygen; jerky pouch buffalo lungs —
It does not surprise me
when he waits patiently for his
grandmother, over her five-hour
painless operation; he has
waited in his isolette
before: the glow in his eyes
is for himself, will and love:
an exclamation of your name:
"Ungie, hi Ungie"; you are saved.

STUDS

Off-color eyes that shine through lobes,
the flesh still uneaten by stickpin,
he was stuck to her; this attachment,
like string from the loops of IUD
caught him unawares, in planes
above the Earth, on plains
near the homestead, on water
which he has touched with his belt

and bow, as a lifeguard,
before he met her.
                        Yes, she could brown
in that sun, the broad shoulders
concealed in flesh for his children,
who grew beyond her; he built a shed
for her tools, the garden, the chain saw —
windows faced toward the southern estuary
where turtles called, for the pond
swelled in the porous ground,
from springs, and she was a spring.

All day he has thought of Seminoles;
all day he has dreamed of the Narragansett;
his children could fit in if the drum
were opened to shells he could use
for the dinner table, and shells
from the sea decorate the walls
of the uterus, mystery of caves
he got lost in on special dates,
January 15 for instance,
now a national holiday;
and April 23, her father's birthday,
and Shakespeare's,
where he read in a long line
at the Library of Congress
after visiting the Capitol
where Martin Luther King, Jr.
stood in consummate black stone.

Now he must ask about diamonds;
how refraction turns into bloodlines
he could choose for band music,
the territory bands
of Count Basie, without charts,
in a beat-up van,
passing for Indians,
passing in the slow lane
through the culture.

He would place her flesh there;
he would ask her to wear these,
diamond studs, in each ear,
to hear his song: to hear his name
come alive in her ears.

MICHAEL S. HARPER

HERE WHERE COLTRANE IS

Soul and race
are private dominions,
memories and modal
songs, a tenor blossoming,
which would paint suffering
a clear color but is not in
this Victorian house
without oil in zero degree
weather and a forty-mile-an-hour wind;
it is all a well-knit family:
a love supreme.
Oak leaves pile up on walkway
and steps, catholic as apples
in a special mist of clear white
children who love my children.
I play "Alabama"
on a warped record player
skipping the scratches
on your faces over the fibrous
conical hairs of plastic
under the wooden floors.

Dreaming on a train from New York
to Philly, you hand out six
notes which become an anthem
to our memories of you:
oak, birch, maple,
apple, cocoa, rubber.
For this reason Martin is dead;
for this reason Malcolm is dead;
for this reason Coltrane is dead;
in the eyes of my first son are the browns
of these men and their music.

Robert Hass

THE IMAGE

The child brought blue clay from the creek
and the woman made two figures: a lady and a deer.
At that season deer came down from the mountain
and fed quietly in the redwood canyons.
The woman and the child regarded the figure of the lady,
the crude roundnesses, the grace, the coloring like shadow.
They were not sure where she came from,
except the child's fetching and the woman's hands
and the lead-blue clay of the creek
where the deer sometimes showed themselves at sundown.

MEDITATION AT LAGUNITAS

All the new thinking is about loss.
In this it resembles all the old thinking.
The idea, for example, that each particular erases
the luminous clarity of a general idea. That the clown-
faced woodpecker probing the dead sculpted trunk
of that black birch is, by his presence,
some tragic falling off from a first world
of undivided light. Or the other notion that,
because there is in this world no one thing
to which the bramble of *blackberry* corresponds,
a word is elegy to what it signifies.
We talked about it late last night and in the voice
of my friend, there was a thin wire of grief, a tone
almost querulous. After a while I understood that,
talking this way, everything dissolves: *justice,
pine, hair, woman, you* and *I.* There was a woman
I made love to and I remembered how, holding
her small shoulders in my hands sometimes,
I felt a violent wonder at her presence
like a thirst for salt, for my childhood river
with its island willows, silly music from the pleasure boat,

muddy places where we caught the little orange-silver fish
called *pumpkinseed*. It hardly had to do with her.
Longing, we say, because desire is full
of endless distances. I must have been the same to her.
But I remember so much, the way her hands dismantled bread,
the thing her father said that hurt her, what
she dreamed. There are moments when the body is as numinous
as words, days that are the good flesh continuing.
Such tenderness, those afternoons and evenings,
saying *blackberry, blackberry, blackberry.*

A STORY ABOUT THE BODY

The young composer, working that summer at an artist's colony, had
watched her for a week. She was Japanese, a painter, almost sixty, and he
thought he was in love with her. He loved her work, and her work was like
the way she moved her body, used her hands, looked at him directly
when she made amused and considered answers to his questions. One
night, walking back from a concert, they came to her door and she
turned to him and said, "I think you would like to have me. I would like
that too, but I must tell you that I have had a double mastectomy," and
when he didn't understand, "I've lost both my breasts." The radiance
that he had carried around in his belly and chest cavity — like music —
withered very quickly, and he made himself look at her when he said,
"I'm sorry. I don't think I could." He walked back to his own cabin
through the pines, and in the morning he found a small blue bowl on the
porch outside his door. It looked to be full of rose petals, but he found
when he picked it up that the rose petals were on top; the rest of the
bowl — she must have swept them from the corners of her studio — was
full of dead bees.

PRIVILEGE OF BEING

Many are making love. Up above, the angels
in the unshaken ether and crystal of human longing
are braiding one another's hair, which is strawberry blond
and the texture of cold rivers. They glance

down from time to time at the awkward ecstasy —
it must look to them like featherless birds
splashing in the spring puddle of a bed —
and then one woman, she is about to come,
peels back the man's shut eyelids and says,
look at me, and he does. Or is it the man
tugging the curtain rope in that dark theater?
Anyway, they do, they look at each other;
two beings with evolved eyes, rapacious,
startled, connected at the belly in an unbelievably sweet
lubricious glue, stare at each other,
and the angels are desolate. They hate it. They shudder pathetically
like lithographs of Victorian beggars
with perfect features and alabaster skin hawking rags
in the lewd alleys of the novel.
All of creation is offended by this distress.
It is like the keening sound the moon makes sometimes,
rising. The lovers especially cannot bear it,
it fills them with unspeakable sadness, so that
they close their eyes again and hold each other, each
feeling the mortal singularity of the body
they have enchanted out of death for an hour or so,
and one day, running at sunset, the woman says to the man,
I woke up feeling so sad this morning because I realized
that you could not, as much as I love you,
dear heart, cure my loneliness,
wherewith she touched his cheek to reassure him
that she did not mean to hurt him with this truth.
And the man is not hurt exactly,
he understands that life has limits, that people
die young, fail at love,
fail of their ambitions. He runs beside her, he thinks
of the sadness they have gasped and crooned their way out of
coming, clutching each other with old, invented
forms of grace and clumsy gratitude, ready
to be alone again, or dissatisfied, or merely
companionable like the couples on the summer beach
reading magazine articles about intimacy between the sexes
to themselves, and to each other,
and to the immense, illiterate, consoling angels.

ROBERT HASS

HAPPINESS

Because yesterday morning from the steamy window
we saw a pair of red foxes across the creek
eating the last windfall apples in the rain;
they looked up at us with their green eyes
long enough to symbolize the wakefulness of living things
and then went back to eating;

and because this morning
when she went into the gazebo with her black pen and yellow pad
to coax an inquisitive soul
from what she thinks of as the reluctance of matter,
I drove into town to drink tea in the cafe
and write notes in a journal; mist rose from the bay
like the luminous and indefinite aspect of intention,
and a small flock of tundra swans
for the second winter in a row were feeding on new grass
in the soaked fields — they symbolize mystery, I suppose,
they are also called whistling swans, are very white,
and their eyes are black —

and because the tea steamed in front of me,
and the notebook, turned to a new page,
was blank except for a faint blue idea of order,
I wrote: *happiness! it is December, very cold,*
we woke early this morning,
and lay in bed kissing,
our eyes squinched up like bats.

OUR LADY OF THE SNOWS

In white,
the unpainted statue of the young girl
on the side altar
made the quality of mercy seem scrupulous and calm.

When my mother was in a hospital drying out,
or drinking at a pace that would put her there soon,
I would slip in the side door,
light an aromatic candle,

and bargain for us both.
Or else I'd stare into the day-moon of that face
and, if I concentrated, fly.

Come down! come down!
she'd call, because I was so high.

Though mostly when I think of myself
at that age, I am standing at my older brother's closet
studying the shirts,
convinced that I could be absolutely transformed
by something I could borrow.
And the days churned by,
navigable sorrow.

SPRING DRAWING 2

A man says *lilacs against white houses, two sparrows, one streaked, in a thinning birch*, and can't find his way to a sentence.

In order to be respectable, Thorstein Veblen said, desperate in Palo Alto, a thing must be wasteful, i.e., "a selective adaptation of forms to the end of conspicuous waste."

So we try to throw nothing away, as Keith, making dinner for us as his grandmother had done in Jamaica, left nothing; the kitchen was as clean at the end as when he started; even the shrimp shells and carrot fronds were part of the process,

and he said, when we tried to admire him, "Listen, I should send you into the chickenyard to look for a rusty nail to add to the soup for iron."

The first temptation of Sakyamuni was desire, but he saw that it led to fulfillment and then to desire, so that one was easy.

Because I have pruned it badly in successive years, the climbing rose has sent out, among the pale pink floribunda, a few wild white roses from the rootstalk.

Suppose, before they said *silver* or *moonlight* or *wet grass*, each poet had to agree to be responsible for the innocence of all the suffering on earth,

because they learned in arithmetic, during the long school days, that if
there was anything left over,

you had to carry it. The wild rose looks weightless, the floribunda are
heavy with the richness and sadness of Europe

as they imitate the dying, petal by petal, of the people who bred them.

You hear pain singing in the nerves of things; it is not a song.

The gazelle's head turned; three jackals are eating his entrails and he is
watching.

FAINT MUSIC

Maybe you need to write a poem about grace.

When everything broken is broken,
and everything dead is dead,
and the hero has looked into the mirror with complete contempt,
and the heroine has studied her face and its defects
remorselessly, and the pain they thought might,
as a token of their earnestness, release them from themselves
has lost its novelty and not released them,
and they have begun to think, kindly and distantly,
watching the others go about their days —
likes and dislikes, reasons, habits, fears —
that self-love is the one weedy stalk
of every human blossoming, and understood,
therefore, why they had been, all their lives,
in such a fury to defend it, and that no one —
except some almost inconceivable saint in his pool
of poverty and silence — can escape this violent, automatic
life's companion ever, maybe then, ordinary light,
faint music under things, a hovering like grace appears.

As in the story a friend told once about the time
he tried to kill himself. His girl had left him.
Bees in the heart, then scorpions, maggots, and then ash.
He climbed onto the jumping girder of the bridge,
the bay side, a blue, lucid afternoon.
And in the salt air he thought about the word "seafood,"

that there was something faintly ridiculous about it.
No one said "landfood." He thought it was degrading to the rainbow
    perch
he'd reeled in gleaming from the cliffs, the black rockbass,
scales like polished carbon, in beds of kelp
along the coast — and he realized that the reason for the word
was crabs, or mussels, clams. Otherwise
the restaurants could just put "fish" up on their signs,
and when he woke — he'd slept for hours, curled up
on the girder like a child — the sun was going down
and he felt a little better, and afraid. He put on the jacket
he'd used for a pillow, climbed over the railing
carefully, and drove home to an empty house.

There was a pair of her lemon yellow panties
hanging on a doorknob. He studied them. Much-washed.
A faint russet in the crotch that made him sick
with rage and grief. He knew more or less
where she was. A flat somewhere on Russian Hill.
They'd have just finished making love. She'd have tears
in her eyes and touch his jawbone gratefully. "God,"
she'd say, "you are so good for me." Winking lights,
a foggy view downhill toward the harbor and the bay.
"You're sad," he'd say. "Yes." "Thinking about Nick?"
"Yes," she'd say and cry. "I tried so hard," sobbing now,
"I really tried so hard." And then he'd hold her for a while —
Guatemalan weavings from his fieldwork on the wall —
and then they'd fuck again, and she would cry some more,
and go to sleep.
                And he, he would play that scene
once only, once and a half, and tell himself
that he was going to carry it for a very long time
and that there was nothing he could do
but carry it. He went out onto the porch, and listened
to the forest in the summer dark, madrone bark
cracking and curling as the cold came up.

It's not the story though, not the friend
leaning toward you, saying "And then I realized — ,"
which is the part of stories one never quite believes.
I had the idea that the world's so full of pain
it must sometimes make a kind of singing.
And that the sequence helps, as much as order helps —
First an ego, and then pain, and then the singing.

Robert Hayden

THOSE WINTER SUNDAYS

Sundays too my father got up early
and put his clothes on in the blueblack cold,
then with cracked hands that ached
from labor in the weekday weather made
banked fires blaze. No one ever thanked him.

I'd wake and hear the cold splintering, breaking.
When the rooms were warm, he'd call,
and slowly I would rise and dress,
fearing the chronic angers of that house,

Speaking indifferently to him,
who had driven out the cold
and polished my good shoes as well.
What did I know, what did I know
of love's austere and lonely offices?

NIGHT, DEATH, MISSISSIPPI

I

A quavering cry. Screech-owl?
Or one of them?
The old man in his reek
and gauntness laughs —

One of them, I bet —
and turns out the kitchen lamp,
limping to the porch to listen
in the windowless night.

Be there with Boy and the rest
if I was well again.

Time was. Time was.
White robes like moonlight

In the sweetgum dark.
Unbucked that one then
and him squealing bloody Jesus
as we cut it off.

Time was. A cry?
A cry all right.
He hawks and spits,
fevered as by groinfire.

Have us a bottle,
Boy and me —
he's earned him a bottle —
when he gets home.

II

Then we beat them, he said,
beat them till our arms was tired
and the big old chains
messy and red.

O Jesus burning on the lily cross

Christ, it was better
than hunting bear
which don't know why
you want him dead.

O night, rawhead and bloodybones night

You kids fetch Paw
some water now so's he
can wash that blood
off him, she said.

O night betrayed by darkness not its own

ROBERT HAYDEN

MIDDLE PASSAGE

I

Jesús, Estrella, Esperanza, Mercy:

> Sails flashing to the wind like weapons,
> sharks following the moans the fever and the dying;
> horror the corposant and compass rose.

Middle Passage:
>   voyage through death
>   to life upon these shores.

> "10 April 1800 —
> Blacks rebellious. Crew uneasy. Our linguist says
> their moaning is a prayer for death,
> ours and their own. Some try to starve themselves.
> Lost three this morning leaped with crazy laughter
> to the waiting sharks, sang as they went under."

Desire, Adventure, Tartar, Ann:

> Standing to America, bringing home
> black gold, black ivory, black seed.

> > *Deep in the festering hold thy father lies,*
> > *of his bones New England pews are made,*
> > *those are altar lights that were his eyes.*

Jesus   Saviour   Pilot   Me
Over   Life's   Tempestuous   Sea

We pray that Thou wilt grant, O Lord,
safe passage to our vessels bringing
heathen souls unto Thy chastening.

Jesus   Saviour

> "8 bells. I cannot sleep, for I am sick
> with fear, but writing eases fear a little
> since still my eyes can see these words take shape
> upon the page & so I write, as one
> would turn to exorcism. 4 days scudding,
> but now the sea is calm again. Misfortune
> follows in our wake like sharks (our grinning

tutelary gods). Which one of us
has killed an albatross? A plague among
our blacks — Ophthalmia: blindness — & we
have jettisoned the blind to no avail.
It spreads, the terrifying sickness spreads.
Its claws have scratched sight from the Capt.'s eyes
& there is blindness in the fo'c'sle
& we must sail 3 weeks before we come
to port."

> *What port awaits us, Davy Jones'*
> *or home? I've heard of slavers drifting, drifting,*
> *playthings of wind and storm and chance, their crews*
> *gone blind, the jungle hatred*
> *crawling up on deck.*

Thou   Who   Walked   On   Galilee

> "Deponent further sayeth *The Bella J*
> left the Guinea Coast
> with cargo of five hundred blacks and odd
> for the barracoons of Florida:

> "That there was hardly room 'tween-decks for half
> the sweltering cattle stowed spoon-fashion there;
> that some went mad of thirst and tore their flesh
> and sucked the blood:

> "That Crew and Captain lusted with the comeliest
> of the savage girls kept naked in the cabins;
> that there was one they called The Guinea Rose
> and they cast lots and fought to lie with her:

> "That when the Bo's'n piped all hands, the flames
> spreading from starboard already were beyond
> control, the negroes howling and their chains
> entangled with the flames:

> "That the burning blacks could not be reached,
> that the Crew abandoned ship,
> leaving their shrieking negresses behind,
> that the Captain perished drunken with the wenches:

> "Further Deponent sayeth not."

Pilot   Oh   Pilot   Me

II

Aye, lad, and I have seen those factories,
Gambia, Rio Pongo, Calabar;
have watched the artful mongos baiting traps
of war wherein the victor and the vanquished

Were caught as prizes for our barracoons.
Have seen the nigger kings whose vanity
and greed turned wild black hides of Fellatah,
Mandingo, Ibo, Kru to gold for us.

And there was one — King Anthracite we named him —
fetish face beneath French parasols
of brass and orange velvet, impudent mouth
whose cups were carven skulls of enemies:

He'd honor us with drum and feast and conjo
and palm-oil-glistening wenches deft in love,
and for tin crowns that shone with paste,
red calico and German-silver trinkets

Would have the drums talk war and send
his warriors to burn the sleeping villages
and kill the sick and old and lead the young
in coffles to our factories.

Twenty years a trader, twenty years,
for there was wealth aplenty to be harvested
from those black fields, and I'd be trading still
but for the fevers melting down my bones.

III

Shuttles in the rocking loom of history,
the dark ships move, the dark ships move,
their bright ironical names
like jests of kindness on a murderer's mouth;
plough through thrashing glister toward
fata morgana's lucent melting shore,
weave toward New World littorals that are
mirage and myth and actual shore.

Voyage through death,
                voyage whose chartings are unlove.

A charnel stench, effluvium of living death
spreads outward from the hold,
where the living and the dead, the horribly dying,
lie interlocked, lie foul with blood and excrement.

    Deep in the festering hold thy father lies,
    the corpse of mercy rots with him,
    rats eat love's rotten gelid eyes.

    But, oh, the living look at you
    with human eyes whose suffering accuses you,
    whose hatred reaches through the swill of dark
    to strike you like a leper's claw.

    You cannot stare that hatred down
    or chain the fear that stalks the watches
    and breathes on you its fetid scorching breath;
    cannot kill the deep immortal human wish,
    the timeless will.

        "But for the storm that flung up barriers
        of wind and wave, *The Amistad*, señores,
        would have reached the port of Príncipe in two,
        three days at most; but for the storm we should
        have been prepared for what befell.
        Swift as the puma's leap it came. There was
        that interval of moonless calm filled only
        with the water's and the rigging's usual sounds,
        then sudden movement, blows and snarling cries
        and they had fallen on us with machete
        and marlinspike. It was as though the very
        air, the night itself were striking us.
        Exhausted by the rigors of the storm,
        we were no match for them. Our men went down
        before the murderous Africans. Our loyal
        Celestino ran from below with gun
        and lantern and I saw, before the cane-
        knife's wounding flash, Cinquez,
        that surly brute who calls himself a prince,
        directing, urging on the ghastly work.
        He hacked the poor mulatto down, and then

he turned on me. The decks were slippery
when daylight finally came. It sickens me
to think of what I saw, of how these apes
threw overboard the butchered bodies of
our men, true Christians all, like so much jetsam.
Enough, enough. The rest is quickly told:
Cinquez was forced to spare the two of us
you see to steer the ship to Africa,
and we like phantoms doomed to rove the sea
voyaged east by day and west by night,
deceiving them, hoping for rescue,
prisoners on our own vessel, till
at length we drifted to the shores of this
your land, America, where we were freed
from our unspeakable misery. Now we
demand, good sirs, the extradition of
Cinquez and his accomplices to La
Havana. And it distresses us to know
there are so many here who seem inclined
to justify the mutiny of these blacks.
We find it paradoxical indeed
that you whose wealth, whose tree of liberty
are rooted in the labor of your slaves
should suffer the august John Quincy Adams
to speak with so much passion of the right
of chattel slaves to kill their lawful masters
and with his Roman rhetoric weave a hero's
garland for Cinquez. I tell you that
we are determined to return to Cuba
with our slaves and there see justice done. Cinquez —
or let us say 'the Prince' — Cinquez shall die."

The deep immortal human wish,
the timeless will:

    Cinquez its deathless primaveral image,
    life that transfigures many lives.

Voyage through death
                to life upon these shores.

BOA Editions (photo Herald)

William Heyen

THE RETURN

I will touch things and things and no more thoughts.
                                    — Robinson Jeffers

My boat slowed on the still water,
stopped in a thatch of lilies.
The moon leaned over the white lilies.

I waited for a sign, and stared
at the hooded water. On the far shore
brush broke, a deer broke cover.

I waited for a sign, and waited.
The moon lit the lilies to candles.
Their light reached down the water

to a dark flame, a fish: it hovered
under the pads, the pond held it
in its dim depths as though in amber.

Green, still, balanced in its own life,
breathing small breaths of light, this
was the world's oldest wonder, the arrow

of thought, the branch that all words
break against, the deep fire, the pure poise
of an object, the pond's presence, the pike.

THE PIGEONS

Audubon watched the flocks beat by for days,
and tried, but could not count them:
their dung fell "like melting flakes of snow,"
the air buzzed until he lost his senses.

215

He heard, he said, their *coo-coo*
and *kee-kee* when they courted, and saw trees
of hundreds of nests, each cradling two
"broadly elliptical pure white eggs."

Over mast, they swept in "rich deep purple
circles," then roosted so thick that high limbs
cracked, and the pigeons avalanched
down the boughs, and had not room to fly,

and died by thousands. Kentucky farmers
fed their hogs on birds
knocked out of the air with poles. No net, stone,
arrow, or bullet could miss one,

so horses drew wagons of them,
and schooners sailed cargoes of them,
and locomotives pulled freightcars of them
to the cities where they sold for one cent each.

When you touched one, its soft
feathers fell away as easily as a puff
of dandelion seeds, and its delicate breastbone seemed to return the pulse of your thumb.

WITNESS

We'd walked into the small warm shed
where spring lambs lay in straw
in the half-dark still smelling of their birth,
of ammonia, the damp grass, dung,
into this world in the middle of a field
where lambs bleating soft songs lifted
their heavy heads toward their mothers,
gentle presences within their wool clouds.
Later, outside, as I watched,
Wenzel wrapped his left arm around a sheep's neck
and struck her with the sledge in his right hand.
The dying sheep, her forehead crushed, cried out,
past pain, for her mortal life. Blood flowed
from her burst skull, over her eyes, her black nose.

Wenzel dropped her to the grass.
When I ran home, I struck my head
on a blossoming apple-bough.
Where was the dead sheep?
What did I hear?
Where is the witness now?

I was nine or ten.
Her cry was terror,
so I lay awake to hear her,
to wonder why she didn't seem to know
her next manger, her golden fields.
Her odors drifted through my screen —
the hay at the roots of her wool,
her urine, the wet graindust under her chin,
her birth fluids hot and flecked with blood.
I could hear her bleat
to her last lamb, hear her heartbeat
in the black air of my room.
Where was the dead sheep?
Why did she cry for her loss?
Where is the witness now?

Not to accept, but to awaken.
Not to understand, to cry terror, but to know
that even a billion years later, now,
we breathe the first circle of light,
and the light curves into us, into the deer's back,
the man's neck, the woman's thigh,
the cat's mouse-mossed tongue, all the ruby
berries ripening in evening air.
The dead elms and chestnuts are of it, and do not
break the curve. The jeweled flies sip it,
and do not break the curve.
Our homes inhabit, and ride the curve.
Our moon, our rivers, the furthest stars blinking blue,
the great named and nameless comets do not break the curve.
The odorous apple-blossom rain does not break the curve.
The struck ewe's broken brainpan does not break the curve.
Wenzel nor this witness breaks the curve.

In the shed's dusk where spring lambs
sang to their mothers, in my dark room
where the dead ewe's odors drifted my sleep,

and now, within these cells where her forehead blood
flows once more into recollection,
the light curves. You and I bear witness, and know this,
and as we do the light curves into this knowledge.
The struck ewe lives in this light,
in this curve of the only unbroken light.

SIMPLE TRUTHS

When a man has grown a body,
a body to carry with him
through nature for as long as he can,
when this body is taken from him
by other men and women who happen to be,
this time, in uniform,
then it is clear he has experienced
an act of barbarism,

and when a man has a wife,
a wife to love for as long as he lives,
when this wife is marked with a yellow star
and driven into a chamber she will never leave alive,
then this is murder,
so much is clear,

and when a woman has hair,
when her hair is shorn and her scalp bleeds,
when a woman has children,
children to love for as long as she lives,
when the children are taken from her,
when a man and his wife and their children
are put to death in a chamber of gas,
or with pistols at close range, or are starved,
or beaten, or injected by the thousands,
or ripped apart, by the thousands, by the millions,
it is clear that where we are
is Europe, in our century, during the years
from nineteen-hundred and thirty-five
to nineteen-hundred and forty-five
after the death of Jesus, who spoke of a different order,
but whose father, who is our father,

WILLIAM HEYEN

if he is our father,
if we must speak of him as father,
watched, and witnessed, and knew,

and when we remember,
when we touch the skin of our own bodies,
when we open our eyes into dream
or within the morning shine of sunlight
and remember what was taken
from these men, from these women,
from these children gassed and starved
and beaten and thrown against walls
and made to walk the valley
of knives and icepicks and otherwise
exterminated in ways appearing to us almost
beyond even the maniacal human imagination,
then it is clear that this is the German Reich,
during approximately ten years of our lord's time,

and when we read a book of these things,
when we hear the names of the camps,
when we see the films of the bulldozed dead
or the film of one boy struck on the head
with a club in the hands
of a German doctor who will wait
some days for the boy's skull to knit, and will enter
the time in his ledger, and then
take up the club to strike the boy again,
and wait some weeks for the boy's skull to knit,
and enter the time in his ledger again,
and strike the boy again,
and so on, until the boy, who,
at the end of the film of his life
can hardly stagger forward toward the doctor,
does die, and the doctor
enters exactly the time of the boy's death in his ledger,

when we read these things or see them,
then it is clear to us that this
happened, and within the lord's allowance, this
work of his minions, his poor
vicious dumb German victims twisted
into the swastika shapes of trees struck by lightning,
on this his earth, if he is our father,

if we must speak of him in this way,
this presence above us, within us, this
mover, this first cause, this spirit, this
curse, this bloodstream and brain-current, this
unfathomable oceanic ignorance of ourselves, this
automatic electric Aryan swerve, this

fortune that you and I were not the victims, this
luck that you and I were not the murderers, this
sense that you and I are clean and understand, this
stupidity that gives him breath, gives him life
as we kill them all, as we killed them all.

BLACKBIRD SPRING

Mid-morning, walking ocean shoreline,
I found a hundred blackbirds
frozen in ice,
only their heads protruding,
black eyes open,
gleaming, most of their sharp beaks still
scissoring in mid-whistle.

Feeding, they'd been caught
in sea-spray, must be —
all males, up north early,
scarlet epaulettes aflame
a few inches under. I chipped
one bird loose with a stone,
held it in gloved hands

under the rising sun until,
until I realized, until I realized
nothing I hadn't known.
The tide retreated & would return.
Within the austere territories
these would have filled with belligerence
& song, spring had begun.

WILLIAM HEYEN

YELLOWJACKETS

How many years past was it I burned out their nest
under the melons? They'd not stung,
but worried me each time I walked among the mounds.
Gasoline, a match, the soft
concussion. I disinterred their charred comb
& found their grotesquely
fat queen exuding translucent eggs & slime from her belly.

Last night I dreamed I died in my office cubicle.
I sensed last rites, then
my corpse laid out on my desk, the space sealed off,
& over the centuries
countless more such rooms, more dead, we
colleagues together until
who knows when the resurrection might or might not be.

From each of its cells our tomb emits a faint light,
my cerements seem
to possess the half life of plutonium, or the stars. From here,
I seem to see almost
everything but cannot find my fruited acre where
yellowjackets flew between
their buried nest & one who could not live with them.

Andrew Hudgins

THE CHINABERRY

I couldn't stand still watching them forever,
but when I moved
             the grackles covering
each branch and twig
                  sprang
                          together into flight
and for a moment in midair they held
the tree's shape,
             the black tree
                          peeling from the green,
as if
      they were its shadow or its soul, before
they scattered,
             circled and
                          re-formed
as grackles heading south for winter grain fields.
Oh, it
      was just a chinaberry tree,
the birds were simply grackles.
                          A miracle
made from this world and where I stood in it.
But you can't know how long
                          I stood there watching.
And you can't know how desperate I'd become
advancing
             each step on the feet of my
advancing shadow,
                  how bitter and afraid I was
matching step after step with the underworld,
my ominous, indistinct and mirror image
darkening with
                  extreme and antic nothings
the ground I walked on,
                          inexact reversals,
elongated and foreshortened parodies
of each
      foot lowering itself
                          onto its shadow.

ANDREW HUDGINS

And you can't know how I had tried to force
the moment, make it happen
                              before it happened —
not necessarily this
                      though this is what I saw:
black birds deserting the tree they had become,
becoming,
            for a moment in midair,
the chinaberry's shadow for a moment
after they had ceased to be
                            the chinaberry,
then scattering:
                  meaning after meaning —
birds strewn across the morning like flung gravel
until
        they found themselves again as grackles,
found each other,
                    found South
                                  and headed there,
while I stood before
                      the green, abandoned tree.

ONE THREW A DIRT CLOD AND IT RAN

One threw a dirt clod and it ran, and when it paused,
another threw a rock and it trotted out of range,
so they pursued it, lobbing rocks and sticks,
just to see it gallop, which was beautiful,
then to keep it running, but when it stumbled on barbed wire
and broke a front leg and crumpled to its knees, entangled,
one hit it with a tree limb and hit it again. It fell
and they, laughing, ran up and kicked it, jumped away,
ran off, ran back and kicked it, till they could stand beside it,
kicking. They cheered when one of them pried loose
a broken fence post. They fought for the fence post
and took turns swinging it until the tangled beast's
slack ribs stopped pumping, heaving. Gasping for breath,
they stared at one another, dropped the post, the stones, the sticks.
They nudged the huge corpse and waited for it to rise,
to rise and gallop over rutted, fenced-off fields
as if there were no ruts, no mudholes, scrub brush, wire,
so they could follow it forever, weeping and hurling stones.

ANDREW HUDGINS

HEAT LIGHTNING IN A TIME OF DROUGHT

My neighbor, drunk, stood on his lawn and yelled,
Want some! Want some! He bellowed it as cops
cuffed him, shoved him in their back seat — *Want some!* —
and drove away. Now I lie here awake,
not by choice, listening to the crickets' high
electric trill, urgent with lust. Heat lightning flashes.
The crickets will not, will not stop. I wish
that I could shut the window, pull the curtain, sleep.
But it's too hot. *Want some!* He screamed it till
I was afraid I'd made him up to scream
what I knew better than to say out loud
although it's August-hot and every move
bathes me in sweat and we are careless,
careless, careless, every one of us,
and when my neighbor screams out in his yard
like one dog howling for another dog,
I call the cops, then lie in my own sweat,
remembering the woman
who, at a party on a night this hot,
walked up to me, propped her chin on my chest,
and sighed. She was a little drunk, the love-light
unshielded in her eyes. We fell in love.
One day at supper the light fixture dropped,
exploded on the table. Glass flew around us,
a low, slow-motion blossoming of razors.
She was unhurt till I reached out my hand
— left hand — to brush glass from her face.
Two drops of blood ran down her cheek.
On TV, I'd seen a teacher dip a rose
in liquid nitrogen. When he withdrew it,
it smoked, frozen solid. He snapped one petal, frail
as isinglass, and then, against the table,
he shattered it. The whole rose blew apart.
Like us. And then one day the doorbell rang.
A salesman said, *Watch this!* He stripped my bed
and vacuumed it. The nozzle sucked up two
full, measured cups of light gray flakes. He said,
That's human skin. I stood, refusing the purchase,
stood staring at her flesh and mine commingled
inside the measuring cup, stood there and thought,
*She's been gone two years, she's married, and all this time
her flesh has been in bed with me.* Don't laugh.

ANDREW HUDGINS

Don't laugh. That's what the Little Moron says
when he arrives home early from a trip
and finds his wife in bed with someone else.
The man runs off. The Little Moron puts
a pistol to his own head, cocks the hammer.
His wife, in bed, sheets pulled up to her breasts,
starts laughing. *Don't you laugh!* he screams. *Don't laugh —*
you're next. It is the wisest joke I know because
the heart's a violent muscle, opening
and closing. Who knows what we might do:
by night, the craziness of dreams; by day,
the craziness of logic. Listen!
My brother told me of a man wheeled, screaming,
into the ward, a large Coke bottle rammed
up his ass. I was awed: there is no telling
what we'll do in our fierce drive to come together.
The heart keeps opening and closing like a mine
where fire still burns, a century underground,
following the veins of black coal, rearing up
to take a barn, a house, a pasture. Although
I wish that it would rain tonight, I fret
about the heat lightning that flicks and glitters
on the horizon as if it promised rain.
It can't. But I walk outside, stand on parched grass,
and watch it hungrily — all light, all dazzle —
remembering how we'd drive out past the town's light,
sit on the hood, and watch great thunderheads
huge as a state — say Delaware — sail past. Branched
lightning jagged, burst the dark from zenith to horizon.
We stared at almost nothing: some live oaks,
the waist-high corn. Slow raindrops smacked the corn,
plopped in the dirt around us, drummed the roof,
and finally reached out, tapped us on the shoulders.
We drove home in the downpour, laughed, made love
— still wet with rain — and slept. But why stop there?
Each happy memory leads me to a sad one:
the friend who helped me through my grief by drinking
all of my liquor. And when, at last, we reached
the wretched mescal, he carefully sliced off
the worm's black face, ate its white body, staggered
onto this very lawn, and racked and heaved
until I helped him up. *You're okay, John.*
You've puked it out. "No, man — you're wrong. That worm
ain't ever coming out." Heat lightning flashes.

No rain falls and no thunder cracks the heat.
No first concussion dwindles to a long
low rolling growl. I go in the house, lie down,
pray, masturbate, drift to the edge of sleep.
I wish my soul were larger than it is.

GRANDMOTHER'S SPIT

To wipe the sleep grains from my eyes or rub
a food smudge from my cheek, Grandmother'd lick
her rough right thumb and order me, *Come here.*
She'd clutch my arm and hold me near her face
while, with that spit-damp thumb, she scrubbed the spot.
I struggled like a kitten being licked,
then leaned into the touch, again cat-like,
helping that fierce thumb scour loose the dirt.
It smelled, her spit, of lipstick and tobacco —
breath-warm, enveloping. She'd hold me at arm's length,
peer hard into my face, and state, *You're clean.*
When she let go, I'd crouch behind the door
and, with my own spit, rub the clean spot raw.

IN

When we first heard from blocks away
the fog truck's blustery roar,
we dropped our toys, leapt from our meals,
and scrambled out the door

into an evening briefly fuzzy.
We yearned to be transformed —
translated past confining flesh
to disembodied spirit. We swarmed

in thick smoke, taking human form
before we blurred again,
turned vague and then invisible,
in temporary heaven.

ANDREW HUDGINS

Freed of bodies by the fog,
we laughed, we sang, we shouted.
We were our voices, nothing else.
Voice was all we wanted.

The white clouds tumbled down our streets
pursued by spellbound children
who chased the most distorting clouds,
ecstatic in the poison.

ASHES

Bill gripped the can in both hands and dashed it upward,
casting into the March air his cousin, a man
I'd met a time or two, but now a cloud
of ash and bone grit launched above the river,
and the wind, which bloweth where it listeth, this time
amused itself to swirl the ashes overhead
and, at the moment I yawned, it slapped them back
across the clustered mourners. I sucked down
a grainy mouthful of fresh death, coughed, gagged,
and everyone surged toward me, hands outstretched.
They swatted at my dusty hair, brushed death's
gray epaulets off my shoulders and thumped my back
furiously, as if this dust were different
from other dust, and it was — or why would I
have dressed in coat and tie, and stood, head bowed,
on the soft bank of the Black Warrior, watching
huge barge trains humped with coal chug to the Gulf
while some young Baptist mumbled pieties?
I hacked death from my lungs and spat death out
and hacked up more. The mourners drummed the loose
death out of me. "I'm okay. Thanks," I said,
but they kept drumming, drumming on my back.
"Leave me alone!" I snapped, and we all glanced,
ashamed, into each other's ash-dappled faces.
We turned back to the river and its commerce,
the sermon and its commerce, the wind's new commerce,
and breathed it in and breathed it out and breathed it in.

ANDREW HUDGINS

SUPPER

We shared our supper with the flames,
or the shadow of the flames — each candle
in the light of the other casting shadows
across the table, dark flickers of a brilliant flicker,
and the grain of rubbed pine swirled with light
and shadow, shoaled and deepened in the soft
inconstancy of candlelight.
                                    With every gesture
the bright flames flinched and then corrected.
Your shrug, my laugh,
                                    my nod, your tilting head
— conveyed on air — invited their response.
They bowed their heads, then snapped upright —
a ripple in the gases' fluted yellow silk,
blue silk, transparent silk. I yearned
to touch the rich untouchable fabric, and finger
the sheen beneath its scorching,
but when I reached, it leaned away
decorously, and I did not pursue it, knowing.

But the dark flames reached out, licked the meat,
licked the plate, the fork, and the knife edge.
They licked our faces and our lips — a dry unfelt tongue,
the shadow of the flame consuming nothing,
but stroking everything as if it could
grasp, hold, take, devour. How ardently it hungers
because it cannot have us.
How chaste the bright flame, because it can.

Richard Hugo

LIVING ALONE

I felt the empty cabin wasn't abandoned.
The axe, for one thing, blood still moist
on the blade. Then, warm coffee on the stove.
God, it blew outside. The owner, I said,
won't last long in this storm. By midnight
I was singing. I knew the cabin was mine.
Fifty years later, he still hadn't returned.

Moss covered the roof by then. I called
the deer by name. Alice, I liked best.
Winslow, next. Reporters came to write me up.
They called me 'animal man' in the feature
in the photogravure. The story said I led
a wonderful life out here. I said clouds
were giant toads but they quoted me wrong.

The coroner identified the bones as woman.
I denied I'd been married and the local
records backed me. Today, they are hunting all over
the world for the previous owner.
I claim the cabin by occupancy rights.
I pray each dawn. How my words climb cedars
like squirrels uttered by God.

DEGREES OF GRAY IN PHILIPSBURG

You might come here Sunday on a whim.
Say your life broke down. The last good kiss
you had was years ago. You walk these streets
laid out by the insane, past hotels
that didn't last, bars that did, the tortured try
of local drivers to accelerate their lives.
Only churches are kept up. The jail

turned 70 this year. The only prisoner
is always in, not knowing what he's done.

The principal supporting business now
is rage. Hatred of the various grays
the mountain sends, hatred of the mill,
The Silver Bill repeal, the best liked girls
who leave each year for Butte. One good
restaurant and bars can't wipe the boredom out.
The 1907 boom, eight going silver mines,
a dance floor built on springs —
all memory resolves itself in gaze,
in panoramic green you know the cattle eat
or two stacks high above the town,
two dead kilns, the huge mill in collapse
for fifty years that won't fall finally down.

Isn't this your life? That ancient kiss
still burning out your eyes? Isn't this defeat
so accurate, the church bell simply seems
a pure announcement: ring and no one comes?
Don't empty houses ring? Are magnesium
and scorn sufficient to support a town,
not just Philipsburg, but towns
of towering blondes, good jazz and booze
the world will never let you have
until the town you came from dies inside?

Say no to yourself. The old man, twenty
when the jail was built, still laughs
although his lips collapse. Someday soon,
he says, I'll go to sleep and not wake up.
You tell him no. You're talking to yourself.
The car that brought you here still runs.
The money you buy lunch with,
no matter where it's mined, is silver
and the girl who serves you food
is slender and her red hair lights the wall.

RICHARD HUGO

A MAP OF MONTANA IN ITALY

for Marjorie Carrier

On this map white. A state thick as a fist
or blunt instrument. Long roads weave and cross
red veins full of rage. Big Canada, map maker's
pink, squats on our backs, planning bad winters
for years, and Glacier Park's green with my envy
of Grizzly Bears. On the right, antelope sail
between strands of barbed wire and never
get hurt, west, I think, of Plevna, say near
Sumatra, or more west, say Shawmut,
anyway, on the right, east on the plains.
The two biggest towns are dull deposits
of men getting along, making money, driving
to church every Sunday, censoring movies and books.
The two most interesting towns, Helena, Butte,
have the good sense to fail. There's too much
schoolboy in bars — I'm tougher than you —
and too much talk about money.
Jails and police are how you dream Poland —
odd charges, bad food and forms you must fill
stating your religion. In Poland say none.
With so few Negroes and Jews we've been reduced
to hating each other, dumping our crud
in our rivers, mistreating the Indians.
Each year, 4000 move, most to the west
where ocean currents keep winter in check.
This map is white, meaning winter, ice
where you are, helping children who may be
already frozen. It's white here too
but back of me, up in the mountains where
the most ferocious animals
are obsequious wolves. No one fights
in the bars filled with pastry. There's no
prison for miles. But last night the Italians
cheered the violence in one of our westerns.

RICHARD HUGO

THE LADY IN KICKING HORSE RESERVOIR

Not my hands but green across you now.
Green tons hold you down, and ten bass curve
teasing in your hair. Summer slime
will pile deep on your breast. Four months of ice
will keep you firm. I hope each spring
to find you tangled in those pads
pulled not quite loose by the spillway pour,
stars in dead reflection off your teeth.

Lie there lily still. The spillway's closed.
Two feet down most lakes are common gray.
This lake is dark from the black blue Mission range
climbing sky like music dying Indians once wailed.
On ocean beaches, mystery fish
are offered to the moon. Your jaws go blue.
Your hands start waving every wind.
Wave to the ocean where we crushed a mile of foam.

We still love there in thundering foam
and love. Whales fall in love with gulls
and tide reclaims the Dolly skeletons
gone with a blast of aching horns to China.
Landlocked in Montana here
the end is limited by light, the final note
will trail off at the farthest point we see,
already faded, lover, where you bloat.

All girls should be nicer. Arrows rain
above us in the Indian wind. My future
should be full of windy gems, my past
will stop this roaring in my dreams.
Sorry. Sorry. Sorry. But the arrows sing:
no way to float her up. The dead sink
from dead weight. The Mission range
turns this water black late afternoons.

One boy slapped the other. Hard.
The slapped boy talked until his dignity
dissolved, screamed a single 'stop'
and went down sobbing in the company pond.
I swam for him all night. My only suit

got wet and factory hands went home.
No one cared the coward disappeared.
Morning then: cold music I had never heard.

Loners like work best on second shift.
No one liked our product and the factory closed.
Off south, the bison multiply so fast
a slaughter's mandatory every spring
and every spring the creeks get fat
and Kicking Horse fills up. My hope is vague.
The far blur of your bones in May
may be nourished by the snow.

The spillway's open and you spill out
into weather, lover down the bright canal
and mother, irrigating crops
dead Indians forgot to plant.
I'm sailing west with arrows to dissolving foam
where waves strand naked Dollys.
Their eyes are white as oriental mountains
and their tongues are teasing oil from whales.

DEATH IN THE AQUARIUM

Praise him for the place he picked.
He shot himself dead in full sight
of the red Irish lord and the rare
albino sea perch. They nosed the glass
and cried to the outside world of air
"he's bleeding" in some salt water tongue.
The flounder dozed on. The octopus
flashed one disapproving eye at the cop.

The cop found no suicide note. The cop found
no I.D. The gun could not be traced.
They questioned everyone there but the fish
who swam around those being questioned.
You'd have wanted to film it, the visitors
with no answers shaken and sad, the red
snapper behind them gasping, the misfit
rock cod proud of his bad looks

and the yellow shiners turning and turning
like beautiful words going nowhere.
What a beautiful picture.
A year later the case was filed unsolved.

And you? Me? Where should we die given
a choice? In a hothouse? Along a remote
seldom traveled dirt road? Isn't some part
of that unidentified man in us all
and wants to die where we started?
Don't we share way back a cold green past
and wouldn't we welcome dying unknown,
unnamed on the floor of the ocean,
our bones ignored by the only clock there,
that slow unrhythmic waver of kelp —
our bones giving off the phosphorus
that collects in pockets and waits,
then one night washes in glowing?
And lovers, lovers would stop making love
and stand there, each suddenly alone
amazed at that gleam riding sand.

LANGAIG

We are what we hear. A well known singer died
yesterday in Spain. Thirty-five years ago
I got fired for sneaking off to hear him. I sobbed
"sorry" at the foreman, fired days later himself.
I cast blue nylon high over water turned black
by peat and light diminished by heavy Highland low sky.
I heard music and lost my job. I've not worked hard since
on anything but words, though I fish all waters
devoted and hum old songs when I fish alone.

I hum "My Heart is Taking Lessons," a song
the dead singer sang. I hum "I Had the Words and You
in My Heart." I remember him singing that.
I hum flat and off key, but that's hardly my fault,
the lack of gift, of training. In this lake (read 'loch'
to be local) trout run black as the water though Scots
like us call them 'browns,' the old Scots, 'Loch Leven!'

RICHARD HUGO

I hum "Makes No Difference Now," the best recording
the dead singer made and he left lots of good records.

To relax, to slide with, ride the forces of whatever
sweeps us along, jokes well timed, phrasing under control —
that was my ideal. I didn't come close in real life.
A soft impulse was proof I was weak. I laughed
at any weak joke, still do, and believed our purpose
to lighten the day, to be tougher than fate.
In reaction to that, I believed we should give in to pathos.
Today I believe: fish hard and hum every tune
I remember hearing the dead singer sing
and leave believing in being like him to others.
Does that make us brothers? Let's be. My bobber
jitters and I know it isn't just wind. I set my line
too soon and lose the black brown. The eagle yells
from the Quirang, "Go easy. Give him time to take it."
I hum "White Christmas," though I never liked it.
Snow on mainland mountains across the minch (if you're
American read 'strait') reminds me I'm fishing
late in the season. I may be breaking Scot law.

Christ, what rain and no real Jesus in it.
No real king. No friend. What lover first inserted a tongue
in a lover's ear? And where? It must have been pre-
Peloponesian war. It must have been pre-all
language and hunger, and located song prior to lyrics.
Fishing preceded song. We know that from instinct,
not records. I've fished this loch often before
and alone with my ghosts felt free to sing.
I've got a brown on. My line is writing a song.

I'm fishing. I'm singing. My heart is not exactly
giving lessons though I've been lucky enough in rare
moments to take heart in some words, and to have
a job teaching others to sing, to locate by game
some word like 'brown' in black water, to cast
hard for that word, then wait a long time to set.
Now the reeling in, the fight, the black trout lovely
on heather, the dead singer in songs
we recover, and hum when alone, and hum wrong.

Arthur Furst

Donald Justice

EARLY POEMS

How fashionably sad those early poems are!
On their clipped lawns and hedges the snows fall.
Rains beat against the tarpaulins of their porches,
Where, Sunday mornings, the bored children sprawl,
Reading the comics before their parents rise.
— The rhymes, the meters, how they paralyze!

Who walks out through their streets tonight?
No one. You know these small towns, how all traffic stops
At ten, the corner streetlamps gathering moths,
And mute, pale mannequins waiting in dark shops,
Undressed, and ready for the dreams of men.
— Now the long silence. Now the beginning again.

FIRST DEATH

June 12, 1933

I saw my grandmother grow weak.
When she died, I kissed her cheek.

I remember the new taste —
Powder mixed with a drying paste.

Down the hallway, on its table,
Lay the family's great Bible.

In the dark, by lamplight stirred,
The Void grew pregnant with the Word.

In black ink they wrote it down.
The older ink was turning brown.

From the woods there came a cry,
The hoot owl asking who not why.

DONALD JUSTICE

The men sat silent on the porch,
Each lighted pipe a friendly torch

Against the unknown and the known.
But the child knew himself alone.

June 13, 1933

The morning sun rose up and stuck.
Sunflower strove with hollyhock.

I ran the worn path past the sty.
Nothing was hidden from God's eye.

The barn door creaked. I walked among
Chaff and wrinkled cakes of dung.

In the dim light I read the dates
On the dusty license plates

Nailed to the wall as souvenirs.
I breathed the dust in of the years.

I circled the abandoned Ford
Before I tried the running board.

At the wheel I felt the heat
Press upward through the springless seat.

And when I touched the silent horn,
Small mice scattered through the corn.

June 14, 1933

I remember the soprano
Fanning herself at the piano,

And the preacher looming large
Above me in his dark blue serge.

My shoes brought in a smell of clay
To mingle with the faint sachet

Of flowers sweating in their vases.
A stranger showed us to our places.

The stiff fan stirred in mother's hand.
Air moved, but only when she fanned.

I wondered how could all her grief
Be squeezed into one small handkerchief.

There was a buzzing on the sill.
It stopped, and everything was still.

We bowed our heads, we closed our eyes
To the mercy of the flies.

CHILDREN WALKING HOME FROM SCHOOL
THROUGH GOOD NEIGHBORHOOD

They are like figures held in some glass ball,
One of those in which, when shaken, snowstorms occur;
But this one is not yet shaken.
       And they go unaccompanied still,
Out along this walkway between two worlds,
This almost swaying bridge.
       October sunlight checkers their path;
It frets their cheeks and bare arms now with shadow
Almost too pure to signify itself.
And they progress slowly, somewhat lingeringly,
Independent, yet moving all together,
Like polyphonic voices that crisscross
In short-lived harmonies.

       Today, a few stragglers.
One, a girl, stands there with hands spaced out, so —
A gesture in a story. Someone's school notebook spills,
And they bend down to gather up the loose pages.
(Bright sweaters knotted at the waist; solemn expressions.)
Not that they would shrink or hold back from what may come,
For now they all at once run to meet it, a little swirl of colors,
Like the leaves already blazing and falling farther north.

DONALD JUSTICE

PSALM AND LAMENT

Hialeah, Florida
in memory of my mother (1897–1974)

The clocks are sorry, the clocks are very sad.
One stops, one goes on striking the wrong hours.

And the grass burns terribly in the sun,
The grass turns yellow secretly at the roots.

Now suddenly the yard chairs look empty, the sky looks empty,
The sky looks vast and empty.

Out on Red Road the traffic continues; everything continues.
Nor does memory sleep; it goes on.

Out spring the butterflies of recollection,
And I think that for the first time I understand

The beautiful ordinary light of this patio
And even perhaps the dark rich earth of a heart.

(The bedclothes, they say, had been pulled down.
I will not describe it. I do not want to describe it.

No, but the sheets were drenched and twisted.
They were the very handkerchiefs of grief.)

Let summer come now with its schoolboy trumpets and fountains.
But the years are gone, the years are finally over.

And there is only
This long desolation of flower-bordered sidewalks

That runs to the corner, turns, and goes on,
That disappears and goes on

Into the black oblivion of a neighborhood and a world
Without billboards or yesterdays.

Sometimes a sad moon comes and waters the roof tiles.
But the years are gone. There are no more years.

DONALD JUSTICE

ABSENCES

It's snowing this afternoon and there are no flowers.
There is only this sound of falling, quiet and remote,
Like the memory of scales descending the white keys
Of a childhood piano — outside the window, palms!
And the heavy head of the cereus, inclining,
Soon to let down its white or yellow-white.

Now, only these poor snow-flowers in a heap,
Like the memory of a white dress cast down . . .
So much has fallen.
         And I, who have listened for a step
All afternoon, hear it now, but already falling away,
Already in memory. And the terrible scales descending
On the silent piano; the snow; and the absent flowers abounding.

MEN AT FORTY

Men at forty
Learn to close softly
The doors to rooms they will not be
Coming back to.

At rest on a stair landing,
They feel it
Moving beneath them now like the deck of a ship,
Though the swell is gentle.

And deep in mirrors
They rediscover
The face of the boy as he practices tying
His father's tie there in secret

And the face of that father,
Still warm with the mystery of lather.
They are more fathers than sons themselves now.
Something is filling them, something

DONALD JUSTICE

That is like the twilight sound
Of the crickets, immense,
Filling the woods at the foot of the slope
Behind their mortgaged houses.

VARIATIONS ON A TEXT BY VALLEJO

Me moriré en Paris con aguacero . . .

I will die in Miami in the sun,
On a day when the sun is very bright,
A day like the days I remember, a day like other days,
A day that nobody knows or remembers yet,
And the sun will be bright then on the dark glasses of strangers
And in the eyes of a few friends from my childhood
And of the surviving cousins by the graveside,
While the diggers, standing apart, in the still shade of the palms,
Rest on their shovels, and smoke,
Speaking in Spanish softly, out of respect.

I think it will be on a Sunday like today,
Except that the sun will be out, the rain will have stopped,
And the wind that today made all the little shrubs kneel down;
And I think it will be a Sunday because today,
When I took out this paper and began to write,
Never before had anything looked so blank,
My life, these words, the paper, the gray Sunday;
And my dog, quivering under a table because of the storm,
Looked up at me, not understanding,
And my son read on without speaking, and my wife slept.

Donald Justice is dead. One Sunday the sun came out,
It shone on the bay, it shone on the white buildings,
The cars moved down the street slowly as always, so many,
Some with their headlights on in spite of the sun,
And after a while the diggers with their shovels
Walked back to the graveside through the sunlight,
And one of them put his blade into the earth
To lift a few clods of dirt, the black marl of Miami,
And scattered the dirt, and spat,
Turning away abruptly, out of respect.

DONALD JUSTICE

IN MEMORY OF THE UNKNOWN POET,
ROBERT BOARDMAN VAUGHN

But the essential advantage for a poet is not, to have a beautiful world with
which to deal: it is to be able to see beneath both beauty and ugliness; to see
the boredom, and the horror, and the glory.

— T. S. Eliot

It was his story. It would always be his story.
It followed him; it overtook him finally —
The boredom, and the horror, and the glory.

Probably at the end he was not yet sorry,
Even as the boots were brutalizing him in the alley.
It was his story. It would always be his story.

Blown on a blue horn, full of sound and fury,
But signifying, O signifying magnificently
The boredom, and the horror, and the glory.

I picture the snow as falling without hurry
To cover the cobbles and the toppled ashcans completely.
It was his story. It would always be his story.

Lately he had wandered between St. Mark's Place and the Bowery,
Already half a spirit, mumbling and muttering sadly.
O the boredom, and the horror, and the glory.

All done now. But I remember the fiery
Hypnotic eye and the raised voice blazing with poetry.
It was his story and would always be his story —
The boredom, and the horror, and the glory.

Galway Kinnell

BLACKBERRY EATING

I love to go out in late September
among the fat, overripe, icy, black blackberries
to eat blackberries for breakfast,
the stalks very prickly, a penalty
they earn for knowing the black art
of blackberry-making; and as I stand among them
lifting the stalks to my mouth, the ripest berries
fall almost unbidden to my tongue,
as words sometimes do, certain peculiar words
like *strengths* or *squinched*,
many-lettered, one-syllabled lumps,
which I squeeze, squinch open, and splurge well
in the silent, startled, icy, black language
of blackberry-eating in late September.

AFTER MAKING LOVE WE HEAR FOOTSTEPS

For I can snore like a bullhorn
or play loud music
or sit up talking with any reasonably sober Irishman
and Fergus will only sink deeper
into his dreamless sleep, which goes by all in one flash,
but let there be that heavy breathing
or a stifled come-cry anywhere in the house
and he will wrench himself awake
and make for it on the run — as now, we lie together,
after making love, quiet, touching along the length of our bodies,
familiar touch of the long-married,
and he appears — in his baseball pajamas, it happens,
the neck opening so small he has to screw them on —
and flops down between us and hugs us and snuggles himself to sleep,
his face gleaming with satisfaction at being this very child.

In the half darkness we look at each other
and smile

and touch arms across this little, startlingly muscled body —
this one whom habit of memory propels to the ground of his making,
sleeper only the mortal sounds can sing awake,
this blessing love gives again into our arms.

THE BEAR

1

In late winter
I sometimes glimpse bits of steam
coming up from
some fault in the old snow
and bend close and see it is lung-colored
and put down my nose
and know
the chilly, enduring odor of bear.

2

I take a wolf's rib and whittle
it sharp at both ends
and coil it up
and freeze it in blubber and place it out
on the fairway of the bears.

And when it has vanished
I move out on the bear tracks,
roaming in circles
until I come to the first, tentative, dark
splash on the earth.

And I set out
running, following the splashes
of blood wandering over the world.
At the cut, gashed resting places
I stop and rest,
at the crawl-marks
where he lay out on his belly
to overpass some stretch of bauchy ice

I lie out
dragging myself forward with bear-knives in my fists.

3

On the third day I begin to starve,
at nightfall I bend down as I knew I would
at a turd sopped in blood,
and hesitate, and pick it up,
and thrust it in my mouth, and gnash it down,
and rise
and go on running.

4

On the seventh day,
living by now on bear blood alone,
I can see his upturned carcass far out ahead, a scraggled,
steamy hulk,
the heavy fur riffling in the wind.

I come up to him
and stare at the narrow-spaced, petty eyes,
the dismayed
face laid back on the shoulder, the nostrils
flared, catching
perhaps the first taint of me as he
died.

I hack
a ravine in his thigh, and eat and drink,
and tear him down his whole length
and open him and climb in
and close him up after me, against the wind,
and sleep.

5

And dream
of lumbering flatfooted
over the tundra,

stabbed twice from within,
splattering a trail behind me,
splattering it out no matter which way I lurch,
no matter which parabola of bear-transcendence,
which dance of solitude I attempt,
which gravity-clutched leap,
which trudge, which groan.

6

Until one day I totter and fall —
fall on this
stomach that has tried so hard to keep up,
to digest the blood as it leaked in,
to break up
and digest the bone itself: and now the breeze
blows over me, blows off
the hideous belches of ill-digested bear blood
and rotted stomach
and the ordinary, wretched odor of bear,

blows across
my sore, lolled tongue a song
or screech, until I think I must rise up
and dance. And I lie still.

7

I awaken I think. Marshlights
reappear, geese
come trailing again up the flyway.
In her ravine under old snow the dam-bear
lies, licking
lumps of smeared fur
and drizzly eyes into shapes
with her tongue. And one
hairy-soled trudge stuck out before me,
the next groaned out,
the next,
the next,
the rest of my days I spend

wandering: wondering
what, anyway,
was that sticky infusion, that rank flavor of blood, that poetry, by which
    I lived?

THE FUNDAMENTAL PROJECT OF TECHNOLOGY

"A flash! A white flash sparkled!"

— Tatsuichiro Akizuki, *Concentric Circles of Death*

Under glass: glass dishes which changed
in color; pieces of transformed beer bottles;
a household iron; bundles of wire become solid
lumps of iron; a pair of pliers; a ring of skull-
bone fused to the inside of a helmet; a pair of eyeglasses
taken off the eyes of an eyewitness, without glass,
which vanished, when a white flash sparkled.

An old man, possibly a soldier back then,
now reduced down to one who soon will die,
sucks at the cigarette dangling from his lip, peers
at the uniform, scorched, of some tiniest schoolboy,
sighs out bluish mists of his own ashes over
a pressed tin lunch box well crushed back then when
the word *future* first learned, in a white flash, to jerk tears.

On the bridge outside, in navy black, a group
of schoolchildren line up, hold it, grin at a flash-pop,
scatter like pigeons across grass, see a stranger, cry
hello! hello! hello! and soon *goodbye! goodbye!*
having pecked up the greetings that fell half unspoken
and the going-sayings that those who went the day
it happened a white flash sparkled did not get to say.

If all a city's faces were to shrink back all at once
from their skulls, would a new sound come into existence,
audible above moans eaves extract from wind that smoothes
the grass on graves, or raspings heart's-blood greases still,
or wails infants trill born already skillful at the grandpa's rattle,

or infra-screams bitter-knowledge's speechlessness
memorized, at that white flash, inside closed-forever mouths?

To de-animalize human mentality, to purge it of obsolete
evolutionary characteristics, in particular of death,
which foreknowledge terrorizes the contents of skulls with,
is the fundamental project of technology; however,
pseudologica fantastica's mechanisms require:
to establish deathlessness it is necessary to eliminate
those who die; a task attempted, when a white flash sparkled.

Unlike the trees of home, which continually evaporate
along the skyline, the trees here have been enticed down
toward world-eternity. No one knows which gods they enshrine.
Does it matter? Awareness of ignorance is as devout
as knowledge of knowledge. Or more so. Even though not knowing,
sometimes we weep, from surplus of gratitude, even though
        knowing,
twice already on earth sparkled a flash, a white flash.

The children go away. By nature they do. And by memory,
in scorched uniforms, holding tiny crushed lunch tins.
All the ecstasy-groans of each night call them back, satori
their ghostliness back into the ashes, in the momentary shrines,
the thankfulness of arms, from which they will go
again and again, until the day flashes and no one lives
to look back and say, a flash, a white flash sparkled.

FLOWER OF FIVE BLOSSOMS

Flower of five blossoms
I have brought you with me here
because you might not still be blossoming when I go back,
and because you might not blossom again.
I watched each of your buds swell up,
like water collected on a child's lid, about to plop,
or the catch in a throat that turns into a sob,
or in a tenor's throat, on some nights into a hundred sobs.
But as the buds
became these blossoms,
I am trying to learn: time suffered

is not necessarily time destroyed.
Outside, snow falls down in big pieces, like petals,
while in here, fire blossoms
out of wood and goes up in flames,
which are not *things dying* but just the *dying*.
Above them on the mantelpiece,
how calm your blossoms appear, austere and orderly, like the faces of
    singers,
but singing in silence, like the child
half-hidden by the pew, who dares only to think the hymns.
Phalaenopsis, sensual Orchidaceae,
sometimes, out of the corner of the eye, your blossoms perched on their
    twigs seem true to your name, "moth-like,"
and there, in the salep risen out of the pot of chipped bark, is the origin
    of your family name, ὄρχις, "testicle."
A few minutes ago, I put on a sonata by Brahms
("Brahms," nearly the sound dwelling on you forms in my mouth)
and I was standing at the mantelpiece
just as the slowest passage began, that moment
when the bow rests nearly immobile on the strings
— as mouths might, on mouths, in stillest kissing,
when a lip could be lying against a tooth in the other mouth, one can't
    say —
the bow's tremblings at what is about to happen
all that shakes any sound out of the strings at all,
and I turned and saw
what everyone else maybe sees at once:
that in each blossom
the calyx's middle petal curves up
and flows over the mons veneris and spreads across the belly,
and the petal on either side rises over the thigh, one edge following the
    ridge of the pelvic bone, which is prominent, for she lies on her
    back,
and the two petals that are set back hold the roundness of her buttocks,
and at the center, in the little crown,
the clitoris leans, above
the vestibule opening into the center of being;
and I wanted to lean close,
without sound, with my lips
touching lightly one of your blossoms,
and find there, like a kiss that has a soft lick in it, like "blossoms,"
the name of this place and speak it.
That's what two keep trying to do,
over and over, at night,

singing,
sometimes together, sometimes alone —
but in a little while they forget, and think they haven't found it,
and what is mute and wet waits again to be sung.
As the sonata ends,
your blossoms fall more profoundly still
— their lavender streaks suddenly empty, like staff-lines before any notes
      have been entered —
have a portion of death in them,
and watch,
intent, unblinking,
like the white, hooded faces of cobras
risen up to mesmerize, or to fling themselves forward into the deadly
      kiss;
though each wears the headdress of Mary.
Or am I myself the spellbinder and the killer?
Alone here, I often find myself thinking of women —
and now your blossoms could stand for five of them —
any five, if I were to try to name them —
one could be she to whom I was married for many years,
or she who merely exchanged a few words with me, across a table, under
      the noise of the conversation of the others,
or that pale, laughing beauty I hugged at the dancing lessons, when we
      were fifteen,
and another could be the woman whose strict intelligence I revere,
      whom I kiss on the forehead, a quarter inch away from the brain, the
      way Plato kissed,
and then the fifth blossom would be my mother, risen up at my bedside,
      wanting to please, but having, the next day or another, to crush —
strange,
for I began by speaking of sexual resemblance,
but not strange, for it was as a sexual creature she seized me into existence,
it was through her vagina, trespassed by a man one way, transpierced by
      three babies the other,
I was dragged out alive, into the dead
of winter — a day
perhaps like this day, sixty years later, when out there earth
draws down on top of herself yet another of her freezing sleeping clothes,
but underneath is awakening . . .
besoming . . . blowsining . . . blissamous . . .
and in here, at the mantelpiece,
bending close to you, praying to you almost, standing almost in flames,
I wonder

what can come of these minutes,
each a hard inner tumbling, as when a key nearly won't turn,
or the note of a piano, clattered or stroked, ringing.
Everyone knows
everything sings and dies.
But it could be, too, everything dies and sings,
and a life is the interlude
when, still humming, we can look up, gawk about, imagine whatever,
    say it,
topple back into singing.
Oh first our voice be done, and then, before and afterwards and all
    around it, that singing.

Carolyn Kizer

THRALL

The room is sparsely furnished:
A chair, a table and a father.

He sits in the chair by the window.
There are books on the table.
The time is always just past lunch.

You tiptoe past as he eats his apple
And reads. He looks up, angry.
He has heard your asthmatic breathing.

He will read for years without looking up
Until your childhood is over:

Smells, untidiness and boring questions;
Blood, from the first skinned knees
To the first stained thighs;
The foolish tears of adolescent love.

One day he looks up, pleased
At the finished product.
Now he is ready to love you!

So he coaxes you in the voice reserved
For reading Keats. You agree to everything.

Drilled in silence and duty,
You will give him no cause for reproach.
He will boast of you to strangers.

When the afternoon is older
Shadows in a smaller room
Fall on the bed, the books, the father.

You read aloud to him
"La Belle Dame sans Merci."

You feed him his medicine.
You tell him you love him.

You wait for his eyes to close at last
So you may write this poem.

THE INTRUDER

My mother — preferring the strange to the tame:
Dove-note, bone marrow, deer dung,
Frog's belly distended with finny young,
Leaf-mould wilderness, hare-bell, toadstool,
Odd, small snakes roving through the leaves,
Metallic beetles rambling over stones: all
Wild and natural! — flashed out her instinctive love, and quick, she
Picked up the fluttering, bleeding bat the cat laid at her feet,
And held the little horror to the mirror, where
He gazed on himself, and shrieked like an old screen door far off.

Depended from her pinched thumb, each wing
Came clattering down like a small black shutter.
Still tranquil, she began, "It's rather sweet. . . ."
The soft mouse body, the hard feral glint
In the caught eyes. Then we saw,
And recoiled: lice, pallid, yellow,
Nested within the wing-pits, cosily sucked and snoozed.
The thing dropped from her hands, and with its thud,
Swiftly, the cat, with a clean careful mouth
Closed on the soiled webs, growling, took them out to the back stoop.

But still, dark blood, a sticky puddle on the floor
Remained, of all my mother's tender, wounding passion
For a whole wild, lost, betrayed and secret life
Among its dens and burrows, its clean stones,
Whose denizens can turn upon the world
With spitting tongue, an odor, talon, claw,
To sting or soil benevolence, alien
As our clumsy traps, our random scatter of shot.
She swept to the kitchen. Turning on the tap,
She washed and washed the pity from her hands.

CAROLYN KIZER

A WIDOW IN WINTERTIME

Last night a baby gargled in the throes
Of a fatal spasm. My children are all grown
Past infant strangles; so, reassured, I knew
Some other baby perished in the snow.
But no. The cat was making love again.

Later, I went down and let her in.
She hung her tail, flagging from her sins.
Though she'd eaten, I forked out another dinner,
Being myself hungry all ways, and thin
From metaphysic famines she knows nothing of,

The feckless beast! Even so, resemblances
Were on my mind: female and feline, though
She preens herself from satisfaction, and does
Not mind lying even in snow. She is
Lofty and bedraggled, without need to choose.

As an ex-animal, I look fondly on
Her excesses and simplicities, and would not return
To them; taking no marks for what I have become,
Merely that my nine lives peal in my ears again
And again, ring in these austerities.

These arbitrary disciplines of mine,
Most of them trivial: like covering
The children on my way to bed, and trying
To live well enough alone, and not to dream
Of grappling in the snow, claws plunged in fur,

Or waken in a caterwaul of dying.

from *PRO FEMINA*

ONE

From Sappho to myself, consider the fate of women.
How unwomanly to discuss it! Like a noose or an albatross necktie
The clinical sobriquet hangs us: cod-piece coveters.

Never mind these epithets; I myself have collected some honeys.
Juvenal set us apart in denouncing our vices
Which had grown, in part, from having been set apart:
Women abused their spouses, cuckolded them, even plotted
To poison them. Sensing, behind the violence of his manner —
"Think I'm crazy or drunk?" — his emotional stake in us,
As we forgive Strindberg and Nietzsche, we forgive all those
Who cannot forget us. We *are* hyenas. Yes, we admit it.

While men have politely debated free will, we have howled for it,
Howl still, pacing the centuries, tragedy heroines.
Some who sat quietly in the corner with their embroidery
Were Defarges, stabbing the wool with the names of their ancient
Oppressors, who ruled by the divine right of the male —
I'm impatient of interruptions! I'm aware there were millions
Of mutes for every Saint Joan or sainted Jane Austen,
Who, vague-eyed and acquiescent, worshiped God as a man.
I'm not concerned with those cabbageheads, not truly feminine
But neutered by labor. I mean real women, like *you* and like *me*.

Freed in fact, not in custom, lifted from furrow and scullery,
Not obliged, now, to be the pot for the annual chicken,
Have we begun to arrive in time? With our well-known
Respect for life because it hurts so much to come out with it;
Disdainful of "sovereignty," "national honor" and other abstractions;
We can say, like the ancient Chinese to successive waves of invaders,
"Relax, and let us absorb you. You can learn temperance
In a more temperate climate." Give us just a few decades
Of grace, to encourage the fine art of acquiescence
And we might save the race. Meanwhile, observe our creative chaos,
Flux, efflorescence — whatever you care to call it!

SEMELE RECYCLED

After you left me forever
I was broken into pieces,
and all the pieces flung into the river.
Then the legs crawled ashore
and aimlessly wandered the dusty cow-track.
They became, for awhile, a simple roadside shrine:
A tiny table set up between the thighs

held a dusty candle, weed and fieldflower chains
placed reverently there by children and old women.
My knees were hung with tin triangular medals
to cure all forms of hysterical disease.

After I died forever in the river,
my torso floated, bloated in the stream,
catching on logs or stones among the eddies.
White water foamed around it, then dislodged it;
after a whirlwind trip it bumped ashore.
A grizzled old man who scavenged along the banks
had already rescued my arms and put them by,
knowing everything has its uses, sooner or later.

When he found my torso, he called it his canoe,
and, using my arms as paddles,
he rowed me up and down the scummy river.
When catfish nibbled my fingers he scooped them up,
and blessed his re-usable bait.
Clumsy but serviceable, that canoe!
The trail of blood that was its wake
attracted the carp and eels, and the river turtle,
easily landed, dazed by my tasty red.

A young lad found my head among the rushes
and placed it on a dry stone.
He carefully combed my hair with a bit of shell
and set small offerings before it
which the birds and rats obligingly stole at night,
so it seemed I ate.
And the breeze wound through my mouth and empty sockets
so my lungs would sigh, and my dead tongue mutter.
Attached to my throat like a sacred necklace
was a circlet of small snails.
Soon the villagers came to consult my oracular head
with its waterweed crown.
Seers found occupation, interpreting sighs,
and their papyrus rolls accumulated.

Meanwhile, young boys retrieved my eyes
they used for marbles in a simple game
— till somebody's pretty sister snatched at them
and set them, for luck, in her bridal diadem.
Poor girl! When her future groom caught sight of her,

all eyes, he crossed himself in horror,
and stumbled away in haste
through her dowered meadows.

When then of my heart and organs,
my sacred slit
which loved you best of all?
They were caught in a fisherman's net
and tossed at night into a pen for swine.
But they shone so by moonlight that the sows stampeded,
trampled each other in fear, to get away.
And the fisherman's wife, who had 13 living children
and was contemptuous of holy love,
raked the rest of me onto the compost heap.

Then in their various places and helpful functions,
the altar, oracle, offal, canoe and oars
learned the wild rumor of your return.
The altar leapt up, and ran to the canoe,
scattering candle grease and wilted grasses.
Arms sprang to their sockets, blind hands with nibbled nails
groped their way, aided by loud lamentation,
to the bed of the bride, snatched up those unlucky eyes
from her discarded veil and diadem,
and rammed them home. O what a bright day it was!
This empty body danced on the river bank.
Hollow, it called and searched among the fields
for those parts that steamed and simmered in the sun,
and never would have found them.

But then your great voice rang out under the skies
my name! — and all those private names
for the parts and places that had loved you best.
And they stirred in their nest of hay and dung.
The distraught old ladies chasing their lost altar,
and the seers pursuing my skull, their lost employment,
and the tumbling boys, who wanted the magic marbles,
and the runaway groom, and the fisherman's 13 children
set up such a clamor, with their cries of "Miracle!"
that our two bodies met like a thunderclap
in mid-day; right at the corner of that wretched field
with its broken fenceposts and startled, skinny cattle.
We fell in a heap on the compost heap
and all our loving parts made love at once,

while the bystanders cheered and prayed and hid their eyes
and then went decently about their business.

And here it is, moonlight again; we've bathed in the river
and are sweet and wholesome once more.
We kneel side-by-side in the sand;
we worship each other in whispers.
But the inner parts remember fermenting hay,
the comfortable odor of dung, the animal incense,
and passion, its bloody labor,
its birth and rebirth and decay.

THE SKEIN

from a poem by Emperor Wu-ti

Moonlight through my gauze curtains
Turns them to nets for snaring wild birds,
Turns them into woven traps, into shrouds.
The old, restless grief keeps me awake.
I wander around, holding a scarf or a shawl;
In the muffled moonlight I wander around
Folding it carefully, shaking it out again.
Everyone says my old lover is happy.
I wish they said he was coming back to me.
I hesitate here, my scarf like a skein of yarn
Binding my two hands loosely
            that would reach for paper and pen.
So I memorize these lines,
Dew on the scarf, dappling my nightdress also.
O love long gone, it is raining in our room!
So I memorize these lines,
            without salutation, without close.

Yusef Komunyakaa

AUDACITY OF THE LOWER GODS

I know salt marshes that move along like one big
trembling wing. I've noticed insects
shiny as gold in a blues singer's teeth
& more keenly calibrated than a railroad watch,
but at heart I'm another breed

The audacity of the lower gods —
whatever we name we own.
Diversiloba, we say, unfolding poison oak.
Lovers go untouched as we lean from bay windows
with telescopes trained on a yellow sky.

I'd rather let the flowers
keep doing what they do best.
Unblessing each petal,
letting go a year's worth of white
death notes, busily unnaming themselves.

BLACKBERRIES

They left my hands like a printer's
Or thief's before a police blotter
& pulled me into early morning's
Terrestrial sweetness, so thick
The damp ground was consecrated
Where they fell among a garland of thorns.

Although I could smell old lime-covered
History, at ten I'd still hold out my hands
& berries fell into them. Eating from one
& filling a half gallon with the other,
I ate the mythology & dreamt
Of pies & cobbler, almost

collective history

Needful as forgiveness. My bird dog Spot
Eyed blue jays & thrashers. The mud frogs
In rich blackness, hid from daylight.
An hour later, beside City Limits Road
I balanced a gleaming can in each hand,
Limboed between worlds, repeating *one dollar.*

The big blue car made me sweat.
Wintertime crawled out of the windows.
When I leaned closer I saw the boy
& girl my age, in the wide back seat
Smirking, & it was then I remembered my fingers
Burning with thorns among berries too ripe to touch.

WORK

I won't look at her.
My body's been one
Solid motion from sunrise,
Leaning into the lawnmower's
Roar through pine needles
& crabgrass. Tiger-colored
Bumblebees nudge pale blossoms
Till they sway like silent bells
Calling. But I won't look.
Her husband's outside Oxford,
Mississippi, bidding on miles
Of timber. I wonder if he's buying
Faulkner's ghost, if he might run
Into Colonel Sartoris
Along some dusty road.
Their teenage daughter & son sped off
An hour ago in a red Corvette
For the tennis courts,
& the cook, Roberta,
Only works a half day
Saturdays. This antebellum house
Looms behind oak & pine
Like a secret, as quail
Flash through branches.
I won't look at her. Nude

On a hammock among elephant ears
& ferns, a pitcher of lemonade
Sweating like our skin.
Afternoon burns on the pool
Till everything's blue,
Till I hear Johnny Mathis
Beside her like a whisper.
I work all the quick hooks
Of light, the same unbroken
Rhythm my father taught me
Years ago: *Always give*
A man a good day's labor.
I won't look. The engine
Pulls me like a dare.
Scent of honeysuckle
Sings black sap through mystery,
Taboo, law, creed, what kills
A fire that is its own heart
Burning open the mouth.
But I won't look
At the insinuation of buds
Tipped with cinnabar.
I'm here, as if I never left,
Stopped in this garden,
Drawn to some Lotus-eater. Pollen
Explodes, but I only smell
Gasoline & oil on my hands,
& can't say why there's this bed
Of crushed narcissus
As if gods wrestled here.

IN THE BACKGROUND OF SILENCE

First, worms begin with a man's mind.
Then they eat away his left shoe
to answer his final question.
His heart turns into a gold thimble of ashes,
his bones remind bees of honeycomb,
he falls back into himself like dirt into a hole,
his soul fits into a matchbox
in the shirt pocket
of his brother's well-tailored uniform.

YUSEF KOMUNYAKAA

Not even a stray dog dares to stir in the plaza,
after the muzzle flash,
after black coffee & Benzedrine,
after the sign of the cross a hundred times,
after sorrow's skirt drops to the floor,
after the soldier pulls off his spit-shined boots
& crawls into bed with the prettiest woman in town.

TU DO STREET

Music divides the evening.
I close my eyes & can see
men drawing lines in the dust.
America pushes through the membrane
of mist & smoke, & I'm a small boy
again in Bogalusa. *White Only*
signs & Hank Snow. But tonight
I walk into a place where bar girls
fade like tropical birds. When
I order a beer, the mama-san
behind the counter acts as if she
can't understand, while her eyes
skirt each white face, as Hank Williams
calls from the psychedelic jukebox.
We have played Judas where
only machine-gun fire brings us
together. Down the street
black GIs hold to their turf also.
An off-limits sign pulls me
deeper into alleys, as I look
for a softness behind these voices
wounded by their beauty & war.
Back in the bush at Dak To
& Khe Sanh, we fought
the brothers of these women
we now run to hold in our arms.
There's more than a nation
inside us, as black & white
soldiers touch the same lovers
minutes apart, tasting
each other's breath,

without knowing these rooms
run into each other like tunnels
leading to the underworld.

THANKS

Thanks for the tree
between me & a sniper's bullet.
I don't know what made the grass
sway seconds before the Viet Cong
raised his soundless rifle.
Some voice always followed,
telling me which foot
to put down first.
Thanks for deflecting the ricochet
against that anarchy of dusk.
I was back in San Francisco
wrapped up in a woman's wild colors,
causing some dark bird's love call
to be shattered by daylight
when my hands reached up
& pulled a branch away
from my face. Thanks
for the vague white flower
that pointed to the gleaming metal
reflecting how it is to be broken
like mist over the grass,
as we played some deadly
game for blind gods.
What made me spot the monarch
writhing on a single thread
tied to a farmer's gate,
holding the day together
like an unfingered guitar string,
is beyond me. Maybe the hills
grew weary & leaned a little in the heat.
Again, thanks for the dud
hand grenade tossed at my feet
outside Chu Lai. I'm still
falling through its silence.
I don't know why the intrepid

sun touched the bayonet,
but I know that something
stood among those lost trees
& moved only when I moved.

BOYS IN DRESSES

We were The Hottentot Venus
Draped in our mothers' dresses,
Wearing rouge & lipstick,
Pillows tucked under floral
& print cloth, the first day of spring,
As we balanced on high heels.
Women sat in a circle talking
About men; the girls off
Somewhere else, in other houses.
We felt the last kisses
Our mothers would give us
On the mouth. Medusa
Wound around our necks
As we wore out the day's
Cantillations. They gazed at us
& looked into their own eyes
Before the water broke, remembering
How we firstborn boys loved
Them from within, cleaved
Like silver on the backs of mirrors.
Would we grow into merciful
Men, less lead in our gloves?
That afternoon lives in the republic
Of our bones, when we were girlish
Women in a hermetic council
Of milky coffee & teacakes.
Dragonflies nudged window screens.
When we stepped out
Wearing an ecstasy of hues,
Faceless wolf whistles
& catcalls heated the air.
Azaleas buzzed as we went
House to house. Soon we'd be
Responsible for the chambered

Rapture honeycombed in flesh
& would mourn something lost.
It was harder than running
Naked down a double line
Of boys in those patriarchal woods,
Belts singing against our skin.

ODE TO THE MAGGOT

Brother of the blowfly
& godhead, you work magic
Over battlefields,
In slabs of bad pork

& flophouses. Yes, you
Go to the root of all things.
You are sound & mathematical.
Jesus Christ, you're merciless

With the truth. Ontological & lustrous,
You cast spells on beggars & kings
Behind the stone door of Caesar's tomb
Or split trench in a field of ragweed.

No decree or creed can outlaw you
As you take every living thing apart. Little
Master of earth, no one gets to heaven
Without going through you first.

*limbo –
in between*

human state of being "stuck"

© Craig Blouin

Maxine Kumin

MORNING SWIM

Into my empty head there come
a cotton beach, a dock wherefrom

I set out, oily and nude
through mist, in chilly solitude.

There was no line, no roof or floor
to tell the water from the air.

Night fog thick as terry cloth
closed me in its fuzzy growth.

I hung my bathrobe on two pegs.
I took the lake between my legs.

Invaded and invader, I
went overhand on that flat sky.

Fish twitched beneath me, quick and tame.
In their green zone they sang my name

and in the rhythm of the swim
I hummed a two-four-time slow hymn.

I hummed *Abide with Me*. The beat
rose in the fine thrash of my feet,

rose in the bubbles I put out
slantwise, trailing through my mouth.

My bones drank water; water fell
through all my doors. I was the well

that fed the lake that met my sea
in which I sang *Abide with Me*.

MAXINE KUMIN

TO SWIM, TO BELIEVE

Centre College, Danville, Kentucky

The beautiful excess of Jesus on the waters
is with me now in the Boles Natatorium.
This bud of me exults, giving witness:

these flippers that rose up to be arms.
These strings drawn to be fingers.
Legs plumped to make my useful fork.

Each time I tear this seam to enter,
all that I carry is taken from me,
shucked in the dive.

Lovers, children, even words go under.
Matters of dogma spin off in the freestyle
earning that mid-pool spurt, like faith.

Where have I come from? Where am I going?
What do I translate, gliding back and forth
erasing my own stitch marks in this lane?

Christ on the lake was not thinking
where the next heel-toe went.
God did him a dangerous favor

whereas Peter, the thinker, sank.
The secret is in the relenting,
the partnership. I let my body work

accepting the dangerous favor
from this king-size pool of waters.
Together I am supplicant. I am bride.

HEAVEN AS ANUS

In the Defense Department there is a shop
where scientists sew the eyelids of rabbits open
lest they blink in the scorch of a nuclear drop

and elsewhere dolphins are being taught to defuse
bombs in the mock-up of a harbor and monkeys
learn to perform the simple tasks of draftees.

It is done with electric shocks. Some mice
who have failed their time tests in the maze
now go to the wire unbidden for their jolts.

Implanting electrodes yields rich results:
alley cats turn from predators into prey.
Show them a sparrow and they cower

while the whitewall labs fill up with the feces of fear
where calves whose hearts have been done away
with walk and bleat on plastic pumps.

And what is any of this to the godhead,
these squeals, whines, writhings, unexpected jumps,
whose children burn alive, booby-trap the dead,
lop ears and testicles, core and disembowel?

It all ends at the hole. No words may enter
the house of excrement. We will meet there
as the sphincter of the good Lord opens wide
and He takes us all inside.

REQUIEM ON I-89

Crow pecks protein from the asphalt smear.
Woodchuck, muskrat, porcupine. The cousins
come. They strut, bicker over the impromptu
feast. Tire marks carry the stain
over the center line: bone shards, red fur
shreds of flesh up, up, up the food chain.
Such sated caws, such croaks of sorrow.

A mile down the median a deer
that chanced the metal barrier
— unforeseen by Darwin — between nature
and the internal combustion engine
lies on its side, burst open. The second

cousins arrive from hayfield, hedgerow.
Such sated caws, such croaks of sorrow.

THE GRACE OF GELDINGS IN RIPE PASTURES

Glutted, half asleep, browsing in
timothy grown so tall I see them
as through a pale-green stage scrim

they circle, nose to rump,
a trio of trained elephants.
It begins to rain, as promised.

Bit by bit they soak up drops
like laundry dampened to be ironed.
Runnels bedeck them. Their sides

drip like the ribs of very broad
umbrellas. And still they graze
and grazing, one by one let down

their immense, indolent penises
to drench the everlasting grass
with the rich nitrogen

that repeats them.

WOODCHUCKS

Gassing the woodchucks didn't turn out right.
The knockout bomb from the Feed and Grain Exchange
was featured as merciful, quick at the bone
and the case we had against them was airtight,
both exits shoehorned shut with puddingstone,
but they had a sub-sub-basement out of range.

Next morning they turned up again, no worse
for the cyanide than we for our cigarettes

and state-store Scotch, all of us up to scratch.
They brought down the marigolds as a matter of course
and then took over the vegetable patch
nipping the broccoli shoots, beheading the carrots.

The food from our mouths, I said, righteously thrilling
to the feel of the .22, the bullets' neat noses.
I, a lapsed pacifist fallen from grace
puffed with Darwinian pieties for killing,
now drew a bead on the littlest woodchuck's face.
He died down in the everbearing roses.

Ten minutes later I dropped the mother. She
flipflopped in the air and fell, her needle teeth
still hooked in a leaf of early Swiss chard.
Another baby next. O one-two-three
the murderer inside me rose up hard,
the hawkeye killer came on stage forthwith.

There's one chuck left. Old wily fellow, he keeps
me cocked and ready day after day after day.
All night I hunt his humped-up form. I dream
I sight along the barrel in my sleep.
If only they'd all consented to die unseen
gassed underground the quiet Nazi way.

THE HIGHWAYMEN

It's true: you wake up one morning and they're gone,
the flock of a hundred redpolls who swept in like Huns
with their tiny red caps and black mustaches,
their breasts freckled and stippled like thrushes',
an irruption of redpolls you haven't seen in a decade
and may never see again in the disorderly parade
of your lifetime. How they intimidated the chickadees,
the titmice, even the needle-nosed nuthatches,
batting your year-round faithfuls away from the feeder.
How they chattered, snatching and flapping, rapacious
yet charming in their little red yarmulkas . . .
you shiver, remembering, refilling the cylinder.
The sunflower seeds glisten like ebony.
O merciless January, where have the highwaymen gone?

MAXINE KUMIN

IN THE PEA PATCH

These as they clack in the wind
saying castanets, saying dance with me,
saying do me, dangle their intricate
nuggety scrota

and these with the light shining through
call up a woman in a gauzy dress
young, with tendrils of hair at her neck,
leaning in a summer doorway

and as the bloom of the lime-green pod
rubs away under the polishing thumb
in the interior
sweet for the taking, nine little fetuses
nod their cloned heads.

IN THE PARK

You have forty-nine days between
death and rebirth if you're a Buddhist.
Even the smallest soul could swim
the English Channel in that time
or climb, like a ten-month-old child,
every step of the Washington Monument
to travel across, up, down, over or through
— you won't know till you get there which to do.

He laid on me for a few seconds
said Roscoe Black, who lived to tell
about his skirmish with a grizzly bear
in Glacier Park. *He laid on me
not doing anything. I could feel
his heart beating against my heart.*
Never mind *lie* and *lay*, the whole world
confuses them. For Roscoe Black you might say
all forty-nine days flew by.

I was raised on the Old Testament.
In it God talks to Moses, Noah,

Samuel, and they answer.
People confer with angels. Certain
animals converse with humans.
It's a simple world, full of crossovers.

Heaven's an airy Somewhere, and God
has a nasty temper when provoked,
but if there's a Hell, little is made of it.
No longtailed Devil, no eternal fire,
and no choosing what to come back as.
When the grizzly bear appears, he lies/lays down
on atheist and zealot. In the pitch-dark
each of us waits for him in Glacier Park.

NURTURE

From a documentary on marsupials I learn
that a pillowcase makes a fine
substitute pouch for an orphaned kangaroo.

I am drawn to such dramas of animal rescue.
They are warm in the throat. I suffer, the critic proclaims,
from an overabundance of maternal genes.

Bring me your fallen fledgling, your bummer lamb,
lead the abused, the starvelings, into my barn.
Advise the hunted deer to leap into my corn.

And had there been a wild child —
filthy and fierce as a ferret, he is called
in one nineteenth-century account —

a wild child to love, it is safe to assume,
given my fireside inked with paw prints,
there would have been room.

Think of the language we two, same and not-same,
might have constructed from sign,
scratch, grimace, grunt, vowel:

Laughter our first noun, and our long verb, howl.

Stanley Kunitz

THE LAYERS

I have walked through many lives,
some of them my own,
and I am not who I was,
though some principle of being
abides, from which I struggle
not to stray.
When I look behind,
as I am compelled to look
before I can gather strength
to proceed on my journey,
I see the milestones dwindling
toward the horizon
and the slow fires trailing
from the abandoned camp-sites,
over which scavenger angels
wheel on heavy wings.
Oh, I have made myself a tribe
out of my true affections,
and my tribe is scattered!
How shall the heart be reconciled
to its feast of losses?
In a rising wind
the manic dust of my friends,
those who fell along the way,
bitterly stings my face.
Yet I turn, I turn,
exulting somewhat,
with my will intact to go
wherever I need to go,
and every stone on the road
precious to me.
In my darkest night,
when the moon was covered
and I roamed through wreckage,
a nimbus-clouded voice
directed me:
"Live in the layers,
not on the litter."

Though I lack the art
to decipher it,
no doubt the next chapter
in my book of transformations
is already written.
I am not done with my changes.

ROBIN REDBREAST

It was the dingiest bird
you ever saw, all the color
washed from him, as if
he had been standing in the rain,
friendless and stiff and cold,
since Eden went wrong.
In the house marked For Sale,
where nobody made a sound,
in the room where I lived
with an empty page, I had heard
the squawking of the jays
under the wild persimmons
tormenting him.
So I scooped him up
after they knocked him down,
in league with that ounce of heart
pounding in my palm,
that dumb beak gaping.
Poor thing! Poor foolish life!
without sense enough to stop
running in desperate circles,
needing my lucky help
to toss him back into his element.
But when I held him high,
fear clutched my hand,
for through the hole in his head,
cut whistle-clean . . .
through the old dried wound
between his eyes
where the hunter's brand
had tunneled out his wits . . .
I caught the cold flash of the blue
unappeasable sky.

STANLEY KUNITZ

THE WELLFLEET WHALE

1

You have your language too,
    an eerie medley of clicks
       and hoots and trills,
location-notes and love calls,
      whistles and grunts. Occasionally,
         it's like furniture being smashed,
or the creaking of a mossy door,
      sounds that all melt into a liquid
        song with endless variations,
as if to compensate
      for the vast loneliness of the sea.
        Sometimes a disembodied voice
breaks in as if from distant reefs,
      and it's as much as one can bear
        to listen to its long mournful cry,
a sorrow without name, both more
      and less than human. It drags
        across the ear like a record
running down.

2

No wind. No waves. No clouds.
    Only the whisper of the tide,
      as it withdrew, stroking the shore,
a lazy drift of gulls overhead,
    and tiny points of light
      bubbling in the channel.
It was the tag-end of summer.
    From the harbor's mouth
      you coasted into sight,
flashing news of your advent,
    the crescent of your dorsal fin
      clipping the diamonded surface.
We cheered at the sign of your greatness
    when the black barrel of your head
      erupted, ramming the water,
and you flowered for us
    in the jet of your spouting.

3

All afternoon you swam
    tirelessly round the bay,
        with such an easy motion,
the slightest downbeat of your tail,
    an almost imperceptible
        undulation of your flippers,
you seemed like something poured,
    not driven; you seemed
        to marry grace with power.
And when you bounded into air,
    slapping your flukes,
        we thrilled to look upon
pure energy incarnate
    as nobility of form.
        You seemed to ask of us
not sympathy, or love,
    or understanding,
        but awe and wonder.

That night we watched you
    swimming in the moon.
        Your back was molten silver.
We guessed your silent passage
    by the phosphorescence in your wake.
        At dawn we found you stranded on the rocks.

4

There came a boy and a man
    and yet other men running, and two
        schoolgirls in yellow halters
and a housewife bedecked
    with curlers, and whole families in beach
        buggies with assorted yelping dogs.
The tide was almost out.
    We could walk around you,
        as you heaved deeper into the shoal,
crushed by your own weight,
    collapsing into yourself,
        your flippers and your flukes
quivering, your blowhole
    spasmodically bubbling, roaring.
        In the pit of your gaping mouth

you bared your fringework of baleen,
    a thicket of horned bristles.
        When the Curator of Mammals
arrived from Boston
    to take samples of your blood
        you were already oozing from below.
Somebody had carved his initials
    in your flank. Hunters of souvenirs
        had peeled off strips of your skin,
a membrane thin as paper.
    You were blistered and cracked by the sun.
        The gulls had been pecking at you.
The sound you made was a hoarse and fitful bleating.

What drew us to the magnet of your dying?
    You made a bond between us,
        the keepers of the nightfall watch,
who gathered in a ring around you,
    boozing in the bonfire light.
        Toward dawn we shared with you
your hour of desolation,
    the huge lingering passion
        of your unearthly outcry,
as you swung your blind head
    toward us and laboriously opened
        a bloodshot, glistening eye,
in which we swam with terror and recognition.

5

Voyager, chief of the pelagic world,
    you brought with you the myth
        of another country, dimly remembered,
where flying reptiles
    lumbered over the steaming marshes
        and trumpeting thunder lizards
wallowed in the reeds.
    While empires rose and fell on land,
        your nation breasted the open main,
rocked in the consoling rhythm
    of the tides. Which ancestor first plunged
        head-down through zones of colored twilight
to scour the bottom of the dark?
    You ranged the North Atlantic track
        from Port-of-Spain to Baffin Bay,

edging between the ice-floes
through the fat of summer,
lob-tailing, breaching, sounding,
grazing in the pastures of the sea
on krill-rich orange plankton
crackling with life.
You prowled down the continental shelf,
guided by the sun and stars
and the taste of alluvial silt
on your way southward
to the warm lagoons,
the tropic of desire,
where the lovers lie belly to belly
in the rub and nuzzle of their sporting;
and you turned, like a god in exile,
out of your wide primeval element,
delivered to the mercy of time.

Master of the whale-roads,
let the white wings of the gulls
spread out their cover.
You have become like us,
disgraced and mortal.

THE ABDUCTION

Some things I do not profess
to understand, perhaps
not wanting to, including
whatever it was they did
with you or you with them
that timeless summer day
when you stumbled out of the wood,
distracted, with your white blouse torn
and a bloodstain on your skirt.
"Do you believe?" you asked.
Between us, through the years,
from bits, from broken clues,
we pieced enough together
to make the story real:
how you encountered on the path

a pack of sleek, grey hounds,
trailed by a dumbshow retinue
in leather shrouds; and how
you were led, through leafy ways,
into the presence of a royal stag,
flaming in his chestnut coat,
who kneeled on a swale of moss
before you; and how you were borne
aloft in triumph through the green,
stretched on his rack of budding horn,
till suddenly you found yourself alone
in a trampled clearing.

That was a long time ago,
almost another age, but even now,
when I hold you in my arms,
I wonder where you are.
Sometimes I wake to hear
the engines of the night thrumming
outside the east bay window
on the lawn spreading to the rose garden.
You lie beside me in elegant repose,
a hint of transport hovering on your lips,
indifferent to the harsh green flares
that swivel through the room,
searchlights controlled by unseen hands.
Out there is childhood country,
bleached faces peering in
with coals for eyes.
Our lives are spinning out
from world to world;
the shapes of things
are shifting in the wind.
What do we know
beyond the rapture and the dread?

THE PORTRAIT

My mother never forgave my father
for killing himself,
especially at such an awkward time

understatement
sounds more like gossip
as opposed to deep
feeling about the event

and in a public park,
that spring
when I was waiting to be born.
She locked his name
in her deepest cabinet
and would not let him out,
though I could hear him thumping.
When I came down from the attic
with the pastel portrait in my hand
of a long-lipped stranger
with a brave moustache
and deep brown level eyes,
she ripped it into shreds
without a single word
and slapped me hard.
In my sixty-fourth year
I can feel my cheek
still burning.

[handwritten: transgressions — public nature of the suicidealmost shames her/him]

[handwritten: fragility/ impermanence]

TOUCH ME

Summer is late, my heart.
Words plucked out of the air
some forty years ago
when I was wild with love
and torn almost in two
scatter like leaves this night
of whistling wind and rain.
It is my heart that's late,
it is my song that's flown.
Outdoors all afternoon
under a gunmetal sky
staking my garden down,
I kneeled to the crickets trilling
underfoot as if about
to burst from their crusty shells;
and like a child again
marveled to hear so clear
and brave a music pour
from such a small machine.
What makes the engine go?

[handwritten: heart?]

STANLEY KUNITZ

Desire, desire, desire.
The longing for the dance
stirs in the buried life.
One season only,
          and it's done.
So let the battered old willow
thrash against the windowpanes
and the house timbers creak.
Darling, do you remember
the man you married? Touch me,
remind me who I am.

short-lived season of love

where does this come from? romantics?

THE LONG BOAT

When his boat snapped loose
from its moorings, under
the screaking of the gulls,
he tried at first to wave
to his dear ones on shore,
but in the rolling fog
they had already lost their faces.
Too tired even to choose
between jumping and calling,
somehow he felt absolved and free
of his burdens, those mottoes
stamped on his name-tag:
conscience, ambition, and all
that caring.
He was content to lie down
with the family ghosts
in the slop of his cradle,
buffeted by the storm,
endlessly drifting.
Peace! Peace!
To be rocked by the Infinite!
As if it didn't matter
which way was home;
as if he didn't know
he loved the earth so much
he wanted to stay forever.

poetry = language under pressure

Courtesy Donna Lee

Li-Young Lee

THE GIFT

To pull the metal splinter from my palm
my father recited a story in a low voice.
I watched his lovely face and not the blade.
Before the story ended, he'd removed
the iron sliver I thought I'd die from.

I can't remember the tale,
but hear his voice still, a well
of dark water, a prayer.
And I recall his hands,
two measures of tenderness
he laid against my face,
the flames of discipline
he raised above my head.

Had you entered that afternoon
you would have thought you saw a man
planting something in a boy's palm,
a silver tear, a tiny flame.
Had you followed that boy
you would have arrived here,
where I bend over my wife's right hand.

Look how I shave her thumbnail down
so carefully she feels no pain.
Watch as I lift the splinter out.
I was seven when my father
took my hand like this,
and I did not hold that shard
between my fingers and think,
Metal that will bury me,
christen it Little Assassin,
Ore Going Deep for My Heart.
And I did not lift up my wound and cry,
Death visited here!
I did what a child does
when he's given something to keep.
I kissed my father.

291

PERSIMMONS

In sixth grade Mrs. Walker
slapped the back of my head
and made me stand in the corner
for not knowing the difference
between *persimmon* and *precision*.
How to choose

persimmons. This is *precision*.
Ripe ones are soft and brown-spotted.
Sniff the bottoms. The sweet one
will be fragrant. How to eat:
put the knife away, lay down newspaper.
Peel the skin tenderly, not to tear the meat.
Chew the skin, suck it,
and swallow. Now, eat
the meat of the fruit,
so sweet,
all of it, to the heart.

Donna undresses, her stomach is white.
In the yard, dewy and shivering
with crickets, we lie naked,
face-up, face-down.
I teach her Chinese.
Crickets: *chiu chiu.* Dew: I've forgotten.
Naked: I've forgotten.
Ni, wo: you and me.
I part her legs,
remember to tell her
she is beautiful as the moon.

Other words
that got me into trouble were
fight and *fright, wren* and *yarn.*
Fight was what I did when I was frightened,
fright was what I felt when I was fighting.
Wrens are small, plain birds,
yarn is what one knits with.
Wrens are soft as yarn.
My mother made birds out of yarn.

Handwritten annotations:
- he might not know the language, but he knows the experience which is more important?
- what does it mean for Mrs. Walker to assume Lee is "unexperienced" because his language is faulty? *see 294
- forgotten heritage
- How to choose — ripeness
- what does this do? heavy ...
- precision of language
- persimmon — sun / Donna — moon / what do those metaphors mean in relation to language and experience?
- confusion, but still logical

I loved to watch her tie the stuff;
a bird, a rabbit, a wee man.

Mrs. Walker brought a persimmon to class
and cut it up — *she was wrong*
so everyone could taste
a *Chinese apple.* Knowing
it wasn't ripe or sweet, I didn't eat
but watched the other faces.

knows the language, but she is unexperienced

— knew how & when to eat it

My mother said every persimmon has a sun
inside, something golden, glowing,
warm as my face.

son

Once, in the cellar, I found two wrapped in newspaper,
forgotten and not yet ripe.
I took them and set both on my bedroom windowsill,
where each morning a cardinal
sang, *The sun, the sun.*

loss

Finally understanding
he was going blind,
my father sat up all one night
waiting for a song, a ghost.
I gave him the persimmons,
swelled, heavy as sadness,
and sweet as love.

loss

— both are invisible

This year, in the muddy lighting
of my parents' cellar, I rummage, looking
for something I lost.
My father sits on the tired, wooden stairs,
black cane between his knees,
hand over hand, gripping the handle.
He's so happy that I've come home.
I ask how his eyes are, a stupid question.
All gone, he answers.

loss

loss ohfather hisfather

loss

Under some blankets, I find a box.
Inside the box I find three scrolls.
I sit beside him and untie
three paintings by my father:
Hibiscus leaf and a white flower.

LI-YOUNG LEE

Handwritten annotations (top): a lot of fruit is ripe when heavy — you pick the one that looks heavy for its size — sadness similar? How does sadness swell, how does (How to Choose / persimmons) loss enlarge / sadness beyond visible recognition?

Handwritten (left margin): heaviness as it relates to loss — loss as heaviness. sadness

Two cats preening.
Two persimmons, so full they want to drop from the cloth.
He knows the heaviness of
He raises both hands to touch the cloth,
asks, *Which is this?*

Handwritten: He knows the heaviness sadness and loss very much. Father, of a sight of or sight. sadness beyond visible recognition?

This is persimmons, Father.

Oh, the feel of the wolftail on the silk,
the strength, the tense
precision in the wrist.
I painted them hundreds of times
(eyes closed.) These I painted (blind.)
Some things never leave a person:
scent of the hair of one you love,
the texture of persimmons,
in your palm, the ripe weight.

Handwritten: difference? what is the ripe right weight

EATING ALONE

I've pulled the last of the year's young onions.
The garden is bare now. The ground is cold,
brown and old. What is left of the day flames
in the maples at the corner of my
eye. I turn, a cardinal vanishes.
By the cellar door, I wash the onions,
then drink from the icy metal spigot.

Once, years back, I walked beside my father
among the windfall pears. I can't recall
our words. We may have strolled in silence. But
I still see him bend that way — left hand braced
on knee, creaky — to lift and hold to my
eye a rotten pear. In it, a hornet
spun crazily, glazed in slow, glistening juice.

It was my father I saw this morning
waving to me from the trees. I almost
called to him, until I came close enough
to see the shovel, leaning where I had
left it, in the flickering, deep green shade.

LI-YOUNG LEE

White rice steaming, almost done. Sweet green peas
fried in onions. Shrimp braised in sesame
oil and garlic. And my own loneliness.
What more could I, a young man, want.

EATING TOGETHER

In the steamer is the trout
seasoned with slivers of ginger,
two sprigs of green onion, and sesame oil.
We shall eat it with rice for lunch,
brothers, sister, my mother who will
taste the sweetest meat of the head,
holding it between her fingers
deftly, the way my father did
weeks ago. Then he lay down
to sleep like a snow-covered road
winding through pines older than him,
without any travelers, and lonely for no one.

MY INDIGO   — *the only one w/o the father*

It's late. I've come
to find the flower which blossoms
like a saint dying upside down.
The rose won't do, nor the iris.
I've come to find the moody one, the shy one,
downcast, grave, and isolated.
Now, blackness gathers in the grass,
and I am on my hands and knees.
What is its name?

Little sister, my indigo,
my secret, vaginal and sweet,
you unfurl yourself shamelessly
toward the ground. You burn. You live
a while in two worlds
at once.

LI-YOUNG LEE

THIS ROOM AND EVERYTHING IN IT

Lie still now
while I prepare for my future,
certain hard days ahead,
when I'll need what I know so clearly this moment.

I am making use
of the one thing I learned
of all the things my father tried to teach me:
the art of memory.

I am letting this room
and everything in it
stand for my ideas about love
and its difficulties.

I'll let your love-cries,
those spacious notes
of a moment ago,
stand for distance.

Your scent,
that scent
of spice and a wound,
I'll let stand for mystery.

Your sunken belly
is the daily cup
of milk I drank
as a boy before morning prayer.

The sun on the face
of the wall
is God, the face
I can't see, my soul,

and so on, each thing
standing for a separate idea,
and those ideas forming the constellation
of my greater idea.
And one day, when I need
to tell myself something intelligent
about love,

[handwritten annotations in margins: "how are memories tied to a place, like a room?", "how to grieve", "memory place", "how to remember"]

I'll close my eyes
and recall this room and everything in it:
My body is estrangement.
This desire, perfection.
Your closed eyes my extinction.
Now I've forgotten my
loss idea. The book
on the windowsill, riffled by wind . . .
the even-numbered pages are
the past, the odd-
numbered pages, the future.
The sun is
God, your body is milk . . .

useless, useless . . .
your cries are song, my body's not me . . .
no good . . . my idea
loss has evaporated . . . your hair is time, your thighs are song . . .
it had something to do
with death . . . it had something
to do with love.

YOU MUST SING

what does changing the pronoun do?

He sings in his father's arms, sings his father
to sleep, all the while seeing how on that face
grown suddenly strange, wasting to shadow,
time moves. Stern time. Sweet time. Because his father

asked, he sings; because they are wholly lost.
How else, in immaculate noon, will each find
each, who are so close now? So close and lost.
His voice stands at windows, runs everywhere.

Was death giant? O, how will he find his
father? They are so close. Was death a guest?
By which door did it come? All the day's doors
are closed. He must go out of those hours, that house,

the enfolding limbs, go burdened to learn:
you must sing to be found; when found, you must sing.

David Geier

Denise Levertov

THE ACOLYTE

The large kitchen is almost dark.
Across the plain of even, diffused light,
copper pans on the wall and the window geranium
tend separate campfires.
Herbs dangle their Spanish moss from rafters.

At the table, floury hands
kneading dough, feet planted
steady on flagstones,
a woman ponders the loaves-to-be.
Yeast and flour, water and salt,
have met in the huge bowl.

It's not
the baked and cooled and cut
bread she's thinking of,
but the way
the dough rises and has a life of its own,

not the oven she's thinking of
but the way
the sour smell changes
to fragrance.

She wants to put
a silver rose or a bell of diamonds
into each loaf;
she wants

to bake a curse into one loaf,
into another, the words that break
evil spells and release
transformed heroes into their selves;
she wants to make
bread that is more than bread.

DENISE LEVERTOV

THE POEM UNWRITTEN

For weeks the poem of your body,
of my hands upon your body
    stroking, sweeping, in the rite
    of worship, going
    their way of wonder down
    from neck-pulse to breast-hair to level
    belly to cock —
for weeks that poem, that prayer,
unwritten.

    The poem unwritten, the act
left in the mind, undone. The years
a forest of giant stones, of fossil stumps,
blocking the altar.

1970

OUR BODIES

Our bodies, still young under
the engraved anxiety of our
faces, and innocently

more expressive than faces:
nipples, navel, and pubic hair
make anyway a

sort of face: or taking
the rounded shadows at
breast, buttock, balls,

the plump of my belly, the
hollow of your
groin, as a constellation,

how it leans from earth to
dawn in a gesture of
play and

DENISE LEVERTOV

(handwritten annotation, left: "spaces broken lines — fantastic movement onjambment ?")

... wise compassion —
nothing like this
comes to pass
in eyes or wistful
mouths.
                I have

a line or groove I love
runs down
my body from breastbone
to waist. It speaks of
eagerness, of
distance. — *(handwritten: "between 2 bodies")*
                Your long back,
the sand color and
how the bones show, say

what sky after sunset
almost white
over a deep woods to which

rooks are homing, says.

(handwritten annotation, right: "overtly sexual (but not mentioned in her bio) — vs. Rich")

THE MUTES

Those groans men use
passing a woman on the street
or on the steps of the subway

to tell her she is a female
and their flesh knows it,

are they a sort of tune,
an ugly enough song, sung
by a bird with a slit tongue

but meant for music?

Or are they the muffled roaring
of deafmutes trapped in a building that is
slowly filling with smoke?

DENISE LEVERTOV

Perhaps both.

Such men most often
look as if groan were all they could do,
yet a woman, in spite of herself,

knows it's a tribute:
if she were lacking all grace
they'd pass her in silence:

so it's not only to say she's
a warm hole. It's a word

in grief-language, nothing to do with
primitive, not an ur-language;
language stricken, sickened, cast down

in decrepitude. She wants to
throw the tribute away, dis-
gusted, and can't,

it goes on buzzing in her ear,
it changes the pace of her walk,
the torn posters in echoing corridors

spell it out, it
quakes and gnashes as the train comes in.
Her pulse sullenly

had picked up speed,
but the cars slow down and
jar to a stop while her understanding

keeps on translating:
'Life after life after life goes by

without poetry,
without seemliness,
without love.'

DENISE LEVERTOV

WEDDING-RING

My wedding-ring lies in a basket
as if at the bottom of a well.
Nothing will come to fish it back up
and onto my finger again.
                              It lies
among keys to abandoned houses,
nails waiting to be needed and hammered
into some wall,
telephone numbers with no names attached,
idle paperclips.
                    It can't be given away
for fear of bringing ill-luck.
                    It can't be sold
for the marriage was good in its own
time, though that time is gone.
                    Could some artificer
beat into it bright stones, transform it
into a dazzling circlet no one could take
for solemn betrothal or to make promises
living will not let them keep? Change it
into a simple gift I could give in friendship?

WHERE IS THE ANGEL?

Where is the angel for me to wrestle?
No driving snow in the glass bubble,
but mild September.

Outside, the stark shadows
menace, and fling their huge arms about
unheard. I breathe

a tepid air, the blur
of asters, of brown fern and gold-dust
seems to murmur,

[handwritten annotations: "anti-complacency"; "Jacob"; "snow globe or bell jar"; "She cannot hear the outside voices"; "protective, romantic scene"; "unheard" circled]

and that's what I hear, only that.
Such clear walls of curved glass:
I see the violent gesticulations

and feel — no, not nothing. But in this
gentle haze, nothing commensurate.
It is pleasant in here. History

mouths, volume turned off. A band of iron,
like they put round a split tree,
circles my heart. In here
it is pleasant, but when I open
my mouth to speak, I too
am soundless. Where is the angel
to wrestle with me and wound
not my thigh but my throat,
so curses and blessings flow storming out

and the glass shatters, and the iron sunders?

Handwritten annotations:
shaking a snowglobe
Protective / Quiet
inside this bubble.
history is "silent" — she is not yet part of it.
wound becomes a symbol for the struggle
the struggle you make
(what doesn't kill you makes you stronger)
b what break will the myth of this masculine-feminine relationship
almost as a "trophy"
nice to be protected, but you are then silenced
recovery
speach / speaking
destruction — is needed but where is it / the angel?

LIFE AT WAR

The disasters numb within us
caught in the chest, rolling
in the brain like pebbles. The feeling
resembles lumps of raw dough

weighing down a child's stomach on baking day.
Or Rilke said it, 'My heart . . .
Could I say of it, it overflows
with bitterness . . . but no, as though

its contents were simply balled into
formless lumps, thus
do I carry it about.'
The same war

DENISE LEVERTOV

continues.
We have breathed the grits of it in, all our lives,
our lungs are pocked with it,
the mucous membrane of our dreams
coated with it, the imagination
filmed over with the gray filth of it:

the knowledge that humankind,

delicate Man, whose flesh
responds to a caress, whose eyes
are flowers that perceive the stars,

whose music excels the music of birds,
whose laughter matches the laughter of dogs,
whose understanding manifests designs
fairer than the spider's most intricate web,

still turns without surprise, with mere regret
to the scheduled breaking open of breasts whose milk
runs out over the entrails of still-alive babies,
transformation of witnessing eyes to pulp-fragments,
implosion of skinned penises into carcass-gulleys.

We are the humans, men who can make;
whose language imagines *mercy*,
lovingkindness; we have believed one another
mirrored forms of a God we felt as good —

who do these acts, who convince ourselves
it is necessary; these acts are done
to our own flesh; burned human flesh
is smelling in Viet Nam as I write.

Yes, this is the knowledge that jostles for space
in our bodies along with all we
go on knowing of joy, of love;

our nerve filaments twitch with its presence
day and night,
nothing we say has not the husky phlegm of it in the saying,
nothing we do has the quickness, the sureness,
the deep intelligence living at peace would have.

① "you"
② narrative form – speaker/characters "on the Birth" &
③ shift from concrete → abstract "The Two"
         "community"
      we labor, we love

*city in decline (industry booms then abandonment)
*enclosure – layering of ownership & tradition
* divide of classes

© Christopher Felver/Corbis

Philip Levine

THE SIMPLE TRUTH

I bought a dollar and a half's worth of small red potatoes,
took them home, boiled them in their jackets
and ate them for dinner with a little butter and salt.
Then I walked through the dried fields
on the edge of town. In middle June the light
hung on in the dark furrows at my feet,
and in the mountain oaks overhead the birds
were gathering for the night, the jays and mockers
squawking back and forth, the finches still darting
into the dusty light. The woman who sold me
the potatoes was from Poland; she was someone
out of my childhood in a pink spangled sweater and sunglasses
praising the perfection of all her fruits and vegetables
at the road-side stand and urging me to taste
even the pale, raw sweet corn trucked all the way,
she swore, from New Jersey. "Eat, eat," she said,
"Even if you don't I'll say you did."
                                    Some things
you know all your life. They are so simple and true
they must be said without elegance, meter and rhyme,
they must be laid on the table beside the salt shaker,
the glass of water, the absence of light gathering
in the shadows of picture frames, they must be
naked and alone, they must stand for themselves.
My friend Henri and I arrived at this together in 1965
before I went away, before he began to kill himself,
and the two of us to betray our love. Can you taste
what I'm saying? It is onions or potatoes, a pinch
of simple salt, the wealth of melting butter, it is obvious,
it stays in the back of your throat like a truth
you never uttered because the time was always wrong,
it stays there for the rest of your life, unspoken,
made of that dirt we call earth, the metal we call salt,
in a form we have no words for, and you live on it.

307

PHILIP LEVINE

ON THE BIRTH OF GOOD & EVIL
DURING THE LONG WINTER OF '28

[handwritten: year he was born (January)]

When the streetcar stalled on Joy Road,
the conductor finished his coffee, puffed
into his overcoat, and went to phone in.
The Hungarian punch press operator wakened
alone, 7000 miles from home, pulled down
his orange cap and set out. If he saw
the winter birds scuffling in the cinders,
if he felt this was the dawn of a new day,
he didn't let on. Where the sidewalks
were unshovelled, he stamped on, raising
his galoshes a little higher with each step.
I came as close as I dared and could hear
only the little gasps as the cold entered
the stained refectory of the breath.
I could see by the way the blue tears squeezed
from the dark of the eyes, by the way
his moustache first dampened and then froze,
that as he turned down Dexter Boulevard,
he considered the hosts of the dead, *[handwritten: how would a "spectator" know / see this]*
and nearest among them, his mother-in-law,
who darkened his table for twenty-seven years
and bruised his wakings. He considered how
before she went off in the winter of '27
she had knitted this cap, knitted so slowly
that Christmas came and went, and now he could
forgive her at last for the twin wool lappets
that closed perfectly on a tiny metal snap
beneath the chin and for making all of it orange.

ANIMALS ARE PASSING FROM OUR LIVES

[handwritten: what does this have to do w/ it?]

It's wonderful how I jog
on four honed-down ivory toes
my massive buttocks slipping
like oiled parts with each light step.

writer's market?
economy?

PHILIP LEVINE

I'm to market. I can smell
the sour, grooved block, I can smell
the blade that opens the hole
and the pudgy white fingers

that shake out the intestines
like a hankie. In my dreams
the snouts drool on the marble,
suffering children, suffering flies,

anger

suffering the consumers
who won't meet their steady eyes
for fear they could see. The boy
who drives me along believes

that any moment I'll fall
on my side and drum my toes
like a typewriter or squeal
and shit like a new housewife

*dehumanizing of the factory line

discovering television,
or that I'll turn like a beast
cleverly to hook his teeth
with my teeth. No. Not this pig.

YOU CAN HAVE IT — *life?*

anger

My brother comes home from work
and climbs the stairs to our room.
I can hear the bed groan and his shoes drop
one by one. You can have it, he says.

The moonlight streams in the window
and his unshaven face is whitened
like the face of the moon. He will sleep
long after noon and waken to find me gone.

Thirty years will pass before I remember
that moment when suddenly I knew each man

PHILIP LEVINE

has one brother who dies when he sleeps
and sleeps when he rises to face this life,
and that together they are only one man
sharing a heart that always labors, hands
yellowed and cracked, a mouth that gasps
for breath and asks, Am I gonna make it?

All night at the ice plant he had fed
the chute its silvery blocks, and then I
stacked cases of orange soda for the children
of Kentucky, one gray boxcar at a time

with always two more waiting. We were twenty
for such a short time and always in
the wrong clothes, crusted with dirt
and sweat. I think now we were never twenty.

In 1948 in the city of Detroit, founded
by de la Mothe Cadillac for the distant purposes
of Henry Ford, no one wakened or died,
no one walked the streets or stoked a furnace,

for there was no such year, and now
that year has fallen off all the old newspapers,
calendars, doctors' appointments, bonds,
wedding certificates, drivers licenses.
The city slept. The snow turned to ice.
The ice to standing pools or rivers
racing in the gutters. Then bright grass rose
between the thousands of cracked squares,

and that grass died. I give you back 1948.
I give you all the years from then
to the coming one. Give me back the moon
with its frail light falling across a face.

Give me back my young brother, hard
and furious, with wide shoulders and a curse
for God and burning eyes that look upon
all creation and say, You can have it.

PHILIP LEVINE

WHAT WORK IS

We stand in the rain in a long line
waiting at Ford Highland Park. For work.
You know what work is — if you're
old enough to read this you know what
work is, although you may not do it.
Forget you. This is about waiting,
shifting from one foot to another.
Feeling the light rain falling like mist
into your hair, blurring your vision
until you think you see your own brother
ahead of you, maybe ten places.
You rub your glasses with your fingers,
and of course it's someone else's brother,
narrower across the shoulders than
yours but with the same sad slouch, the grin
that does not hide the stubbornness,
the sad refusal to give in to
rain, to the hours wasted waiting,
to the knowledge that somewhere ahead
a man is waiting who will say, "No,
we're not hiring today," for any
reason he wants. You love your brother,
now suddenly you can hardly stand
the love flooding you for your brother,
who's not beside you or behind or
ahead because he's home trying to
sleep off a miserable night shift
at Cadillac so he can get up
before noon to study his German.
Works eight hours a night so he can sing
Wagner, the opera you hate most,
the worst music ever invented.
How long has it been since you told him
you loved him, held his wide shoulders,
opened your eyes wide and said those words,
and maybe kissed his cheek? You've never
done something so simple, so obvious,
not because you're too young or too dumb,
not because you're jealous or even mean
or incapable of crying in
the presence of another man, no,
just because you don't know what work is.

PHILIP LEVINE

I WAS BORN IN LUCERNE

Everyone says otherwise. They take me
to a flat on Pingree in Detroit
and say, Up there, the second floor. I say,
No, in a small Italian hotel overlooking
the lake. No doctor, no nurse. Just
a beautiful single woman who preferred
to remain that way and raise me to
the proper height, weight, and level of audacity.
They show me a slip of paper that says,
"Ford Hospital, Dr. Smear, male," and all
the rest of the clichés I could have lived by.
All that afternoon my mother held me close
to her side and watched the slow fog lift
and the water and sky blue all at once,
then darken to a deeper blue that turned
black at last, as I faced the longest night
of my life with tight fists and closed eyes
beside a woman of independence and courage
who sang the peasant songs of her region.
Later she recited the names of small mountain
villages like a litany that would protect
us against the rise of darkness and the fall
of hundreds of desperate men no longer
willing to pull in the fields or the factories
of Torino for a few lire and a Thank You.
She told me of those men, my uncles
and cousins, with names like water pouring
from stone jugs. Primo, Grunwald,
Carlo Finzi, Mario Antonio Todesco, Beniamino
Levi, my grandfather. They would die,
she said, as my father had died, because all
of these lands of ours were angered. No one
remembered the simple beauty of a clear dawn
and how snow fell covering the streets
littered with lies. Toward dawn she rose
and watched the light graying the still waters
and held me to the window and bobbed me up
and down until I awakened a moment to
see the golden sun splashed upon the eye
of the world. You wonder why I am
impossible, why I stand in the bus station

PHILIP LEVINE

in Toledo baying No! No! and hurling
the luggage of strangers every which way,
why I refuse to climb ladders or descend into
cellars of coal dust and dead mice or eat
like a good boy or change my dirty clothes
no matter who complains. Look in my eyes!
They have stared into the burning eyes of earth,
molten metals, the first sun, a woman's face,
they have seen the snow covering it all
and a new day breaking over the mother sea.
I breathed the truth. I was born in Lucerne.

THEY FEED THEY LION

Rebellion

Out of burlap sacks, out of bearing butter,
Out of black bean and wet slate bread,
Out of the acids of rage, the candor of tar,
Out of creosote, gasoline, drive shafts, wooden dollies,
They Lion grow.
                    Out of the gray hills
Of industrial barns, out of rain, out of bus ride,
West Virginia to Kiss My Ass, out of buried aunties,
Mothers hardening like pounded stumps, out of stumps,
Out of the bones' need to sharpen and the muscles' to stretch,
They Lion grow.
                    Earth is eating trees, fence posts,
Gutted cars, earth is calling in her little ones,
"Come home, Come home!" From pig balls,
From the ferocity of pig driven to holiness,
From the furred ear and the full jowl come
The repose of the hung belly, from the purpose
They Lion grow.
                    From the sweet glues of the trotters
Come the sweet kinks of the fist, from the full flower
Of the hams the thorax of caves,
From "Bow Down" come "Rise Up,"
Come they Lion from the reeds of shovels,
The grained arm that pulls the hands,
They Lion grow.
                    From my five arms and all my hands,
From all my white sins forgiven, they feed,

From my car passing under the stars,
They Lion, from my children inherit,
From the oak turned to a wall, they Lion,
From they sack and they belly opened
And all that was hidden burning on the oil-stained earth
They feed they Lion and he comes.

THE TWO

narrative

When he gets off work at Packard, they meet
outside a diner on Grand Boulevard. He's tired,
a bit depressed, and smelling the exhaustion
on his own breath, he kisses her carefully
on her left cheek. Early April, and the weather
has not decided if this is spring, winter, or what.
The two gaze upward at the sky, which gives
nothing away: the low clouds break here and there
and let in tiny slices of a pure blue heaven.
The day is like us, she thinks; it hasn't decided
what to become. The traffic light at Linwood
goes from red to green and the trucks start up,
so that when he says, "Would you like to eat?"
she hears a jumble of words that means nothing,
though spiced with things she cannot believe,
"wooden Jew" and "lucky meat." He's been up
late, she thinks, he's tired of the job, perhaps tired
of their morning meetings, but then he bows
from the waist and holds the door open
for her to enter the diner, and the thick
odor of bacon frying and new potatoes
greets them both, and taking heart she enters
to peer through the thick cloud of tobacco smoke
to see if "their booth" is available.
F. Scott Fitzgerald wrote that there were no
second acts in America, but he knew neither
this man nor this woman and no one else
like them unless he stayed late at the office
to test his famous one-liner, "We keep you clean
in Muscatine," on the woman emptying
his wastebasket. Fitzgerald never wrote
with someone present, except for this woman

love

never became lovers

working class

PHILIP LEVINE

in a gray uniform whose comings and goings
went unnoticed even on those December evenings
she worked late while the snow fell silently
on the windowsills and the new fluorescent lights
blinked on and off. Get back to the two, you say.
Not who ordered poached eggs, who ordered
only toast and coffee, who shared the bacon
with the other, but what became of the two
when this poem ended, whose arms held whom,
who first said "I love you" and truly meant it,
and who misunderstood the words, so longed
for and yet still so unexpected, and began
suddenly to scream and curse until the waitress
asked them both to leave. The Packard plant closed
years before I left Detroit, the diner was burned
to the ground in '67, two years before my oldest son
fled to Sweden to escape the American dream.
"And the lovers?" you ask. I wrote nothing about lovers.
Take a look. Clouds, trucks, traffic lights, a diner, work,
a wooden shoe, East Moline, poached eggs, the perfume
of frying bacon, the chaos of language, the spices
of spent breath after eight hours of night work.
Can you hear all I feared and never dared to write?
Why the two are more real than either you or me,
why I never returned to keep them in my life,
how little I now mean to myself or anyone else,
what any of this could mean, where you found
the patience to endure these truths and confusions?

uniquely positioned to change poetry b/c he was born well-known; talented, but very public

acceptance/ giving high priority" Q: at bottom of ? find page

a: "For the Union Dead" – decay – Aquarium – in history
b: "Skunk Hour" – decay/decline
c: decay/decline (buildings)

decline – decay – in nature (buildings)
in the mind
in relationships

Rollie McKenna

Does this have anything to do w/ his adherence to → rejection of form? Letting mistakes happen, form getting looser.

Robert Lowell

MEMORIES OF WEST STREET AND LEPKE

Only teaching on Tuesdays, book-worming
in pajamas fresh from the washer each morning,
I hog a whole house on Boston's
"hardly passionate Marlborough Street,"
where even the man
scavenging filth in the back alley trash cans,
has two children, a beach wagon, a helpmate,
and is a "young Republican."
I have a nine months' daughter,
young enough to be my granddaughter.
Like the sun she rises in her flame-flamingo infants' wear.

These are the tranquillized *Fifties*,
and I am forty. Ought I to regret my seedtime?
I was a fire-breathing Catholic C.O.,
and made my manic statement,
telling off the state and president, and then
sat waiting sentence in the bull pen
beside a Negro boy with curlicues
of marijuana in his hair.

Given a year,
I walked on the roof of the West Street Jail, a short
enclosure like my school soccer court,
and saw the Hudson River once a day
through sooty clothesline entanglements
and bleaching khaki tenements.
Strolling, I yammered metaphysics with Abramowitz,
a jaundice-yellow ("it's really tan")
and fly-weight pacifist,
so vegetarian,
he wore rope shoes and preferred fallen fruit.
He tried to convert Bioff and Brown,
the Hollywood pimps, to his diet.
Hairy, muscular, suburban,
wearing chocolate double-breasted suits,
they blew their tops and beat him black and blue.

I was so out of things, I'd never heard
of the Jehovah's Witnesses.
"Are you a C.O.?" I asked a fellow jailbird.
"No," he answered, "I'm a J.W."
He taught me the "hospital tuck,"
and pointed out the T-shirted back
of *Murder Incorporated's* Czar Lepke,
there piling towels on a rack,
or dawdling off to his little segregated cell full
of things forbidden the common man:
a portable radio, a dresser, two toy American
flags tied together with a ribbon of Easter palm.
Flabby, bald, lobotomized,
he drifted in a sheepish calm,
where no agonizing reappraisal
jarred his concentration on the electric chair —
hanging like an oasis in his air
of lost connections. . . .

"TO SPEAK OF WOE THAT IS IN MARRIAGE"

*It is the future generation that presses into being by means of these
exuberant feelings and supersensible soap bubbles of ours.*

— Schopenhauer

"The hot night makes us keep our bedroom windows open.
Our magnolia blossoms. Life begins to happen.
My hopped up husband drops his home disputes,
and hits the streets to cruise for prostitutes,
free-lancing out along the razor's edge.
This screwball might kill his wife, then take the pledge.
Oh the monotonous meanness of his lust. . . .
It's the injustice . . . he is so unjust —
whiskey-blind, swaggering home at five.
My only thought is how to keep alive.
What makes him tick? Each night now I tie
ten dollars and his car key to my thigh. . . .
Gored by the climacteric of his want,
he stalls above me like an elephant."

SKUNK HOUR

[for Elizabeth Bishop]

Nautilus Island's hermit
heiress still lives through winter in her Spartan cottage;
her sheep still graze above the sea.
Her son's a bishop. Her farmer
is first selectman in our village;
she's in her dotage.

Thirsting for
the hierarchic privacy
of Queen Victoria's century,
she buys up all
the eyesores facing her shore,
and lets them fall.

The season's ill —
we've lost our summer millionaire,
who seemed to leap from an L. L. Bean
catalogue. His nine-knot yawl
was auctioned off to lobstermen.
A red fox stain covers Blue Hill.

And now our fairy
decorator brightens his shop for fall;
his fishnet's filled with orange cork,
orange, his cobbler's bench and awl;
there is no money in his work,
he'd rather marry.

One dark night,
my Tudor Ford climbed the hill's skull;
I watched for love-cars. Lights turned down,
they lay together, hull to hull,
where the graveyard shelves on the town. . . .
My mind's not right.

A car radio bleats,
"Love, O careless Love. . . ." I hear
my ill-spirit sob in each blood cell,
as if my hand were at its throat. . . .

I myself am hell;
nobody's here —

only skunks, that search
in the moonlight for a bite to eat.
They march on their soles up Main Street:
white stripes, moonstruck eyes' red fire
under the chalk-dry and spar spire
of the Trinitarian Church.

I stand on top
of our back steps and breathe the rich air —
a mother skunk with her column of kittens swills the garbage pail.
She jabs her wedge-head in a cup
of sour cream, drops her ostrich tail,
and will not scare.

[handwritten annotations: "lower class" / "scavengers are 'ok'"; "trash (decay?)"; "(not scared of)/(at the same level as)/(prosperous through) humans"]

EYE AND TOOTH

My whole eye was sunset red,
the old cut cornea throbbed,
I saw things darkly,
as through an unwashed goldfish globe.

I lay all day on my bed.
I chain-smoked through the night,
learning to flinch
at the flash of the matchlight.

Outside, the summer rain,
a simmer of rot and renewal,
fell in pinpricks.
Even new life is fuel.

My eyes throb.
Nothing can dislodge
the house with my first tooth
noosed in a knot to the doorknob.

Nothing can dislodge
the triangular blotch

of rot on the red roof,
a cedar hedge, or the shade of a hedge.

No ease from the eye
of the sharp-shinned hawk in the birdbook there,
with reddish-brown buffalo hair
on its shanks, one ascetic talon

clasping the abstract imperial sky.
It says:
an eye for an eye,
a tooth for a tooth.

No ease for the boy at the keyhole,
his telescope,
when the women's white bodies flashed
in the bathroom. Young, my eyes began to fail.

decay?   *where does this ???*

Nothing! No oil
for the eye, nothing to pour
on those waters or flames.
I am tired. Everyone's tired of my turmoil.

FOR THE UNION DEAD

ancestor's poetic inscription on statue   *commemorating American history*

"Relinquunt Omnia Servare Rem Publicam."

Lowell : He gives up everything to serve the republic

The old South Boston Aquarium stands
in a Sahara of snow now. Its broken windows are boarded.   *decay ①*
The bronze weathervane cod has lost half its scales.
The airy tanks are dry.

Once my nose crawled like a snail on the glass;
my hand tingled
to burst the bubbles
drifting from the noses of the cowed, compliant fish.

My hand draws back. I often sigh still
for the dark downward and vegetating kingdom
of the fish and reptile. One morning last March,
I pressed against the new barbed and galvanized

builds on history; ironizes it a bit; co-opts it; makes it "fruitless."

fence on the Boston Common. Behind their cage,
yellow dinosaur steamshovels were grunting
as they cropped up tons of mush and grass
to gouge their underworld garage.

Parking spaces luxuriate like civic
sandpiles in the heart of Boston.
A girdle of orange, Puritan-pumpkin colored girders
braces the tingling Statehouse,

shaking over the excavations, as it faces Colonel Shaw
and his bell-cheeked Negro infantry
on St. Gaudens' shaking Civil War relief,
propped by a plank splint against the garage's earthquake.

Two months after marching through Boston,
half the regiment was dead;
at the dedication,
William James could almost hear the bronze Negroes breathe.

Their monument sticks like a fishbone
in the city's throat.
Its Colonel is as lean
as a compass-needle.

He has an angry wrenlike vigilance,
a greyhound's gentle tautness;
he seems to wince at pleasure,
and suffocate for privacy.

He is out of bounds now. He rejoices in man's lovely,
peculiar power to choose life and die —
when he leads his black soldiers to death,
he cannot bend his back.

On a thousand small town New England greens,
the old white churches hold their air
of sparse, sincere rebellion; frayed flags
quilt the graveyards of the Grand Army of the Republic.

The stone statues of the abstract Union Soldier
grow slimmer and younger each year —
wasp-waisted, they doze over muskets
and muse through their sideburns . . .

Shaw's father wanted no monument
except the ditch,
where his son's body was thrown
and lost with his "niggers."

The ditch is nearer.
There are no statues for the last war here;
on Boylston Street, a commercial photograph
shows Hiroshima boiling

over a Mosler Safe, the "Rock of Ages"
that survived the blast. Space is nearer.
When I crouch to my television set,
the drained faces of Negro school-children rise like balloons.

Colonel Shaw
is riding on his bubble,
he waits
for the blessèd break.

The Aquarium is gone. Everywhere,
giant finned cars nose forward like fish;
a savage servility
slides by on grease.

William Matthews

MEN AT MY FATHER'S FUNERAL

The ones his age who shook my hand
on their way out sent fear along
my arm like heroin. These weren't
men mute about their feelings,
or what's a body language for?

And I, the glib one, who'd stood
with my back to my father's body
and praised the heart that attacked him?
I'd made my stab at elegy,
the flesh made word: the very spit

in my mouth was sour with ruth
and eloquence. What could be worse?
Silence, the anthem of my father's
new country. And thus this babble,
like a dial tone, from our bodies.

HOUSEWORK

How precise it seems, like a dollhouse,
and look: the tiniest socks ever knit
are crumpled on a chair in your bedroom.
And how still, like the air inside a church
or basketball. How you could have lived
your boyhood here is hard to know,

unless the blandishing lilacs
and slant rain stippling the lamplight
sustained you, and the friendship of dogs,
and the secrecy that flourishes in vacant lots.
For who would sleep, like a cat in a drawer,
in this house memory is always dusting,

unless it be you? I'd hear you on the stairs,
an avalanche of sneakers, and then the sift
of your absence and then I'd begin to rub
the house like a lantern until you came back
and grew up to be me, wondering how to sleep
in this lie of memory unless it be made clean.

IN MEMORY OF THE UTAH STARS

Each of them must have terrified
his parents by being so big, obsessive
and exact so young, already gone
and leaving, like a big tipper,
that huge changeling's body in his place.
The prince of bone spurs and bad knees.

The year I first saw them play
Malone was a high school freshman,
already too big for any bed,
14, a natural resource.
You have to learn not to
apologize, a form of vanity.
You flare up in the lane, exotic
anywhere else. You roll the ball
off fingers twice as long as your
girlfriend's. Great touch for a big man,
says some jerk. Now they're defunct
and Moses Malone, boy wonder at 19,
rises at 20 from the St. Louis bench,
his pet of a body grown sullen
as fast as it grew up.

Something in you remembers every
time the ball left your fingertips
wrong and nothing the ball
can do in the air will change that.
You watch it set, stupid moon,
the way you watch yourself
in a recurring dream.
You never lose your touch
or forget how taxed bodies

go at the same pace they owe,
how brutally well the universe
works to be beautiful,
how we metabolize loss
as fast as we have to.

PISSING OFF THE BACK OF THE BOAT
INTO THE NIVERNAIS CANAL

It's so cold my cock is furled
like a nutmeat and cold,
for all its warm aspirations
and traffic of urine. 37
years old and it takes me a second
to find it, the poor pink slug,
so far from the brash volunteer
of the boudoir. I arc a few
finishing stutters into the water.
Already they're converted,
opaque and chill. How com-
modious the dark universe is,
and companionable the stars.
How drunk I am. I shake
my shriveled nozzle and three
drops lurk out like syllables
from before there were languages. Snug
in my pants it will leak a whole sentence
in Latin. How like a lock-keeper's
life a penis biography would be,
bucolic and dull. What the penis
knows of sex is only arithmetic.
The tongue can kiss and tell.
But the imagination has,
as usual, most of the fun.
It makes discriminations,
bad jokes. It knows itself
to be tragic and thereby silly.
And it can tell a dull story well,
drop by reluctant drop.
What it can't do is be a body
nor survive time's acid work

on the body it enlivens,
I think as I try not to pitch
my wine-dulled body and wary
imagination with it into the inky
canal by the small force
of tugging my zipper up.
How much damage to themselves
the body and imagination
can absorb, I think as I drizzle
to sleep, and how much
the imagination makes
of its body of work
a place to recover itself.

MOVING AGAIN

At night the mountains look like huge
dim hens. In a few geological eras
new mountains may
shatter the earth's shell
and poke up like stone wings.
Each part must serve for a whole.
I bring my sons to the base
of the foothills and we go up.
From a scruff of ponderosa
pines we startle gaudy swerves
of magpies that settle in our rising
wake. Then there's a blooming
prickly pear. "Jesus, Dad, what's that?"
Willy asks. It's like a yellow tulip
grafted to a cactus: it's a beautiful
wound the cactus puts out
to bear fruit and be healed.
If I lived with my sons
all year I'd be less sentimental
about them. We go up
to the mesa top and look down
at our new hometown. The thin air
warps in the melting light
like the aura before a migraine.

The boys are tired. A tiny magpie
fluffs into a pine far below
and farther down in the valley
of child support and lights
people are opening drawers.
One of them finds a yellowing
patch of newsprint with a phone
number penciled on it
from Illinois, from before they moved, before
Nicky was born. Memory
is our root system.
"Verna," he says to himself
because his wife's in another room,
"whose number do you suppose this is?"

GRIEF

E detto l'ho perché doler ti debbia!
         — *Inferno, xxiv, 151*

Snow coming in parallel to the street,
a cab spinning its tires (a rising whine
like a domestic argument, and then
the words get said that never get forgot),

slush and backed-up runoff waters at each
corner, clogged buses smelling of wet wool . . .
The acrid anger of the homeless swells
like wet rice. *This slop is where I live, bitch,*

a sogged panhandler shrieks to whom it may
concern. But none of us slows down for scorn;
there's someone's misery in all we earn.
But like a bur in a dog's coat his rage

has borrowed legs. We bring it home. It lives
like kin among the angers of the house,
and leaves the same sharp zinc taste in the mouth:
And I have told you this to make you grieve.

WILLIAM MATTHEWS

THE CLOISTER

The last light of a July evening drained
into the streets below. My love and I had hard
things to say and hear, and we sat over
wine, faltering, picking our words carefully.

The afternoon before I had lain across
my bed and my cat leapt up to lie
alongside me, purring and slowly
growing dozy. By this ritual I could

clear some clutter from my baroque brain.
And into that brief vacancy the image
of a horse cantered, coming straight to me,
and I knew it brought hard talk and hurt

and fear. How did we do? A medium job,
which is well above average. But because
she had opened her heart to me as far
as she did, I saw her fierce privacy,

like a gnarled, luxuriant tree all hung
with disappointments, and I knew
that to love her I must love the tree
and the nothing it cares for me.

ONIONS

How easily happiness begins by
dicing onions. A lump of sweet butter
slithers and swirls across the floor
of the sauté pan, especially if its
errant path crosses a tiny slick
of olive oil. Then a tumble of onions.

This could mean soup or risotto
or chutney (from the Sanskrit
chatni, to lick). Slowly the onions
go limp and then nacreous

WILLIAM MATTHEWS

and then what cookbooks call clear,
though if they were eyes you could see

clearly the cataracts in them.
It's true it can make you weep
to peel them, to unfurl and to tease
from the taut ball first the brittle,
caramel-colored and decrepit
papery outside layer, the least

recent the reticent onion
wrapped around its growing body,
for there's nothing to an onion
but skin, and it's true you can go on
weeping as you go on in, through
the moist middle skins, the sweetest

and thickest, and you can go on
in to the core, to the bud-like,
acrid, fibrous skins densely
clustered there, stalky and in-
complete, and these are the most
pungent, like the nuggets of nightmare

and rage and murmury animal
comfort that infant humans secrete.
This is the best domestic perfume.
You sit down to eat with a rumor
of onions still on your twice-washed
hands and lift to your mouth a hint

of a story about loam and usual
endurance. It's there when you clean up
and rinse the wine glasses and make
a joke, and you leave the minutest
whiff of it on the light switch,
later, when you climb the stairs.

James Merrill

THE OCTOPUS

There are many monsters that a glassen surface
Restrains. And none more sinister
Than vision asleep in the eye's tight translucence.
Rarely it seeks now to unloose
Its diamonds. Having divined how drab a prison
The purest mortal tissue is,
Rarely it wakes. Unless, coaxed out by lusters
Extraordinary, like the octopus
From the gloom of its tank half-swimming half-drifting
Toward anything fair, a handkerchief
Or child's face dreaming near the glass, the writher
Advances in a godlike wreath
Of its own wrath. Chilled by such fragile reeling
A hundred blows of a boot-heel
Shall not quell, the dreamer wakes and hungers.
Percussive pulses, drum or gong,
Build in his skull their loud entrancement,
Volutions of a Hindu dance.
His hands move clumsily in the first conventional
Gestures of assent.
He is willing to undergo the volition and fervor
Of many fleshlike arms, observe
These in their holiness of indirection
Destroy, adore, evolve, reject —
Till on glass rigid with his own seizure
At length the sucking jewels freeze.

LABORATORY POEM

Charles used to watch Naomi, taking heart
And a steel saw, open up turtles, live.
While she swore they felt nothing, he would gag
At blood, at the blind twitching, even after
The murky dawn of entrails cleared, revealing
Contours he knew, egg-yellows like lamps paling.

Well then. She carried off the beating heart
To the kymograph and rigged it there, a rag
In fitful wind, now made to strain, now stopped
By her solutions tonic or malign
Alternately in which it would be steeped.
What the heart bore, she noted on a chart,

For work did not stop only with the heart.
He thought of certain human hearts, their climb
Through violence into exquisite disciplines
Of which, as it now appeared, they all expired.
Soon she would fetch another and start over,
Easy in the presence of her lover.

CHARLES ON FIRE

Another evening we sprawled about discussing
Appearances. And it was the consensus
That while uncommon physical good looks
Continued to launch one, as before, in life
(Among its vaporous eddies and false calms),
Still, as one of us said into his beard,
"Without your intellectual and spiritual
Values, man, you are sunk." No one but squared
The shoulders of his own unloveliness.
Long-suffering Charles, having cooked and served the meal,
Now brought out little tumblers finely etched
He filled with amber liquor and then passed.
"Say," said the same young man, "in Paris, France,
They do it this way" — bounding to his feet
And touching a lit match to our host's full glass.
A blue flame, gentle, beautiful, came, went
Above the surface. In a hush that fell
We heard the vessel crack. The contents drained
As who should step down from a crystal coach.
Steward of spirits, Charles's glistening hand
All at once gloved itself in eeriness.
The moment passed. He made two quick sweeps and
Was flesh again. "It couldn't matter less,"
He said, but with a shocked, unconscious glance
Into the mirror. Finding nothing changed,
He filled a fresh glass and sank down among us.

JAMES MERRILL

THE MAD SCENE

Again last night I dreamed the dream called Laundry.
In it, the sheets and towels of a life we were going to share,
The milk-stiff bibs, the shroud, each rag to be ever
Trampled or soiled, bled on or groped for blindly,
Came swooning out of an enormous willow hamper
Onto moon-marbly boards. We had just met. I watched
From outer darkness. I had dressed myself in clothes
Of a new fiber that never stains or wrinkles, never
Wears thin. The opera house sparkled with tiers
And tiers of eyes, like mine enlarged by belladonna,
Trained inward. There I saw the cloud-clot, gust by gust,
Form, and the lightning bite, and the roan mane unloosen.
Fingers were running in panic over the flute's nine gates.
Why did I flinch? I loved you. And in the downpour laughed
To have us wrung white, gnarled together, one
Topmost mordent of wisteria,
As the lean tree burst into grief.

A RENEWAL

Having used every subterfuge
To shake you, lies, fatigue, or even that of passion,
Now I see no way but a clean break.
I add that I am willing to bear the guilt.

You nod assent. Autumn turns windy, huge,
A clear vase of dry leaves vibrating on and on.
We sit, watching. When I next speak
Love buries itself in me, up to the hilt.

THE KIMONO

When I returned from lovers' lane
My hair was white as snow.
Joy, incomprehension, pain
I'd seen like seasons come and go.

How I got home again
Frozen half dead, perhaps you know.

You hide a smile and quote a text:
Desires ungratified
Persist from one life to the next.
Hearths we strip ourselves beside
Long, long ago were x'd
On blueprints of "consuming pride."

Times out of mind, the bubble-gleam
To our charred level drew
April back. A sudden beam . . .
— Keep talking while I change into
The pattern of a stream
Bordered with rushes white on blue.

VOICES FROM THE OTHER WORLD

Presently at our touch the teacup stirred,
Then circled lazily about
From A to Z. The first voice heard
(If they are voices, these mute spellers-out)
Was that of an engineer

Originally from Cologne.
Dead in his 22nd year
Of cholera in Cairo, he had KNOWN
NO HAPPINESS. He once met Goethe, though.
Goethe had told him: PERSEVERE.

Our blind hound whined. With that, a horde
Of voices gathered above the Ouija board,
Some childish and, you might say, blurred
By sleep; one little boy
Named Will, reluctant possibly in a ruff

Like a large-lidded page out of El Greco, pulled
Back the arras for that next voice,
Cold and portentous: ALL IS LOST.

FLEE THIS HOUSE. OTTO VON THURN UND TAXIS.
OBEY. YOU HAVE NO CHOICE.

Frightened, we stopped; but tossed
Till sunrise striped the rumpled sheets with gold.
Each night since then, the moon waxes,
Small insects flit round a cold torch
We light, that sends them pattering to the porch . . .

But no real Sign. New voices come,
Dictate addresses, begging us to write;
Some warn of lives misspent, and all of doom
In ways that so exhilarate
We are sleeping sound of late.

Last night the teacup shattered in a rage.
Indeed, we have grown nonchalant
Towards the other world. In the gloom here,
Our elbows on the cleared
Table, we talk and smoke, pleased to be stirred

Rather by buzzings in the jasmine, by the drone
Of our own voices and poor blind Rover's wheeze,
Than by those clamoring overhead,
Obsessed or piteous, for a commitment
We still have wit to postpone

Because, once looked at lit
By the cold reflections of the dead
Risen extinct but irresistible,
Our lives have never seemed more full, more real,
Nor the full moon more quick to chill.

A DOWNWARD LOOK

Seen from above, the sky
Is deep. Clouds float down there,

Foam on a long, luxurious bath.
Their shadows over limbs submerged in "air,"

Over protuberances, faults,
A delta thicket, glide. On high, the love

That drew the bath and scattered it with salts

Still radiates new projects old as day,
And hardly registers the tug

When, far beneath, a wrinkled, baby hand
Happens upon the plug.

b o d y

Look closely at the letters. Can you see,
entering (stage right), then floating full,
then heading off — so soon —
how like a little kohl-rimmed moon
o plots her course from b to d

— as y, unanswered, knocks at the stage door?
Looked at too long, words fail,
phase out. Ask, now that body shines
no longer, by what light you learn these lines
and what the b and d stood for.

AN UPWARD LOOK

O heart green acre   sown with salt
by the departing   occupier

lay down your gallant   spears of wheat
Salt of the earth   each stellar pinch

flung in blind   defiance backwards
now takes its toll   Up from his quieted

quarry the lover   colder and wiser
hauling himself   finds the world turning

JAMES MERRILL

toys triumphs   toxins into
this vast facility   the living come
dearest to die in   How did it happen

In bright alternation   minutely mirrored
within the thinking   of each and every

mortal creature   halves of a clue
approach the earthlights   Morning star

evening star   salt of the sky
First the grave   dissolving into dawn

then the crucial   recrystallizing
from inmost depths   of clear dark blue

W. S. Merwin

THE POEM

Coming late, as always,
I try to remember what I almost heard.
The light avoids my eye.

How many times have I heard the locks close
And the lark take the keys
And hang them in heaven.

HOW WE ARE SPARED

At midsummer before dawn an orange light returns to the mountains
Like a great weight and the small birds cry out
And bear it up

FOR THE ANNIVERSARY OF MY DEATH

Every year without knowing it I have passed the day
When the last fires will wave to me
And the silence will set out
Tireless traveller
Like the beam of a lightless star

Then I will no longer
Find myself in life as in a strange garment
Surprised at the earth
And the love of one woman
And the shamelessness of men
As today writing after three days of rain
Hearing the wren sing and the falling cease
And bowing not knowing to what

W. S. MERWIN

DEAD HAND

Temptations still nest in it like basilisks.
Hang it up till the rings fall.

THE CHAFF

Those who cannot love the heavens or the earth
beaten from the heavens and the earth
eat each other
those who cannot love each other
beaten from each other
eat themselves
those who cannot love themselves
beaten from themselves
eat a terrible bread
kneaded in the morning shrouded all day
baked in the dark
whose sweet smell brings the chaff flying like empty hands
through the turning sky night after night
calling with voices of young birds
to its wheat

FIELD MUSHROOMS

I never gave a thought to them at first
with their white heads
cut into slices
under a water of plastic on a blue
section of carpet
or even hanging in a scale
like the piled ruins of a foot

I was shown that when the right time came
you could overturn a dry cow pat
by the edge of a long green swamp
late on a cold

autumn afternoon
as the sun was going down
and there underneath
the real white heads were still growing

I went on finding them
always at evening
coming to recognize a depth
in the shade of oaks and chestnuts
a quickening in the moss year after year
a suggestion of burning
signs of something already there in its own place
a texture of flesh
scarcely born
full of the knowledge of darkness

THE ROSE BEETLE

It is said that you came from China
but you never saw China
you eat up the leaves here

your ancestors travelled blind in eggs
you arrive just after dark from underground
with a clicking whir in the first night
knowing by the smell what leaves to eat here
where you have wakened for the first time

the strawberry leaves foreign as you
the beans the orchid tree the eggplant
the old leaves of the heliconia the banana some palms
and the roses from everywhere but here
and the hibiscus from here the abutilons
the royal ilima

in the night you turn them into lace
into an arid net
into sky

like the sky long ago over China

W. S. MERWIN

FOG-HORN

Surely that moan is not the thing
That men thought they were making, when they
Put it there, for their own necessities.
That throat does not call to anything human
But to something men had forgotten,
That stirs under fog. Who wounded that beast
Incurably, or from whose pasture
Was it lost, full grown, and time closed round it
With no way back? Who tethered its tongue
So that its voice could never come
To speak out in the light of clear day,
But only when the shifting blindness
Descends and is acknowledged among us,
As though from under a floor it is heard,
Or as though from behind a wall, always
Nearer than we had remembered? If it
Was we that gave tongue to this cry
What does it bespeak in us, repeating
And repeating, insisting on something
That we never meant? We only put it there
To give warning of something we dare not
Ignore, lest we should come upon it
Too suddenly, recognize it too late,
As our cries were swallowed up and all hands lost.

ST VINCENT'S

Thinking of rain clouds that rose over the city
on the first day of the year

in the same month
I consider that I have lived daily and with
eyes open and ears to hear
these years across from St Vincent's Hospital
above whose roof those clouds rose

its bricks by day a French red under
cross facing south

W. S. MERWIN

blown-up neo-classic facades the tall
dark openings between columns at
the dawn of history
exploded into many windows
in a mortised face

inside it the ambulances have unloaded
after sirens' howling nearer through traffic on
Seventh Avenue long
ago I learned not to hear them
even when the sirens stop

they turn to back in
few passers-by stay to look
and neither do I

at night two long blue
windows and one short one on the top floor
burn all night
many nights when most of the others are out
on what floor do they have
anything

I have seen the building drift moonlit through geraniums
late at night when trucks were few
moon just past the full
upper windows parts of the sky
as long as I looked
I watched it at Christmas and New Year
early in the morning I have seen the nurses ray out through
arterial streets
in the evening have noticed interns blocks away
on doorsteps one foot in the door

I have come upon the men in gloves taking out
the garbage at all hours
piling up mountains of
plastic bags white strata with green intermingled and
black
I have seen one pile
catch fire and studied the cloud
at the ends of the jets of the hoses
the fire engines as near as that

red beacons and
machine-throb heard by the whole body
I have noticed molded containers stacked outside
a delivery entrance on Twelfth Street
whether meals from a meal factory made up with those
mummified for long journeys by plane
or specimens for laboratory
examination sealed at the prescribed temperatures
either way closed delivery

and approached faces staring from above
crutches or tubular clamps
out for tentative walks
have paused for turtling wheel-chairs
heard visitors talking in wind on each corner
while the lights changed and
hot dogs were handed over at the curb
in the middle of afternoon
mustard ketchup onions and relish
and police smelling of ether and laundry
were going back

and I have known them all less than the papers of our days
smoke rises from the chimneys do they have an incinerator
what for
how warm do they believe they have to maintain the air
in there
several of the windows appear
to be made of tin
but it may be the light reflected
I have imagined bees coming and going
on those sills though I have never seen them

who was St Vincent

WHEN YOU GO AWAY

for Dido

When you go away the wind clicks around to the north
The painters work all day but at sundown the paint falls
Showing the black walls

The clock goes back to striking the same hour
That has no place in the years

And at night wrapped in the bed of ashes
In one breath I wake
It is the time when the beards of the dead get their growth
I remember that I am falling
That I am the reason
And that my words are the garment of what I shall never be
Like the tucked sleeve of a one-armed boy

AIR

Naturally it is night.
Under the overturned lute with its
One string I am going my way
Which has a strange sound.

This way the dust, that way the dust.
I listen to both sides
But I keep right on.
I remember the leaves sitting in judgment
And then winter.

I remember the rain with its bundle of roads.
The rain taking all its roads.
Nowhere.

Young as I am, old as I am,

I forget tomorrow, the blind man.
I forget the life among the buried windows.
The eyes in the curtains.
The wall
Growing through the immortelles.
I forget silence
The owner of the smile.

This must be what I wanted to be doing,
Walking at night between the two deserts,
Singing.

Marilyn Nelson

Marilyn Nelson

A WREATH FOR EMMETT TILL

R.I.P. Emmett Louis Till, 1941–1955

I.

Rosemary for remembrance, Shakespeare wrote:
a speech for poor Ophelia, who went mad
when her love killed her father. Flowers had
a language then. Rose petals in a note
said *I love you*; a sheaf of bearded oat
said *Your music enchants me.* Goldenrod:
Be careful. Weeping-willow twigs: *I'm sad.*
What should my wreath for Emmett Till denote?
First, heliotrope, for *Justice shall be done.*
Daisies and white lilacs, for *Innocence.*
Then mandrake: *Horror* (wearing a white hood,
or bare-faced, laughing). For grief, more than one,
for one is not enough: rue, yew, cypress.
Forget-me-nots. Though if I could, I would.

II.

Forget him not. Though if I could, I would
forget much of that racial memory.
No: I remember, like a haunted tree
set off from other trees in the wildwood
by one bare bough. If trees could speak, it could
describe, in words beyond words, make us see
the strange fruit which still ghosts its reverie,
misty companion of its solitude.
Dendrochronology could give its age
in centuries, by counting annual rings:
seasons of drought and rain. But one night blood,
spilled at its roots, blighted its foliage.
Pith outward, it has been slowly dying,
pierced by the screams of a shortened childhood.

III.

Pierced by the screams of a shortened childhood,
my heartwood has been scarred for fifty years

349

by what I heard, with hundreds of green ears.
That jackal laughter. Two hundred years I stood
listening to small struggles to find food,
to the songs of creature life, which disappears
and comes again, to the music of the spheres.
Two hundred years of deaths I understood.
Then slaughter axed one quiet summer night,
shivering the deep silence of the stars.
A running boy, five men in close pursuit.
One dark, five pale faces in the moonlight.
Noise, silence, back-slaps. One match, five cigars.
Emmett Till's name still catches in the throat.

IV.

Emmett Till's name still catches in my throat,
like syllables waylaid in a stutterer's mouth.
A fourteen-year old stutterer, in the South
to visit relatives, and to be taught
the family's ways. His mother had finally bought
that White Sox cap; she'd made him swear an oath
to be careful around white folks. She'd told him the truth
of many a Mississippi anecdote:
Some white folks have blind souls. In his suitcase
she'd packed dungarees, t-shirts, underwear
and comic books. She'd given him a note
for the conductor, waved to his chubby face,
wondered if he'd remember to brush his hair.
Her only child. A body left to bloat.

V.

Your only child a body thrown to bloat,
mother of sorrows, of justice denied.
Surely you must have thought of suicide,
seeing his gray flesh, chains around his throat.
Surely you didn't know you would devote
the rest of your changed life to dignified
public remembrance of how Emmett died,
innocence slaughtered by the hands of hate.
If sudden loving light proclaimed you blest
would you bow your head in humility,
your healed heart overflow with gratitude?
Would you say yes, like the mother of Christ?

MARILYN NELSON

Or would you say no to your destiny,
mother of a boy martyr, if you could?

VI.

Mutilated boy martyr, if I could,
I'd put you in a parallel universe,
give you a better fate. There is none worse.
I'd let you live through a happy boyhood,
let your gifts bloom into a livelihood
on a planet which didn't bear Cain's curse.
I'd put you in a nice, safe universe,
not like this one. A universe where you'd
surpass your mother's dreams. But parallel
realities may have terrorists, too.
Evil multiplies to infinitude,
like mirrors facing each other in hell.
You were a wormhole history passed through,
transformed by the memory of your victimhood.

VII.

Erase the memory of Emmett's victimhood.
Let's write the obituary of a life
lived well and wisely, mourned by a loving wife
or partner, friends, and a vast multitude.
Remember the high purpose he pursued.
Remember how he earned a nation's grief.
Remember accomplishments beyond belief,
honors enough to make us *ooh* slack-jawed,
as if we looked up at a meteor shower
or were children watching a fireworks display.
Let America remember what he taught.
Or at least let him die in a World Trade Tower
rescuing others, that unforgettable day,
that memory of monsters, that bleak thought.

VIII.

The memory of monsters: That bleak thought
should be confined to a horror-movie world.
A horror classic, in which a blind girl
hears, one by one, the windows broken out,

an axe at the front door. In the onslaught
of terror, as a hate-filled body hurls
itself against her door, her senses swirl
around one prayer: Please, God, forget me not.
The body-snatchers jiggle the doorknob,
werewolves and vampires slaver after blood,
the circus of nightmares is here. She screams,
he screams, neighbors with names he knows, a mob
heartless and heedless, answering to no god,
tears through the patchwork drapery of our dreams.

IX.

Tears, through the patchwork drapery of dream,
for the hanging bodies, the men on flaming pyres,
the crowds standing around like devil choirs,
the children's eyes lit by the fire's gleams
filled with the delight of licking ice cream,
men who hear hog screams as a man expires,
watch fob good-luck charms teeth pulled out with pliers,
sinners I can't believe Christ's death redeems,
your ash hair Shulamith, Emmett your eye,
machetes, piles of shoes, bull-dozed mass graves,
the broken towers, the air filled with last breaths,
the blasphemies pronounced to justify
the profane, obscene theft of human lives.
Let me gather spring flowers for a wreath.

X.

Let me gather spring flowers for a wreath.
Not lilacs from the door-yard, but wild-flowers
I'd search for in the greening woods for hours
of solitude, meditating on death.
Let me wander through pathless woods, beneath
the choirs of small birds trumpeting their powers
at the intruder trampling through their bowers,
disturbing their peace. I cling to the faith
that innocence lives on, that a blind soul
can see again. That miracles do exist.
In my house, there is still something called grace,
which melts ice-shards of hate, and makes hearts whole.
I bear arm-loads of flowers home, to twist
into a circle: Trillium, Queen Anne's lace . . .

XI.

Trillium, apple-blossoms, Queen Anne's lace,
woven with oak twigs, for sincerity . . .
Thousands of oak trees around this country
groaned with the weight of men slain for their race,
their murderers acquitted in almost every case.
One night five black men died on the same tree,
with toeless feet, in this Land of the Free.
This country we love has a Janus-face:
One mouth speaks with forked tongue, the other reads
the Constitution. My country, 'tis of both
thy nightmare history and thy grand dream,
thy centuries of good and evil deeds,
I sing. Thy fruited plain, thy undergrowth
of mandrake, which flowers white as moonbeams.

XII.

Indian-pipe, bloodroot. White as moonbeams,
their flowers. Picked, one blackens, and one bleeds
a thick red sap. Indian-pipe, a weed
which thrives on rot, is held in disesteem,
though it does have its use in nature's scheme,
unlike the rose. The bloodroot poppy needs
no explanation here: Its red sap pleads
the case for its inclusion in the theme
of a wreath for the memory of Emmett Till.
Though the white poppy means *forgetfulness*,
who could forget, when red sap on a wreath
recalls the brown boy five white monsters killed?
Forgetting would call for consciencelessness.
Like the full moon, which smiled calmly on his death.

XIII.

Like the full moon which smiled calmly on his death.
Like the stars which fluttered their quicksilver wings.
Like the unbroken song creation sings
while humankind tramples the grapes of wrath.
Like wildflowers growing along the path
a boy was dragged along, blood spattering
their white petals as he, abandoning

all hope, gasped his agonizing last breath.
Like a nation sending its children off to fight
our faceless enemy, immortal fear,
the most feared enemy of the human race.
Like a plague of not knowing wrong from right.
Like the consciencelessness of the atmosphere.
Like a gouged eye, watching boots kick a face.

XIV.

Like his gouged eye, which watched boots kick his face,
we must bear witness to atrocity.
But we are whole: We can speak what we see.
People may disappear leaving no trace
unless we stand before the populace,
orators denouncing the slavery
to fear. For the lynchers feared the lynchee,
what he might do, being of another race,
a great unknown. They feared because they saw
their own inner shadows, their vicious dreams,
the farthest horizons of their own thought,
their jungles immune to the rule of law.
We can speak now, or bear unforgettable shame.
Rosemary for remembrance, Shakespeare wrote.

XV.

Rosemary for remembrance, Shakespeare wrote.
If I could forget, believe me, I would.
Pierced by the screams of a shortened childhood,
Emmett Till's name still catches in my throat.
Mamie's one child a body thrown to bloat,
Mutilated boy martyr. If I could
Erase the memory of Emmett's victimhood,
The memory of monsters . . . That bleak thought
Tears through the patchwork drapery of dreams.
Let me gather spring flowers for a wreath:
Trillium, apple-blossoms, Queen Anne's lace,
Indian-pipe, bloodroot, white as moonbeams,
Like the full moon which smiled calmly on his death,
Like his gouged eye, which watched boots kick his face.

MARILYN NELSON

MINOR MIRACLE

Which reminds me of another knock-on-wood
memory. I was cycling with a male friend,
through a small midwestern town. We came to a 4-way
stop and stopped, chatting. As we started again,
a rusty old pick-up truck, ignoring the stop sign,
hurricaned past scant inches from our front wheels.
My partner called, "Hey, that was a 4-way stop!"
The truck driver, stringy blond hair a long fringe
under his brand-name beer cap, looked back and yelled,
        "You fucking niggers!"
And sped off.
My friend and I looked at each other and shook our heads.
We remounted our bikes and headed out of town.
We were pedaling through a clear blue afternoon
between two fields of almost-ripened wheat
bordered by cornflowers and Queen Anne's lace
when we heard an unmuffled motor, a honk-honking.
We stopped, closed ranks, made fists.
It was the same truck. It pulled over.
A tall, very much in shape young white guy slid out:
greasy jeans, homemade finger tattoos, probably
a Marine Corps boot-camp footlockerful
of martial arts techniques.

"What did you say back there!" he shouted.
My friend said, "I said it was a 4-way stop.
You went through it."
"And what did I say?" the white guy asked.
"You said: 'You fucking niggers.'"
The afternoon froze.

"Well," said the white guy,
shoving his hands into his pockets
and pushing dirt around with the pointed toe of his boot,
"I just want to say I'm sorry."
He climbed back into his truck
and drove away.

Naomi Shihab Nye

VOCABULARY OF DEARNESS

How a single word
may shimmer and rise
off the page, a wafer of
syllabic light, a bulb
of glowing meaning,
whatever the word,
try "tempestuous" or "suffer,"
any word you have held
or traded so it lives a new life
the size of two worlds.
Say you carried it
up a hill and it helped you
move. Without this
the days would be thin sticks
thrown down in a clutter of leaves,
and where is the rake?

STEPS

A man letters the sign for his grocery in Arabic and English.
Paint dries more quickly in English.
The thick swoops and curls of Arabic letters stay moist
and glistening till tomorrow when the children show up
jingling their dimes.

They have learned the currency of the New World,
carrying wishes for gum and candies shaped like fish.
They float through the streets, diving deep to the bottom,
nosing rich layers of crusted shell.

One of these children will tell a story that keeps her people
alive. We don't know yet which one she is.
Girl in the red sweater dangling a book bag,
sister with eyes pinned to the barrel of pumpkin seeds.
They are lettering the sidewalk with their steps.

They are separate and together and a little bit late.
Carrying a creased note, "Don't forget."
Who wrote it? They've already forgotten.
A purple fish sticks to the back of the throat.
Their long laughs are boats they will ride and ride,
making the shadows that cross each other's smiles.

ARABIC

(Jordan, 1992)

The man with laughing eyes stopped smiling
to say, "Until you speak Arabic —
— you will not understand pain."

Something to do with the back of the head,
an Arab carries sorrow in the back of the head
that only language cracks, the thrum of stones

weeping, grating hinge on an old metal gate.
"Once you know," he whispered, "you can enter the room
whenever you need to. Music you heard from a distance,

the slapped drum of a stranger's wedding,
wells up inside your skin, inside rain, a thousand
pulsing tongues. You are changed."

Outside, the snow had finally stopped.
In a land where snow rarely falls,
we had felt our days grow white and still.

I thought pain had no tongue. Or every tongue
at once, supreme translator, sieve. I admit my
shame. To live on the brink of Arabic, tugging

its rich threads without understanding
how to weave the rug . . . I have no gift.
The sound, but not the sense.

I kept looking over his shoulder for someone else
to talk to, recalling my dying friend who only scrawled
I can't write. What good would any grammar have been

to her then? I touched his arm, held it hard,
which sometimes you don't do in the Middle East, and said,
I'll work on it, feeling sad

for his good strict heart, but later in the slick street
hailed a taxi by shouting *Pain!* and it stopped
in every language and opened its doors.

THE SMALL VASES FROM HEBRON

Tip their mouths open to the sky.
Turquoise, amber,
the deep green with fluted handle,
pitcher the size of two thumbs,
tiny lip and graceful waist.

Here we place the smallest flower
which could have lived invisibly
in loose soil beside the road,
sprig of succulent rosemary,
bowing mint.

They grow deeper in the center of the table.

Here we entrust the small life,
thread, fragment, breath.
And it bends. It waits all day.
As the bread cools and the children
open their gray copybooks
to shape the letter that looks like
a chimney rising out of a house.

And what do the headlines say?

Nothing of the smaller petal
perfectly arranged inside the larger petal
or the way tinted glass filters light.
Men and boys, praying when they died,
fall out of their skins.
The whole alphabet of living,
heads and tails of words,

sentences, the way they said,
"Ya'Allah!" when astonished,
or "ya'ani" for "I mean" —
a crushed glass under the feet
still shines.
But the child of Hebron sleeps
with the thud of her brothers falling
and the long sorrow of the color red.

THE SHAPES OF MOUTHS AT PARTIES

A mouth like a hammer
pounding out its own tale.
Sometimes I float among the mouths
carrying my own like an unpicked plum.
The man who tells about crashing in an airplane
does not need my "Oh really?" for his story to go on.
As if we were standing at some coast,
things continue without our help,
the predictable waves, the smooth-backed shells,
and the mouths like jellyfish swelling . . .
As if the mouth were the opening
most suited to knowledge and communication,
more than the weightless eye,
landing carefully on each occupied chair,
the fluent nose, vibrantly awake
before the mouth names what it is eating,
or the hand, the articulate hand,
which comes undressed to every party,
opens easily to receive wine or cake,
and secretly converses with the rug, the dog, the air.

MORNING PAPER, SOCIETY PAGE

I can never see fashion models,
lean angular cheeks, strutting hips
and blooming hair, without thinking of
the skulls at the catacombs in Lima, Peru.

How we climbed down from blurred markets
to find a thousand unnamed friends smiling at us
as if they too could advertise
a coming style.

WHAT BRINGS US OUT

Something about pumpkins caused
the man who had not spoken in three years
to lean forward, cough, open his mouth.
How the room heaved into silence,
his words enormous in that air:
"I won't . . . be . . . afraid . . .
of my . . . father . . . anymore."
And what silence followed,
as if each heart had spoken
its most secret terror,
had combed the tangled clump
for the hardest line
and pulled it, intact,
from the mass.

I bless that man forever
for his courage, his voice
which started with one thing
and went to many, opening up and up
to the rim of the world.
So much silence had given him
a wisdom which held us all at bay,
amazed. Sometimes when I see
mountains of pumpkins by the roadside,
or watermelons, a hill of autumn gourds
piled lavishly on crates, I think
perhaps this one, or that, were it to
strike someone right,
this curl of hardened stalk,
this pleated skin . . .
or, on an old bureau drawer,
the vegetable-like roundness of a glass knob
that the baby turns and turns
emerging, later, from a complicated dream . . .

the huge navigational face of a radio
which never worked while I was alive
but gave me more to go on than most sounds:
how what brings us out may be
small as that black arrow, swinging
the wide arc, the numbers where silent voices lived,
how fast you had to turn to make it move.

THE LAST DAY OF AUGUST

A man in a lawn chair
with a book on his lap

realizes pears are falling
from the tree right beside him.

Each makes a round,
full sound in the grass.

Perhaps the stem takes an hour
to loosen and let go.

This man who has recently written words
to his father forty years in the birthing:

I was always afraid of you.
When would you explode next?

has sudden reverence for the pears.
If a dark bruise rises,

if ants inhabit the juicy crack,
or the body remains firm, unscarred,

remains secret till tomorrow . . .
By then the letter to his father

may be lying open on a table.
We gather pears in baskets, sacks.

What will we do with everything
that has been given us? Ginger pears, pear pies,

fingers weighing flesh.
Which will be perfect under the skin?

It is hard not to love the pile of peelings
growing on the counter next to the knife.

THE TRAVELING ONION

*It is believed that the onion originally came from India. In
Egypt it was an object of worship — why I haven't been able
to find out. From Egypt the onion entered Greece and on to
Italy, thence into all of Europe.*

— *Better Living Cookbook*

When I think how far the onion has traveled
just to enter my stew today, I could kneel and praise
all small forgotten miracles,
crackly paper peeling on the drainboard,
pearly layers in smooth agreement,
the way knife enters onion
and onion falls apart on the chopping block,
a history revealed.

And I would never scold the onion
for causing tears.
It is right that tears fall
for something small and forgotten.
How at meal, we sit to eat,
commenting on texture of meat or herbal aroma
but never on the translucence of onion,
now limp, now divided,
or its traditionally honorable career:
For the sake of others,
disappear.

Renate Ponsold

Frank O'Hara

WHY I AM NOT A PAINTER

I am not a painter, I am a poet.
Why? I think I would rather be
a painter, but I am not. Well,

for instance, Mike Goldberg
is starting a painting. I drop in.
"Sit down and have a drink" he
says. I drink; we drink. I look up.
"You have SARDINES in it."
"Yes, it needed something there."
"Oh." I go and the days go by
and I drop in again. The painting is
going on, and I go, and the days
go by. I drop in. The painting is
finished. "Where's SARDINES?"
All that's left is just
letters, "It was too much," Mike says.

But me? One day I am thinking of
a color: orange. I write a line
about orange. Pretty soon it is a
whole page of words, not lines.
Then another page. There should be
so much more, not of orange, of
words, of how terrible orange is
and life. Days go by. It is even in
prose, I am a real poet. My poem
is finished and I haven't mentioned
orange yet. It's twelve poems, I call
it ORANGES. And one day in a gallery
I see Mike's painting, called SARDINES.

FRANK O'HARA

POEM

I don't know as I get what D. H. Lawrence is driving at
when he writes of lust springing from the bowels
or do I
it could be the bowels of the earth
to lie flat on the earth in spring, summer or winter is sexy
you feel it stirring deep down slowly up to you
and sometimes it gives you a little nudge in the crotch
that's very sexy
and when someone looks sort of raggedy and dirty like Paulette Goddard
in *Modern Times* it's exciting, it isn't usual or attractive
perhaps D.H.L. is thinking of the darkness
certainly the crotch is light
and I suppose
any part of us that can only be seen by others
is a dark part
I feel that about the small of my back, too and the nape of my neck
they are dark
they are erotic zones as in the tropics
whereas Paris is straightforward and bright about it all
a coal miner has kind of a sexy occupation
though I'm sure it's painful down there
but so is lust
of light we can never have enough
but how would we find it
unless the darkness urged us on and into it
and I am dark
except when now and then it all comes clear
and I can see myself
as others luckily sometimes see me
in a good light

PERSONAL POEM

Now when I walk around at lunchtime
I have only two charms in my pocket
an old Roman coin Mike Kanemitsu gave me
and a bolt-head that broke off a packing case
when I was in Madrid the others never

brought me too much luck though they did
help keep me in New York against coercion
but now I'm happy for a time and interested

I walk through the luminous humidity
passing the House of Seagram with its wet
and its loungers and the construction to
the left that closed the sidewalk if
I ever get to be a construction worker
I'd like to have a silver hat please
and get to Moriarty's where I wait for
LeRoi and hear who wants to be a mover and
shaker the last five years my batting average
is .016 that's that, and LeRoi comes in
and tells me Miles Davis was clubbed 12
times last night outside BIRDLAND by a cop
a lady asks us for a nickel for a terrible
disease but we don't give her one we
don't like terrible diseases, then

we go eat some fish and some ale it's
cool but crowded we don't like Lionel Trilling
we decide, we like Don Allen we don't like
Henry James so much we like Herman Melville
we don't want to be in the poets' walk in
San Francisco even we just want to be rich
and walk on girders in our silver hats
I wonder if one person out of the 8,000,000 is
thinking of me as I shake hands with LeRoi
and buy a strap for my wristwatch and go
back to work happy at the thought possibly so

STEPS

How funny you are today New York
like Ginger Rogers in *Swingtime*
and St. Bridget's steeple leaning a little to the left

here I have just jumped out of a bed full of V-days
(I got tired of D-days) and blue you there still
accepts me foolish and free

all I want is a room up there
and you in it
and even the traffic halt so thick is a way
for people to rub up against each other
and when their surgical appliances lock
they stay together
for the rest of the day (what a day)
I go by to check a slide and I say
that painting's not so blue

where's Lana Turner
she's out eating
and Garbo's backstage at the Met
everyone's taking their coat off
so they can show a rib-cage to the rib-watchers
and the park's full of dancers with their tights and shoes
in little bags
who are often mistaken for worker-outers at the West Side Y
why not
the Pittsburgh Pirates shout because they won
and in a sense we're all winning
we're alive

the apartment was vacated by a gay couple
who moved to the country for fun
they moved a day too soon
even the stabbings are helping the population explosion
though in the wrong country
and all those liars have left the UN
the Seagram Building's no longer rivalled in interest
not that we need liquor (we just like it)

and the little box is out on the sidewalk
next to the delicatessen
so the old man can sit on it and drink beer
and get knocked off it by his wife later in the day
while the sun is still shining

oh god it's wonderful
to get out of bed
and drink too much coffee
and smoke too many cigarettes
and love you so much

POEM

Lana Turner has collapsed!
I was trotting along and suddenly
it started raining and snowing
and you said it was hailing
but hailing hits you on the head
hard so it was really snowing and
raining and I was in such a hurry
to meet you but the traffic
was acting exactly like the sky
and suddenly I see a headline
LANA TURNER HAS COLLAPSED!
there is no snow in Hollywood
there is no rain in California
I have been to lots of parties
and acted perfectly disgraceful
but I never actually collapsed
oh Lana Turner we love you get up

FOR GRACE, AFTER A PARTY

You do not always know what I am feeling.
Last night in the warm spring air while I was
blazing my tirade against someone who doesn't
interest
            me, it was love for you that set me
afire,
        and isn't it odd? for in rooms full of
strangers my most tender feelings
                                    writhe and
bear the fruit of screaming. Put out your hand,
isn't there
            an ashtray, suddenly, there? beside
the bed? And someone you love enters the room
and says wouldn't
                    you like the eggs a little
different today?
                And when they arrive they are
just plain scrambled eggs and the warm weather
is holding.

FRANK O'HARA

THE DAY LADY DIED

It is 12:20 in New York a Friday
three days after Bastille day, yes
it is 1959 and I go get a shoeshine
because I will get off the 4:19 in Easthampton
at 7:15 and then go straight to dinner
and I don't know the people who will feed me

I walk up the muggy street beginning to sun
and have a hamburger and a malted and buy
an ugly NEW WORLD WRITING to see what the poets
in Ghana are doing these days
                                    I go on to the bank
and Miss Stillwagon (first name Linda I once heard)
doesn't even look up my balance for once in her life
and in the GOLDEN GRIFFIN I get a little Verlaine
for Patsy with drawings by Bonnard although I do
think of Hesiod, trans. Richmond Lattimore or
Brendan Behan's new play or *Le Balcon* or *Les Nègres*
of Genet, but I don't, I stick with Verlaine
after practically going to sleep with quandariness

and for Mike I just stroll into the PARK LANE
Liquor Store and ask for a bottle of Strega and
then I go back where I came from to 6th Avenue
and the tobacconist in the Ziegfeld Theatre and
casually ask for a carton of Gauloises and a carton
of Picayunes, and a NEW YORK POST with her face on it

and I am sweating a lot by now and thinking of
leaning on the john door in the 5 SPOT
while she whispered a song along the keyboard
to Mal Waldron and everyone and I stopped breathing

GETTING UP AHEAD OF SOMEONE (SUN)

I cough a lot (sinus?) so I
get up and have some tea with cognac
it is dawn
                the light flows evenly along the lawn

in chilly Southampton and I smoke
and hours and hours go by I read
van Vechten's *Spider Boy* then a short
story by Patsy Southgate and a poem
by myself it is cold and I shiver a little
in white shorts the day begun
so oddly not tired not nervous I
am for once truly awake letting it all
start slowly as I watch instead of
grabbing on late as usual

          where did it go
          it's not really awake yet
          I will wait

and the house wakes up and goes
to get the dog in Sag Harbor I make
myself a bourbon and commence
to write one of my "I do this I do that"
poems in a sketch pad

          it is tomorrow
though only six hours have gone by
each day's light has more significance these days

Sharon Olds

MONARCHS

All morning, as I sit thinking of you,
the Monarchs are passing. Seven stories up,
to the left of the river, they are making their way
south, their wings the dark red of
your hands like butchers' hands, the raised
veins of their wings like your scars.
I could scarcely feel your massive rough
palms on me, your touch was so light,
the delicate chapped scrape of an insect's leg
across my breast. No one had ever
touched me before. I didn't know enough to
open my legs, but felt your thighs,
feathered with red-gold hairs,
        opening
between my legs like a
pair of wings.
The hinged print of my blood on your thigh —
a winged creature pinned there —
and then you left, as you were to leave
over and over, the butterflies moving
in masses past my window, floating
south to their transformation, crossing over
borders in the night, the diffuse blood-red
cloud of them, my body under yours,
the beauty and silence of the great migrations.

A WOMAN IN HEAT WIPING HERSELF

High in the inner regions of my body
this gloss is spun, high up
under the overhanging ledge where the
light pours down on the cliff night and day.
No workers stand around in the
camaraderie of workers,
no one lays the color down on the

lip of the braid, there is only the light,
bands and folds of light, and the clean
sand at the edge, the working surface — there is
no one around for miles, no one hungry,
no one being fed. Just as in the side of the
lamb no one is tending the hole where the
light pours out, no one is folding or
carding while the gold grease of the floss
flows through the follicle, beading and rippling back and
curving forward in solemn spillage.
Things done with no reference to the human.
Most things are done with no reference to the human
even if they happen inside us, in our
body that is far beyond our powers, that we could
never invent. Deep in my sex, the
glittering threads are thrown outward and thrown outward
the way the sea lifts up the whole edge of its body,
the rim, the slit where once or twice in a lifetime
you can look through and see the other world —
it is this world, without us,
this earth and our bodies
without us watching.

EARLY IMAGES OF HEAVEN

It amazed me that the shapes of penises,
their sizes, and angles, everything about them
was the way I would have designed them if I had
invented them. The skin, the way the skin
thickens and thins, its suppleness,
the way the head barely fits in the throat,
its mouth almost touching the valve of the stomach —
and the hair, which lifts, or crinkles, delicate
and free — I could not get over all this,
the passion for it as intense in me
as if it were made to my order, or my
desire made to its order — as if I had
known it before I was born, as if
I remembered coming through it, like God
the Father all around me.

SHARON OLDS

THE POPE'S PENIS

It hangs deep in his robes, a delicate
clapper at the center of a bell.
It moves when he moves, a ghostly fish in a
halo of silver seaweed, the hair
swaying in the dark and the heat — and at night,
while his eyes sleep, it stands up
in praise of God.

THE ELDER SISTER

When I look at my elder sister now
I think how she had to go first, down through the
birth canal, to force her way
head-first through the tiny channel,
the pressure of Mother's muscles on her brain,
the tight walls scraping her skin.
Her face is still narrow from it, the long
hollow cheeks of a Crusader on a tomb,
and her inky eyes have the look of someone who has
been in prison a long time and
knows they can send her back. I look at her
body and think how her breasts were the first to
rise, slowly, like swans on a pond.
By the time mine came along, they were just
two more birds in the flock, and when the hair
rose on the white mound of her flesh, like
threads of water out of the ground, it was the
first time, but when mine came
they knew about it. I used to think
only in terms of her harshness, sitting and
pissing on me in bed, but now I
see I had her before me always
like a shield. I look at her wrinkles, her clenched
jaws, her frown-lines — I see they are
the dents on my shield, the blows that did not reach me.
She protected me, not as a mother
protects a child, with love, but as a

hostage protects the one who makes her
escape as I made my escape, with my sister's
body held in front of me.

THE LIFTING

Suddenly my father lifted up his nightie, I
turned my head away but he cried out
Shar!, my nickname, so I turned and looked.
He was sitting in the high cranked-up hospital bed with the
gown up, around his neck,
to show me the weight he had lost. I looked
where his solid ruddy stomach had been
and I saw the skin fallen into loose
soft hairy rippled folds
lying in a pool of folds
down at the base of his abdomen,
the gaunt torso of a big man
who will die soon. Right away
I saw how much his hips are like mine,
the long, white angles, and then
how much his pelvis is shaped like my daughter's,
a chambered whelk-shell hollowed out,
I saw the folds of skin like something
poured, a thick batter, I saw
his rueful smile, the cast-up eyes as he
shows me his old body, he knows
I will be interested, he knows I will find him
appealing. If anyone had told me I would sit
by him and he would pull up his nightie and I would look
at him, his naked body, the thick
bud of his glans, his penis in all that
dark hair, look at him
in affection and uneasy wonder
I would not have believed it. But now I can still
see the tiny snowflakes, white and
night-blue, on the cotton of the gown as it
rises the way we were promised at death it would rise,
the veils would fall from our eyes, we would know everything.

SHARON OLDS

THE GLASS

I think of it with wonder now,
the glass of mucus that stood on the table
next to my father all weekend. The cancer is
growing fast in his throat now,
and as it grows it sends out pus like the
sun sending out solar flares, those
pouring tongues of fire. So my father has to
gargle, hack, cough, and spit a
mouth full of thick stuff
into the glass every ten minutes or so,
scraping the glass up his lower lip to
get the last bit off his skin, then he
sets the glass down on the table and it
sits there, shiny and faintly
gold like a glass of beer foam, he
gurgles and reaches for it again and
gets the heavy sputum out,
full of bubbles and moving around like yeast — he is
like some god producing dark food from his own mouth.
He himself can eat nothing anymore,
just a swallow of milk sometimes,
cut with water, and even then it
can't always get past the tumor,
and the next time the saliva comes up it's
chalkish and ropey, he has to roll it a
long time in his throat like a ball of
clay to form it and get it up and dis-
gorge the elliptical globule into the cup —
and the wonder to me is that it did not disgust me,
that glass of phlegm that stood there all day and
filled slowly with compound globes and then I'd
empty it and it would fill again and
shimmer there on the table until the
room seemed to turn around it
in an orderly way, like a model of the solar system
turning around the gold sun,
my father like the dark earth that
used to be the center of the universe, now
turning with the rest of us
around his death — bright glass of
spit on the table, these last mouthfuls of his life.

SHARON OLDS

MAY 1968

When the Dean said we could not cross campus
until the students gave up the buildings,
we lay down, in the street,
we said the cops will enter this gate
over us. Lying back on the cobbles,
I saw the buildings of New York City
from dirt level, they soared up
and stopped, chopped off — above them, the sky,
the night air over the island.
The mounted police moved, near us,
while we sang, and then I began to count,
12, 13, 14, 15,
I counted again, 15, 16, one
month since the day on that deserted beach,
17, 18, my mouth fell open,
my hair on the street,
if my period did not come tonight
I was pregnant. I could see the sole of a cop's
shoe, the gelding's belly, its genitals —
if they took me to Women's Detention and did
the exam on me, the speculum,
the fingers — I gazed into the horse's tail
like a comet-train. All week, I had
thought about getting arrested, half-longed
to give myself away. On the tar —
one brain in my head, another,
in the making, near the base of my tail —
I looked at the steel arc of the horse's
shoe, the curve of its belly, the cop's
nightstick, the buildings streaming up
away from the earth. I knew I should get up
and leave, but I lay there looking at the space
above us, until it turned deep blue and then
ashy, colorless, *Give me this one
night,* I thought, *and I'll give this child
the rest of my life,* the horses' heads,
this time, drooping, dipping, until
they slept in a circle around my body and my daughter.

SHARON OLDS

GOOD WILL

Sorting clothes, I find our son's old
jeans, the dirt worn so deeply in
they are almost tan, worked as a palimpsest,
the nub down to a flat gloss,
the metal of the rivets soured to ochre,
the back pockets curved like shields,
their stitching is like water far from land,
a long continuous swell. *Lee,*
the pants say in auric print,
LEE, they say in letters branded
in leather on the waistband, like the voice of a boy's
pants, the snap's rattle, the rough
descending and ascending scale of the zipper,
the coin-slot pocket inside the front pocket.
He had waited inside me so many years, his
egg in my side before I was born,
and he sprang fresh in his father that morning,
I had seen it long ago in science,
I shake out the jeans, and there are the knees
exploded, the white threads hanging
outside the body, the frail, torn,
blue knee open, singing of the boy.

Mary Oliver

WHERE DOES THE DANCE BEGIN,
WHERE DOES IT END?

Don't call this world adorable, or useful, that's not it.
It's frisky, and a theater for more than fair winds.
The eyelash of lightning is neither good nor evil.
The struck tree burns like a pillar of gold.

But the blue rain sinks, straight to the white
        feet of the trees
whose mouths open.
Doesn't the wind, turning in circles, invent the dance?
Haven't the flowers moved, slowly, across Asia, then Europe,
        until at last, now, they shine
                in your own yard?

Don't call this world an explanation, or even an education.

When the Sufi poet whirled, was he looking
outward, to the mountains so solidly there
in a white-capped ring, or was he looking

to the center of everything: the seed, the egg, the idea
that was also there,
beautiful as a thumb
curved and touching the finger, tenderly,
little love-ring,

as he whirled,
oh jug of breath,
in the garden of dust?

SLEEPING IN THE FOREST

I thought the earth
remembered me, she
took me back so tenderly, arranging
her dark skirts, her pockets
full of lichens and seeds. I slept

MARY OLIVER

as never before, a stone
on the riverbed, nothing
between me and the white fire of the stars
but my thoughts, and they floated
light as moths among the branches
of the perfect trees. All night
I heard the small kingdoms breathing
around me, the insects, and the birds
who do their work in the darkness. All night
I rose and fell, as if in water, grappling
with a luminous doom. By morning
I had vanished at least a dozen times
into something better.

SPRING AZURES

In spring the blue azures bow down
at the edges of shallow puddles
to drink the black rain water.
Then they rise and float away into the fields.

Sometimes the great bones of my life feel so heavy,
and all the tricks my body knows —
the opposable thumbs, the kneecaps,
and the mind clicking and clicking —

don't seem enough to carry me through this world
and I think: how I would like

to have wings —
blue ones —
ribbons of flame.

How I would like to open them, and rise
from the black rain water.

And then I think of Blake, in the dirt and sweat of London — a boy
staring through the window, when God came
fluttering up.

Of course, he screamed,
seeing the bobbin of God's blue body
leaning on the sill,
and the thousand-faceted eyes.

Well, who knows.
Who knows what hung, fluttering, at the window
between him and the darkness.

Anyway, Blake the hosier's son stood up
and turned away from the sooty sill and the dark city —
turned away forever
from the factories, the personal strivings,

to a life of the imagination.

LITTLE OWL WHO LIVES IN THE ORCHARD

His beak could open a bottle,
and his eyes — when he lifts their soft lids —
go on reading something
just beyond your shoulder —
Blake, maybe,
or the Book of Revelation.

Never mind that he eats only
the black-smocked crickets,
and dragonflies if they happen
to be out late over the ponds, and of course
the occasional festal mouse.
Never mind that he is only a memo
from the offices of fear —

it's not size but surge that tells us
when we're in touch with something real,
and when I hear him in the orchard
fluttering
down the little aluminum
ladder of his scream —
when I see his wings open, like two black ferns,

a flurry of palpitations
as cold as sleet
rackets across the marshlands
of my heart,
like a wild spring day.

Somewhere in the universe,
in the gallery of important things,

the babyish owl, ruffled and rakish,
sits on its pedestal.
Dear, dark dapple of plush!
A message, reads the label,
from that mysterious conglomerate:
Oblivion and Co.
The hooked head stares
from its blouse of dark, feathery lace.
It could be a valentine.

UNIVERSITY HOSPITAL, BOSTON

The trees on the hospital lawn
are lush and thriving. They too
are getting the best of care,
like you, and the anonymous many,
in the clean rooms high above this city,
where day and night the doctors keep
arriving, where intricate machines
chart with cool devotion
the murmur of the blood,
the slow patching-up of bone,
the despair of the mind.

When I come to visit and we walk out
into the light of a summer day,
we sit under the trees —
buckeyes, a sycamore and one
black walnut brooding
high over a hedge of lilacs
as old as the red-brick building
behind them, the original
hospital built before the Civil War.
We sit on the lawn together, holding hands
while you tell me: you are better.

How many young men, I wonder,
came here, wheeled on cots off the slow trains
from the red and hideous battlefields
to lie all summer in the small and stuffy chambers
while doctors did what they could, longing
for tools still unimagined, medicines still unfound,
wisdoms still unguessed at, and how many died

staring at the leaves of the trees, blind
to the terrible effort around them to keep them alive?
I look into your eyes

which are sometimes green and sometimes gray,
and sometimes full of humor, but often not,
and tell myself, you are better,
because my life without you would be
a place of parched and broken trees.
Later, walking the corridors down to the street,
I turn and step inside an empty room.
Yesterday someone was here with a gasping face.
Now the bed is made all new,
the machines have been rolled away. The silence
continues, deep and neutral,
as I stand there, loving you.

IN BLACKWATER WOODS

Look, the trees
are turning
their own bodies
into pillars

of light,
are giving off the rich
fragrance of cinnamon
and fulfillment,

the long tapers
of cattails
are bursting and floating away over
the blue shoulders

of the ponds,
and every pond,
no matter what its
name is, is

nameless now.
Every year
everything
I have ever learned

in my lifetime
leads back to this: the fires
and the black river of loss
whose other side

is salvation,
whose meaning
none of us will ever know.
To live in this world

you must be able
to do three things:
to love what is mortal;
to hold it

against your bones knowing
your own life depends on it;
and, when the time comes to let it go,
to let it go.

THE SUMMER DAY

Who made the world?
Who made the swan, and the black bear?
Who made the grasshopper?
This grasshopper, I mean —
the one who has flung herself out of the grass,
the one who is eating sugar out of my hand,
who is moving her jaws back and forth instead of up and down —
who is gazing around with her enormous and complicated eyes.
Now she lifts her pale forearms and thoroughly washes her face.
Now she snaps her wings open, and floats away.
I don't know exactly what a prayer is.
I do know how to pay attention, how to fall down
into the grass, how to kneel down in the grass,
how to be idle and blessed, how to stroll through the fields,
which is what I have been doing all day.
Tell me, what else should I have done?
Doesn't everything die at last, and too soon?
Tell me, what is it you plan to do
with your one wild and precious life?

MARY OLIVER

SINGAPORE

In Singapore, in the airport,
a darkness was ripped from my eyes.
In the women's restroom, one compartment stood open.
A woman knelt there, washing something
    in the white bowl.

Disgust argued in my stomach
and I felt, in my pocket, for my ticket.

A poem should always have birds in it.
Kingfishers, say, with their bold eyes and gaudy wings.
Rivers are pleasant, and of course trees.
A waterfall, or if that's not possible, a fountain
    rising and falling.
A person wants to stand in a happy place, in a poem.

When the woman turned I could not answer her face.
Her beauty and her embarrassment struggled together, and
    neither could win.
She smiled and I smiled. What kind of nonsense is this?
Everybody needs a job.

Yes, a person wants to stand in a happy place, in a poem.
But first we must watch her as she stares down at her labor,
    which is dull enough.
She is washing the tops of the airport ashtrays, as big as
    hubcaps, with a blue rag.
Her small hands turn the metal, scrubbing and rinsing.
She does not work slowly, nor quickly, but like a river.
Her dark hair is like the wing of a bird.

I don't doubt for a moment that she loves her life.
And I want her to rise up from the crust and the slop
    and fly down to the river.
This probably won't happen.
But maybe it will.
If the world were only pain and logic, who would want it?

Of course, it isn't.
Neither do I mean anything miraculous, but only
the light that can shine out of a life. I mean
the way she unfolded and refolded the blue cloth,
the way her smile was only for my sake; I mean
the way this poem is filled with trees, and birds.

Michael Palmer

I DO NOT

"Je ne sais pas l'anglais."
— Georges Hugnet

I do not know English.

I do not know English, and therefore I can have nothing to
    say about this latest war, flowering through a night-scope
    in the evening sky.

I do not know English and therefore, when hungry, can do no
    more than point repeatedly to my mouth.

Yet such a gesture might be taken to mean any number of things.

I do not know English and therefore cannot seek the requisite
    permissions, as outlined in the recent protocol.

Such as: May I utter a term of endearment; may I now proceed
    to put my arm or arms around you and apply gentle pressure;
    may I now kiss you directly on the lips; now on the left tendon
    of the neck; now on the nipple of each breast? And so on.

Would not in any case be able to decipher her response.

I do not know English. Therefore I have no way of communicating
    that I prefer this painting of nothing to that one of something.

No way to speak of my past or hopes for the future, of my glasses
    mysteriously shattered in Rotterdam, the statue of Eros and
    Psyche in the Summer Garden, the sudden, shrill cries in the
    streets of São Paulo, a watch abruptly stopping in Paris.

No way to tell the joke about the rabbi and the parrot, the
    bartender and the duck, the Pope and the porte-cochère.

You will understand why you have received no letters from me
and why yours have gone unread.

Those, that is, where you write so precisely of the confluence
of the visible universe with the invisible, and of the lens of
dark matter.

No way to differentiate the hall of mirrors from the meadow of
mullein, the beetlebung from the pinkletink, the kettlehole
from the ventifact.

Nor can I utter the words science, seance, silence, language
and languish.

Nor can I tell of the aboreal shadows elongated and shifting
along the wall as the sun's angle approaches maximum
hibernal declination.

Cannot tell of the almond-eyed face that peered from the well,
the ship of stone whose sail was a tongue.

And I cannot report that this rose has twenty-four petals, one
slightly cancred.

Cannot tell how I dismantled it myself at this desk.

Cannot ask the name of this rose.

I cannot repeat the words of the Recording Angel or those of
the Angle of Erasure.

Can speak neither of things abounding nor of things
disappearing.

Still the games continue. A muscular man waves a stick at a
ball. A woman in white, arms outstretched, carves a true
circle in space. A village turns to dust in the chalk hills.

Because I do not know English I have been variously called
Mr. Twisted, The One Undone, The Nonrespondent, The
Truly Lost Boy, and Laughed-At-By-Horses.

The war is declared ended, almost before it has begun.

MICHAEL PALMER

They have named it The Ultimate Combat between Nearness and
Distance.

I do not know English.

SUN

Write this. We have burned all their villages

Write this. We have burned all the villages and the people in them

Write this. We have adopted their customs and their manner of dress

Write this. A word may be shaped like a bed, a basket of tears or an X

In the notebook it says, It is the time of mutations, laughter at jokes,
secrets beyond the boundaries of speech

I now turn to my use of suffixes and punctuation, closing Mr. Circle with
a single stroke, tearing the canvas from its wall, joined to her, experienc-
ing the same thoughts at the same moment, inscribing them on a loquat
leaf

Write this. We have begun to have bodies, a now here and a now gone,
a past long ago and one still to come

Let go of me for I have died and am in a novel and was a lyric poet, certainly, who attracted crowds to mountaintops. For a nickel I will appear
from this box. For a dollar I will have text with you and answer three
questions

First question. We entered the forest, followed its winding paths, and
emerged blind

Second question. My townhouse, of the Jugendstil, lies by Darmstadt

Third question. He knows he will wake from this dream, conducted in the
mother-tongue

Third question. He knows his breathing organs are manipulated by God,
so that he is compelled to scream

Third question. I will converse with no one on those days of the week which end in *y*

Write this. There is pleasure and pain and there are marks and signs. A word may be shaped like a fig or a pig, an effigy or an egg
                                                                    but
there is only time for fasting and desire, device and design, there is only time to swerve without limbs, organs or face into a
                                                    scientific
silence, pinhole of light

Say this. I was born on an island among the dead. I learned language on this island but did not speak on this island. I am writing to you from this island. I am writing to the dancers from this island. The writers do not dance on this island

Say this. There is a sentence in my mouth, there is a chariot in my mouth. There is a ladder. There is a lamp whose light fills empty space and a space which swallows light

A word is beside itself. Here the poem is called What Speaking Means to Say
      though I have no memory of my name

Here the poem is called Theory of the Real, its name is Let's Call This, and its name is called A Wooden Stick. It goes yes-yes, no-no. It goes one and one

I have been writing a book, not in my native language, about violins and smoke, lines and dots, free to speak and become the things we speak, pages which sit up, look around and row resolutely toward the setting sun

Pages torn from their spines and added to the pyre, so that they will resemble thought

Pages which accept no ink

Pages we've never seen — first called Narrow Street, then Half a Fragment, Plain of Jars or Plain of Reeds, taking each syllable into her mouth, shifting position and passing it to him

Let me say this. Neak Luong is a blur. It is Tuesday in the hardwood forest. I am a visitor here, with a notebook

MICHAEL PALMER

The notebook lists My New Words and Flag above White. It claims to have no inside
  only characters like A-against-Herself, B, C, L and
N, Sam, Hans Magnus, T. Sphere, all speaking in the dark with their hands
  G for Gramsci or Goebbels, blue hills, cities, cities with hills,
modern and at the end of time

        F for alphabet, Z for A, an H in an
arbor, shadow, silent wreckage, W or M among stars

What last. Lapwing. Tesseract. X perhaps for X. The villages are known as
These Lettters — humid, sunless. The writing occurs on their walls

DEAREST READER

He painted the mountain over and over again
from his place in the cave, agape
at the light, its absence, the mantled
skull with blue-tinted hollows, wrenlike bird plucking berries from the fire
her hair alight and so on
lemon grass in cafe in clear glass.
Dearest reader there were trees
formed of wire, broad entryways
beneath balconies beneath spires
youthful head come to rest in meadow
beside bend in gravel road, still
body of milky liquid
her hair alight and so on
successive halls, flowered carpets and doors
or the photograph of nothing but pigeons
and grackles by the shadow of a fountain.

UNTITLED

O you in that little bark
What is the relation of the painting to its title

The painting bears no relation to its title
The tiny boat bears

nameless people across
water that is infinitely dark

darker even than snow on paving stones
darker than faces in shadow on a boat

The boat is called Blunder, or Nothing, or Parallel Lines
The poem was called I Forget, then Empire, then Game of Cards

a game played yesterday in milky light
light which played across the players' faces

and the arcane faces of the cards
There is no relation between the painting and its title

The painting came first then its title
The players are playing cards in a little boat

They are asleep and it is dark
Their dream is called The Orderly Electrons

One traveler dreams she does not belong
Another dreams with his eyes wide open

like a solemn philosopher
dead from an act of thought

Two more lie with limbs intertwined
The painting has no title

though it has been signed Keeper of the Book
the signature obviously forged

for D.S.

"or anything resembling it"

The hills like burnt pages
Where does this door lead

Like burnt pages
Then we fall into something still called the sea

MICHAEL PALMER

A mirrored door
And the hills covered with burnt pages

With words burned into the pages
The trees like musical instruments attempt to read

Here between idea and object
Otherwise a clear even completely clear winter day

Sometimes the least memorable lines will ring in your ears
The disappearing pages

Our bodies twisted into unnatural shapes
To exact maximum pleasure

From the view of what is in any case long gone and never was
A war might be playing itself out beyond the horizon

An argument over the future-past enacted in the present
Which is an invisible present

Neva streaming by outside the casement
Piazza resculpted with bricolage

Which way will the tanks turn their guns
You ask a woman with whom you hope to make love

In this very apartment
Should time allow

What I would describe as a dark blue dress with silver threads
And an overturned lamp in the form of a swan

A cluster of birches represents negativity
Flakes of ash continue to descend

We offer a city with its name crossed out
To those who say we are burning the pages

Carl Phillips

GLADS

Three, at the most four days later,
they're dying, knuckled
over at whichever flower has bloomed

largest. The way everything beautiful
finally breaks because of, from it.
As if this were necessary. The reason,

maybe, why the loveliest things are always
also the most ruined:
a man's aging breast falling until,

naturally, brassieres come to mind;
or why, given any crumbled wall, nobody
thinks to ask where did they go to,

bring them back, all those
missing pieces.
The difference between a cock at plain

rest, for once longing to put itself
nowhere special,
and one that, just done thirsting,

collapses, curls slowly back in on
itself.
In Renaissance Italy,

when depicting the saints and Christ
in mid-torment was all the rage,
the painters chose for their backdrops

the most unremarkable buildings,
landscapes stranded in neutral, people
doing the dull things they still do —

plowing, benchwarming a small hill,
idly swinging a staff at livestock,
or at nothing, gone fishing.

The idea was to throw up into relief,
in its rawest form, sheer affliction.
The motto was

No distractions from suffering, hence
the skies: in general, clear
or just clearing, washed of anything

like rescue birds hope clouds mercy.

OUR LADY

In the final hour, our lady — Of
the electric rosary, Of the highway,
by then Of the snows mostly — was

the man he'd always been really,
though, yes, we'd sometimes forgotten.
Still, even while he lay fanning,

as one might any spent flame, where
it was hot, between his legs, and
saying it didn't much matter anymore

about dying, what came of having
come too often, perhaps, to what in
the end had fallen short of divine

always, he said that more than the
bare-chested dancers and all-conquering
bass-line that had marked his every

sudden, strobe-lit appearance, at
precisely the same moment, in all of
the city's best clubs; more than

the just-heated towels and the water
he'd called holy in those windowless,
too thinly-walled, now all but

abandoned bath-houses, he regretted
the fine gowns that he'd made, just
by wearing them, famous; and then,

CARL PHILLIPS

half, it seemed, to remind us, half
himself, he recreated the old shrug,
slowly raising from his hospital

robe — not green, he insisted, but
two shades, maybe three, shy of
turquoise — one shoulder to show

the words still tattooed there:
Adore me; for a moment, it was
possible to see it, the once

extraordinary beauty, the heated
grace for which we'd all of us,
once, so eagerly sought him.

LUNA MOTH

No eye that sees could fail to remark you:
like any leaf the rain leaves fixed to and
flat against the barn's gray shingle. But

what leaf, this time of year, is so pale,
the pale of leaves when they've lost just
enough green to become the green that *means*

loss and more loss, approaching? Give up
the flesh enough times, and whatever is lost
gets forgotten: that was the thought that I

woke to, those words in my head. I rose,
I did not dress, I left no particular body
sleeping and, stepping into the hour, I saw

you, strange sign, at once transparent and
impossible to entirely see through, and how
still: the still of being unmoved, and then

the still of no longer being able to be
moved. If I think of a heart, his, as I've
found it. . . . If I think of, increasingly, my

own. . . . If I look at you now, as from above,
and see the diva when she is caught in mid-
triumph, arms half-raised, the body as if

set at last free of the green sheath that has —
how many nights? — held her, it is not
without remembering another I once saw:

like you, except that something, a bird, some
wild and necessary hunger, had gotten to it;
and like the diva, but now broken, splayed

and torn, the green torn piecemeal from her.
I remember the hands, and — how small they
seemed, bringing the small ripped thing to me.

TOYS

Seeing them like this,
arranged according to size,
sectioned off by color,

I think it's not so much their being
made mostly for men, nor anything in
their being man-made; it's what

they are made *of* disturbs me: rubber
and urethane, plastic aiming for
the plastic of flesh,

and just missing. Growing up, I was
told once that, somewhere in the Vatican,
there's a room still, where —

ordered and numbered, as if
awaiting recall — lie all the phalluses
of stone, granite, tufa, fine marble,

that were removed from pagan statues
for lacking what any leaf, it seems,
can provide: some decorum.

I've never seen them, but their beauty,
I imagine, is twofold: what they're
made of, for one — what, in cracking,

suggests more than just the body that
came first, but the peril,
the vulnerability

that is all the flesh means to say,
singing; then, what even these
imitations before me — lesser somehow

but, to the eye and to touch, finally
more accurate, in being true
to an absurdity that is always there

in the real thing — even these seem
like wanting to tell about beauty,
that it also comes this way, in parts.

PARABLE

There was a saint once,
he had but to ring across
water a small bell, all

manner of fish
rose, as answer, he was
that holy, persuasive,

both, or the fish
perhaps merely
hungry, their bodies

a-shimmer with
that hope especially that
hunger brings, whatever

the reason, the fish
coming unassigned, in
schools coming

into the saint's hand and,
instead of getting,
becoming food.

I have thought, since, of
your body — as I first came
to know it, how it still

can be, with mine,
sometimes. I think on
that immediate and last gesture

of the fish leaving water
for flesh, for guarantee
they will die, and I cannot

rest on what to call it.
Not generosity, or
a blindness, trust, brute

stupidity. Not the soul
distracted from its natural
prayer, which is attention,

for in the story they are
paying attention. They
lose themselves eyes open.

AUBADE: SOME PEACHES, AFTER STORM

So that each
is its own, now — each a fallen, blond stillness.
Closer, above them,
the damselflies pass as they would over water,
if the fruit were water,
or as bees would, if they weren't
somewhere else, had the fruit found
already a point more steep
in rot, as soon it must, if
none shall lift it from the grass whose damp only
softens further those parts where flesh
goes soft.

There are those
whom no amount of patience looks likely
to improve ever, I always said, meaning
gift is random,
assigned here,
here withheld — almost always
correctly,
as it's turned out: how your hands clear
easily the wreckage;
how you stand — like a building for a time condemned,
then deemed historic. Yes. You
will be saved.

SINGING

Overheard,
late, this morning: *Don't blame*
me, if I am everything your heart
has led to.

Hazel trees;
ghost-moths in the hazel branches.
Why not stay?

It's a dream I've had
twice now: God is real, as
the difference between
having squandered faith and having lost it
is real. He's straightforward:

when he says *Look at me when I'm speaking,*
it means he's speaking.
He's not unreasonable:

because I've asked, he shows me his mercy —
a complicated arrangement
of holes and

hooks, buckles. *What else did you think*
mercy looked like,

he says and, demonstrating, he straps it on, then takes it off.

Sylvia Plath

STILLBORN

These poems do not live: it's a sad diagnosis.
They grew their toes and fingers well enough,
Their little foreheads bulged with concentration.
If they missed out on walking about like people
It wasn't for any lack of mother-love.

O I cannot understand what happened to them!
They are proper in shape and number and every part.
They sit so nicely in the pickling fluid!
They smile and smile and smile and smile at me.
And still the lungs won't fill and the heart won't start.

They are not pigs, they are not even fish,
Though they have a piggy and a fishy air —
It would be better if they were alive, and that's what they were.
But they are dead, and their mother near dead with distraction,
And they stupidly stare, and do not speak of her.

[Handwritten annotations: "They existed; they were created"; "perfected verse"; "fish"; "Preservation (anaerobic fermentation)"; "when?"; "at something? or randomly?"]

CROSSING THE WATER

Black lake, black boat, two black, cut-paper people.
Where do the black trees go that drink here?
Their shadows must cover Canada.

A little light is filtering from the water flowers.
Their leaves do not wish us to hurry:
They are round and flat and full of dark advice.

Cold worlds shake from the oar.
The spirit of blackness is in us, it is in the fishes.
A snag is lifting a valedictory, pale hand;

Stars open among the lilies.
Are you not blinded by such expressionless sirens?
This is the silence of astounded souls.

[Handwritten annotations: "fishing, sea, very Bishop"; "fish"]

405

SYLVIA PLATH

DADDY

You do not do, you do not do
Any more, black shoe
In which I have lived like a foot
For thirty years, poor and white,
Barely daring to breathe or Achoo.

Daddy, I have had to kill you.
You died before I had time ——
Marble-heavy, a bag full of God,
Ghastly statue with one gray toe
Big as a Frisco seal

And a head in the freakish Atlantic
Where it pours bean green over blue
In the waters off beautiful Nauset.
I used to pray to recover you.
Ach, du.

sea

In the German tongue, in the Polish town
Scraped flat by the roller
Of wars, wars, wars.
But the name of the town is common.
My Polack friend

Says there are a dozen or two.
So I never could tell where you
Put your foot, your root,
I never could talk to you.
The tongue stuck in my jaw.

internal slant rhymes

It stuck in a barb wire snare.
Ich, ich, ich, ich,
I could hardly speak.
I thought every German was you.
And the language obscene

An engine, an engine
Chuffing me off like a Jew.
A Jew to Dachau, Auschwitz, Belsen.
I began to talk like a Jew.
I think I may well be a Jew.

The snows of the Tyrol, the clear beer of Vienna
Are not very pure or true.
With my gipsy ancestress and my weird luck
And my Taroc pack and my Taroc pack
I may be a bit of a Jew.

I have always been scared of *you*,
With your Luftwaffe, your gobbledygoo.
And your neat mustache
And your Aryan eye, bright blue.
Panzer-man, panzer-man, O You ——

*fuller comparison
to Hitler*

Not God but a swastika
So black no sky could squeak through.
Every woman adores a Fascist,
The boot in the face, the brute
Brute heart of a brute like you.

You stand at the blackboard, daddy,
In the picture I have of you,
A cleft in your chin instead of your foot
But no less a devil for that, no not
Any less the black man who

Bit my pretty red heart in two.
I was ten when they buried you.
At twenty I tried to die
And get back, back, back to you.
I thought even the bones would do.

But they pulled me out of the sack,
And they stuck me together with glue.
And then I knew what to do.
I made a model of you,
A man in black with a Meinkampf look

And a love of the rack and the screw.
And I said I do, I do.
So daddy, I'm finally through.
The black telephone's off at the root,
The voices just can't worm through.

If I've killed one man, I've killed two ——
The vampire who said he was you
And drank my blood for a year,

Seven years, if you want to know.
Daddy, you can lie back now.

There's a stake in your fat black heart
And the villagers never liked you.
They are dancing and stamping on you.
They always *knew* it was you.
Daddy, daddy, you bastard, I'm through.

CUT

For Susan O'Neill Roe

What a thrill ——
My thumb instead of an onion.
The top quite gone
Except for a sort of a hinge

Of skin,
A flap like a hat,
Dead white.
Then that red plush.

Little pilgrim,
The Indian's axed your scalp.
Your turkey wattle
Carpet rolls

Straight from the heart.
I step on it,
Clutching my bottle
Of pink fizz.

A celebration, this is.
Out of a gap
A million soldiers run,
Redcoats, every one.

Whose side are they on?
O my
Homunculus, I am ill.
I have taken a pill to kill

The thin
Papery feeling.

Saboteur,
Kamikaze man —

The stain on your
Gauze Ku Klux Klan
Babushka
Darkens and tarnishes and when

The balled
Pulp of your heart
Confronts its small
Mill of silence

How you jump —
Trepanned veteran,
Dirty girl,
Thumb stump.

[handwritten: — white cloak]
[handwritten: hankerchief]
[handwritten: Black comedy — compare to Lazarus — not risen story]

LADY LAZARUS

I have done it again.
One year in every ten
I manage it —

A sort of walking miracle, my skin
Bright as a Nazi lampshade,
My right foot

A paperweight,
My face a featureless, fine
Jew linen.

Peel off the napkin
O my enemy.
Do I terrify? —

The nose, the eye pits, the full set of teeth?
The sour breath
Will vanish in a day.

Soon, soon the flesh
The grave cave ate will be
At home on me

[handwritten annotations: "1", "2", "6", "9", "10", "6" line numbers; "preservation"; "what does this rhyme scheme do?"; "who removes Lazarus' shroud/cloth?"; "internal rhymes"]

And I a smiling woman.
I am only thirty.
And like the cat I have nine times to die.

This is Number Three.
What a trash
To annihilate each decade.

What a million filaments.
The peanut-crunching crowd
Shoves in to see

Them unwrap me hand and foot ——
The big strip tease.
Gentlemen, ladies

These are my hands
My knees.
I may be skin and bone,

Nevertheless, I am the same, identical woman.
The first time it happened I was ten.
It was an accident.

The second time I meant
To last it out and not come back at all.
I rocked shut

As a seashell.
They had to call and call
And pick the worms off me like sticky pearls.

Dying
Is an art, like everything else.
I do it exceptionally well.

I do it so it feels like hell.
I do it so it feels real.
I guess you could say I've a call.

It's easy enough to do it in a cell.
It's easy enough to do it and stay put.
It's the theatrical

Comeback in broad day
To the same place, the same face, the same brute
Amused shout:

'A miracle!'
That knocks me out.
There is a charge ——

For the eyeing of my scars, there is a charge ——
For the hearing of my heart ——
It really goes.

And there is a charge, a very large charge
For a word or a touch
Or a bit of blood

Or a piece of my hair or my clothes.
So, so, Herr Doktor.
So, Herr Enemy.

I am your opus,
I am your valuable,
The pure gold baby

That melts to a shriek.
I turn and burn.
Do not think I underestimate your great concern.

Ash, ash —
You poke and stir.
Flesh, bone, there is nothing there ——

A cake of soap,
A wedding ring,
A gold filling.

Herr God, Herr Lucifer
Beware
Beware.

Out of the ash
I rise with my red hair
And I eat men like air.

Adrienne Rich

POWER

Living   in the earth-deposits   of our history

Today a backhoe divulged   out of a crumbling flank of earth
one bottle   amber   perfect   a hundred-year-old
cure for fever   or melancholy   a tonic
for living on this earth   in the winters of this climate

Today I was reading about Marie Curie:
she must have known she suffered   from radiation sickness
her body bombarded for years   by the element
(she had purified)
It seems she denied to the end
the source of the cataracts on her eyes
the cracked and suppurating skin   of her finger-ends
till she could no longer hold   a test-tube or a pencil

She died   a famous woman   denying
her wounds
denying
her wounds   came   from the same source as her power

PLANETARIUM

Thinking of Caroline Herschel (1750–1848)
astronomer, sister of William; and others.

A woman in the shape of a monster
a monster in the shape of a woman
the skies are full of them

a woman   'in the snow
among the Clocks and instruments
or measuring the ground with poles'

in her 98 years to discover
8 comets

she whom the moon ruled — *cycles*
like us
levitating into the night sky
riding the polished lenses

Galaxies of women, there
doing penance for impetuousness
ribs chilled
in those spaces   of the mind

An eye,

        'virile, precise and absolutely certain'
        from the mad webs of Uranusborg

                    encountering the NOVA

every impulse of light exploding
from the core
as life flies out of us

        Tycho whispering at last
        'Let me not seem to have lived in vain'

What we see, we see
and seeing is changing

the light that shrivels a mountain
and leaves a man alive

Heartbeat of the pulsar
heart sweating through my body

The radio impulse
pouring in from Taurus

        I am bombarded yet   I stand

I have been standing all my life in the
direct path of a battery of signals
the most accurately transmitted most
untranslatable language in the universe
I am a galactic cloud so deep   so invo-
luted that a light wave could take 15
years to travel through me   And has

taken (I am an instrument) in the shape
of a woman trying to translate pulsations
into images   for the relief of the body
and the reconstruction of the mind.

[handwritten: instrument]

DIVING INTO THE WRECK

First having read the book of myths,
and loaded the camera,
and checked the edge of the knife-blade,
I put on
the body-armor of black rubber
the absurd flippers
the grave and awkward mask.
I am having to do this
not like Cousteau with his
assiduous team
aboard the sun-flooded schooner
but here alone.

There is a ladder.
The ladder is always there
hanging innocently
close to the side of the schooner.
We know what it is for,
we who have used it.
Otherwise
it's a piece of maritime floss
some sundry equipment.

[handwritten: journey? transformation]

I go down.
Rung after rung and still
the oxygen immerses me
the blue light
the clear atoms
of our human air.
I go down.
My flippers cripple me,
I crawl like an insect down the ladder
and there is no one
to tell me when the ocean
will begin.

[handwritten: descent — an exploration, of tragedy? disappointment disaster,]

[handwritten: enjambment]

First the air is blue and then
it is bluer and then green and then
black I am blacking out and yet
my mask is powerful
it pumps my blood with power
the sea is another story
the sea is not a question of power
I have to learn alone
to turn my body without force
in the deep element.

And now: it is easy to forget
what I came for
among so many who have always
lived here
swaying their crenellated fans
between the reefs
and besides
you breathe differently down here.

I came to explore the wreck.
The words are purposes.
The words are maps.
I came to see the damage that was done
and the treasures that prevail.
I stroke the beam of my lamp
slowly along the flank
of something more permanent
than fish or weed

the thing I came for:
the wreck and not the story of the wreck
the thing itself and not the myth
the drowned face always staring
toward the sun
the evidence of damage
worn by salt and sway into this threadbare beauty
the ribs of the disaster
curving their assertion
among the tentative haunters.

This is the place.
And I am here, the mermaid whose dark hair
streams black, the merman in his armored body

ADRIENNE RICH

We circle silently
about the wreck
we dive into the hold.
I am she: I am he

whose drowned face sleeps with open eyes
whose breasts still bear the stress
whose silver, copper, vermeil cargo lies
obscurely inside barrels
half-wedged and left to rot
we are the half-destroyed instruments
that once held to a course
the water-eaten log
the fouled compass

We are, I am, you are
by cowardice or courage
the one who find our way
back to this scene
carrying a knife, a camera
a book of myths
in which
our names do not appear.

fortress

collective narrative of exploration

instruments

history — misrecording

missed opportunities?

reflection?

THE NOVEL

All winter you went to bed early, drugging yourself on *War and Peace*
Prince Andrei's cold eyes taking in the sky from the battlefield
were your eyes, you went walking wrapped in his wound
like a padded coat against the winds from the two rivers
You went walking in the streets as if you were ordinary
as if you hadn't been pulling with your raw mittened hand
on the slight strand that held your tattered mind
blown like an old stocking from a wire
on the wind between two rivers.   *first stop*
                                    All winter you asked nothing
of that book though it lay heavy on your knees
you asked only for a shed skin, many skins in which to walk
you were old woman, child, commander
you watched Natasha grow into a neutered thing
you felt your heart go still while your eyes swept the pages

you felt the pages thickening to the left and on the right-
hand growing few, you knew the end was coming
you knew beyond the ending lay
your own, unwritten life

ONE LIFE

A woman walking in a walker on the cliffs
recalls great bodily joys, much pain.
Nothing in her is apt to say
My heart aches, though she read those words
in a battered college text, this morning
as the sun rose. It is all too
mixed, the heart too mixed with laughter
raucousing the grief, her life
too mixed, she shakes her heavy
silvered hair at all the fixed
declarations of baggage. I should be dead and I'm alive
don't ask me how; I don't eat like I should
and still I like how the drop of vodka
hits the tongue. I was a worker and a mother,
that means a worker and a worker ———   "instrument"
but for one you don't pay union dues
or get a pension; for the other
the men ran the union, we ran the home.
It was terrible and good, we had more than half a life,
I had four lives at least, one out of marriage
when I kicked up all the dust I could
before I knew what I was doing.
One life with the girls on the line during the war,
yes, painting our legs and jitterbugging together
one life with a husband, not the worst,
one with your children, none of it just what you'd thought.
None of it what it could have been, if we'd known.
We took what we could.
But even this is a life, I'm reading a lot of books
I never read, my daughter brought home from school,
plays where you can almost hear them talking,
Romantic poets, Isaac Babel. A lot of lives
worse and better than what I knew. I'm walking again.
My heart doesn't ache; sometimes though it rages.

ADRIENNE RICH

THE SCHOOL AMONG THE RUINS

Beirut.Baghdad.Sarajevo.Bethlehem.Kabul. Not of course here.

1

Teaching the first lesson and the last
— great falling light of summer will you last
longer than schooltime?
When children flow
in columns at the doors
BOYS GIRLS and the busy teachers

open or close high windows
with hooked poles   drawing darkgreen shades

closets unlocked, locked
questions unasked, asked, when

love of the fresh impeccable
sharp-pencilled   yes
order without cruelty

a street on earth   neither heaven nor hell
busy with commerce and worship
young teachers walking to school

fresh bread and early-open foodstalls

2

When the offensive rocks the sky when nightglare
misconstrues day and night when lived-in
rooms from the upper city
tumble cratering lower streets

cornices of olden ornament   human debris
when fear vacuums out the streets

When the whole town flinches
blood on the undersole thickening to glass

Whoever crosses   hunched   knees bent   a contested zone
knows why she does this suicidal thing

School's now in session day and night
children sleep
in the classrooms   teachers rolled close

3

How the good teacher loved
his school   the students
the lunchroom with fresh sandwiches

lemonade and milk
the classroom   glass cages
of moss and turtles
teaching responsibility

A morning breaks without bread or fresh-poured milk
parents or lessons plans

diarrhea first question of the day
children shivering   it's September
Second question: where is my mother?

4

One: I don't know where your mother
is   Two: I don't know
why they are trying to hurt us
Three: or the latitude and longitude
of their hatred   Four: I don't know if we
hate them as much   I think there's more toilet paper
in the supply closet   I'm going to break it open

Today this is your lesson:
write as clearly as you can
your name   home street   and number
down on this page
No you can't go home yet
but you aren't lost
this is our school

I'm not sure what we'll eat
we'll look for healthy roots and greens
searching for water though the pipes are broken

5

There's a young cat sticking
her head through window bars
she's hungry like us
but can feed on mice
her bronze erupting fur
speaks of a life already wild

her golden eyes
don't give quarter   She'll teach us   Let's call her
Sister
when we get milk we'll give her some

6

I've told you, let's try to sleep in this funny camp
All night pitiless pilotless things go shrieking
above us to somewhere

Don't let your faces turn to stone
Don't stop asking me why
Let's pay attention to our cat   she needs us

Maybe tomorrow the bakers can fix their ovens

7

"We sang them to naps   told stories   made
shadow-animals with our hands

wiped human debris off boots and coats
sat learning by heart the names
some were too young to write
some had forgotten how"

2001

Theodore Roethke

MY PAPA'S WALTZ

The whiskey on your breath
Could make a small boy dizzy;
But I hung on like death:
Such waltzing was not easy.

We romped until the pans
Slid from the kitchen shelf;
My mother's countenance
Could not unfrown itself.

The hand that held my wrist
Was battered on one knuckle;
At every step you missed
My right ear scraped a buckle.

You beat time on my head
With a palm caked hard by dirt,
Then waltzed me off to bed
Still clinging to your shirt.

[handwritten annotations: rhyme; staccato; Staggering waltz — swinging movement, but ...]

ROOT CELLAR

[handwritten annotation: alliteration]

Nothing would sleep in that cellar, dank as a ditch,
Bulbs broke out of boxes hunting for chinks in the dark,
Shoots dangled and drooped,
Lolling obscenely from mildewed crates,
Hung down long yellow evil necks, like tropical snakes.
And what a congress of stinks! —
Roots ripe as old bait,
Pulpy stems, rank, silo-rich,
Leaf-mold, manure, lime, piled against slippery planks.
Nothing would give up life:
Even the dirt kept breathing a small breath.

[handwritten annotations: encountering the dark and seeing it as passion — not just succumbing to it.; vocabulary leads to a strong, almost disturbed reading]

THEODORE ROETHKE

CUTTINGS

(later)

alliteration

This urge, wrestle, resurrection of dry sticks,
Cut stems struggling to put down feet,
What saint strained so much,
Rose on such lopped limbs to a new life?

I can hear, underground, that sucking and sobbing,
In my veins, in my bones I feel it, —
The small waters seeping upward,
The tight grains parting at last.
When sprouts break out,
Slippery as fish,
I quail, lean to beginnings, sheath-wet.

THE LOST SON

1. *The Flight*

At Woodlawn I heard the dead cry:
I was lulled by the slamming of iron,
A slow drip over stones,
Toads brooding wells.
All the leaves stuck out their tongues;
I shook the softening chalk of my bones,
Saying,
Snail, snail, glister me forward,
Bird, soft-sigh me home,
Worm, be with me.
This is my hard time.

Fished in an old wound,
The soft pond of repose;
Nothing nibbled my line,
Not even the minnows came.

Sat in an empty house
Watching shadows crawl,
Scratching.
There was one fly.

Voice, come out of the silence.
Say something.
Appear in the form of a spider
Or a moth beating the curtain.

Tell me:
Which is the way I take;
Out of what door do I go,
Where and to whom?

Dark hollows said, lee to the wind,
The moon said, back of an eel,
The salt said, look by the sea,
Your tears are not enough praise,
You will find no comfort here,
In the kingdom of bang and blab.

Running lightly over spongy ground,
Past the pasture of flat stones,
The three elms,
The sheep strewn on a field,
Over a rickety bridge
Toward the quick-water, wrinkling and rippling.

Hunting along the river,
Down among the rubbish, the bug-riddled foliage,
By the muddy pond-edge, by the bog-holes,
By the shrunken lake, hunting, in the heat of summer.

The shape of a rat?
It's bigger than that.
It's less than a leg
And more than a nose,
Just under the water
It usually goes.

Is it soft like a mouse?
Can it wrinkle its nose?
Could it come in the house
On the tips of its toes?

Take the skin of a cat
And the back of an eel,
Then roll them in grease, —
That's the way it would feel.

It's sleek as an otter
With wide webby toes
Just under the water
It usually goes.

2. *The Pit*

Where do the roots go?
    Look down under the leaves.
Who put the moss there?
    These stones have been here too long.
Who stunned the dirt into noise?
    Ask the mole, he knows.
I feel the slime of a wet nest.
    Beware Mother Mildew.
Nibble again, fish nerves.

3. *The Gibber*

At the wood's mouth,
By the cave's door,
I listened to something
I had heard before.

Dogs of the groin
Barked and howled,
The sun was against me,
The moon would not have me.

The weeds whined,
The snakes cried,
The cows and briars
Said to me: Die.

What a small song. What slow clouds. What dark water.
Hath the rain a father? All the caves are ice. Only the snow's here.
I'm cold. I'm cold all over. Rub me in father and mother.
Fear was my father, Father Fear.
His look drained the stones.

        What gliding shape
        Beckoning through halls,
        Stood poised on the stair,
        Fell dreamily down?

From the mouths of jugs
Perched on many shelves,
I saw substance flowing
That cold morning.

Like a slither of eels
That watery cheek
As my own tongue kissed
My lips awake.

Is this the storm's heart? The ground is unstilling itself.
My veins are running nowhere. Do the bones cast out their fire?
Is the seed leaving the old bed? These buds are live as birds.
Where, where are the tears of the world?
Let the kisses resound, flat like a butcher's palm;
Let the gestures freeze; our doom is already decided.
All the windows are burning! What's left of my life?
I want the old rage, the lash of primordial milk!
Goodbye, goodbye, old stones, the time-order is going,
I have married my hands to perpetual agitation,
I run, I run to the whistle of money.

Money money money
Water water water

How cool the grass is.
Has the bird left?
The stalk still sways.
Has the worm a shadow?
What do the clouds say?

These sweeps of light undo me.
Look, look, the ditch is running white!
I've more veins than a tree!
Kiss me, ashes, I'm falling through a dark swirl.

4. *The Return*

The way to the boiler was dark,
Dark all the way,
Over slippery cinders
Through the long greenhouse.

The roses kept breathing in the dark.
They had many mouths to breathe with.

My knees made little winds underneath
Where the weeds slept.

There was always a single light
Swinging by the fire-pit,
Where the fireman pulled out roses,
The big roses, the big bloody clinkers.

Once I stayed all night.
The light in the morning came slowly over the white
Snow.
There were many kinds of cool
Air.
Then came steam.

Pipe-knock.

Scurry of warm over small plants.
Ordnung! ordnung!
Papa is coming!

A fine haze moved off the leaves;
Frost melted on far panes;
The rose, the chrysanthemum turned toward the light.
Even the hushed forms, the bent yellowy weeds
Moved in a slow up-sway.

5. *"It was beginning winter"*

It was beginning winter,
An in-between time,
The landscape still partly brown:
The bones of weeds kept swinging in the wind,
Above the blue snow.

It was beginning winter,
The light moved slowly over the frozen field,
Over the dry seed-crowns,
The beautiful surviving bones
Swinging in the wind.

Light traveled over the wide field;
Stayed.
The weeds stopped swinging.
The mind moved, not alone,
Through the clear air, in the silence.

THEODORE ROETHKE

Was it light?
Was it light within?
Was it light within light?
Stillness becoming alive,
Yet still?

A lively understandable spirit
Once entertained you.
It will come again.
Be still.
Wait.

IN A DARK TIME

In a dark time, the eye begins to see,
I meet my shadow in the deepening shade;
I hear my echo in the echoing wood —
A lord of nature weeping to a tree.
I live between the heron and the wren,
Beasts of the hill and serpents of the den.

What's madness but nobility of soul
At odds with circumstance? The day's on fire!
I know the purity of pure despair,
My shadow pinned against a sweating wall.
That place among the rocks — is it a cave,
Or winding path? The edge is what I have.

A steady storm of correspondences!
A night flowing with birds, a ragged moon,
And in broad day the midnight come again!
A man goes far to find out what he is —
Death of the self in a long, tearless night,
All natural shapes blazing unnatural light.

Dark, dark my light, and darker my desire.
My soul, like some heat-maddened summer fly,
Keeps buzzing at the sill. Which I is I?
A fallen man, I climb out of my fear.
The mind enters itself, and God the mind,
And one is One, free in the tearing wind.

Hirsch: from reading assignment —
   * a moment in time that erases history
     and context for the poet
   * a character who seems very close to the poet,
     but is not the poet.

Anne Sexton

HER KIND

I have gone out, a possessed witch,
haunting the black air, braver at night;
dreaming evil, I have done my hitch
over the plain houses, light by light:
lonely thing, twelve-fingered, out of mind.
A woman like that is not a woman, quite.
I have been her kind.

I have found the warm caves in the woods,
filled them with skillets, carvings, shelves,
closets, silks, innumerable goods;
fixed the suppers for the worms and the elves:
whining, rearranging the disaligned.
A woman like that is misunderstood.
I have been her kind.

I have ridden in your cart, driver,
waved my nude arms at villages going by,
learning the last bright routes, survivor
where your flames still bite my thigh
and my ribs crack where your wheels wind.
A woman like that is not ashamed to die.
I have been her kind.

WITH MERCY FOR THE GREEDY

*For my friend, Ruth, who urges me to make an
appointment for the Sacrament of Confession*

Concerning your letter in which you ask
me to call a priest and in which you ask
me to wear The Cross that you enclose;
your own cross,
your dog-bitten cross,
no larger than a thumb,
small and wooden, no thorns, this rose —

431

I pray to its shadow,
that gray place
where it lies on your letter . . . deep, deep.
I detest my sins and I try to believe
in The Cross. I touch its tender hips, its dark jawed face,
its solid neck, its brown sleep.

True. There is
a beautiful Jesus.
He is frozen to his bones like a chunk of beef.
How desperately he wanted to pull his arms in!
How desperately I touch his vertical and horizontal axes!
But I can't. Need is not quite belief.

All morning long
I have worn
your cross, hung with package string around my throat.
It tapped me lightly as a child's heart might,
tapping secondhand, softly waiting to be born.
Ruth, I cherish the letter you wrote.

My friend, my friend, I was born
doing reference work in sin, and born
confessing it. This is what poems are:
with mercy
for the greedy,
they are the tongue's wrangle,
the world's pottage, the rat's star.

TO A FRIEND WHOSE WORK HAS COME TO TRIUMPH

Consider Icarus, pasting those sticky wings on,
testing that strange little tug at his shoulder blade,
and think of that first flawless moment over the lawn
of the labyrinth. Think of the difference it made!
There below are the trees, as awkward as camels;
and here are the shocked starlings pumping past
and think of innocent Icarus who is doing quite well:
larger than a sail, over the fog and the blast
of the plushy ocean, he goes. Admire his wings!

Feel the fire at his neck and see how casually
he glances up and is caught, wondrously tunneling
into that hot eye. Who cares that he fell back to the sea?
See him acclaiming the sun and come plunging down
while his sensible daddy goes straight into town.

THE ABORTION

Somebody who should have been born
is gone.

Just as the earth puckered its mouth,
each bud puffing out from its knot,
I changed my shoes, and then drove south.

Up past the Blue Mountains, where
Pennsylvania humps on endlessly,
wearing, like a crayoned cat, its green hair,

its roads sunken in like a gray washboard;
where, in truth, the ground cracks evilly,
a dark socket from which the coal has poured,

Somebody who should have been born
is gone.

the grass as bristly and stout as chives,
and me wondering when the ground would break,
and me wondering how anything fragile survives;

up in Pennsylvania, I met a little man,
not Rumpelstiltskin, at all, at all . . .
he took the fullness that love began.

Returning north, even the sky grew thin
like a high window looking nowhere.
The road was as flat as a sheet of tin.

Somebody who should have been born
is gone.

ANNE SEXTON

2

Yes, woman, such logic will lead
to loss without death. Or say what you meant,
you coward . . . this baby that I bleed.

— Bishop-esque
(write it!)

MAN AND WIFE

To speke of wo
that is in mariage . . .

We are not lovers.
We do not even know each other.
We look alike
but we have nothing to say.
We are like pigeons . . .

that pair who came to the suburbs
by mistake,
forsaking Boston where they bumped
their small heads against a blind wall,
having worn out the fruit stalls in the North End,
the amethyst windows of Louisburg Square,
the seats on the Common
And the traffic that kept stamping
and stamping.

Now there is green rain for everyone
as common as eyewash.
Now they are together
like strangers in a two-seater outhouse,
eating and squatting together.
They have teeth and knees
but they do not speak.
A soldier is forced to stay with a soldier
because they share the same dirt
and the same blows.

They are exiles
soiled by the same sweat and the drunkard's dream.
As it is they can only hang on,
their red claws wound like bracelets
around the same limb.

ANNE SEXTON

Even their song is not a sure thing.
It is not a language;
it is a kind of breathing.
They are two asthmatics
whose breath sobs in and out
through a small fuzzy pipe.

Like them
we neither talk nor clear our throats.
Oh darling,
we gasp in unison beside our window pane,
drunk on the drunkard's dream.
Like them
we can only hang on.

But they would pierce our heart
if they could only fly the distance.

IN CELEBRATION OF MY UTERUS

Everyone in me is a bird.
I am beating all my wings.
They wanted to cut you out
but they will not.
They said you were immeasurably empty
but you are not.
They said you were sick unto dying
but they were wrong.
You are singing like a school girl.
You are not torn.

Sweet weight,
in celebration of the woman I am
and of the soul of the woman I am
and of the central creature and its delight
I sing for you. I dare to live.
Hello, spirit. Hello, cup.
Fasten, cover. Cover that does contain.
Hello to the soil of the fields.
Welcome, roots.

*b/c it is "empty"
does not mean
it is useless*

ANNE SEXTON

Each cell has a life.
There is enough here to please a nation.
It is enough that the populace own these goods.
Any person, any commonwealth would say of it,
"It is good this year that we may plant again
and think forward to a harvest.
A blight had been forecast and has been cast out."
Many women are singing together of this:
one is in a shoe factory cursing the machine,
one is at the aquarium tending a seal,
one is dull at the wheel of her Ford,
one is at the toll gate collecting,
one is tying the cord of a calf in Arizona,
one is straddling a cello in Russia,
one is shifting pots on the stove in Egypt,
one is painting her bedroom walls moon color,
one is dying but remembering a breakfast,
one is stretching on her mat in Thailand,
one is wiping the ass of her child,
one is staring out the window of a train
in the middle of Wyoming and one is
anywhere and some are everywhere and all
seem to be singing, although some can not
sing a note.

community

Sweet weight,
in celebration of the woman I am
let me carry a ten-foot scarf,
let me drum for the nineteen-year-olds,
let me carry bowls for the offering
(if that is my part).
Let me study the cardiovascular tissue,
let me examine the angular distance of meteors,
let me suck on the stems of flowers
(if that is my part).
Let me make certain tribal figures
(if that is my part).
For this thing the body needs
let me sing
for the supper,
for the kissing,
for the correct
yes.

ANNE SEXTON

THE ROOM OF MY LIFE

Here,
in the room of my life
the objects keep changing.
Ashtrays to cry into,
the suffering brother of the wood walls,
the forty-eight keys of the typewriter
each an eyeball that is never shut,
the books, each a contestant in a beauty contest,
the black chair, a dog coffin made of Naugahyde,
the sockets on the wall
waiting like a cave of bees,
the gold rug
a conversation of heels and toes,
the fireplace
a knife waiting for someone to pick it up,
the sofa, exhausted with the exertion of a whore,
the phone
two flowers taking root in its crotch,
the doors
opening and closing like sea clams,
the lights
poking at me,
lighting up both the soil and the laugh.
The windows,
the starving windows
that drive the trees like nails into my heart.
Each day I feed the world out there
although birds explode
right and left.
I feed the world in here too,
offering the desk puppy biscuits.
However, nothing is just what it seems to be.
My objects dream and wear new costumes,
compelled to, it seems, but all the words in my hands
and the sea that bangs in my throat.

Charles Simic

CHARLES SIMIC

Charles Simic is a sentence.
A sentence has a beginning and an end.

Is he a simple or compound sentence?
It depends on the weather,
It depends on the stars above.

What is the subject of the sentence?
The subject is your beloved Charles Simic.

How many verbs are there in the sentence?
Eating, sleeping and fucking are some of its verbs.

What is the object of the sentence?
The object, my little ones,
Is not yet in sight.

And who is writing this awkward sentence?
A blackmailer, a girl in love,
And an applicant for a job.

Will they end with a period or a question mark?
They'll end with an exclamation point and an ink spot.

POEM WITHOUT A TITLE

I say to the lead
Why did you let yourself
Be cast into a bullet?
Have you forgotten the alchemists?
Have you given up hope
Of turning into gold?

Nobody answers.
Lead. Bullet.
With names like that
The sleep is deep and long.

CHARLES SIMIC

FEBRUARY

The one who lights the wood stove
Gets up in the dark.

How cold the iron is to the hand
Groping to open the flue,
The hand that will draw back
At the roar of the wind outside.

The wood that no longer smells of the woods;
The wood that smells of rats and mice —
And the matches which are always so loud
In the glacial stillness.

By its flare you'll see her squat;
Gaunt, wide-eyed;
Her lips saying the stark headlines
Going up in flames.

POEM

Every morning I forget how it is.
I watch the smoke mount
In great strides above the city.
I belong to no one.

Then, I remember my shoes,
How I have to put them on,
How bending over to tie them up
I will look into the earth.

STONE

Go inside a stone
That would be my way.
Let somebody else become a dove
Or gnash with a tiger's tooth.
I am happy to be a stone.

From the outside the stone is a riddle:
No one knows how to answer it.
Yet within, it must be cool and quiet
Even though a cow steps on it full weight,
Even though a child throws it in a river;
The stone sinks, slow, unperturbed
To the river bottom
Where the fishes come to knock on it
And listen.

I have seen sparks fly out
When two stones are rubbed,
So perhaps it is not dark inside after all;
Perhaps there is a moon shining
From somewhere, as though behind a hill —
Just enough light to make out
The strange writings, the star-charts
On the inner walls.

FORK

This strange thing must have crept
Right out of hell.
It resembles a bird's foot
Worn around the cannibal's neck.

As you hold it in your hand,
As you stab with it into a piece of meat,
It is possible to imagine the rest of the bird:
Its head which like your fist
Is large, bald, beakless and blind.

SOLITUDE

There now, where the first crumb
Falls from the table
You think no one hears it
As it hits the floor

But somewhere already
The ants are putting on
Their Quakers' hats
And setting out to visit you.

FEAR

Fear passes from man to man
Unknowing,
As one leaf passes its shudder
To another.

All at once the whole tree is trembling
And there is no sign of the wind.

CLASSIC BALLROOM DANCES

Grandmothers who wring the necks
Of chickens; old nuns
With names like Theresa, Marianne,
Who pull schoolboys by the ear;

The intricate steps of pickpockets
Working the crowd of the curious
At the scene of an accident; the slow shuffle
Of the evangelist with a sandwich-board;

The hesitation of the early morning customer
Peeking through the window-grille
Of a pawnshop; the weave of a little kid
Who is walking to school with eyes closed;

And the ancient lovers, cheek to cheek,
On the dancefloor of the Union Hall,
Where they also hold charity raffles
On rainy Monday nights of an eternal November.

CHARLES SIMIC

THE OLD WORLD

for Dan and Jeanne

I believe in the soul; so far
It hasn't made much difference.
I remember an afternoon in Sicily.
The ruins of some temple.
Columns fallen in the grass like naked lovers.

The olives and goat cheese tasted delicious
And so did the wine
With which I toasted the coming night,
The darting swallows,
The Saracen wind and moon.

It got darker. There was something
Long before there were words:
The evening meal of shepherds . . .
A fleeting whiteness among the trees . . .
Eternity eavesdropping on time.

The goddess going to bathe in the sea.
She must not be followed.
These rocks, these cypress trees,
May be her old lovers.
Oh to be one of them, the wine whispered to me.

ENTERTAINING THE CANARY

Yellow feathers,
Is it true
You chirp to the cop
On the beat?

Desist. Turn your
Nervous gaze
At the open bathroom door
Where I'm soaping

My love's back
And putting my chin on her shoulder
So I can do the same for her
Breasts and crotch.

Sing. Flutter your wings
As if you were applauding,
Or I'll throw her black slip
Over your gilded cage.

USED BOOK STORE

Lovers hold hands in never-opened novels.
The page with a recipe for cucumber soup is missing.
A dead man writes of his happy childhood on a farm,
Of riding in a balloon over Lake Erie.

A sudden draft shuts his book in my hand,
While a philosopher asks how is it possible
To maintain the theologically orthodox doctrine
Of eternal punishment of the damned?

Let's see. There may be sand among the pages
Of a travel guide to Egypt or even a dead flea
That once bit the ass of the mysterious Abigail
Who scribbled her name teasingly with an eye pencil.

MY NOISELESS ENTOURAGE

We were never formally introduced.
I had no idea of their number.
It was like a discreet entourage
Of homegrown angels and demons
All of whom I had met before
And had since largely forgotten.

In time of danger, they made themselves scarce.
Where did they all go?

I asked some felon one night
While he held a knife to my throat,
But he was spooked too,
Letting me go without a word,

It was disconcerting, downright frightening
To be reminded of one's solitude,
Like opening a children's book —
With nothing better to do — reading about stars,
How they can afford to spend centuries
Traveling our way on a glint of light.

errata

Where it says snow
read teeth-marks of a virgin
Where it says knife read
you passed through my bones
like a police-whistle
Where it says table read horse
Where it says horse read my migrant's bundle
Apples are to remain apples
Each time a hat appears
think of Isaac Newton
reading the Old Testament
Remove all periods
They are scars made by words
I couldn't bring myself to say
Put a finger over each sunrise
it will blind you otherwise
That damn ant is still stirring
Will there be time left to list
all errors to replace
all hands guns owls plates
all cigars ponds woods and reach
that beer-bottle my greatest mistake
the word I allowed to be written
when I should have shouted
her name

John Keating

Louis Simpson

WORKING LATE

A light is on in my father's study.
"Still up?" he says, and we are silent,
looking at the harbor lights,
listening to the surf
and the creak of coconut boughs.

He is working late on cases.
No impassioned speech! He argues from evidence,
actually pacing out and measuring,
while the fans revolving on the ceiling
winnow the true from the false.

Once he passed a brass curtain rod
through a head made out of plaster
and showed the jury the angle of fire —
where the murderer must have stood.
For years, all through my childhood,
if I opened a closet . . . bang!
There would be the dead man's head
with a black hole in the forehead.

All the arguing in the world
will not stay the moon.
She has come all the way from Russia
to gaze for a while in a mango tree
and light the wall of a veranda,
before resuming her interrupted journey
beyond the harbor and the lighthouse
at Port Royal, turning away
from land to the open sea.

Yet, nothing in nature changes, from that day to this,
she is still the mother of us all.
I can see the drifting offshore lights,
black posts where the pelicans brood.
And the light that used to shine
at night in my father's study
now shines as late in mine.

LOUIS SIMPSON

RIVERSIDE DRIVE

I have been staring at a sentence
for fifteen minutes. The mind
was not made for social science.

I take my overcoat and go.

Night has fallen on Riverside Drive . . .
the sign for Spry shining
across the Hudson: "Spry for Frying ****
for Baking."

I am thinking of Rilke
and "Who if I cried would hear me
among the angelic orders?"

It seems that we are here to say
names like "Spry" and "Riverside Drive" . . .
to carry the names of places
and things with us, into the night

glimmering with stars and constellations.

QUIET DESPERATION

At the post office he sees Joe McInnes.
Joe says, "We're having some people over.
It'll be informal. Come as you are."

She is in the middle
of preparing dinner. Tonight
she is trying an experiment:
Hal Burgonyaual — Fish-Potato Casserole.
She has cooked and drained the potatoes
and cut the fish in pieces.
Now she has to "mash potatoes,
add butter and hot milk," et cetera.

He relays Joe's invitation.
"No," she says, "not on your life.
Muriel McInnes is no friend of mine."

It appears that she told Muriel
that the Goldins live above their means,
and Muriel told Mary Goldin.

He listens carefully, to get things right.
The feud between the Andersons and the Kellys
began with Ruth Anderson calling Mike Kelly
a reckless driver. Finally
the Andersons had to sell their house and move.

Social life is no joke.
It can be the only life there is.

*

In the living room the battle of Iwo Jima
is in progress, watched by his son.
Men are dying on the beach,
pinned down by a machine gun.

The marine carrying the satchel charge
falls. Then Sergeant Stryker
picks up the charge and starts running.

Now you are with the enemy machine gun
firing out of the pillbox
as Stryker comes running,
bullets at his heels kicking up dust.
He makes it to the base of the pillbox,
lights the charge, raises up,
and heaves it through the opening.
The pillbox explodes . . .
the NCO's wave, "Move out!"

And he rises to his feet.
He's seen the movie. Stryker gets killed
just as they're raising the flag.

*

A feeling of pressure . . .
There is something that needs to be done
immediately.
           But there is nothing,
only himself. His life is passing,

and afterwards there will be eternity,
silence, and infinite space.

He thinks, "Firewood!" —
and goes to the basement,
takes the Swede-saw off the wall,
and goes outside, to the woodpile.

He carries an armful to the sawhorse
and saws the logs into smaller pieces.
In twenty minutes he has a pile of firewood
cut just the right length.
He carries the cut logs into the house
and arranges them in a neat pile
next to the fireplace.

Then looks around for something else to do,
to relieve the feeling of pressure.

The dog!
He will take the dog for a walk.

＊

They make a futile procession . . .
he commanding her to "Heel!" —
she dragging back or straining ahead.

The leaves are turning yellow.
Between the trunks of the trees
the cove is blue, with ripples.
The swans — this year there are seven —
are sailing line astern.

But when you come closer
the rocks above the shore are littered
with daggers of broken glass
where the boys sat on summer nights
and broke beer bottles afterwards.

And the beach is littered, with cans,
containers, heaps of garbage,
newspaper wadded against the sea-wall.
Someone has even dumped a mattress . . .
a definite success!

Some daring guy, some Stryker
in the pickup speeding away.

He cannot bear the sun
going over and going down . . .
the trees and houses vanishing
in quiet every day.

IN THE SUBURBS

There's no way out.
You were born to waste your life.
You were born to this middleclass life

As others before you
Were born to walk in procession
To the temple, singing.

PHYSICAL UNIVERSE

He woke at five and, unable
to go back to sleep,
went downstairs.

A book was lying on the table
where his son had done his homework.
He took it into the kitchen,
made coffee, poured himself a cup,
and settled down to read.

"There was a local eddy in the swirling gas
of the primordial galaxy,
and a cloud was formed, the protosun,
as wide as the present solar system.

"This contracted. Some of the gas
formed a diffuse, spherical nebula,
a thin disk, that cooled and flattened.

Pulled one way by its own gravity,
the other way by the sun,
it broke, forming smaller clouds,
the protoplanets. Earth
was 2,000 times as wide as it is now."

The earth was without form, and void,
and darkness was upon the face of the deep.

*

"Then the sun began to shine,
dispelling the gases and vapors,
shrinking the planets, melting earth,
separating iron and silicate
to form the core and mantle.
Continents appeared . . ."

history, civilization,
the discovery of America
and the settling of Green Harbor,
bringing us to Tuesday, the seventh of July.

Tuesday, the day they pick up the garbage!
He leapt into action,
took the garbage bag out of its container,
tied it with a twist of wire,
and carried it out to the toolshed,
taking care not to let the screen door slam,
and put it in the large garbage can
that was three-quarters full.
He kept it in the toolshed so the raccoons
couldn't get at it.

He carried the can out to the road,
then went back into the house
and walked around, picking up newspapers
and fliers for: "Thompson Seedless Grapes,
California's finest sweet eating";

"Scott Bathroom Tissue";

"Legislative report from Senator Ken LaValle."

He put all this paper in a box,
and emptied the waste baskets in the two
downstairs bathrooms,
and the basket in the study.

He carried the box out to the road,
taking care not to let the screen door slam,
and placed the box next to the garbage.

Now let the garbage men come!

*

He went back upstairs.
Mary said, "Did you put out the garbage?"
But her eyes were closed.
She was sleeping, yet could speak in her sleep,
ask a question, even answer one.

"Yes," he said, and climbed into bed.
She turned around to face him,
with her eyes still closed.

He thought, perhaps she's an oracle,
speaking from the Collective Unconscious.
He said to her, "Do you agree with Darwin
that people and monkeys have a common ancestor?
Or should we stick to the Bible?"
She said, "Did you take out the garbage?"

"Yes," he said, for the second time.
Then thought about it. Her answer
had something in it of the sublime.
Like a *koan* . . . the kind of irrelevance
a Zen master says to the disciple
who is asking riddles of the universe.

He put his arm around her,
and she continued to breathe evenly
from the depths of sleep.

Dave Smith

FIDDLERS

Black mudbank pushes them out like hotel fire.
Some at water's edge seem to wait for transport.
Others sweat, pale, scattered on the shining beach.
All keep closed the mighty arms of God's damage,
waving at shadows and movements made by the sun.
Desire, the dragging arm, sifts, picks, tastes, untastes
endlessly the civic occasions the tide brings in.
Surely floods, cold fronts, embolisms of dreams
drive them in where the earth's brain hums. They
clasp, breed. They glare upward in rooms where the moon
slips its question. Daylong they spout, fume, command.
Biblical as kinsmen with a son they must kill.
Nouns, verbs couple like years. Water comes, listens.

BLOWFISH AND MUDTOAD

Held the wrong way either will take the finger
that clamps the casual pen, changing your words,
its rows of teeth like a serrated bread knife.
Moss-covered as bottom rock, wearing the brown
scum of salt water settlers, current-fluttered
flags of weed, eyes like glass pitted by age,
each reads steadily the downdrifted offerings
its tongue ticks for: crawlers, wings, limbs, all
the great current gathers to sweep away at last.
Our line sinkered into that steep wants a sleek
one to claim us — big Blue, Striper, Thor-like Drum.
Not these nibbling small-town preachers, Mudtoad's
black ambush, or Blowfish, resurrection and rage.

NIGHT FISHING FOR BLUES

At Fortress Monroe, Virginia,
the big-jawed Bluefish, ravenous, sleek muscle slamming
at rock, at pier legs, drives into Chesapeake shallows,

convoys rank after rank, wheeling through
flume and flute of blood, something
like hunger's throb hooking
until you hear it and know them there,
the family.
                    Tonight, not far from where Jefferson Davis
hunched in a harrowing cell, gray eyes quick
as crab's nubs, I come back over planks
deep drummed under boots years ago, tufts of hair

floating at my eyes, thinking it is right
                    to pitch through tideturn and mudslur
                    for fish with teeth like snapped sabers.
                    In blue crescents of base lights, I cast hooks

baited with Smithfield ham: they reel, zing,
plummet, coil in corrosive swirls, bump on
scum-skinned rocks. No skin divers prowl here,
                    visibility an arm's length, my visions

hand-to-hand in the line's warp. A meat-baited
lure limps through limbs nippling the muck,
silhouettes, shoots forward, catches a cruising Blue
sentry's eye, snags, and sets

case-hardened barbs. Suddenly, I am not alone:
            three negroes plump down in lawn chairs, shudder,
            cast quick into the black pod slopping under us. One

            ripples with age, a grandmotherly obelisk,

her breath puffing like a coal stove. She swivels
heavily, chewing her dark nut, humming gospel,
then spits thick juice like a careful chum.

            When I yank the first Blue
she mumbles, her eyes roll far out on the black
blue billowing of the sea. I hear her cant
            to Africa, a cluck in her throat, a chain

song from the fisherman's house. I cannot
understand her yet. Bluefish pour at me in squads.
I haul two, three at a time, torpedoes, moon-shiners,
jamming my feet into the splintered floor, battling

whatever comes. Fathers, we have waited
a whole life for this minute. Dreams

       graven on cold cell walls, Blues walk over

our heads, ground on back-wings, grind their teeth.
They splash rings of blue and silver around us, chevrons
of lost battalions. I can smell the salt of many ocean
runners, and now she hollers *I ain't doing so bad
for an old queen!* No time to answer. Two

      car-hoods down her descendents swing

moonsleek arms, exotic butterflies: I hear them
pop beer cans, the whoosh released like stale breath
through a noose no one remembers. We hang
fast flat casts, artless, no teasing fishers,
beyond the book-bred lures, the pristine streams,
speeded-up, hungry, almost machines wound
too far, belts slipped, gears gone, momentum

      hauling us to race at each other, winging

wildly as howitzers. Incredibly it happens: I feel
the hook hammer and shake and throw my entire weight
to dragging, as if have caught the goddamndest

      Blue in the Atlantic. She screams: *Oh my God!*
Four of us fumbling in beamed headlight and blue
arcs overhead cut the hook from her face. Gnats
nag us: I put it in deep and it must be gouged out
like old hate. When it is free, I hear Blues

not dead flop softly. I whisper it's luck
she could see us. She mops blood blued over
gold-lined teeth and opens her arms so her dress
      billows like a caftan. She wants

nothing but to fish. I hand her a pole, then cast
as far as I can. She pumps, wings a sinker and hooks
into flashing slop and reels hard. In one instant both

      our lines leap rigid as daguerreotypes. We

have caught each other but keep on, pushed by blue
ghosts that thrash in the brain's deep cull.

We reel shadows until we see there is nothing,
then sit on the shaky pier like prisoners. Coil
by coil we trace the path of Bluefish-knots backward,
        unlooping, feeling for holes, testing,

slapping gnats like small fears. Harried, unbound,
at last we leap to fish again. But now a gray glow
shreds with the cloud curtain, an old belly-fire
        guts the night. Already the tide humps

on itself. Lights flicker like campfires in duty windows
at Ft. Monroe. She hooks up, saying *Sons they done
let us go.* I cast once more but nothing bites.

        Everywhere the circle of Blues stiffens

in flecks of blood. We kneel, stuff styrofoam
boxes with blankets of ice, break their backs
to keep them cold and sweet, the woman
showing us what to do. By dawn the stink has passed
        out of our noses. We drink beer like family.

All the way home thousands of Blues fall from my head,
falling with the gray Atlantic, and a pale veiny light
fills the road with sea-shadows that drift in figure

        eights, knot and snarl and draw me forward.

2000

It's always been nineteen something for me.
Nineteen for my father all his life,
nineteen for my grandmother who went,
nineteen for my sister who wanders,
nineteen for my grandfathers who won't make it,
nineteen for my wife who will, our children,
and, for all I know, yours, and theirs.
Nineteen is a lot of sad, dirty numbers
and something that reports to none of us.

What good are words in the face of numbers?
They keep the shadow under a boat rotting

where I crawled as a child, they hide
the pitted spoon of dreams, they deliver
wind in tunes over the reed-heads of home.
They turn my father's face to a thin plank
where I cross the creek over fallen stars.
They are the zeroes of sorrow something says.

I want to pick up my ears like a tired dog
when the whistling comes over the fences.
I want to lie down and dream of God counting
my sins until in anger he sounds sexual
as a Peterbilt diesel in a fishing scow.
I want to watch the words: nineteen something.
They'll loop out of sight like a slow worm
and I won't even try to read the slime,
the dirt, or the revolutions of the moon.

PINE CONES

Any way you hold them, they hurt.
What's the use, then?

Once in our backyard, by a sparrow's hidden
tremor there in the green wish of spruce,
a full but unfolded body hung.

It bore every color of the world and was sweet
beyond measure. The canyon wind banged
at this then went elsewhere.

Something happened that night.
The sparrow seems to have seen what it was.

Look at him huddled, mistakably some other shadow,
the sly outlines of his body almost blue as spruce,
the sun like a big wall nearby,

and you stepping through it, big, so big
he would almost give up his only wish.

Almost. Almost. Almost.

DAVE SMITH

Isn't this the way hearts beat in the world,
the way pine cones fall in the night
until they don't?

When you pick them up, as children do,
the tiny spot appears in your palm,
red as the sun's first blink
of love.

And that sticking, unabidable tar.

ALLEGHENY HAPPINESS

When we were done she said it burned. Love can, I said,
hearing the push and pull of hours, the years grind.
The girl, a guy's wife in Pittsburgh, red dress on toilet door,
made a noise in her throat, soft, but ugly all the same.
Face pale, underwear glowing on chair, soul in a hurry,
dusk shivering down on buds, azaleas, jonquils, tulips.
I was happy, Cumberland left behind. No, she said, I mean
you've torn me, I wasn't ready. Don't you know anything yet?

Be always ready, I knew what those words hurried to mean.
I'd told her I drove train diesels. I watched one in my head
tearing the darkness, not caring what came next. But
I felt my legs start to burn like they did tucked up
so I could lean way out of the cab as it climbed.
I felt her knees bumping mine under the sheets.
Rain came, brittle at the window, then quiet, thickening.
I was afraid to touch her again, I said what do you mean?

The usual thing, a man won't wait, afraid of the dark.
You can't help it, pushing, taking it too fast, not seeing.
I kept hearing the way she said *a man*. Off in the yard,
a diesel's horn wailed, its B&O face pinched, light
swelling bigger, speed balling to weight I couldn't feel,
somebody inside, I knew, squinting at blurred signals,
looking for mistakes. My job was to see into that dark.

Don't rush, my father said, take time, go easy, come back.
Nothing terrible had hurt me yet, my lunch tin was full,
thermos wet with whiskey, streets shining below,

late dawn snow somewhere ahead. Hungry, I'd eat,
lean out of my cab, coffee churned to burning flecks
on my skin when curves came. I might think about her.
I wouldn't fail, brakes would hold the dark off. No problem.

Ahead of me the clank and shriek of the B&O's couplings.
Coal ash now on green lawns. I smelled roses in her hair.
You don't know so much, she said. *A man.* She said that, too.

THE TIRE HANGS IN THE YARD

1

First it was the secret place where I went to dream, end
of the childhood road, deep-tracked, the dark
behind my best friend's house, blackberry
thickets of darkness, and later where
we stared, with willing girls, into the sky.

Past that hedgerow, past fields turned to houses, past
the crows we shot in our bored pleasure, I drive
bathed by green dashlight and the sun's blood
glinting on leaves just parted, then see

again the road's dead-end in woods, its deep stillness
ticking like throat-wheeze — and Jesus Christ
look at the beer cans, the traffic, even
hung on a berry vine somebody's rubber,
and wouldn't you know it that tire still hangs.

2

On the Churchland Baptist Church the hot ivy hung, smelled
of dust, our mouths lifting their black holes
like a tire I kept dreaming. Clenched
by mother and father who stank sweetly in sweat,

I sang and sang until the black ceiling
of our house seemed to sway and crack
and the tire skulled against my eyes
in time with the great clock in the far hall.
Hanging in darkness, like my sex, it made me listen.

3

One summer night here I came to fistfight Jim Jenrett,
whose house she had gone to, who is now no more
than a frail hand remembered on cheek, and I
was beer-brave, nearly wild with all
the dozen piling from cars. Jesus,
look at us in the ghost-flare of headlights,
pissing, taunting, boy-shadows, me hung
in the tire of my best friend spitting final threats.

So we passed, blinded, into the years, into the trees
holding their scars, half-healed, into the dark
where Jim, dunned by our words, went out
near dawn and stepped in the tire
and shied up the electric extension cord, noosed,
by the rope whose tire, burdened, ticked slowly.

4

Ghost-heart of this place, of dreams, I give you a shove
and sure enough I hear the tick and all that was
is, and a girl straightening her skirt walks
smack against you and screams. You know
who laughs, smoking in the shadows, don't you?

There are no headlights now, only the arc of blackness
gathering the hung world in its gullet. Blink
and maybe he's there, his great feet jammed
halfway in the hole of your heart,
gone halfway.

5

Where do they go who were with us on this dream road,
who flung themselves like seed under berry-black
nights, those faces black-clustered,
who could lean down and tell us
what love is and mercy and why now

I imagine a girl, mouth open in the sexual O, her hair
gone dull as soap scum, the husband grunting

as his fist smacks again, her scream
not out yet, nor the promise
she could never love anyone else.

I climb in the tire, swinging like a secret in the dark
woods surrounded by homelights of strangers.
She swore she loved me best.

In the church I imagined this place left forever behind
but it's with me as I try to see the road begin.
Blackberries on both sides blackly hang.
Trees, in blackness, leaned down at me.
When will they come, the headlights
washing over me like revelation,
the cars ticking and swirling like souls?

Once when my mother could not find me, they came here.
They said, "So this is it, the place." It was dark,
or nearly, and they said I might have died.
I asked them what being dead was like.
Like swinging at night, they joked, in the trees.

I shove my foot at the dirt, lifting off in blackness.
The whine of the rope is like a distant scream.
I think, so this is it. Really it.

for Robert Penn Warren

W. D. Snodgrass

VIEWING THE BODY

Flowers like a gangster's funeral;
    Eyeshadow like a whore.
They all say isn't she beautiful.
    She, who never wore

Lipstick or such a dress,
    Never got taken out,
Was scarcely looked at, much less
    Wanted or talked about;

Who, gray as a mouse, crept
    The dark halls at her mother's
Or snuggled, soft, and slept
    Alone in the dim bedcovers.

Today at last she holds
    All eyes and a place of honor
Till the obscene red folds
    Of satin close down on her.

[handwritten: confessional poem — patient zero]
[handwritten: personal & unpoetic theme: Divorce and trying to be a father to his 3 yo. daughter]

from *HEART'S NEEDLE*

9

I get numb and go in
though the dry ground will not hold
    the few dry swirls of snow
and it must not be very cold.
A friend asks how you've been
    and I don't know

or see much right to ask.
Or what use it could be to know.
    In three months since you came
the leaves have fallen and the snow;

your pictures pinned above my desk
seem much the same.

Somehow I come to find
myself upstairs in the third floor
museum's halls,
walking to kill my time once more
among the enduring and resigned
stuffed animals,

where, through a century's
caprice, displacement and
known treachery between
its wars, they hear some old command
and in their peaceable kingdoms freeze
to this still scene,

Nature Morte. Here
by the door, its guardian,
the patchwork dodo stands
where you and your stepsister ran
laughing and pointing. Here, last year,
you pulled my hands

[handwritten annotation: uselessness (as a father) → trying to blend the families]

and had your first, worst quarrel,
so toys were put up on your shelves.
Here in the first glass cage
the little bobcats arch themselves,
still practicing their snarl
of constant rage.

The bison, here, immense,
shoves at his calf, brow to brow,
and looks it in the eye
to see what is it thinking now.
I forced you to obedience;
I don't know why.

Still the lean lioness
beyond them, on her jutting ledge
of shale and desert shrub,
stands watching always at the edge,
stands hard and tanned and envious
above her cub;

W. D. SNODGRASS

with horns locked in tall heather,
two great Olympian Elk stand bound,
    fixed in their lasting hate
till hunger brings them both to ground.
Whom equal weakness binds together
    none shall separate.

    Yet separate in the ocean
of broken ice, the white bear reels
    beyond the leathery groups
of scattered, drab Arctic seals
arrested here in violent motion
    like Napoleon's troops.

    Our states have stood so long
at war, shaken with hate and dread,
    they are paralyzed at bay;
once we were out of reach, we said,
we would grow reasonable and strong.
    Some other day.

    Like the cold men of Rome,
we have won costly fields to sow
    in salt, our only seed.
Nothing but injury will grow.
I write you only the bitter poems
    that you can't read.

    Onan who would not breed
a child to take his brother's bread
    and be his brother's birth,
rose up and left his lawful bed,
went out and spilled his seed
    in the cold earth.

    I stand by the unborn,
by putty-colored children curled
    in jars of alcohol,
that waken to no other world,
unchanging, where no eye shall mourn.
    I see the caul

    that wrapped a kitten, dead.
I see the branching, doubled throat

of a two-headed foal;
I see the hydrocephalic goat;
here is the curled and swollen head,
      there, the burst skull;

    skin of a limbless calf;
a horse's foetus, mummified;
    mounted and joined forever,
the Siamese twin dogs that ride
belly to belly, half and half,
      that none shall sever.

    I walk among the growths,
by gangrenous tissue, goiter, cysts,
    by fistulas and cancers,
where the malignancy man loathes
is held suspended and persists.
      And I don't know the answers.

    The window's turning white.
The world moves like a diseased heart
    packed with ice and snow.
Three months now we have been apart
less than a mile. I cannot fight
    or let you go.

"AFTER EXPERIENCE TAUGHT ME . . ."

After experience taught me that all the ordinary
Surroundings of social life are futile and vain;

    I'm going to show you something very
    Ugly: someday, it might save your life.

Seeing that none of the things I feared contain
In themselves anything either good or bad

    What if you get caught without a knife;
    Nothing — even a loop of piano wire;

Excepting only in the effect they had
Upon my mind, I resolved to inquire

W. D. SNODGRASS

Take the first two fingers of this hand;
Fork them out — kind of a "V for Victory" —

Whether there might be something whose discovery
Would grant me supreme, unending happiness.

And jam them into the eyes of your enemy.
You have to do this hard. Very hard. Then press

No virtue can be thought to have priority
Over this endeavor to preserve one's being.

Both fingers down around the cheekbone
And setting your foot high into the chest

No man can desire to act rightly, to be blessed,
To live rightly, without simultaneously

You must call up every strength you own
And you can rip off the whole facial mask.

Wishing to be, to act, to live. He must ask
First, in other words, to actually exist.

And you, whiner, who wastes your time
Dawdling over the remorseless earth,
What evil, what unspeakable crime
Have you made your life worth?

OLD APPLE TREES

Like battered old millhands, they stand in the orchard —
Like drunk legionnaires, heaving themselves up,
Lurching to attention. Not one of them wobbles
The same way as another. Uniforms won't fit them —
All those cramps, humps, bulges. Here, a limb's gone;
There, rain and corruption have eaten the whole core.
They've all grown too tall, too thick, or too something.
Like men bent too long over desks, engines, benches,
Or bent under mailsacks, under loss.
They've seen too much history and bad weather, grown

Around rocks, into high winds, diseases, grown
Too long to be willful, too long to be changed.

Oh, I could replant, bulldoze the lot,
Get nursery stock, all the latest ornamentals,
Make the whole place look like a suburb,
Each limb sleek as a teeny bopper's — pink
To the very crotch — each trunk smoothed, ideal
As the fantasy life of an adman.
We might just own the Arboreal Muscle Beach:
Each tree disguised as its neighbor. Or each disguised
As if not its neighbor — each doing its own thing
Like executives' children.

                            At least I could prune,
At least I should trim the dead wood; fill holes
Where rain collects and decay starts. Well, I should;
I should. There's a red squirrel nests here someplace.
I live in the hope of hearing one saw-whet owl.
Then, too, they're right about Spring. Bees hum
Through these branches like lascivious intentions. The white
Petals drift down, sift across the ground; this air's so rich
No man should come here except on a working pass;
No man should leave here without going to confession.
All Fall, apples nearly crack the boughs;
They hang here red as candles in the
White oncoming snow.

Tonight we'll drive down to the bad part of town
To the New Hungarian Bar or the Klub Polski,
To the Old Hellas where we'll eat the new spring lamb;
Drink good *mavrodaphne*, say, at the Laikon Bar,
Send drinks to the dancers, those meatcutters and laborers
Who move in their native dances, the archaic forms.
Maybe we'll still find our old crone selling chestnuts,
Whose toothless gums can spit out fifteen languages,
Who turns, there, late at night, in the center of the floor,
Her ancient dry hips wheeling their slow, slow *tsamikos*;
We'll stomp under the tables, whistle, we'll all hiss
Till even the belly dancer leaves, disgraced.

We'll drive back, lushed and vacant, in the first dawn;
Out of the light gray mists may rise our flowering
Orchard, the rough trunks holding their formations

Like elders of Colonus, the old men of Thebes
Tossing their white hair, almost whispering,
Soon, each one of us will be taken
By dark powers under this ground
That drove us here, that warped us.
Not one of us got it his own way.
Nothing like any one of us
Will be seen again, forever.
Each of us held some noble shape in mind.
It seemed better that we kept alive.

LOVE LAMP

There's our candle, on the bedstand still,
That served, warm nights, for lovelight
And the rays of its glass panels played
On our entangled legs and shoulders
Like some sailor's red and blue tattoos
Or as cathedral stained glass alters
Congregated flesh to things less
Carnal, tinged by its enfolding glow.

What could that frail lamp seem
To prowlers outside — the fox, say, the owl,
Or to some smaller creature, shrieking,
Pierced in the clutch of tooth and claw
That interrupted love's enactments?
Our glancing flashlight, though, showed
Only scattered grey fur, some broken
Feathers, bloodstained, on the lawn.

Scuttling back to bed, a little
Chilled from the wet grass, we scratched
A match restoring our small gleam
To see there, sinking in soft wax,
The wings and swimming dark limbs
Of that moth — still there, hardened
By the years like amber. While I remember
The scathing fire-points of his eyes.

Gary Snyder

"ONE SHOULD NOT TALK TO A SKILLED HUNTER ABOUT WHAT IS FORBIDDEN BY THE BUDDHA"

— Hsiang-yen

A gray fox, female, nine pounds three ounces.
39 5/8" long with tail.
Peeling skin back (Kai
reminded us to chant the *Shingyo* first)
cold pelt. crinkle; and musky smell
mixed with dead-body odor starting.

Stomach content: a whole ground squirrel well chewed
plus one lizard foot
and somewhere from inside the ground squirrel
a bit of aluminum foil.

The secret.
and the secret hidden deep in that.

BUBBS CREEK HAIRCUT

High ceilinged and the double mirrors, the
     calendar a splendid alpine scene — scab barber —
in stained white barber gown, alone, sat down, old man
a summer fog gray San Francisco day
I walked right in. On Howard Street
               haircut a dollar twenty-five.
Just clip it close as it will go.
     "Now why you want your hair cut back like that."
     — Well I'm going to the Sierras for a while
Bubbs Creek and on across to upper Kern.
         He wriggled clippers
"Well I been up there, I built the cabin
     up at Cedar Grove. In nineteen five."
         Old haircut smell.

Next door, Goodwill
        where I came out.
A search for sweater and a stroll
        in the board & concrete room of
        unfixed junk downstairs —
all emblems of the past — too close —
        heaped up in chilly dust and bare-bulb glare
of tables, wheelchairs, battered trunks & lamps
& pots that boiled up coffee nineteen ten, things
swimming on their own & finally freed
                from human need. Or?
        Waiting a final flicker of desire
to tote them out once more. Some freakish use.
The Master of the limbo drag-legged watches
                making prices
        to the people seldom buy.
The sag-asst rocker has to make it now. Alone.

                A few days later drove with Locke
down San Joaquin, us barefoot in the heat
stopping for beer and melon on the way
        the Giant Orange,
rubber shreds of cast truck retreads on the pebble
shoulder, highway 99.
                Sierras marked by cumulus in the east.
Car coughing in the groves, six thousand feet
down to Kings River Canyon; camped at Cedar Grove.
        Hard granite canyon walls that
        leave no scree.

Once tried a haircut at the Barber College too —
sat half an hour before they told me
        white men use the other side.
Goodwill, St. Vincent de Paul,
        Salvation Army up the coast
for mackinaws and boots and heavy socks
        — Seattle has the best for logger gear
once found a pair of good tricouni boots
        at the under-the-public market store,
        Mark Tobey's scene,
                torn down I hear —
and Filson jacket with a birdblood stain.

A.G. and me got winter clothes for almost nothing
    at Lake Union, telling the old gal
      we was on our way
to work the winter out up in B.C.
         hitchhiking home the
green hat got a ride (of that more later).

Hiking up Bubbs Creek saw the trail crew tent
in a scraggly grove of creekside lodgepole pine
      talked to the guy, he says

"If you see McCool on the other trail crew over there
tell him Moorehead says to go to hell."
Late snow that summer. Crossing the scarred bare
      shed of Forester Pass
   the winding rock-braced switchbacks
dive in snowbanks, we climb on where
      pack trains have to dig or wait.
A half-iced-over lake, twelve thousand feet
      its sterile boulder bank
but filled with leaping trout:
      reflections wobble in the
mingling circles always spreading out
    the crazy web of wavelets makes sense
    seen from high above.
A deva world of sorts — it's high
      — a view that few men see, a point
   bare sunlight
   on the spaces
empty sky
      molding to fit the shape of what ice left
of fire-thrust, or of tilted, twisted, faulted
      cast-out from this lava belly globe.

The boulder in my mind's eye is a chair.
        . . . why was the man drag-legged?
King of Hell
   or is it a paradise of sorts, thus freed
from acting out the function some
      creator / carpenter
thrust on a thing to think he made, himself,
    an object always "chair"?
      Sinister ritual histories.
   Is the Mountain God a gimp?

The halting metrics   and the ritual limp,
           Good   Will?

Daughter of mountains, stooped
      moon breast Parvati

      mountain thunder speaks
      hair tingling static as the lightning lashes
      is neither word of love nor wisdom;
      though this be danger: hence thee fear.
              Some flowing girl
      whose slippery dance
      en trances Shiva
                — the valley spirit / Anahita,
                    Sarasvati,
      dark and female gate of all the world
      water that cuts back quartzflake sand
              soft is the dance that melts the
      mat-haired mountain sitter
                      to leap in fire
      & make of sand a tree
          of tree a board, of board (ideas!)
          somebody's rocking chair.
      A room of empty sun of peaks and ridges
      a universe of junk, all left alone.

The hat I always take on mountains:
When we came back down through Oregon
              (three years before)
at nightfall in the Siskiyou few cars pass.

A big truck stopped a hundred yards above
      "Siskiyou Stoneware" on the side
the driver said
he recognized my old green hat.
I'd had a ride
          with him two years before
a whole state north
          when hitching down to Portland
              from Warm Springs.

Allen in the rear on straw
forgot salami and we went on south
all night — in many cars — to Berkeley in the dawn.

Upper Kern River country now after nine days walk
it finally rain.
     We ran on that other trail crew
setting up new camp in the drizzly pine
cussing & slapping bugs, four days from road,
we saw McCool, & he said tell that Moorehead
    kiss my ass.

We squatted smoking by the fire.
    "I'll never get a green hat now"
the foreman says fifty mosquitoes sitting on the brim

       they must like green.
& two more days of thundershower and cold
    (on Whitney hair on end
    hail stinging bare legs in the blast of wind
    but yodel off the summit echoes clean)

    all this comes after:

purity of the mountains and goodwills.
The diamond drill of racing icemelt waters
    and bumming trucks & watching

buildings raze
    the garbage acres burning at the Bay
    the girl who was the skid-row
cripple's daughter —

    out of the memory of smoking pine
the lotion and the spittoon glitter rises
chair turns and in the double mirror waver
the old man cranks me down and cracks a chuckle

    "Your Bubbs Creek haircut, boy."

HAY FOR THE HORSES

He had driven half the night
From far down San Joaquin
Through Mariposa, up the

Dangerous mountain roads,
And pulled in at eight a.m.
With his big truckload of hay
    behind the barn.
With winch and ropes and hooks
We stacked the bales up clean
To splintery redwood rafters
High in the dark, flecks of alfalfa
Whirling through shingle-cracks of light,
Itch of haydust in the
    sweaty shirt and shoes.
At lunchtime under Black oak
Out in the hot corral,
  — The old mare nosing lunchpails,
Grasshoppers crackling in the weeds —
"I'm sixty-eight" he said,
"I first bucked hay when I was seventeen.
I thought, that day I started,
I sure would hate to do this all my life.
And dammit, that's just what
I've gone and done."

THE BATH

Washing Kai in the sauna,
The kerosene lantern set on a box
    outside the ground-level window,
Lights up the edge of the iron stove and the
    washtub down on the slab
Steaming air and crackle of waterdrops
    brushed by on the pile of rocks on top
He stands in warm water
Soap all over the smooth of his thigh and stomach
    "Gary don't soap my hair!"
    — his eye-sting fear —
    the soapy hand feeling
    through and around the globes and curves of his body
    up in the crotch,
And washing-tickling out the scrotum, little anus,
    his penis curving up and getting hard
    as I pull back skin and try to wash it

Laughing and jumping, flinging arms around,
    I squat all naked too,
                    is this our body?

Sweating and panting in the stove-steam hot-stone
    cedar-planking wooden bucket water-splashing
    kerosene lantern-flicker wind-in-the-pines-out
    sierra forest ridges night —
Masa comes in, letting fresh cool air
    sweep down from the door
    a deep sweet breath
And she tips him over gripping neatly, one knee down
    her hair falling hiding one whole side of
    shoulder, breast, and belly,
Washes deftly Kai's head-hair
    as he gets mad and yells —
The body of my lady, the winding valley spine,
    the space between the thighs I reach through,
    cup her curving vulva arch and hold it from behind,
    a soapy tickle   a hand of grail
The gates of Awe
That open back a turning double-mirror world of
    wombs in wombs, in rings,
    that start in music,
                    is this our body?

The hidden place of seed
The veins net flow across the ribs, that gathers
    milk and peaks up in a nipple — fits
    our mouth —
The sucking milk from this our body sends through
    jolts of light; the son, the father,
    sharing mother's joy
That brings a softness to the flower of the awesome
    open curling lotus gate I cup and kiss
As Kai laughs at his mother's breast he now is weaned
    from, we
    wash each other,
                    this our body

Kai's little scrotum up close to his groin,
    the seed still tucked away, that moved from us to him
In flows that lifted with the same joys forces
    as his nursing Masa later,
    playing with her breast,

Or me within her,
Or him emerging,

        this is our body:

Clean, and rinsed, and sweating more, we stretch
    out on the redwood benches hearts all beating
Quiet to the simmer of the stove,
    the scent of cedar
And then turn over,
    murmuring gossip of the grasses,
    talking firewood,
Wondering how Gen's napping, how to bring him in
    soon wash him too —
These boys who love their mother
    who loves men, who passes on
    her sons to other women;

The cloud across the sky. The windy pines.
    the trickle gurgle in the swampy meadow

    this is our body.

Fire inside and boiling water on the stove
We sigh and slide ourselves down from the benches
    wrap the babies, step outside,

black night & all the stars.

Pour cold water on the back and thighs
Go in the house — stand steaming by the center fire
Kai scampers on the sheepskin
Gen standing hanging on and shouting,

"Bao! bao! bao! bao! bao!"

This is our body. Drawn up crosslegged by the flames
    drinking icy water
    hugging babies, kissing bellies,

Laughing on the Great Earth

Come out from the bath.

GARY SNYDER

AXE HANDLES

One afternoon the last week in April
Showing Kai how to throw a hatchet
One-half turn and it sticks in a stump.
He recalls the hatchet-head
Without a handle, in the shop
And go gets it, and wants it for his own.
A broken-off axe handle behind the door
Is long enough for a hatchet,
We cut it to length and take it
With the hatchet head
And working hatchet, to the wood block.
There I begin to shape the old handle
With the hatchet, and the phrase
First learned from Ezra Pound
Rings in my ears!
"When making an axe handle
            the pattern is not far off."
And I say this to Kai
"Look: We'll shape the handle
By checking the handle
Of the axe we cut with — "
And he sees. And I hear it again:
It's in Lu Ji's *Wên Fu*, fourth century
A.D. "Essay on Literature" — in the
Preface: "In making the handle
Of an axe
By cutting wood with an axe
The model is indeed near at hand."
My teacher Shih-hsiang Chen
Translated that and taught it years ago
And I see: Pound was an axe,
Chen was an axe, I am an axe
And my son a handle, soon
To be shaping again, model
And tool, craft of culture,
How we go on.

Gary Soto

BLACK HAIR

At eight I was brilliant with my body.
In July, that ring of heat
We all jumped through, I sat in the bleachers
Of Romain Playground, in the lengthening
Shade that rose from our dirty feet.
The game before us was more than baseball. *American dream as a mexican*
It was a figure — Hector Moreno — *mexican*
Quick and hard with turned muscles,
His crouch the one I assumed before an altar
Of worn baseball cards, in my room.

I came here because I was Mexican, a stick
Of brown light in love with those
Who could do it — the triple and hard slide,
The gloves eating balls into double plays.
What could I do with 50 pounds, my shyness,
My black torch of hair, about to go out?
Father was dead, his face no longer
Hanging over the table or our sleep,
And mother was the terror of mouths
Twisting hurt by butter knives. — *dull*

In the bleachers I was brilliant with my body,
Waving players in and stomping my feet,
Growing sweaty in the presence of white shirts.
I chewed sunflower seeds. I drank water
And bit my arm through the late innings.
When Hector lined balls into deep
Center, in my mind I rounded the bases
With him, my face flared, my hair lifting
Beautifully, because we were coming home
To the arms of brown people.

GARY SOTO

ENVYING THE CHILDREN OF SAN FRANCISCO

At a city square
Children laugh in the red
Sweaters of Catholics,
As they walk home between trucks
And sunlight angled off buildings that end in points.
I'm holding an apple, among shoppers
Clutching bags big enough to sleep in,
And the air is warm for October —
Torn pieces of paper
Scuttling like roaches, a burst at a time.

The children are blond,
Shiny, and careful at the lights —
The sister with her brother's hand.
They cross looking
At their watches, and I cross too.
I want to know where
They're going, what door they'll push
Open and call home —
The TV coming on,
Milk, a cookie for each hand.

As a kid I wanted to live
In the city, in a building that rose above it all,
The gray streets burst open, a rattle
Of jackhammers. I wanted to
Stare down from the eighteenth floor, and let things go —
My homework for one, a paper plane
With a half-drawn heart and a girl's name.
I wanted to say that I ate
And slept, ate and slept in a building
That faced other buildings, a sliver of sea
Blue in the distance.

I wanted to hear voices
Behind walls, the *click-click* of a poodle
Strolling to his bowl — a violin like fingers
Running down a blackboard.
I wanted to warm my hands at a teakettle
And comb my hair in an elevator, my mouth
Still rolling with cereal, as I started off

[handwritten annotation: wanting to be a part of something — but not quite dream]

GARY SOTO

For school, a row of pens in my shirt pocket.
Back home at the window
I wanted it to be December —
Flags and honking cars,
A Santa Claus with his pot, a single red
Balloon let go and racing skyward,
And the tiny mothers who would come around
Buildings, disappear, and come around again,
Hugging bags for all they were worth to children.

ORANGES

The first time I walked
With a girl, I was twelve,
Cold, and weighted down
With two oranges in my jacket.
December. Frost cracking
Beneath my steps, my breath
Before me, then gone,
As I walked toward
Her house, the one whose
Porch light burned yellow
Night and day, in any weather.
A dog barked at me, until
She came out pulling
At her gloves, face bright
With rouge. I smiled,
Touched her shoulder, and led
Her down the street, across
A used car lot and a line
Of newly planted trees, —— *in a newly developed neighborhood*
Until we were breathing
Before a drugstore. We
Entered, the tiny bell
Bringing a saleslady
Down a narrow aisle of goods.
I turned to the candies
Tiered like bleachers,
And asked what she wanted —
Light in her eyes, a smile
Starting at the corners

Of her mouth. I fingered
A nickel in my pocket,
And when she lifted a chocolate
That cost a dime,
I didn't say anything.
I took the nickel from
My pocket, then an orange,
And set them quietly on
The counter. When I looked up,
The lady's eyes met mine,
And held them, knowing
Very well what it was all
About.

    Outside,
A few cars hissing past,
Fog hanging like old
Coats between the trees.
I took my girl's hand
in mine for two blocks,
Then released it to let
Her unwrap the chocolate.
I peeled my orange
That was so bright against
The gray of December
That, from some distance,
Someone might have thought
I was making a fire in my hands.

MEXICANS BEGIN JOGGING

At the factory I worked
In the fleck of rubber, under the press
Of an oven yellow with flame,
Until the border patrol opened
Their vans and my boss waved for us to run.
"Over the fence, Soto," he shouted,
And I shouted that I was American.
"No time for lies," he said, and pressed
A dollar in my palm, hurrying me
Through the back door.

Since I was on his time, I ran
And became the wag to a short tail of Mexicans —
Ran past the amazed crowds that lined
The street and blurred like photographs, in rain.
I ran from that industrial road to the soft
Houses where people paled at the turn of an autumn sky.
What could I do but yell *vivas*
To baseball, milkshakes, and those sociologists
Who would clock me
As I jog into the next century
On the power of a great, silly grin.

THE TALE OF SUNLIGHT

Listen, nephew.
When I opened the cantina
At noon
A triangle of sunlight
Was stretched out
On the floor
Like a rug
Like a tired cat.
It flared in
From the window
Through a small hole
Shaped like a yawn.
Strange I thought
And placed my hand
Before the opening,
But the sunlight
Did not vanish.
I pulled back
The shutters
And the room glowed,
But this pyramid
Of whiteness
Was simply brighter.
The sunlight around it
Appeared soiled
Like the bed sheet
Of a borracho.

Amazed, I locked the door,
Closed the windows.
Workers, in from
The fields, knocked
To be let in,
Children peeked
Through the shutters,
But I remained silent.
I poured a beer,
At a table
Shuffled a pack
Of old cards,
And watched it
Cross the floor,
Hang on the wall
Like a portrait
Like a calendar
Without numbers.
When a fly settled
In the sunlight
And disappeared
In a wreath of smoke,
I tapped it with the broom,
Spat on it.
The broom vanished.
The spit sizzled.
It is the truth, little one.
I stood eye to blank eye
And by misfortune
This finger
This pink stump
Entered the sunlight,
Snapped off
With a dry sneeze,
And fell to the floor
As a gift
To the ants
Who know me
For what I gave.

GARY SOTO

FAILING IN THE PRESENCE OF ANTS

We live to some purpose, daughter.
Across the park, among
The trees that give the eye
Something to do, let's spread
A blanket on the ground
And examine the ants, loose
Thread to an old coat.
Perhaps they are more human than we are.
They live for the female, *matriarchal, supportive,*
Rescue their hurt, and fall earthward
For their small cause. And
Us? We live for our bellies, *gluttony,*
The big O of our mouths. *greed,*
Give me, give me, they say,
And many people, whole countries,
May go under because we desire TV
And chilled drinks, clothes *material*
That hang well on our bodies —
Desire sofas and angled lamps,
Hair the sea may envy
On a slow day.
It is hurtful to sweep
Ants into a frenzy, blow
Chemicals into their eyes —
Those austere marchers who will lift
Their heads to rumor — seed,
Wafer of leaf, dropped apple —
And start off, over this
And that, between sloppy feet
And staggered chairs, for no
Purpose other than it might be good.

Elizabeth Spires

THE BEDS

London

Each day, I take the lift from the sublet down to the ground floor.
Out on the street, I pass the shop that sells the beds,
the sumptuous beds, made up each morning anew, afresh,
by smiling clerks who please their own moods,
doing the beds up one day in flaming sunrise and sunset tones,
and the next, in shades of white on white, with satin piping,
pillowcases expertly threaded with ribbons and bows,
like a bride's too-delicate underclothes.
And yet, nobody sleeps in the beds, makes love in the beds.
They wait, like a young girl with too much imagination,
to be taken away for a weekend in the country,
to a great house where lovers flirt and scheme
in preliminary maneuvering, but know, in the end,
what beds are for. Know, no matter what they do,
all will be plumped and tucked and smoothed,
all made as it was, by knowing maids the morning after.

The anxious clerks stare out at the soiled street,
the racing cars and taxis, the passersby, waiting for money
to stop, walk in the door, and ask to buy a bed.
There are circles under their eyes,
as if they've been sleeping badly.
Beds must make way for other beds,
pillows for other pillows, new sheets, new lives!
The seconds tick on the big clock
a block from the bed shop, the minute hand moves
with a jerk, and suddenly whole hours have flown, the day vanishes,
pulled by an unseen hand through a small hole in the sky
somewhere in the darkening East End.

Night falls so quickly on this street of Dream Merchandise!
Now all of us reverse ourselves and change direction
to come home to well-intentioned stews with husbands and wives,
yesterday's leftovers made to stretch so economically,
my heels on the sidewalk clicking in silver tones
like the small change in my pocket falling end over end over end,
all that remains of a day's hard buying.

491

Already the new moon is backlighting the city's towers and spires,
illuminating shadowy shop windows up and down Fulham Road.
It drapes itself casually across the beds,
like the misplaced towel or bathrobe
of a woman who has just stepped out for the evening,
wearing new evening clothes, made up so carefully
she can't be recognized, who secretly knows
she will not be coming back until morning
to sleep, if she sleeps then,
in the perfect bed of her own making.

SUNDAY AFTERNOON AT FULHAM PALACE

Putney Bridge, London

A Sunday afternoon in late September, one of the last
good weekends before the long dark, old couples
taking the air along the Thames, sunning themselves,
their arms and legs so pale, *exposed*,
eyes closed against the slanting autumn light,
while the young press forward, carry us
along in the crowd to the fair at Fulham Palace
where a few people have already spread blankets and tablecloths
for the picnics they've brought, laughing and talking
as they wait for the music to begin at three o'clock.
Inside the palace gates, a man inflates
a room-size, brightly painted rubber castle,
the children impatiently waiting for walls and turrets to go up,
the spongy floor they like to jump on.
The palace is empty. The Bishop gone.
Now overfed goldfish swim slowly round and round
in the crumbling courtyard fountain, and farther on,
a white peacock stands still as a statue,
still as a stone, whether in pride or sorrow
at being the last of its kind here I don't know.
A low door opens into the Bishop's walled garden, but once
inside nothing miraculous or forbidden tempts us,
just a few flowers and herbs among weeds
(unlike those illuminated scenes in books of hours),
the past passing away too quickly to catch or recognize.

ELIZABETH SPIRES

Out on the other side, we pick our way
among booths put up for the day,
one woman, predictably, passing out pamphlets
on nuclear winter and cruise missiles, as if she could stop it alone.
The Fulham Band takes its place on the platform,
the conductor announcing as the overture
"Those Magnificent Men in Their Flying Machines,"
the crossed shadow of coincidence, of airplanes from Gatwick
passing over at two-minute intervals, touching us
for a moment before they fly into the day's
unplanned pattern of connections, the music
attracting more of a crowd, men, women, and children
making their entrances like extras in a movie,
in pairs, in families, no one alone that I can see
except one girl, no more than ten,
lagging behind the others, lost completely
in a vivid, invisible daydream until her mother finds her,
brings her back with a touch on the arm,
and the daughter says, unbelievably,
"I was thinking about what kind of anesthesia
they'll give me when I have my first baby."

The future expands, then contracts, like an eye's iris opening
        and closing,
walling me into a room where light and sound come and go,
first near, then far, as if I had vertigo.
It is easy, too easy, to imagine the world ending
on a day like today, the sun shining and the band playing,
the players dreamily moving now into Ellington's "Mood Indigo."
Easy to see the great gray plane hovering briefly overhead,
the gray metal belly opening and the bomb dropping,
a flash, a light "like a thousand suns,"
and then the long winter.
The white peacock. Erased. The goldfish in the fountain
swimming crazily as the water boils up around them, evaporates.
The children's castle. Gone. The children. The mothers and the fathers.
As if a hand had suddenly erased a huge blackboard.
Thank God you don't know what I'm thinking.
You press my hand as if to ask, "Am I here with you?
Do you want to go?" pulling me back to this moment,
to this music we are just coming to know, the crowd around us
growing denser, just wanting to live their lives,
each person a *nerve*, thinking and feeling
too much as sensation pours over them

in a ceaseless flow, the music, as we move to go,
jumping far back in time, the conductor oddly choosing
something devotional, a coronet solo
composed, and probably played here, by Purcell three centuries ago.
All is as it was as we make our way back along the Thames
to Putney Bridge, the old souls still sleeping unaware,
hands lightly touching, as the river bends in a gentle arc
around them. Mood indigo. The white peacock.
The walled garden and the low door.
As if, if it did happen, we could bow our heads
and ask, once more, to enter that innocent first world.

THE FIRST DAY

The ward is quiet, the mothers delivered,
except in one a woman labors still and calls,
with a sharp cry, that she is dying.
She is not dying but cannot know it now.
Trapped in the birthstorm, I did not cry,
but saw my body as the enemy
I could not accommodate, could not deny.
Morning arrived, and my daughter.
That's how it is in this world, birth, death,
matter-of-fact, happening like that.
The room was warm. The room was full of flowers,
her face all petals and leaves, a flower
resembling such as I had never seen.
All day she slept beside me, eyes darting
beneath bruised blue eyelids, retracing the journey,
dreaming the birth dream over and over
until it held no fear for her.
I dared not wake her. The hours passed.
I rested as her soul poured in her body,
the way clear water, poured from a height,
takes the shape of a flaring vase or glass, or light
fills a room's corners on a brilliant winter morning.
Slowly, she opened her eyes, a second waking,
taking me by surprise, a bright being
peering out from behind dark eyes,
as if she already knew what sights would be seen,
what marvels lay ahead of her, weariness and woe,

the joists and beams, the underpinnings of the world
shifting a little to make room for her.
The first day was over forever. Tranced,
I picked up the pen, the paper, and wrote:
I have had a child. Now I must live with death.

THE CELESTIAL

Korean Buddhists traditionally keep this breed of carp in temple ponds.

When God made the angels, a man made me,
turning my gaze heavenward for a purpose
I know and do not know. The world
is a sphere that mirrors my pond, all things
have order here: the sun rushes
across the sky, pulling the moon
on a pale fishing line, and I see myself
printed among the stars, a great fish
swimming in the night's black sea.
Weeks pass into months, the year going
from warm to cool, bright to dull,
ginkgo leaves drifting down,
down, to slowly settle on pondbottom,
like pieces of ragged gold foil. I, too,
am streaked with gold along my spine and tail
but am valued for my eyes, bulging
blue-green globes larger than my soul,
a small clear bubble wrapped around the purity
of nothing. It slips with each breath
from my astonished mouth and flies rapidly upward
— as prayers will sometimes —
but always catches on the pond's rough skin.
I twin until there are many of me.
I begin and begin.

O Ghosts of the Upper World,
don't we see you in your shimmering robes,
peering through seven watery veils
that, lifted, reveal nothing behind the curtain?
Don't we hear you chanting?
Bells call you to the temple and you hurry away,
orange robes streaming, as if

you were running headlong into a violent wind.
We do not hurry as we take the world in
through our mouths, as sensation
passes through us, unconcerned
to be swimming toward where we've already been.
To be, not do: that is the lesson
we try to teach you.
We have heard of an underworld where fire
is the transforming element and water burns
quickly away to vapor,
but will not see it ever.

Our gaze is upward and forever.

"IN HEAVEN IT IS ALWAYS AUTUMN"

John Donne

In heaven it is always autumn. The leaves are always near
to falling there but never fall, and pairs of souls out walking
heaven's paths no longer feel the weight of years upon them.
Safe in heaven's calm, they take each other's arm,
the light shining through them, all joy and terror gone.
But we are far from heaven here, in a garden ragged and unkept
as Eden would be with the walls knocked down, the paths littered
with the unswept leaves of many years, bright keepsakes
for children of the Fall. The light is gold, the sun pulling
the long shadow soul out of each thing, disclosing an outcome.
The last roses of the year nod their frail heads,
like listeners listening to all that's said, to ask,
What brought us here? What seed? What rain? What light?
What forced us upwards through dark earth? What made us bloom?
What wind shall take us soon, sweeping the garden bare?
Their voiceless voices hang there, as ours might,
if we were roses, too. Their beds are blanketed with leaves,
tended by an absent gardener whose life is elsewhere.
It is the last of many last days. Is it enough? To rest in this moment?
To turn our faces to the sun? To watch the lineaments of a world
    passing?
To feel the metal of a black iron chair, cool and eternal,
press against our skin? To apprehend a chill as clouds pass
overhead, turning us to shivering shade and shadow?

And then to be restored, small miracle, the sun shining brightly
as before? We go on, you leading the way, a figure
leaning on a cane that leaves its mark on the earth.
My friend, you have led me farther than I have ever been.
To a garden in autumn. To a heaven of impermanence
where the final falling off is slow, a slow and radiant happening.
The light is gold. And while we're here, I think it must be heaven.

GLASS-BOTTOM BOAT

Key West

In the Cubano diner, tiny cups
of black, black coffee, hot and sweet,
and chipped blue china plates
of black beans and yellowtail,
fished by the fishermen
as the sun came up this morning.

Yesterday out on the reef,
we looked through the floor of the boat,
through layers of clear, clean water —
windows looking into other windows —
down to the floor of the world,
shallow, pliant, and shifting.
There, schools of yellowtail
swam through the living coral,
bright as stained glass,
cast into underwater constellations
both strange and familiar:
a flower, a brain, a cathedral.
Suddenly a shadow parted the school —
as if a cloud had just blotted the sun —
a barracuda swerving as they swerved,
and nothing they could do.
After it fed, the two halves joined,
the missing ones unmourned,
all as it was before.

If I could live for a thousand years,
ten thousand, would ever I see
the great family of men, women, and children,

both preying and preyed-upon,
swimming as freely as the yellowtail?
Would that be heaven or hell?
Each naked human face a candle
joining other candles in a procession
spanning many centuries, entering
the cathedral of live stone
whose heavy doors are cast
with scenes from our own lives,
moving as moving pictures move,
until the reel runs out.
In that world-without-end hour,
will the future read us in relief,
blindly touching each raised
and burnished scene with fingertips,
the ejaculate word forming on their lips,
an *O!* and then again an *O!*
of terror and astonishment?
O how will they sing knowing what they know?
Streaming through time, they see
our approach, we are plotted
in space, our light outlives our lives
and sends a signal far into
the future: *the past is alive!*
Dead and dark for a long time,
we are as stars to them,
stars wishing to be wished on.

CEMETERY REEF

Grand Cayman Island

Walking down the beach, I took your arm.
The treatments were over. Your hair was growing back.
For a week, time lay suspended. And yet, too fast,
too soon, everything was changing to memory.
But your arm was real when I touched it, real flesh and blood.
We were talking about doctors when I saw the blowfish,
green as the greenest apple, puffed-up and bobbing in the shallows.
But when I looked again, it was only a pair of bathing trunks,
ballooning out, aimlessly knocked back and forth by the tide.
Ahead, the cruise ships lay at anchor in the harbor.
At noon they'd slip away, like days we couldn't hold onto,

dropping over the blurred blue horizon to other ports of call.
The hotels we were passing all looked out to water,
a thousand beach chairs in the sand looked out to water,
but no one sat there early in the morning. And no one
slept in the empty hammock at the Governor's House,
where workmen in gray coveralls raked the seaweed into piles,
until the sand was white and smooth, like paper not yet written on.

All lies in retrospect now: how, each afternoon,
we put on masks and fins and swam to Cemetery Reef.
The coral looked like brains and flowers, like unreal cities
of melted peaks and towers, pointing up to where the sun,
flat and round as a host, lay dissolving on the water.
Schools of fish, bright as neon, ragged as flags,
drifted directionless with the tide, or swerved
and hid from our reaching hands in beds of waving kelp.
We breathed through snorkels, did the dead man's float,
the hollow rushing sound we heard inside our heads
our own frail breath going slowly *in* and *out*. Farther out,
the shallow reef dropped off to chasm, the waves
choppy and thick, the calm clear water darkening to ink.
How far could we swim before exhaustion took us,
before a shark or barracuda rounded a cornerless corner
to meet us eye to eye? My mind circled back to our dinner
in the Chinese restaurant: the waiter bringing six cookies
on a plate, alike in every way, except that one, just one,
contained a different fate. *Wealth*, *long life*, *happiness*,
the plate was passed around. Then your turn came.
You chose one, broke it open, read aloud,
Soon you will cross the great water, dropping it, as if stung.

And then, too quickly, it was the last day.
Dreaming, we all came to. We were back at Cemetery Reef,
walking a narrow path of broken shells toward the shining water.
Off to one side, a low stone wall squared off the cemetery,
the dead buried aboveground in white weathered slabs,
their plots neatly surrounded by smooth white stones.
Morning of all mornings, you swam out to the reef alone,
came back. Gathering our things to go, what made me say,
When we come back. . . . All lies unanswered now.
I remember how the flowers on the graves were red
and white plastic, the color of flesh and blood, of regret,
of paper not yet written on. Put there, *In Memory*.
In a colder place, we would soon — unwilling, stunned —
remember you with the kind that always die.

David St. John

GIN

There's a mystery
By the river, in one of the cabins
Shuttered with planks, its lock
Twisted; a bunch of magazines flipped open,
A body. A blanket stuffed with leaves
Or lengths of rope, an empty gin bottle.
Put down your newspaper. Look out
Beyond the bluffs, a coal barge is passing,
Its deck nearly
Level with the water, where it comes back riding
High. You start talking about nothing,
Or that famous party, where you went dressed
As a river. They listen,
The man beside you touching his odd face
In the countertop, the woman stirring tonic
In your glass. Down the bar the talk's divorce,
The docks, the nets
Filling with branches and sour fish. Listen,
I knew a woman who'd poke a hole in an egg, suck
It clean and fill the shell with gin,
Then walk around all day disgusting people
Until she was so drunk
The globe of gin broke in her hand. She'd stay
Alone at night on the boat, come back
Looking for another egg. That appeals to you, rocking
For hours carving at a hollow stone. Or finding
A trail by accident, walking the bluff's
Face. You know, your friends complain. They say
You give up only the vaguest news, and give a bakery
As your phone. Even your stories
Have no point, just lots of detail: The room
Was long and bright, small and close, angering Gaston;
They turned away to embrace him; She wore
The color out of season,
She wore hardly anything at all; Nobody died; Saturday.
These disguises of omission. Like forgetting
To say obtuse when you talk about the sun, leaving
Off the buttons as you're sewing up the coat. So,

501

People take the little
They know to make a marvelous stew;
Sometimes, it even resembles you. It's not so much
You cover your tracks, as that they bloom
In such false directions. This way friends who awaken
At night, beside you, awaken alone.

THE SWAN AT SHEFFIELD PARK

It is a dim April
Though perhaps no dimmer than any
London April my friend says
As we turn our backs
To the crooked Thames to the stark
London skyline
                        walking up the hill's
Mild slope to one of the paths
And prospects of Kew
He introduces
The various and gathered families
Of trees then every subtle
Shift of design along the grounds
The carefully laid views and pools
The chapel-sized orangery
Where citrus in their huge trolley tubs
Were wheeled behind the glass walls
And spared each winter
Fresh lime grapefruit and orange
That's what a queen wants
That's what the orangery says
Now April's skies grow a little
More forgiving
Breaking into these tall columns
Of white clouds
                        the kinds of elaborate
Shapes that children call God's Swans
Here in the country an hour
South of London
                        where Gibbon finished
Decline and Fall in Lord Sheffield's library
In the manor house I can see just there

DAVID ST. JOHN

In the trees
                as I walk with my friend along
The road that passes by his cottage
At the edge of the grounds of Sheffield Park
Once again
                the sky's high pillars collect
Into one flat unrelieved blanket
Above these shivering leaves
And bent blades   ·
                        a curtaining mist
Materializes out of the air
As we stop for a moment
On a stone bridge over the small falls
Between two of the lakes
And from the center of one of the lakes
A single swan glides toward us
Its wake a perfect spreading V
Widening along the water
                        as each arm
Of the V begins to break against
The lake's shores
                        the swan holds its head
And neck in a classical question mark
The crook of an old man's
Walking stick its eyes fixed on us
As it spreads its wings
In this exact feathery symmetry
Though it does not fly
                        simply lifting
Its head until the orange beak
Almost touches the apex of the stone
Arch of the bridge
Waiting for whatever crumbs we might
Have thought to bring
For a swan
                that now turns from us
Gliding with those same effortless gestures
Away without a glance back over
Its smooth shoulder
                        the mist
Thickens as the clouds drop lower
And the rain threading the branches and leaves
Grows darker and more dense
Until I can barely see the swan on the water

DAVID ST. JOHN

Moving slowly as smoke through this haze
Covering the surface of the lake
That white smudge sailing
To whatever shelter it can find and as
I look again there's nothing
                              only
The rain pocking the empty table
Of the lake
                    so even the swan knows
Better than I to get out of the rain
The way it curled white as breath and rose
To nothing along the wind
                              tonight
By the wood stove of the cottage
Drinking and talking with my friend
I'll tell him about the two women
I saw last week in Chelsea
One of them wrapped in a jumpsuit of wet
Black plastic
                    her hair coal
Black greased and twirled into spikes
That fell like fingers onto her shoulders
But more alarming
                              those lines she'd drawn
Out from her mouth with an eyebrow pencil
Along her pale cheeks the perfect
Curved whiskers of a cat
And the other one
                          her friend dressed
In white canvas painter's pants white leather
Boots and a cellophane blouse
                                    who'd dyed
Her hair utterly white then teased it
So that it rose
Or fell in the breeze lightly and stiffly
As feathers who'd painted her mouth
The same hard rubbery orange as a swan's
And even to a person of no great humor
Or imagination they were
                                    these two
In the silent path they cut in the air
Along King's Road in every way
Beautiful
            and for the rest

DAVID ST. JOHN

Of the day I was so shaken I made
Myself stop for a drink in Soho
A strip joint called *The Blade*
I'd stumbled into and judging from my
Welcome not a place for the delicate
But I stuck it out through enough Scotch
To make me drunk fearless
And screaming through the first show
When at its end the final stripper
Stepped from the small stage right onto the bar top
Everyone clearing away the glasses and bottles
From the polished copper in front of them
As she threw off everything strutting
Down the narrow bar except
A white boa G-string
Shivering against her thighs as she
Kicked her silver high heels to either side
Then lay down in front of me
Her bare back and shoulders pressed flat
To the copper as it steamed and smudged beneath
Her body's heat
              the catcalls and hollers
Rising as she lifted each leg
Pointing her toes to the spotlights scattered
Across the ceiling
              her legs held in a pale V
The silver sequins of her high heels
Glittering in the lights but
Then she stood abruptly
And stepped back onto the stage not
Waiting a moment before turning her back
To the hoarse cheers
          disappearing
In the sheer misty gauze of the old curtains
And as the lights came up there was
Where she'd been
Just the trails and webs of cigarette smoke
Those long curlicues in a tattoo of light
Those ghosts and feathers of dust
Still drifting down onto the bare tables
The glistening bar
             onto the empty veiled stage
Of wood warped gently as waves

DAVID ST. JOHN

LUCIFER IN STARLIGHT

> *Tired of his dark dominion . . .*
> — *George Meredith*

It was something I'd overheard
One evening at a party; a man I liked enormously
      Saying to a mutual friend, a woman
Wearing a vest embroidered with scarlet and violet tulips
      That belled below each breast, "Well, I've always
Preferred Athens; Greece seems to me a country
      Of the day — Rome, I'm afraid, strikes me
As being a city of the night . . ."
      Of course, I knew instantly just what he meant —
      Not simply because I love
Standing on the terrace of my apartment on a clear evening
      As the constellations pulse low in the Roman sky,
The whole mind of night that I know so well
      Shimmering in its elaborate webs of infinite,
Almost divine irony. No, and it wasn't only that Rome
      Was *my* city of the night, that it was here I'd chosen
      To live when I grew tired of my ancient life
As the Underground Man. And it wasn't that Rome's darkness
      Was of the kind that consoles so many
      Vacancies of the soul; my Rome, with its endless history
Of falls . . . No, it was that this dark was the deep, sensual dark
      Of the dreamer; this dark was like the violet fur
Spread to reveal the illuminated nipples of
      The She-Wolf — all the sequins above in sequence,
The white buds lost in those fields of ever-deepening gentians,
      A dark like the polished back of a mirror,
      The pool of the night scalloped and hanging
Above me, the inverted reflection of a last,
                  Odd Narcissus . . .

      One night my friend Nico came by
Close to three A.M. — As we drank a little wine, I could see
      The black of her pupils blown wide,
The spread ripples of the opiate night . . . And Nico
      Pulled herself close to me, her mouth almost
      Touching my mouth, as she sighed, "Look . . . ,"
And deep within the pupil of her left eye,
      Almost like the mirage of a ship's distant, hanging

DAVID ST. JOHN

Lantern rocking with the waves,
I could see, at the most remote end of the receding,
      Circular hallway of her eye, there, at its doorway,
At the small aperture of the black telescope of the pupil,
      A tiny, dangling crucifix —
Silver, lit by the ragged shards of starlight, reflecting
      In her as quietly as pain, as simply as pain . . .
Some years later, I saw Nico on stage in New York, singing
      Inside loosed sheets of shattered light, a fluid
Kaleidoscope washing over her — the way any naked,
      Emerging Venus steps up along the scalloped lip
Of her shell, innocent and raw as fate, slowly
Obscured by a florescence that reveals her simple, deadly
      Love of sexual sincerity . . .
      I didn't bother to say hello. I decided to remember
The way in Rome, out driving at night, she'd laugh as she let
      Her head fall back against the cracked, red leather
      Of my old Lancia's seats, the soft black wind
Fanning her pale, chalky hair out along its currents,
      Ivory waves of starlight breaking above us in the leaves;
The sad, lucent malevolence of the heavens, falling . . .
      Both of us racing silently as light. Nowhere,
Then forever . . .
      Into the mind of the Roman night.

LAST NIGHT WITH RAFAELLA

Last night, with Rafaella,

I sat at one of the outside tables
At *Rosati* watching the *ragazzi* on Vespas
Scream through the Piazza del Popolo

And talked again about changing my life,

Doing something meaningful — perhaps
Exploring a continent or discovering a vaccine,
Falling in love or over the white falls
Of a dramatic South American river! —
And Rafaella
Stroked the back of my wrist as I talked,

DAVID ST. JOHN

Smoothing the hairs until they lay as quietly
As wheat before the old authoritarian wind.

Rafaella had just returned from Milano
Where she'd supervised the Spring collection
Of a famous, even notorious, young designer —

A man whose name brought tears to the eyes
Of contessas, movie stars, and diplomats' wives
Along the Via Condotti or the Rue
Du Faubourg-St-Honoré.

So I felt comfortable there, with Rafaella,
Discussing these many important things, I mean
The spiritual life, and my own
Long disenchantment with the ordinary world.

Comfortable because I knew she was a sophisticated,
Well-traveled woman, so impossible
To shock. A friend who'd
Often rub the opal on her finger so slowly

It made your mouth water,

The whole while telling you what it would be like
To feel her tongue addressing your ear.

And how could I not trust the advice
Of a woman who, with the ball of her exquisite thumb,
Carefully flared rouge along the white cheekbones
Of the most beautiful women in the world?

Last night, as we lay in the dark,
The windows of her bedroom open to the cypress,
To the stars, to the wind knocking at those stiff
Umbrella pines along her garden's edge,
I noticed as she turned slowly in the moonlight

A small tattoo just above her hip bone —

It was a dove in flight or an angel with its
Head tucked beneath its wing,
I couldn't tell in the shadows . . .

DAVID ST. JOHN

And as I kissed this new illumination of her body
Rafaella said, *Do you know how to tell a model?*
In fashion, they wear tattoos like singular beads
Along their hips,
                    but artists' models
Wear them like badges against the daily nakedness,
The way Celestine has above one nipple that
Minute yellow bee and above
The other an elaborate, cupped poppy . . .

I thought about this,
Pouring myself a little wine and listening
To the owls marking the distances, the geometries
Of the dark.
                Rafaella's skin was
Slightly damp as I ran my fingertip
Along each delicate winged ridge of her
Collarbone, running the harp length of ribs
Before circling the shy angel . . .

And slowly, as the stars
Shifted in their rack of black complexities above,

Along my shoulder, Rafaella's hair fell in coils,

Like the frayed silk of some ancient tapestry,
Like the spun cocoons of the Orient —
Like a fragile ladder

To some whole other level of the breath.

(Rome)

William Stafford

HOW THE REAL BIBLE IS WRITTEN

Once we painted our house and went into it.
Today, after years, I remember that color
under the new paint now old.
I look out of the windows dangerously
and begin to know more. Now when I
walk through this town there are
too many turns before the turn
I need. Listen, birds and cicadas
still trying to tell me surface things:
I have learned how the paint goes on,
and then other things — how the real Bible is
written, downward through the pages,
carved, hacked, and molded, like the faces
of saints or the planks ripped aside
by steady centuries of weather, deeper than
dust, under the moles, caught by the
inspiration in an old badger's shoulder
that bores for grizzled secrets in the ground.

AT FOURTH AND MAIN IN LIBERAL, KANSAS, 1932

An instant sprang at me, a winter instant,
a thin gray panel of evening. Slanted
shadows leaned from a line of trees where rain
had slicked the sidewalk. No one was there —
it was only a quick flash of a scene,
unplanned, without connection to anything
that meant more than itself, but I carried it
onward like a gift from a child who knows
that the giving is what is important, the paper, the ribbon,
the holding of breath and surprise, the friends around,
and God holding it out to you, even a rock
or a slice of evening, and behind it the whole world.

WILLIAM STAFFORD

GROWING UP

One of my wings beat faster,
I couldn't help it —
the one away from the light.

It hurt to be told all the time
how I loved that terrible flame.

ASK ME

Some time when the river is ice ask me
mistakes I have made. Ask me whether
what I have done is my life. Others
have come in their slow way into
my thought, and some have tried to help
or to hurt: ask me what difference
their strongest love or hate has made.

I will listen to what you say.
You and I can turn and look
at the silent river and wait. We know
the current is there, hidden; and there
are comings and goings from miles away
that hold the stillness exactly before us.
What the river says, that is what I say.

CEREMONY

On the third finger of my left hand
under the bank of the Ninnescah
a muskrat whirled and bit to the bone.
The mangled hand made the water red.

That was something the ocean would remember:
I saw me in the current flowing through the land,
rolling, touching roots, the world incarnadined,
and the river richer by a kind of marriage.

WILLIAM STAFFORD

While in the woods an owl started quavering
with drops like tears I raised my arm.
Under the bank a muskrat was trembling
with meaning my hand would wear forever.

In that river my blood flowed on.

TRAVELING THROUGH THE DARK

Traveling through the dark I found a deer
dead on the edge of the Wilson River road.
It is usually best to roll them into the canyon:
that road is narrow; to swerve might make more dead.

By glow of the tail-light I stumbled back of the car
and stood by the heap, a doe, a recent killing;
she had stiffened already, almost cold.
I dragged her off; she was large in the belly.

My fingers touching her side brought me the reason —
her side was warm; her fawn lay there waiting,
alive, still, never to be born.
Beside that mountain road I hesitated.

The car aimed ahead its lowered parking lights;
under the hood purred the steady engine.
I stood in the glare of the warm exhaust turning red;
around our group I could hear the wilderness listen.

I thought hard for us all — my only swerving — ,
then pushed her over the edge into the river.

VOCATION

This dream the world is having about itself
includes a trace on the plains of the Oregon trail,
a groove in the grass my father showed us all
one day while meadowlarks were trying to tell
something better about to happen.

WILLIAM STAFFORD

I dreamed the trace to the mountains, over the hills,
and there a girl who belonged wherever she was.
But then my mother called us back to the car:
she was afraid; she always blamed the place,
the time, anything my father planned.

Now both of my parents, the long line through the plain,
the meadowlarks, the sky, the world's whole dream
remain, and I hear him say while I stand between the two,
helpless, both of them part of me:
"Your job is to find what the world is trying to be."

ADULTS ONLY

Animals own a fur world;
people own worlds that are variously, pleasingly, bare.
And the way these worlds *are* once arrived for us kids with a jolt,
that night when the wild woman danced
in the giant cage we found we were all in
at the state fair.

Better women exist, no doubt, than that one,
and occasions more edifying, too, I suppose.
But we have to witness for ourselves what comes for us,
nor be distracted by barkers of irrelevant ware;
and a pretty good world, I say, arrived that night
when that woman came farming right out of her clothes,
by God,

At the state fair.

FIFTEEN

South of the bridge on Seventeenth
I found back of the willows one summer
day a motorcycle with engine running

as it lay on its side, ticking over
slowly in the high grass. I was fifteen.

I admired all that pulsing gleam, the
shiny flanks, the demure headlights
fringed where it lay; I led it gently
to the road and stood with that
companion, ready and friendly. I was fifteen.

We could find the end of a road, meet
the sky on out Seventeenth. I thought about
hills, and patting the handle got back a
confident opinion. On the bridge we indulged
a forward feeling, a tremble. I was fifteen.

Thinking, back farther in the grass I found
the owner, just coming to, where he had flipped
over the rail. He had blood on his hand, was pale —
I helped him walk to his machine. He ran his hand
over it, called me good man, roared away.

I stood there, fifteen.

WIDOW

On the first day when light came through the curtain
a mosquito thought was bothering her — what if
I am important? She wandered the house — the forgiving
table, the surprised-looking bed. Dishes
in the rack needed putting away, and she helped
them. But afterward she regretted — maybe nothing
should move, maybe this day the stillness begins.
She looked out a front window and held every
neighborhood shadow exactly where it was. Then
she carefully X'd out the calendar that had waited
all year for this date. She held out her hand
in a shaft of sun and flexed her fingers, in case
time had passed, in case her body was already gone.

WILLIAM STAFFORD

THE LIGHT BY THE BARN

The light by the barn that shines all night
pales at dawn when a little breeze comes.

A little breeze comes breathing the fields
from their sleep and waking the slow windmill.

The slow windmill sings the long day
about anguish and loss to the chickens at work.

The little breeze follows the slow windmill
and the chickens at work till the sun goes down —

Then the light by the barn again.

A WIND FROM A WING

Something outside my window in the dark
whispers a message. Maybe it is
a prayer sent by one of those friends
forgiving me the years when I sat out their war.
It flared, you know, generating
its own reasons for being, its heroes
anyone killed by an enemy. They looked up
and met fame on a bullet awarded so fast
their souls remained stuck in their bodies,
and then their names, caught on flypaper
citation, couldn't escape. Their families eat that
carrion, and like it. That is their punishment.

In a sky as distant and clear as Pascal's
nightmare, and immediate as our sweat
when God shakes us from sleep, my fate
shudders me awake. Little squeals
of the unborn fly past in the wind. It is midnight
and a motel, and nobody but me remembers
my mother, my father, and that hidden key
they left by our door when I was out late.

WILLIAM STAFFORD

WITH KIT, AGE 7, AT THE BEACH

We would climb the highest dune,
from there to gaze and come down:
the ocean was performing;
we contributed our climb.

Waves leapfrogged and came
straight out of the storm.
What should our gaze mean?
Kit waited for me to decide.

Standing on such a hill,
what would you tell your child?
That was an absolute vista.
Those waves raced far, and cold.

"How far could you swim, Daddy,
in such a storm?"
"As far as was needed," I said,
and as I talked, I swam.

NEAR

Walking along in this not quite prose way
we both know it is not quite prose we speak,
and it is time to notice this intolerable snow
innumerably touching, before we sink.

It is time to notice, I say, the freezing snow
hesitating toward us from its gray heaven;
listen — it is falling not quite silently
and under it still you and I are walking.

Maybe there are trumpets in the houses we pass
and a redbird watching from an evergreen —
but nothing will happen until we pause
to flame what we know, before any signal's given.

① How do these animals save him? How do the animals star for him
② Expansive U.S. ⟷ Europe (Eastern) for him
(counterparts) "two universes intertwined" huma ?
③ soap = humans

Martin J. Desht

Gerald Stern

I REMEMBER GALILEO

I remember Galileo describing the mind
as a piece of paper blown around by the wind, — *not sure where it's going — where it's going to land w/o purpose*
and I loved the sight of it sticking to a tree
or jumping into the backseat of a car,
and for years I watched paper leap through my cities;
but yesterday I saw the mind was a squirrel caught crossing
Route 80 between the wheels of a giant truck,
dancing back and forth like a thin leaf, — *w/ purpose*
or a frightened string, for only two seconds living
on the white concrete before he got away,
his life shortened by all that terror, his head
jerking, his yellow teeth ground down to dust.

It was the speed of the squirrel and his lowness to the ground,
his great purpose and the alertness of his dancing,
that showed me the difference between him and paper.
Paper will do in theory, when there is time
to sit back in a metal chair and study shadows;
but for this life I need a squirrel,   *squirrel*
his clawed feet spread, his whole soul quivering,
the hot wind rushing through his hair,
the loud noise shaking him from head to tail.
   O philosophical mind, O mind of paper, I need a squirrel
finishing his wild dash across the highway,
rushing up his green ungoverned hillside.

THE DANCING

In all these rotten shops, in all this broken furniture
and wrinkled ties and baseball trophies and coffee pots
I have never seen a postwar Philco
with the automatic eye
nor heard Ravel's "Bolero" the way I did   *prophetic*
in 1945 in that tiny living room
on Beechwood Boulevard, nor danced as I did

519

then, my knives all flashing, my hair all streaming,
my mother red with laughter, my father cupping
his left hand under his armpit, doing the dance
of old Ukraine, the sound of his skin half drum,
half fart, the world at last a meadow,
the three of us whirling and singing, the three of us
screaming and falling, as if we were dying,
as if we could never stop — in 1945 —
in Pittsburgh, beautiful filthy Pittsburgh, home
of the evil Mellons, 5,000 miles away
from the other dancing — in Poland and Germany —
oh God of mercy, oh wild God.

SOAP

Here is a green Jew
with thin black lips.
I stole him from the men's room
of the Amelia Earhart and wrapped him in toilet paper.
Up the street in *Parfumes*
are Austrian Jews and Hungarian,
without memories really,
holding their noses in the midst of that
paradise of theirs.
There is a woman outside
who hesitates because it is almost Christmas.
"I think I'll go in and buy a Jew," she says.
"I mean some soap, some nice new lilac or lily
to soothe me over the hard parts,
some Zest, some Fleur de Loo, some Wild Gardenia."

And here is a blue Jew.
It is his color, you know,
and he feels better buried in it, imprisoned
in all that sky, the land of death and plenty.
If he is an old one he dances,
or he sits stiffly,
listening to the meek words and admiring the vile actions
of first the Goths and then the Ostrogoths.
Inside is a lovely young girl,

GERALD STERN

a Dane, who gave good comfort
and sad support to soap of all kinds and sorts
during the war and during the occupation.
She touches my hand with unguents and salves.
She puts one under my nose all wrapped in tissue,
and squeezes his cheeks.

I buy a black Romanian for my shelf.
I use him for hair and beard,
and even for teeth when things get bitter and sad.
He had one dream, this piece of soap,
if I'm getting it right,
he wanted to live in Wien
and sit behind a hedge on Sunday afternoon
listening to music and eating a tender schnitzel.
That was delirium. Other than that he'd dream
of America sometimes, but he was a kind of cynic,
and kind of lazy — conservative — even in his dream,
and for this he would pay, he paid for his lack of dream.
The Germans killed him because he didn't dream
enough, because he had no vision.

I buy a brush for my back, a simple plastic
handle with gentle bristles. I buy some dust
to sweeten my body. I buy a yellow cream
for my hairy face. From time to time I meet
a piece of soap on Broadway, a sliver really,
without much on him, sometimes I meet two friends
stuck together the way those slivers get
and bow a little, I bow to hide my horror,
my grief, sometimes the soap is so thin
the light goes through it, these are the thin old men
and thin old women the light goes through, these are
the Jews who were born in 1865
or 1870, for them I cringe, for them
I whimper a little, they are the ones who remember
the eighteenth century, they are the ones who listened
to heavenly voices, they were lied to and cheated.

My counterpart was born in 1925
in a city in Poland — I don't like to see him born
in a little village fifty miles from Kiev
and have to fight so wildly just for access

to books, I don't want to see him struggle
half his life to see a painting or just to
sit in one of the plush chairs listening to music.
He was dragged away in 1940
and turned to some use in 1941,
although he may have fought a little, piled
some bricks up or poured some dirty gasoline
over a German truck. His color was rose
and he floated for me for days and days; I love
the way he smelled the air, I love how he looked,
how his eyes lighted up, how his cheeks were almost pink
when he was happy. I love how he dreamed, how he almost
disappeared when he was in thought. For him
I write this poem, for my little brother, if I
should call him that — maybe he is the ghost
that lives in the place I have forgotten, that dear one
that died instead of me — oh ghost, forgive me! —
Maybe he stayed so I could leave, the *older* one
who stayed so I could leave — oh live forever!
forever! — Maybe he is a Being from the other
world, his left arm agate, his left eye crystal,
and he has come back again for the twentieth time,
this time to Poland, to Warsaw or Bialystok,
to see what hell is like. I think it's that,
he has come back to live in our hell, if he could
even prick his agate arm or even weep
with his crystal eye — oh weep with your crystal eye,
dear helpless Being, dear helpless Being. I'm writing this
in Iowa and Pennsylvania and New York City,
in time for Christmas, 1982,
the odor of Irish Spring, the stench of Ivory.

THE BULL-ROARER

I

I only saw my father's face in butchery
once — it was a horror — there were ten men
surrounding a calf, their faces were red, my father's
eyes were shining; there might have been fewer than ten,

some were farmers, some were my father's friends
down from the city. I was nine, maybe eight;
I remember we slept a few hours and left
at four in the morning, there were two cars, or three,
I think it was West Virginia. I remember
the pasture, the calf was screaming, his two eyes
where white with terror, there was blood and slaver
mixed, he was spread-eagled, there was a rope
still hanging from his neck, they all had knives
or ice picks — is that possible? — they were beery,
drunk, the blood was pouring from the throat
but they were stabbing him, one of them bellowed
as if he were a bull, he was the god
of the hunters, dressed in overalls and boots,
the king of animals; they seemed to know —
some of them seemed to know — the tendons and bones,
they were already cutting and slicing, pulling
the skin off, or maybe that was later, I stood there
staring at them, my father with a knife;
we didn't even have a dog — my mother froze
whenever she saw one — we were living in Beechview,
we had the newest car on the street, it was
an ugly suburb, everything was decent,
there was a little woods, but it was locust,
it would be covered with houses, we didn't even have
a parrot, my father left at eight in the morning
and drove his car downtown, he always wore
a suit and tie, his shoes were polished, he spent
the day with customers, he ate his lunch
at a little booth, I often sat with him,
with him and his friends, I had to show off, I drew
their likenesses, I drew the tables and chairs,
it was the Depression, none of them had brass rings
hanging from their ears, they all wore socks,
and long-sleeved shirts, they ate and drank with passion.

II

My mother is eighty-seven, she remembers
the visit to the farm, there was her brother,
my uncle Simon, and there was his friend, MacBride,
Lou MacBride, he was the connection, he was

a friend of the farmer's, maybe a cousin. I asked her
about the killing — "that is the way those farmers
got their meat, they lived like that, they butchered
whatever they needed." I asked if she could remember
anything strange, was she nervous or frightened?
"There was the tail, they cut the tail off
and chased each other; it was like pinning the tail
to the donkey." Both of us laughed. I didn't have the heart
to mention my father's face, or mention the knife —
and, most of all, my pain. What did I want?
That he should stay forever locked inside
his gold-flecked suits? That he should get up in the dark
and put his shoes on with a silver knife?
That he should unbutton his shirts and stuff the cardboard
into a chute? That he should always tie
his tie with three full loops, his own true version
of the Windsor knot? And what did I want for myself?
Some childish thing, that no one would ever leave me?
That there would always be logic — and loyalty?
— I think that tail goes back to the Paleolithic.
I think our game has gory roots — some cave,
or field, they chased each other — or they were grimmer,
pinning that tail, some power was amassed,
as well as something ludicrous, always that,
the tail was different from the horns, or paws,
it was the seat of shame — and there was envy,
not just contempt, but envy — horns a man has,
and he has furry hands and he has a mane,
but never a tail. I remember dimly
a toy we had, a kind of flattened stone,
curved at the sides, with a long rope at one end
we whirled around to make a thundering noise.
This was a "bull-roarer"; we made thunder
and felt the power in our shoulders and legs.
I saw this toy in southern Italy;
I saw children throwing it over their heads
as if they were in central Australia
or ancient Europe somewhere, in a meadow,
forcing the gods to roar. They call it Uranic,
a heavenly force, sometimes almost a voice,
locked up in that whirling stone, dear father.

GERALD STERN

ANOTHER INSANE DEVOTION

cat

This was gruesome — fighting over a ham sandwich
with one of the tiny cats of Rome, he leaped
on my arm and half hung on to the food and half
hung on to my shirt and coat. I tore it apart
and let him have his portion, I think I lifted him
down, sandwich and all, on the sidewalk and sat
with my own sandwich beside him, maybe I petted
his bony head and felt him shiver. I have
told this story over and over; some things
root in the mind; his boldness, of course, was frightening
and unexpected — his stubbornness — though hunger
drove him mad. It was the breaking of boundaries,
the sudden invasion, but not only that, it was
the sharing of food and the sharing of space; he didn't
run into an alley or into a cellar,
he sat beside me, eating, and I didn't run
into a trattoria, say, shaking,
with food on my lips and blood on my cheek, sobbing;
but not only that, I had gone there to eat
and wait for someone. I had maybe an hour
before she would come and I was full of hope
and excitement. I have resisted for years
interpreting this, but now I think I was given
a clue, or I was giving myself a clue,
across the street from the glass sandwich shop.
That was my last night with her, the next day
I would leave on the train for Paris and she would
meet her husband. Thirty-five years ago
I ate my sandwich and moaned in her arms, we were
dying together; we never met again
although she was pregnant when I left her — I have
a daughter or son somewhere, darling grandchildren
in Norwich, Connecticut, or Canton, Ohio.
Every five years I think about her again
and plan on looking her up. The last time
I was sitting in New Brunswick, New Jersey,
and heard that her husband was teaching at Princeton,
if she was still married, or still alive, and tried
calling. I went that far. We lived
in Florence and Rome. We rowed in the bay of Naples
and floated, naked, on the boards. I started

to think of her again today. I still
am horrified by the cat's hunger. I still
am puzzled by the connection. This is another
insane devotion, there must be hundreds, although
it isn't just that, there is no pain, and the thought
is fleeting and sweet. I think it's my own dumb boyhood,
walking around with Slavic cheeks and burning
stupid eyes. I think I gave the cat
half of my sandwich to buy my life, I think
I broke it in half as a decent sacrifice.
It was this I bought, the red coleus,
the split rocking chair, the silk lampshade.
Happiness. I watched him with pleasure.
I bought memory. I could have lost it.
How crazy it sounds. His face twisted with cunning.
The wind blowing through his hair. His jaws working.

Whitman

LILACS FOR GINSBERG

I was most interested in what they looked like dead
and I could learn to love them so I waited
for three or four days until the brown set in
and there was a certain reverse curl to the leaf by
which in putting my finger on the main artery
beside the throat I knew the blood had passed on
to someplace else and he was talking to two
demons from the afterlife although it was
just like the mountains in New York State since there was
smoke in the sky and they were yelping and he was
speaking in his telltale New Jersey English
and saying the same thing over and over the way he
did when he was on stage and his white shirt was
perfect and the lack of air and of light
aged the lilacs but he was sitting on a lily
in one or two seconds and he forgot about Eighth Street
and fame and cancer and bent down to pick a loose
diamond but more important than that he talked
to the demons in French and sang with his tinny voice
nor did he go on about his yellowing sickness
but counted the clusters and said they were only stars
and there were two universes intertwined, the

GERALD STERN

white and the purple, or they were just crumbs or specks
that he could sprinkle on his pie nor could he
exactly remember his sorrow except when he pressed
the lilacs to his face or when he stooped
to bury himself in the bush, then for a moment
he almost did, for lilacs clear the mind
and all the elaborations are possible in their
dear smell and even his death which was so
good and thoughtful became, for a moment, sorrowful.

SHE WAS A DOVE

Red are her eyes, for she was a dove once,
and green was her neck and blue and gray her throat,
croon was her cry and noisy flutter her wing once
going for water, or reaching up for another note.

And yellow her bill, though white some, and red her feet,
though not to match her eyes, for they were more suave,
those feet, and he who bore down above her
his feathers dropped around her like chaff from wheat.

And black was her mood, consider a dove that black,
as if some avian fury had overcome her
and overtaken my own oh lackadaisical state,
for she was the one I loved and I abused her.

Blue we lived in, blue was our country seat,
and wrote our letters out on battered plates
and fought injustice and once or twice French-kissed there
and took each other out on desperate dates.

And it was a question always should we soar —
like eagles, you know — or should we land and stay,
the battle I fought for sixty years or more
and still go over every day.

And there was a spot of orange above the bone
that bore a wing, though I could never explain
how that was what I lived and died for
or that it blossomed in the brain.

Mark Strand

KEEPING THINGS WHOLE

In a field
I am the absence
of field.
This is
always the case.
Wherever I am
I am what is missing.

When I walk
I part the air
and always
the air moves in
to fill the spaces
where my body's been.

We all have reasons
for moving.
I move
to keep things whole.

THE DRESS

Lie down on the bright hill
with the moon's hand on your cheek,
your flesh deep in the white folds of your dress,
and you will not hear the passionate mole
extending the length of his darkness,
or the owl arranging all of the night,
which is his wisdom, or the poem
filling your pillow with its blue feathers.
But if you step out of your dress and move into the shade,
the mole will find you, so will the owl, and so will the poem,
and you will fall into another darkness, one you will find
yourself making and remaking until it is perfect.

MARK STRAND

THE PREDICTION

That night the moon drifted over the pond,
turning the water to milk, and under
the boughs of the trees, the blue trees,
a young woman walked, and for an instant

the future came to her:
rain falling on her husband's grave, rain falling
on the lawns of her children, her own mouth
filling with cold air, strangers moving into her house,

a man in her room writing a poem, the moon drifting into it,
a woman strolling under its trees, thinking of death,
thinking of him thinking of her, and the wind rising
and taking the moon and leaving the paper dark.

MY LIFE BY SOMEBODY ELSE

I have done what I could but you avoid me.
I left a bowl of milk on the desk to tempt you.
Nothing happened. I left my wallet there, full of money.
You must have hated me for that. You never came.

I sat at my typewriter naked, hoping you would wrestle me
to the floor. I played with myself just to arouse you.
Boredom drove me to sleep. I offered you my wife.
I sat her on the desk and spread her legs. I waited.

The days drag on. The exhausted light falls like a bandage
over my eyes. Is it because I am ugly? Was anyone
ever so sad? It is pointless to slash my wrists. My hands
would fall off. And then what hope would I have?

Why do you never come? Must I have you by being
somebody else? Must I write *My Life* by somebody else?
My Death by somebody else? Are you listening?
Somebody else has arrived. Somebody else is writing.

MARK STRAND

A MORNING

I have carried it with me each day: that morning I took
my uncle's boat from the brown water cove
and headed for Mosher Island.
Small waves splashed against the hull
and the hollow creek of oarlock and oar
rose into the woods of black pine crusted with lichen.
I moved like a dark star, drifting over the drowned
other half of the world until, by a distant prompting,
I looked over the gunwale and saw beneath the surface
a luminous room, a light-filled grave, saw for the first time
the one clear place given to us when we are alone.

THE IDEA

for Nolan Miller

For us, too, there was a wish to possess
Something beyond the world we knew, beyond ourselves,
Beyond our power to imagine, something nevertheless
In which we might see ourselves; and this desire
Came always in passing, in waning light, and in such cold
That ice on the valley's lakes cracked and rolled,
And blowing snow covered what earth we saw,
And scenes from the past, when they surfaced again,
Looked not as they had, but ghostly and white
Among false curves and hidden erasures;
And never once did we feel we were close
Until the night wind said, "Why do this,
Especially now? Go back to the place you belong;"
And there appeared, with its windows glowing, small,
In the distance, in the frozen reaches, a cabin;
And we stood before it, amazed at its being there,
And would have gone forward and opened the door,
And stepped into the glow and warmed ourselves there,
But that it was ours by not being ours,
And should remain empty. That was the idea.

MARK STRAND

A. M.

for Lee Rust Brown

. . . And here the dark infinitive to feel,
Which would endure and have the earth be still
And the star-strewn night pour down the mountains
Into the hissing fields and silent towns until the last
Insomniac turned in, must end, and early risers see
The scarlet clouds break up and golden plumes of smoke
From uniform dark homes turn white, and so on down
To the smallest blade of grass and fallen leaf
Touched by the arriving light. Another day has come,
Another fabulous escape from the damages of night,
So even the gulls, in the ragged circle of their flight,
Above the sea's long lanes that flash and fall, scream
Their approval. How well the sun's rays probe
The rotting carcass of a skate, how well
They show the worms and swarming flies at work,
How well they shine upon the fatal sprawl
Of everything on earth. How well they love us all.

from *DARK HARBOR*

XXX

There is a road through the canyon,
A river beside the road, a forest.
If there is more, I haven't seen it yet.

Still, it is possible to say this has been
An amazing century for fashion if for nothing else;
The way brave models held back their tears

When thinking of the millions of Jews and Serbs
That Hitler killed, and how the photographer
Steadied his hand when he considered

The Muzhiks that Stalin took care of.
The way skirts went up and down; how breasts
Were in, then out; and the long and the short of hair.

But the road that winds through the canyon
Is covered with snow, and the river flows
Under the ice. Cross-country skiers are moving

Like secrets between the trees of the glassed-in forest.
The day has made a fabulous cage of cold around
My face. Whenever I take a breath I hear cracking.

XXXIX

When after a long silence one picks up the pen
And leans over the paper and says to himself:
Today I shall consider Marsyas

Whose body was flayed to excess,
Who made no crime that would square
With what he was made to suffer.

Today I shall consider the shredded remains of Marsyas —
What do they mean as they gather the sunlight
That falls in pieces through the trees,

As in Titian's late painting? Poor Marsyas,
A body, a body of work as it turns and falls
Into suffering, becoming the flesh of light,

Which is fed to onlookers centuries later.
Can this be the cost of encompassing pain?
After a long silence, would I, whose body

Is whole, sheltered, kept in the dark by a mind
That prefers it that way, know what I'd done
And what its worth was? Or is a body scraped

From the bone of experience, the chart of suffering
To be read in such ways that all flesh might be redeemed,
At least for the moment, the moment it passes into song.

XLV

I am sure you would find it misty here,
With lots of stone cottages badly needing repair.
Groups of souls, wrapped in cloaks, sit in the fields

Or stroll the winding unpaved roads. They are polite,
And oblivious to their bodies, which the wind passes through,
Making a shushing sound. Not long ago,

I stopped to rest in a place where an especially
Thick mist swirled up from the river. Someone,
Who claimed to have known me years before,

Approached, saying there were many poets
Wandering around who wished to be alive again.
They were ready to say the words they had been unable to say —

Words whose absence had been the silence of love,
Of pain, and even of pleasure. Then he joined a small group,
Gathered beside a fire. I believe I recognized

Some of the faces, but as I approached they tucked
Their heads under their wings. I looked away to the hills
Above the river, where the golden lights of sunset

And sunrise are one and the same, and saw something flying
Back and forth, fluttering its wings. Then it stopped in mid-air.
It was an angel, one of the good ones, about to sing.

THE NIGHT, THE PORCH

To stare at nothing is to learn by heart
What all of us will be swept into, and baring oneself
To the wind is feeling the ungraspable somewhere close by.
Trees can sway or be still. Day or night can be what they wish.
What we desire, more than a season or weather, is the comfort
Of being strangers, at least to ourselves. This is the crux
Of the matter, which is why even now we seem to be waiting
For something whose appearance would be its vanishing —
The sound, say, of a few leaves falling, or just one leaf,
Or less. There is no end to what we can learn. The book out there
Tells us as much, and was never written with us in mind.

A PIECE OF THE STORM

for Sharon Horvath

From the shadow of domes in the city of domes,
A snowflake, a blizzard of one, weightless, entered your room
And made its way to the arm of the chair where you, looking up
From your book, saw it the moment it landed. That's all

There was to it. No more than a solemn waking
To brevity, to the lifting and falling away of attention, swiftly,
A time between times, a flowerless funeral. No more than that
Except for the feeling that this piece of the storm,
Which turned into nothing before your eyes, would come back,
That someone years hence, sitting as you are now, might say:
"It's time. The air is ready. The sky has an opening."

LEOPARDI

The night is warm and clear and without wind.
The stone-white moon waits above the rooftops
and above the nearby river. Every street is still
and the corner lights shine down only upon the hunched shapes of cars.
You are asleep. And sleep gathers in your room
and nothing at this moment bothers you. Jules,
an old wound has opened and I feel the pain of it again.
While you sleep I have gone outside to pay my late respects
to the sky that seems so gentle
and to the world that is not and that says to me:
"I do not give you any hope. Not even hope."
Down the street there is the voice of a drunk
singing an unrecognizable song
and a car a few blocks off.
Things pass and leave no trace,
and tomorrow will come and the day after,
and whatever our ancestors knew time has taken away.
They are gone and their children are gone
and the great nations are gone.
And the armies are gone that sent clouds of dust and smoke
rolling across Europe. The world is still and we do not hear them.
Once when I was a boy, and the birthday I had waited for
was over, I lay on my bed, awake and miserable, and very late
that night the sound of someone's voice singing down a side street,
dying little by little into the distance,
wounded me, as this does now.

Jean Valentine

ANNUNCIATION

I saw my soul become flesh   breaking open
the linseed oil breaking over the paper
running down   pouring
no one to catch it   my life breaking open
no one to contain it   my
pelvis thinning out into God

DECEMBER 21ST

How will I think of you
"God-with-us"
a name: a word

and trees paths stars this earth
how will I think of them

and the dead I love   and all absent friends
here-with-me

and table: hand: white coffee mug:
a northern still life:

and you
without a body

quietness

and the infant's red-brown mouth   a star
at the star of a girl's nipple . . .

JEAN VALENTINE

AMERICAN RIVER SKY ALCOHOL FATHER

What is pornography? What is dream?
American River Sky Alcohol Father,
forty years ago, four lifetimes ago,
brown as bourbon, warm, you said to me,
"Sorry sorry sorry sorry sorry."
Then: "You're killing your mother."
And she: "You're killing your father."
What do men want? What do fathers want?
Why won't they go to the mothers?
(What do the mothers want.)
American River Sky Alcohol Father,
your warm hand. Your glass. Your bedside table gun.
The dock, the water, the fragile, tough beach grass.
Your hand. I wouldn't swim. I wouldn't fly.

THE MESSENGER

I / THE FATHER

In the strange house
in the strange town
going barefoot past the parents' empty room
I hear the horses   the fire   the wheel   bone wings
your voice.

I make my corners:
this table
this letter
this walk.

The night you died
by the time I got there to the Peter Bent Brigham Hospital
the guard said, It's no use your going up.
That was the first time you spoke to me dead —
from the high corner of the lobby.

The next night a friend said, Well these deaths
bring our own deaths, close.

But now, this is your voice
younger than mine; leaning over — say goodbye —
the fake gold Navy officer's sword
the square real gun.

Every night the freight train crossed the grown-over road
at the foot of the Neilsens' field, trailing its rusty
whistle. The fire, the wheel; fireflies.
The wall of stars. Real horses. I could go
anywhere. I could go to where you are.
I lie under the bank, my face on the wall of wet grass.
I can't go anywhere, No such thing my dear.

My mother has flour on her hands,
on her cheekbone. My father smiles his one smile
gray and white on the wall. She pushes
her hair back from her eyes. His eyes
settle. On us.

II / THE MESSENGER

You are the messenger
my half-brother, I have seen you before,
you have visited me before,
in the hallways of a school, a hospital,
in a narrow hotel room once,
once on a dirt road in August.

I lean on the oak grain of this desk,
the grain of your body, your hair,
your long back. This plum
is darker than your mouth
I drink its salty sweetness   its leaf-smell
from your tongue. Sleep;
your dark head at my breasts

       turns
to a boy's head, you are Allan   my brother
Johnny DeSoto, nine
Philip   my brother
David

Your hand is my father's sure, square hand,
it is not too late, digging down through the sand
to show me the water

You turn, say something in your sleep

You are my sister   I hold you warm in my hand   her breast
You trace my breasts

My eyes were clenched, they are opening . . .
everything, nothing . . .
We aren't afraid.
The earth drips through us

Now I want to live forever
Now I could scatter my body easily
if it was any use

now that the earth
has rained through us
green   white
green green grass.

You say you came to say if I live without you
I'll live. That's always been your story.

III / THE HILL

The dogwood blossoms stand in still, horizontal planes
at the window. In mist. Small gray figures
climb away up the green hill. Carrying precision tools wrapped in
    oilcloth.
Some push their bicycles. — Wait, I'm coming, no this time I mean it

now I could scatter my body
if it was any use

saying again
if you do not teach me I shall not learn

— First, you see, you must be still. Touch nothing.
Here, in this room. To look at nothing, to listen to nothing.
A long time. First, you see, you must open your clenched hands.
You must carry your mother and your father at your breasts.

I stand on all fours, my fur
is warm; warm organs, the male and the female.

The earth is light and warm around us.
We lick our cracked old worries
like blood away from our faces, our haunches, we
nudge each other, all our white fur, goodbye, goodbye . . .

saying again there is a last
even of last times

I wake up with one hand holding hard to the other hand.
My head rests on oilcloth. A quiet voice laughs, and says again,

— You were going to go without me?
That was always your story.

SNOW LANDSCAPE, IN A GLASS GLOBE

In memory of Elizabeth Bishop

A thumb's-length landscape: Snow, on a hill
in China. I turn the glass ball over in my hand,
and watch the snow
blow around the Chinese woman,
calm at her work,
carrying her heavy yoke
uphill, towards the distant house.
Looking out through the thick glass ball
she would see the lines of my hand,
unearthly winter trees, unmoving, behind the snow . . .

No more elders.
The Boston snow grays and softens
the streets where you were . . .
Trees older than you, alive.

The snow is over and the sky is light.
Pale, pale blue distance . . .
Is there an east? A west? A river?
There, can we live right?

I look back in through the glass. You,
in China, I can talk to you.
The snow has settled; but it's cold
there, where you are.

What are you carrying?
For the sake of what? through such hard wind
and light.
            — And you look out to me,
and you say, "Only the same as everyone; your breath,
your words, move with mine,
under and over this glass; we who were born
and lived on the living earth."

THE UNDER VOICE

I saw streaming up out of the sidewalk the homeless women and men
the East side of Broadway fruit and flowers and bourbon
the homeless men like dull knives gray-lipped the homeless women
connected to no one streaming no one to no one
more like light than like people, blue neon,
blue the most fugitive of all the colors

Then I looked and saw our bodies
not near but not far out,
lying together, our whiteness

And the under voice said, Stars you are mine,
you have always been mine; I remember the minute on the birth table
when you were born, I riding with my feet up in the wide silver-blue
       stirrups,
I came and came and came, little baby and woman, where were you
       taking me?
Everyone else may leave you, I will never leave you, fugitive.

SKATE

Now a year after your death, fish-mother, skate,
you swim up off the surface of the earth:
your other-worldly face
not saying anything
face I can never meet
inside the inside face

not since the land came wet
out of the water, face
under all the pieces of light,
how could I get to you?
Never leave you. Please you!
Teacher, spine in my spine:
the spelling of the world
kneels down before the skate.

LETTER

The hornet holds on to the curtain, winter
sleep. Rubs her legs. Climbs the curtain.
Behind her the cedars sleep lightly,

like guests. But I am the guest.
The ghost cars climb the ghost highway. Even my hand
over the page   adds to the 'room tone': the little

constant wind. The effort of becoming. These words
are my life. The effort
of loving the un-become. To make the suffering

visible. The un-become love: What we
lost, a leaf, what we cherish, a leaf.
One leaf of grass. I'm sending you this seed-pod,

this red ribbon, my tongue,
these two red ribbons, my mouth, my other mouth,

— but the other world — blindly I guzzle
the swimming milk of *its* seed field flower —

Ellen Bryant Voigt

JANUARY

After days of putting down my poem
to wipe the chair, I see
the skin of the room is oozing pitch.
Steep as a church, a bishop's hat,
the roof is lined with spruce,
and this close to the stove
the heat has opened the sapline
at each dark flaw, as though it tapped
a living tree. Everyday, a pure emanation,
the syrup bleeds to the surface of the wood.

Now, a length of softwood in its craw,
the stove crackles with resin,
and the room itself
stretches and cracks with heat, cold,
the walls' mediation between them.
There are three pale coins of resin
in the usual place on the arm of the chair.
And the momentary flies,
hatched behind the wallboard
or in the pores of the old beams,
stagger down the window's white page.

If I think I am apart from this, I am a fool.
And if I think the black engine of the stove
can raise in me the same luminous waking,
I am still a fool,
since I am the one who keeps the fire.

THE HEN

The neck lodged under a stick,
the stick under her foot,
she held the full white breast
with both hands, yanked up and out,

and the head was delivered of the body.
Brain stuck like a lens; the profile
fringed with red feathers.
Deposed, abstracted,
the head lay on the ground like a coin.
But the rest, released into the yard,
language and direction wrung from it,
flapped the insufficient wings
and staggered forward, convulsed, instinctive —
I thought it was sobbing to see it hump the dust,
pulsing out those muddy juices,
as if something, deep in the gizzard,
in the sack of soft nuggets,
drove it toward the amputated member.
Even then, watching it litter the ground
with snowy refusals, I knew it was this
that held life, gave life,
and not the head with its hard contemplative eye.

THE TRUST

Something was killing sheep
but it was sheep this dog attended on the farm —
a black-and-white border collie, patrolling his fold
like a parish priest. The second time the neighbor came,
claiming to have spotted the dog at night, a crouched figure
slithering toward the pen on the far side of the county,
the farmer let him witness how the dog,
alert and steady, mended the frayed
edge of the flock, the clumped sheep calm
as they drifted together along the stony hill.
But still more sheep across the glen were slaughtered,
and the man returned more confident. This time,
the master called his dog forward,
and stroking the eager head, prized open the mouth to find,
wound around the base of the back teeth — squat molars
the paws can't reach to clean — small coils of wool,
fine and stiff, like threads from his own jacket.
So he took down the rifle from the rack
and shot the dog and buried him,
his best companion in the field for seven years.
Once satisfied, the appetite is never dulled again.

ELLEN BRYANT VOIGT

Night after night, its sweet insistent promise
drives the animal under the rail fence and miles away
for a fresh kill; and with guilty cunning brings him back
to his familiar charges, just now stirring in the early light,
brings him home to his proud husbandry.

WOMAN WHO WEEPS

Up from the valley, ten children working the fields
and three in the ground, plus four who'd slipped like fish
from a faulty seine, she wept to the priest:
    Father, I saw the Virgin on a hill,
    she was a lion, lying on her side,
    grooming her blond shoulders with her tongue.

Six months weeping as she hulled the corn,
gathered late fruit and milked the goats,
planted grain and watched the hillside blossom,
before she went to the Bishop, kissed his ring.
    Father, I saw Our Lady in a tree,
    swaddled in black, she was a raven,
    on one leg, on one bent claw
    she hunched in the tree but she was the tree,
    charred trunk in a thicket of green.

After seven years of weeping,
not as other stunned old women weep,
she baked flat bread, washed the cooking stones,
cut a staff from a sapling by the road.
The Holy Father sat in a gilded chair:
    Father, I saw Christ's Mother in a stream,
    she was a rock, the water
    parted on either side of her,
    from one stream she made two —
    two tresses loosened across her collarbone —
    until the pouring water met at her breast
    and made a single stream again —
Then from the marketplace, from the busiest stall
she stole five ripened figs
and carried her weeping back to the countryside,
with a cloth sack, with a beggar's cup,
village to village and into the smoky huts,
her soul a well, an eye, an open door.

ELLEN BRYANT VOIGT

THE LOTUS FLOWERS

The surface of the pond was mostly green —
bright green algae reaching out from the banks,
then the mass of waterlilies, their broad round leaves
rim to rim, each white flower spreading
from the center of a green saucer.
We teased and argued, choosing the largest,
the sweetest bloom, but when the rowboat
lumbered through and rearranged them,
we found the plants were anchored, the separate
muscular stems descending in the dense water —
only the most determined put her hand
into that frog-slimed pond
to wrestle with a flower. Back and forth
we pumped across the water, in twos and threes,
full of brave adventure. On the marshy shore,
the others hollered for their turns,
or at the hem of where we pitched the tents
gathered firewood —
                                        this was wilderness,
although the pond was less than half an acre
and we could still see the grand magnolias
in the village cemetery, their waxy
white conical blossoms gleaming in the foliage.
A dozen girls, the oldest only twelve, two sisters
with their long braids, my shy neighbor,
someone squealing without interruption:
all we didn't know about the world buoyed us,
as the frightful water sustained and moved the flowers
tethered at a depth we couldn't see.

In the late afternoon, before they'd folded
into candles on the dark water,
I went to fill the bucket at the spring.
Deep in the pines, exposed tree roots
formed a natural arch, a cave of black loam.
I raked off the skin of leaves and needles,
leaving a pool so clear and shallow
I could count the pebbles
on the studded floor. The sudden cold
splashing up from the bucket to my hands
made me want to plunge my hand in —
and I held it under, feeling the shock that wakes

and deadens, watching first my fingers,
then the ledge beyond me,
the snake submerged and motionless,
the head propped on its coils the way a girl
crosses her arms before her on the sill
and rests her chin there.
                              Lugging the bucket
back to the noisy clearing, I found nothing changed,
the boat still rocked across the pond,
the fire straggled and cracked as we fed it
branches and debris into the night,
leaning back on our pallets —
spokes in a wheel — learning the names of the many
constellations, learning how each fixed
cluster took its name:
not from the strongest light, but from the pattern
made by stars of lesser magnitude,
so like the smaller stars we rowed among.

TWO TREES

At first, for the man and woman,
everything was beautiful.
Which is to say there was no beauty,
since there was not its opposite, its absence.
Every tree was "pleasant to the sight,"
the cattle also, and every creeping thing.

But at the center, foreground of the painting,
God put two trees, different from the others.
One was shrubby, spreading near the ground
lithe branches, like a fountain,
studded with fruit and thorns.
When the woman saw
this tree was good for food
and a tree to be desired to make one wise,
she ate,
            and also saw
the other, even more to be desired,
tallest in the garden, its leaves
a deeper green than all the others',
its boughs, shapely and proportionate,

hung with sweet fruit that never fell,
fruit that made the birds nesting there
graceful, brightly plumed and musical,
yet when they pecked it showed no scar.

To eat from both these trees was to be a god.
So God kept them from the second fruit,
and sent them into thistles and violent weather,
wearing the skins of lesser beasts —
let them garden dust and stony ground,
let them bear a child who was beautiful,
as they had been, and also bear a child
marked and hateful as they would become,
and bring these forth from the body's
stink and sorrow while the mind cried out
for that addictive tree it had tasted,
and for that other, crown still visible
over the wall.

HARVESTING THE COWS

Stringy, skittery, thistle-burred, rib-etched,
        they're like a pack of wolves lacking a sheep
                but also lacking the speed, the teeth, the wits —

they're heifers culled from the herd, not worth the cost
        of feeding and breeding and milking, let loose on a hill
                one-third rock, one-third blackberry bramble.

And now, the scrub stung black by hard frost,
        here come the young farmer and his father,
                one earnest, one wizened, wind-whipped, sun-whipped,

who make at the gate, from strewn boards and boughs,
        a pen, and park at its near end the compact
                silver trailer, designed for two horses —

it waits at the mouth of the rutted tractor-trail
        descending through trees, an artificial gulley.
                Up goes Junior, hooting, driving them down.

ELLEN BRYANT VOIGT

So much bigger than wolves, these sixteen cows:
        head to flank or flank to scrawny flank,
                they can't turn around; but what they know is *no:*

some splash over the walls of the small corral,
        one, wall-eyed, giddy, smashes away
                the warped plank that's propped on the far side,

crashing across alders and wet windfall
        in a plausible though explosive dance, which prompts
                another to aim herself at the same hole,

too late: the plank's back up, she's turned to the clump
        and soon swimming among them, their white necks
                extended like the necks of hissing geese,

but so much bigger than geese. When the younger man
        wraps one neck in his arms, the cow rears up
                and he goes down, plaid wool in shit-slicked mud.

So then the elder takes her by the nose —
        I mean, he puts two fingers and a thumb
                inside the nostrils, pulls her into the trailer.

The rest shy and bunch away from the gate;
        a tail lifts for a stream of piss; one beast
                mounts another — panic that looks erotic —

and the herdsmen try guile, a pail of grain
        kept low, which keeps the head of the lead cow low
                as though resigned, ready for the gallows.

The silver loaf opens, swallows them in,
        two by two by two, and takes them away —
                Hams need to be smoked, turkeys to be dressed out

here in Arcadia, where a fine cold spit
        needles the air, and the birch and beech let go
                at last their last tattered golden rags.

Rollie McKenna

Richard Wilbur

THE RIDE

The horse beneath me seemed
To know what course to steer
Through the horror of snow I dreamed,
And so I had no fear,

Nor was I chilled to death
By the wind's white shudders, thanks
To the veils of his patient breath
And the mist of sweat from his flanks.

It seemed that all night through,
Within my hand no rein
And nothing in my view
But the pillar of his mane,

I rode with magic ease
At a quick, unstumbling trot
Through shattering vacancies
On into what was not,

Till the weave of the storm grew thin,
With a threading of cedar-smoke,
And the ice-blind pane of an inn
Shimmered, and I awoke.

How shall I now get back
To the inn-yard where he stands,
Burdened with every lack,
And waken the stable-hands

To give him, before I think
That there was no horse at all,
Some hay, some water to drink,
A blanket and a stall?

RICHARD WILBUR

LOVE CALLS US TO THE THINGS OF THIS WORLD

The eyes open to a cry of pulleys,
And spirited from sleep, the astounded soul
Hangs for a moment bodiless and simple
As false dawn.
                    Outside the open window
The morning air is all awash with angels.

Some are in bed-sheets, some are in blouses,
Some are in smocks: but truly there they are.
Now they are rising together in calm swells
Of halcyon feeling, filling whatever they wear
With the deep joy of their impersonal breathing;

Now they are flying in place, conveying
The terrible speed of their omnipresence, moving
And staying like white water; and now of a sudden
They swoon down into so rapt a quiet
That nobody seems to be there.
                              The soul shrinks

From all that it is about to remember,
From the punctual rape of every blessèd day,
And cries,
            "Oh, let there be nothing on earth but laundry,
Nothing but rosy hands in the rising steam
And clear dances done in the sight of heaven."

Yet, as the sun acknowledges
With a warm look the world's hunks and colors,
The soul descends once more in bitter love
To accept the waking body, saying now
In a changed voice as the man yawns and rises,

"Bring them down from their ruddy gallows;
Let there be clean linen for the backs of thieves;
Let lovers go fresh and sweet to be undone,
And the heaviest nuns walk in a pure floating
Of dark habits,
                keeping their difficult balance."

PLAYBOY

High on his stockroom ladder like a dunce
The stock-boy sits, and studies like a sage
The subject matter of one glossy page,
As lost in curves as Archimedes once.

Sometimes, without a glance, he feeds himself.
The left hand, like a mother-bird in flight,
Brings him a sandwich for a sidelong bite,
And then returns it to a dusty shelf.

What so engrosses him? The wild décor
Of this pink-papered alcove into which
A naked girl has stumbled, with its rich
Welter of pelts and pillows on the floor,

Amidst which, kneeling in a supple pose,
She lifts a goblet in her farther hand,
As if about to toast a flower-stand
Above which hovers an exploding rose

Fired from a long-necked crystal vase that rests
Upon a tasseled and vermillion cloth
One taste of which would shrivel up a moth?
Or is he pondering her perfect breasts?

Nothing escapes him of her body's grace
Or of her floodlit skin, so sleek and warm
And yet so strangely like a uniform,
But what now grips his fancy is her face,

And how the cunning picture holds her still
At just that smiling instant when her soul,
Grown sweetly faint, and swept beyond control,
Consents to his inexorable will.

COTTAGE STREET, 1953

Framed in her phoenix fire-screen, Edna Ward
Bends to the tray of Canton, pouring tea
For frightened Mrs. Plath; then, turning toward
The pale, slumped daughter, and my wife, and me,

Asks if we would prefer it weak or strong.
Will we have milk or lemon, she enquires?
The visit seems already strained and long.
Each in his turn, we tell her our desires.

It is my office to exemplify
The published poet in his happiness,
Thus cheering Sylvia, who has wished to die;
But half-ashamed, and impotent to bless,

I am a stupid life-guard who has found,
Swept to his shallows by the tide, a girl
Who, far from shore, has been immensely drowned,
And stares through water now with eyes of pearl.

How large is her refusal; and how slight
The genteel chat whereby we recommend
Life, of a summer afternoon, despite
The brewing dusk which hints that it may end.

And Edna Ward shall die in fifteen years,
After her eight-and-eighty summers of
Such grace and courage as permit no tears,
The thin hand reaching out, the last word *love*,

Outliving Sylvia who, condemned to live,
Shall study for a decade, as she must,
To state at last her brilliant negative
In poems free and helpless and unjust.

THE WRITER

In her room at the prow of the house
Where light breaks, and the windows are tossed with linden,
My daughter is writing a story.

I pause in the stairwell, hearing
From her shut door a commotion of typewriter-keys
Like a chain hauled over a gunwale.

Young as she is, the stuff
Of her life is a great cargo, and some of it heavy:
I wish her a lucky passage.

RICHARD WILBUR

But now it is she who pauses,
As if to reject my thought and its easy figure.
A stillness greatens, in which

The whole house seems to be thinking,
And then she is at it again with a bunched clamor
Of strokes, and again is silent.

I remember the dazed starling
Which was trapped in that very room, two years ago;
How we stole in, lifted a sash

And retreated, not to affright it;
And how for a helpless hour, through the crack of the door,
We watched the sleek, wild, dark

And iridescent creature
Batter against the brilliance, drop like a glove
To the hard floor, or the desk-top,

And wait then, humped and bloody,
For the wits to try it again; and how our spirits
Rose when, suddenly sure,

It lifted off from a chair-back,
Beating a smooth course for the right window
And clearing the sill of the world.

It is always a matter, my darling,
Of life or death, as I had forgotten. I wish
What I wished you before, but harder.

IN TRACKLESS WOODS

In trackless woods, it puzzled me to find
Four great rock maples seemingly aligned,
As if they had been set out in a row
Before some house a century ago,
To edge the property and lend some shade.
I looked to see if ancient wheels had made
Old ruts to which these trees ran parallel,

RICHARD WILBUR

But there were none, so far as I could tell —
There'd been no roadway. Nor could I find the square
Depression of a cellar anywhere,
And so I tramped on further, to survey
Amazing patterns in a hornbeam spray
Or spirals in a pinecone, under trees
Not subject to our stiff geometries.

THE LILACS

Those laden lilacs
    at the lawn's end
Came stark, spindly,
     and in staggered file,
Like walking wounded
     from the dead of winter.
We watched them waken
     in the brusque weather
To rot and rootbreak,
    to ripped branches,
And saw them shiver
    as the memory swept them
Of night and numbness
     and the taste of nothing.
Out of present pain
    and from past terror
Their bullet-shaped buds
     came quick and bursting,
As if they aimed
    to be open with us!
But the sun suddenly
    settled about them,
And green and grateful
    the lilacs grew,
Healed in that hush,
    that hospital quiet.
These lacquered leaves
    where the light paddles
And the big blooms
    buzzing among them

RICHARD WILBUR

Have kept their counsel,
                  conveying nothing
Of their mortal message,
                      unless one should measure
The depth and dumbness
                of death's kingdom
By the pure power
           of this perfume.

MAYFLIES

In sombre forest, when the sun was low,
I saw from unseen pools a mist of flies
    In their quadrillions rise
And animate a ragged patch of glow
With sudden glittering — as when a crowd
    Of stars appear
Through a brief gap in black and driven cloud,
One arc of their great round-dance showing clear.

It was no muddled swarm I witnessed, for
In entrechats each fluttering insect there
    Rose two steep yards in air,
Then slowly floated down to climb once more,
So that they all composed a manifold
    And figured scene,
And seemed the weavers of some cloth of gold,
Or the fine pistons of some bright machine.

Watching those lifelong dancers of a day
As night closed in, I felt myself alone
    In a life too much my own,
More mortal in my separateness than they —
Unless, I thought, I had been called to be
    Not fly or star
But one whose task is joyfully to see
How fair the fiats of the caller are.

C. K. Williams

BLADES

When I was about eight, I once stabbed somebody, another kid, a little
    girl.
I'd been hanging around in front of the supermarket near our house
and when she walked by, I let her have it, right in the gap between her
    shirt and her shorts
with a piece of broken-off car antenna I used to carry around in my
    pocket.
It happened so fast I still don't know how I did it: I was as shocked as she
    was
except she squealed and started yelling as though I'd plunged a knife in
    her
and everybody in the neighborhood gathered around us, then they called
    the cops,
then the girl's mother came running out of the store saying "What hap-
    pened? What happened?"
and the girl screamed, "He stabbed me!" and I screamed back, "I did
    not!" and she you did too
and me I didn't and we were both crying hysterically by that time.
Somebody pulled her shirt up and it was just a scratch but we went on
    and on
and the mother, standing between us, seemed to be absolutely terrified.
I still remember how she watched first one of us and then the other with
    a look of complete horror —
You did too! I did not! — as though we were both strangers, as though it
    was some natural disaster
she was beholding that was beyond any mode of comprehension so all
    she could do
was stare speechlessly at us, and then another expression came over her
    face,
one that I'd never seen before, that made me think she was going to cry
    herself
and sweep both of us, the girl and me, into her arms to hold us against
    her.
The police came just then, though, quieted everyone down, put the girl
    and the mother
into a squad-car to take to the hospital and me in another to take to jail
except they really only took me around the corner and let me go because
    the mother and daughter were black

561

and in those days you had to do something pretty terrible to get into trouble
    that way.

I don't understand how we twist these things or how we get them straight
    again
but I relived that day I don't know how many times before I realized I had
    it all wrong.
The boy wasn't me at all, he was another kid: I was just there.
And it wasn't the girl who was black, but him. The mother was real,
    though.
I really had thought she was going to embrace them both
and I had dreams about her for years afterwards: that I'd be being born
    again
and she'd be lifting me with that same wounded sorrow or she would
    suddenly appear out of nowhere,
blotting out everything but a single, blazing wing of holiness.
Who knows the rest? I can still remember how it felt the old way.
How I make my little thrust, how she crushes us against her, how I turn
    and snarl
at the cold circle of faces around us because something's torn in me,
some ancient cloak of terror we keep on ourselves because we'll do any-
    thing,
anything, not to know how silently we knell in the mouth of death
and not to obliterate the forgiveness and the lies we offer one another and
    call innocence.
This is innocence. I touch her, we kiss.
And this. I'm here or not here. I can't tell. I stab her. I stab her again. I
    still can't.

FROM MY WINDOW

Spring: the first morning when that one true block of sweet, laminar,
    complex scent arrives
from somewhere west and I keep coming to lean on the sill, glorying in
    the end of the wretched winter.
The scabby-barked sycamores ringing the empty lot across the way are
    budded — I hadn't noticed —
and the thick spikes of the unlikely urban crocuses have already broken
    the gritty soil.
Up the street, some surveyors with tripods are waving each other left and
    right the way they do.
A girl in a gym suit jogged by a while ago, some kids passed, playing
    hooky, I imagine,

C. K. WILLIAMS

and now the paraplegic Vietnam vet who lives in a half-converted ware-
house down the block
and the friend who stays with him and seems to help him out come
weaving towards me,
their battered wheelchair lurching uncertainly from one edge of the sidewalk to the other.
I know where they're going — to the "Legion": once, when I was putting
something out, they stopped,
both drunk that time, too, both reeking — it wasn't ten o'clock — and we
chatted for a bit.
I don't know how they stay alive — on benefits most likely. I wonder if
they're lovers?
They don't look it. Right now, in fact, they look a wreck, careening hap-
hazardly along,
contriving, as they reach beneath me, to dip a wheel from the curb so
that the chair skewers, teeters,
tips, and they both tumble, the one slowly, almost gracefully sliding in
stages from his seat,
his expression hardly marking it, the other staggering over him, spinning
heavily down,
to lie on the asphalt, his mouth working, his feet shoving weakly and
fruitlessly against the curb.
In the storefront office on the corner, Reed and Son, Real Estate, have
come to see the show.
Gazing through the golden letters of their name, they're not, at least,
thank god, laughing.
Now the buddy, grabbing at a hydrant, gets himself erect and stands there
for a moment, panting.
Now he has to lift the other one, who lies utterly still, a forearm shielding
his eyes from the sun.
He hauls him partly upright, then hefts him almost all the way into the
chair, but a dangling foot
catches a support-plate, jerking everything around so that he has to put
him down,
set the chair to rights, and hoist him again and as he does he jerks the
grimy jeans right off him.
No drawers, shrunken, blotchy thighs: under the thick, white coils of
belly blubber,
the poor, blunt pud, tiny, terrified, retracted, is almost invisible in the
sparse genital hair,
then his friend pulls his pants up, he slumps wholly back as though he
were, at last, to be let be,
and the friend leans against the cyclone fence, suddenly staring up at me
as though he'd known,

all along, that I was watching and I can't help wondering if he knows that in the winter, too,

I watched, the night he went out to the lot and walked, paced rather, almost ran, for how many hours.

It was snowing, the city in that holy silence, the last we have, when the storm takes hold,

and he was making patterns that I thought at first were circles, then realized made a figure eight,

what must have been to him a perfect symmetry but which, from where I was, shivered, bent,

and lay on its side: a warped, unclear infinity, slowly, as the snow came faster, going out.

Over and over again, his head lowered to the task, he slogged the path he'd blazed,

but the race was lost, his prints were filling faster than he made them now and I looked away,

up across the skeletal trees to the tall center city buildings, some, though it was midnight,

with all their offices still gleaming, their scarlet warning beacons signaling erratically

against the thickening flakes, their smoldering auras softening portions of the dim, milky sky.

In the morning, nothing: every trace of him effaced, all the field pure white,

its surface glittering, the dawn, glancing from its glaze, oblique, relentless, unadorned.

THE GAS STATION

This is before I'd read Nietzsche. Before Kant or Kierkegaard, even before Whitman and Yeats.

I don't think there were three words in my head yet. I knew, perhaps, that I should suffer,

I can remember I almost cried for this or for that, nothing special, nothing to speak of.

Probably I was mad with grief for the loss of my childhood, but I wouldn't have known that.

It's dawn. A gas station. Route twenty-two. I remember exactly: route twenty-two curved,

there was a squat, striped concrete divider they'd put in after a plague of collisions.

The gas station? Texaco, Esso — I don't know. They were just words anyway then, just what their signs said.

I wouldn't have understood the first thing about monopoly or imperialist
 or oppression.
It's dawn. It's so late. Even then, when I was never tired, I'm just holding on.
Slumped on my friend's shoulder, I watch the relentless, wordless misery
 of the route twenty-two sky
that seems to be filming my face with a grainy oil I keep trying to rub off
 or in.
Why are we here? Because one of my friends, in the men's room over
 there, has blue balls.
He has to jerk off. I don't know what that means, "blue balls," or why he
 has to do that —
it must be important to have to stop here after this long night, but I
 don't ask.
I'm just trying, I think, to keep my head as empty as I can for as long as
 I can.
One of my other friends is asleep. He's so ugly, his mouth hanging, slack
 and wet.
Another — I'll never see this one again — stares from the window as
 though he were frightened.
Here's what we've done. We were in Times Square, a pimp found us, cor-
 ralled us, led us somewhere,
down a dark street, another dark street, up dark stairs, dark hall, dark
 apartment,
where his whore, his girl or his wife or his mother for all I know dragged
 herself from her sleep,
propped herself on an elbow, gazed into the dark hall, and agreed, for two
 dollars each, to take care of us.
Take care of us. Some of the words that come through me now seem to
 stay, to hook in.
My friend in the bathroom is taking so long. The filthy sky must be starting to lighten.
It took me a long time, too, with the woman, I mean. Did I mention that
 she, the woman, the whore or mother,
was having her time and all she would deign do was to blow us? Did I say
 that? Deign? Blow?
What a joy, though, the idea was in those days. Blown! What a thing to
 tell the next day.
She only deigned, though, no more. She was like a machine. When I lift
 her back to me now,
there's nothing there but that dark, curly head, working, a machine, up
 and down, and now,
Freud, Marx, Fathers, tell me, what am I, doing this, telling this, on her,
 on myself,

hammering it down, cementing it, sealing it in, but a machine, too? *Why
    am I doing this?*
I still haven't read Augustine. I don't understand Chomsky that well.
    Should I?
My friend at last comes back. Maybe the right words were there all along.
    Complicity. Wonder.
How pure we were then, before Rimbaud, before Blake. *Grace. Love. Take
    care of us. Please.*

BONE

An erratic, complicated shape, like a tool for some obsolete task:
the hipbone and half the gnawed shank of a small, unrecognizable animal
        on the pavement in front of the entrance to the museum;
grimy, black with tire-dust, soot, the blackness from our shoes, our ink, the
        grit that sifts out of our air.

Still, something devoured all but this much, and if you look more
        closely,
you can see tiny creatures still gnawing at the shreds of decomposing meat,
        sucking at the all but putrefying bone.

Decades it must be on their scale that they harvest it, dwell and generate
        and age and die on it.
Where will they transport the essence of it when they're done?
How far beneath the asphalt, sewers, subways, mains and conduits is the
        living earth to which at last they'll once again descend?
Which intellect will register in its neurons the great fortune of this ex-
        ceptional adventure? Which poet sing it?
Such sweetness, such savor: luxury, satiety, and no repentance, no regret.

But Maman won't let you keep it.
"Maman, please . . ."
"It's filthy. Drop it. *Drop it! Drop it! Drop it!*"

THE SINGING

I was walking home down a hill near our house on a balmy afternoon
        under the blossoms
Of the pear trees that go flamboyantly mad here every spring with their
        burgeoning forth

C. K. WILLIAMS

When a young man turned in from a corner singing no it was more of a
    cadenced shouting
Most of which I couldn't catch I thought because the young man was
    black speaking black

It didn't matter I could tell he was making his song up which pleased me
    he was nice-looking
Husky dressed in some style of big pants obviously full of himself hence
    his lyrical flowing over

We went along in the same direction then he noticed me there almost
    beside him and "Big"
He shouted-sang "Big" and I thought how droll to have my height incor-
    porated in his song

So I smiled but the face of the young man showed nothing he looked in
    fact pointedly away
And his song changed "I'm not a nice person" he chanted "I'm not I'm
    not a nice person"

No menace was meant I gathered no particular threat but he did want to
    be certain I knew
That if my smile implied I conceived of anything like concord between
    us I should forget it

That's all nothing else happened his song became indecipherable to me
    again he arrived
Where he was going a house where a girl in braids waited for him on the
    porch that was all

No one saw no one heard all the unasked and unanswered questions were
    left where they were
It occurred to me to sing back "I'm not a nice person either" but I couldn't
    come up with a tune

Besides I wouldn't have meant it nor he have believed it both of us knew
    just where we were
In the duet we composed the equation we made the conventions to
    which we were condemned

Sometimes it feels even when no one is there that someone something is
    watching and listening
Someone to rectify redo remake this time again though no one saw nor
    heard no one was there

C. D. Wright

THE SECRET LIFE OF MUSICAL INSTRUMENTS

Between midnight and Reno
the world borders on a dune.
The bus does not stop.

The boys in the band have their heads on the rest.
They dream like so-and-sos.

The woman smokes
one after another.
She is humming "Strange Fruit."
There is smoke in her clothes, her voice,
but her hair never smells.

She blows white petals off her lapel,
tastes salt.
It is a copacetic moon.

The instruments do not sleep in their dark cribs.
They keep cool, meditate.
They have speech with strangers:

Come all ye faithless
young and crazy victims of love.
Come the lowlife and the highborn
all ye upside-down shitasses.

Bring your own light.
Come in. Be lost. Be still.
If you miss us at home
we'll be on our way to the reckoning.

for Claudia Burson

WAGES OF LOVE

The house is watched, the watchers only planets.

Very near the lilac
                        a woman leaves her night soil
to be stepped in. Like other animals.
                        Steam lifts off her mess.

They have power, but not water.
                        Pregnant. She must be.

The world is all that is the case.

You can hear the strike of the broom, a fan
                        slicing overhead light.
At the table the woman stares at a dish
                        of peaches, plums; black ants
filing down the sill to bear away the fly.

Everywhere in America is summer. The young
                        unaware they are young, their minds
on other wounds or the new music.

The heart some bruised fruit
knocked loose by a long stick
                        aches at the stem.
It's not forbidden to fall out of love
                        like from a tree.

As for the tenants whose waters
                        will break in this bed,
May they live through the great pain;
may their offspring change everything —

                        because everything must change.

The man joins the woman in the kitchen. They touch
                        the soft place of their fruit.
They enter in, tell their side, and pass through.

C. D. WRIGHT

MORE BLUES AND THE ABSTRACT TRUTH

I back the car over a soft, large object;
hair appears on my chest in dreams.
The paperboy comes to collect
with a pit bull. Call Grandmother
and she says, Well you know
death is death and none other.

In the mornings we're in the dark;
even at the end of June
the zucchini keep on the sill.
Ring Grandmother for advice
and she says, O you know
I used to grow so many things.

Then there's the frequent bleeding,
the tender nipples, and the rot
under the floormat. If I'm not seeing
a cold-eyed doctor it is
another gouging mechanic.
Grandmother says, Thanks to the blue rugs
and Eileen Briscoe's elms
the house keeps cool.

Well. Then. You say Grandmother
let me just ask you this:
How does a body rise up again and rinse
her mouth from the tap. And how
does a body put in a plum tree
or lie again on top of another body
or string a trellis. Or go on drying
the flatware. Fix rainbow trout. Grout the tile.
Buy a bag of onions. Beat an egg stiff. Yes,
how does the cat continue
to lick itself from toenail to tailhole.
And how does a body break
bread with the word when the word
has broken. Again. And. Again.
With the wine. And the loaf.
And the excellent glass
of the body. And she says,
Even. If. The. Sky. Is. Falling.
My. Peace. Rose. Is. In. Bloom.

C. D. WRIGHT

WHY RALPH REFUSES TO DANCE

He would have to put out his smoke.
    At this time of year the snakes are slow and sorry-acting
His ice would melt. He'd lose his seat.
    you don't take chances once in a while you still see
He does not feel the beat.
    a coontail tied to an aerial, but don't look
His pocket could be picked. His trousers rip.
    for signs keep your black shoes on the floor
He could break a major bone.
    burn every tick you pull off your head
He remembers the last time he stepped out on the floor.
    roll a set of steel balls around in your fist
Who do you think I am, she said, a broom.
    looking at the moon's punched-out face
No, he mumbled, saxophone.
    think about Lily coming down the staircase
At the tables they whispered about him.
    her crushed-velvet chairs
He would begin to smell of baby shrimp.
    her pearled brown toes
The music could stop in the middle of his action.
    that time with the three of them in a boat
What would he do with his hands.
    and him throwing up in the river
The women his age are spoken for.
    as she stood up to skim his hat into the shallows
After sitting out so long, his heart could give out.
    and tomorrow would unleash another spell of spare-rib theology
People will be stepped on. A fight ensue.
    aw shuddup somebody clapped a hand on his shoulder
The cats in the band will lose respect.
    aw shuddup he was getting the heavy hand again
He will bring dishonor to his family name.
    are you going to dance or not, just say
good-night, no thanks, hallelujah yourself, go to hell.

C. D. WRIGHT

PLANKS

While we are all together under burring bulbs we would do well
to remember the wild rose in the pelvis bone. Albumen.
The accoutrements and utensils of love. And labor.
A soft robe. A solid teapot. Our talking guitar.
Why not go to a green field. Barefooted, hair unbound. And fill
our belly with short sweet grass. Cover the shorn shoulders
with new wool. Rid the body of its white implacability.
Bite down and hold on. Remember string light.

Remember lives on the periphery: the Indian in handcuffs.
The twin sisters who man the mausoleum. Or just standing in line
we could shut our eyes. Stop counting. Imagine:
the color Naomi Trosper wanted to paint West Memphis;
now picture West Memphis, gentian violet.
While we are starching our coats for their steel constructions
we could be shining the particulars; emery boards,
grasshoppers . . . , remembering the birth of our boy. The giant hibiscus.

The first feces, meconium. Forever bearing in mind why
we have been assembled. Remember pain. The night Yolanda lost her
    baby.
Bite down and hold on. Be ourselves chastened,
doing away with engraved gifts, boxes of miscellany.
Ignore the butcherbirds. The aims of the ruthless. Bad endings.
Breakfasts of Coca-Cola and cigarette smoke. Sabotage. Stay
down and let go. Of vain love. The frayed light. All together now.
The night Esmerelda came to town and laid an egg. Forget pain.

Alone and awake in our cells like a bird left without a blanket,
we would do well to find the wild rose in the pelvis bone; turn
our back on the figure in the undergrowth, the felo-de-se,
his draining face. Albumen. Let us go back to the green field. And lie
    down.

Eliminate strategies. The key to the handcuffs. Singing nail file.
    Acrididae.
Bury Yolanda's placenta. The pain. Esmerelda's egg. The pain.
Naomi's violet city. Childbirth. Our talking guitar. We must bite down
and hold on. Never mind learning to draw. The giant hibiscus.

SO FAR OFF AND YET HERE

Because I know this is going to be painful
I can feel the pain before it acquires a shape

Now nearer to me

How at night it is just audible
like mice in the insulation

So windows snow and pears soften
an old house settles into its infested studs

Always there is more inside
than outside in the open

Where I came to be identified with
your scars and green limbs

Now nearer to me

What in the meantime happened to my eyes
they shone   at least   they seemed capable   of shine

But a poem on a page by itself
does not penetrate the retina of fear

Now nearer to me

So the mind dispels us
radiators gasp and washers wear out

Your left middle finger sinks inside me
the nail of love just holds

SONG OF THE GOURD

In gardening I continued to sit on my side of the car: to
drive whenever possible at the usual level of distraction:
in gardening I shat nails glass contaminated dirt and
threw up on the new shoots: in gardening I learned to
praise things I had dreaded: I pushed the hair out of my
face: I felt less responsible for one man's death one
woman's long-term isolation: my bones softened: in

gardening I lost nickels and ring settings I uncovered
buttons and marbles: I laid half the worm aside and
sought the rest: I sought myself in the bucket and wondered why I came into being in the first place: in gardening I turned away from the television and went
around smelling of offal the inedible parts of the
chicken: in gardening I said excelsior: in gardening I required no company I had to forgive my own failure to
perceive how things were: I went out barelegged at
dusk and dug and dug and dug: I hit rock my ovaries
softened: in gardening I was protean as in no other
realm before or since: I longed to torch my old belongings and belch a little flame of satisfaction: in gardening
I longed to stroll farther into soundlessness: I could almost forget what happened many swift years ago in
arkansas: I felt like a god from down under: chthonian:
in gardening I thought this is it body and soul I am
home at last: excelsior: praise the grass: in gardening I
fled the fold that supported the war: only in gardening
could I stop shrieking: stop: stop the slaughter: only in
gardening could I press my ear to the ground to hear
my soul let out an unyielding noise: my lines softened: I
turned the water onto the joy-filled boychild: only in
gardening did I feel fit to partake to go on trembling in
the last light: I confess the abject urge to weed your
beds while the bittersweet overwhelmed my daylilies: I
summoned the courage to grin: I climbed the hill with
my bucket and slept like a dipper in the cool of your
body: besotted with growth: shot through by green

GIRL FRIEND POEM #3

She was white and flown
as a kleenex turning into a swan.
I lifted her veil; the face disappeared.
As if I had exposed some film
to sun. Twirling our skirts.
Laughing until the clouds sopped up
the light. And the peaches fell down around us.

for Sharon

Nancy Crampton

Charles Wright

REUNION

Already one day has detached itself from all the rest up ahead.
It has my photograph in its soft pocket.
It wants to carry my breath into the past in its bag of wind.

I write poems to untie myself, to do penance and disappear
Through the upper right-hand corner of things, to say grace.

GRACE

Its hair is a fine weed,
Matted, where something has lain,
Or fallen repeatedly:

Its arms are rivers that sink
Suddenly under the earth,
Elbow and wristbone: cold sleeve:

Its face is a long soliloquy,
A language of numerals,
Impossible to erase.

SNOW

If we, as we are, are dust, and dust, as it will, rises,
Then we will rise, and recongregate
In the wind, in the cloud, and be their issue,

Things in a fall in a world of fall, and slip
Through the spiked branches and snapped joints of the evergreens,
White ants, white ants and the little ribs.

CHARLES WRIGHT

HIM

His sorrow hangs like a heart in the star-flowered boundary tree.
It mirrors the endless wind.

He feeds on the lunar differences and flies up at the dawn.

When he lies down, the waters will lie down with him,
And all that walks and all that stands still, and sleep through the thunder.

It's for him that the willow bleeds.

Look for him high in the flat black of the northern Pacific sky,
Released in his suit of lights,
                              lifted and laid clear.

CALIFORNIA DREAMING

We are not born yet, and everything's crystal under our feet.
We are not brethren, we are not underlings.
We are another nation,
                              living by voices that you will never hear,
Caught in the net of splendor
                              of time-to-come on the earth.
We shine in our distant chambers, we are golden.

———————

Midmorning, and Darvon dustfall off the Pacific
Stuns us to ecstasy,
                    October sun
Stuck like a tack on the eastern drift of the sky,
The idea of God on the other,
                              body by body
Rinsed in the Sunday prayer-light, draining away
Into the undercoating and slow sparks of the west,
                              which is our solitude and our joy.

———————

I've looked at this ridge of lights for six years now
                                        and still don't like it,
Strung out like Good Friday along a cliff
That Easters down to the ocean,

CHARLES WRIGHT

A dark wing with ruffled feathers as far out as Catalina
Fallen from some sky,
                         ruffled and laid back by the wind,
Santa Ana that lisps its hot breath
                              on the neck of everything.

———————

What if the soul indeed is outside the body,
                         a little rainfall of light
Moistening our every step, prismatic, apotheosizic?
What if inside the body another shape is waiting to come out,
White as a quilt, loose as a fever,
                        and sways in the easy tides there?
What other anagoge in this life but the self?
What other ladder to Paradise
                 but the smooth handholds of the rib cage?
High in the palm tree the orioles twitter and grieve.
We twitter and grieve, the spider twirls the honey bee,
Who twitters and grieves, around in her net,
                    then draws it by one leg
Up to the fishbone fern leaves inside the pepper tree
                       swaddled in silk
And turns it again and again until it is shining.

———————

Some nights, when the rock-and-roll band next door has quit playing,
And the last helicopter has thwonked back to the Marine base,
And the dark lets all its weight down
                 to within a half inch of the ground,
I sit outside in the gold lamé of the moon
                 as the town sleeps and the country sleeps
Like flung confetti around me,
And wonder just what in the hell I'm doing out here
So many thousands of miles away from what I know best.
And what I know best
                 has nothing to do with Point Conception
And Avalon and the long erasure of ocean
Out there where the landscape ends.
What I know best is a little thing.
It sits on the far side of the simile,
                 the like that's like the like.

———————

Today is sweet stuff on the tongue.
The question of how we should live our lives in this world

CHARLES WRIGHT

Will find no answer from us
                              this morning,
Sunflick, the ocean humping its back
Beneath us, shivering out
                              wave after wave we fall from
And cut through in a white scar of healed waters,
Our wet suits glossed slick as seals,
                              our boards grown sharp as cries.
We rise and fall like the sun.

———————

Ghost of the Muse and her dogsbody
Suspended above the beach, November 25,
Sun like a Valium disc, smog like rust in the trees.
White-hooded and friar-backed,
                              a gull choir eyeballs the wave reach.
Invisibly pistoned, the sea keeps it up,
                    plunges and draws back, plunges and draws back,
Yesterday hung like a porcelain cup behind the eyes,
Sonorous valves, insistent extremities,
                    the worm creeping out of the heart . . .

———————

Who are these people we pretend to be,
                    untouched by the setting sun?
They stand less stiffly than we do, and handsomer,
First on the left foot, and then the right.
Just for a moment we see ourselves inside them,
                                        peering out,
And then they go their own way and we go ours,
Back to the window seat above the driveway,
Christmas lights in the pepper tree,
                              black Madonna
Gazing out from the alicanthus.
Chalk eyes downcast, heavy with weeping and bitterness,
Her time has come round again.

———————

Piece by small piece the world falls away from us like spores
From a milkweed pod,
                              and everything we have known,
And everyone we have known,
Is taken away by the wind to forgetfulness,
Somebody always humming,
                              California dreaming . . .

CHARLES WRIGHT

NIGHT JOURNAL

— I think of Issa, a man of few words:
The world of dew
Is the world of dew.
And yet . . .
And yet . . .

— Three words contain
                                all that we know for sure of the next life
Or the last one: Close your eyes.
Everything else is gossip,
                                false mirrors, trick windows
Flashing like Dutch glass
In the undiminishable sun.

— I write it down in visible ink,
Black words that disappear when held up to the light —
I write it down
                        not to remember but to forget,
Words like thousands of pieces of shot film
                                        exposed to the sun.
I never see anything but the ground.

— Everyone wants to tell his story.
The Chinese say we live in the world of the 10,000 things,
Each of the 10,000 things
                                crying out to us
Precisely nothing,
A silence whose tune we've come to understand,
Words like birthmarks,
                        embolic sunsets drying behind the tongue.
If we were as eloquent,
If what we say could spread the good news the way that dogwood does,
Its votive candles
                        phosphorous and articulate in the green haze
Of spring, surely something would hear us.

— Even a chip of beauty
                                is beauty intractable in the mind,
Words the color of wind
Moving across the fields there
                                wind-addled and wind-sprung,

CHARLES WRIGHT

Abstracted as water glints,
The fields lion-colored and rope-colored,
As in a picture of Paradise,
                              the bodies languishing over the sky
Trailing their dark identities
That drift off and sieve away to the nothingness
Behind them
                  moving across the fields there
As words move, slowly, trailing their dark identities.

— Our words, like blown kisses, are swallowed by ghosts
Along the way,
                  their destinations bereft
In a rub of brightness unending:
How distant everything always is,
                              and yet how close,
Music starting to rise like smoke from under the trees.

— Birds sing an atonal row
                        unsyncopated
From tree to tree,
                  dew chants
Whose songs have no words
                        from tree to tree
When night puts her dark lens in,
One on this limb, two others back there.

— Words, like all things, are caught in their finitude.
They start here, they finish here
No matter how high they rise —
                              my judgment is that I know this
And never love anything hard enough
That would stamp me
                  and sink me suddenly into bliss.

RELICS

After a time, Hoss, it makes such little difference
What anyone writes —
Relics, it seems, of the thing
                        are always stronger than the thing itself.

Palimpsest and pentimento, for instance, saint's bones
Or saint's blood,
Transcendent architecture of what was possible, say,
                                        once upon a time.

The dogwoods bloom, the pink ones and the white ones, in blots
And splotches across the dusk.
                        Like clouds, perhaps. Mock clouds
In a mock heaven,
The faint odor of something unworldly, or otherworldly,
Lingering in the darkness, then not.
As though some saint had passed by the side yard,
                                the odor of Paradise,

As Aldo Buzzi has it,
Odor of Heaven, the faithful say.
And what is this odor like? someone who'd smelled it was asked once.
He had no answer, and said,
"It doesn't resemble any flower or any bloom or spice on this earth.
I wouldn't know how to describe it."
                        Lingering as the dark comes on.

St. Gaspare Del Bufalo was one of these fragrant saints,
Buzzi continues,
St. Gaspare, who walked in the rain without an umbrella and still stayed
    dry.
Miraculous gift.
He knew, he added, one of the saint's relatives, a pianist,
                        who served him an osso buco once
In a penthouse in Milan.

Let's see. A cold spring in Charlottesville,
End of April, 2000 —
If you can't say what you've got to say in three lines,
                        better change your style.
Nobody's born redeemed, nobody's moonlight, golden fuse in the
    deadly trees.
White wind through black wires,
                        humming a speech we do not speak.
Listen for us in the dark hours, listen for us in our need.

Gerald Malanga

James Wright

AUTUMN BEGINS IN MARTINS FERRY, OHIO

In the Shreve High football stadium,
I think of Polacks nursing long beers in Tiltonsville,
And gray faces of Negroes in the blast furnace at Benwood,
And the ruptured night watchman of Wheeling Steel,
Dreaming of heroes.

All the proud fathers are ashamed to go home.
Their women cluck like starved pullets,
Dying for love.

Therefore,
Their sons grow suicidally beautiful
At the beginning of October,
And gallop terribly against each other's bodies.

LYING IN A HAMMOCK AT WILLIAM DUFFY'S FARM
IN PINE ISLAND, MINNESOTA

Over my head, I see the bronze butterfly,
Asleep on the black trunk,
Blowing like a leaf in green shadow.
Down the ravine behind the empty house,
The cowbells follow one another
Into the distances of the afternoon.
To my right,
In a field of sunlight between two pines,
The droppings of last year's horses
Blaze up into golden stones.
I lean back, as the evening darkens and comes on.
A chicken hawk floats over, looking for home.
I have wasted my life.

585

JAMES WRIGHT

THE MINNEAPOLIS POEM

1

[handwritten: "the unnamed poor" in part 7]

I wonder how many old men last winter
Hungry and frightened by namelessness prowled
The Mississippi shore
Lashed blind by the wind, dreaming
Of suicide in the river.
The police remove their cadavers by daybreak
And turn them in somewhere.
Where?
How does the city keep lists of its fathers
Who have no names?
By Nicollet Island I gaze down at the dark water
So beautifully slow.
And I wish my brothers good luck
And a warm grave.

[handwritten: — patriarchy vs.]

[handwritten: communion]

2

The Chippewa young men
Stab one another shrieking
Jesus Christ.
Split-lipped homosexuals limp in terror of assault.
High school backfields search under benches
Near the Post Office. Their faces are the rich
Raw bacon without eyes.
The Walker Art Center crowd stare
At the Guthrie Theater.

3

Tall Negro girls from Chicago
Listen to light songs.
They know when the supposed patron
Is a plainclothesman.
A cop's palm
Is a roach dangling down the scorched fangs
Of a light bulb.
The soul of a cop's eyes

[handwritten: hand extending out — interconnected help]

Is an eternity of Sunday daybreak in the suburbs
Of Juárez, Mexico.

4

The legless beggars are gone, carried away *part 7*
By white birds.
The Artificial Limbs Exchange is gutted
And sown with lime.
The whalebone crutches and hand-me-down trusses
Huddle together dreaming in a desolation
Of dry groins.
I think of poor men astonished to waken
Exposed in broad daylight by the blade
Of a strange plough.

5

All over the walls of comb cells
Automobiles perfumed and blindered
Consent with a mutter of high good humor
To take their two naps a day.
Without sound windows glide back
Into dusk.
The sockets of a thousand blind bee graves tier upon tier
Tower not quite toppling.
There are men in this city who labor dawn after dawn
To sell me my death.

6

But I could not bear
To allow my poor brother my body to die
In Minneapolis.
The old man Walt Whitman our countryman
Is now in America our country
Dead.
But he was not buried in Minneapolis
At least.
And no more may I be
Please God.

7

I want to be lifted up
By some great white bird unknown to the police,
And soar for a thousand miles and be carefully hidden
Modest and golden as one last corn grain,
Stored with the secrets of the wheat and the mysterious lives
Of the unnamed poor.

**IN RESPONSE TO A RUMOR THAT THE OLDEST
WHOREHOUSE IN WHEELING, WEST VIRGINIA,
HAS BEEN CONDEMNED**

I will grieve alone,
As I strolled alone, years ago, down along
The Ohio shore.
I hid in the hobo jungle weeds
Upstream from the sewer main,
Pondering, gazing.

I saw, down river,
At Twenty-third and Water Streets
By the vinegar works,
The doors open in early evening.
Swinging their purses, the women
Poured down the long street to the river
And into the river.

I do not know how it was
They could drown every evening.
What time near dawn did they climb up the other shore,
Drying their wings?

For the river at Wheeling, West Virginia,
Has only two shores:
The one in hell, the other
In Bridgeport, Ohio.

And nobody would commit suicide, only
To find beyond death
Bridgeport, Ohio.

JAMES WRIGHT

THE YOUNG GOOD MAN

1

The young good man walked out savoring
His own tongue instead of the lips
Of the wild crab apple.
You will believe this,

[handwritten: is this enjambment / an exploration / space? / raunch / seedy]

But there used to be places just on the other side
Of Cadiz, Ohio, where you could slip in
Without anybody knowing,
And find them sweet.

Everybody I knew, loved, and respected,
Like Charlie Duff, my cousin Dave,
George Ellis, Gene Turner from Bellaire
Who tackled me twice, and even I swear to Christ
John Shunk, the one man all the way from Pittsburgh
To Cincinnati who knew how to use
A diving suit and who got his name
In the newspapers all the time for
Dragging up the drowned boys,

Said leave them crab apples alone,
They taste so bitter you pucker
Two days at least. You bite one,
You'll be sorry.

[handwritten, circled: prostitutes]

2

I don't know why,
One evening in August something illuminated my body
And I got sick of laying my cold
Hands on myself.
I lied to my family I was going for a walk uptown.
When I got to that hill,
Which now, I hear, Bluehart has sold to the Hanna
Strip Mine Company, it was no trouble at all to me.
Within fifteen yards of his charged fence I found me
A wild crab apple.

"Room to "make (?) choices" ↑ or ↓

I licked it all over.
You are going to believe this.
It tasted sweet.

I know what would have happened to my tongue
If I had bitten. The people who love me
Are sure as hell no fools.

="crab apple"? 3 Anne Sexton?

You and I could not have been simple married lovers.
There are so many reasons I can't count them,
But here are some few:
You are much more intelligent and learned than I am.
I have a very quick felicity of tongue.
Sooner or later I would have bitten your heart
With some snide witty remark or other.
And you wouldn't stand for it.
Our lives being what we are,
We didn't have a chance.

I wish we had had.
I have written this poem to you before I die.
And I don't mean to die
For some good time yet.

THE OLD WPA SWIMMING POOL
IN MARTINS FERRY, OHIO

I am almost afraid to write down
This thing. I must have been,
Say, seven years old. That afternoon,
The families of the WPA had come out
To have a good time celebrating
A long gouge in the ground,
That the fierce husbands
Had filled with concrete.

We knew even then the Ohio
River was dying. *drying up*

JAMES WRIGHT

Most of the good men who lived along that shore
Wanted to be in love and give good love
To beautiful women, who weren't pretty,
And to small children like me who wondered,
What the hell is this?

When people don't have quite enough to eat
In August, and the river,
That is supposed to be some holiness, *baptism*
Starts dying,

They swim in the earth. Uncle Sherman, *in / down?*
Uncle Willie, Uncle Emerson, and my father
Helped dig that hole in the ground. — *WPA pool*

I had seen by that time two or three
Holes in the ground, ————— *underground*
And you know what they were.

But this one was not the usual, cheap
Economics, it was not the solitary
Scar on a poor man's face, that respectable
Hole in the ground you used to be able to buy *grave*
After you died for seventy-five dollars and
Your wages tached for six months by the Heslop
Brothers.

Brothers, dear God.

No, this hole was filled with water,
And suddenly I flung myself into the water.
All I had on was a jockstrap my brother stole
From a miserable football team. *not a baptism*

Oh never mind, Jesus Christ, my father
And my uncles dug a hole in the ground,
No grave for once. It is going to be hard
For you to believe; when I rose from that water,

A little girl who belonged to somebody else,
A face thin and haunted appeared
Over my left shoulder, and whispered, Take care now, *(???)*
Be patient, and live.

JAMES WRIGHT

I have loved you all this time,
And didn't even know
I am alive.

A BLESSING

Just off the highway to Rochester, Minnesota,
Twilight bounds softly forth on the grass.
And the eyes of those two Indian ponies
Darken with kindness.
They have come gladly out of the willows
To welcome my friend and me.
We step over the barbed wire into the pasture
Where they have been grazing all day, alone.
They ripple tensely, they can hardly contain their happiness
That we have come.
They bow shyly as wet swans. They love each other.
There is no loneliness like theirs.
At home once more,
They begin munching the young tufts of spring in the darkness.
I would like to hold the slenderer one in my arms,
For she has walked over to me
And nuzzled my left hand.
She is black and white,
Her mane falls wild on her forehead,
And the light breeze moves me to caress her long ear
That is delicate as the skin over a girl's wrist.
Suddenly I realize
That if I stepped out of my body I would break
Into blossom.

THE JOURNEY

Anghiari is medieval, a sleeve sloping down
A steep hill, suddenly sweeping out
To the edge of a cliff, and dwindling.
But far up the mountain, behind the town,
We too were swept out, out by the wind,
Alone with the Tuscan grass.

JAMES WRIGHT

Wind had been blowing across the hills
For days, and everything now was graying gold
With dust, everything we saw, even
Some small children scampering along a road,
Twittering Italian to a small caged bird.
We sat beside them to rest in some brushwood,
And I leaned down to rinse the dust from my face.

I found the spider web there, whose hinges
Reeled heavily and crazily with the dust,
Whole mounds and cemeteries of it, sagging
And scattering shadows among shells and wings.
And then she stepped into the center of air
Slender and fastidious, the golden hair
Of daylight along her shoulders, she poised there,
While ruins crumbled on every side of her.
Free of the dust, as though a moment before
She had stepped inside the earth, to bathe herself.

I gazed, close to her, till at last she stepped
Away in her own good time.

Many men
Have searched all over Tuscany and never found
What I found there, the heart of the light
Itself shelled and leaved, balancing
On filaments themselves falling. The secret
Of this journey is to let the wind
Blow its dust all over your body,
To let it go on blowing, to step lightly, lightly
All the way through your ruins, and not to lose
Any sleep over the dead, who surely
Will bury their own, don't worry.

[handwritten annotations:]

?

don't worry about what came before

"Theory and Play of the Duende" — garcía Lorca
spirit of death which hovers over the artist ⇒ creates deep feeling — gives life to work.

Notes on the Poets

This section offers information on the life and work of the poets in *Contemporary American Poetry*. Each note includes a selected bibliography.

AI (1947)

Born Florence Anthony in Albany, Texas, Ai attended the University of Arizona and the University of California at Irvine. "One-half Japanese, one-eighth Choctaw, one-fourth Black, and one-sixteenth Irish," she has said that "the history of my family is itself a history of America." Her chosen name, Ai, means "love" in Japanese. The recipient of Guggenheim and Radcliffe Fellowships, she received the Lamont Poetry Award from the Academy of American Poets for *Killing Floor* (1978), the American Book Award for *Sin* (1987), and the National Book Award for *Vice: New and Selected Poems* (1999). She teaches at Oklahoma State University in Stillwater.

Ai's early, compressed dramatic monologues give voice to characters whose lives have been stripped to their bare essentials: hunger, sex, and survival. Murderers, wife-beaters, prostitutes, and molesters of the dead and the living inhabit these poems, enacting principles of social Darwinism against barren desert landscapes. Like Stephen Crane's *Maggie*, Ai's poems attempt "to show that environment is a tremendous thing in this world, and often shapes lives regardless." In graphic, unadorned language, her narrators relate their stories matter-of-factly, their struggle for existence characterized by its fundamental condition: violence. The titles of her books emphasize the oppressive nature of the fallen state: *Cruelty*, *Sin*, *Fate*, *Greed*, *Vice*, *Dread*. Though her poems refuse consolation, their confrontational stance suggests an attempt at exorcism.

Her recent work implies the inexorable movement of violence from private lives to the public realm. Monologues by cultural icons such as Marilyn Monroe and James Dean and by political figures such as John Kennedy and J. Edgar Hoover, as well as by anonymous journalists and paparazzi, extend the range of her concerns by demonstrating again and again how personal tragedy can transform itself into national, even global, malaise. No one escapes complicity, and the violence of our age, witnessed not only in the Los Angeles riots of 1992 but also in Vietnam and Rwanda, begins its blossoming in the hardscrabble lives of individuals eking out their existence on the ragged edges of any republic.

Poetry: *Cruelty* (1973). *Killing Floor* (1979). *Sin* (1986). *Fate* (1991). *Greed* (1993). *Vice: New and Selected Poems* (1999). *Dread* (2003).

JOHN ASHBERY (1927)

John Ashbery was born in Rochester, New York. A graduate of Harvard and Columbia, he lived in France for many years, and he was editor of *Art News*. He currently teaches at Bard College. The recipient of MacArthur and Fulbright Fellowships (among many other honors), Ashbery was awarded the Pulitzer Prize, the National Book Award, and the National Book Critics Circle Award in 1975 for *Self-Portrait in a Convex Mirror*. In 2001, he received the Wallace Stevens Award from the Academy of American Poets, and in 2002, he was awarded the French Legion of Honor.

With the publication of *The Tennis Court Oath*, Ashbery was recognized as one of the most experimental and, at times, one of the most exasperating poets of his generation: his montages of words and unrelated, juxtaposed images threatened the reader to attention, but then these fragments slipped away like verbal hallucinations, leaving the atmosphere charged with an emotional haze. Critics recognized the possible influences of Wallace Stevens, the French symbolists, and New York action painters; however, even the most unorthodox tools of criticism were blunted by this enigmatic poetry whose syntax refused to yield a recognizable sense of development or sustained meaning. While Ashbery's recent poems have become ostensibly more accessible and translucent, most critics continue to be baffled and to venture complex interpretations that, by comparison, make Ashbery's poems sound utterly transparent.

One critic has observed that Ashbery's largest aesthetic principle is the discovery that the world consents, every day, to being shaped into a poem. Ashbery himself has modified this view by asserting that there are no traditional subjects or themes in his poetry: "Most of my poems," he has said in an interview, "are about the experience of experience . . . and the particular experience is of lesser interest to me than the way it filters through to me. I believe this is the way in which it happens with most people, and I'm trying to record a kind of generalized transcript of what's really going on in our minds all day long."

Before the publication of *Three Poems* — long prose poems that may be viewed, at least in part, as an extended statement of poetics — Ashbery offered a somewhat minimal key to his enigmatic poetics when he wrote, "the carnivorous / Way of these lines is to devour their own nature, leaving / Nothing but a bitter impression of absence, which as we know involves presence, but still, / Nevertheless these are fundamental absences, struggling to get up and be off themselves." And the more one reads Ashbery's work, the more it is clear that these "absences" in his poetry — as in the work of Rilke — are the consequences of the innocent eye confronting experience: the lingering pain of loss.

Poetry: *Turandot and Other Poems* (1953). *Some Trees* (1956). *The Tennis Court Oath* (1962). *Rivers and Mountains* (1966). *The Double Dream of Spring* (1970).

Three Poems (1972). *The Vermont Notebook* (1975). *Self-Portrait in a Convex Mirror* (1975). *Houseboat Days* (1977). *As We Know* (1979). *Shadow Train* (1981). *A Wave* (1984). *Selected Poems* (1985). *April Galleons* (1987). *Flow Chart* (1991). *Three Books: Houseboat Days, Shadow Train, A Wave* (1993). *Hotel Lautramont* (1994). *And the Stars Were Shining* (1994). *Can You Hear, Bird* (1995). *The Mooring of Starting Out* (1998). *Wakefulness* (1998). *Girls on the Run* (1999). *Your Name Here* (2000). *As Umbrellas Follow Rain* (2001). *Chinese Whispers* (2002). *Where Shall I Wander* (2005).

Prose: *A Nest of Ninnies*, a novel, with James Schuyler (1969). *Three Plays* (1978). *Reported Sightings: Art Chronicles 1957–1987*, edited by D. Bergman (1989). *Other Traditions* (2000). *Selected Prose* (2004).

MARVIN BELL (1937)

Born in New York City, Marvin Bell attended Alfred University, Syracuse University, the University of Chicago, and the University of Iowa, where he taught for many years in the Writers' Workshop. His book *A Probable Volume of Dreams* was the 1969 Lamont Poetry Selection of the Academy of American Poets, and he has been awarded fellowships by the National Endowment for the Arts and the Guggenheim Foundation.

Because Bell is committed to enlarging the experiment of American free verse, the surface quality of his poems can be deceptively laconic. But they amply demonstrate the fact that the "freer" poetry seems to be, the more carefully crafted it is. (Of course, the obverse is equally true: the more carefully crafted a poem is, the freer it seems.) The effectiveness of his seemingly straightforward but somewhat strange love poem "To Dorothy," for example, is highly controlled by Bell's drawing on the centuries-old tradition of love lyrics using gardens and flowers as metaphors for the loved one. The power of "To an Adolescent Weeping Willow," on the other hand, depends in part on a careful blending of concentric and intraconnecting images, rhythms, and syntactical repetitions.

On a philosophical level, Bell's subjects include love; desire; the nature of reality, knowledge, and belief; the existential nature of truth and of the human condition; courage; and a pursuit of truths behind appearances that is peculiarly American. Those philosophical subjects, however, are rooted in the day-to-day human experiences of a father and lover, remembering World War II or clover in moonlight, discovering a potter's sponge in a foreign country, and especially, trying to understand the inner nature of his vocation and his craft and to capture the ecstasy at the heart of metaphor — or the metaphor at the heart of ecstasy.

What is also remarkable about much of Bell's work is that, by fully *doing* what it *says*, a poem is not only "about" the immediate subject at hand but also is its own statement of poetics — just as Robert Frost's "Birches" is as much a poem about the nature of poetic craft as it is a poem about trees.

A few other poets of this generation have written poems that are their own statement of poetics: Heyen's "The Return," Creeley's "The Language," and Kunitz's "The Layers" come to mind. However, perhaps no poet has pursued the philosophical and ecstatic dimensions of aesthetics in so many individual poems as rigorously as Bell has. The rewards of that quest have been abundant and rich, as much for his readers as for Bell.

Although it isn't possible to devise a full-fledged system of aesthetics from Bell's poetry (that isn't what poetry does), it is possible to suggest a few of the touchstones that inform Marvin Bell's vibrant vision: a vigorous life of the imagination leads to much the same depth of knowledge as that offered by the pursuit of history, mathematics, and physics and the exploration of unknown frontiers ("Sevens (Version 3): In the Closed Iris of Creation"); commitment to one's art demands the same painful, self-effacing mortification and loneliness as any other quest for genuine excellence ("The Self and the Mulberry"); and human beings, born to be makers and lovers, realize that the ultimate source of meaningful loving and making is that ever-endless chain of honorable human labor — "because men and women had sown green grass, / and flowered to my eye in man-made light, / and to some would be as fire in the body / and to others a light in the mind. . . ."

Poetry: *Things We Dreamt We Died For* (1966). *A Probable Volume of Dreams* (1969). *The Escape into You: A Sequence* (1971). *Residue of Song* (1974). *Stars Which See, Stars Which Do Not See* (1977). *These Green-Going-to-Yellow* (1981). *Segues: A Correspondence in Poetry,* with William Stafford (1983). *Drawn by Stones, by Earth, by Things That Have Been in the Fire* (1984). *New and Selected Poems* (1987). *Iris of Creation* (1990). *The Book of the Dead Man* (1994). *Ardor: The Book of the Dead Man, Vol. II* (1997). *Wednesday: Selected Poems* (1998). *Nightworks, Poems 1962–2000* (2000). *Rampant* (2004).

Prose and Poetry: *Old Snow Just Melting: Essays and Interviews* (1983). *A Marvin Bell Reader: Selected Poetry and Prose* (1994).

JOHN BERRYMAN (1914–1972)

John Berryman graduated from Columbia and Clare College (Cambridge). He taught at Brown, Harvard, Princeton, and the University of Minnesota. A recipient of Rockefeller and Guggenheim Fellowships and of a special grant from the National Arts Council, he also won the Pulitzer Prize and the National Book Award. On January 7, 1972, John Berryman committed suicide.

In the course of his career, Berryman wrote not only a distinguished long poem in homage to Anne Bradstreet but also an equally notable sonnet sequence. However, his major work is his sequence of 385 *Dream Songs,* for which he may well be recognized as one of the truly great poets of the century. The scope, depth, daring, and craftsmanship of these poems have caused critics to compare Berryman with Homer, Dante, and Whitman.

The Dream Songs constitutes a loose narrative about a multidimensional figure most often called Henry Pussycat. Berryman wrote that Henry is "an imaginary character (not the poet . . .), a white American in early middle age, sometimes in blackface, who has suffered an irreversible loss and talks to himself sometimes in the first person, sometimes in the third, sometimes even in the second; he has a friend, never named, who addresses him as Mr Bones and variants thereof." There are moments in *The Dream Songs* when Henry, Mr Bones, and the poet are barely distinguishable from one another — and are not meant to be distinguishable. Thus, Berryman attempts and achieves a linear- multidimensional vision — maneuvered by a dazzling shift of pronouns — which is a verbal equivalent to what Picasso achieved in his Cubist period.

Like Odysseus, Henry Pussycat undergoes a fantastic range of experience. He even dies and comes back to life. His emotions shift from incredible panic, horror, and self-pity to sheer joy and self-deprecating slapstick. If Henry gets out of hand, his friend and conscience, his sidekick and minstrel chorus are always there either to cut him down to size or to support him through despair. At the end of his journey, which takes him across spiritual as well as spatial and historical boundaries, Henry, the schizophrenic Odysseus of the atomic age, returns to his wife and child, scarred but bearing that most ancient and essential knowledge: to be human is to suffer.

Poetry: *Poems* (1942). *The Dispossessed* (1948). *Homage to Mistress Bradstreet* (1956). *Short Poems* (1964). *77 Dream Songs* (1967). *His Toy, His Dream, His Rest* (1968). *The Dream Songs* (1969). *Love & Fame* (1970, revised 1972). *Delusions, Etc.* (1972). *Henry's Fate & Other Poems, 1967–1972* (1977). *Collected Poems 1937–1971*, edited by C. Thornbury (1989).

Prose: *Stephen Crane*, a biography (1950). *Recovery*, a novel (1973). *The Freedom of the Poet*, essays and stories (1976). *We Dream of Honour: John Berryman's Letters to His Mother* (1987).

ELIZABETH BISHOP (1911–1979)

A native of Worcester, Massachusetts, Elizabeth Bishop received her formal education at Vassar. She lived in Brazil for many years but also taught in the United States at Harvard and elsewhere and was Consultant in Poetry at the Library of Congress. Her many awards included the Pulitzer Prize, the National Book Award, and the Order of Rio Branco (Brazil).

Although Bishop was far less prolific than most poets of her generation, she was one of the few poets about whom it could be said that each new book — indeed each new poem — was an "event." One reason may be that she was far less predictable than many of her contemporaries; that is, readers of poetry did not come to expect a particular kind of poem from Bishop the way that they had come to expect a certain kind of poem from Anne Sexton or Robert Lowell.

Another reason why Bishop's poems are rare moments of delight and epiphany stems from her stunning perceptions and reconstruction of the details of physical reality. As Randall Jarrell says in *Poetry and the Age,* "all her poems have written underneath, *I have seen it.*" Whether the matter at hand is the exotic rainbow glow of a tremendous fish or the common-place sheen of oil in a dingy filling station, Bishop knows that poetry and vision are rooted, first of all, in what Archibald MacLeish has called "the shine of the world." In her better poems, Bishop amply demonstrates that the perception of sensible objects and moral vision, for the poet, may be one and the same experience.

Ralph J. Mills, Jr., has rightfully noted another, more ambitious dimension of Bishop's achievement. In addition to her graceful use of fairly strict forms — and the unmistakable presence of a formalist approach even in the freer verse — Bishop's poems are distinguished by what Mills calls a "total accomplishment of language, technique, music, and imagery working simultaneously, or (in T. S. Eliot's phrase) 'the complete consort dancing together.'"

Poetry: *North and South* (1946). *Poems: North and South — A Cold Spring* (1955). *Questions of Travel* (1965). *Selected Poems* (1967). *The Ballad of the Burglar of Babylon* (1968). *The Complete Poems* (1969/1979). *Geography III* (1976). *The Complete Poems 1927–1979* (1983). *Collected Poems,* edited by F. Bidart and D. Gewanter (2003).

Prose: *Brazil* (1962). *The Collected Prose,* edited by R. Giroux (1984). *One Art: Letters,* edited by R. Giroux (1994).

Translations: *The Diary of Helena Morley* (1957). *Anthology of Contemporary Brazilian Poetry,* editor and translator, with others (1972).

ROBERT BLY (1926)

For the 1975 edition of *Contemporary Poets,* Robert Bly wrote, "I earn my living giving readings at American colleges and universities, and by translating." More than thirty years later, to a large extent, he still does, with the hiatus of the phenomenal success of his book for and about the men's movement, *Iron John.* Bly graduated from Harvard and — though he hates to admit it — the University of Iowa Writers' Workshop. The founder of the influential journal and small press called *The Fifties, The Sixties* . . . to *The Thousands,* Bly has received fellowships from several foundations and won the National Book Award.

Influenced by the thought of the seventeenth-century German theosophist Jacob Boehme, and the techniques of such twentieth-century Spanish surrealists as Lorca and Neruda, Bly's poems tend to be almost purely phenomenological. Revolting against the rationalism and empiricism of his century, Boehme emphasized an intuitive perception of the outer tangible world of humans and things as a symbol of the corresponding and truer inner spiritual world. The outward man is asleep, Boehme wrote; he is only the husk of the real inner man. Like the American Romantic Transcendentalist Emerson, Boehme insisted that men neither see nor respond to that inner spiritual world: "The wise of this world . . . have shut and locked us up in their art and rationality, so that we have had to see with their eyes."

Bly himself has written that American poetry took a wrong turn, moving in "a destructive motion outward" rather than a "plunge inward, trying for a great (spiritual and imaginative) intensity." In his revolt against Eliot's theory of the "objective correlative" and against Pound's practice in the *Cantos* of "eating up more and more of the outer world, with less and less life at the center," Bly has fashioned his poems after the work of Rilke, Trakl, and twentieth-century Spanish surrealists. In them, he seems to have found a poetics that corresponds to Boehme's mysticism, enabling him to plunge beneath the phenomenology of surfaces and find images and words to suggest the inner reality and spiritual intensity of experience. Moreover, many of Bly's poems continue to be implicit reaffirmations of a statement that appeared on the flyleaf of *The Lion's Tail and Eyes* in which he suggests that his poems come from "the part of the personality which is nourished by notice of things that are growing" and simultaneously that they "resist the Puritan insistence on being busy, the need to think of everything in terms of work."

Poetry: *The Lion's Tail and Eyes: Poems Written Out of Laziness and Silence,* with James Wright and William Duffy (1962). *Silence in the Snowy Fields* (1962). *The Light Around the Body* (1967). *The Morning Glory* (1969; expanded edition, 1975). *The Teeth Mother Naked at Last* (1970). *Jumping Out of Bed* (1973; revised and expanded edition, 1988). *Sleepers Joining Hands* (1973). *Point Reyes Poems* (1974/1989). *Old Man Rubbing His Eyes* (1975). *This Body Is Made of Camphor and Gopherwood* (1977). *This Tree Will Be Here for a Thousand Years* (1979). *The Man in the Black Coat Turns* (1981). *Loving a Woman in Two Worlds* (1985). *Selected Poems* (1986). *Angels of Pompeii* (1991). *What Have I Ever Lost by Dying* (1992). *Meditations on the Insatiable Soul* (1994). *Morning Poems* (1997). *Eating the Honey of Words: New and Selected Poems* (1999). *The Night Abraham Called to the Stars* (2001). *The Insanity of Empire: A Book of Poems Against the Iraq War* (2004).

Prose: *Leaping Poetry: An Idea with Poems and Translations* (1975). *Talking All Morning: Collected Interviews and Conversations* (1979). *The Eight Stages of Translation* (1983). *A Little Book on the Human Shadow,* edited by W. Booth (1988). *American Poetry: Wildness and Domesticity,* critical essays (1990). *Remembering James Wright* (1991). *Iron John* (1992). *The Sibling Society* (1996). *The Maiden King,* with M. Woodman (1999).

Translations and Versions: POETRY: *Twenty Poems of Georg Trakl*, with J. Wright (1961). *Twenty Poems of César Vallejo*, with J. Knoepfle and J. Wright (1962). *Juan Ramon Jiménez: Forty Poems* (1967). *Late Arrival on Earth: Selected Poems of Gunnar Ekelöf*, with C. Paulston (1967). *Pablo Neruda: Twenty Poems*, with J. Wright (1967). *Tomas Tranströmer: Twenty Poems* (1970). *Neruda and Vallejo: Selected Poems*, with J. Knoepfle and J. Wright (1971). *Night Visions*, poems by Tomas Tranströmer (1971). *Bashó* (1972). *Lorca and Jiménez: Selected Poems* (1973). *Blase de Otero and Miguel Hernandez: Selected Poems* (1974). *Friends, You Drank Some Darkness: Three Swedish Poets: Martinson, Ekelöf and Tranströmer* (1976). *The Kabir Book: 44 of the Ecstatic Poems of Kabir* (1977). *Vicente Alexandre: Twenty Poems*, with L. Hyde (1977). *Rolf Jacobsen: Twenty Poems* (1977). *Rainer Maria Rilke: The Voices* (1977). *I Never Wanted Fame: Ten Poems and Proverbs*, by Antonio Machado (1979). *Mirabai: Six Versions* (1980). *Rumi: Night and Sleep*, with C. Barks (1980). *Canciones*, by Antonio Machado (1980). *Truth Barriers: Poems by Tomas Tranströmer* (1980). *Selected Poems of Rainer Maria Rilke* (1981). *When Grapes Turn to Wine: Versions of Rumi* (1983). *Time Alone: Selected Poems of Antonio Machado* (1983). *Twenty Poems of Olav Hauge* (1987). *Ten Poems of Francis Ponge Translated by Robert Bly and Ten Poems of Robert Bly Inspired by Francis Ponge* (1990). *The Roads Have Come to an End Now: Selected and Last Poems*, by Rolf Jacobsen, with R. Greenwald and R. Hedin (2000). *The Half-Finished Heaven: The Best Poems of Tomas Tranströmer* (2001). *Ecstatic Poems*, by Kabir (2004). *The Winged Energy of Delight: Selected Translations* (2004).

GWENDOLYN BROOKS (1917–2000)

A graduate of Wilson Junior College in Chicago, Gwendolyn Brooks began her professional career in 1941 with Inez Boulton's poetry workshop at the South Side Community Art Center in Chicago. She was awarded two Guggenheim Fellowships, a grant from the National Institute of Arts and Letters, and the Pulitzer Prize for her second book of poems, *Annie Allen*. In 1969, Brooks was named Poet Laureate of the State of Illinois, an honor formerly held by Carl Sandburg. More recent honors include the National Book Foundation's medal for Distinguished Contribution to American Letters (1994).

Brooks's poems are often marked by direct and bold social observation and by language that precedes — indeed foreshadows — much of the poetry written by younger African-American poets today. Her African-American hero's assertion "I helped to save them . . . / Even if I had to kick their law into their teeth in order to do that for them" might well have been written in the 1960s or 1990s rather than in the 1940s. In those poems addressed specifically to the horror of the African-American experience in America, she is also capable of a range of emotions: brutal anger, wry satire, and visionary serenity.

Informed by the spectrum of the African-American experience and by emotional objectivity, some of her poems are also marked by the simplicity, quiet, and gentility of a private sensibility. Yet in a poem like "the mother," she also demonstrates the kind of fierce emotion that other women poets like Anne Sexton and Adrienne Rich have displayed in more consciously personal or political poems. Gentle or fierce, personal or social, her poems consistently affirm the common denominator of human experience in poetry and in the human community.

Poetry: *A Street in Bronzeville* (1945). *Annie Allen* (1949). *Bronzeville Boys and Girls* (1956). *Selected Poems* (1963). *In the Time of Detachment, in the Time of Cold* (1965). *In the Mecca: Poems* (1968). *Riot* (1969). *The Wall* (nd). *Family Pictures* (1970). *Aloneness* (1971). *Beckonings* (1975). *To Disembark* (1981). *The Near-Johannesburg Boy and Other Poems* (1986). *Blacks* [collected poems] (1987). *Gottschalk and the Grande Tarantelle* (1988). *Children Coming Home* (1991).

Prose: *Maud Martha*, a novel (1953). *Report from Part One: An Autobiography* (1972). *The World of Gwendolyn Brooks* (1972). *Primer for Blacks* (1980).

OLGA BROUMAS (1949)

Born in Syros, Greece, Olga Broumas published her first book there in 1967. That same year she came to the United States to study architecture and dance at the University of Pennsylvania, then creative writing at the University of Oregon. Her first book in English, *Beginning with O* (1977), received the Yale Younger Poets Award. A licensed bodywork therapist, she has received fellowships from the Guggenheim Foundation and the National Endowment for the Arts, and the Witter Bynner Award of the American Academy and Institute of Arts and Letters. She has taught at Boston University and is currently Poet-in-Residence at Brandeis University.

The sensuous lyrics of Olga Broumas have their source in the Sapphic tradition of her native country, and her poems celebrate lust while exploring the politics of desire. Her subject is the body in its various configurations — omphalos, sanctuary, and muse — and her conflation of flesh and landscape, their common salts, gives an ecstatic, feminist slant to "the eyes of fire, the nostrils of air, the mouth of water, the beard of earth" drawn by William Blake. Broumas populates her land- and seascapes with goddesses ancient — perhaps ancestral — and contemporary; they bathe in the visionary light of her gaze.

Unabashedly explicit, Broumas's poems reenact versions of mythology and fable to extend (and return) their provenance to the communal body: "We came together / like months / in a lunar year, measured in nights, dividing / perfectly into female phases. Like women anywhere / living in groups we had synchronous menses. And had / no need of a wound, a puncture, to seal our bond." Broumas's fascination with linguistic roots, her compulsive tracings of words to their Greek and Latin sources, reaffirms the classical role of the poet for our time. She renders her alphabet in the service of praise.

Poetry: *Beginning with O* (1977). *Soie Sauvage* (1979). *Pastoral Jazz* (1983). *Perpetua* (1989). *The Choir* (1989–1991). *Rave: Poems 1975–1999* (1999).

Collaborations: *Black Holes, Black Stockings,* with Jane Miller (1985). *Sappho's Gymnasium,* with T Begley (1994). *Ithaca: Little Summer in Winter,* with T Begley (1996).

Translations: *What I Love: Poems,* by Odysseas Elytis (1986). *The Little Mariner,* by Odysseas Elytis (1988). *Open Papers,* by Odysseas Elytis, trans. with T Begley (1995). *Eros, Eros, Eros: Selected & Last Poems,* by Odysseas Elytis (1998).

LUCILLE CLIFTON (1936)

Lucille Clifton was born in Depew, New York, and educated at the State University of New York at Fredonia. Currently teaching at St. Mary's College in Maryland, she has also held distinguished posts at a number of other colleges and universities. Clifton's awards and distinctions as a poet, fiction writer, and screenplay writer include creative writing fellowships from the National Endowment for the Arts, an Emmy, and two nominations for the Pulitzer Prize for poetry, and the National Book Award for *Blessing the Boats: New and Selected Poems 1988–2000.*

Clifton's entire comment on her work in the third edition of *Contemporary Poets* (1980) consists of one brief sentence: "I am a Black woman poet, and I sound like one." And yet, after reading even a short selection of her poems, we quickly realize that Clifton's description of herself does not explain why she is one of the most unique voices of her generation. Of course, like numerous other women writers, she explores the dimensions of her sexual identity and her role as daughter, as mother, as lover, as woman; like many other African-American poets (men and women), she too addresses herself to the quality of the African-American experience in America, just as she too makes full use of the African-American idiom. But no other poet of her generation (regardless of gender or race) *sounds* quite like Clifton. Why that is, however, is rather difficult to identify in the standard language of literary criticism.

Clifton's subjects and themes run the gamut of human experience. She laments the loss of an aborted child, and she celebrates her own mature body and sexuality with wonderful verve. She admonishes children to "come home from the movies" and face the responsibilities of everyday life, but she also recalls the pain and terror of her own growth into adult responsibility. She engages in social criticism and in criticism of individual human beings, but she also affirms "the bond of live things everywhere." She feels religious doubts, but she is nonetheless a profoundly religious spirit whose sensibility encompasses both the Judeo-Christian tradition and a primal sense of spiritualism and magic. Despite the high seriousness of many of her poems, she also obviously revels in a vibrant sense of humor that she directs not only at others but also at herself and her craft. She can poke gentle fun at herself because "she is a poet / she don't have no sense," but after the joy and celebration, after the anguish and despair, after the doubt and struggle to believe, she also can assert, "I am left with plain hands and / nothing to give you but poems."

One of the striking characteristics of Clifton's poems is their distilled brevity. Like Emily Dickinson, Clifton rarely offers any but the most essential elaborations on experience. However, for a clue to the sound of Clifton's poems, we have to turn elsewhere: African-American spirituals and secular folksongs; the rich history of rhythm and blues; the rhythms and sounds of an African-American fundamentalist revival meeting and of magical incantations; the phrasing and timing of classic African-American humorists; an utterly physical sense of language (somehow we can *see* how these poems incorporate a range of bodily movements); a belief in the power of idiom to give voice to the human heart as much by transcending individual race and culture as by affirming it; a belief in the language of poetry, not as a threat of further social and human alienation but as a bridge of reconciliation; a belief in the power of song and in the impotency of slogans; a belief in tongues.

Poetry: *Good Times* (1969). *Good News About the Earth* (1972). *An Ordinary Woman* (1974). *Two-Headed Woman* (1980). *Good Woman: Poems and a Memoir 1969–1980* (1987). *Next: New Poems* (1987). *Quilting: Poems 1987–1990* (1991). *The Book of Light* (1993). *The Terrible Stories* (1996). *Blessing the Boats: New and Selected Poems 1988–2000* (2000). *Mercy* (2004).

Prose: *Generations: A Memoir* (1976).

BILLY COLLINS (1941)

Born in New York, Billy Collins attended Holy Cross College and the University of California at Riverside. The recipient of fellowships from the New York Foundation for the Arts, the National Endowment for the Arts, and the Guggenheim Foundation, as well numerous prizes from *Poetry* magazine, Collins served as Poet Laureate of the United States during 2001–2003. He teaches at Lehman College of the City University of New York.

Superbly self-conscious, Billy Collins often writes from the point of view of a poet living in suburbia, "a creature with a full stomach — / something you don't hear much about in poetry, / that sanctuary of hunger and deprivation," and his poems at times resemble nineteenth-century French *plein air* paintings in which, for verisimilitude's sake, the artist paints himself at his easel in the lower right-hand corner, then reproduces yet another version of his painting and himself on that miniature easel, and so on until the image dissolves. Collins's poems seem effortless — their simple diction and breezy exhalations balancing them on that edge of dissolution— yet his craft lies in making poetry less an argument with oneself than a whimsical inventory "of the plentiful imagery of the world" through which he might more fully know himself. "I think my work has to do with a sense that we are

attempting, all the time, to create a logical, rational path through the day,"
Collins told the *New York Times* in 1999. "To the left and right there are
an amazing set of distractions that we usually can't afford to follow. But
the poet is willing to stop anywhere. . . . And it's that willingness to slow
down and examine the mysterious bits of fluff in our lives that is the
poet's interest."

A master of tone, Collins discards the poet's usual tools — those literary
devices that often announce *a poem* — to allow his work its accessibility and
humor, and to tweak, at times, the literary pretensions of poetasters while
muting the more serious concerns underpinning his lines: the struggle to
love in a time of spiritual ennui, the failure of language to provide consolation, and the inability to progress beyond "the hoop of myself" to a place
"where longing and heartache will find an end." Collins's purpose, then,
is to discover life's "secret marrow," and he insists that it may be found in
poetry: "I listen to myself saying it."

Poetry: *Pokerface* (1977). *Video Poems* (1980). *The Apple That Astonished Paris*
(1988). *Questions About Angels* (1991). *The Art of Drowning* (1995). *Picnic, Lighting* (1998). *Sailing Alone Around the Room: New and Selected Poems* (2001).
Nine Horses (2002).

ROBERT CREELEY (1926–2005)

A New Englander by birth and sensibility, Robert Creeley was born in
Arlington, Massachusetts, and was educated at Harvard, Black Mountain
College, and the University of New Mexico. He has traveled widely and
has taught at the University of New Mexico, at Black Mountain College
where he also edited the influential journal *Black Mountain Review*, and
at the State University of New York at Buffalo. He won the Bolligen Prize
in 1999, a Before Columbus Lifetime Achievement Award in 2000, and a
Lannan Lifetime Achievement Award in 2001.

Generally associated with the "Projectivists" and poets of the Black
Mountain School, Creeley nevertheless is a Puritan at heart — Emily
Dickinson's cool, hip, one-eyed, and unvirginal nephew. Like all good
Puritans, Creeley is "hung up": "I think I grow tensions / like flowers . . ."
("The Flower"). Pain is central to his work — a sharp, stinging pain evoked
in such images as "Each wound is perfect, / encloses itself in a tiny / imperceptible blossom, / making pain." In other poems, such as "Something," a
Puritan sensibility surfaces more explicitly, as it does in the very structure
and substance of collections such as *A Day Book* and *Hello* — sustained
attempts at recording and discovering the "meaning" of diurnal events, an
implicit quest for signs of salvation, especially love. "I love you. / Do you
love me. / What to say / when you see me" ("A Form of Women") might
be a summary of one of Creeley's central concerns.

No critical essay or explanatory statement reveals Creeley's poetics as precisely as his own poems, especially "The Language," in which he states simply, "Locate *I* . . ." The position of the *I* — as locus, as viewer, and as speaker — largely determines the form and the direction of the poem. The position of words on the page results from the location of this I, who, by arranging the poem as it is, speaks not only in grammatical units but also in linear units. In other words, Creeley's poems evolve on both a sequential grammatical level and on a cumulative linear level, with each individual line reaffirming or modifying the sense of the sentence and of the poem. And such contrapuntal tension in the very structure of Creeley's poems — perhaps more than the sparse, occasionally hesistant language — reflects the contemporary struggle with those forces that would make us all inarticulate.

Poetry: *Le Fou* (1952). *The Kind of Act of* (1953). *The Immoral Proposition* (1953). *All That Is Lovely in Men* (1955). A *Form of Women* (1959). *For Love: Poems 1950–1960* (1962). *Words* (1967). *The Charm: Early and Uncollected Poems* (1967/1969). *Pieces* (1968). *A Day Book* (1972). *Presences,* with Marisol (1976). *Selected Poems* (1976). *Hello: A Journal* (1978). *Later* (1979). *The Collected Poems of Robert Creeley 1945–1975* (1983). *Mirrors* (1983). *Memory Gardens* (1986). *Windows* (1990). *Selected Poems* (1991). *Echoes* (1994). *So There: Poems 1976–83* (1998). *Day Book of a Virtual Poet* (1998). *Life & Death* (1998). *Just in Time: Poems 1984–1994* (2001). *If I Were Writing This* (2003).

Prose: ESSAYS AND CRITICISM: A *Quick Graph: Collected Notes and Essays* (1970). *Contexts of Poetry: Interviews 1961–1971,* edited by D. M. Allen (1973). *Was That a Real Poem & Other Essays,* edited by D. M. Allen (1979). *Charles Olson & Robert Creeley: The Complete Correspondence,* edited by G. F. Butterick (1983). *Collected Essays* (1989). *Autobiography* (1990). *Tales Out of School: Selected Interviews* (1994). FICTION: *The Island* (1963). *The Gold Diggers and Other Stories* (1965). *Mabel: A Story* (1976). *The Collected Prose of Robert Creeley* (1984).

JAMES DICKEY (1923–1997)

James Dickey received his bachelor's and master's degrees from Vanderbilt University. He was a night fighter pilot during both World War II and the Korean War; as a civilian, he worked as an advertising executive; and he taught at a variety of universities, including the University of South Carolina. In 1966, Dickey received the National Book Award for poetry and was appointed Consultant in Poetry at the Library of Congress.

One of the less ostensibly "academic" poets of his generation, Dickey, in poems that are often disarmingly frank in subject matter and in "moral tone," has refused to assume those moral postures often expected of today's poets: during Vietnam, he did not write antiwar poetry but rather, as in "The Firebombing," he confronted his own understanding of and sympathy with the pilot whose mission was to drop napalm on enemy villages without the luxury of questioning the morality of such an act. In several other poems, he has explored varieties of sexual experiences, including implicit and explicit sexual encounters between humans and animals, as in "The Sheep Child."

Dickey's poems are marked by an exuberant language and by a primal energy, passion, and ritual. Probing the elemental, his poems often trace a human's mythic subconscious and paradoxical evolution to a primitive level where humans and animals become companions and mates in the same irrational but holy species. Moreover, at the heart of Dickey's vision, poetry is the tongue articulating the consciousness of all creation on this planet, from the mute stone up the earthly chain of being to humankind. And in this way, his poems often recall Whitman's poetry and vision.

Simultaneously, many of Dickey's poems are also marked by a Southern Puritanism similar to that found in the work of William Faulkner and Flannery O'Connor. His characters are grotesque — physically and spiritually wounded. They are violent creatures; their brutal sexuality is immersed in pain and death. And they move about in a world churning with violence and profound evil that is as much inherent in the human condition as it is man-made. Dickey's vision, then, includes the polarities of light and grace, darkness and sin. The total impact of his poems is often the drama of Adam, shimmering with primal light, awakening to guilt, and finding it magical.

Poetry: *Into the Stone and Other Poems*, in *Poets of Today VII* (1960). *Drowning with Others* (1962). *Helmets* (1964). *Buckdancer's Choice* (1965). *Poems 1957–1967* (1967). *The Eye-Beaters, Blood, Victory, Madness, Buckhead and Mercy* (1970). *The Zodiac* (1976). *The Enemy from Eden* (1978). *The Strength of Fields* (1979). *The Early Motion: Drowning with Others and Helmets* (1981). *Falling, May Day Sermon, and Other Poems* (1981). *Puella* (1982). *The Central Motion: Poems 1968–1979* (1983). *The Eagle's Mile* (1990). *The Whole Motion: Collected Poems 1945–1992* (1992). *The Selected Poems*, edited by R. Kirschten (1998). *The James Dickey Reader*, edited by H. Hart (1999).

Prose: ESSAYS, CRITICISM AND LETTERS: *The Suspect in Poetry* (1964). *Babel to Byzantium: Poets & Poetry Now* (1968). *Self-Interviews*, edited by B. and J. Reiss (1970/1984). *Sorties: Journals and New Essays* (1971). *Crux: The Letters of James Dickey*, edited by M. J. Bruccoli and J. S. Baughman (1999). FICTION AND OTHER PROSE: *Deliverance* (1970). *The Poet Turns on Himself* (1982). *Night Hurdling* (1983). *Alnilam* (1988). *To the White Sea* (1994).

STEPHEN DOBYNS (1941)

Born in East Orange, New Jersey, Stephen Dobyns was raised in several states, moving every year or two. He never graduated from high school, but attended Shimer College, Wayne State University, and the University of Iowa. He has taught at several universities and in the MFA Program at Warren Wilson College, and has worked as a reporter for the Detroit *News*. He currently teaches at Sarah Lawrence. Dobyns's first book, *Concurring Beasts* (1972), was the Lamont Poetry Selection of the Academy of American Poets. *Black Dog, Red Dog* (1984) was the winner of the National

Poetry Series competition, and *Cemetery Nights* (1987) was chosen for the Poetry Society of America's Melville Cane Award. The author of twenty novels in addition to his books of poetry, Dobyns has been the recipient of fellowships from the Guggenheim Foundation and the National Endowment for the Arts.

"How hard to love the world; we must love the world," Dobyns has written, and this dichotomy, its terse imperative, informs his work. In muscular lines and insistent rhythms, his narratives function as metaphysical monologues, darkly comic in their bleak and sometimes absurd vision of the human condition. The humorous veneer, however, barely conceals the desperation of his characters. Violence, spiritual destitution, and a contagious impotence — sexual, political, psychological — ravage their suburban landscape. "The speaker in Dobyns's poems," critic Peter Stitt has noted, "is obsessed by the futility of human life, by its meaninglessness; obsessed by our inability to know what is going on, our inability to control it; obsessed by our frail and imperfect bodies, by the certainty that they will die and turn to dust."

Dobyns's consolation is the creative act, any gesture of communication that dispels tension between individuals, that expresses tenderness: "A poem is a window that hangs between two or more human beings who otherwise live in darkened rooms." Underlying his existential fables (his recent books of poems are titled *Common Carnage* and *Pallbearers Envying the One Who Rides*, respectively) is the desire to grasp anything, "fragments of language, / fragments of blue sky," that might kindle compassion.

Poetry: *Concurring Beasts* (1972). *Griffon* (1976). *Heat Death* (1980). *The Balthus Poems* (1982). *Black Dog, Red Dog* (1984). *Cemetery Nights* (1987). *Body Traffic* (1990). *Velocities: New and Selected Poems, 1966–1992* (1994). *Common Carnage* (1996). *Pallbearers Envying the One Who Rides* (1999). *The Porcupine's Kisses* (2002). *Mystery, So Long* (2005).

Prose: ESSAYS: *Best Words, Best Order* (1996). NOVELS: *A Man of Little Evils* (1973). *Saratoga Longshot* (1976). *Saratoga Swimmer* (1981). *Dancer with One Leg* (1983). *Saratoga Headhunter* (1985). *Cold Dog Soup* (1985). *Saratoga Snapper* (1986). *A Boat Off the Coast* (1987). *Two Deaths of Senora Puccini* (1988). *Saratoga Bestiary* (1988). *The House on Alexandrine* (1990). *Saratoga Hexameter* (1990). *After Shocks/Near Escapes* (1991). *Saratoga Haunting* (1993). *The Wrestler's Cruel Study* (1993). *Saratoga Backtalk* (1994). *Saratoga Fleshpot* (1995). *The Church of Dead Girls* (1997). *Saratoga Strongbox* (1998). *Boy in the Water* (1999). SHORT FICTION: *Eating Naked* (2000).

RITA DOVE (1952)

Rita Dove was born in Akron, Ohio. She received a BA from Miami University, studied modern European literature at the University of Tübingen, and received an MFA from the University of Iowa. A professor of English at the University of Virginia, Dove's literary honors include grants and fellowships from the National Endowment for the Arts and the General Electric Foundation. In 1987, she was awarded the Pulitzer Prize for poetry.

Many of Dove's poems are deeply rooted in moments of intimate personal experience: a child marvels at the power of language; an adolescent girl fantasizes the arrival of a dreamed-of lover; a young mother teaches her daughter the truth and mystery of her vagina. And many of her poems — most notably the book-length sequence, *Thomas and Beulah* — find their source in extended family history.

Dove is not a personal-confessional poet. No doubt there is suffering and anguish in her poems, often revealed in haunting images (as in "Crab-Boil," where the crabs suffocating in the pot, "the scratch, / shell on tin, of their distress," underscore the African-American narrator's discomfort on the whites-only beach in Ft. Myers, Florida, in 1962), but there is no sense of personal evil to confess or to exorcise. Rather, Dove is what might be called a "fictive" poet, in whose work autobiography and family history are transformed into a lyrical fiction, into a larger drama in which the reader participates. This communal drama does not borrow from established myth for its resonance; instead, it strives to become archetype, to be its own myth.

Even when she uses traditional myth, Dove seems compelled to retell it from her own perspective — the terrifying rediscovery of the garden of Eden in Mississippi — thereby implicitly reaffirming her assertion that "each god is empty / without us. . . ." But whether focusing on personal experience, family history, or communal archetype, Dove's poems not only erect verbal silos — "the ribs of the modern world" — at the heart of the American myth; they are also carefully structured circles of images, layers of metaphors that re-create an epiphanal moment irrevocably sculpted in words.

Poetry: *Ten Poems* (1977). *The Yellow House on the Corner* (1980). *Museum* (1983). *Thomas and Beulah* (1986). *Grace Notes* (1989). *Selected Poems* (1993). *The Darker Face of the Earth* (verse play) (1994). *Mother Love* (1995). *On the Bus with Rosa Parks* (1999). *American Smooth* (2004).

Prose: *Fifth Sunday*, short stories (1985). *Through the Ivory Gate*, a novel (1992). *The Poet's World* (1995).

STEPHEN DUNN (1939)

Born in New York City, Stephen Dunn attended Hofstra University, the New School, and Syracuse University. The recipient of the 2001 Pulitzer Prize for *Different Hours*, Dunn has also received fellowships from the National Endowment for the Arts and the Guggenheim Foundation, the Levinson Award from *Poetry* magazine, and an Academy Award in Literature from the American Academy of Arts and Letters. Having taught and held residencies at several universities, including Columbia, Princeton, Wichita State, and the University of Michigan, he divides his time between

Frostburg, Maryland, and Pomona, New Jersey, where he is Distinguished Professor of Creative Writing at Richard Stockton College.

"Tainted with charm" and "rotten with virtue," the poetry of Stephen Dunn often charts the course of the erotic life upon its modern map of restraint and domesticity with dialectic compulsion and self-deprecatory humor. "Urge and urge and urge," yawped Whitman, but Dunn, a self-described "urban moralist," responds with modesty and indirection. In a 2000 interview with Philip Dacey, he states: "Poetry is, in large part, manipulation and seduction." Depictions of love, work, and beauty, especially as they charge and transform human relationships, inform his poems, which have progressed from the often image-driven narratives of earlier books to the more expansive and philosophically discursive lyrics of recent volumes. "I love to find strategies for getting away with the abstract," he has stated. "I've been refining how to write the poem of mind. I've tried for a poem of clear surfaces in service . . . of the elusive, the difficult to say."

Although Dunn has suggested that his work might prove "disappointing to those looking for politics," his poems have long centered on the hegemonies of desire, and recent historical exigencies — the fall of the Berlin Wall and of Eastern European communism, the Oklahoma City bombing, the attacks on the World Trade Center — have found their way into work that still managers to hold its "secret," the "you / who were always here," at its core: "Can this still turn out to be a love poem?" In language that "structure[s] meaning," that attempts to give it both "a rhythm and a frame," Dunn creates suspended stairways surrounded by practical houses, "built two-by-four by / two-by-four, slat by slat, without ornament."

Poetry: *Looking for Holes in the Ceiling* (1974). *Full of Lust and Good Usage* (1976). *A Circus of Needs* (1978). *Work and Love* (1981). *Not Dancing* (1984). *Local Time* (1986). *Between Angels* (1989). *Landscape at the End of the Century* (1991). *New & Selected Poems: 1974–1994* (1994). *Loosestrife* (1996). *Different Hours* (2000). *Local Visitations* (2003). *The Insistence of Beauty* (2004).

Prose: *Walking Light: Essays & Memoirs* (1993; expanded edition, 2001). *Riffs & Reciprocities: Prose Pairs* (1998).

LOUISE ERDRICH (1954)

"My father used to give me a nickel for every story I wrote, and my mother wove strips of construction paper together and stapled them into book covers. So at an early age I felt myself to be a published author earning substantial royalties," Louise Erdrich told *Contemporary Authors*. Born in Little Falls, Minnesota, and raised in Wahpeton, North Dakota, by a French Ojibwe mother and a German-American father, both of whom worked at the Bureau of Indian Affairs School, Louise Erdrich is a member of the Turtle Mountain Band of Chippewa. She attended Dartmouth

College and The Johns Hopkins University, working between degrees at a series of low-wage jobs. Known primarily as a fiction writer, Erdrich received the National Book Critics Circle Award, the American Book Award, and the *Los Angeles Times* Award for her first novel, *Love Medicine*, and has been awarded fellowship by the National Endowment for the Arts and the Guggenheim Foundation. She lives in Minneapolis, Minnesota.

Storytelling is crucial to Louise Erdrich's art. "The Ojibwe have been telling stories through and in spite of immense hardship, dispossession, and anguish," she told *The Atlantic Monthly* in 2001. "In fact, Ojibwe narrative has grown rich and subtle on the ironies of conflict. . . . I write in English, and so I suppose I function as an emissary of the between-world, that increasingly common margin where cultures mix and collide." Such tensions between Christian iconographies and Native American mythologies, between Catholic rituals and Ojibwe traditional practices, inform her poems as they draw upon narrative powers to convey fully the frustrations of America's disenfranchised and disinherited. In "Dear John Wayne," Erdrich comments incisively on that actor's Hollywood-cowboy persona and its embodiment of manifest destiny: "his disease was the idea of taking everything." Such knowledge may not help, though, as his voice trails the audience of "Indians" even after the film has ended and the drive-in, "this wide screen beneath the sign of the bear," has closed: "*Come on, boys, we got them / where we want them, drunk, running.*" To counter such dominant, cultural, and stereotypical representation, Erdrich evokes both common and otherworldly creatures, deer and antelope and "*the ghosts of the tree people,*" and reaffirms her belief in elemental, non-Christian rituals such as "the heron dance" and the marriage with "the dark firs." By doing so, she is able to reconvene undiminished communities — the dead and the living, the non-human and all-too-human — that "move freely within me as words."

Poetry: *Jacklight* (1984). *Baptism of Desire* (1989). *Original Fire: Selected and New Poems* (2003).

Prose: *Love Medicine* (1984; revised and expanded edition, 1993). *The Beet Queen* (1986). *Tracks* (1988). *The Crown of Columbus*, with M. Dorris (1991). *The Bingo Palace*, short stories (1994). *The Blue Jay's Dance: A Birth Year*, memoir (1995). *Tales of Burning Love* (1996). *The Antelope Wife* (1998). *The Last Report on the Miracles at Little No Horse* (2002). *Books and Islands in Ojibwe Country*, travel memoir (2003). *The Master Butchers Singing Club* (2003). *Four Souls* (2004).

CAROL FROST (1948)

Born in Lowell, Massachusetts, Carol Frost was educated at the Sorbonne, the State University College at Oneonta, New York, and Syracuse University. She has been Distinguished Writer-in-residence at Wichita State University and Visiting Writer at Washington University in St. Louis.

Currently Writer-in-residence at Hartwick College, she has directed the Catskill Poetry Workshop since 1988 and divides her time between upstate New York and Cedar Key, Florida. Among her awards are fellowships from the National Endowment for the Arts and three Pushcart Prizes.

Frost's lyrics are distinguished by their meditative tone, rigorous intellect, and erotic appetite. Often short, her poems achieve density through their use of Yeats's "passionate syntax," idiosyncratic punctuation, and casual abstraction. In *Pure* (1994), she developed a free-verse form, a truncated sonnet of eleven lines, that makes use of traditional method — the singular focus, the quick turn — while subverting traditional structure. Unsentimental, her poems emphasize the vicissitudes of love and lust, reveling in the sensual pleasure of their language and the integrity of their lines.

Drawn toward purity, particularly in an age that celebrates Whitman's "urge and urge and urge" and favors Darwinian principle, Frost's poems examine the impossibility of divesting oneself of the philosophical import and moral underpinnings of language and gesture. The epigraph to *Day of the Body* (1986), " . . . *thou among the wastes of time must go*," with its biblical injunction and implicit call to purpose, informs her reverent meditations on the nature of the soul's passage through the physical world, "a little in awe of everything." Her poems reach back to the glimmerings of consciousness in early man — the origins of desire "where / the beauty of relation begins" — and focus, through Time, on "people and animals / ripening in dark / green garden where the world is / made." Her lyrics explore myth and archetype to consider "the difference between . . . early ideals — / a garden where plums and peaches grew well and tasted wild / and they were unembarrassed by genitals — and what had become of them." Domestic tension and muted humor infuse such lines. Carol Frost, unlike so many of her contemporaries, deemphasizes the Self to assume her place within "the harmony and breaking down / of such harmony that is the passing world."

Poetry: *Liar's Dice* (1978). *The Fearful Child* (1983). *Day of the Body* (1986). *Chimera* (1990). *Pure* (1994). *Venus and Don Juan* (1996). *Love and Scorn: New and Selected Poems* (2000). *I Will Say Beauty* (2003). *The Queen's Desertion* (2006).

ALLEN GINSBERG (1926–1997)

Born in Newark, New Jersey, Allen Ginsberg attended Columbia University and was dismissed, but returned later to receive his BA in 1948. A leader of the Beat Movement and the San Francisco Renaissance, in 1954 he married Peter Orlovsky. He was the recipient of grants from the Guggenheim Foundation, the National Endowment for the Arts, and the National Institute of Arts and Letters. In 1974, with Adrienne Rich, he was cowinner of the National Book Award.

In his poem "Ego Confession," Ginsberg asserts, "I want to be known as the most brilliant man in America . . . / I want to be the spectacle of Poesy triumphant over trickery of the world. . . ." Poet, guru, world traveler, prophet, and visionary Uncle Sam of the Flower-Acid-Rock Generation, Ginsberg may well have been the planet's most renowned poet. And if Ginsberg's notoriety as a sociocultural *enfant terrible* obscured his power as a poet, he is nevertheless recognized by his contemporaries as one of the most influential post-1945 poets. His first major poem, "Howl," is a milestone, perhaps as significant a poem and document for his genera-tion as "The Waste Land" was for Eliot's.

At once intimate and prophetic, hilarious and terrifying, profoundly religious and, at times, commensurately outrageous, Ginsberg's poetry encompasses a myriad of experiences, ranges over the full spectrum of human life on this planet, and — like the poetry of Whitman — is a com-bination of incredible power and drivel. Clearly, in technique, scope, and intent, Whitman is Ginsberg's model and mentor; like him, Ginsberg is attempting to re-create not only the world but also the full dimensions of a human's physical and spiritual odyssey through a given moment in history — with the crucial difference being that Whitman's poems were hefty songs and Ginsberg's are often reverberating lamentations.

Part of Ginsberg's impact results from his prophetic stance as a man and as a poet, sustained by the vital spirit of William Blake and the prophets of the Old Testament. A modern-day Isaiah, whose public personality often betrayed the depth and range of his erudition, Ginsberg was the public conscience of the nation — if not of the species — lamenting the impon-derable evil humankind has perpetrated against life. But like Isaiah, Blake, and Whitman, he was also moved by a profound belief in the holiness of life and by a vision of a new Jerusalem, a new world.

Poetry: *Howl and Other Poems* (1956). *Empty Mirror: Early Poems* (1961). *Kad-dish and Other Poems* (1961). *Reality Sandwiches* (1963). *Airplane Dreams: Com-positions from Journals* (1968/1969). *Ankor-Wat* (1968). *Planet News, 1961–1967* (1968). *The Gates of Wrath: Rhymed Poems, 1948–1952* (1972). *The Fall of Amer-ica: Poems of These States, 1965–1971* (1973). *Iron Horse* (1973). *First Blues* (1975). *Mind Breaths: Poems 1972–1977* (1978). *Plutonium Ode: Poems 1977–1980* (1982). *Collected Poems: 1947–1980* (1984). *White Shroud: Poems 1980–1985* (1986). *Cosmopolitan Greetings: Poems 1986–1992* (1994). *Selected Poems: 1947–1995* (1997). *Death and Fame: Last Poems 1993–1997* (1999). *Poems for the Nation* (2000).

Prose: *The Yage Letters*, with William Burroughs (1963). *Indian Journals* (1970). *Improvised Poetics*, edited by M. Robinson (1971). *Allen Verbatim: Lectures on Poetry, Politics, Consciousness*, edited by G. Ball (1974). *To Eberhart from Ginsberg: A Letter About Howl 1956* (1976). *As Ever: The Collected Correspondence of Allen Ginsberg & Neal Cassady*, edited by B. Gifford (1977). *Journals: Early Fifties Early Sixties*, edited by G. Ball (1977). *Composed on the Tongue*, edited by D. Allen (1980). *Straight Hearts Delight: Love Poems and Selected Letters 1974–1980*, with Peter Orlovsky, edited by W. Layland (1980). *Your Reason and Blake's System*

(1988). *Deliberate Prose: Selected Essays, 1952–1995*, edited by B. Morgan (2000). *Spontaneous Mind: Selected Interviews, 1958–1998*, edited by D. Carter (2001). *Family Business: Selected Letters Between Father and Son*, by Allen Ginsberg and Louis Ginsberg, edited by M. Schumacher (2001).

LOUISE GLÜCK (1943)

Born in New York City and raised on Long Island, Louise Glück attended Sarah Lawrence and Columbia, where she studied with Stanley Kunitz. She has taught at many colleges and universities and has been awarded fellowships from the National Endowment for the Arts and the Guggenheim Foundation. Her books of poetry also have won the National Book Critics Circle Award and the Pulitzer Prize. During 2003–2004, she served as U.S. Poet Laureate.

"I have always been too at ease with extremes," writes Louise Glück. Whether those extremes are life and death, love and pain, possession and release, or illusion and reality, it is from the tension between them that many of her most moving poems draw their force. But because of her skill with the striking image, the canny tonal shift, and the poetic line, the weight of her themes never overwhelms the poem. Whether writing in her early dense, near-surrealistic mode ("Fish bones walked the waves off Hatteras") or in the looser, more conversational style of her later work ("I have a friend who still believes in heaven"), she controls the rhythm of the poetic line the way a skilled rider handles the reins, alternately tightening and loosening to keep the desired momentum.

Though aspects of autobiography are present in Glück's poems, they rarely serve an expiational purpose. Rather, her self-scrutiny is linked to a wider search for meaning and value, and above all for what it means to be human. It is that exploration of human existence — the "hard loss" of birth, the "thrust and ache" of male/female relations — that may account for the frequent presence in her poems of ancient Greek characters, themes, and images. Taking to heart the Sophoclean edict that "Man is the measure of all things," she seems to forswear both a specifically Christian redemption and a generically spiritual transcendence. In "Celestial Music," a friend who believes in God tells her to look up: "When I look up, nothing. / Only clouds, snow, a white business in the trees."

If the gods long ago "sank down to human shape with longing" — if there is no supernatural world — Glück's poetry seems all the more urgent regarding the question of what makes us human: the part that loves or the part that is mortal? That is the common denominator in her poetry — to be human is to love, to long, to suffer, and to know you will die. Not that Glück would seem to want it otherwise, for "There is always something to be made of pain."

Poetry: *Firstborn* (1968/1981). *The Home on Marshland* (1975). *Descending Figure* (1980). *The Triumph of Achilles* (1985). *Ararat* (1990). *The Wild Iris* (1992). *The First Four Books of Poems* (1996). *Meadowlands* (1996). *Vita Nova* (1999). *The Seven Ages* (2001). *October* (2004).

Prose: *Proofs and Theories: Essays on Poetry* (1994).

ALBERT GOLDBARTH (1948)

Born in Chicago, Albert Goldbarth was educated at the University of Illinois–Chicago, the University of Iowa, and the University of Utah. He has taught at Cornell, Syracuse, the University of Texas, and Wichita State University, where he is Distinguished Professor of the Humanities. Among his numerous awards are fellowships from the Guggenheim Foundation and the National Endowment for the Arts, two National Book Critics Circle Awards, and the Center for the Study of Science Fiction Theodore Sturgeon Memorial Award.

Wildly prolific and unabashedly enthusiastic, Albert Goldbarth is, according to David Barber in *Poetry*, "American poetry's consummate showman . . . whose sensibility conceivably owes as much to Barnum as to Whitman." Like Barnum, Goldbarth is an impresario of the wonders of the New World, an entrepreneur of American culture, boyish, breathless, and awestruck. Like Whitman, he renders his bustling scenarios in "the blab of the pave," tossing slang, vulgarity, jargon, prayer, Yiddish phrases, and neologisms, the whole potpourri of American language, into a mixed stew, a linguistic melting pot of overbrimming abundance. Nothing is ever wasted. His poems respond to the barrage of stimulation, the technological overkill that forces the mind to shuffle detail upon detail toward significance. His purpose, in Joseph Conrad's phrase, is "to render the highest possible justice to the visible world," and perhaps more than any other contemporary poet, Goldbarth conveys the sense of what it means to live in America at the turn of the millennium.

A hip, comic, self-styled Adam whose incumbent task is to name everything, Goldbarth layers the surfaces of his poems with talk-show dross and junk-mail salesmanship as well as scholarly erudition. Underneath his voracious appetite for knowledge and full-throttle narrative momentum, however, lies an abiding tenderness, a concern for the consolations of faith in an age that has come to rely on technology. His poems draw on family, his Jewish heritage, and the common aspects of love as much as they draw on ancient history, archeology, and popular culture. He recognizes that the comic books, mechanical toys, and bric-a-brac of one century will provide the detritus through which future generations might sift for meaning, and that personal relationships exist against the backdrop of a historic and cosmological continuum. His ambitious and seemingly inexhaustible catalogs, his playful, vertiginous sermons, and his vast generosity of spirit allow us to view the world, and those who inhabit it, "wholly, culture-wide, cross-time."

Poetry: *Coprolites* (1973). *Jan. 31* (1974). *Opticks* (1974). *Keeping* (1975). *A Year of Happy* (1976). *Comings Back* (1976). *Different Fleshes* (1979). *Who Gathered and Whispered Behind Me* (1981). *Faith* (1982). *Original Light: New & Selected Poems 1973–1983* (1983). *Arts & Sciences* (1986). *Popular Culture* (1989). *Heaven and Earth: A Cosmology* (1991). *The Gods* (1993). *Across the Layers: poems old and new* (1993). *Marriage, and Other Science Fiction* (1994). *A Lineage of Ragpickers* (1996). *Adventures in Ancient Egypt* (1996). *Beyond* (1998). *Troubled Lovers in History* (1999). *Saving Lives* (2001). *Combinations of the Universe* (2003). *Budget Travel Through Space and Time* (2005).

Prose: *A Sympathy of Souls* (1990). *Great Topics of the World* (1995). *Dark Waves and Light Matter* (1999). *Many Circles: New and Selected Essays* (2001). *Pieces of Payne*, a novel (2003).

KIMIKO HAHN (1955)

Born in Mt. Kisco, New York, Kimiko Hahn, the daughter of two artists, attended the University of Iowa and Columbia University. She has taught at the Poetry Project at St. Mark's Church, the Parsons School of Design, Sarah Lawrence College, and Yale University, and currently teaches at Queens College/CUNY and at the University of Houston. Among her awards are the Theodore Roethke Memorial Poetry Prize and an Association of Asian American Studies Literature Award for *Earshot* (1992), an American Book Award for *The Unbearable Heart* (1995), a Lila Wallace–Readers Digest Writers Award, and fellowships from the New York Foundation for the Arts and the National Endowment for the Arts. In 1995, she wrote ten "portraits" of women for the HBO special, "Ain't Nuthin' but a She Thing."

Asian as well as American literary traditions inform the poems of Kimiko Hahn. A poet of exile even on her familiar New York streets, she relies on storytelling to center herself and to ward off grief, fully realized and/or potential — the loss of her mother who was "broadsided by an Arab kid fleeing a car of white kids with baseball bats," the violence intimated in the consonantal harshness "of boys in the empty lot" that penetrates her daughters' bedroom. For Hahn, the creative act, the engaged *process*, often becomes a means of attaining solace as the poem extends itself organically, finding its true subject through shifts of consciousness and verbal improvisation. In "The Izu Dancer," her attempt to recall Japanese, to "resume the journey inside words / I had begun as a child," by reading the Kawabata tale is undercut by unbidden and intrusive recollections of lust for an American professor who drove a red Volkswagen: "Perhaps I did not want the language enough." Yet that hint of betrayal, as well as the play of the mind across such disparate and cross-cultural elements, allows the poet to translate the past and interpret desire, "flesh / and emblem," with fluency. "I can only speak for myself," she realizes.

Kimiko Hahn's poems portray "someone tearing the past apart," Adrienne Rich has written, "and rebuilding with naked raw hands." Her elegiac and passionate voice, sustained by "the unbearable heart" that gives her work its human measure, unfurls in a New World of its own making.

Poetry: *We Stand Our Ground*, with Susan Sherman and Gale Jackson (1988). *Air Pocket* (1989). *Earshot* (1992). *The Unbearable Heart* (1995). *Volatile* (1999). *Mosquito and Ant* (1999). *The Artist's Daughter* (2002).

DONALD HALL (1928)

Born in New Haven, Connecticut, Donald Hall is a graduate of Harvard and Oxford. He taught for several years at the University of Michigan before returning to his family's farm in New Hampshire, where he now lives and writes. In 1954, his book *Exiles and Marriages* was the Academy of American Poets' Lamont Poetry Selection. His other literary awards include the Lenore Marshall Prize, the National Book Critics Circle Award, and appointment as Poet Laureate of New Hampshire.

Hall's many other accomplishments include monographs on Marianne Moore and Henry Moore, and such noted textbooks as *Writing Well* and *To Read Literature*. He also has edited many anthologies, including *Contemporary American Poetry* (1962).

In a variety of statements — and especially in his dazzling essay "Goatfoot, Milktongue, Twinbird: The Psychic Origins of Poetic Form" — Hall has repeatedly affirmed that the essential beauty of poetry lies in the sensual body of the poem — the sheer physical pleasure that a poem offers. That physical pleasure, Hall observes, "reaches us through our mouths (Milktongue) . . . in the muscles of our legs (Goatfoot) . . . in the resolution of dance and noise (Twinbird)." Hall's quest for the sensual body of his own poems was originally in more traditional forms; later, his poems became less formal, more expansive, and more sensual — without losing the control and discipline learned in the atelier of formalism.

Moreover, Hall's quest for the sensual body of poetry hasn't been the aesthete's pursuit of pleasure. Hall knows all too well: "Milktongue also remembers hunger, and the cry without answer. Goatfoot remembers falling, and the ache that bent the night. Twinbird remembers the loss of the brother, so long he believed in abandonment forever." At the heart of Hall's own poetry are the ever-present ache and modulated cry of abandonment, of grief over loss that is also at the heart of human experience.

The sense of loss in Hall's poems is often complemented and perhaps surpassed by a joyous reconciliation with personal history, a discovery of the redemptive power inherent in all cycles of existence. Thus, twenty-five years after the grandfather's body has slid into the ground like snow melting on the roof of the sap-house, his grandchildren dip their fingers in the maple syrup the dead man preserved in his cellar. Thus, Hall himself can exclaim, "Oh, this delicious falling into the arms of leaves, / into the soft laps of leaves! . . . / Now I leap and fall, exultant, recovering / from death, on account of death, in accord with the dead. . . ." More recently, Hall has struggled to transform his grief over the death of his wife, the poet Jane Kenyon, into poetic sequences notable for their unflinching candor and aesthetic restraint. And thus he evokes still another ancient image of the sensual pleasure of poetry in the myth of Philomel, magically transformed into a nightingale whose torn tongue makes song, makes music, out of grief.

Poetry: *Exiles and Marriages* (1955). *The Dark Houses* (1958). A *Roof of Tiger Lilies* (1964). *The Alligator Bride: Poems New and Selected* (1969). *The Yellow Room: Love Poems* (1971). *The Town of Hill* (1975). *Kicking the Leaves* (1978). *The Happy Man* (1986). *The One Day. A Poem in Three Parts* (1988). *Old and New Poems, 1947–1990* (1990). *The Museum of Clear Ideas: New Poems* (1993). *The Old Life* (1996). *Without* (1998). *The Painted Bed* (2002).

Prose: FICTION: *The Ideal Bakery* (1987). *Willow Temple: New and Selected Stories* (2004). CRITICISM: *Goatfoot Milktongue Twinbird: Interviews, Essays, and Notes on Poetry 1970–76* (1978). *To Keep Moving: Essays 1959–69* (1980). *The Weather for Poetry: Essays, Reviews, and Notes on Poetry 1977–81* (1983). *Poetry and Ambition: Essays 1982–1988* (1990). *Breakfast Served Any Time All Day: Essays on Poetry New and Selected* (2004). MEMOIRS AND OTHER: *String Too Short To Be Saved: Childhood Reminiscences* (1961/1979). *Dock Ellis in the Country of Baseball* (1976). *Remembering Poets: Reminiscences and Opinions* (1978). *Fathers Playing Catch with Sons: Essays on Sports* (1985). *Seasons at Eagle Pond* (1987). *Daylilies at Eagle Pond* (1990). *Here at Eagle Pond* (1990). *Their Ancient Glittering Eyes: Remembering Poets and More Poets* (1992). *Life Work* (1993). *The Best Day The Worst Day: Life with Jane Kenyon* (2005).

MICHAEL S. HARPER (1938)

Michael Harper was born in Brooklyn and educated at California State in Los Angeles and at the University of Iowa. He has taught at various universities, including Brown, where he is I. J. Kapstein Professor of English. In addition to fellowships and grants from the National Endowment for the Arts and the National Institute of Arts and Letters, Harper also has received the Black Academy of Arts and Letters Award.

The titles of Michael Harper's books are genuine flags of his substantive and sustained concerns. Many of his poems are indeed "images of kin": the woman to whom he is married, their living children, their children who died as infants, his own parents and grandparents. But in Harper's poems kinship also expands in time and space to include historical figures, ranging from Frederick Douglass to Martin Luther King, Jr., and Malcolm X, as well as members of the artistic community — jazz musicians such as John Coltrane, Charlie Parker, Bessie Smith, and Billie Holiday and writers such as Richard Wright and, especially among his contemporaries, Robert Hayden.

Moreover, the focus of Harper's concern is a powerful sense of kinship as shared history. Such a vision, then, begins by asserting that "history is your own heartbeat," but it necessarily expands in ever-widening circles of kinship, generated by the pulse that is at the heart of the human family. Full and active participation in those human bonds, Harper knows, may often result in considerable pain and anguish, for to be fully human often necessitates recognizing the nightmare of our condition and accepting its necessary consequence: "nightmare begins responsibility."

Harper is also one of the poets of his generation whose poetry and sensibility have been influenced by the work and presence of the classic American jazz musicians. In his poems they assume the dimensions and implications of larger figures from ancient myths. But they are more than just mythical presences, for in their work Harper has searched for and learned what he calls "the cadence of street talk in the inner ear of the great musicians, the great blues singers." And as Ralph J. Mills, Jr., has noted, Harper's poetry is infused with "a complex jazz of sudden leaps, silences, long rides." No less important, Harper reflects that rich tradition of making music out of fundamental human suffering, whether it be personal, racial, or historical. The conscious transmutation of suffering into song is at once an assertion of our humanity and an affirmation of our freedom. But in one of his essays Harper also tells the story of how John Coltrane tried to find an especially soft reed that would alleviate his pain as he played his horn in search of a particular tone. Coltrane eventually gave up looking for such a reed, regardless of how painful it was for him to make music. "There was no easy way to get that sound," Harper concludes: "play through the pain to *a love supreme*" — the phrase that appears most frequently in Harper's work. No wonder Michael Harper's poems are such "healing songs."

Poetry: *Dear John, Dear Coltrane* (1970). *History Is Your Own Heartbeat* (1971). *Photographs: Negatives: History as Apple Tree* (1972). *Song: I Want a Witness* (1972). *Debridement* (1973). *Nightmare Begins Responsibility* (1975). *Images of Kin: New and Selected Poems* (1977). *Healing Song for the Inner Ear* (1985). *Spiritual Warfare* (1984). *Rhode Island: Eight Poems* (1985). *Honorable Amendments* (1995). *Songlines in Michaeltree* (2000).

ROBERT HASS (1941)

Born in San Francisco and raised in San Rafael, California, Robert Hass received a BA from St. Mary's College and a PhD from Stanford University. He has taught at the State University of New York at Buffalo, St. Mary's

College, and since 1989, at the University of California at Berkeley. The recipient of a Guggenheim Fellowship, Hass also won the Yale Series of Younger Poets Award, the National Book Critics Circle Award for criticism, and a distinguished John D. and Catherine T. MacArthur Fellowship. In 1995, he was appointed Poet Laureate of the United States.

Representing the second generation of poets since 1945, Hass is both heir to and active participant in the restlessness and eclectic spirit of contemporary American poetry. In his early work there is the unmistakable and vibrant influence of the previous generation of poets who helped shape the aesthetics of the late sixties and early seventies. In many poems the Chinese and Japanese aesthetics that so influenced Gary Snyder are present. By contrast, the imagery, tone, structure, and closure of other poems vividly call to mind Robert Bly's and Louis Simpson's earlier experiments in North American neosurrealism. A poem like "Bookbuying in the Tenderloin," meanwhile, reflects the aesthetic and thematic sensibilities of poets such as Robert Lowell and John Logan: the deterioration of Judeo-Christian spiritual values, commensurate with commerce in sex, and the deterioration of sexual mores and values foreshadow the death of western civilization — expressed in rhymed, occasional couplets: "The sky glowers. My God, it is a test, / this riding out the dying of the West."

Peculiar to Hass's poetry is the obsession with the relationship between language and the physical world — between word and thing. This tension, never fully resolved, is explored both explicitly ("a word is elegy to what it signifies") and implicitly through the joy Hass takes in simply naming things ("Tall Buttercup. Wild Vetch"; "*silver* or *moonlight* or *wet grass*"). If images of decay ("The dead with their black lips are heaped / on one another, intimate as lovers") are central to Hass's early poems, so too is the belief in "the magic of names and poems" and in the vision that "our words are clear / and our movements give off light." And it is a sustained belief in such magic that enables Hass in later poems — most of them written in long, lyrical lines — to wrestle with "All the new thinking . . . about loss," to affirm "moments when the body is as numinous as words, days that are the good flesh continuing," and to celebrate the physical, sensual, and transcendent pleasures of this world (such as food and language): "Such tenderness, these afternoons and evenings, / saying *blackberry, blackberry, blackberry.*"

Poetry: *Field Guide* (1973). *Praise* (1979). *Human Wishes* (1989). *Sun Under Wood* (1996).

Prose: *Twentieth Century Pleasures: Prose on Poetry*, essays (1984).

Translations: *The Separate Notebooks*, poems by Czeslaw Milosz, with R. Gorcynski and R. Pinsky (1984). *Unattainable Earth*, poems by Czeslaw Milosz, with the author (1986). *Collected Poems*, by Czeslaw Milosz, with the author and others (1989). *Provinces: Poems 1987–1991*, by Czeslaw Milosz, with the author (1991). *The Essential Haiku* (1994). *Facing the River*, by Czeslaw Milosz, with the author (1995). *Road-Side Dog*, by Czeslaw Milosz, with the author (1998). *Selected Poems 1954–1986*, by Tomas Tranströmer (1999). *A Treatise on Poetry*, by Czeslaw Milosz (2001).

ROBERT HAYDEN (1913–1980)

A native of Detroit, Robert Hayden received a BA from Wayne State University and an MA from the University of Michigan. He taught at Fisk, Louisville, and Washington, and he was professor of English at the University of Michigan. He was a staff member of the Breadloaf Writers Conference, and from 1976 to 1978 he served as Consultant in Poetry at the Library of Congress. His honors and awards included a Rosenwald Fellowship, a Ford Foundation grant, and the First World Festival of Negro Arts Prize for Poetry, Dakar, Senegal, in 1966.

From the publication of his first book in 1940, Hayden's poetry consistently reflected a sensibility informed by a vital awareness of and participation in the broad spectrum of the African-American experience. He explored dimensions of his own childhood and personal life, he focused on central historical and cultural figures and events, and he re-created such immeasurable horrors as an African-American man's castration at the hands of the Ku Klux Klan. No less important, while eschewing political rhetoric, he recognized that much the same moral poison infected the air of both Selma and Saigon, that the ashes in the pits at Dachau resulted from a fire not unlike that which burned on lawns in innumerable American towns.

Hayden's moral vision is all the more powerful because his work reveals that he is equally conscious of the broader aesthetic traditions in the art of poetry and of the obvious — but often overlooked — fact that the wellsprings of poetry run more deeply and serendipitously than even the most active pools of political or racial experience. The depths of horror in "Night, Death, Mississippi" are intensified by the delicate and exquisite lyrical qualities of much of Hayden's work.

In short, Robert Hayden's poems are themselves vibrant "lives grown out of his life, the lives / fleshing his dream of *the beautiful, needful thing.*"

Poetry: *Heart-Shape in the Dust* (1940). *The Lion and the Archer*, with Myron O'Higgins (1948). *Figures of Time: Poems* (1955). *A Ballad of Remembrance* (1962). *Selected Poems* (1966). *Words in the Mourning Time* (1970). *The Night-Blooming Cereus* (1975). *Angle of Ascent: New and Selected Poems* (1975). *American Journal* (1978/1982). *Robert Hayden: Collected Poems* (1985).

Prose: *The Collected Prose of Robert Hayden* (1984).

WILLIAM HEYEN (1940)

Born in Brooklyn, New York, William Heyen grew up on then-rural Long Island. He attended the State University of New York at Brockport and Ohio University, and taught at the former from 1967 until his recent retirement. He has been a Senior Fulbright Lecturer in American Literature at Hannover University in Germany and the recipient of fellowships from the National Endowment for the Arts, the Guggenheim Foundation, and the New York Foundation for the Arts. In 1982, he was awarded the Witter Bynner Prize from the American Academy and Institute of Arts and Letters. His *Crazy Horse in Stillness* (1996) received the National Small Press Book Award.

Prolific, obsessive, and fiercely intelligent, Heyen has managed an impressive body of work in both traditional and unconventional, even unique, modes. Finding it impossible, it would seem, to write only a single poem on a particular topic, Heyen instead exhausts his vast knowledge of the subject by composing long sequences of poems that provide multiple perspectives, that attempt to see "from all sides at once." He has written such sequences on the rural Long Island of his boyhood, the Holocaust, the history of the American chestnut tree, the Gulf War, Crazy Horse and Custer, even the Royal Family. This latter sequence, *Diana, Charles, & the Queen* (1998), consists of 324 separate poems, each "two quatrains, / usually rhymed." Yet his narrowly focused though wildly diverse topics allow him an ambitious, inclusive range. The poems in *Crazy Horse in Stillness*, for example, circle widely enough around their subject to draw upon pop culture and cyberspace. Despite such eccentric gestures, Heyen's visionary lyricism remains constant, rooted in the Emersonian transcendentalism of the nineteenth century.

Heyen's poetry remains aware of its moral function as it confronts history and serves as the conscience of a still-developing democracy. His poems on Nature extend their tradition by evincing ecological and environmental concerns, sometimes uncomfortably so. Whatever the object of attention, Heyen wields a formidable intellect and lyric intensity upon his sometimes deceptively simple surfaces. "Prune for shade," reads his shortest poem, and that epigrammatic imperative could serve as a description of this poet's particular craft.

Poetry: *Depth of Field* (1970). *Noise in the Trees: Poems and a Memoir* (1974). *The Swastika Poems* (1977). *Long Island Light: Poems and a Memoir* (1979). *The City Parables* (1980). *Lord Dragonfly: Five Sequences* (1981). *Erika: Poems of the Holocaust* (1984). *The Chestnut Rain: A Poem* (1986). *Brockport, New York: Beginning with 'And'* (1988). *Falling from Heaven: Holocaust Poems*, with Louis Daniel Brodsky (1991). *Pterodactyl Rose: Poems of Ecology* (1991). *Ribbons: The Gulf War* (1991). *The Host: Selected Poems 1965–1990* (1994). *Crazy Horse in Stillness*

(1996). *Diana, Charles, & the Queen* (1998). *The Rope* (2003). *Shoah Train* (2004). *The Confessions of Doc Williams* (2005).

Prose: FICTION: *Vic Holyfield and the Class of 1957: A Romance* (1986). *The Hummingbird Corporation* (2003). ESSAYS: *With Me Far Away: A Memoir* (1994). *Pig Notes & Dumb Music: Prose on Poetry* (1998). *Home: Autobiographies, Etc.* (2005). *Titanic & Iceberg: Early Essays and Reviews* (2005).

ANDREW HUDGINS (1951)

Born in Killeen, Texas, Andrew Hudgins attended Sidney Lanier High School in Montgomery, Alabama, where the football team was named the Poets. He attended Huntingdon College, the University of Alabama, Syracuse University, and the University of Iowa, and in 1984 was a Wallace Stegner Fellow at Stanford University. He has taught at Baylor University, the University of Cincinnati, and Ohio State University. In 1989–1990, he held the Alfred Hodder Fellowship at Princeton. His honors include the Witter Bynner Award of the American Academy and Institute of Arts and Letters, the Poets' Prize for *After the Lost War* (1988), and fellowships from the Ingram Merrill Foundation and the National Endowment for the Arts.

Rooted in his Southern Baptist upbringing, the poems of Andrew Hudgins, though not religious in the conventional sense, focus on fundamentalism as a backdrop for human behavior to illustrate the disparity between biblical injunction and Darwinian imperative. In *Saints and Strangers* (1985), naked adolescents cavort in a baptismal font and one boy sings "Amazing Grace" in the cartoon voice of Donald Duck. Such irreverence, however, doesn't mitigate the overarching presence of "God's clear flesh beneath / its human dying." The poems admit the oppression as well as the ecstasy inherent in religious (and southern) iconography and reflect this duality in their comic desperation, their repetitious rituals of absolution and violence, and their plainspoken, at times scatological, language arranged within the formal cadences of blank verse.

Hudgins's second volume, the ambitious, book-length narrative *After the Lost War* (1988), has been described by the poet as "a historical novel in verse that masquerades as a biography of the Civil War veteran and poet Sidney Lanier." The sequence questions the validity and power of the romantic imagination confronted by the landscape of the defeated South and anticipates Hudgins's later work in which his characters, often unwillingly, test their faith — in themselves, in God — against commonplace horrors. "I wish my soul were larger than it is," prays one narrator as racism, sexual violence, and death course through these poems. "This world, / this world is home," insists another. "But it / will never feel like home."

Poetry: *Saints and Strangers* (1985). *After the Lost War: A Narrative* (1988). *The Never-Ending* (1991). *The Glass Hammer: A Southern Childhood* (1994). *Babylon in a Jar* (1998). *Ecstatic in the Poison* (2003).

Prose: *The Glass Anvil* (1997).

RICHARD HUGO (1923–1982)

Richard Hugo was born in Seattle and educated at the University of Washington. He was a bombardier in the U.S. Army Air Corps during World War II and subsequently worked for the Boeing Company for twelve years. He later was director of the creative writing program at the University of Montana (Missoula) and served as editor of the Yale Series of Younger Poets. His awards included the Theodore Roethke Memorial Poetry Prize and fellowships from the Rockefeller and Guggenheim Foundations.

Perhaps more than the work of any other poet of his generation, Hugo's poetry is rooted in and mines a specific, identifiable landscape — the American Far West. However, Hugo's landscape isn't the breathtaking panorama of a Grand Canyon or spectacular hills and plains against a blazing sunset of romantic American western movies. The landscape in his poetry is suggested in Hugo's comment: "Usually I find a poem is triggered by something, a small town or an abandoned house, that I feel others would ignore." Thus, the geographic, human, and moral landscape in Hugo's poems is a bleak and threatening panorama in which one finds those small, dry, and blistered towns where all life and human constructs decay too soon — and where perhaps nothing dies soon enough.

If, like Wallace Stevens, Hugo understands the extent to which "the soil is man's intelligence," he nevertheless does not succumb to easy fatalism. In poems whose language and texture assert their own organic shapes and rhythms, as if in defiance of the odds of lunar dust, Hugo affirms the things of this earth and of his poetic landscape. Just as Rilke could assert, "Maybe we're here only to say: *house, / bridge, well, gate, jug, olive tree, window* — / at most, *pillar, tower* . . . but to say them, remember, / oh, to say them in a way that the things themselves / never dreamed of existing so intensely," so Hugo can assert, "To live good, keep your life and the scene. / Cow, brook, hay; these are names of coins."

"A part of the West belongs to Hugo," William Stafford has written. "By telling over and over again its places and people, he reclaims it from the very bleakness he confronts; and it all begins to loom as a great intense abode that we can't neglect, that we can't bear to let go." Thus, Richard Hugo's intense love of the things of *his* earth keeps them and us alive at a level of intensity and joy we could not know without the melancholy and redemptive beauty of his poems.

Poetry: A *Run of Jacks* (1961). *Five Poets of the Pacific Northwest*, with Kenneth Hanson, Carolyn Kizer, William Stafford, and David Wagoner (1964). *Death of the Kapowsin Tavern* (1965). *Good Luck in Cracked Italian* (1969). *The Lady in Kicking Horse Reservoir* (1973). *Rain Five Days and I Love It* (1975). *What Thou Lovest Well, Remains American* (1975). *Duwamish Head* (1976). *31 Letters and 13 Dreams* (1977). *Road Ends at Tahola* (1978). *Selected Poems* (1979). *White Center* (1980). *The Right Madness of Skye* (1980). *Making Certain It Goes On: The Collected Poems of Richard Hugo* (1983). *Sea Lanes Out* (1983).

Prose: *The Triggering Town: Lectures and Essays on Poetry and Writing* (1979). *Death and the Good Life*, a novel (1981). *The Real West Marginal Way: A Poet's Autobiography* (1986).

DONALD JUSTICE (1925–2004)

Donald Justice was born in Miami, Florida. He attended the University of Miami, the University of North Carolina at Chapel Hill, Stanford University, and the University of Iowa. He taught at the University of Missouri, Syracuse University, the University of California, and the University of Iowa. Justice was the recipient of grants, awards, and fellowships from the Ford and Guggenheim Foundations, the National Endowment for the Arts, and the National Institute of Arts and Letters. In 1980, he was awarded the Pulitzer Prize for his *Selected Poems*.

Many of Justice's poems generate much the same kind of emotional center and aura as Edward Hopper's well-known paintings (such as *Nighthawks*): the figures, landscapes, and dramatic situations reflect the depth of loneliness, the isolation, and the spiritual desolation at the heart of twentieth-century experience. Any number of these people or situations could suddenly turn up in our own nightmares or in our living rooms. However, while Hopper achieves his effects by means of bold colors, thick strokes, and stark contrasts, the surface texture of Justice's poems is far more delicate and subtle — the restrained turn of a phrase (as in "Men at Forty"), the carefully controlled but haunting repetitions of lines (as in the villanelle "In Memory of the Unknown Poet, Robert Boardman Vaughn").

Given a list of some of Justice's subjects — loneliness, isolation, madness, despair, terror — he might be wrongfully associated with some of the personal-confessional poets. His poems, however, do not suggest any of the verbal or emotional sensationalism that occasionally may be ascribed to some of those other poets. Rightfully celebrated for his work's formal qualities, Justice is a master of sparse elegance. His poems are not the result of emotional or technical self-indulgence; rather, they are moving because of his consummate linguistic, tonal, and formal exactitude.

If Justice's commitment to the "well-made poem" suggests his formal schooling among the New Critics, he is also one of the obvious emotional-spiritual heirs of T. S. Eliot — that is, of the vision found in Eliot's earlier poems, before his conversion to Christianity. Like the work of other poets of his generation, Justice's poems flesh out in more intimate and sustained detail the figures and states of being that Eliot only sketched in poems like "The Love Song of J. Alfred Prufrock," "Preludes," and "The Waste Land." What further distinguishes Justice's work is not only his unrelieved sense of loss ("But the years are gone. There are no more years.") but also his profound acceptance of (*not* resignation to) the human condition as he finds it. But if Donald Justice's poems are elegies of loss, they are also unswerving and powerful affirmations that to be human is to make poetry of "the boredom, and the horror, and the glory."

Poetry: *The Summer Anniversaries* (1960). A *Local Storm* (1963). *Four Poets*, with others (1963). *Night Light* (1967). *Sixteen Poems* (1970). *From a Notebook* (1972). *Departures* (1973). *Selected Poems* (1979). *The Sunset Maker: Poems/Stories/A Memoir* (1987). *New and Selected Poems* (1995). *Collected Poems* (2004).

Prose and Poetry: *Platonic Scripts*, essays (1984). A *Donald Justice Reader: Selected Poetry and Prose* (1991). *Oblivion: On Writers & Writing* (1999).

Translations: *The Man Closing Up*, poems by Guillevic (1973).

GALWAY KINNELL (1927)

Galway Kinnell is a graduate of Princeton and the University of Rochester. He was a Fulbright Fellow in Paris, served in the U.S. Navy, and was a field worker for the Congress of Racial Equality. He has traveled widely in the Middle East and in Europe, where he taught at the universities of Grenoble and Nice (France). Formerly Erich Maria Remarque Professor of Creative Writing at New York University, Kinnell has received several awards and fellowships, including the Brandeis University Creative Arts Award, the National Book Award, and the Pulitzer Prize.

Kinnell's earlier poems were both traditionally formal and informed by a traditional Christian sensibility. However, while retaining an essentially religious and sacramental dimension, his later work — as he has said in an interview — has become an increasing "struggle against the desire for heaven," as well as a movement toward a freer verse that takes more risks and in which "there is the chance of finding that great thing you might be after, of finding glory."

Confronted by a constant threat of extinction, Kinnell is capable of witnessing even the most elemental energy as an affirmation of life. Perhaps human life is a participation in the ultimate madness of a universe flinging itself into emptiness; the image of fire often reappearing in his poems may not be the flame of the phoenix. Thus, Kinnell insists that for man, "as he goes up in flames, his own work / is / to open himself, to *be* / the flames."

In their language and substance, Kinnell's poems achieve that rhythm and solemnity often found in a shaman's chant. And yet his poems are also intensely personal, reflecting an attempt to strip away personality, to go deeper into the self "until," he says, "you're just a person. If you could keep going deeper and deeper, you'd finally not be a person either; you'd be an animal; and if you kept going deeper and deeper, you'd be a blade of grass or ultimately perhaps a stone. And if a stone could read, [poetry] would speak for it." For Kinnell, then, poetry is primal experience and myth, the most elemental kind of prayer, or a "paradigm of what people might wish to say in addressing the cosmos."

Poetry: *What a Kingdom It Was* (1960). *Flower Herding on Mount Monadnock* (1964). *Body Rags* (1968). *First Poems: 1946–54* (1971). *The Book of Nightmares* (1971). *The Avenue Bearing the Initial of Christ into the New World: Poems 1946–64* (1974). *Mortal Acts, Mortal Words* (1980). *Selected Poems* (1982). *The Past* (1985). *When One Has Lived a Long Time Alone* (1990). *Three Books: Body Rags, Mortal Acts, Mortal Words, The Past* (1993). *Imperfect Thirst* (1994). *A New Selected Poems* (2000).

Prose: *Black Light,* novel (1966; revised edition, 1981). *Walking Down the Stairs: Selections from Interviews* (1978).

Translations: POETRY: *The Poems of François Villon* (1965; revised version, 1977). *On the Motion and Immobility of Douve,* by Yves Bonnefoy (1968). *Lackawanna Elegy,* by Yvan Goll (1970). *Early Poems 1947–1959,* by Yvan Goll; with R. Pevear (1990). *The Essential Rilke,* with H. Liebmann (1999). FICTION: *Bitter Victory,* by Rene Hardy (1965).

CAROLYN KIZER (1925)

Born in Spokane, Washington, Carolyn Kizer graduated from Sarah Lawrence College and was a fellow of the Chinese government in comparative literature at Columbia University, followed by a year of study in Nationalist China. The founder of the quarterly *Poetry Northwest,* in 1964–1965 she was a Specialist in Literature for the U.S. State Department in Pakistan, and from 1966 to 1970 she served as the first director of the Literature Program for the newly established National Endowment for the Arts. The recipient of the Pulitzer Prize for *Yin* (1984), she currently lives in Sonoma, California.

With the publication of her first book-length collection of poems Carolyn Kizer staked out the diverse technical and thematic territories of her art. Whether she is working with free verse, with more formal verse, or with combinations of free verse and occasional slant rhymes, Kizer's poetry is always remarkable for its consummate grace and control. (She is one member of her generation who continues to explore the possibilities and power of strict form.) The intellectual credibility and emotional impact of her poems are further enhanced by her unique intellectual wit and hearty, often stinging, sense of humor. Indeed, Kizer was one of the first poets to approach feminist subjects and themes with a measure of healthy humor and sophisticated wit, which are an integral part of her sensibility rather than merely the device of poetic irony.

Kizer's concern for the cause of feminism has been at the heart of her poetry from the very start of her career — for the most fundamental of reasons: ". . . we are the custodians of the world's best-kept secret: / Merely the private lives of one-half of humanity." And it's important to note that the composition of "Pro Femina" dates back to the mid-1950s, before feminism was an issue of general consciousness. But Kizer's interest isn't limited to feminism as a sociopolitical cause; rather, what generally rivets her attention is the quality of representative women's diurnal experiences. "The Great Blue Heron," for example, is a meditation on the "invisible wires" that connect mother and daughter; "A Widow in Wintertime" is a portrait of repressed sexuality, disciplined loneliness, and "metaphysic famines."

However, Kizer doesn't limit herself to the "famines" of experience, either, for also at the heart of her poetry is her vision of the profound patterns of physical and metaphysical life: change, transformation, and transubstantiation in nature and in the spirit, for good or ill; birth, death, and rebirth of love, the self, the soul, as in "Semele Recycled," where "the inner parts remember . . . / the comfortable odor of dung, the animal incense, / and passion, its bloody labor, / its birth and rebirth and decay." In short, without sacrificing their feminist edge, Kizer's poems are powerful, mythmaking hymns in celebration of "we who invented dying / And the whole alchemy of resurrection."

Poetry: *Poems* (1959). *The Ungrateful Garden* (1961/1999). *Five Poets of the Pacific Northwest*, with Kenneth Hanson, Richard Hugo, William Stafford, and David Wagoner; edited by R. Skelton (1964). *Knock Upon Silence* (1965/1966). *Midnight Was My Cry: New and Selected Poems* (1971). *Mermaids in the Basement: Poems for Women* (1984). *Yin: New Poems* (1984). *The Nearness of You* (1986). *Harping On: Poems 1985–1995* (1996). *Cool, Calm and Collected: Poems 1960–2000* (2001).

Prose: *Proses: On Poems & Poets* (1993). *Picking and Choosing: Essays on Prose* (1996).

Translations: *Carrying Over: Poems from the Chinese, Urdu, Macedonian, Yiddish, and French African* (1988). *A Splintered Mirror: Contemporary Chinese Poets*, with D. Finkel (1990).

YUSEF KOMUNYAKAA (1947)

Yusef Komunyakaa was born and raised in Bogalusa, Louisiana. After graduating from the University of Colorado, Colorado State University, and the University of California at Irvine, he held a fellowship in poetry at the Provincetown Fine Arts Work Center. He teaches at Princeton University.

His awards and distinctions include fellowships from the National Endowment for the Arts, the Thomas Forcade Award for Literature and Art Dedicated to the Healing of Vietnam in America, and the Pulitzer Prize.

From the primal experience of the African veldts, in which he speaks of having "eaten handfuls of fire / back to the bright sea / of my first breath . . . ," to the German Third Reich that produced the "Nazi Doll" with a heart that hums "the song of dust / like a sweet beehive," from his childhood experiences as one of the boys wearing their mothers' clothes in afternoons that live in the republic of their bones, to the horror of the war in Vietnam, where the cry "from the hills / belongs to a girl still burning / inside my head . . ." — history courses through the poetry of Yusef Komunyakaa like a great Nile of the imagination.

The aesthetics at work in Komunyakaa's poetry are not so much that of the Harlem Renaissance as that of the European Renaissance, which influenced American poetry down into the twentieth century. And this poet's strength in large part is his ability to couple a near-mystical African-American superstition with a glimpse of a Wallace Stevens image of eleven black birds on a power line, "a luminous / message. . . ." He knows that poetry and its music are "a bridge, / more than a ledger of bones" that links Villon and Leadbelly. And he knows that the Muse with whom he sleeps is silence, "my impossible white wife." Thus, "the tongue even lies to itself, / gathering wildfire for songs of gibe."

Poetry: *Dedications and Other Darkhorses* (1977). *Lost in the Bonewheel Factory* (1979). *Copacetic* (1984). *Toys in a Field* (1986). *I Apologize for the Eyes in My Head* (1986). *Dien Cai Dau* (1988). *February in Sydney* (1989). *Magic City* (1992). *Neon Vernacular: New and Selected Poems* (1993). *Thieves of Paradise* (1998). *Pleasure Dome: New and Collected Poems, 1975–1999* (1999). *Talking Dirty to the Gods* (2000). *Taboo* (2004).

Prose: *Blue Notes: Essays, Interviews, and Commentaries*, edited by R. Clytus (2000).

MAXINE KUMIN (1925)

Maxine Kumin was born in Philadelphia and educated at Radcliffe. The author of several children's books (three of them written with Anne Sexton), she has taught at Tufts, the University of Massachusetts, and Princeton. An officer of the Radcliffe Institute's Society of Fellows, Kumin was awarded the Pulitzer Prize in 1973 for *Up Country* and the Ruth Lilly Prize in 1999. She lives in rural New Hampshire, where she raises horses.

One of Kumin's critics has faulted her work for often being "the poetry of a special world, unmistakably upper middle-class, comfortable, urbane, safe in its place at the center of things." To suggest that such arenas of experience may not be legitimate or "worthy" concerns of poetry in this century and country is nonsense, of course. Besides, when Eliot posited his dictum "Redeem the time," he didn't specify that it had to be an urban and industrial time fraught with its unique sets of psychic and physical terrors. Moreover, if Kumin's poetry does focus on the middle-class experience, like Louis Simpson, she too is "taking part in a great experiment — / whether writers can live peacefully in the suburbs / and not be bored to death."

Kumin's personal experiment as a poet also has an edge of intensity that goes considerably beyond mere survival of boredom. Because of her powerful sense of observation and her masterful handling of technique, the objects and experiences of suburban life in Kumin's poetry assume a greater hum and buzz of emblematic implication of the direction of the human soul.

Consequently, the ordinary task of ridding one's garden of woodchucks suggests a greater kind of historical extermination. Beneath the ostensible safety of suburban life lies the nightmare of a cleansing fire all inhabitants must pass through. No less important, one senses in Kumin's poetry a conscious urgency to discover in the natural world not only emblems of endurance, survival, and continuity but also momentary symbols of that more human longing for the possibility of transcendence. With remarkable grace and wit, the poems of Maxine Kumin redeem the personal and communal time and space in which she lives, in which most of us measure the worth of our lives.

Poetry: *Halfway* (1961). *The Privilege* (1965). *The Nightmare Factory* (1970). *Up Country* (1972). *House, Bridge, Fountain, Gate* (1975). *The Retrieval System* (1978). *Our Ground Time Here Will Be Brief: New and Selected Poems* (1982). *The Long Approach* (1985). *Nurture: Poems* (1989). *Looking for Luck* (1992). *Connecting the Dots* (1996). *Selected Poems, 1960–1990* (1997). *The Long Marriage* (2001). *Bringing Together: Uncollected Early Poems 1958–1988* (2003). *Jack and Other New Poems* (2005).

Prose: ESSAYS: *To Make a Prairie: Essays on Poets, Poetry, and Country Living* (1979). *In Deep: Country Essays* (1988). *Always Beginning: Essays on a Life in Poetry* (2000). FICTION: *Through Dooms of Love* (1965). *The Passions of Uxport* (1968). *The Abduction* (1971). *The Designated Heir* (1974). *Why Can't We Live Together Like Civilized Human Beings?* (1982). *Women, Animals, and Vegetables* (1994). *Quit Monks or Die!* (1999). MEMOIR: *Inside the Halo and Beyond* (2000).

STANLEY KUNITZ (1905)

Born in Worcester, Massachusetts, and educated at Harvard, Stanley Kunitz has taught at Bennington, Brandeis, Columbia, and Yale. He also has been a Cultural Exchange Scholar in the Soviet Union and Poland. From 1969 to 1976, he was editor of the Yale Series of Younger Poets; from 1974 to 1976, he served as Consultant in Poetry at the Library of Congress. The recipient of grants from the Guggenheim and Ford Foundations, the

Academy of American Poets, and the National Institute of Arts and Letters, he was awarded the Pulitzer Prize in 1959 and the National Book Award in 1995.

After the publication of *The Testing-Tree* in 1971, Stanley Kunitz wrote, "I am no more reconciled than I ever was to the world's wrongs and the injustice of time." Among the wrongs and injustices present in Kunitz's poetry are the memories of a painful childhood that seemingly cannot be redeemed or reshaped, inevitable participation in the scientific and technological violence against the human spirit; and — despite the moments of beauty's hope — the inescapable promise of "a dusty finger on my lip."

Throughout his career, Kunitz's measure of emotional and moral energy has been further intensified by his equally passionate reverence for and use of form. In his poems, more than in the work of most poets of his generation, one senses that any experience or vision — regardless of how intense it might have been in itself — has consistently been forged by the white heat of a metaphysical sensibility. Thus, Kunitz's poems have a physical presence and quality that are verbal equivalents of graceful sculptures forged out of the toughest metal — just as the works of certain contemporary metalsmiths are intricate sculptures of iron and steel that seem to be leaping toward pure sound.

Poetry: *Intellectual Things* (1930). *Passport to the War: A Selection of Poems* (1944). *Selected Poems 1928–1958* (1958). *The Testing-Tree: Poems* (1971). *The Lincoln Relics: A Poem* (1979). *The Poems of Stanley Kunitz 1928–1978* (1979). *The Wellfleet Whale and Companion Poems* (1983). *Next-to-Last Things: New Poems and Essays* (1985). *Passing Through: The Later Poems, New and Selected* (1995). *The Collected Poems* (2000).

Prose: *A Kind of Order, A Kind of Folly: Essays and Conversations* (1975). *The Art of Poetry: Interviews with Stanley Kunitz* (1989). *The Wild Braid*, with G. Lentine (2005).

Translations: *Poems of Akhmatova*, with M. Hayward (1973).

LI-YOUNG LEE (1957)

Li-Young Lee was born in Jakarta, Indonesia, of Chinese parents. In 1959, his father, after spending a year as a political prisoner in President Sukarno's jails, fled Indonesia with his family. Between 1959 and 1964 they traveled in Hong Kong, Macau, and Japan, until arriving in America. Li-Young Lee has studied at the University of Pittsburgh, the University of Arizona, and the State University of New York, College at Brockport. His many awards include fellowships from the Guggenheim and Whiting Foundations and the National Endowment for the Arts, as well as awards from the Academy of American Poets and the Lannan Foundation.

Clearly one of the most gripping voices to have emerged in American poetry since the late 1980s, Li-Young Lee is also a master of modulation.

While maintaining his unmistakable voice, he is capable of being lyrical ("My Indigo"), elegaic ("Eating Alone"), as well as meditative and religious ("This Room and Everything in It"); moreover, in a poem like "Persimmons," he becomes almost operatic in much the same way as Whitman. Lee can be gentle, reverential, passionate, and musical. And although he is first and foremost an American poet, his rich Asian experience and upbringing weave through his voice and poetry like a contrapuntal thread generating extraordinary harmony.

Family is at the heart of much of Lee's poetry: his mother and grandmother singing together "like young girls" and conjuring vivid images of Peking or the Summer Palace; his brother, "in heavy boots . . . walking / through bare rooms over my head . . . / what could he possibly need there in heaven?" And finally, his father, who is both the source of pain and his greatest inspiration; the father, who pulls "the metal splinter from my palm," which, seen from another viewpoint, "you would have thought you saw a man / planting something in a boy's palm, / a silver tear, a tiny flame." It is that tear and it is that flame which serve as tangible epiphanies of pain and light that lead him to affirm "you must sing to be found; when found, you must sing."

Poetry: *Rose* (1986). *The City in Which I Love You* (1990). *Book of My Nights* (2001).

Prose: *The Winged Seed* (1995).

DENISE LEVERTOV (1923–1997)

Born in Essex, England, Denise Levertov was privately educated, served as a nurse during World War II, and emigrated to the United States in 1948. She taught at Vassar, Drew, City College of New York, MIT, and Tufts University. A scholar at the Radcliffe Institute for Independent Study, Levertov also received the Morton Dauwen Zabel Award, a fellowship from the Guggenheim Foundation, an award from the National Institute of Arts and Letters, and a Senior Fellowship from the National Endowment for the Arts.

Influenced by William Carlos Williams and the Black Mountain School — or simply their natural aesthetic compatriot — Denise Levertov wrote poems that are nevertheless charged by an unmistakably distinctive voice, capable of ranging from a tough to a tender lyricism that is proportionately intense. Her poems fully explore and — with assurance, pleasure, or grief — celebrate the multifaceted experience of the contemporary woman. By so doing, they invite all of us into a celebration of the full range of human experience.

In an early interview Levertov said, "I believe in writing about what lies under the hand, in a sense. . . . Not necessarily in the visual world — the external world — it can be an inner experience — but it must be something true." And in one poem Levertov wrote, "The best work is made / from hard, strong materials, / obstinately precise. . . ." Her own poems repeatedly assert that the most obstinate and hard materials — even in that kind of natural lyrical poem she mastered — are not onyx and steel, but rather the small, at times elusive, materials of daily human life.

An antiwar poem such as "Life at War" affirms the inestimable power of the simple but sacred human gesture over "the gray filth" that can coat our dreams and drab the imagination "The same war / continues," Levertov wrote in the sixties, and if the war in Vietnam has been relegated to history, her poem remains relevant to whatever war America may be waging now. But so much of her work also reminds us that each new poem is that difficult and laborious Jacob's ladder between the facts of the diurnal and the bid for the eternal; each poem carves the physical details and quality of our daily communal experience in the unyielding onyx and steel of a cosmic history that would obliterate us.

Poetry: *The Double Image* (1946). *Here and Now* (1957). *Overland to the Islands* (1958). *With Eyes at the Back of Our Heads* (1959). *The Jacob's Ladder* (1961). *O Taste and See: New Poems* (1964). *The Sorrow Dance* (1967). *A Tree Telling of Orpheus* (1968). *Relearning the Alphabet* (1970). *To Stay Alive* (1971). *Footprints* (1972). *The Freeing of the Dust* (1975). *Life in the Forest* (1978). *Collected Earlier Poems 1940–1960* (1979). *Candles in Babylon* (1982). *Poems 1960–1967* (1983). *Oblique Prayers* (1984). *Poems 1968–1972* (1987). *Breathing the Water* (1988). *A Door in the Hive* (1989). *Evening Train* (1992). *Sands of the Well* (1996). *The Life Around Us: Selected Poems on Ecological Themes* (1997). *The Stream and the Sapphire: Selected Poems on Religious Themes* (1999). *This Great Unknowing: Last Poems* (1999). *Poems 1972–1982* (2001). *Selected Poems* (2002).

Prose: *The Poet in the World,* essays (1973). *Light Up the Cave,* essays (1981). *New & Selected Essays* (1992). *Selected Criticism* (1993). *Tesserae: Memories and Suppositions* (1995). *Conversations with Denise Levertov,* edited by J. S. Brooker (1998). *The Letters of Denise Levertov and William Carlos Williams* (1998).

Translations: *In Praise of Krishna: Songs from the Bengali,* with E. R. Dimmock, Jr. (1968). *Selected Poems of Guillevic* (1969). *Black Iris,* poems by Jean Joubert (1988).

PHILIP LEVINE (1928)

Philip Levine was born in Detroit. He received a BA and an MA from Wayne State University and an MFA from the University of Iowa. Subsequently, he held a fellowship in poetry at Stanford University. From 1958 until his retirement, he taught at California State University, Fresno. He has received grants from the National Endowment for the Arts, the National Institute of Arts and Letters, and the Guggenheim Foundation, and he has been awarded the National Book Award and the Pulitzer Prize.

Critics can't seem to agree on what Levine's central theme is. One says it's a "rogue's gallery of drunks, draft-dodgers, boxers, Hell's Angels, midgets, poor neighbors." Another asserts that his themes include "Hiroshima, the torture of Algerian prisoners, soldiers in eye-to-eye combat, generalized and brutal bigotry . . . man's cruelty to man." Still another critic argues that Levine's "fields of exploration" include "experiences which manifest themselves in irrational, dreamlike, fantastic or visionary forms." In fact, all these observations are true, for what is consistently striking about Levine's poetry is precisely his wide range of themes.

Levine himself has written, "I try to pay homage to the people who taught me my life was a holy thing, who convinced me that my formal education was a lie. . . . These people, both Black and white, were mainly rural people, and the horror of the modern world was clearer to them than to me, and the beauty and value of the world was something they knew in a way I did not, first hand." No less important in his poetry is the vital role of Levine's own sense of place — especially the bleak, dirty, and threatening industrial cityscape of Levine's childhood in Detroit; more recently one notes references to Levine's own personal life and background, especially members of his family.

Equally striking — although not immediately noticeable to the more casual reader — is Levine's mastery of a range of forms, from the most ostensible manipulation of tighter forms, through the freer lyric, to the more surrealistic and incantatory poems. Levine displays a seemingly contradictory range of emotional, moral, and often profoundly religious responses to the horror and beauty in the world around him — and inside us all.

Reading the body of Levine's work, one senses a fiercely honest exploration of the totality of a complex human life and a particular personality moving about the crucial arenas of our common experience. One also senses a complex, intense, and disciplined sensibility's response — in pity and in condemnation, in anger and in awe, in lamentation and in song — to the conflicting phenomena of contemporary life that offer us these choices: to sit on the father's shoulders and awaken in another world, to pray to become all we'll never be, or to offer ourselves as sacrificial animals in the slaughterhouse of a blasphemous industrial liturgy of annihilation. Philip Levine's answer to the last alternative continues to be a resounding "No. Not this pig."

Poetry: *On the Edge* (1963). *Silent in America: Vivas for Those Who Failed* (1965). *Not This Pig* (1968). *Five Detroits* (1970). *Pili's Wall* (1971). *Red Dust* (1971). *They Feed They Lion* (1972). *1933* (1974). *The Names of the Lost* (1976). *Ashes: Poems Old and New* (1979). *7 Years from Somewhere* (1979). *One for the Rose* (1981). *Selected Poems* (1984). *Sweet Will* (1985). *A Walk with Tom Jefferson* (1988). *What Work Is* (1991). *New Selected Poems* (1991). *The Simple Truth* (1994). *Unselected Poems* (1997). *They Feed They Lion and The Names of the Lost* (1999). *The Mercy* (1999). *Breath* (2004).

Prose: *Don't Ask*, interviews (1981). *The Bread of Time: Toward an Autobiography* (1994). *So Ask* (2003).

Translations: *Tarumba: The Selected Poems of Jaime Sabines*, with E. Trejo (1979). *Off the Map: Selected Poems of Gloria Fuertes*, with A. Long (1984).

ROBERT LOWELL (1917–1977)

Born in Boston, Robert Lowell attended Harvard and graduated from Kenyon College. A conscientious objector during World War II, he spent several months in prison. He taught at various universities, including Harvard and the University of Iowa, and he served as Consultant in Poetry at the Library of Congress. His many awards included the Pulitzer Prize, the National Book Award, the Copernicus Award, and the Bollingen Poetry Translation Award.

Lowell's career seems to have evolved in three stages. His early poems, written under the tutelage of John Crowe Ransom and Allen Tate, were intricately wrought and complex, clearly reflecting the dictates of the New Criticism. Emerging out of a Christian spiritual tradition, an English poetic tradition influenced by the French symbolists, and a New England historical and ethical tradition, they were poems written by a young man whose sensibilities and talent began to mature at a time when T. S. Eliot was an overpowering presence in American poetry.

In *Life Studies* — perhaps his most brilliant and significant book, and the result of an encounter with W. D. Snodgrass — Lowell implicitly renounced many of the New Critics' formal demands and Eliot's cultural and spiritual vision. These poems were less consciously wrought and extremely intimate. As M. L. Rosenthal has observed, the orchestration of *Life Studies* traced the deterioration of Western civilization, the U.S. republic, Lowell's own family, and his very self. In the powerful concluding poem, "Skunk Hour," Lowell asserted, "The season's ill . . . / My mind's not right." And in this cultural and personal wasteland, he found no kingfisher, no Christ diving in fire.

"I am tired. Everyone's tired of my turmoil," Lowell wrote in *For the Union Dead*, and this realization marked the start of a third phase in his career. The poems grew more serenely formal, less intricate, and surely less hysterical. In *Near the Ocean*, he turned to muted couplets; his *Notebook* and *History*, though tracing intimate aspects of his life, were sonnet sequences. Although their central theme of the desolation and deterioration of humans and their world remained, Lowell was able to view that drama with a measure of objectivity, distance, and — at times — a detachment that bordered on ennui. In his last book, *Day by Day*, Lowell returned once again to the lyrical and personal modes; however, despite the intimacy of subject matter, the poems continued to be marked by a kind of intellectual detachment.

Poetry: *Land of Unlikeness* (1944). *Lord Weary's Castle* (1946). *The Mills of the Kavanaughs* (1951). *Life Studies* (1959). *Imitations* (1961). *For the Union Dead*

(1964). *The Old Glory*, verse drama (1965; expanded edition, 1968). *Near the Ocean* (1967). *Notebook 1967–1968* (1969). *Notebook* (augmented edition, 1970). *For Lizzie and Harriet* (1973). *History* (1973). *The Dolphin* (1973). *Selected Poems* (1976). *Day by Day* (1977). *Collected Poems* (2000).

Prose: *Robert Lowell: Interviews and Memoirs*, edited by J. Myers (1987). *Collected Prose*, edited by R. Giroux (1990). *The Letters of Robert Lowell*, edited by S. Hamilton (2005).

Translations: POETRY: *The Voyage and Other Versions of Poems by Baudelaire* (1968). VERSE DRAMA: *Phaedra*, by Racine (1961). *Prometheus*, by Aeschylus (1969). *The Oresteia of Aeschylus* (1979).

WILLIAM MATTHEWS (1942–1997)

Born in Cincinnati, Ohio, William Matthews was a graduate of Yale University and the University of North Carolina at Chapel Hill. He began his teaching career at Wells College and subsequently taught at Cornell, the University of Colorado, the University of Washington, Columbia University, and City College of New York. Cofounding editor of Lillabulero Press and its magazine from 1966 to 1974, Matthews received grants and fellowships from the National Endowment for the Arts and the Guggenheim and Ingram Merrill Foundations. In 1996, he was the recipient of the National Book Critics Circle Award, and in 1997 received the Modern Poetry Association's Ruth Lilly Award.

Like the work of other poets whose first books appeared in the late 1960s and early 1970s, William Matthews's early poems reflect both a direct and indirect involvement in the continuing aesthetic ferment of the time, wrestling with fundamental assumptions regarding the use of symbol, irony, and artistic detachment. Matthews's range of subjects and themes is as broad and challenging as the aesthetic and cultural strands that shaped his work. But whether the ostensible subject is basketball, onions, or hiking with his sons, a Matthews poem is always "about" much more. If "Men at My Father's Funeral" and "Grief" probe the source of the creative impulse, "the flesh made word," "Moving Again" and "The Cloister" question its purpose, its "fierce privacy." In the latter poem, Matthews quarrels with his muse and accepts the rigorous self-discipline and essential loneliness imposed upon any serious practitioner of the craft. "Pissing off the Back of the Boat in the Nivernais Canal" begins as a funny take on the drunken poet's penis but draws the reader into a meditation on the relationship between penis and tongue as they concern sex and the artistic process; it is a poem about flesh and the imagination, and, ultimately, it is a poem about poetry itself.

If "Pissing off the Back of the Boat" affirms the inseparability of desire and linguistic creation in Matthews's poetry, it also signals his abiding search for profundity within humor and lightness at the core of the profound.

Indeed, his poems consistently seek to unite perceived dualities. "Each emotion lusts for its opposite," Matthews wrote. Thus, there is truth at the heart of fiction; excellence uncoils with a "sweet ferocity"; and, despite "death's old sweet song . . . / [a] relentless joy infests the blues all day."

Poetry: *Ruining the New Road* (1970). *Sleek for the Long Flight* (1972). *Sticks and Stones* (1975). *Rising and Falling* (1979). *Flood* (1982). A *Happy Childhood* (1984). *Foreseeable Futures* (1987). *Blues If You Want* (1989). *Selected Poems and Translations* (1992). *Time & Money* (1995). *After All: Last Poems* (1998). *Search Party: The Collected Poems*, edited by S. Matthews and S. Plumly (2004).

Prose: *Curiosities*, essays (1989). *The Poetry Blues* (2001).

Translations: A *World Rich in Anniversaries*, prose poems by Jean Follain, with M. Feeney (1979). *The Mortal City: 100 Epigrams of Martial* (1995).

JAMES MERRILL (1926–1995)

James Merrill was born in New York City. He attended Lawrenceville School, graduated from Amherst College, and served in the U.S. Army. Unlike most of his contemporaries, James Merrill did not seek a professional teaching career. His many awards and distinctions included the Pulitzer Prize, the National Book Award, and the Rebekah Bobbitt National Prize for Poetry awarded by the Library of Congress.

Most critics would agree that James Merrill's poetry has consistently reflected the influence of New Criticism and that his mentor is more likely W. H. Auden than William Carlos Williams. Indeed, in Merrill's long trilogy *The Changing Light at Sandover*, Auden's spirit is Merrill's "guide." Clearly, Merrill was a masterful formalist whose manipulation of metrics and of sound — especially end rhymes — revealed the range of startling and subtle nuances in language in much the same way as Rothko unveils the nuances of color in painting. Even in what seem to be more personal poems, one is never quite sure whether the speaker is Merrill or a persona. Most of his poems are marked by a tone edged with a measure of ironic detachment that, in some literary circles — where irony is blasphemy and guts rule — might be considered indicative of high, albeit elegant, decadence.

When so many poets of his generation lead their readers into the bedlam of their tortured souls and the bedrooms of their monstrous marriages — and, indeed, into their very own and much-used beds — one emerges from the surroundings of Merrill's poetry with the heady sense of having lingered in a rather rarefied atmosphere. (Indeed, as a son of Charles Merrill, the cofounder of the Merrill Lynch stock brokerage house, James Merrill was born into enormous wealth and privilege.) This is the physical, moral, and aesthetic world as perceived by Proust rather than by Baudelaire, by Henry James rather than by Walt Whitman. This is the world where, in Merrill's words, "Light into the olive entered / And was oil," an arena of human experience where it does seem that "the world beneath the world is brightening."

And yet, despite the seeming orderliness of his poems, Merrill's Weltanschauung and aesthetic often lead him — and us — to the very edge of chaos. Merrill's persona in "Laboratory Poem" knows that the heart must climb "through violence into exquisite disciplines." And whatever entrances into immortality that art may offer, it leaves us *and* the artist with that unnerving realization that "the life it asks of us is a dog's life." Thus, if poetry, if speech "is but a mouth pressed / Lightly and humbly against the angel's hand" in a Rilkean attempt to impress the angel with the things of this world, it's distinctly possible that this very angel "does not want even these few lines written." In short, in a society where "Art, Public Spirit / Ignorance, Economics, Love of Self / Hatred of Self" are earnestly dedicated to "*sparing* us the worst" and just as earnestly *inspire* the worst, Merrill's poems stand on the edge of chaos, radiant attempts to survive its meanings — and our own.

Poetry: *The Black Swan* (1946). *First Poems* (1951). *The Country of a Thousand Years of Peace and Other Poems* (1959; revised edition, 1970). *Water Street* (1962). *Nights and Days* (1966). *The Fire Screen* (1969). *Braving the Elements* (1972). *The Yellow Pages* (1974). *Divine Comedies* (1976). *Mirabell: Book of Numbers* (1978). *Scripts for the Pageant* (1980). *From the First Nine: Poems 1946–1976* (1982). *The Changing Light at Sandover* (1982). *Late Settings* (1985). *The Inner Room* (1988). *Selected Poems* (1992). *A Scattering of Salts* (1995). *Collected Poems* (2002).

Prose: FICTION: *The Seraglio* (1957). *The (Diblos) Notebook* (1965). *Collected Novels and Plays*, edited by J. D. McClatchy and S. Yenser (2002). *Collected Prose*, edited by J. D. McClatchy and S. Yenser (2004). ESSAYS: *Recitative: Prose*, edited and with an introduction by J. D. McClatchy (1986). AUTOBIOGRAPHY: *A Different Person: A Memoir* (1993).

W. S. MERWIN (1927)

W. S. Merwin was born in New York City and educated at Princeton. He was tutor to Robert Graves's son for a year, but — unlike most of his contemporaries — he has not had a teaching career. Since 1951, he has devoted time to his writings and translations and, more recently, to ecological concerns. He currently resides in Hawaii. In addition to the Pulitzer Prize and the Shelley Memorial Award, he has received grants from the National Endowment for the Arts, the Rockefeller Foundation, the Academy of American Poets, the National Institute of Arts and Letters, and the Arts Council of Great Britain.

One of the most prolific poets and translators of his generation, Merwin is among those contemporary poets (others include Adrienne Rich and James Wright) whose talents were originally shaped by New Criticism and whose styles underwent a radical change in the course of their careers. His early poems were elegant, controlled, symmetrical, and often concerned with myth and archetype. However, the appearance of *The Drunk in the Furnace* suggested a dissatisfaction with old techniques: his forms were looser; his language appeared less contrived and closer to the spoken word. Like other poets of the period, he turned to family history and individual suffering in search of larger, more immediate patterns of human experience.

Merwin's most radical departure — and most exciting style — appeared still later in *The Moving Target*. Open and terse, these surrealistic poems — and most of the poems that Merwin has published since — are controlled not as much by a craftsman's delicate hand as by a powerful imagination. And they rise out of the depths of a more personal, sometimes enigmatic necessity. Merwin's aesthetics are clear in the statement that he wrote for *Naked Poetry* (edited by Stephen Berg and Robert Mezey): "In an age when time and technique encroach hourly, or appear to, on the source itself of poetry, it seems as though what is needed for any particular nebulous hope that may become a poem is not a manipulable, more or less predictably recurring pattern, but an unduplicatable resonance, something that would be like an echo except that it is repeating no sound. Something that always belonged to it: its sense and its conformation before it entered words."

Throughout his career, one of Merwin's dominant concerns has been death — or perhaps more specifically, extinction. The journey motif that critics have recognized in Merwin's poetry is emblematic of all life's motion toward death. However, in later poems, this concern doesn't necessarily focus on any sudden or cataclysmic end of life — although many of his later poems are clearly laments for the destruction of our ecology and, thus, our society and culture. Rather, it is more manifest in powerful and menacing shadows surrounding frail light, in sound struggling against the tyranny of silence, in the slow but seemingly inevitable transformation of all organic life into inert matter. And if Merwin agrees with Berryman that the individual has undertaken the biggest job of all — *son fin* — Merwin has also erected a powerful emblem of his vision in his prose piece, "Tergvinder's Stone." In the presence of a mysterious, almost mystical stone in the middle of his living room and his life, Merwin's central character kneels in the darkness of the stone, converses with the stone, and even in the silence of the stone "knows that it is peace."

Poetry: *A Mask for Janus* (1952). *The Dancing Bears,* (1954). *Green with Beasts* (1956). *The Drunk in the Furnace* (1960). *The Moving Target* (1963). *The Lice* (1967). *Animae: Poems* (1969). *The Carrier of Ladders* (1970). *Writings to an Unfinished Accompaniment* (1973). *The First Four Books of Poems* (1975). *The Compass Flower* (1977). *Finding the Islands* (1982). *Opening the Hand* (1983). *Selected Poems* (1988). *The Rain in the Trees* (1988). *Travels* (1993). *The Second Four Books* *of Poems* (1993). *The Vixen* (1995). *Flower & Hand: Poems 1977–1983: The Compass Flower: Opening the Hand: Feathers from the Hill* (1997). *Folding Cliffs: A Narrative* (1998). *The River Sound* (1999). *Pupil* (2001). *Migration: New and Selected Poems* (2005).

Prose: FICTION: *A New Right Arm* (1969). *The Miner's Pale Children* (1970). *Houses and Travellers* (1977). AUTOBIOGRAPHY: *Unframed Originals* (1982). ESSAYS: *Regions of Memory: Uncollected Prose 1949–1982*, edited by E. Folsom and C. Nelson (1987). *The Lost Upland* (1992). *The Mays of Ventadorn* (2002). *The Ends of the Earth* (2004).

Translations: POETRY: *The Poem of the Cid* (1959). *Spanish Ballads* (1961). *The Song of Roland* (1963). *Selected Translations 1948–1968* (1968). *Transparence of the World*, by Jean Follain (1969). *Voices*, by Antonio Porchia (1969/1988). *Twenty Love Poems and a Song of Despair*, by Pablo Neruda (1969). *Chinese Figures: Second Series* (1971). *Japanese Figures* (1971). *Asian Figures* (1973). *Selected Poems of Osip Mandelstam*, with C. Brown (1974). *Vertical Poetry*, by Roberto Juarroz (1977/1988). *Selected Translations 1968–1978* (1979). *The Peacock's Egg: Love Poems from Ancient India*, with J. M. Masson (1981). *From the Spanish Morning* (1985). *Sun at Midnight*, by Muso Soseki (1989). *Pieces of Shadow: Selected Poems of Jaime Sabines* (1996). *East Window: The Asian Translations* (1999). PROSE: *The Satires of Perseus* (1960). *The Life of Lazarillo de Tormes: His Fortunes and Adversities* (1962). *Products of the Perfected Civilization*, by Sebastian Chamfort (1969). DRAMA: *Iphigenia at Aulis*, by Euripides; with G. E. Dimmock, Jr. (1977). *Four French Plays* (1985).

MARILYN NELSON (1946)

Born in Cleveland, Ohio, Marilyn Nelson was educated at the University of California–Davis, the University of Pennsylvania, and the University of Minnesota. She has taught at Lane Community College (Oregon), the Norre Nissum Seminary Fellowship in Denmark, Saint Olaf College (Minnesota), and since 1978, the University of Connecticut. She has been the recipient of the Annisfield-Wolf Award and a fellowship from the National Endowment for the Arts.

A poet of domestic plenitude and spiritual bounty, Marilyn Nelson writes from the African-American literary tradition that acknowledges, without much bitterness, "the fact of oppression" and tempers rage with intergenerational love, humor, and religious sensibility. To her, "the body" represents community rather than the individual, and the self remains only an extension of that hub, that central "homeplace" from which the poet engages social and theological issues. Biblical allusions, family history, and folk wisdom intertwine in affirmative sequences that honor the past while deepening the present. "I had originally intended 'Mama' of my second book, *Mama's Promises* [1985], to be not only myself, my mother, and other mothers whose stories I snitched for the poems, but also the Divine Mother, the feminine face of God," she has stated. This movement outward from a central source toward communal imagination becomes a redemptive element not only in the lives of those embraced but also in the process that re-creates those lives. Nelson's third book, *The Homeplace* (1990), gives play to this idea of *elevation*, serving as an homage to her father and his comrades, the black World War II aviators known as the Tuskegee Airmen.

The "Abba Jacob" poems of *Magnificat* (1994) and *The Fields of Praise: New and Selected Poems* (1997) "imitate the format of the apothegms of the Desert Fathers, the earlier Christian monks," Nelson has noted, and their subject, the discipline required to approach spiritual wisdom, had been anticipated by the taut lines and nods to traditional forms — sonnets, villanelles, and ballads — that began to appear in her work in *The Homeplace*. Such discipline has its own requirements, though, and in poems that confront racial violence at home and abroad, Nelson reconfigures her terms of affirmation in the light of "the atrocities we commit and bear," placing faith in the power of language, its incantatory and restorative spell: "*Justice* I willed myself *peace* to unknow / *conscience* the evil I saw *dignity* / pinpricked in her *faith* blue *humanity* eyes."

Poetry: *For the Body* (1978). *Mama's Promises* (1985). *The Homeplace* (1990). *Magnificat* (1994). *The Fields of Praise: New and Selected Poems* (1997). *Carver: A Life in Poems* (2000). *Fortune's Bones: The Manumission Requiem* (2004). *The Cachoeira Tales, and Other Poems* (2005). *A Wreath for Emmett Till* (2005).

NAOMI SHIHAB NYE (1952)

Naomi Shihab Nye, born of a Palestinian father and an American mother, grew up in St. Louis, Missouri; Jerusalem; and San Antonio, Texas, graduating from Trinity University in 1974. Nye has been a visiting writer at a wide variety of universities, including Berkeley and Hawaii. She has participated in three Arts America tours in the Middle East and Asia, and her awards include the I. B. Lavin Award from the Academy of American Poets, a Guggenheim Fellowship, and four Pushcart Prizes.

A friend and informal student of William Stafford, Naomi Nye probes that vein of poetry unearthed by that modest poet. Hers is a quiet, gentle voice that can celebrate the beauty of such simple items as melons, bananas, and peppers through which she can learn the "secrets of dying, / how to do it gracefully . . . softening in silence . . . / finely tuned to its own skin." Nye understands that even in the life of the imagination and deeper into the life of memories, therefore history, the dust-covered things of this and other worlds "have only to be touched lightly / to shine."

Her Middle Eastern heritage is also vibrant in her poems. It is the texture of experience: her father balancing a tray of coffee which becomes the center of the flower of guests. It is the source of anguish and her understanding of it, "the man with laughing eyes" who reminds her, "until you speak Arabic — / you will not understand pain." And what seems to be a somewhat simplified view of experience turns into epiphany when she goes out into the slick street to hail a cab "by shouting *Pain!* and it stopped / in every language." Her faith in such consolation, the "Vocabulary of Dearness," remains evident throughout her work. In "Steps," the "thick swoops and curls of [newly painted] Arabic letters stay moist / and glistening till tomorrow when the children show up," and it's "One of these children [who] will tell a story that keeps her people / alive."

Poetry: *Different Ways to Pray* (1980). *Hugging the Jukebox* (1982). *The Yellow Glove* (1986). *Red Suitcase* (1994). *Words Under the Words: Selected Poems* (1995). *Fuel* (1998). *Mint Snowball* (2001). *19 Varieties of Gazelle: Poems of the Middle East* (2002). *You and Yours* (2005).

Prose: PARAGRAPHS: *Mint* (1991). ESSAYS: *Never in a Hurry* (1996).

FRANK O'HARA (1926–1966)

Before his untimely, accidental death on Fire Island, Frank O'Hara was associate curator and then curator of the international program at the Museum of Modern Art in New York and an editorial associate for *Art News*. Born in Baltimore, O'Hara was educated at the New England Conservatory of Music, Harvard, and the University of Michigan. He collaborated in various projects involving poetry and the visual arts, and in 1956 was awarded a Ford Fellowship for drama.

Before the publication of his *Collected Poems* (and the companion volume, *Poems Retrieved*), O'Hara was almost a closet poet, the product and hero of a pop-camp imagination whose seeming antipoems were often light and chatty, marked by a spontaneity, exuberance, and wit that were characteristic of his contemporaries in the visual arts. His most memorable poems, like the paintings of Oldenburg and Warhol, focused on the all-too-obvious things of our urban and suburban world: hamburgers, malts, cigarettes, instant coffee. Looming above that world were its own godly artifacts: Lichtenstein's suprahuman heroes of the comic strips and Warhol's movie stars. Their mythic proportions were — and continue to be — the dimensions of contemporary human fantasies and dreams of redemption. Moreover, in O'Hara's poems there is the stinging, if somewhat hysterical, crackle of a melancholy comment on the absurdity of such hollow rites.

It now seems clear that O'Hara's scope and power as a poet extend far beyond the circumscribed world of a merely campy and gay subculture. One leaves the body of O'Hara's poetry — and his sense of what constitutes the identifiable substance and quality of our communal experience — with a verbal-emotional equivalent of Kandinsky's acute perception of "the particular spiritual perfume of the triangle." One also leaves the existential world of O'Hara's poems with a fuller understanding of the truth of Cocteau's rejection of history: "*J'ai une tres mauvaise memoire de l'avenir.*"

Poetry: A *City Winter and Other Poems* (1952). *Meditations in an Emergency* (1957). *Hartigan and Rivers with O'Hara: An Exhibition of Pictures, with Poems* (1959). *Second Avenue* (1960). *Odes* (1960). *Lunch Poems* (1964). *Love Poems: Tentative Title* (1965). *In Memory of My Feelings: A Selection of Poems*, edited by B. Berkson (1967). *Odes* (1969). *The Collected Poems of Frank O'Hara*, edited by D. Allen (1971). *The Selected Poems of Frank O'Hara*, edited by D. Allen (1974). *Hymns of St. Bridget*, with Bill Berkson (1974). *Early Poems 1946–1951*, edited by D. Allen (1976). *Poems Retrieved*, edited by D. Allen (1977). *To Be True to a City*, edited by J. Elledge (1990).

Prose: *Jackson Pollock* (1959). A *Frank O'Hara Miscellany* (1974). *Art Chronicles 1954–1966* (1975). *Standing Still and Walking in New York*, notes and essays, edited by D. Allen (1975). *Early Writing*, edited by D. Allen (1977). *Selected Plays* (1978).

SHARON OLDS (1942)

Born in San Francisco in 1942, Sharon Olds was educated at Stanford University and Columbia University. Her first book, *Satan Says* (1980), was the recipient of the inaugural San Francisco Poetry Center Award, and her second, *The Dead and the Living* (1984), received both the Lamont Prize from the Academy of American Poets and the National Book Critics Circle Award. She has received fellowships from the Guggenheim Foundation and the National Endowment for the Arts. Olds teaches at New York University and at Goldwater Hospital on Roosevelt Island in New York.

Critics have commented on the influence of Sylvia Plath's poems on Olds's work, and certainly Olds has written in the Confessional mode, though the author and her narrators should not be confused. Whoever speaks them, her poems have a startling power and urgency, even a breathlessness, as if any momentary hesitation on the speaker's part, any self-censorship, would inhibit the work and disallow its existence. Her narrative thrust seems unable to restrain itself and often suits the brutal revelations of the poems. Richard Wilbur has described Plath's work, her "brilliant negative," as "free and helpless and unjust," suggesting that Plath writes out of only one aspect of personality, and such description might apply to some of Olds's work as well. Yet Olds's insistence on formerly taboo subjects, her intensely personal emphases and erotic self-absorption, convey a politics, sexual and otherwise, that opens her poems to a more inclusive perspective.

Her subject is the body and the space it inhabits, as well as the violations of that space. For Olds, the body offers a defining sense of self against the father's psychological abuse, and becomes, like language, a source of cathartic pleasure, a means of escape from domestic dysfunction. Her sexual imagery and blunt, at times vulgar, vocabulary preserve an essential privacy by claiming selfhood, and allow love to evolve despite its history of lack. Her poems for her children, especially, display a disarming vulnerability that extends from the "egg in my side before I was born" to the larger, communal body of frailty and ceaseless regeneration.

Poetry: *Satan Says* (1980). *The Dead and the Living* (1984). *The Gold Cell* (1987). *The Father* (1992). *The Wellspring* (1995). *Blood, Tin, Straw* (1999). *The Unswept Room* (2002). *Strike Sparks: Selected Poems, 1980–2002* (2004).

MARY OLIVER (1935)

Born in Cleveland and educated at Ohio State University and Vassar College, Mary Oliver has been visiting professor in creative writing and poet-in-residence at Case Western Reserve, Sweet Briar College, Duke University, and Bennington College as well as a member of the writing staff at the Fine Arts Work Center in Provincetown, Massachusetts, where she lives. Her awards include the Achievement Award from the American Academy and Institute of Arts and Letters, a Guggenheim Fellowship, the Alice Fay di Castagnola Award from the Poetry Society of America, and a creative writing fellowship from the Literature Program of the National Endowment for the Arts. She was awarded the Pulitzer Prize in 1984 and the National Book Award in 1992.

To read Oliver's poems is to immerse oneself in a world of intense physical sensation made doubly acute by the emotional transformation that Oliver achieves while registering the impact of the physical world on the world of her feelings: the "icy kick" of water, "the small kingdoms" of birds and insects breathing in the dark, the fish at spawning time following "the fragrance spilling / from her old birth pond," "the crows, plump / As black rocks in the cold trees" in winter. Reminiscent of the poetry of Theodore Roethke, James Wright, and Emily Dickinson in the precise observations of the things of this world, Oliver's poems have a physical impact like "the dark thorns of the wild grapes / on the unsuspecting tongue."

Although somewhat ambiguous, that image of pleasure and pain is also central to Oliver's hard-earned vision profoundly accepting an essential tension between the polarities that define the boundaries of all experience — whether in the physical world, in the realm of human relationships, or in the self. There is great pleasure and beauty and joy in the poems of Mary Oliver, but there is also a commensurate (though muted) measure of pain resulting from the recognition of one's full awareness of those elements of the natural and human world that transport and transform us, giving us a glimpse of eternity, perhaps, or of some kind of immortality — a recognition that also gives us a fuller awareness of the world's, and of our own, mortality.

The acceptance of the hard truths of mortal existence is at the heart and boundaries of Oliver's poems. If thrown into the water and told to sink or swim, what we learn isn't necessarily how to swim but rather "How to put off, one by one, / Dreams and pity, love and grace, — / How to survive in any place." Art in itself is no escape. While the beauty of music may be a "lick of flame" that transports and transforms the audience, for the artist it is only a momentary stay against "the duties of flesh and home," perhaps against "the knife at the throat," and in fact, against that very "death in the metronome." "To live in this world," Oliver reminds us, requires three measures of acceptance: "to love what is mortal; / to hold it / against your bones knowing / your own life depends on it; / and, when the time comes to let it go, / to let it go." If life, love, and work do not negate our mortality, then our acceptance of it may allow us to view our daily deaths as repeated vanishings "into something better." In Mary Oliver's poems, such acceptance is epiphany.

Poetry: *No Voyage and Other Poems* (1965). *The River Styx, Ohio and Other Poems* (1972). *The Night Traveler* (1978). *Sleeping in the Forest* (1979). *Twelve Moons* (1979). *American Primitive* (1983). *Dreamwork* (1986). *House of Light* (1990). *New and Selected Poems* (1992). *White Pine* (1996). *West Wind* (1997). *The Leaf and the Cloud* (2000). *Owls and Other Fantasies* (2003). *What Do We Know* (2003). *Why I Wake Early* (2004).

Prose: *A Poetry Handbook* (1994). *Blue Pastures* (1995). *Rules for the Dance* (1998). *Winter Hours* (1999). *Blue Iris* (2004). *Long Life* (2004).

MICHAEL PALMER (1943)

I think Michael Palmer was delivered two blocks astray in 1943 because he was aborted at our address two months before. Now he has arrived I think a long way from the Rhinelander Apartments in Greenwich Village with a poetry addressed to occupant to refund the Indians for the Manhattan sell. So wrote poet Robert Duncan for the biographical note to Palmer's first full-length book, though the publisher replaced it with the more conventional *Michael Palmer was born in New York City in 1943. He was educated at Harvard University and now lives and works in San Francisco.* Such evasiveness, playfulness, and collaboration remain at the heart of Palmer's poetry. A choreographer as well as a writer, Palmer has been the recipient of fellowships from the National Endowment for the Arts and the Guggenheim Foundation and of awards from the Lila Wallace–Reader's Digest Fund and the Poetry Society of America. In 1999, he was appointed Chancellor of the Academy of American Poets.

"But the truth is that the linguistic field is never entirely stable," Palmer has stated, so for him poetry is "a site of slippages and folds, of irrational commands from the *Melos*, where a multiplicity of meanings may be joined in a word, and where the *nothing* beneath is never far from the surface." Often associated with the "Language" poets, Palmer combines gestures of dance — "In the poem he learns to turn and turn" — with theatrical polyphonies toward emphasizing the dislocations and absences that characterize his craft: "I became a painter of paintings briefly // then I eliminated paint," and "I have no way of communicating that I prefer this painting of nothing to that one of something." Yet qualities of the traditional lyric often infuse his work, and if his poems purposefully lack a central core or triggering source, it is because language itself, torn from narrative and fractured of meaning, offers a momentary stay against leaden social and political discourse and reenacts sensual pleasure — not only that of childhood in its word-making but also that of adulthood in its implicit beckoning: "as is the case with absence generally, a trace of the erotic had lingered in the atmosphere."

Coolly abstract, erudite, filled with clues and intimations toward some central truth at which we can never fully arrive, and gorgeous in their "ungovernable" musings, Palmer's poems celebrate their own making. In a time when meaning seems dictated by political agency, each poem then becomes an act of resistance, a civil disobedience, "Pages torn from their spines and added to the pyre, so that they will resemble thought."

Poetry: *Plan of the City of O* (1971). *Blake's Newton* (1972). *C's Song* (1973). *The Circular Gates* (1974). *Without Music* (1977). *Alogon* (1980). *Transparency of the Mirror* (1980). *Notes for Echo Lake* (1981). *First Figure* (1984). *Songs for Sarah*, with I. Petlin ((1987). *For a Reading* (1988). *Sun* (1988). *An Alphabet Underground* (1993). *At Passages* (1995). *The Lion Bridge: Selected Poems 1972–1995* (1998). *The Promises of Glass* (2000). *Codes Appearing: Poems 1979–1988* (2001). *Company of Moths* (2005).

Prose: *The Danish Notebook* (1999).

Translations: *Voyelles*, by Arthur Rimbaud (1980). *Jonah Who Will Be 25 in the Year 2000*, by Alain Tanner and John Berger (1983). *The Surrealists Look at Art*, with N. Cole (1990). *Blue Vitriol*, by Alexei Parshchikov, with J. High and M. Molnar (1994). *Theory of Tables*, by Emmanuel Hocquard (1996). *Three Moral Tales*, by Emmanuel Hocquard (1996).

CARL PHILLIPS (1959)

Born in Everett, Washington, Carl Phillips attended Harvard, the University of Massachusetts at Amherst, and Harvard again to study classical philology before pursuing an advanced degree in creative writing at Boston University. "I consider the study of Classics to have been the most significant influence on my writing," he has stated. "I believe I learned most about poetry from reading — in the original Latin and Greek — the political speeches of Cicero and those that occur in the historical writings of Thucydides, respectively." He has been the recipient of the Morse Poetry Prize for his first volume, *In the Blood* (1992), an Academy of American Poets Prize, fellowships from the Library of Congress and the Guggenheim

Foundation, and the Kingsley Tufts Award. Phillips taught high school Latin for eight years and, more recently, has taught at Harvard, the University of Iowa, and Washington University in St. Louis.

In an interview with Charles H. Rowell in *Callaloo*, Carl Phillips names his subjects: "hunger, loss, devotion" and "the nature of desire." Avoiding traditional narrative and conventional syntax, he trusts instead intuition and its associative imagery, combined with densely textured phrases, to convey an erotic and spiritual intellect in the flux of ceaseless self-examination. Oddly Puritan in measure and restraint, austere enough in language so that each word bears its particular weight, his poems seem hushed and reverential, barely spoken, the hesitant shifts of the mind given utterance and eloquence. "I think of writing as prayer," Phillips told Rowell, then added, "And sex is also prayer." This sexual element in his work, homo-erotic and coolly passionate, infuses his philosophical musings with moral urgency: "the yearnings of the body," Phillips told David Dykes in *Excerpt*, "can serve as metaphors or parallels for the yearnings of the soul." In un-assuming yet profoundly moving meditations on hunger for man and God, loss of human love and heavenly dispensation, and devotion to the sacraments of desire, Phillips delineates those planes where the profane and sacred intersect in numinous coupling.

Poetry: *In the Blood* (1992). *Cortege* (1995). *From the Devotions* (1998). *Pastoral* (2000). *The Tether* (2001). *Rock Harbor* (2002). *The Rest of Love* (2004). *Riding Westward* (2006).

Prose: *Coin of the Realm* (2004).

Translation: *Philoctetes*, by Sophocles (2003).

SYLVIA PLATH (1932–1963)

A native of Boston and a graduate of Smith College, in 1955 Sylvia Plath won a Fulbright Scholarship to Newnham College, Cambridge. While in England, she met and married the British poet Ted Hughes. After she taught for a year at Smith (1957–1958), the couple returned to England where in 1960 she published her first book of poems and subsequently completed her novel, *The Bell Jar*. On February 11, 1963, Sylvia Plath committed suicide.

A friend of Anne Sexton and student of Robert Lowell, Sylvia Plath wrote poems that were intended to sound and to feel brutally personal, almost unbearably painful. Her poems are not merely *about* acute mental and emotional suffering; their very structure — the controlled flow of images, the insistent appositives — draws the reader fully into that suffering. Indeed, her later poems are so well crafted that some critics have argued, wrongheadedly, that she seemed engaged in "a murderous art" — that after writing such frighteningly honest and painfully personal poems, her suicide was virtually inevitable. As a *critical premise*, such an argument is utter nonsense, its absurdity manifestly clear when transferred to another artist and to his or her work. If Plath virtually had no choice but to commit suicide after writing the poems in *Ariel*, then what inevitable choice did Melville have after writing *Moby Dick?*

What makes Plath interesting as a poet is not primarily her ostensible subject matter and tone; rather, the success of the poems depends largely on her precision of observation, imagination, and language — as well as on the mastery of her craftsmanship. For example, the onion simile in "Cut" not only accurately describes the swirls of a thumb print but also serves as the entire poem's controlling metaphor. Moreover, in such poems as "Cut" and "Lady Lazarus," or even in a celebrated poem such as "Daddy," there is also a strong measure of wit and humor — albeit black — often conveyed through resuscitated clichés that manage to rescue the poems from pathos.

On more than one occasion, Plath insisted that even the most personal poetry cannot be merely a *cri de coeur*; it must be informed by and partici-pate in a greater historical drama. Her own poems participate fully in the vibrant Puritan tradition, not only through her preoccupation with evil (which is utterly distinct from personal suffering) but also through her meta-physical and emblematic technique. They also occur against a constant his-torical drama, especially the contemporary phenomenon of Nazi Germany out of which she fabricates a modern myth. In short, the pain, the suffer-ing, the fine edge of madness — all are ultimately crafted and controlled by the poet's reasoned and careful hand flashing a measure of genius.

Poetry: *The Colossus* (1962). *Uncollected Poems* (1965). *Ariel* (1966; restored edition, 2004). *Crossing the Water: Transitional Poems* (1971). *Crystal Gazer and Other Poems* (1971). *Lyonesse: Poems* (1971). *Winter Trees* (1972). *The Collected Poems of Sylvia Plath*, edited by T. Hughes (1981). *Stings*, original drafts of the poem in facsimile, with an essay by S. R. Van Dyne (1982). *The Voice of the Poet*, edited by J. D. McClatchy (1999).

Prose: *The Bell Jar*, novel (under the pseudonym Victoria Lucas, 1963; under the name Sylvia Plath, 1971). *Letters Home*, edited by A. Plath (1975). *Johnny Panic and the Bible of Dreams: Short Stories, Prose, and Diary Excerpts*, edited by T. Hughes (1979). *The Journals of Sylvia Plath*, edited by T. Hughes and F. McCullough (1982). *The Unabridged Journals of Sylvia Plath: 1950–1962*, edited by K. V. Kukil (2000).

ADRIENNE RICH (1929)

Adrienne Rich's first book of poems won the Yale Series of Younger Poets award while she was an undergraduate at Radcliffe. She has taught at Bran-deis, Swarthmore, Harvard, and Columbia, and her many honors include the Dorothea Tanning Prize for "mastery in the art of poetry" from the

Academy of American Poets, the MacArthur Fellowship, the Ruth Lilly
Poetry Prize, and the Poets' Prize. In 1974, Rich and Allen Ginsberg were
cowinners of the National Book Award for poetry. Rich rejected her share
as a personal award, but in a statement she wrote with the two other
women nominated that year, she accepted the award in the name of all
women. In 1997, she declined the National Medal for the Arts. Rich's
letter, reprinted in the *New York Times*, stated: "I could not accept such an
award from President Clinton or this White House because the very
meaning of art, as I understand it, is incompatible with the cynical politics
of this administration. . . . [A]rt means nothing if it simply decorates the
dinner-table of power which holds it hostage. The radical disparities of
wealth and power in America are widening at a devastating rate. A President cannot meaningfully honor certain token artists while the people at
large are so dishonored."

Adrienne Rich has described her poems written since the late 1970s
as "a coming-home to the darkest and richest source of my poetry: sex,
sexuality, sexual wounds, sexual identity, sexual politics: many names for
pieces of one whole. I feel [this poetry] continues the work I've been trying
to do — breaking down the artificial barriers between private and public,
between Vietnam and the lovers' bed, between the deepest images we
carry out of our dreams and the most daylight events 'out in the world.'
This is the intention and longing behind everything I write."

Sexual identity and its profound political implications are indeed
among the substantial sources of Rich's work, especially in her courageous
and beautiful sequence of love poems addressed to another woman — a
theme that reappears in *The Dream of a Common Language*. Moreover,
even as she speaks about and for women, her poetry is informed by a vigorous intelligence that transcends any unilateral sense of sexuality and
politics; her poetry reaches beyond the limited periphery of any "movement" to become a profoundly personal statement forged into a powerful
description of our common condition.

If some of Rich's poems can be read as a "diving into the wreck," it is
crucial to realize that her purpose is not only "to see the damage that was
done" but also to catch a glimpse of "the treasures that prevail." Like the
astronomer in "Planetarium," she is "a woman trying to translate pulsations / into images," not only for their own sake, not only for her own
sake, but "for the relief of the body / and the reconstruction of the mind."
Meanwhile, having found the courage to utter, "I choose to love this time
for once / with all my intelligence," she also can assert and demonstrate
a whole new poetry beginning here.

Poetry: *A Change of World* (1951). *The Diamond Cutters* (1955). *Snapshots of a
Daughter-in-Law: Poems 1954–1962* (1963; revised edition, 1967). *Necessities of
Life: Poems 1962–1965* (1966). *Leaflets: Poems 1965–1968* (1969). *The Will to
Change: Poems 1968–1970* (1971). *Diving into the Wreck: Poems 1971–1972*
(1973). *Poems: Selected and New, 1950–1974* (1975). *Twenty-one Love Poems*

(1976). *The Dream of a Common Language: Poems 1974–1977* (1978). *A Wild Patience Has Taken Me This Far: Poems 1978–1981* (1981). *Sources* (1983). *The Fact of a Doorframe: Poems Selected and New 1950–1984* (1985). *Your Native Land, Your Life* (1986). *Time's Power: Poems 1985–1988* (1989). *An Atlas of the Difficult World: Poems 1988–1991* (1991). *Collected Early Poems* (1993). *Dark Fields of the Republic: Poems 1991–1995* (1995). *Midnight Salvage: Poems 1995–1998* (1999). *Fox: Poems 1998–2000* (2001). *The School Among the Ruins: Poems 2000–2004* (2004).

Prose: *Of Woman Born: Motherhood as Experience and Institution* (1976). *On Lies, Secrets and Silence: Selected Prose 1966–1978* (1979). *Compulsory Heterosexuality and Lesbian Experience* (1982). *Women and Honor: Some Notes on Lying* (1982). *Blood, Bread, and Poetry: Selected Prose 1979–1985* (1986). *What Is Found There* (1993/2003). *Arts of the Possible: Essays and Conversations* (2001).

THEODORE ROETHKE (1908–1963)

Theodore Roethke was born in Saginaw, Michigan. The son of a florist, he received a bachelor's and a master's degree from the University of Michigan. He taught at Lafayette College (where he was also tennis coach and director of public relations), Michigan State, and Bennington. He also taught at the University of Washington where, after fifteen years of teaching and having received every major literary award in this country, he was eventually appointed poet-in-residence in 1962. Roethke's awards included two Guggenheim Foundation Fellowships, the Pulitzer Prize, the National Book Award twice, and the Bollingen Prize in Poetry.

In his notebook, Roethke repeatedly insisted on — and demonstrated with incredible brilliance — the crucial need for the poet to *look* to be a good reporter, and to record even the most minute details of the physical world. His poems reflect not only attention to but also reverence for the glory and terror of the physical world: "Hair on a narrow wrist bone." But Roethke also insisted that it is not enough just to look and report; the poet also must learn: "It's the poet's business to be more, not less, than a man."

The range of Roethke's poems amply demonstrates his own dictum. In addition to his often masterful control of form, his poems are marked by a precise observation of natural phenomena and include a gentle, lilting humor or ironic eroticism; a quiet horror in the face of an inevitable annihilation; and a contrapuntal tension between existential despair and the hope for transcendence. If throughout much of his life Roethke was a man who walked the void, his poems are finally a prayer and an affirmation that, although the "dark comes down on what we do," the human spirit finally cannot be overwhelmed by time.

Poetry: *Open House* (1941). *The Lost Son and Other Poems* (1948). *Praise to the End!* (1951). *The Waking: Poems 1933–1953* (1953). *Words for the Wind: The Collected Verse of Theodore Roethke* (1958). *Sequence, Sometimes Metaphysical* (1963). *The Far Field* (1964). *The Collected Poems of Theodore Roethke* (1966).

Prose: *On the Poet and His Craft: Selected Prose of Theodore Roethke*, edited by
R. J. Mills, Jr. (1965). *Selected Letters of Theodore Roethke*, edited by R. J. Mills, Jr.
(1968). *Straw for the Fire: From the Notebooks of Theodore Roethke*, selected and
arranged by D. Wagoner (1972).

ANNE SEXTON (1928–1974)

Anne Sexton was born in Newton, Massachusetts. According to the short
autobiographical note she wrote for *A Controversy of Poets* (1965), Anne
Sexton received "no visible education." However, with Sylvia Plath and
George Starbuck, she did attend seminars by Robert Lowell at Boston Uni-
versity; she participated in a summer seminar taught by W. D. Snodgrass at
Antioch College; and she was a scholar at the Radcliffe Institute. In addi-
tion to her several books of poetry, she wrote three children's books with
Maxine Kumin. Her many awards included fellowships from the American
Academy of Arts and Letters, the Radcliffe Institute, and the Ford Founda-
tion; she was awarded the Pulitzer Prize; and she was elected a fellow of the
Royal Society of Literature in London. On October 4, 1974, Anne Sexton
committed suicide.

Possibly the most famous of the personal-confessional poets, Anne
Sexton confessed to more than any of her contemporaries, re-creating experiences with unabashed honesty. Indeed, it is probable that she "confessed" to a number of events that she simply invented. In "With Mercy for
the Greedy" she wrote, "I was born / doing reference work in sin, and
born / confessing it." Like other confessional Puritans, she did just that. But
in various interviews, she also insisted that poetry is as much fabrication
as it is confession — that even the most brutal truth is shaped by imagination's energy and the artisan's hand. Moreover, doing research in sin, by
necessity, must involve a commensurate search for grace, for God. That
combination, for Sexton, was absolute — and as risky as Russian roulette.

When it wasn't yet fashionable for women to write poems about
being a woman, Sexton wrote them — openly, unashamedly, and without resorting to political rhetoric. She knew all along that the victimized
woman is "misunderstood" and "not a woman, quite." But, like Hester
Prynne, the first liberated woman in American literature, Sexton also
knew that a relationship between a man and woman could make them
gods. And she knew that she could be the ultimate survivor: "A woman like
that is not ashamed to die."

Like Sylvia Plath and John Berryman, Anne Sexton chose the moment
of her death. But before doing so — as Maxine Kumin has reported — she
found the signs of grace and hope spelled out on her typewriter keys. Sexton
knew full well that, regardless of how painful it might seem, each poem is
an affirmation and celebration of life — as is all poetry.

Poetry: *To Bedlam and Part Way Back* (1960). *All My Pretty Ones* (1962). *Live or Die* (1966). *Love Poems* (1969). *Transformations* (1971). *The Book of Folly* (1972). *The Death Notebooks* (1974). *The Awful Rowing Toward God* (1975). *45 Mercy Street*, edited by L. G. Sexton (1976). *Words for Dr. Y: Uncollected Poems with Three Stories*, edited by L. G. Sexton (1978). *Anne Sexton: The Complete Poems*, edited by L. G. Sexton, with a foreword by M. Kumin (1981). *Selected Poems of Anne Sexton*, edited with an introduction by D. W. Middlebrook and D. H. George (1988).

Prose: *Anne Sexton: A Self-Portrait in Letters*, edited by L. G. Sexton and L. Ames (1977). *No Evil Star: Selected Essays, Interviews, Prose*, edited by S. E. Colburn (1985).

CHARLES SIMIC (1938)

Charles Simic was born in Belgrade, Yugoslavia; raised in Paris, Chicago, and New York City; and received a BA from New York University. He has worked as a bookkeeper, accountant, house painter, and shirt salesman; he served in the U.S. Army from 1961 to 1963; and he has taught at California State University at Hayward. Since 1973, he has been teaching at the University of New Hampshire. He has received several PEN Translation Awards; fellowships from the National Endowment for the Arts and the Guggenheim, Ingram Merrill, and MacArthur Foundations; and the Pulitzer Prize for Poetry.

Charles Simic has described himself as "a realist *and* a surrealist, always drawn between the two." Thus, for some readers, reading Simic's poetry for the first time may be a little like walking into a landscape designed by Salvador Dali ("a meadow / Where the grass was silence / And the flowers / Words") and populated by Hieronymous Bosch ("Grandmothers who wring the necks / Of chickens; old nuns . . . / Who pull schoolboys by the ear"). This rare combination may be partly accounted for by Simic's childhood and early adolescence in wartime Yugoslavia — where, in his own words, "Hitler and Stalin fought over my soul, my destiny . . ." and his essential imagination was shaped — and by his education in the United States, where he learned the first literature he knew, American literature. Whatever the reasons, clearly this is not the realism of high seriousness found in the poetry of someone like Robert Lowell; neither is it the kind of stark and dark surrealism found in the work of poets like Mark Strand. Rather, throughout Simic's poetry, even in scenes that are emotionally devastating, there are almost always threads of humor, ranging from ironic, sophisticated mordancies to cunning peasant wit.

Moreover, in Simic's world, where old women sniff the air for snow and silence is some enormous animal to be dismantled, the real and the surreal coexist and have value primarily as image and substance and not as idea and abstraction. In "A Letter," a friend insists, "'We reach the real by overcoming the seduction of images.'" Simic answers, "Such abstinence will never be possible for me," because "trees with an infinity of tragic shapes / . . . make thinking difficult." Perhaps that accounts for the seemingly total absence of the pursuit of transcendence in his work. For Simic, salvation, as it were, is "To breakfast on slices of watermelon / In the company of naked gods and goddesses / On a patch of last night's snow."

Simic's persistent humor (which may suggest a sense of the absurdity of human existence, as in Beckett's play *Waiting for Godot*) and the absence of traditional transcendence (which might suggest the commensurate absence of spirituality) do not preclude a profound moral commitment. In "Poem Without a Title," he laments the consequences of industrial technology: "I say to the lead / Why did you let yourself / Be cast into a bullet?" "Fear" speaks of the nameless dread inherent in the human condition. "I believe in the soul," Simic insists in "The Old World"; "so far / It hasn't made much difference."

The great themes of literature are all present in Charles Simic's work, but they are incarnate in the images of the simple and the small. It is the drama of a life found in a bit of thread; it is the sudden discovery of a poem not when the poet looks up at the sky, but when he bends over to tie his shoes and looks into the earth. It is to stare steadily into the small pieces of this fractured world, "So that briefly, in that one spell, / Your heartache hushes at the beauty of it."

Poetry: *What the Grass Says* (1967). *Somewhere Among Us a Stone Is Taking Notes* (1969). *Dismantling the Silence* (1971). *Return to a Place Lit by a Glass of Milk* (1974). *Charon's Cosmology* (1977). *Classic Ballroom Dances* (1980). *Austerities* (1982). *Weather Forecast for Utopia and Vicinity* (1983). *Selected Poems 1963–1983* (1985, revised and expanded edition, 1990). *Unending Blues* (1986). *The World Doesn't End* (1989). *The Book of Gods and Devils* (1990). *Hotel Insomnia* (1992). A *Wedding in Hell* (1994). *Walking the Black Cat* (1996). *Jackstraws* (1999). *Selected Early Poems* (1999). *Night Picnic* (2001). *The Voice at 3:00 A.M.: Selected Late & New Poems* (2003). *Aunt Lettuce, I Want to Peek Under Your Skirt*, with Howie Michels (2005). *My Noiseless Entourage* (2005).

Prose: *The Uncertain Certainty*, essays (1986). *Wonderful Words, Silent Truth*, essays (1990). *Dimestore Alchemy (The Art of Joseph Cornell)* (1992). *The Unemployed Fortune-Teller: Essays & Memoirs* (1994). *Orphan Factory: Essays and Memoirs* (1998). A *Fly in the Soup: Memoirs* (2000). *Charles Simic in Conversation*, with Michael Hulse (2002). *Metaphysician in the Dark* (2003).

Translations: POETRY: *Fire Gardens*, by Ivan V. Lalic; with C. W. Truesdale (1970). *Four Modern Yugoslav Poets* (1970). *The Little Box*, by Vasko Popa (1970). *Homage to the Lame Wolf*, by Vasko Popa (1979; expanded edition, 1987). *Atlantis*, by Slavko Mihalic; with P. Kastmiler (1987). *Roll Call of Mirrors*, selected poems of Ivan V. Lalic (1987). *Selected Poems of Tomaz Salamun* (1988). *Some Other Wine and Light*, by Aleksandar Ristovic (1989). *The Bandit Wind*, by Slavko Janevski (1991). *Night Mail: Selected Poems*, by Nicola Tadic (1992). *Devil's Lunch: Selected Poems*, by Aleksandar Ristovic (2000).

LOUIS SIMPSON (1923)

Educated at Munro College (Jamaica, West Indies) and at Columbia, where he received his doctorate, Louis Simpson has taught at Columbia, the University of California at Berkeley, and the State University of New York at Stony Brook. With Donald Hall and Robert Pack, he edited the celebrated anthology *New Poets of England and America* (1957), and he is the author and editor of the textbook *An Introduction to Poetry* (1968). He has received the Rome Fellowship of the American Academy of Arts and Letters, a *Hudson Review* Fellowship, a Guggenheim Foundation Fellowship, and the Pulitzer Prize.

Like many other poets of his generation, Simpson began his poetic career as a formalist and gradually worked toward a verse in which content primarily determines form. In the process, his own language has become increasingly natural and closer to the colloquial idiom of American speech — a language "closely related to the language in which men actually think and speak." At the same time, both his language and his view of the American experience — the root source of much of his poetry — have retained an educated and literate edge that informs his poems with a fully conscious sense of history and tradition.

Reading Simpson's poetry, one might be reminded of Robert Frost's famous aphorism about his lover's-quarrel with the world. No less a lover, Simpson quarrels, more specifically, with America. It is an ongoing struggle to come to grips with the pathetic or tragic failure of the American dream and myth — especially as announced by Whitman. "Where are you, Walt? / The Open Road goes to the used-car lot," he says in "Walt Whitman at Bear Mountain." The open road also leads to the suburbs where, it seems, "You were born to waste your life." Yet it is in the daily routines of suburban living — driving to the mall, walking the dog, taking out the trash — that Simpson insists on looking for some semblance of a peculiarly American spiritual and intellectual life.

Poetry: *The Arrivistes: Poems 1940–1949* (1949). *Good News of Death and Other Poems*, in *Poets of Today II*, with Norma Faber and Robert Pack (1955). *A Dream of Governors* (1959). *At the End of the Open Road* (1963). *Selected Poems* (1965). *Adventures of the Letter I* (1971). *Searching for the Ox* (1976). *Armidale* (1980). *Caviare at the Funeral* (1980). *The Best Hour of the Night* (1983). *People Live Here: Selected Poems 1949–1983* (1983). *Collected Poems* (1988). *In the Room We Share* (1990). *There You Are* (1995). *The Owner of the House: New Collected Poems 1940–2001* (2003).

Prose: *James Hogg: A Critical Study* (1962). *Riverside Drive*, a novel (1962). *North of Jamaica*, autobiography (1972). *Three on the Tower: The Lives and Works of Ezra Pound, T. S. Eliot and William Carlos Williams* (1975). *A Revolution in Taste: Studies of Dylan Thomas, Allen Ginsberg, Sylvia Plath and Robert Lowell* (1978). *A Company of Poets* (1981). *The Character of the Poet* (1986). *Selected Prose,* autobiography, fiction, literary criticism (1989). *The King My Father's Wreck*, autobiography (1994). *Ships Going into the Blue* (1995).

Translation: *Modern Poets of France* (1997). *The Legacy and The Testament*, by François Villon (2000).

DAVE SMITH (1942)

Born in Portsmouth, Virginia, Dave Smith attended the University of Virginia and Southern Illinois University before serving in the U.S. Air Force. He completed his academic education at Ohio University and then taught at the University of Utah, SUNY–Binghamton, the University of Florida, Virginia Commonwealth University, and Louisiana State University, where he was coeditor of *The Southern Review*. The recipient of numerous awards, including fellowships from the National Endowment for the Arts, the Guggenheim Foundation, and the Lyndhurst Foundation, he is currently Elliot Coleman Professor of Poetry at The Johns Hopkins University in Baltimore.

"No place is more home than Poquoson," Dave Smith has written. "Its citizens have always been watermen, American renegades with hard hands, bowed backs, salty tongues, a tribal capacity for loyalty, courage, and admiration for the work a man or woman could do." More so than most poets of his generation, Smith has been a poet of place, situating himself mostly — though not solely — in Tidewater Virginia, its landscape of crab pots, oyster shells, and unsalvaged boats a *locus* where the rural South still seethes under its burden of tradition. Like the work of fellow southerner Yusef Komunyakaa, Smith's poems often conflate images of labor and violence — the legacy of man in his fallen state — with nature's plenitude and the beckoning yet often broken promises of redemption. "In Poquoson I began to write," he goes on, "[and] . . . the opposition of Poqouson and Charlottesville [site of the University of Virginia] forecast the long, unresolvable struggle of the physical and the intellectual in my poems."

Smith's early influences, ranging from Old English poetry to the narrative expansiveness of James Dickey and Robert Penn Warren, allow his poems their horizontal thrust, clumps of words cast out like fishing line to troll for meaning as strata of history and myth — Smith is a cracker-barrel storyteller — layer themselves vertically down the page. Racial clashes, adolescent cruelties, desperate endeavors, and the helpless complicities inherent in social and historical entanglements consume the narrators of these quasi-biblical tales. While aware of the comforts of writing within literary traditions — the Romantic, the Agrarian — Smith constantly seeks ways to expand and subvert those traditions in his poetry. Having established himself as a poet of muscular Anglo-Saxon cadences, knotty syntax, and complex narratives, Smith in 1996 published a book-length sequence, *Fate's Kite*, consisting of ninety thirteen-line poems. These loose sonnets meditate on the melancholies of aging and desire with lyrical pessimism occasionally tempered by self-deprecatory humor. Smith's poetry is rife with such pleasurable tensions. "Great poetry must be responsible and serious," Smith insists, and he has unabashedly assumed the task — often successfully — of attempting to write such poetry.

Poetry: *Mean Rufus Throw Down* (1973). *The Fisherman's Whore* (1974). *Cumberland Station* (1977). *Goshawk, Antelope* (1979). *Dream Flights* (1981). *Homage to Edgar Allan Poe* (1981). *In the House of the Judge* (1983). *Gray Soldiers* (1984). *The Roundhouse Voices: Selected and New Poems* (1985). *Cuba Night* (1990). *Night Pleasures: New and Selected Poems* (1992). *Fate's Kite: Poems 1991–1995* (1995). *Floating on Solitude: Three Books of Poems* (1997). *The Wick of Memory: New and Selected Poems 1970–2000* (2000). *Little Boats, Unsalvaged: Poems 1992–2004* (2005).

Prose: *Onliness*, novel (1981). *Southern Delights*, stories (1984). *Local Assays: On Contemporary American Poetry*, essays (1985).

W. D. SNODGRASS (1926)

Born in Wilkinsburg, Pennsylvania, and educated at Geneva College and at the University of Iowa, W. D. Snodgrass has taught at the University of Rochester, Wayne State, Syracuse, Old Dominion, and the University of Delaware. He has received fellowships from the Guggenheim and Ingram Merrill Foundations, the Academy of American Poets, the National Institute of Arts and Letters, and the National Endowment for the Arts. His first book of poems won the Pulitzer Prize in 1960.

Until the late 1970s, Snodgrass was known primarily as a personal-confessional poet; indeed, he, rather than Robert Lowell, was probably responsible for the emergence of that mode of poetry in the late 1950s and early 1960s. Unlike Lowell, Plath, and Sexton, Snodgrass made poetry not out of madness and sensationally violent suffering but rather out of the daily neuroses and everyday failures of a man — a husband, father, and teacher. Snodgrass also saw such domestic suffering as occurring against a backdrop of a more universal suffering inherent in the whole of human experience. In *Heart's Needle*, he stated *and* demonstrated, "We need the landscape to repeat us." Snodgrass also shared that fundamental concern of his generation announced by Albert Camus: "There is but one truly serious philosophical problem, and that is suicide." In "April Inventory," he wrote, "I have not learned how often I / Can win, can love, but choose to die."

Although noted for their candor, Snodgrass's early poems were also controlled by an unmistakable sense of irony, directed by a highly literate imagination shaped by the New Critics, and organized by a consciously formal craftsmanship. Consequently, Snodgrass achieves a good measure of distance between himself as subject and himself as poem; thus the speaker of a "personal" Snodgrass poem often sounds more like a personal-confessional "persona."

In any case, little in Snodgrass's early poetry foreshadowed the appearance of *The Führer Bunker*. A cycle of dramatic monologues, these poems are spoken by leading figures of the Nazi regime during the last days of the Third Reich — including Albert Speer, Martin Bormann, Joseph Goebbels, Magda Goebbels, Eva Braun, and Adolf Hitler. Displaying an even more powerful range of dazzling craftsmanship in *The Führer Bunker* — which unfolds like a modern-day *Inferno* — Snodgrass zeroes in on the historical and moral landscape that modern humankind seems intent or fated to repeat. The power and the horror of this cycle do not depend on what Snodgrass has to say about the historical figures and events *per se*; he knows all too well that there is little that can be said. Rather, the emotional and moral impact of this cycle emerges out of the fact that, like the dark and suffering creatures Dante encountered in hell, the personages in this Nazi *Götterdämmerung* are not the monsters we have met in the history books. They are all too recognizable, all too human.

Poetry: *Heart's Needle* (1959). *After Experience* (1967). *Remains* (under the pseudonym S. S. Gardons, 1970; revised edition under the name W. D. Snodgrass, with a foreword by A. Poulin, Jr., 1985). *The Führer Bunker: A Cycle of Poems in Progress* (1977). *If Birds Build with Your Hair* (1979). *The Boy Made of Meat* (1983). *A Locked House* (1986). *Selected Poems: 1957–1987* (1987). *W. D.'s Midnight Carnival*, in collaboration with the painter DeLoss McGraw (1988). *The Death of Cock Robin*, in collaboration with the painter DeLoss McGraw (1989). *Each in His Season* (1993). *The Führer Bunker: The Complete Cycle* (1995). *De-Compositions*, poetry/criticism (2001). *Not for Specialists: New and Selected Poems* (2006).

Prose: *In Radical Pursuit: Critical Essays and Lectures* (1975). *After-Images: Autobiographical Sketches* (1999). *To Sound Like Yourself: Essays on Poetry* (2002).

Translations: *Gallows Songs*, poems by Christian Morgenstern, translated with L. Segal (1967). *Six Troubadour Songs* (1977). *Traditional Hungarian Songs* (1978). *Six Minnesinger Songs* (1983). *Antonio Vivaldi: The Four Seasons* (1984). *Star and Other Poems*, by Mihai Eminescu (1990). *Selected Translations* (1998).

GARY SNYDER (1930)

Born in San Francisco, Gary Snyder received a bachelor's degree in literature and anthropology from Reed College. He did further study in languages at the University of California at Berkeley and later studied Zen Buddhism in a monastery in Kyoto, Japan. He has worked as a seaman, logger, and forester, and he has taught at Berkeley and the University of

California at Davis. The recipient of a Bollingen Foundation grant for Buddhist Studies, a grant from the National Institute of Arts and Letters, and a Guggenheim Foundation Fellowship, he was awarded the Pulitzer Prize in 1975.

In *Six San Francisco Poets* (1969), David Kherdian quotes Snyder as saying, "As much as the books I've read, the jobs I've had have been significant in shaping me. My sense of body and language and the knowledge that intelligence and insight, sensitivity, awareness, and brilliance are not limited to educated people, or anything like it." Many of Snyder's poems are direct and simple, marked by an elemental reverence for life and salvaging poetry from the most basic human experience.

The simplicity, however, is not simplistic, for it reflects the profound influence of Zen on Snyder's sensibility and thought. As Snyder has said, "A poet faces two directions: one is the world of people and language and society, and the other is the nonhuman, nonverbal world, which is nature. . . ." For Snyder, "nature" refers to the natural world and "the inner world . . . before language, before custom, before culture. There's no words in that realm."

Snyder's response to both the inner and outer worlds has resulted in the quest for a primitive identification with nature and a contemporary concern for the ecological consequences of progress and civilization. "As a poet," Snyder has said, "I hold the most archaic values on earth. They go back to the late Paleolithic: the fertility of the soil, the magic of animals, the power-vision in solitude, the terrifying initiation and rebirth, the love and ecstasy of the dance, the common work of the tribe. I try to hold history and wilderness in mind, that my poems may approach the true measure of things and stand against the unbalance and ignorance of our times."

Among the "archaic values" that Snyder has attempted to erect "against the unbalance and ignorance of our times" are a vital and sacred reintegration of human sexuality and a full celebration of the whole sexual self. Few poets of his generation have celebrated heterosexual love as vividly as Snyder has. "The Bath," for example, extols the pleasurable glory of the male and female bodies with unabashed and reverential joy.

Poetry: *Riprap* (1959/1990). *Myths and Texts* (1960/1978). *Riprap and Cold Mountain Poems* (1965). *Six Sections from Mountains and Rivers Without End* (1965). *A Range of Poems* (1966). *Three Worlds. Three Realms. Six Roads* (1966). *The Back Country* (1968). *The Blue Sky* (1969). *Regarding Wave* (1970). *Manzanita* (1972). *Fudo Trilogy* (1973). *Turtle Island* (1974). *Axe Handles* (1983). *Left Out in the Rain: Poems 1947–1984* (1986). *No Nature: New and Selected Poems* (1992). *Mountains and Rivers Without End* (1996). *The Gary Snyder Reader: Prose, Poetry, and Translations 1952–1998* (1999). *Danger on Peaks* (2004).

Prose: ESSAYS AND INTERVIEWS: *Earth House Hold: Technical Notes and Queries to Fellow Dharma Revolutionaries* (1969). *The Old Ways* (1977). *He Who Hunted*

Birds in His Father's Village: Dimensions of a Haida Myth (1979). *The Real Work: Interviews & Talks 1964–1979,* edited by S. McLean (1980). *Good Wild Sacred* (1984). *A Passage Through India* (1984). *The Practice of the Wild* (1990). *A Place in Space: Ethics, Aesthetics, and Watersheds* (1996). *Look Out: A Selection of Writings* (2002).

GARY SOTO (1952)

Born and raised in Fresno, California, Gary Soto received a BA from California State University–Fresno and an MFA from the University of California–Irvine. While in college, he worked at a number of odd jobs, such as chopping beets or cotton and picking grapes. The author of numerous books for children and young adults, he has taught at Wayne State University, the University of Cincinnati, and the University of California–Riverside. He has received fellowships from the Guggenheim Foundation and the National Endowment for the Arts in addition to receiving the American Book Award from the Before Columbus Foundation.

The stuff of Gary's Soto's poems — especially his early lyrics — is the stuff that makes up the life of the migrant worker, the tenant farmer, the men and women who are hired on a day-to-day basis to work the fields of California: sweat, dust, and more dust. "And next summer . . . ?" Soto asks. The answer is obvious: "Boredom, / in early June, will settle / on the eyelash shading your pupil from dust. . . ." Soto's poems also give us brief glimpses of life in the barrio. In "Mexicans Begin Jogging," the factory boss insists he flee the border patrol despite Soto's telling him there's no need: "I was American."

His journey, then, is in the pursuit of the American dream, sometimes by ridiculing it, sometimes by sneering at the values it propagates. Sometimes, it is in the recognition of having been envious of "the children of San Francisco [who] are blond, / shiny, and careful at the lights. . . ." This journey is a spiritual one; it is that quest for identity which is at the heart of the American melting pot experience, and it is undertaken at some cost: "many people, whole countries," Soto tells his daughter, "May go under because we desire TV / And chilled drinks. . . ." It is also the pilgrimage that we all must make: "We are [those] passengers, the old and the young alike. / Who will know us when we breathe through the grass?"

Poetry: *The Elements of San Joaquin* (1977). *The Tale of Sunlight* (1978). *Where Sparrows Work Hard* (1981). *Black Hair* (1985). *A Fire in My Hands* (1990). *Who Will Know Us?* (1990). *Home Course in Religion* (1991). *Neighborhood Odes* (1992). *Canto Familiar* (1995). *New and Selected Poems* (1995). *Junior College* (1997). *A Natural Man* (1999). *One Kind of Faith* (2003).

Prose: ESSAYS: *Living Up the Street* (1992). *The Effects of Knut Hamsun on a Fresno Boy: Recollections and Short Essays* (2000).

ELIZABETH SPIRES (1952)

Born in Lancaster, Ohio, and raised in nearby Circleville, where, she told interviewer A. V Christie in 1993, she "had indiscriminately read the books in the Children's Room of the Circleville Public Library, including about three hundred sappy biographies," Elizabeth Spires was educated at Vassar College and The Johns Hopkins University. The Amy Lowell Travelling Poetry Scholar in 1986–1987, she has received fellowships from the Ingram Merrill, Guggenheim and Whiting Foundations and from the National Endowment for the Arts, and she was awarded the Witter Bynner Prize by the American Academy of Arts and Letters. The author of several books for children, she has taught at Washington College in Chestertown, Maryland, in the Writing Seminars at Johns Hopkins, and at Goucher College in Baltimore.

Like Elizabeth Bishop, whom she interviewed for *The Paris Review* in 1977 and to whom she has been compared for her austere vocabulary, elegant diction, imaginative play, and meditative decorum, Elizabeth Spires has built an impressive body of work poem by poem, focusing, according to Christie, on the "tension . . . between the immediate and the visionary." Her attraction to the themes of the Metaphysical Poets has been evident since her first volume, *Globe* (1981), and has deepened in subsequent volumes. "I suppose the poems I care about the most," she has stated, "are the ones that see the pattern and the connections between people, between the living and the dead, how the past, the present, and the future connect with each other."

Her subject, then, is Time, its circularity rather than its linear progression, birth as much as death, and images of circles fill her poems: globes, islands, sundials, coins, eggs, the mouths of goldfish "frozen over O-shaped syllables of air." The poems themselves engage in circular patterns, often using repetition, strict stanzaic structure, and slant rhyme, as ghosts and souls drift through her fluid lines. Her circular imagery also suggests isolation and the need for self-sufficiency, so the poems become self-reflexive, as much about artistic discipline and the act of creation as about their ostensible subjects. Her purpose as a poet (and, more recently, as a mother) is to challenge the inevitable: "Only when we are 'in the process' do we lose our sense of time rapidly passing and, for a little while, escape death."

Poetry: *Globe* (1981). *Swan's Island* (1985). *Annonciade* (1989). *Worldling* (1995). *Now the Green Blade Rises* (2002).

DAVID ST. JOHN (1949)

Born in Fresno, California, David St. John was educated at California State University–Fresno and the University of Iowa Writers' Workshop. He has taught at Oberlin College and The Johns Hopkins University.

Presently he is Professor of English at the University of Southern California. St. John has received grants and fellowships from the Guggenheim and Ingram Merrill Foundations and the National Endowment for the Arts. In 1984, he received the Prix de Rome Fellowship awarded by the American Academy and Institute of Arts and Letters, and he has been Visiting Scholar at the Getty Research Institute for the History of Art and the Humanities.

In his early poem "Gin," St. John writes: "You know, your friends complain. They say / you give up only the vaguest news, and give a bakery / As your phone. Even your stories / Have no point, just lots of detail." His work is characterized by such "disguises of omission," and his method often makes use of elision, fragmentation, collage, and fierce understatement. His elegant, precisely detailed surfaces, such gorgeous veneer, belie an undercurrent of decadence, an atmospheric *noir* that slowly surfaces to reveal decay at the heart of glamour. Love, alienation, and degradation commingle as his characters waver between nihilism and the muted promises of desire.

Critics have commented upon St. John's European influences, especially Baudelaire and Mallarmé, and Floyd Collins has noted that St. John, "like Poe and the French Symbolists before him, deliberately debases the corporeal in a fervent desire for the spiritual." In their assumption that transcendence, if possible, may be approached through unconventional measures, his poems resist moralizing. Like the photographic stills from nonexistent films created by Cindy Sherman, or the scores to nonexistent films composed by Brian Eno, St. John's poems suggest larger narratives, those abandoned novels populated with the ghosts of romance whose lives touched upon momentary grandeur before flaring into oblivion.

Poetry: *Hush* (1976). *The Shore* (1980). *No Heaven* (1985). *Terraces of Rain: An Italian Sketchbook* (1991). *Study for the World's Body: New and Selected Poems* (1994). *In the Pines: Lost Poems, 1972–1997* (1999). *The Red Leaves of Night* (1999). *Prism* (2002). *The Face: A Novella in Verse* (2004).

Prose: *Where the Angels Come Toward Us: Selected Essays, Reviews, and Interviews* (1995).

WILLIAM STAFFORD (1914–1993)

William Stafford received his BA and MA from the University of Kansas and his PhD from the University of Iowa, where he was also a member of the Writers' Workshop. A conscientious objector during World War II and active in pacifist organizations, he taught at Manchester College, San Jose State College, and Lewis and Clark College, where he was professor emeritus. From 1970 to 1971, he was Consultant in Poetry at the Library of Congress. In addition to being awarded a fellowship from the Guggenheim

Foundation, a grant from the National Endowment for the Arts, the Shelley Memorial Award, and the Melville Cane Award, he also received the National Book Award.

In a statement for William J. Martz's *The Distinctive Voice* (1966), William Stafford wrote, "When you make a poem you merely speak or write the language of every day, capturing as many bonuses as possible and economizing on the losses; that is, you come awake to what always goes on in the language, and you use it to the limit of your ability and your power of attention at the moment." Part of what is truly distinctive about Stafford's poetry is his sustained ability to make each poem sound as though it were, in fact, the language of everyday. But it's clear that his power as a poet arises equally out of his ability to capture an extraordinary number of bonuses — the intensity of feeling that daily speech cannot maintain. By so doing, he achieves what he considered to be the meaningful opportunity in the social process of language: "to become more aware of what being alive means."

To a large extent, this awareness also may be the primary thematic focus of Stafford's work: "Your job is to find out what the world is trying to be," he writes in his poem "Vocation." Thus, his poetry reflects his attempt not only to capture the possibilities of everyday language but also to maintain "the worth of local things": the plains and small towns of the midwestern and western landscape, the often overlooked experiences of everyday life, and his relationship with his family. Stafford's is also a highly personal poetry, but one which is neither self-torturing nor confessional; rather, it is calm and gentle while remaining honest and firm. Moreover, while neither ostensibly religious nor trailing remnants of the kind of Puritanism inherent in the work of many of his contemporaries, Stafford's poems — as Richard Howard notes in *Alone with America* (1969) — occur within a *paysage moralise* and are informed by an equally powerful moral vision.

Poetry: *Traveling Through the Dark* (1961). *West of Your City* (1961). *Five Poets of the Pacific Northwest*, with Kenneth Hanson, Richard Hugo, Carolyn Kizer, and David Wagoner; edited by R. Skelton (1964). *The Rescued Year* (1966). *Eleven Untitled Poems* (1968). *Weather* (1969). *Allegiances* (1970). *Temporary Facts* (1970). *In the Clock of Reason* (1973). *Someday, Maybe* (1973). *That Other Alone, Poems* (1973). *Going Places* (1974). *North by West* (1975). *Braided Apart*, with Kim Stafford (1976). *Late, Passing Prairie Farm* (1976). *The Design on the Oriole* (1977). *Stories That Could Be True: New and Collected Poems* (1977). *All About Light* (1978). A *Meeting with Disma Tumminello and William Stafford*, poems by William Stafford, photographs of Disma Tumminello's sculptures (1978). *Smoke's Way* (1978). *Tuft by Puff* (1978). *Tuned in Late One Night* (1978). *Two About Music* (1978). *The Quiet of the Land* (1979). *Around You, Your House & A Catechism* (1979). *Things That Happen Where There Aren't Any People* (1980). *Wyoming Circuit* (1980). *Sometimes a Legend: Puget Sound Country* (1981). *A Glass Face in the Rain* (1982). *Segues: A Conversation in Poetry*, with Marvin Bell (1983). *Smoke's Way: Poems from Limited Editions 1968–1981* (1983). *Roving*

Across Fields: A Conversation and Uncollected Poems 1942–1982 (1983). *Stories and Storms and Strangers* (1984). *Listening Deep* (1984). *Wyoming* (1985). *Brother Wind* (1986). *An Oregon Message* (1987). *You and Some Other Character* (1987). *Annie Over*, with Marvin Bell (1988). *Fin, Feather, Fur* (1989). *How to Hold Your Arms When It Rains* (1990). *Passwords* (1991). *My Name Is William Tell* (1992). *The Darkness Around Us Is Deep*, edited by R. Bly (1993). *The Way It Is: New and Selected Poems* (1998). *Every War Has Two Losers: On Peace and War*, edited by K. Stafford (2003).

Prose: *Down in My Heart*, a memoir (1947/1971/1985). *The Achievement of Brother Antoninus* (1967). *Leftovers, a Care Package: Two Lectures* (1973). *Writing the Australian Crawl: Views of the Writer's Vocation* (1978). *You Must Revise Your Life*, essays (1986). *Crossing Unmarked Snow* (1997). *The Answers Are Inside the Mountains: Meditations on the Writing Life*, edited by P. Merchant and V. Wixon (2004).

GERALD STERN (1925)

Born in Pittsburgh, Gerald Stern was educated at the University of Pittsburgh and at Columbia. He served in the U.S. Army Air Corps and subsequently traveled widely and taught high school English in Europe. In this country he has taught at several colleges and universities, including the University of Pittsburgh and the University Iowa. Stern's book *Lucky Life* was the Academy of American Poets' Lamont Poetry selection for 1977. He also has been the recipient of the Poetry Society of America's Melville Cane Award, creative writing fellowships from the National Endowment for the Arts, and the National Book Award.

Compared with many of today's poets, who publish their first books when they are in their early twenties, Gerald Stern came to poetry relatively late in life; he was forty-six when his first book was published. The wait, the years of seeming silence, the apprenticeship proved to be worthwhile, for Stern has grown into a unique presence in contemporary poetry.

Reading Stern's poems and being moved by the persuasive rhythms of their exhilaration or by the resonating cadences of their sorrow, one may exclaim quite spontaneously, "Wonderful! Wonderful!" (At their best, Stern's poems warrant a *physical* response.) But the specific reasons for the poems' effectiveness or for our response may not be identified quite so spontaneously. Clearly, the cultural and literary "influences" are all there: the biblical prophets and psalmists, William Blake and Walt Whitman, Allen Ginsberg and Frank O'Hara. Those influences, however, are more like translucent flags or crystalline signals rather than prescriptive aesthetic or moral imperatives. Enigmatically, Stern seems to combine Ginsberg's visionary moral stance and O'Hara's chatty urban sophistication, but in the process sounds entirely unique. In an interview published in *American*

Poetry Review in early 1984, Stern offered a more personal explanation for his voice: "Everything depends on your signature, your breath, your person. Maybe your rhythm. Your peculiarity, your uniqueness. Your crankiness. That thumb print of yours."

Perhaps the seeming enigma lies more deeply in the expansiveness of Stern's imagination, for he is a poet whose work not only includes, but also attempts to reconcile, the emotional, moral, and existential polarities of experience into a more integrally human whole. Thus, his poems encompass the urban experience as much as the rural experience, Cavafy's Alexandria as much as O'Hara's Bickford's, Dionysian joy as much as Judaic anguish. "Lilacs for Ginsberg" begins on a level of straightforward realism and suddenly blooms into a lovely surrealistic lyric while "The Dancing" begins with reminiscence and celebration, then suddenly shifts from "whirling and singing" to the darker "screaming and falling" that connects the family, safe in Pittsburgh in 1945, with victims of the Holocaust. In the same interview, Stern said, "Poets are witnesses, living proof of the uniqueness of the individual soul, of the unforgivable sadness of its perishing, of its immortality. . . . The more living the poet, the more unbearable the death; the greater the poem, the more it ransoms." To that end, this poet understands the essential need for the reconciliation of polarities: "stretching my body and turning on my left side / for music, / humming to myself and turning on my right side / for words."

Poetry: *The Pineys* (1971). *The Name of Beasts and Other Poems* (1972). *Rejoicings* (1973; reprinted as *Rejoicings: Poems 1966–1972*, 1984). *Lucky Life* (1977). *The Red Coal* (1981). *Paradise Poems* (1984). *Lovesick* (1987). *Leaving Another Kingdom: Selected Poems* (1990). *Two Long Poems* (1990). *Bread Without Sugar* (1992). *Odd Mercy* (1995). *This Time: New and Selected Poems* (1998). *Last Blue* (2000). *American Sonnets* (2002). *Everything Is Burning* (2005).

Prose: *What I Can't Bear Losing*, memoir (2004). *Not God After All* (2004).

MARK STRAND (1934)

Mark Strand was born of American parents in Summerside, Prince Edward Island, Canada. He holds degrees from Antioch, Yale, and the University of Iowa and was a Fulbright Fellow in Florence, Italy. Strand has taught at many universities, including Iowa, Yale, Wesleyan, Utah, and Johns Hopkins, and he currently teaches in the Committee on Social Thought at the University of Chicago. A former Poet Laureate of the United States, he has received fellowships from the National Endowment for the Arts and the MacArthur Foundation, and his prizes include the National Institute of Arts and Letters Award and the Pulitzer Prize.

The development and impact of Mark Strand's poems, like those of Elizabeth Bishop, depend in large part on the straightforward technique of reportage: a seemingly simple presentation of surface facts. What differentiates Strand's poetry from that of others who employ this technique, however, is that Strand doesn't report only the factual images of the perceived physical world, but especially the figures, contours, and dramatic configurations of dreams and of nonconscious states — what Jung termed the archetypal symbols of the collective unconscious. Even when they address themselves to recognizable figures and situations of the tangible world, Strand's poems continue to generate an aura of the dream world.

Strand's work is further differentiated — not only from the work of other poets who use the technique of reportage but also from the work of those who, like Robert Bly, use the unconscious as a source of imagery — by the measure of irony that suffuses so many of his poems. Given the dramatic situation of a Strand poem, the speaker seems to bring a very conscious intelligence to bear on his reporting; that conscious intelligence directs the development of the action and choreographs the emotional impact of the images, thereby harnessing the full surge of the subconscious — occasionally with an edge of humor. Thus, one of Strand's unique characteristics is that many of his poems reflect a controlling sensibility that might be termed *ironic surrealism*.

Another characteristic that is almost entirely unique to the poetry of Mark Strand is the extent to which the personality of the speaker of his poems seems to be the result of a conscious obliteration of all traces of the surface texture of personality. In other words, these poems offer us a personality of absence rather than of presence. This personality suggests, "Wherever I am / I am what is missing." But such absence — the fact of absence, the threat of absence, the longing for absence — is also one of Strand's central themes. And so there's a startling but also wonderful irony at work when Strand asserts, "More is less. / I long for more." Should some readers fault Strand's poems for the personality of its speakers and theme of absence, it is important to note Strand's own realization that, confronted by such absence, it is possible to see "the blaze of promise everywhere."

Poetry: *Sleeping with One Eye Open* (1964). *Reasons for Moving* (1968). *Darker* (1970). *The Sargentville Notebook* (1973). *The Story of Our Lives* (1973). *The Late Hour* (1978). *Selected Poems* (1980). *The Continuous Life* (1990). *Reasons for Moving, Darker, & The Sargentville Notebook* (1992). *Dark Harbor* (1993). *Blizzard of One* (1998). *Chicken, Shadow, Moon & More* (2000).

Prose: *The Monument* (1978). *Art of the Real* (1983). *Mr. & Mrs. Baby*, fiction (1985). *William Bailey* (1987). *Hopper* (1993). *The Weather of Words: Poetic Invention* (2000).

Translations: POETRY: *18 Poems from the Quechua* (1971). *The Owl's Insomnia: Selected Poems of Rafael Alberti* (1973). *Souvenir of the Ancient World,* by Carlos

Drummond de Andrade (1976). *Travelling in the Family*, by Carlos Drummond de Andrade, with Thomas Colchie (1986). PROSE: *Texas*, by Jorge Luis Borges (1975).

JEAN VALENTINE (1934)

Born in Chicago, Jean Valentine earned a BA degree from Radcliffe College. In 1965, her first volume, *Dream Barker*, won the Yale Younger Poets Award, and in 2004, *Door in the Mountain: New and Collected Poems 1965–2003* was the recipient of the National Book Award. Valentine has received numerous fellowships, including those from the Guggenheim Foundation, the National Endowment for the Arts, the Bunting Institute, the Rockefeller Foundation, and the New York Foundation for the Arts, as well as the 2000 Shelley Memorial Prize from the Poetry Society of America. She has taught at Sarah Lawrence, Columbia, New York University, and the 92nd Street Y in Manhattan.

Jean Valentine is a poet of the palimpsest: "Here's the letter I wrote, / and the ghost letter, underneath — / that's my work in life." Her austere and eloquent lyrics, read horizontally, poem by poem, across her books create a continuum of unfolding, with the creative process itself often her true subject: "The effort of becoming. These words / *are* my life." As bonsai in their miniature plots can evoke provinces, her spare and intuitive poems scroll moral landscapes often ravaged by alcoholism and AIDS and undergoing spiritual and political turmoil. Her sparse vocabulary, with its constant doubling, functions always as an extension of (re)vision — "To make the suffering / visible" — and the repetitions contribute to the dreamlike quality of her work. Richard Jackson has remarked that her poems seem to be "based upon fragments, shifts in perspective, traces, frayings . . . a world of deferrals, discontinuities, differences, gaps." Oddly, such absences situate Valentine's poems, allowing them simplicity and resonance: "The known and familiar become one with the mysterious and half-wild, at the place where consciousness and the subliminal meet," notes Adrienne Rich.

Brimming with spiritual hunger and populated with the dead as well as the living — friends and lovers, mother and father, Orpheus and Eurydice, the vital and nurturing community of poets — Valentine's poems exist on the edge of dissolution, there and not-there, letter and ghost letter, as the poet yearns for some purposeful and transcendent dispersal: "Now I could scatter my body easily / if it was any use." Such notions of sacrifice and effacement, endlessly mirrored in the poems' white spaces and in their isolated words and phrases, floating pronouns, and dissolving syntaxes, give voice to a vast, interior life in the process of "breaking open / no one to contain it   my / pelvis thinning out into God."

Poetry: *Dream Barker* (1965). *Pilgrims* (1969). *Ordinary Things* (1974). *The Messenger* (1979). *Home Deep Blue: New and Selected Poems* (1989). *The River at*

Wolf (1992). *The Under Voice: Selected Poems* (1995). *Growing Darkness, Growing Light* (1997). *The Cradle of the Real Life* (2000). *Door in the Mountain: New and Collected Poems 1965–2003* (2004).

ELLEN BRYANT VOIGT (1943)

Born in Danville, Virginia, Ellen Bryant Voigt attended Converse College in South Carolina and the University of Iowa. A former faculty member at Goddard College and the Massachusetts Institute of Technology, she currently teaches in the Warren Wilson College low-residency MFA Program for Writers. Currently the Vermont State Poet, she has received fellowships from the Guggenheim and Lila Wallace Foundations and the National Endowment for the Arts.

Landscape has played a formative role in the poetic development of Ellen Bryant Voigt. As a child in the rural South and as an adult in New England, she learned to accept the world on its own terms, not turning away from its natural violence or ignoring its lessons of trust and betrayal. In poems of quiet, celebratory power, she addresses family bonds and domestic struggles, "summer and winter, youth and age, / as though the forces of plenty and of loss / played equally on the human soul." Darkness inhabits many of these poems — the deaths of children and parents, marital tension, mastectomy, suicide — yet Voigt always attempts to strike a balance, "to fix / some truth beyond all change." In "At the Movie: Virginia, 1956," the narrator remembers the segregated theater of her adolescence, the "sullen glamor" of the balcony, and the drawn lines and "stringent rule" that limited the future of both races, one "that would try to be invisible" and the other, "not knowing how to see," that owned "everything / but easy passage out of there." For these children, the only "lit horizon" is the movie screen where images of suffocation — *King Solomon's Mines* and the undersea continent of Atlantis — flicker and beckon.

Critics have praised the linguistic density of Voigt's poems and commented upon their lucid and unsentimental evocations of the past. In *Kyrie* (1995), Voigt has written a book-length sequence on the influenza pandemic of 1918–1919. Its loose sonnets with their overlapping voices, grief-stricken yet at times mordantly funny, create a swelling *chorale* of the living that serves both as elegy for those lost and as thanksgiving for survival. Set against the backdrop of World War I, the book speaks to incomprehensible devastation at a time when AIDS ravages the globe, and remains more powerful for its muted metaphor. Such restraint characterizes Voigt's passionate eloquence.

Poetry: *Claiming Kin* (1976). *The Forces of Plenty* (1983). *The Lotus Flowers* (1987). *Two Trees* (1992). *Kyrie* (1995). *Shadow of Heaven* (2002).

Prose: *The Flexible Lyric* (1999).

RICHARD WILBUR (1921)

A graduate of Amherst and Harvard, Richard Wilbur has taught at Harvard, Wellesley, Wesleyan, and Smith. In addition to having served as Poet Laureate, he has been awarded Guggenheim and Ford Foundation Fellowships, the Prix de Rome, the National Book Award and, twice, the Pulitzer Prize.

Among poets whose sensibilities were shaped by the New Critics, Wilbur continues to be the consummate artist. His poetry is marked by grace, wit, and a kind of masterful craftsmanship equaled by few of his contemporaries. In his statement for John Ciardi's *Mid-Century American Poets* (1950), Wilbur affirmed the poet's need for form, for "artistry," saying that "limitation makes for power: the strength of the genie comes of his being confined in a bottle." Elsewhere he has stated that the poet must move "to attempt a maximum range" and to do so "without apparent strain." At his best, Wilbur's mastery of language and form is not merely without strain — it is dazzling and breathtaking.

The precision of sensuous detail and the verbal entrechats in Wilbur's poems are formal affirmations of his profound humanism, his belief in potential natural grace in this "world of sensible objects." In an era when many other poets have loitered around the deterioration of social, psychic, and personal fabrics and have proclaimed us and our world absurd, Wilbur has consistently sought for "a reconciliation between joy and pleasure, between acceptance and transcendence" — often against strenuous odds. And he has succeeded. By so doing, his poems have found and continue to offer the possibility of human beauty and grace.

Poetry: *The Beautiful Changes and Other Poems* (1947). *Ceremony and Other Poems* (1950). *Things of This World: Poems* (1956). *Advice to a Prophet and Other Poems* (1961). *The Poems of Richard Wilbur* (1963). *Walking to Sleep: New Poems and Translations* (1969). *The Mind-Reader: New Poems* (1976). *Opposites: Poems and Drawings* (1979). *Seven Poems* (1981). *New and Collected Poems* (1988). *More Opposites: Poems and Drawings* (1991). *Mayflies: New Poems and Translations* (2000). *Collected Poems 1943–2004* (2004).

Prose: *Responses: Prose Pieces 1953–1976*, essays (1976; expanded edition, 2000).

Translations: POETRY: *The Whale and Other Uncollected Translations* (1982). VERSE DRAMA: *The Misanthrope*, by Molière (1955). *Tartuffe*, by Molière (1963). *The School for Wives*, by Molière (1971). *The Learned Ladies*, by Molière (1978). *Andromache*, by Racine (1982). *Four Comedies*, by Molière (1982). *Phaedra*, by Racine (1986).

C. K. WILLIAMS (1936)

Born in Newark, New Jersey, and educated at Bucknell and the University of Pennsylvania, C. K. Williams has engaged in a wide range of professional activities. He established a program of poetry-therapy for the emotionally disturbed in Philadelphia, where he was also a group therapist for disturbed adolescents. He has been an editor and ghostwriter of articles, booklets, and speeches in the fields of psychiatry and architecture. And he has taught creative writing at Drexel, Irvine, Columbia, George Mason, and Princeton. In addition to receiving a Guggenheim Fellowship, Williams has been awarded the *Paris Review*'s Bernard F. Connor Prize and the National Book Critics Circle Award. In 2000, he received the Pulitzer Prize for *Repair.*

Reading the poems of C. K. Williams, we are quickly struck by how much pain and grief are harbored in their stark lines. Perhaps no other postwar poet in the United States has confronted so unswervingly and relentlessly the levels and dimensions of anguish as the fulcrum of human experience. Moreover, unlike many of his contemporaries, Williams has explored suffering without the seeming intellectual comfort of a formal philosophical system such as existentialism (W. D. Snodgrass), without even a precarious solace of faith or of a theological framework (John Berryman), and certainly without the emotional-aesthetic buffer of a strong ironic sense in the service of sustained artifice (Sylvia Plath). Whether confronting inner states of psychic pain in earlier poems or more external constructs of human anguish in later poems, Williams's poetry has as its heart the fundamental and essentially unconsoled vision announced in "It Is This Way with Men": "They are pounded into the earth / like nails; move an inch, / they are driven down again. / The earth is sore with them."

The anguish of our common condition, in an age that threatens annihilation on all sides, also seems to have rendered Williams commensurately unsympathetic to the kinds of artifices we have come to expect from poetry. Thus, in his earlier poems he seemed intent on stripping language down to its most essential syntax and then stripping it even further of most signs of syntax's own formal artifice. Consider the intense aesthetic and syntactical starkness of these lines: "if you told him god lived in his own penis / he'd bite into it / and tear like a carnivore / this is how men renounce / this is how we obliterate." Clearly, the visual aesthetic equivalent of such lines would be found more in Käthe Kollwitz's hauntingly sparse but blunt depictions of pain than in the more complex, inventive, and often witty depictions by Hieronymous Bosch.

In his fifth book, *Tar,* Williams introduced a long tonal line that may well be unique in postwar American poetry. Williams's lines may look like Ginsberg's, but they are not marked by the incantatory quality in many of Ginsberg's poems. And while their tone is very conversational, like many of Simpson's recent poems, Williams's tone isn't marked by the crackling terseness found in them. Approaching the quality of a highly refined, sparse prose, Williams's new tonal lines continue to accommodate his dark vision but also enable him to be more experientially, intellectually, and aesthetically expansive. These new poems also reflect a maturation of

Williams's vision: the pain, the anguish, the annihilation are still present and unconsoled, but that vision is also counterpointed by the recognition of the possibility of beauty: "all the field pure white, / its surface glittering, the dawn, glancing from its glaze, oblique, relentless, unadorned."

Poetry: A Day for Anne Frank (1968). Lies (1969). I Am the Bitter Name (1972). With Ignorance (1977). Tar (1983). Flesh and Blood (1987). Poems 1963–1983 (1988). A Dream of Mind (1992). Selected Poems (1994). The Vigil (1997). Repair (1999). The Singing (2003).

Prose: Poetry and Consciousness: Selected Essays (1998). Misgivings, memoir (2000).

Translations: POETRY: The Lark. The Thrush. The Starling, by Issa (1983). Canvas, by Adam Zagajewski, with R. Gorczynski and B. Ivry (1991). Selected Poems of Francis Ponge, with J. Montague and M. Guiton (1994). VERSE DRAMA: Women of Trachis, by Sophocles; with G. Dickerson (1978). The Bacchae, by Euripides (1990).

C. D. WRIGHT (1949)

Born in the Ozark town of Mountain Home, Arkansas, and educated at Memphis State University and the University of Arkansas, C. D. Wright has received fellowships from the National Endowment for the Arts, the Guggenheim Foundation, the Bunting Institute, and the MacArthur Foundation as well as a Whiting Writers Award and the Witter Bynner Prize from the American Academy and Institute of Arts and Letters. Her collaborative project (with photographer Deborah Luster), One Big Self: Prisoners of Louisiana, won the Lange-Taylor Prize from the Center for Documentary Studies at Duke University. She teaches at Brown University and coedits Lost Roads Publishers.

Suppressed and disjunctive narratives, cinematic cut-ups, and collage techniques — both aural and visual — quicken the associative and often erotic imagery charging the poems of C. D. Wright. Natural abundance and Southern lushness provide the backdrop for violent as well as spiritual reckoning, a "spare-rib theology" expressed in an American idiom that encompasses the improvisatory rhythms of sermons, jazz, yarn spinning, list making, and sex, its diction ranging from "hallelujah" to "go to hell," often in a single line. "Even in religious fervor," wrote Walt Whitman, "there is a touch of animal heat," and Wright's constant dislocations and blues-fused progressions serve to remind us that systems of belief can rub up against social and political sympathies: "A poetry / of shine could come of this."

The forfeiture and ruin that center her work scroll outwardly from biblical and personal elements, conflating the mythical ("The heart some bruised fruit / knocked loose by a long stick") and the confessional ("in gardening . . . I felt less responsible for one man's death one woman's long-term isolation") in order to gather "tokens of loss and recovery." The voices that surge forth to "have speech with strangers" have been shaped by fear and pain, a chorus of the wounded, those "lives on the periphery" struggling to "go back to the green field. And lie down." In poem after poem wrought with an implacable seriousness of purpose, Wright places her hard-bitten faith in language despite its history of imprecision and its failure to offer more than momentary consolation: "And how does a body break / bread with the word when the word / has broken. Again. And. Again."

Poetry: *Translations of the Gospel Back into Tongues* (1982). *Further Adventures with You* (1986). *String Light* (1991). *Just Whistle: a valentine* (1993). *Tremble* (1996). *Deepstep Come Shining* (1998). *One Big Self: Prisoners of Louisiana*, with D. Luster (2002). *Steal Away: selected and new poems* (2002). *Scar Tissue* (2006).

Prose: *Cooling Time: An American Poetry Vigil* (2005).

CHARLES WRIGHT (1935)

Born in Pickwick Dam, Tennessee, Charles Wright was educated at David-son College, the University of Iowa, and the University of Rome, where he was a Fulbright fellow. He served in the U.S. Army Intelligence Service and has taught in Italy as well as at Iowa, Princeton, Columbia, and the University of Virginia. Wright has received fellowships from the National Endowment for the Arts, the Ingram Merrill Foundation, and the Academy of American Poets, and has been the recipient of the PEN Translation Prize, the National Book Award, the National Book Critics Circle Award, and the Pulitzer Prize.

Because they are carefully, delicately crafted and because they often rely more on links of the imagination than on narrative and other surface connections, some of Wright's poems may seem less immediately accessible than the work of other poets. It's no wonder that one critic has asserted that Wright's poetry struggles to render the connections between his life and his poems "tenuous, often invisible" and characterized Wright's poems as being "unanchored to incident," thus "resisting description" and "defying exposition." However, on closer examination it is clear that the range of Wright's concerns is fully rooted in the range of recognizable and shared experience. His work includes poems of place energized by the spirit of that place, Blackwater Mountain in Tennessee, for example, and it in-cludes poems of the natural, physical world with its splendors and horrors.

What is also striking about the work of Charles Wright is its strong and consistent religious nature; Wright is one of the few poets of his generation who continues to wrestle openly with the traditional values (if not the work-ing tenets) of the Judeo-Christian tradition and to use the symbols, saints, and metaphors of that tradition as an integral part of his sensibility and vocabulary. The poem "Snow" uses as its launching point the biblical statement "Dust thou art, and unto dust shalt thou return"; "California Dreaming," whose very tone resonates with biblical rhythms and whose language incorporates traditional religious phrases and concepts, is a profound exploration of the possibility of a tradition-oriented spirituality within the boundaries and texture of contemporary experience. What if, in his quest for transcendence, Wright recognizes that "The ache for anything is a thick dust in the heart," that transcendence may be no more than being "Released as a glint, as a flash, as a spark"? Of the people and places in his world, past and present, he asserts, "I am their music"; of his music, he ventures, "I write poems to untie myself, to do penance and disappear / Through the upper right-hand corner of things, to say grace."

Poetry: *The Grave of the Right Hand* (1970). *The Venice Notebook* (1971). *Hard Freight* (1973). *Bloodlines* (1975). *China Trace* (1977). *The Southern Cross* (1981). *Country Music: Selected Early Poems* (1982). *The Other Side of the River* (1984). *Zone Journals* (1988). *The World of the Ten Thousand Things: Poems 1980–1990* (1990). *Xionia* (1990). *Chickamauga* (1995). *Black Zodiac* (1997). *Appalachia* (1999). *Negative Blue: Selected Later Poems* (2000). *A Short History of the Shadow* (2002). *Buffalo Yoga* (2004). *The Wrong End of the Rainbow* (2005). *Scar Tissue* (2006).

Prose: *Halflife: Improvisations and Interviews* (1988). *Quarter Notes: Improvisations and Interviews* (1995).

Translations: *The Storm and Other Poems*, by Eugenio Montale (1978). *The Motets*, poems by Eugenio Montale (1981). *Orphic Songs*, poems by Dino Campana (1984).

JAMES WRIGHT (1927–1980)

James Wright was born in the steel town of Martin's Ferry, Ohio — a place he subsequently transformed into a literary landmark in the contemporary imagination. He received his BA from Kenyon College and his MA and PhD from the University of Washington and attended the University of Vienna as a Fulbright Scholar. The recipient of several awards for poetry — including the Pulitzer Prize — he taught at Macalester College, the University of Minnesota, and Hunter College.

Like the styles of many other poets of his generation, James Wright's underwent significant changes in the course of his career. With the publication of his first book, Wright stated that he "wanted to make [his] poems say something humanly important" and pointed to Robert Frost and E. A. Robinson as his models. Thus, his early poems are often concerned with his response to the life and suffering of others. After his second book, however, he asserted, "Whatever I write from now on will be entirely different."

According to Robert Bly, Wright's decision was largely the result of his having read — and translated — the work of the German poet Georg Trakl, a contemporary of Rilke. "In Trakl," Bly writes, "a series of images makes a series of events. Because these events appear out of their 'natural' order, without the connection we have learned to expect from reading newspapers, doors silently open to unused parts of the brain." In Wright's poems such as "Lying in a Hammock . . . ," and "A Blessing" — generally written between 1960 and 1970 — the doors open to startling images, strange but emotionally precise. More personal than his earlier poems, these discover in his own subconscious and imagination the secret pools of human fear and joy. Moreover, the poems themselves seem to evolve quietly through layers of images until they surface with the quick thrust of a striking final image and epiphany.

Poetry: *The Green Wall* (1957). *Saint Judas* (1959). *The Lion's Tail and Eyes: Poems Written Out of Laziness and Silence*, with Robert Bly and William Duffy (1962). *The Branch Will Not Break* (1963). *Shall We Gather at the River* (1968). *Collected Poems* (1971). *Two Citizens* (1973). *Moments of the Italian Summer* (1976). *To a Blossoming Pear Tree* (1977). *A Reply to Matthew Arnold*, edited by A. Wright (1981). *Leave It to the Sunlight*, edited by A. Wright (1981). *This Journey*, edited by A. Wright (1981). *The Shape of Light*, edited by A. Wright (1986). *Above the River: The Complete Poems*, edited by A. Wright (1990). *Selected Poems*, edited by R. Bly and A. Wright (2005).

Prose: *Collected Prose*, essays, edited by A. Wright (1982). *Against the Exile*, letters to Wayne Burns, edited by J. R. Doheny (1985). *The Delicacy and Strength of Lace*, letters between James Wright and Leslie Marmon Silko, edited by A. Wright (1985). *A Secret Field: Selections from the Final Journals*, edited by A. Wright (1985).

Translations: *Twenty Poems of Georg Trakl*, with R. Bly (1961). *Twenty Poems of César Vallejo*, with R. Bly (1962). *The Rider on the White Horse: Selected Short Fiction of Theodor Storm* (1964). *Pablo Neruda: Twenty Poems*, with R. Bly (1967). *Poems by Hermann Hesse* (1970). *Neruda and Vallejo: Selected Poems*, with R. Bly and J. Knoepfle (1971). *Wandering: Notes and Sketches by Hermann Hesse*, with F. Wright (1972).

Criticism: A Selected Bibliography

Most of the following books and pamphlets contain substantial discussions of the work of individual poets, especially those represented in this book; some also include critical essays or statements of poetics by these poets. A few books in this bibliography, however, are primarily concerned with poetry in the United States before 1960; still others focus on various aspects of the art of poetry in the twentieth century.

Advanced students of poetry will want to turn to book-length bibliographies devoted to individual poets, as well as to such standard bibliographical sources as *Contemporary Poets* (St. Martin's Press); *Contemporary Authors* (Gale Research Company); *Dictionary of Literary Biography* (Gale Research Company); the annual bibliographies published in *PMLA*, *American Literature*, and *Journal of Modern Literature*; the regular bibliographies in *Twentieth Century Literature*; and *Contemporary Literary Criticism* (Gale Research Company), an annual volume of critical excerpts. Of course, many of the books listed here also include their own individual bibliographies.

Readers should be aware that several of the earlier, seminal books of criticism devoted to post-1960 U.S. poetry are now out of print and available only in larger libraries.

Lastly, books of criticism by poets represented in this volume are listed in the Notes on the Poets.

D. M. Allen and W. Tallman, eds., *The Poetics of the New American Poetry* (1973).
C. Altieri, *Enlarging the Temple: New Directions in American Poetry During the 1960's* (1979).
D. Baker, *Heresy and the Ideal: On Contemporary Poetry* (2000).
H. A. Baker, Jr., *Afro-American Poets* (1988).
J. D. Bellamy, ed., *American Poetry Observed: Poets on Their Work* (1984).
M. K. Blasing, *American Poetry: The Rhetoric of Its Forms* (1988).
J. E. B. Breslin, *From Modern to Contemporary: American Poetry 1945–1965* (1984).
P. Carroll, *The Poem in Its Skin* (1968).
S. Charters, *Some Poems/Poets: Poets and Poetry* (1971).
J. Clausen, *A Movement of Poets: Thoughts on Poetry & Feminism* (1983).
M. Davidson, *The San Francisco Renaissance: Poetics and Community at Mid-Century* (1989).
C. Dennis, *Poetry as Persuasion* (2001).
T. M. Disch, *The Castle of Indolence* (1995).
W. Dodd, *Toward the End of the Century: Essays into Poetry* (1992).
M. Duberman, *Black Mountain: An Experiment in Community* (1972).
E. Faas, ed., *Towards a New American Poetics: Essays and Interviews* (1978).
R. Frank and H. Sayre, eds., *The Line in Postmodern Poetry* (1989).
S. Fredman, *Poet's Prose: The Crisis in American Verse* (1983).
S. Friebert and D. Young, eds., *A Field Guide to Contemporary Poetry and Poetics* (1980).
T. Gardner, *Discovering Ourselves in Whitman: The Contemporary American Long Poem* (1988).
A. Gayle, *The Black Aesthetic* (1971).
D. Gioia, *Can Poetry Matter? Essays on Poetry and American Culture* (1992).

D. Gioia, *Disappearing Ink: Poetry at the End of Print Culture* (2004).

P. Goodman, *Speaking and Language: A Defense of Poetry* (1971).

J. Gould, *Modern American Women Poets* (1984).

J. Grahn, *The Highest Apple: Sappho and the Lesbian Poetic Tradition* (1985).

D. Hall, ed., *Claims for Poetry* (1982).

M. Harris and K. Aguero, eds., *A Gift of Tongues: Critical Challenges in Contemporary Poetry* (1988).

S. Henderson, ed., *Understanding the New Black Poetry: Black Speech and Black Music as Poetic Reference* (1973).

W. Heyen, ed., *American Poets in 1976* (1975).

H. L. Hix, *As Easy as Lying* (2002).

J. Holden, *The Old Formalism: Character in Contemporary American Poetry* (2000).

J. Holden, *The Rhetoric of the Contemporary Lyric* (1980).

R. Howard, *Alone with America: Essays on the Art of Poetry in the United States Since 1950* (1969; enlarged edition, 1980).

E. B. Hungerford, *Poets in Progress: Critical Prefaces to Thirteen Modern American Poets* (1967).

R. Jackson, *Acts of Mind: Conversations with Contemporary Poets* (1983).

R. Jackson, *The Dismantling of Time in Contemporary Poetry* (1988).

M. Jarman, *The Secret of Poetry* (2001).

M. Jarman and R. McDowell, *The Reaper Essays* (1996).

D. Kalstone, *Five Temperaments: Elizabeth Bishop, Robert Lowell, James Merrill, Adrienne Rich, John Ashbery* (1977).

L. Keller, *Remaking It New: Contemporary Poetry and the Modern Feminist* (1989).

L. Keller and C. Miller, eds., *Feminist Measures: Soundings in Poetry and Theory* (1994).

D. Kherdian, *Six San Francisco Poets* (1969).

H. Kohl, *A Grain of Poetry* (1999).

R. Kostelanetz, *The Old Poetries and the New* (1981).

G. Kuzma, ed., *A Book of Rereadings in Recent American Poetry* (1980).

H. Lazer, *What Is a Poet?* (1987).

D. Lehman, ed., *Ecstatic Occasions, Expedient Forms: Sixty-Five Leading Contemporary Poets Select and Comment on Their Poems* (1988).

G. Lensing and R. Moran, *Four Poets and the Emotive Imagination: Robert Bly, James Wright, Louis Simpson and William Stafford* (1976).

L. Lieberman, *Unassigned Frequencies: American Poetry in Review* (1977).

K. Malkoff, *Crowell's Handbook of Contemporary American Poetry: A Critical Handbook of American Poetry Since 1940* (1973).

K. Malkoff, *Escape from the Self* (1977).

P. Mariani, *A Useable Past: Essays on Modern and Contemporary Poetry* (1984).

R. K. Martin, *The Homosexual Tradition in American Poetry* (1979).

D. Mason, *The Poetry of Life and the Life of Poetry* (2000).

J. Mazzaro, ed., *Modern American Poetry: Essays in Criticism* (1970).

J. Mazzaro, *Postmodern American Poetry* (1980).

J. D. McClatchy, *White Paper: On Contemporary American Poetry* (1987).

M. McQuade, ed., *By Herself: Women Reclaim Poetry* (2000).

M. McQuade, *Stealing Glimpses* (1999).

D. Meltzer, *The San Francisco Poets* (1971).

D. M. Middlebrook and M. Yalom, eds., *Coming to Light: American Women Poets in the Twentieth Century* (1985).

R. J. Mills, Jr., *Creation's Very Self: On the Personal Element in Recent American Poetry* (1969).

R. J. Mills, Jr., *Cry of the Human: Essays on Contemporary American Poetry* (1974).

C. Molesworth, *The Fierce Embrace: A Study of Contemporary American Poetry* (1979).

C. Nelson, *Our Last First Poets: Vision and History in Contemporary American Poetry* (1984).

H. Nemerov, ed., *Poets on Poetry* (1961).

H. Nemerov, *Reflections on Poetry & Poets* (1972).

A. Oberg, *Modern American Lyric* (1978).

D. Ossman, *The Sullen Art: Interviews by David Ossman with Modern American Poets* (1963).

A. Ostriker, *Stealing the Language: The Emergence of Women's Poetry in America* (1986).

A. Ostroff, ed., *The Contemporary Poet as Artist and Critic* (1964).

G. Owen, ed., *Modern American Poetry: Essays in Criticism* (1972).

W. Packard, ed., *The Craft of Poetry: Interviews from the* New York Quarterly (1974).

J. Parini, *The Columbia History of American Poetry* (1994).

T. Parkinson, ed., *A Casebook on the Beat* (1961).

T. Parkinson, *Poets, Poems, Movements* (1988).

R. Phillips, *The Confessional Poets* (1973).

R. H. Pierce, *The Continuity of American Poetry* (1973).

R. Pinsky, *The Situation of Poetry: Contemporary Poetry and Its Traditions* (1977).

G. Plimpton, ed., *Poets at Work* (1989).

W. Prunty, *Fallen from the Symboled World: Precedents for the New Formalism* (1990).

K. Rexroth, *American Poetry in the Twentieth Century* (1973).

S. Rodman, *Tongues of Fallen Angels,* interviews (1984).

M. L. Rosenthal, *The Modern Poetic Sequence: The Genius of Modern Poetry* (1983).

M. L. Rosenthal, *The Modern Poets: A Critical Introduction* (1962).

M. L. Rosenthal, *The New Poets: American and British Poetry Since World War II* (1967).

M. L. Rosenthal, *Poetry and the Common Life* (1974; revised edition, 1984).

M. L. Rosenthal, *The Poet's Art* (1989).

M. Ryan, *A Difficult Grace* (2000).

S. Santos, *A Poetry of Two Minds* (2000).

R. B. Shaw, ed., *American Poetry Since 1960: Some Critical Perspectives* (1974).

M. Sienicka, *The Making of a New American Poem: Some Tendencies in the Post–World War II American Poetry* (1972).

E. Simpson, *Poets in Their Youth: A Memoir* (1982).

T. Steele, *Missing Measures: Modern Poetry and the Revolt Against Meter* (1990).

S. Stepanchev, *American Poetry Since 1945: A Critical Survey* (1965).

J. Sternberg, ed., *The Writer on Her Work* (1980).

P. Stitt, *Uncertainty & Plenitude: Five Contemporary Poets* (1997).

P. Stitt, *The World's Hieroglyphic Beauty: Five American Poets* (1987).

L. P. Turco, *Visions and Revisions in American Poetry* (1986).

H. Vendler, *The Music of What Happens: Poems, Poets, Critics* (1989).

H. Vendler, *Part of Nature, Part of Us* (1980).

H. Vendler, *Soul Says: On Recent Poetry* (1995).

J. Vinson, ed., *Contemporary Poets* (1985).

R. Von Hallberg, *American Poetry and Culture: 1945–1980* (1988).

A. Williamson, *Eloquence and Mere Life: Essays on the Art of Poetry* (1994).

A. Williamson, *Introspection and Contemporary Poetry* (1984).

D. Wojahn, *Strange Good Fortune* (2001).

Writers at Work: The Paris Review Interviews (First Series, 1958; Second Series, 1963; Third Series, 1967; Fourth Series, 1976; Fifth Series, 1981).

Notes on the Editors

A. POULIN, JR. (1938–1996)

A. Poulin, Jr., was born of immigrant Québécois parents in Lisbon, Maine. He received a BA from St. Francis College, an MA from Loyola University (Chicago), and an MFA from the University of Iowa. He taught for the European Division of the University of Maryland, at the University of New Hampshire, and at St. Francis College, where he was chairman of the Division of Humanities. In 1971, Poulin joined the faculty at the State University of New York, College at Brockport, where he was Professor of English. In 1980, he was Visiting Fulbright Lecturer in Contemporary American Poetry at the University of Athens and the University of Thessaloniki in Greece.

A poet, translator, and editor, Poulin wrote a number of books and chapbooks of poetry, including *In Advent* (1972), *The Widow's Taboo: Poems After the Catawba* (1977), *The Nameless Garden* (1978), *A Nest of Sonnets* (1986), *A Momentary Order* (1987), and *Cave Dwellers* (1991). *Selected Poems*, edited by Michael Waters, was published posthumously in 2001. His books of translations include *Selected Poems* (1987) and *Day Has No Equal but Night* (1994) by the Québécois poet Anne Hébert, Rainer Maria Rilke's *Duino Elegies and The Sonnets to Orpheus* (1977) and *The Complete French Poems of Rainer Maria Rilke* (1986). Poulin also edited *A Ballet for the Ear: Interviews, Essays, and Reviews* by John Logan (1983) and, with David A. DeTurk, coedited *The American Folk Scene: Dimensions of the Folksong Revival* (1967).

For his poetry and translations, Poulin received both a creative writing fellowship and translator's grant from the National Endowment for the Arts, as well as a poetry fellowship from the New York Foundation for the Arts, two translation awards from Columbia University's Translation Center, and a Faculty Enrichment Programme grant for research and translation from the Embassy of Canada. In 1989, Poulin was awarded an honorary Doctorate of Humane Letters by the University of New England.

A. Poulin, Jr., was also the founding editor and publisher of BOA Editions, Ltd., now in its third decade, a nonprofit publishing house devoted to the publication of poetry and of poetry in translation.

MICHAEL WATERS (1949)

Michael Waters was born in New York City. He attended the State University of New York at Brockport (BA, MA), the University of Nottingham (England), the University of Iowa (MFA), and Ohio University, where he received a PhD in American Literature. He taught in the Creative Writing Programs at Ohio University and the University of Maryland and has been Visiting Professor of American Literature at the University of Athens, Greece; Banister Writer-in-Residence at Sweet Briar College; Stadler Poet-in-Residence at Bucknell University; and Distinguished Poet-in-Residence at Wichita State University. He has also taught in several summer programs, including the Catskill Poetry Workshop at Hartwick College, the Writers' Center at Chautauqua, the West Virginia Writers' Workshop, and the Prague Summer Program. Waters teaches in the New England College MFA Program and, since 1978, at Salisbury University in Maryland, where he is Professor of English.

Waters's books of poems include *Fish Light* (1975), *Not Just Any Death* (1979), *Anniversary of the Air* (1985), *The Burden Lifters* (1989), *Bountiful* (1992), *Green Ash, Red Maple, Black Gum* (1997), *Parthenopi: New and Selected Poems* (2001), and *Darling Vulgarity* (2006). He has edited *Dissolve to Island: On the Poetry of John Logan* (1984) and *Selected Poems* by A. Poulin, Jr. (2001) and has coedited (with Robert Hedin) *Perfect in Their Art: Poems on Boxing from Homer to Ali* (2003).

For his poetry, Waters has received a fellowship in creative writing from the National Endowment for the Arts, several Individual Artist Awards from the Maryland State Arts Council, and three Pushcart Prizes. He has been a resident fellow at Yaddo, the MacDowell Colony, the Virginia Center for the Creative Arts, the Anderson Center for Interdisciplinary Studies, the Tyrone Guthrie Centre at Annaghmakerrig (Ireland), Le Chateau de Lavigny (Switzerland), and the St. James Cavalier Centre (Malta). Waters has read his poems at universities and other venues in the United States and abroad, including the Al-Merbid Poetry Festival in Baghdad, the "Mapping American Space" Conference at the University of Toulouse-Le Mirail, and the Museums for Romanian Literature in Bucharest and Iasi.

Michael Waters currently resides in Salisbury, on the Eastern Shore of Maryland, with his wife, the translator Mihaela Moscaliuc, and his daughter, Kiernan.

Acknowledgments

ACKNOWLEDGMENTS

Carol Frost: "Chimera," "Homo Sapiens," "Sexual Jealousy," "Laws," "Fury," "Scorn," "To Kill a Deer," "The St. Louis Zoo," "The Undressing," all from *Love and Scorn: New and Selected Poems* by Carol Frost. Copyright © 2000 by Carol Frost. Published 2000 by TriQuarterly Books/Northwestern University Press. All rights reserved. "The Part of the Bee's Body Embedded in the Flesh," from *I Will Say Beauty* by Carol Frost. Copyright © 2003 by Carol Frost. Published by TriQuarterly Books/Northwestern University Press. All rights reserved. "Telling the Bees." Reprinted by author's permission.

Allen Ginsberg: "Howl — Part I," "America," and "Ode to Failure" from *Collected Poems 1947–1980* by Allen Ginsberg. Copyright © 1955, 1956, 1959, 1984 by Allen Ginsberg. Reprinted by permission of HarperCollins Publishers Inc.

Louise Glück: "Nostos," "Midnight," and "Parable of Flight" from *Meadowlands* by Louise Glück. Copyright © 1996 by Louise Glück. Reprinted by permission of HarperCollins Publishers Inc. "The Mirror" from *Descending Figure* from *The First Four Books of Poems* by Louise Glück. Copyright 1968, 1971, 1972, 1973, 1974, 1975, 1976, 1977, 1978, 1979, 1980, 1985, 1995 by Louise Glück. Reprinted by permission of HarperCollins Publishers Inc. "Mock Orange" from *The Triumph of Achilles* from *The First Four Books of Poems* by Louise Glück. Copyright 1968, 1971, 1972, 1973, 1974, 1975, 1976, 1977, 1978, 1979, 1980, 1985, 1995 by Louise Glück. Reprinted by permission of HarperCollins Publishers Inc. "Retreating Wind," "The White Rose," and "Vespers" from *The Wild Iris* by Louise Glück. Copyright © 1993 by Louise Glück. Reprinted by permission of HarperCollins Publishers Inc. "Celestial Music" from *Ararat* by Louise Glück. Copyright © 1990 by Louise Glück. Reprinted by permission of HarperCollins Publishers Inc. "The Balcony" from *The Seven Ages* by Louise Glück. Copyright © 2001 by Louise Glück. Reprinted by permission of HarperCollins Publishers Inc.

Albert Goldbarth: "The Talk Show," "Reality Organization," and "The Whole Earth Catalogue" from *Heaven and Earth: A Cosmology* by Albert Goldbarth, The University of Georgia Press, 1991. Reprinted with permission of The University of Georgia Press. "*Ancestored-Back* Is the Overpresiding Spirit of This Poem" from *Troubled Lovers in History*, 1999. "Arguing Bartusiak" from *Marriage, and Other Science Fiction*, 1994. Reprinted with permission from Ohio State University Press.

Kimiko Hahn: "The Shower," reprinted from *Volatile* © 1999 by Kimiko Hahn, by permission of Hanging Loose Press. "The Izu Dancer" and "The Older Child" reprinted from *Earshot* © 1992 by Kimiko Hahn, by permission of Hanging Loose Press. "Reckless Sonnet 4," "The Artist's Daughter," from *The Artist's Daughter* by Kimiko Hahn. Copyright © 2002 by Kimiko Hahn. Used by permission of W. W. Norton & Company, Inc.

Donald Hall: "Maple Syrup," "Digging," and "In the Kitchen of the Old House" from *Old and New Poems* by Donald Hall. Copyright © 1990 by Donald Hall. Reprinted by permission of Houghton Mifflin Company. All rights reserved. "When the Young Husband" from *The Museum of Clear Ideas* by Donald Hall. Copyright © 1993 by Donald Hall. Reprinted by permission of Houghton Mifflin Company. All rights reserved. "The Porcelain Couple," from *Without: Poems* by Donald Hall. Copyright © 1998 by Donald Hall. Reprinted by permission of Houghton Mifflin Company. All rights reserved. "Ardor" from *The Painted Bed: Poems* by Donald Hall. Copyright © 2002 by Donald Hall. Reprinted by permission of Houghton Mifflin Company. All rights reserved.

Michael S. Harper: "We Assume: On the Death of Our Son, Reuben Masai Harper," "Reuben, Reuben," "Dear John, Dear Coltrane," "Love Medley: Patrice Cuchulain," "This Is My Son's Song: '*Ungie, Hi Ungie*,'" "Studs," and "Here Where Coltrane Is," from *Songlines in Michaeltree: New and Collected Poems*. Copyright 2000 by Michael S. Harper. Used with permission of the poet and the University of Illinois Press.

Robert Hass: "Spring Drawing 2," "Privilege of Being," and "A Story About the Body," from *Human Wishes* by Robert Hass. Copyright © 1989 by Robert Hass. Reprinted by permission of HarperCollins Publishers Inc. "Happiness," "Our Lady of the Snows," and "Faint Music" from *Sun Under Wood* by Robert Hass. Copyright © 1996 by Robert Hass.

Reprinted by permission of HarperCollins Publishers Inc. "The Image" and "Meditation at Lagunitas" from *Praise* by Robert Hass. Copyright © 1979 by Robert Hass. Reprinted by permission of HarperCollins Publishers Inc.

Robert Hayden: "Those Winter Sundays." Copyright © 1966 by Robert Hayden. "Night, Death, Mississippi." Copyright © 1962, 1966 by Robert Hayden. "Middle Passage." Copyright © 1962, 1966 by Robert Hayden, from *Collected Poems of Robert Hayden* by Robert Hayden, edited by Frederick Glaysher. Used by permission of Liveright Publishing Corporation.

William Heyen: "The Pigeons," "The Return," "Simple Truths," and "Witness" are from *The Host: Selected Poems 1965–1990*, by William Heyen. Copyright © 1994 by Time Being Books. Reprinted by permission of Time Being Press. "Blackbird Spring" and "Yellow-jackets" in *Ontario Review*; © William Heyen. Reprinted by permission of the author.

Andrew Hudgins: "The Chinaberry," "One Threw a Dirt Clod and It Ran," "Ashes," and "Supper" from *Babylon In A Jar: New Poems* by Andrew Hudgins. Copyright © 1998 by Andrew Hudgins. Reprinted by permission of Houghton Mifflin Company. All rights reserved. "Heat Lightning in a Time of Drought" from *The Never-Ending: New Poems* by Andrew Hudgins. Copyright © 1991 by Andrew Hudgins. Reprinted by permission of Houghton Mifflin Company. All rights reserved. "Grandmother's Spit" from *The Glass Hammer: Poems* by Andrew Hudgins. Copyright © 1994 by Andrew Hudgins. Reprinted by permission of Houghton Mifflin Company. All rights reserved. "In" from the book *Ecstatic in the Poison*. Copyright © 2003 by Andrew Hudgins. Reprinted with permission of The Overlook Press.

Richard Hugo: "Degrees of Gray in Philipsburg." Copyright © 1973 by Richard Hugo. "Death in the Aquarium," "The Lady in Kicking Horse Reservoir." Copyright © 1973 by Richard Hugo. "Living Alone," "A Map of Montana in Italy," "Langaig," from *Making Certain It Goes On: Collected Poems of Richard Hugo* by Richard Hugo. Copyright © 1984 by The Estate of Richard Hugo. Used by permission of W. W. Norton & Company, Inc.

Donald Justice: "Early Poems," "First Death," "Children Walking Home from School Through Good Neighborhood," "Psalm and Lament," "Absences," "Men at Forty," "Variations on a Text by Vallejo," "In Memory of the Unknown Poet, Robert Boardman Vaughn," all from *New and Selected Poems* by Donald Justice, Copyright © 1995 by Donald Justice. Used by permission of Alfred A. Knopf, a division of Random House, Inc.

Galway Kinnell: "The Fundamental Project of Technology" from *The Past* by Galway Kinnell. Copyright © 1985 by Galway Kinnell. Reprinted by permission of Houghton Mifflin Company. All rights reserved. "The Bear" and "Blackberry Eating," from *Three Books* by Galway Kinnell. Copyright © 1993 by Galway Kinnell. Reprinted by permission of Houghton Mifflin Company. All rights reserved. "After Making Love We Hear Footsteps" from *Mortal Acts, Mortal Words* by Galway Kinnell. Copyright © 1980 by Galway Kinnell. Reprinted by permission of Houghton Mifflin Company. All rights reserved. "Flower of Five Blossoms" from *When One Has Lived a Long Time Alone* by Galway Kinnell. Copyright © 1990 by Galway Kinnell. Used by permission of Alfred A. Knopf, a division of Random House, Inc.

Carolyn Kizer: "Thrall," "The Intruder," "A Widow in Wintertime," "Pro Femina" (Part One), and "The Skein" from *Cool, Calm & Collected: Poems 1960–2000*. Copyright © 2001 by Carolyn Kizer. Reprinted with the permission of Copper Canyon Press, P.O. Box 271, Port Townsend, WA 98368-0271. "Semele Recycled" from *Yin*. Copyright © 1984 by Carolyn Kizer. Reprinted with the permission of BOA Editions, Ltd., www.BOAEditions.org.

Yusef Komunyakaa: "Ode to the Maggot" from *Talking Dirty to the Gods* by Yusef Komunyakaa. Copyright © 2000 by Yusef Komunyakaa. Reprinted by permission of Farrar, Straus and Giroux, LLC. "Audacity of the Lower Gods," "Blackberries," "Work," "In the Background of Silence," "Tu Do Street," and "Thanks" from *Neon Vernacular*, 1993. "Boys in Dresses" from *Magic City*, © 1992 by Yusef Komunyakaa, Wesleyan University Press, reprinted by permission of University Press of New England.

"Voices from the Other World," from *Collected Poems* by James Merrill and J. D. McClatchy and Stephen Yenser, editors. Copyright © 2001 by the Literary Estate of James Merrill at Washington University. Used by permission of Alfred A. Knopf, a division of Random House, Inc.

W. S. Merwin: "Field Mushrooms" from *Travels* by W. S. Merwin, Copyright © 1992 by W. S. Merwin. "The Rose Beetle" from *The Rain in the Trees* by W. S. Merwin, Copyright © 1988 by W. S. Merwin. Used by permission of Alfred A. Knopf, a division of Random House, Inc. "When You Go Away," © 1967, "The Poem," "How We Are Spared," "For the Anniversary of My Death," "Dead Hand," "The Chaff," "Fog-Horn," "St Vincent's," and "Air" © 1988 by W. S. Merwin, reprinted with the permission of the Wylie Agency, Inc.

Marilyn Nelson: "Minor Miracle," reprinted by permission of Louisiana State University Press from *The Fields of Praise: New and Selected Poems* by Marilyn Nelson. Copyright © 1997 by Marilyn Nelson. "A Wreath for Emmett Till," from *A Wreath For Emmett Till* by Marilyn Nelson. Text copyright © 2005 by Marilyn Nelson. Reprinted by permission of Houghton Mifflin Company. All rights reserved.

Naomi Shihab Nye: "The Traveling Onion" by Naomi Shihab Nye from *Words Under the Words: Selected Poems*, 1995. By permission of the author, Naomi Shihab Nye, 2005. "Arabic," "Morning Paper, Society Page," and "What Brings Us Out" from *Red Suitcase*. Copyright © 1995 by Naomi Shihab Nye. Reprinted with the permission of BOA Editions, Ltd., www.BOAEditions.org. Naomi Shihab Nye, "Vocabulary of Dearness," "Steps," "The Small Vases from Hebron," and "The Last Day of August" from *Fuel*. Copyright © 1998 by Naomi Shihab Nye. Reprinted with the permission of BOA Editions, Ltd., www.BOAEditions.org. "The Shapes of Mouths at Parties," from *Hugging the Jukebox* (Dutton, 1982). Reprinted with the permission of the poet.

Frank O'Hara: "Why I Am Not a Painter," "Poem [I don't know as I get what D. H. Lawrence is driving at]," "For Grace, After a Party," and "Getting Up Ahead of Someone (Sun)," all from *Collected Poems* by Frank O'Hara, Copyright © 1971 by Maureen Granville-Smith, Administratrix of the Estate of Frank O'Hara. Used by permission of Alfred A. Knopf, a division of Random House, Inc. "Poem [Lana Turner has collapsed]," "Steps," "The Day Lady Died," and "Personal Poem" from *Lunch Poems*. Copyright © 1964 by Frank O'Hara. Reprinted by permission of City Lights.

Sharon Olds: "Good Will," from *The Wellspring* by Sharon Olds. Copyright © 1996 by Sharon Olds. Used by permission of Alfred A. Knopf, a division of Random House, Inc. "Monarchs" from *Satan Says*, by Sharon Olds, © 1980 by Sharon Olds. Reprinted by permission of the University of Pittsburgh Press. "A Woman in Heat Wiping Herself" and "The Pope's Penis" from *The Gold Cell* by Sharon Olds. Copyright © 1987 by Sharon Olds. "The Elder Sister" from *The Dead and the Living* by Sharon Olds. Copyright © 1987 by Sharon Olds. "Early Images of Heaven" and "May 1968" from *The Wellspring* by Sharon Olds. Copyright © 1996 by Sharon Olds. "The Lifting" and "The Glass" from *The Father* by Sharon Olds. Copyright © 1992 by Sharon Olds. Used by permission of Alfred A. Knopf, a division of Random House, Inc.

Mary Oliver: "Where Does the Dance Begin, Where Does It End?" from *Why I Wake Early* by Mary Oliver. Copyright © 2004 by Mary Oliver. Reprinted by permission of Beacon Press, Boston. "Spring Azures," from *New and Selected Poems* by Mary Oliver. Copyright © 1992 by Mary Oliver. Reprinted by permission of Beacon Press, Boston. "Little Owl Who Lives in the Orchard," "The Summer Day," and "Singapore" from *House of Light* by Mary Oliver. Copyright © 1990 by Mary Oliver. Reprinted by permission of Beacon Press, Boston. "University Hospital, Boston" and "In Blackwater Woods" from *American Primitive* by Mary Oliver. Copyright © 1978, 1979, 1980, 1981, 1982, 1983 by Mary Oliver. By permission of Little, Brown and Co., Inc. "Sleeping in the Forest" from *Twelve Moons* by Mary Oliver. Copyright © 1972, 1973, 1974, 1976, 1977, 1978, 1979 by Mary Oliver. By permission of Little, Brown and Co., Inc.

ACKNOWLEDGMENTS

Michael Palmer: "Sun," "Dearest Reader," "Untitled," and "'or anything resembling it,'" by Michael Palmer, from *The Lion Bridge*, copyright © 1998 by Michael Palmer. Reprinted by permission of New Directions Publishing Corp. "I Do Not," by Michael Palmer, from *The Promises of Glass*, copyright © 1999 by Michael Palmer. Reprinted by permission of New Directions Publishing Corp.

Carl Phillips: "Aubade: Some Peaches, After Storm" and "Singing" from *The Rest of Love* by Carl Phillips. Copyright © 2004 by Carl Phillips. Reprinted by permission of Farrar, Straus and Giroux, LLC. "Glads," "Toys," and "Our Lady" Copyright 1995 by Carl Phillips. Reprinted from *Cortege* with the permission of Graywolf Press, Saint Paul, Minnesota. "Luna Moth" Copyright 1998 by Carl Phillips. Reprinted from *From the Devotions* with the permission of Graywolf Press, Saint Paul, Minnesota. "Parable" Copyright 2000 by Carl Phillips. Reprinted from *Pastoral* with the permission of Graywolf Press, Saint Paul, Minnesota.

Sylvia Plath: "Stillborn" and "Crossing the Water" from *Crossing the Water* by Sylvia Plath. Copyright © 1971 by Ted Hughes. Reprinted by permission of HarperCollins Publishers Inc. "Daddy," "Cut," and "Lady Lazarus" from *Ariel* by Sylvia Plath. Copyright © 1963 by Ted Hughes. Reprinted by permission of HarperCollins Publishers Inc.

Adrienne Rich: "The Novel," "One Life," from *Time's Power: Poems 1985–1988* by Adrienne Rich. Copyright © 1989 by Adrienne Rich. Used by permission of the author and W. W. Norton & Company, Inc. "Power." Copyright © 2002 by Adrienne Rich. Copyright © 1978 by W. W. Norton & Company, Inc. "Planetarium." Copyright © 2002 by Adrienne Rich. Copyright © 1971 by W. W. Norton & Company, Inc., "Diving into the Wreck." Copyright © 2002 by Adrienne Rich. Copyright © 1973 by W. W. Norton & Company, Inc., from *The Fact of a Doorframe: Selected Poems 1950–2001* by Adrienne Rich. Used by permission of the author and W. W. Norton & Company, Inc. "The School Among the Ruins," from *The School Among the Ruins: Poems 2000–2004* by Adrienne Rich. Copyright © 2004 by Adrienne Rich. Used by permission of the author and W. W. Norton & Company, Inc.

Theodore Roethke: "My Papa's Waltz," Copyright 1942 by Hearst Magazines, Inc., "Root Cellar," Copyright 1943 by Modern Poetry Association, Inc., "Cuttings (*later*)," Copyright 1948 by Theodore Roethke, "The Lost Son," Copyright 1947 by Theodore Roethke, "In A Dark Time," Copyright © 1960 by Beatrice Roethke, Administratrix of The Estate of Theodore Roethke, from *The Collected Poems* by Theodore Roethke. Used by permission of Doubleday, a division of Random House, Inc.

Anne Sexton: "Her Kind" from *To Bedlam and Part Way Back* by Anne Sexton. Copyright © 1960 by Anne Sexton, renewed 1988 by Linda G. Sexton. Reprinted by permission of Houghton Mifflin Company. All rights reserved. "With Mercy for the Greedy," "To a Friend Whose Work Has Come to Triumph," and "The Abortion," from *All My Pretty Ones* by Anne Sexton. Copyright © 1962 by Anne Sexton, renewed 1990 by Linda G. Sexton. Reprinted by permission of Houghton Mifflin Company. All rights reserved. "Man and Wife," from *Live or Die* by Anne Sexton. Copyright © 1966 by Anne Sexton, renewed 1994 by Linda G. Sexton. Reprinted by permission of Houghton Mifflin Company. All rights reserved. "In Celebration of My Uterus," from *Love Poems* by Anne Sexton. Copyright © 1967, 1968, 1969 by Anne Sexton. Reprinted by permission of Houghton Mifflin Company. All rights reserved. "The Room of My Life," from *The Awful Rowing Toward God* by Anne Sexton. Copyright © 1975 by Loring Conant, Jr., Executor of the Estate of Anne Sexton. Reprinted by permission of Houghton Mifflin Company. All rights reserved.

Charles Simic: "Charles Simic," "Poem Without a Title," "February," "Poem," "Stone," "Fork," "Solitude," "Fear," "Classic Ballroom Dances," and "*errata*," from *Charles Simic: Selected Early Poems*. Reprinted by permission from George Braziller, Inc. "The Old World" from *Hotel Insomnia*, copyright © 1992 by Charles Simic, reprinted by permission of Harcourt, Inc. "Entertaining the Canary" from *Walking the Black Cat*, copyright © 1992 by Charles Simic, reprinted by permission of Harcourt, Inc. "Used Book Store" and "My

Noiseless Entourage" from *My Noiseless Entourage,* copyright © 2005 by Charles Simic, reprinted by permission of Harcourt, Inc.

Louis Simpson: "Quiet Desperation," "In the Suburbs," "Physical Universe" from *Collected Poems* (Paragon House, 1990). "Working Late" and "Riverside Drive" from *In the Room That We Share* (Paragon House, 1990). Poems by Louis Simpson reprinted by permission of the author. Copyright © Louis Simpson.

Dave Smith: "Allegheny Happiness," from *Little Boats, Unsalvaged* by Dave Smith, published by Louisiana State University Press, © 2005. Reprinted with permission of Louisiana State University Press. "Fiddlers," "Blowfish and Mudtoad," "Night Fishing for Blues," "2000," "Pine Cones," and "The Tire Hangs in the Yard," from *The Wick of Memory* by Dave Smith. Copyright © 2000 by Dave Smith. Reprinted by permission of Louisiana State University Press.

W. D. Snodgrass: "Love Lamp" from *Each in His Own Season.* Copyright © 1993 by W. D. Snodgrass. Reprinted with the permission of BOA Editions, Ltd., www.BOAEditions. org. "Viewing the Body," "*Heart's Needle* 9 [I get numb and go in]," "'After Experience Taught Me . . . ,'" and "Old Apple Trees," from *Selected Poems: 1957–1987.* Copyright © by W. D. Snodgrass. Reprinted by permission of the author.

Gary Snyder: "Hay for the Horses" from *Riprap and Cold Mountain Poems,* and "Axe Handles" from *Axe Handles.* Copyright Gary Snyder, 1958, 1983. Reprinted with permission. "Bubbs Creek Haircut" from *Mountains and Rivers Without End* by Gary Snyder. Copyright © 1996 by Gary Snyder. Reprinted by permission of Counterpoint Press, a member of Perseus Books, L.L.C. "'One Should Not Talk to a Skilled Hunter About What Is Forbidden by the Buddha'" and "The Bath," by Gary Snyder, from *Turtle Island,* copyright © 1974 by Gary Snyder. Reprinted by permission of New Directions Publishing Corp.

Gary Soto: "Black Hair," "Envying the Children of San Francisco," "Oranges," and "Failing in the Presence of Ants," from *Black Hair.* "Mexicans Begin Jogging," from *Where Sparrows Work Hard.* "The Tale of Sunlight," from *The Tale of Sunlight.* From *New and Selected Poems* © 1995 by Gary Soto. Used with permission of Chronicle Books LLC, San Francisco. Visit ChronicleBooks.com.

Elizabeth Spires: "The Beds," "Sunday Afternoon at Fulham Palace," "The Celestial," "Glass-Bottom Boat," from *Annonciade* by Elizabeth Spires, copyright © 1985, 1986, 1987, 1988, 1989 by Elizabeth Spires. Used by permission of Viking Penguin, a division of Penguin Group (USA) Inc. "Cemetery Reef," from *Now the Green Blade Rises: Poems* by Elizabeth Spires. Copyright © 2002 by Elizabeth Spires. Used by permission of W. W. Norton & Company, Inc. "The First Day," from *Worldling* by Elizabeth Spires. Copyright © 1995 by Elizabeth Spires. Used by permission of the author and W. W. Norton & Company, Inc. "'In Heaven It Is Always Autumn,'" copyright 1996 by Elizabeth Spires. Reprinted by permission of the poet.

David St. John: "Gin," "The Swan at Sheffield Park," "Lucifer in Starlight," and "Last Night with Rafaella," from *Study for the World's Body: New and Selected Poems* (HarperCollins, 1994), © 1994, David St. John. Reprinted by permission of the author.

William Stafford: "Widow" and "A Wind from a Wing" are reprinted with the permission of Confluence Press from *My Name is William Tell,* copyright 1992 by William Stafford. "Near," "Ceremony," "Traveling Through the Dark," "Adults Only," "Vocation," "Fifteen," "With Kit, Age 7, at the Beach," "Growing Up," "Ask Me," "The Light by the Barn," "How the Real Bible Is Written," "At Fourth and Main in Liberal, Kansas, 1932." Copyright 1954, 1960, 1962, 1966, 1970, 1977 1991, 1998 by The Estate of William Stafford. Reprinted from *The Way It Is: New & Selected Poems* with the permission of Graywolf Press, Saint Paul, Minnesota.

Gerald Stern: "The Bull-Roarer," from *Bread Without Sugar* by Gerald Stern. Copyright © 1992 by Gerald Stern. Used by permission of W. W. Norton & Company, Inc. "I Remember Galileo," "The Dancing," "Soap," "Another Insane Devotion," "Lilacs for Ginsberg," from *This Time: New and Selected Poems* by Gerald Stern. Copyright © 1998 by

ACKNOWLEDGMENTS

Gerald Stern. Used by permission of W. W. Norton & Company, Inc. "She Was a Dove," from *Everything Is Burning* by Gerald Stern. Copyright © 2005 by Gerald Stern. Used by permission of W. W. Norton & Company, Inc.

   Mark Strand: "The Idea" and "A. M." from *The Continuous Life* by Mark Strand, Copyright © 1990 by Mark Strand. "XXX," "XXXIX," and "XLV" from *The Dark Harbor* by Mark Strand, Copyright © 1993 by Mark Strand. "Keeping Things Whole," "The Dress," "The Prediction," "My Life by Somebody Else," "A Morning," and "Leopardi" from *Selected Poems* by Mark Strand, copyright © 1979, 1980 by Mark Strand. "The Night, The Porch," and "A Piece of the Storm" from *Blizzard of One* by Mark Strand, Copyright © 1998 by Mark Strand. Used by permission of Alfred A. Knopf, a division of Random House, Inc.

   Jean Valentine: "Annunciation," "December 21st," "American River Sky Alcohol Father," "The Messenger," "Snow Landscape, in a Glass Globe," "The Under Voice," "Skate," and "Letter," from *Door in the Mountain: New and Collected Poems, 1965–2003* © 2004 by Jean Valentine and reprinted by permission of Wesleyan University Press.

   Ellen Bryant Voigt: "Woman Who Weeps," from *Two Trees* by Ellen Bryant Voigt. Copyright © 1992 by Ellen Bryant Voigt. Used by permission of W. W. Norton & Company, Inc. "Two Trees," from *Two Trees* by Ellen Bryant Voigt. Copyright © 1992 by Ellen Bryant Voigt. Used by permission of W. W. Norton & Company, Inc. "Harvesting the Cows" by Ellen Bryant Voigt. First published in *The Kenyon Review*—New Series, Volume XXVII, Number 1, Winter 2005. Reprinted with permission of Ellen Bryant Voigt and *The Kenyon Review*. "The Hen," from *Claiming Kin.* © 1978 by Ellen Bryant Voigt, Wesleyan University Press, reprinted by permission of University Press of New England. "January," from *The Forces of Plenty* by Ellen Bryant Voigt (Norton, 1983). "The Trust" and "The Lotus Flowers," from *The Lotus Flowers* by Ellen Bryant Voigt (Norton, 1987). Reprinted with permission of the poet.

   Richard Wilbur: "In Trackless Woods," *The New Yorker*, March 31, 2003. Copyright © Richard Wilbur. "Love Calls Us to the Things of This World" from *Things of This World*, copyright © 1956 and renewed 1984 by Richard Wilbur, reprinted by permission of Harcourt, Inc. "The Lilacs" from *Walking to Sleep: New Poems and Translations*, copyright © 1963 and renewed 1991 by Richard Wilbur, reprinted by permission of Harcourt, Inc. "Playboy" from *Walking to Sleep: New Poems and Translations*, copyright © 1968 and renewed 1996 by Richard Wilbur, reprinted by permission of Harcourt, Inc. "The Writer" from *The Mind-Reader*, copyright © 1971 by Richard Wilbur, reprinted by permission of Harcourt, Inc. "The Ride" from *New and Collected Poems*, copyright © 1982 by Richard Wilbur, reprinted by permission of Harcourt, Inc. "Mayflies" from *Mayflies: New Poems and Translations*, Copyright © 2000 by Richard Wilbur. Reprinted by permission of Harcourt, Inc. "Cottage Street, 1953," from *The Mind-Reader*, copyright © 1972 by Richard Wilbur, reprinted by permission of Harcourt, Inc.

   C. K. Williams: "Blades," "From My Window," and "The Gas Station," from *Poems 1963–1983* by C. K. Williams. Copyright © 1988 by C. K. Williams. "Bone," from *Repair* by C. K. Williams. Copyright © 1998 by C. K. Williams. "The Singing," from *The Singing* by C. K. Williams. Copyright © 2003 by C. K. Williams. Reprinted by permission of Farrar, Straus and Giroux, LLC.

   C. D. Wright: "The Secret Life of Musical Instruments," "Wages of Love," "More Blues and the Abstract Truth," "Why Ralph Refuses to Dance," "Planks," "So Far Off and Yet Here," "Song of the Gourd," and "Girl Friend Poem #3," from *Stealing Away: Selected and New Poems.* Copyright © 2002 C. D. Wright. Reprinted with the permission of Copper Canyon Press, P.O. Box 271, Port Townsend, WA 98368-0271.

   Charles Wright: "Relics" from *A Short History of The Shadow* by Charles Wright. Copyright © 2002 by Charles Wright. "Night Journal" from *Zone Journals* by Charles Wright. Copyright © 1988 by Charles Wright. Reprinted by permission of Farrar, Straus and Giroux, LLC. "California Dreaming" from *The World of the Ten Thousand Things: Poems 1980–1990* by Charles Wright. Copyright © 1990 by Charles Wright. Reprinted by

ACKNOWLEDGMENTS

permission of Farrar, Straus and Giroux, LLC. "Reunion," "Grace," "Him," and "Snow" by Charles Wright, from *Country Music: Selected Early Poems* (Wesleyan University Press, 1982). © 1982 by Charles Wright. Reprinted with the permission of Wesleyan University Press.

James Wright: "Autumn Begins in Martins Ferry, Ohio," "Lying in a Hammock at William Duffy's Farm in Pine Island, Minnesota," "The Minneapolis Poem," "In Response to a Rumor That the Oldest Whorehouse in Wheeling, West Virginia, Has Been Condemned," and "A Blessing" by James Wright, from *Above the River: The Complete Poems* (Wesleyan University Press, 1990). © 1990 by James Wright. Reprinted with the permission of Wesleyan University Press. "The Journey" from *This Journey*, 1981. Reprinted with permission of Edith Anne Wright. "The Young Good Man" and "The Old WPA Swimming Pool in Martins Ferry, Ohio" from *Above the River: The Complete Poems* by James Wright. Copyright © 1990 by Anne Wright. Reprinted by permission of Farrar, Straus and Giroux, LLC.